The Dartnell

Sales Manager's

Handbook

DARTNELL is a publisher serving the world of business with books, manuals, newsletters, bulletins, and other training materials for executives, managers, supervisors, sales representatives, financial officers, personnel executives and office employees. In addition, Dartnell produces management and sales training films and audio cassettes, publishes many useful business forms, and has many of its materials and films available in languages other than English. Dartnell, established in 1917, serves the world's whole business community. For details, catalogs, and product information, address: DARTNELL, 4660 N. Ravenswood Avenue, Chicago, Illinois 60640, USA.
Phone (312) 561-4000. FAX (312) 561-3801.

OTHER DARTNELL HANDBOOKS

Advertising Manager's Handbook
Direct Mail and Mail Order Handbook
Marketing Manager's Handbook
Office Administration Handbook
Personnel Administration Handbook
Public Relations Handbook
Sales Promotion Handbook

The Dartnell Sales Manager's Handbook

John P. Steinbrink, Editor

 THE DARTNELL CORPORATION
CHICAGO · BOSTON · LONDON

First Edition—1934
Second Edition—1937
Third Edition—1940
Fourth Edition—1945
Fifth Edition—1947
Sixth Edition—1949
Seventh Edition—1956
Eighth Edition—1959
Ninth Edition—1962
Tenth Edition—1965
Eleventh Edition—1968
Twelfth Edition—1977
Thirteenth Edition—1980
Second Printing—1982
Third Printing—1985
Fourteenth Edition—1989
Second Printing—1990

International Standard Book Number: 0-85013-162-6
Library of Congress Catalog Card Number: 56-59050

Printed in the United States of America by Dartnell Press, Chicago, Illinois 60640-4595

Dedication

This fourteenth edition of Dartnell's Sales Manager's Handbook *is dedicated to all sales managers. More than any other professional group, you have done the most to keep the wheels of commerce turning. Without your continuing efforts — past, present, and future — the standard of living we all enjoy, and too frequently take for granted, would be just an unrealized dream. It is fervently hoped that this book will help guide you through the many challenges you will encounter in your continuing quest to be the best.*

Contents

Foreword

Today's fast-paced world is creating more new and exciting challenges for the sales manager than ever before. Over the past few years, many changes have taken place which have had a profound impact on our businesses. Production and manufacturing methods have changed ... the computer has become an indispensable business tool ... our markets have expanded to include the entire world ... and even our time-honored approach to selling has undergone rethinking.

With this in mind, it shouldn't come as too much of a shock to discover that the sales management function has been in just as dramatic a transition period as every other aspect of business. Believe me, if you're managing the sales team in the same way you did just 36 months ago, you may be in trouble! What's more, a recent study found that when companies failed to achieve their full sales potential, more often than not the cause was *poor sales management and not problems with the salespeople themselves.*

This new edition of Dartnell's *Sales Manager's Handook,* revised and rewritten to reflect our changing world, is designed to ensure that you keep pace. In total, this book gives you a complete picture of what it takes to be a successful sales manager. In this book, you have at your fingertips the knowledge possessed by the world's best sales managers — their skills, tools, activities, and methods distilled into a form you can use.

As before, the Dartnell *Sales Manager's Handbook* remains a nuts-and-bolts, day-to-day resource tool. But the new concepts, the improved systems, and the enhanced and updated material give you new and unique insights into what it takes to be the best at leading, motivating, and managing the sales team.

To get the most benefit from this book, you — the sales manager — must understand your role, and you must understand the role of your salespeople. The number-one priority of your salespeople today must be to *identify and then satisfy customer needs ... profitably*. Their understanding of this premise will dictate how they sell. For example, many of the top-producing salespeople rarely discuss "product" on the initial sales contact. Rather, they believe their first priority is to identify the prospect's needs.

It is just as important that you understand your role. In the past decade, most sales managers functioned as a super salesperson and performed many of the activities their salespeople performed. In short, these sales managers *sold.*

That's just not the way it is today — or will be tomorrow. The role of the successful sales manager is to *coach and train salespeople to identify and then satisfy customer needs ... profitably.* Those skills, tools, and techniques are conveniently documented and detailed in this book.

The top sales producers in the 1990s will rarely talk product on the initial sales contact, rarely ask the prospect to "pick something from the catalog," and will rarely measure their performance only by what they earn. Other measures, such as market share at the territory level, will increase in importance. Sales managers will spend a great deal of time in the field with their salespeople and they will motivate not with money and hype, but rather with challenge and expertise. The transition from cheerleader, policeman, and superman to the more sophisticated developer of people has already started.

In the next decade, the total number of sales managers with these skills and this capability will increase tenfold. Use the Dartnell *Sales Manager's Handbook* often and well to help yourself to be one of those sales managers. I guarantee you will need this information to keep pace.

D.W. Beveridge, Jr.
CEO
Beveridge Business Systems, Inc.

Preface

The job of sales management has been, and will remain, one of the most important management responsibilities in business. It is underscored by Arthur "Red" Motley's truism — "Nothing happens until a sale is made." Sales are the basis and the sustaining force of business. Personal sales contact is, and will continue to be, one of the most important tools of marketing.

Today's sales managers have responsibilities that extend far beyond the basic function of concern with the field sales force. In many companies, particularly the smaller ones, they assume tasks usually reserved for the marketing executive in the specialized fields of sales promotion, market research, advertising, product planning and design, and physical distribution, to name a few.

Additionally, the scope of markets has expanded from domestic geographical boundaries into global possibilities. This includes exporting American products and services as well as establishing manufacturing and distribution in other countries. The expanded revision of Chapter 35 provides help and guidance for such profitable ventures that extend the horizons of sales possibilities.

This revised edition of the *Handbook* is presented in a logical and sequential manner to discuss the contemporary scene of sales and marketing, organization and management of the sales function, sales planning and control, sales policies, marketing channels, and, perhaps most importantly, management of the sales force. New chapters on telemarketing, trade shows, sales promotion, direct marketing, new product considerations, and trends in distribution channels have been included.

Thus, this *Handbook* serves as a central source of vital information in the many aspects of sales management. It serves the experienced sales manager as a refresher course in ongoing practices as well as a well-rounded guide to assigned responsibilities. It serves newly appointed sales managers as a basic foundation and approach to their job duties.

As in previous editions, the present-day sales practices and policies of American companies of every size and the practical experiences of successful executives are included. We are indebted to the many companies, corporate officers, sales and marketing executives, business and trade organizations, business publications and management consultants for their generous cooperation and contributions. The various divisions of the Department of Commerce, Department of Labor, and the Small Business Administration provided invaluable data and statistics.

Many of Dartnell's comprehensive surveys, reports, and publications were of immeasurable help in the preparation of this new, up-to-date edition. A virtual gold mine of information, with appropriate, pertinent data, is presented in the handy Ready-Reference section.

It has been a pleasure and a privilege to conduct the planning, research, and execution of this *Handbook,* which is dedicated to the continued growth of the American economy through improved methods and practices of professional sales management.

JOHN P. STEINBRINK

Introduction

You hold in your hands a real treasure: the fourteenth edition of Dartnell's *Sales Manager's Handbook*. I call it a real treasure because, through its fourteen editions, that is what it has been fondly called by the literally thousands of sales executives — like yourself — who have turned to it and found the facts, ideas, and stimulation needed to become successful sales managers.

I say the above with some justification and authority, for in my background are many years spent as a Director of Sales for a major manufacturing company. In that capacity, it was to Dartnell's *Sales Manager's Handbook* that I looked for the direction to do my job better.

What is the history of this remarkable book?

The first edition was published in 1934, the work of John Cameron Aspley, the founder and president of The Dartnell Corporation. Surely no one was better qualified to write such a book than Mr. Aspley for he was long identified as America's top sales authority with the writing ability to make complex subjects both interesting and understandable. The company he founded was the only one in the world devoted to serving the needs of sales managers by gathering and disseminating sales information.

As you might expect, the first edition of the *Sales Manager's Handbook* was an immediate success and quickly became a best seller. Over the years, the book has grown in influence and impact through the efforts of a number of outstanding sales authorities — individuals like John Cousty Harkness and Ovid Riso — who have edited and authored succeeding editions.

The resulting books each made a valuable and unique contribution to the study of sales management. Although exact figures are unknown, it is estimated that over a half-million copies of Dartnell's *Sales Manager's Handbook* in its various editions have been sold. How many copies have been "passed along" to other aspiring sales managers is impossible to even estimate. Suffice it to say that this book has been responsible for the success of more sales managers than any other book on sales management ever published.

And now in your hands is the just published fourteenth edition, this time the work of John P. Steinbrink who, in addition to his many years as senior vice president and editorial director of The Dartnell Corporation, has lectured on sales and sales management throughout the world. He is genuinely a sales authority.

So there you have it — the whys and wherefores of Dartnell's *Sales Manager's Handbook.* As Chairman of The Dartnell Corporation, I'm proud of it — and trust that it will serve you as that earlier edition first served me when I was a Sales Executive.

WM. HARRISON FETRIDGE
Chairman
The Dartnell Corporation

About the Editor

This 14th edition of Dartnell's highly praised *Sales Manager's Handbook* has been completely reorganized and updated by John P. Steinbrink, former senior vice president and editorial director of The Dartnell Corporation. Steinbrink is well-qualified to have undertaken a project of this magnitude. He has logged over 40 years of diversified managerial experience in both business research and educational publishing, including eight years in a sales management capacity.

In addition, he is a nationally known expert in sales force compensation, and the author of the 23rd edition of Dartnell's *Sales Force Compensation* survey published in 1986. He has written hundreds of articles and reports on various aspects of sales management, including a *Harvard Business Review* article that was translated for the premier Spanish edition.

Steinbrink is a past president of the Sales and Marketing Executives Association of Chicago and was vice president/corporate support of Sales and Marketing Executives International, where he also served on the finance and executive committees. He holds an MBA degree through the Executive Program of the University of Chicago. Steinbrink is currently president of his own sales management consulting group, JPS Associates, in Niles, Illinois.

Chapter 1

The Changing Marketplace

"In the successful marketing strategies of many diversified companies, a single thread winds through them and links them all together. That thread is *change;* it is the quickening pace of change—of new demands and the great opportunities that change is creating for the sales and marketing executive," said a marketing expert.

Television, air-conditioning, antibiotics, latex paint, health insurance, credit cards, aluminum baseball bats, enriched bread, social security, personal computers, pensions, the birth-control pill, robotics, prepared baby food, Federal Housing Authority mortgages, automated teller machines, computerized inventory control, polio vaccines, safety belts, disposable diapers, power mowers, transparent tape.

Prefabricated houses, the jogging bra, answering machines, indoor soccer, Silly Putty, quadrophonic sound, Disneyland, styling mousse, beepers, the shower massage, air travel, Polaroid camera, self-correcting typewriters, word processors, laser beams, compact discs, frozen foods.

This is quite a list, but just a few of the 100,000 products and services made available in the past 50 years "that significantly transcended the rather everyday quality of the marketplace to earn a place in the history of consumption," according to Rhoda Karpatkin in a study by Consumers Union.

Sales and marketing have played an important role in making these products and services "household names" in the past 50 years, and this listing presents a challenge for marketing in the next 50 years. The key word is "change." Marketing faces the formidable task of translating the inventions, improvements, innovations, and ideas of the future into useful products and services. Sales and marketing will be the catalyst for the next "100,000 wonders of the American world."

PART 1

Sales and
Marketing Today

What Is "Marketing"?

We've gone from the era of product orientation characterized by industrial development and a "sell whatever the factory produces" attitude through a period of sales orientation—the recognition of salesmanship—to the current stage of market orientation, where the interest of the customer comes first.

Definitions of marketing and the marketing concept abound. Let's look at some of them.

- "The process of planning and executing the conception, pricing, promotion and distribution of ideas, goods, and services to create exchanges that satisfy individual and organizational objectives."

  —*American Marketing Association*

- "Selling is the management of the present, while marketing is the management of the future. This means, simply, that sales involves current activities designed to persuade customers to buy products or services. Marketing, on the other hand, manages sales developments of the future through application of such disciplines as market research, analysis of purchasing trends, study of changing customer habits and long-range planning. Thus sales is a part of marketing, and an important part, but not vice versa.

  "While we maintain a distinction between these two pursuits at Pitney Bowes, we do acknowledge the need for bringing selling and marketing together at higher levels of our management. We believe strongly that our marketing of the future can be most effectively planned and managed by people who have a thorough understanding of our current customers' wants and needs. These are the people with sales backgrounds.

  "So, while selling and marketing represent different but related career fields, the marketing manager needs sales experience to make correct decisions affecting the marketing function."

  —*Michael O'Connor,*
  Vice President, Field Operations
  Pitney Bowes

- "Marketing includes all business activities that determine the needs and wants of customers, develop new markets, aid in product development, estimate potentials, forecast and aid in production planning; that operate a marketing organization, determine marketing strategy, select channels of distribution, inform and motivate customers, price, sell, and provide marketing services, including order entry, customer financing, credit and collection, and both customer and product services; that provide for physical distribution, including packaging, transportation, field warehousing of finished goods, and delivery; that contribute to overall corporate planning and that plan and control this entire operation."

  —*George Risley,*
  Modern Industrial Marketing

- "There are three key phases to this matter of keeping pace: 1) Anticipating the needs and desires of the market and satisfying them as quickly as possible; 2) then being quick to recognize when the market has changed, or is about to change, and 3) being ready to meet that change with a corresponding shift in product or service.

  "If a company can manage to do well in each phase, it should be strong and successful; if not, sooner or later it will find itself in trouble."

  —*William F. May,*
  Business Executive

An executive in the Maytag Company outlined marketing basics including the following functions: as 1) recognizing the need for a product, 2) building a product to fulfill that need, 3) exposing the product, 4) "hooking up" the product with a prospect, 5) writing the order, and 6) standing behind the product and making certain it performs exactly as represented.

Since the objective of nearly all businesses is to "market" goods and services, and thereby make a profit, the whole of business may be said to be a marketing enterprise, in which case marketing becomes the *sole* activity of business. This, of course, would be the broadest possible interpretation of the term "marketing." But such an interpretation would not be helpful in an exploration of the problems of the marketing function, for obviously engineering, manufacturing, purchasing—and possibly product research and development—while contributing to the marketing objectives of a business, are not, of themselves, part of the responsibility of the marketing department.

Some companies are very broad in assigning responsibility to the marketing function; some are more restrictive. Because of the diversity in the structure of firms and in accounting practices, the extent of the responsibilities of the marketing entity within a given company will vary considerably. In many smaller companies, sales managers perform many of the functions usually reserved for the marketing department in larger companies. In this regard, the sales management function is not a separate entity from marketing, but rather both functions are closely interrelated and dependent upon each other. For that reason, many of what might, in some companies, be called pure marketing functions are covered in this Handbook inasmuch as the sales manager is either directly responsible for them or has a voice in formulating related policies and decisions.

The State of Ferment

The marketplace is dynamic—always changing with advances, new techniques, and shifting emphases and ideas. A look at some of these innovations will stimulate the marketing and sales executive to keep pace by keeping abreast of what's happening and what will happen in the future.

An example of marketing advances is consumer-interactive electronic transaction devices, cited by the American Marketing Association (AMA) as the second in its series of commendations for Great Marketing Ideas in the Decade of Marketing. "Breakthroughs in communications have led to a new generation of marketing services," stated the AMA's Great Marketing Ideas Task Force, a panel of 11 marketing experts including both executives and educators. Two-way electronic devices are cited for changing the ways consumers bank, shop, invest, and receive and transmit information.

Joseph M. Kamen, professor of marketing at Indiana University Northwest, Gary, named the automatic teller machines (ATMs) as a "prototype illustration of devices already in widespread use." "The product is banking services, not the machines or cash," Kamen stated. "It took marketing minds to envision the service, design the package, measure the potential, interpret the benefits, and educate the consumer on using ATMs."

Among the marketing services provided by consumer-interactive transaction devices are in-home shopping and banking via personal computer, in-store merchandising kiosks, directory and information services in public places, literature searches, securities and investment purchases, auction participation, college registration, medical diagnosis, and direct electronic ordering by industrial customers.

Task force member Alden G. Clayton, president of the Marketing Science Institute, Cambridge, Massachusetts, described computer hardware and software as technology while the applications often come from marketing. His example: "High-capacity computers make possible system-wide airline scheduling, but also provide many customer comfort, convenience, and economic benefits." Think of services, such as special fares, preprinted boarding passes, programmed selection of seats, choice of meals, and, of course, frequent-flier programs.

Segmenting the Market

Moore Business Forms, Inc. plans selling strategies according to customer size: very large accounts, middle market accounts, and small accounts.

"Each of these account sizes has different implications in terms of coverage, or how they are called on, and the kinds of services needed to provide to them," stated Thomas J. McKiernan, vice-president of sales and marketing. He continued:

"The primary marketing strategy is direct sales coverage. The strategies employed at the high end of the market are also employed, with some modifications and refinements, in the middle market. In addition, coverage of the middle market is enhanced by various means and other channels of distribution that we also employ to reach the low end of the market.

"In addition to segmenting the market according to size, the market is segmented vocationally—by industries that have some peculiarities or characteristics that lend themselves to specialization. The health care and financial services markets are two good examples.

"The low end of the market does not justify the cost of direct coverage to get at this market. Therefore, a variety of ways to purchase products through several channels of distribution is offered:

- regional telemarketing centers

- direct mail

- catalogs

- retail stores

- association programs

- office products dealers

- mutual marketing programs.

"Underlying all of this, however, is a recognition that there are no clear-cut lines of demarcation for all of these differing markets and how they can or should be reached.

"Many of the marketing techniques employed are used for both the upper and middle markets, or both the middle and lower markets, or a combination of all three. There is often a blending of strategies up and down the line, just as there is a blending of market characteristics.

"The key is to continually take the pulse of your market and the changes taking place there. If you do, you will be aware of the significant opportunities that are unfolding as these changes take place.

"It's like the old sign placed at railroad crossing—STOP, ¯LOOK, and LISTEN. If you stop and you really look at your market and you really listen to your customers, you'll be able to take advantage of the opportunities that are going to develop in the next several years as a result of technological change and the need your customers have to contain their own costs, so that they, too, can remain competitive and healthy."

Quality Is Number One Issue

There has been much discussion about the less-than-satisfactory "quality level" of American-made products. The high number of recalls by the automotive industry and the constantly told tale that "it only lasts until the day after the warranty expires" contribute to this image. Japanese and West German factories and mills were flattened during World War II and were rebuilt with new, modern equipment. This added to the perception that foreign-made products were of a better quality than U.S. products, despite the fact that the components of many American products are manufactured overseas and assembled in the United States.

Executives agree that product and service quality is the most critical issue facing American business in the next decade, but many are naive about how to achieve it, a Gallup poll showed. Of 608 executives surveyed, 64 percent chose customer complaints to determine the quality of products and services, instead of relying on the preventive measures of their quality departments. Only 29 percent of the executives professed strong confidence in the quality of U.S. products and services. Seventy percent estimated the cost of poor quality (warranties, recall, rework, etc.) at 10 percent or less of gross sales, but 23 percent were not aware of the costs associated with producing a quality product or service.

Tomorrow's Distribution

In a presentation to The Conference Board Marketing Conference, Wendell M. Stewart, Kearney Management Consultants, stated: "The future belongs to those marketing executives who can lead their companies to significantly improved productivity of the human, physical, financial, and technological resources devoted to the business.

"It is said that the keys to marketing success are

- Selection of the right channel structure, both for selling and delivering the goods;

- Tailor-making physical distribution operations to the needs of the customer within acceptable cost and investment limitations;

- Establishing the necessary facilitating marketing institutions, such as credit and service, and finally,

- Actual marketing, or the integration of needs, wants, and purchasing power.

"Sears Roebuck and Company long has been cited as an example of an organization that has been able to successfully blend the above four keys into a highly profitable and effective corporate system.

"In viewing the distribution process, management is becoming increasingly concerned over customer service. By this we mean the level of inventory reliability or, if you prefer, the level of stockout that is acceptable to customers. Customer service also implies order cycle time and the dependability of that cycle time. Customer service is the critical customer-supplier interface, the moment of truth that makes or breaks all of the demand-generation effort that has gone before it. Superior customer service can help to increase sales and market share; inferior customer service can lose sales and erode share. But higher customer service usually increases inventories and operating costs, thus decreasing productivity and creating a tradeoff to consider.

"Next is distribution strategy. Having defined the service goals necessary to be successful in the marketplace, it is critical to determine what combination of channels and inventory deployment schemes will minimize distribution investment and operating costs within acceptable service constraints. Channel selection and inventory deployment are key elements of distribution strategy. Again, strategies that require too much inventory and/or marketing operations cost tend to decrease productivity.

"The third concern is with the materials management plan. How can materials be flowed through the distribution facility network, as defined by the distribution strategy, in a way that satisfies customer service goals with minimum inventory in the distribution pipeline? The integrated planning and control of the flow of materials from raw suppliers to final consumers is the heart of the distribution process, or as some are beginning to call it, the 'logistics process.'

"The fourth area of concern is the actual physical distribution

9

(PD) operations of order processing, transportation, warehousing, and delivery. PD operations act to move the materials through the network of facilities in a way that satisfies customers at minimum operating expense. Anything that can be done to take work out of the system, or to eliminate cost or investment, will improve productivity. Perhaps the most dynamic area of management concern is the area of information systems. There is more happening today in the exploding technology of information transmission and processing than in almost any other area of business. As a result, managers are increasingly asking themselves questions such as: What kind of information do I need? Where do I get it? How can I process it most economically? And the proliferation of hardware, telecommunications equipment, and software programs will continue to multiply almost exponentially over the next few years, making this whole area even more complex. Information processing holds much promise as a means of improving productivity, both by speeding up marketing operations and by helping management to make better decisions faster.

"And finally, management is concerned about organization—people in the distribution process and their relationships, their motivation, their recognition, and their reward systems. Management is especially concerned because many of the traditional reward systems are counter-productive to good, cost-effective distribution practice. Decentralizing a multi-product, multi-channel company into autonomous business units, for example, can seriously impair corporate distribution productivity, even though it may simplify the management process.

"So, in total, although today's distribution manager has a number of key areas with which he must concern himself, he is primarily concerned with using information to effectively operate distribution activities to satisfy customers' service requirements. It all seems so simple, yet in reality this function can be frustratingly complex.

"The bad news begins with government regulation. In its infinite wisdom, the government (federal, state, and local) apparently believes that it must intrude at every juncture in the course of business. There are many indications that this will get worse. If you are a manufacturer, this can mean anything from loss of exclusive use of your long-established trademark to further erosion of your ability to control distribution at the wholesale and retail levels. If you are a wholesaler or a retailer, it can mean slow strangulation in record keeping, government reporting, and conforming with a proliferation of regulations designed to protect everyone but the business person.

"The key areas to watch are

1. Regulation of monopolistic control
   • Market control
   • Collusive practices
   • Market exclusion tactics

2. Regulation of product characteristics
   • Product standards
   • Product quality
   • Packaging and conditions of sale

3. Regulation of price competition
   • Price discrimination
   • Resale price maintenance
   • Price control (minimum, maximum)

4. Regulation of channels of distribution
   • Operating features of marketing institutions
   • Relations between buyers and sellers

5. Regulation of unfair competition
   • Advertising
   • Nonadvertising promotional methods
   • Trademarks and trade names

"It is important to realize that the Department of Justice and the Federal Trade Commission are using new criteria to define and test for competition. Profit, market share, product-line extensions, advertising expenditures, rate of return, and channel strategies—the very heart of the marketing plan—are now part of the tests for competition.

"There have been several technological advances in distribution that have contributed directly to increased productivity. Some of these, like warehouse automation, have yet to provide the full measure of promised benefits, but as direct labor becomes more and more of a fixed cost, we may have no choice but to move toward further automation in order to avoid putting people on the distribution payroll who can never be removed. Here again, there is a trade-off to keep in mind. Multi-marketing, or the use of different channels to sell the same products, can undermine the economic feasibility of warehouse automation by decentralizing the workload.

"Interorganizational coordination is simply the cooperation of various elements in the distribution process to bridge the gaps or the barriers that typically exist at those points where title to the goods passes down the distribution channel from supplier to customer. Examples in this area are:

- Development of the Universal Product Code
- The automated ordering system in the wholesale drug industry linking wholesalers and manufacturers
- The food industry's evaluation of the feasibility of computer-to-computer ordering between suppliers and retailers.

"Vertical integration within channels is increasing and probably will continue to increase, although this will perhaps be more prevalent in consumer goods, as for example, those in the do-it-yourself home improvement industry. There will be forward integration by manufacturers and wholesalers to establish an aligned group of retail outlets. Retail chains, however, will continue to integrate backup stream by establishing their own wholesale buying and distribution organizations and, in some instances, their own manufacturing operations. The intention is control, price and cost stability, and assured volume.

"Catalog operations are booming, reflecting the consumer desire for lower prices on branded merchandise. Basically, it's a more productive way of reaching the customer.

"Specialty distributors and retailers are emerging as a potent force in distribution. It could be that some of the mass merchandisers have reached the point where they are encountering *dis*economics of scale due to their size. It could also be that customers for certain types of products are willing to pay for the personalized attention provided by specialty outlets, attention that is lacking in the self-service stores.

"The future of the stocking wholesaler is also in doubt. In many categories of goods the wholesalers are being bypassed with increasing frequency because:

- The increasing strength of chain retailers makes the independent wholesaler redundant;
- Many manufacturers believe that they can obtain better control over sales with their own sales forces.

"The emerging pattern in this regard is unclear, however, because in some industries, the wholesalers are stronger than ever.

"In the years ahead, the main thrust will be to further reduce total inventories in all stages of the distribution pipeline by realigning them (between vendors, manufacturers, wholesalers, and retailers) to provide maximum inventory utilization, which is a good example of the interorganizational coordination referred to earlier.

"Finally, in the future, market segment profitability and return on investment measurement will be the primary focus. We are coming to realize that the customer order is the ultimate profit center and only by flowing *all* costs forward to the order and comparing it with net revenues can we determine the real source of our net operating profit or loss. This type of information will form the foundation for market planning, pricing, establishment of distribution policies, and customer service goals."

The Changing Role
Of the Salesperson

It has been suggested by many sources that a salesperson will become a marketing manager at the micro level. In an article in *Marketing News,* Marvin A. Jolson stated that this transformation began in the 1970s and will intensify in the current and future decades. The emerging "marketing manager at the micro level" will be quite different from the salespeople of the 1960s who were described by one expert as "persons who were recruited, hired, fired up, and evaluated in terms of how many orders they bring in."

Jolson further says that that description is probably still true, if one examines the attitudes of many managers, educators, public policy-makers, consumers, and even salespeople. Indeed, the buyer-seller relationship has long been described as a competitive battleground where someone wins and another person loses.

"But with the advent of the marketing concept," Jolson says, "a reincarnation of salesmanship is taking place. The personal selling function has become much more professional, especially in terms of planning and coordinating the firm's sales strategies with the needs of the marketplace.

"The 'new salesperson' is becoming a caterer to existing attitudes and needs, rather than an influencer and changer of attitudes and behavior—a value creator rather than a need creator. In effect, the selling emphasis is on finding prospects who have needs, rather than on creating new needs by aggressive and persuasive methods.

"Salespersons in the 1970s were categorized as problem-solvers or managers of assigned territories. They had the dual responsibility of simultaneously representing both the customer and the selling organization.

"In the decades to come, however, the salesperson will be one who searches for and locates people or organizations with needs, describes how his or her firm's product or service will diminish or remove those needs and, following acceptance by the prospect, assume responsibility for monitoring and maintaining the performance of the product or service in order to ensure continuing customer satisfaction.

"Thus, the minimal responsibilities of the new salespeople are to

- Search for and recognize market opportunities;

- Determine the precise nature of prospects' needs and desires;

- Offer and describe their firm's products in a need-satisfying context;

- Ensure that the recommended products/services fulfill these need-satisfying goals on an ongoing basis.

Tomorrow's Sales Force

In analyzing a study from the Bureau of Labor Statistics in *Sales and Marketing Management,* Thayer C. Taylor concludes that the sales force of the future will be older, decidedly more female, and more productive.

Taylor states that marketers mapping long-range sales strategies through the mid-1990s will have to reckon with a sales force whose complexion will change markedly. Mostly, marketers can expect to have more women calling on prospects and accounts. They will also benefit from healthy productivity gains by their salespeople and experience considerable difficulty in hiring younger trainees.

These trends will be triggered by the aging of the baby boom generation and the baby bust group that followed it, says Taylor. The effects of this maturation process are at the core of the federal government's new long-range projections, developed by the Bureau of Labor Statistics' Office of Economic Growth and Employment Projections (OEGEP), that cover the economy, labor force, industry, and occupations.*

Taylor says that while the total labor force (people with jobs plus those looking for work) will increase 15.6 million (13.8 percent) between 1984 and 1995, two-thirds of the newcomers will be women. John Lukasiewicz, OEGEP economist, states that considering that the total number of salesworkers is projected to increase at a faster-than-average 20 percent rate, the more rapid growth rate implies that marketers will have to hire women to a greater degree to keep their sales forces expanding. (Table 1, page 16).

Marketers can be encouraged by the changed mix of tomorrow's work force. "Nearly three-fourths of the 1995 labor force will be in the prime working ages (25-54 years), compared with two-thirds in 1984," notes Howard N. Fullerton, demographic statistician in OEGEP. This is illustrated in Figure 1, page 17.

In fact, prime age workers will swell 21 million, while younger (16-

---

* The Bureau of Labor Statistics developed three scenarios of future growth: low trend, with an annual 2.2 percent growth in gross national product (GNP); moderate trend, 2.9 percent, and high trend, 3.5 percent. GNP grew 2.6 percent in 1977-84.

Table 1. Sales Force Outlook: Above-Average Growth

Marketing & Sales Occupations (000)	1984	1995 Low Trend	1995 Moderate Trend	1995 High Trend	1984-95 % Increase Moderate Trend
Total	11,173	12,697	13,393	13,990	+20%
Retail salespersons	2,732	2,916	3,075	3,213	13
Cashiers	1,902	2,343	2,469	2,579	30
Wholesale trade salesworkers[1]	1,248	1,536	1,617	1,688	30
Stock clerks, sales floor	574	607	641	670	12
Manufacturing salesworkers[1]	**547**	**569**	**598**	**623**	**9**
Insurance salesworkers	371	384	405	422	9
Real estate agents & brokers	363	396	415	432	14
Brokers, real estate	43	48	50	52	16
Sales agents, real estate	320	348	365	380	14
Counter & rental clerks	96	93	98	101	2
Securities & Financial services salesworkers	81	107	113	118	39
Travel agents	72	98	103	108	44
Real estate appraisers	38	42	45	46	19

[1]Wage and salary workers only; does not include self-employed.
Source: Bureau of Labor Statistics, *Monthly Labor Review.*
©Sales and Marketing Management.

24) and older (55 and up) workers will decline 3.7 million and 1.6 million, respectively.

For marketers, this means sales forces will be tilted more toward older and, ergo, more experienced professionals, says Taylor. Hence productivity gains should slant upwards.

However, Taylor cautions, a big unknown hovers over this prospect: namely, the greater number of women who, because of their recent entrance into the sales picture, will be on the early phase of their learning curve. Their productivity gains will be influenced by the encouragement they receive in realizing their potential and by the depth of their commitment to a sales career.

The ascendancy of the prime working age group promises a big plus for marketers in the consumer buying area. The changed age mix means that more workers will be in their peak earning years, thus lifting more consumer buying units into the upper income brackets.

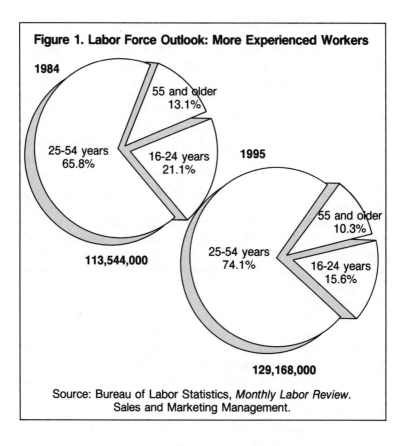

Figure 1. Labor Force Outlook: More Experienced Workers

1984

55 and older
13.1%

25-54 years
65.8%

16-24 years
21.1%

1995

113,544,000

55 and older
10.3%

25-54 years
74.1%

16-24 years
15.6%

129,168,000

Source: Bureau of Labor Statistics, *Monthly Labor Review.*
Sales and Marketing Management.

   To be sure, Taylor says, there's a cloud to the age mix's silver lining. The slippage in the 16-24 age group means a shrinking reservoir from which sales trainees are traditionally drawn. Marketers will thus face considerable pressure to raise compensation levels for new recruits, retain older salespeople for longer periods, or depend more on outright raiding. Thus, the complexities of staffing tomorrow's sales forces may be as challenging as the strategies they'll be executing.

Spiraling Selling Costs

A growing number of large manufacturers are reaching customers through distributors and other middlemen, rather than through their own sales staffs, according to a major Conference Board study.

The study, covering 214 major manufacturers, shows that the primary reason manufacturers are turning to individual distrubutors, wholesalers, and retailers is to control spiraling sales costs. Nearly half of the surveyed companies (49 percent) are now using wholesalers, with 42 percent depending on distributors and 39 percent relying on independent retailers. Five years from now, more than one-fifth of the surveyed firms say that they will be relying even more heavily on all three of these outlets.

The study also finds a growing use of telemarketing. Some 25 percent of the surveyed companies are now using the telephone as a direct sales weapon, and 25 percent say they will become more dependent on this technique over the next five years. The two major forces behind this trend are a growing corporate need to reach new customers and to service small-order customers more effectively.

"Although most manufacturers still rely on a direct sales force, many are trying to find ways to use this resource more efficiently," declares Howard Sutton, a marketing and sales specialist at The Conference Board and author of the study. "If the costs of direct selling continue to rise as fast as they have in recent years, some companies may consider the possibility of eliminating the traditional field sales force entirely."

Two other key findings in the study were as follows:

- More firms are installing computer-to-computer ordering systems to speed deliveries and cut selling costs. Under these systems, customers make purchases via their own computer terminals; orders are instantly transmitted by telephone cable and then processed in suppliers' offices. Although only a small number of firms now have the necessary hardware and software, this technique has enormous potential for saving both time and money. About 12 percent of the surveyed firms now feature computer-to-computer ordering; 20 percent predict that this technique will become more widely used during the next five years.

- Corporate sales forces are becoming more and more specialized. While 58 percent of the surveyed companies say their sales staffs now consist primarily of generalists, about half of the companies expect to rely more on specialists over the next five years. These new specialists are increasingly likely to spend less time selling and more time providing customers with technical advice and helping them solve problems.

The final users of manufacturers' products are steadily relying on fewer and fewer suppliers. They are also demanding that supplies, parts, and materials be delivered on specific days and even at specific times to cut storage and handling costs.

Since few manufacturers are equipped to make "just-in-time" deliveries throughout the country, many companies are likely to depend more heavily on their distributors. They especially will be turning to distributors with solid track records in managing warehouse and transportation operations, the study predicts.

"Those manufacturers that lead the way into these closer alliances may be in a better position to compete," notes The Conference Board's Sutton.

Stronger links between American manufacturers and distributors could strengthen this country's competitive base. "If manufacturers develop loyal partnerships with distributors in this country, they can hold off or neutralize foreign competition," explains one prominent marketing executive. "I'm not sure a lot of manufacturers appreciate that, but it's a very viable defense."

Consumer Market/Industrial Sales Outlook

The trend for both the consumer market and industrial sales through 1995 is comfortably upward. The Bureau of Labor Statistics *Monthly Labor Review* data for the consumer market predict a 30 percent increase in disposable income, with a healthy 35 percent, 23 percent and 45 percent increase in personal consumption of durables, nondurables, and services respectively. The complete data are shown in Table 2, page 20.

Comparable data for the industrial sales outlook are shown in Table 3, page 21.

Table 2. Consumer Market Outlook: Services the Spur

	1984	1995 Low Trend	1995 Moderate Trend	1995 High Trend	1984-95 % Increase Moderate Trend
Key Indicators (Bil. of 1977 dollars)					
Gross national product	$2,367.3	$3,006.4	$3,240.5	$3,550.9	+37%
Disposable personal income	1,630.3	2,055.7	2,114.6	2,125.5	30
Per capita income	**$6,888**	**$7,921**	**$8,147**	**$8,190**	18
Personal consumption	1,522.2	1,929.2	2,053.5	2,257.9	35
Durables	237.2	299.9	320.6	363.7	35
Nondurables	572.2	659.7	702.5	763.0	23
Services	712.8	969.6	1,030.4	1,131.2	45
Households (Thous.)	84,985	102,446	102,446	102,446	21
Family	61,996	72,250	72,250	72,250	17
Nonfamily	22,989	30,196	10,196	30,196	31

Sources: Bureau of Labor Statistics, *Monthly Labor Review;* income data provided by Betty W. Su, Office of Economic Growth and Employment Projections.

Consumer Attitudes

"Consumers are taking a more realistic attitude towards their quality of life, towards their future and towards what they purchase," said Robert Shulman, president of Yankelovich Clancy Shulman as reported in *Inside Print*. According to Shulman, consumers are willing to shop strategically and delay spending in order to obtain the quality they have come to feel they deserve.

These observations are based on the *Yankelovich Monitor* survey, which revealed new trends in the consumer marketplace for the 1980s and beyond. The trend of shifting American consumer values is summarized in Table 4, page 22.

As for the consequences of these findings for advertisers, Shulman said, "the marketers who succeed in the years ahead will be those who can adjust to this new realism and speak in the neotraditionalist language customers want to hear."

Major Sectors (Bil. of 1977 dollars)	1984	1995 Low Trend	1995 Moderate Trend	High Trend	1984-95 % Increase Moderate Trend
Agriculture	$ 65.9	$73.5	$80.7	$88.5	+ 23%
Mining	55.0	57.5	64.8	72.6	18
Construction	85.7	107.3	113.3	118.2	32
Manufacturing	533.9	669.3	738.6	827.4	38
Durables	324.5	426.5	472.3	532.2	46
Nondurables	209.4	242.8	266.3	295.2	27
Transportation, communications & public utilities	202.8	286.3	31.05	341.0	53
Transportation	69.8	83.6	90.6	99.0	30
Communications	75.0	134.7	145.8	160.6	94
Public Utilities	58.0	68.0	74.1	81.4	28
Trade	411.6	494.1	532.3	584.0	29
Wholesale	187.0	220.5	240.4	263.6	29
Retail	224.6	273.6	291.9	320.4	30
Finance, insurance, & real estate	347.8	493.2	523.1	576.8	50
Services	315.5	430.8	461.9	503.7	46
Government enterprises	29.4	36.2	38.8	42.6	32

Table 3. Industrial Sales Outlook: Communications the Frontrunner

Source: Bureau of Labor Statistics, *Monthly Labor Review.*
©Sales and Marketing Management.

Global Marketing on the Rise

Still another force very much on the scene is that of world trade. And for the truly ambitious sales manager or company, this force may hold the greatest challenge. There will be debate, argument, dissension; there could be anger and walkouts. Yet, inevitably, the age-old trade barriers will begin to crumble. It will be a result of sheer selfishness as well as of the recognition of the dire necessity of gaining new markets and sources of supply.

Whether your market areas are in a few nations or cover entire hemispheres, this will mean new markets and new competition. It will bring new customers, who have different needs and respond to different appeals. Of its very nature, it will mean a broader and very much more challenging world of opportunity.

One footnote must be added: As today we see many of our compa-

> **Table 4. Shifting American Consumer Values**
>
> **Traditional values: late 1940s-1950s**
> **Goals:** Upward mobility signaled by material possessions
> **Means:** Protestant ethic, conformity, self-denial, personal morality
> **Consumer behavior:** Conformity, brand/store loyalty, career consumers, mass markets
>
> **New values: 1960s-1970s**
> **Goals:** Self-fulfillment, self-expression, experience, hedonism, having it all, pluralism
> **Means:** Focus-on-self, focus on public morality
> **Consumer behavior:** Instant gratification—"Have It All," personalization/product proliferation, breakdown of hierarchies and brand loyalties
>
> **Adaptive/pragmatic values: early 1980s**
> **Goal:** The "new" materialism and personal choice fulfillment
> **Means:** Pragmatism—"what works," winning, competition, personal control
> **Consumer behavior:** Strategic consumer emerges, quality as "moral" issue, beat the system, tradition/heritage re-emerge, take control
>
> **Late 1980s**
> **Outlook:** Strategic consumer commitment continues, pragmatism coming up short, hunger for something beyond shopping smart, emotional as well as pragmatic needs
> **Values:** A need for principles, rules and guidelines, priorities still based on personal choice, neotraditional and strategic approach to consuming
> **New consumer behavior:** Values planning, disciplines self in order to contain costs and minimize penalties, consumer sets rules, works out personal solutions, confident that he/she can do it, takes advantage of options, choices, is willing to "beat the system," emphasizes self-reliance but open to service, sets priorities for expenditures of three important resources—time, money, effort

Concerns with upward mobility in the 1950s gave way to an emphasis on self-fulfillment in the 1960s and 1970s. The materialism of the early 1980s is expected to be tempered with concern for emotional fulfillment by decade's end.

nies sweep beyond our continent and around the world, we note the similarities in market development. We see, for example, European and Asian countries now accepting convenience foods and products; South America in need of hardware and durables; and Africa crying for the basic necessities. All that has been learned in U.S.A.-style marketing (after all, we *are* the greatest test market of all) can be applied with full vigor in these developing world markets.

Changing patterns of competition not only are altering the role of U.S. industry in the world picture but also are changing the structure of American business. With mergers with and buyouts by foreign companies, management may be placed in the hands of people who are not U.S. citizens. Also, as technology speeds forward, new products may be developed that become obsolete before they can be marketed. It becomes imperative for executives of U.S. companies to equip themselves to compete in the world arena. They must pay particular attention to the ever-changing tides of international trade. Moreover, there will be an increasing need for experts on foreign trade on company payrolls.

Strategic Marketing

"Strategic marketing" is the new buzzword among top executives who are moving toward greater professionalism and integration in corporate operations. This is suggested in a study by management consultants at the accounting firm of Coopers and Lybrand and reported in *Marketing News*.

The study, performed in conjunction with researchers at Yankelovich, Skelly and White, indicates that marketing finally is getting its due in the executive suite. While only 29 percent of executives believed marketing was the most important management area in 1983, 64 percent now hold that opinion, concludes the study based on personal interviews with 140 chief executive officers (CEOs) and other top executives.

"Strategic marketing, marketing strategies, and market plans which help corporations hold or develop a competitive advantage have become paramount management challenges and major unresolved business issues," write the authors.

The majority of those surveyed said they planned significant increases in marketing research to help them reach the right market niches in the most cost-effective manner possible. Additionally, 62 percent of high-tech firms and 40 percent of industrial and services companies plan to increase budgets for market planning staffs and corporate marketing programs.

Chief executives have assumed hands-on control of strategic planning, but they plan to leave marketing strategy to the professionals. However, those professionals are being drawn from the marketing ranks only in the consumer products sector; industrial and services companies are apt to tap marketing leaders from other sectors of the management team, rather than hire marketing experts from other economic sectors.

Among consumer goods companies, the shift is on from mature, less profitable "big brands" toward a multitude of new products with high profit margins targeted at specific groups. "Managers at consumer product companies need to decide what to do with their mature brands," observed Samuel A. Ruello, partner in charge of Coopers & Lybrand's New York office. "As they look beyond their mature brands, they're making severe fundamental changes in their marketing function."

Some firms are scrapping brand management in favor of greater centralization, allowing senior marketing managers to allocate resources as they see fit. Funds are being marshaled on a need and opportunity basis, rather than as a proportion of brand revenues.

Others are seeking market niches which are reachable through existing distribution channels and affluent enough to warrant special attention. Still others are using collaborative arrangements, strategic acquisitions, and other outside resources to speed development and production of new products.

Unlike industrial and services firms, consumer goods companies have institutionalized marketing research as part of their marketing programs, Ruello pointed out, routinely using research to track sales, register market share shifts, track consumer attitude changes, and predict market acceptance of new products before full rollout.

Customers' needs, wants, and desires long have been management concerns at consumer goods firms, and that same marketing focus is becoming the standard at high-tech, industrial, and services firms, as well. "All the industry groups we studied were encumbered by traditional management and marketing practices that stunt long-term growth and reduce potential profit levels," said Ruello. "CEOs are now becoming aware that they need to redefine and improve their marketing and market planning orientations—or suffer the consequences."

CEOs intend to get closer to their customers by forging a closer link between marketing and strategic planning, thereby elevating marketing to equal status with other corporate functions in the process.

Two-thirds of consumer and industrial companies plan to increase their new-product development budgets; 33 percent of industrial and high-tech firms and 50 percent of consumer and services companies intend to boost product-specific advertising and promotions. Development projects are being subjected to more rigorous scrutiny from a marketing and financial perspective, Ruello said, with fewer firms giving free reign to engineering and research and development.

Blueprints for Marketing Success

We've looked at many factors having an impact and influence on the changing marketplace. Now let's look at some guidelines and thoughts expressed by sales and marketing professionals for making the whole thing work.

"At least six indispensable ingredients are necessary for marketing effectiveness and success" according to an economic and marketing research expert.

- *People* are the most important part of an aggressive organization. They must be creative, confident, and courageous, and routinely exercise sound judgment.

- *Products* must be appealing to future customers and establish an image of uniqueness and superior quality over competitive entries.

- *Productivity* (a key to profits) needs to maximize the efficient use of both labor and capital, including foreign sourcing where the cost-saving factors outweigh the elements of risk and distance.

- *Places* are vital in that products must be readily available both where and when customers want them.

Table 5. What Factors are the Most Important in Running a Quality Selling Operation?

Characteristics	% Saying	
	Extremely Important	Very Important
Reputation among customers	**76.9%**	19.2%
Holding old accounts	**61.5**	36.1
Quality of management	**51.5**	40.7
Ability to keep top salespeople	**44.6**	43.1
Product/technical knowledge	**37.7**	46.1
Innovativeness	**37.7**	38.4
Quality of training	**34.6**	54.6
Opening new accounts	**33.8**	48.8
Meeting sales targets	**26.9**	46.9
Frequency of calls/territory coverage	**14.6**	41.5

- *Prices* should be at a level that will be considered a good value by customers and at the same time be profitable at reasonable volumes to producers and to the distributions system.

- *Promotions* should include "attention-getting" and "action-stimulating" advertising, as well as "newsworthy" public relations and exhibits.

"An effective mixture of these six indispensable ingredients will add up to greater long-range *profits!*"

Qualities of a Solid Sales Operation

Finally, what characteristics are the most important in the making of a top-notch sales force?

"Reputation among customers" and "holding old accounts" ranked highest in a Best Sales Force survey conducted by *Sales and Marketing Management*. The results are graphically displayed in Table 5, above.

One respondent, a director of marketing, defined "reputation" as "identifying the product, the quality of service. It's kind of an all-inclusive category."

If the responses of "extremely important" and "very important" categories are combined, we find that "reputation among customers," "holding old accounts" and "quality of management" all scored above the 90 percent level. All are key factors in making and maintaining a solid sales operation now and in the future.

Chapter 2

The Sales Manager's Job

Management of the sales organization provides one of the most complex, varied and challenging opportunities in the modern company.

As marketing management evolved, a significantly broader meaning has been attached to sales management to the extent that it encompasses two broad areas:

1. *Managing the sales function,* including sales planning and control, sales policies, distribution methods and channels, and market analysis and planning;

2. *Managing the sales force,* including recruiting and selection, training, motivating, compensating, and directing of salespeople.

To this end, this *Handbook* treats each broad area separately and extensively.

Sales, and the revenue and profits that they generate, are the life blood, the *raison d'etre,* of a company. The sales manager is, in fact, the spearhead for the company's major objective—*profit making.*

Wide Scope of Responsibilities

As already stated, the changing marketplace had demanded a broader scope of responsibilities, thus blurring the lines between marketing and sales management functions in many companies. This is evidenced in the results of a survey by Sales and Marketing Executives–International. This organization surveyed its membership in a wide cross-section of American business on the functions with which they are personally concerned. The following list of these functions (compiled in the study) shows the wide scope of the sales manager's job today:

- Sales estimates and sales quotas
- Sales control; control of volume, margins, and expenses
- Sales territories and routing
- Supervision of field sales organization
- Selecting channels of distribution
- Pricing and pricing policies
- Sales budgeting
- Market research and planning
- Liaison between sales and other departments
- Supervision of headquarter's sales organization
- Product policy
- Discount policy
- Advertising
- Special selling terms
- Dealer aids and other promotional programs
- Guaranty and service policies
- Branding and trademark policies
- Style and design policy
- Materials used in product
- Containers and packaging

In this regard, it is worth noting the results of a survey of 900 first-line sales managers in 15 different businesses conducted by Jerry Harrison, a distinguished member of the National Society of Sales Training Executives. The sales forces involved had an average number of 15 to 20 salespeople per manager.

It was found that the average total time spent in coaching/developing salespeople was 10 percent. Assuming a 40-hour week with 20 salespeople, this allowed *12 minutes per person per week.* Assuming a 60-hour week, time allowed increased six minutes or *18 minutes per person per week.*

In answer to the obvious question as to why more time could not be allotted to working directly with salespeople, 12 reasons or job duty roles were cited as the time-consumers:

- Market manager
- Planner/forecaster
- Company spokesman
- Task force leader
- Financial manager
- Product department coordinator
- Recruiter
- Product service complaint handler
- Order expediter
- Report writer
- Competitive action analyzer
- Personal sales quota

A further analysis identified the following factors or influences contributing to the field sales manager's "problem perspective":

- Recruiting
- Quota allocation
- Late reports
- Lack of prospects
- Product service
- Customer complaints
- Wrong products

- Order processing
- Expenses up
- People conflicts
- Competition
- Sales planning
- Training
- Paperwork

And what does the chief executive expect from his top marketer? A chairman of the board and former president of a national consumer products company outlined his requirements as follows.

- My top marketing person must be smart enough to know his or her objectives and strong enough not to be distracted from them.

- He or she must be a bold innovator—not only sensitive to changes in the marketplace but also capable of anticipating the unstated needs of the consumer.

- He or she must have the courage to make decisions in the face of uncertainty, and defend them against criticism and second guessing from others, including myself.

- How do you judge the marketing person in action? Looking hard at this question, one word comes to my mind — *results.* But certain questions can be asked about any marketing operation:

- How long does it take to move from the idea to the product to the marketplace? Are we doing this faster than competition?

- How well-positioned are we to make strategic adjustments within the marketing program to meet competitive actions?

- Do we beat competition to the punch a fair share of the time? That is, do we develop our share of product 'firsts'?

- Is the long-range marketing plan clearly defined? In other words, do we know just what we're trying to achieve and how we expect to do so?

- While I would expect marketing objectives to be in practical alignment with business trends, I would also expect marketing objectives to be sprinkled with imaginative thinking about the shape of things to come.

- It has been said that a marketing genius is one who shoots at something no one else can see—and hits it. This portrays the successful marketing executive. He or she is possessed with the ability to imagine and do the unexpected. And I believe it is the duty of the chief executive officer to create an atmosphere for bold innovation.

All of these views highlight the diversity and wide span of responsibilities of the sales manager as a company executive. This diversity is dependent upon the type of organization, the product(s) or service(s) sold, and the method of distribution used.

Job Summary and Duties

The following job description illustrates the diverse responsibilities typically assigned to the sales manager.

JOB SUMMARY

Plans, controls, and directs activities of the field sales personnel to obtain maximum sales volume, achieve plans, and to develop maximum potential volume from the markets for the corporation's products. Acts within the scope of corporate objectives and policies to accomplish assigned goals. Plans, controls, and directs financial planning and budgets that correspond to volume goals at most profitable levels. Includes manpower complement. Ensures adequate distribution of the product line with a minimum out-of-stock position. Responsible for the selection and training of personnel to ensure long-term employment and department effectiveness.

JOB DUTIES

Specific duties of a sales manager include the following:

1. Directs all field sales personnel within limits of corporate and sales department policies, to achieve assigned sales objectives.

2. Formulates and recommends policies and objectives to ensure the most effective operation of field sales activities. Sees that approved policies and objectives are fully understood by all personnel under his or her direction.

3. Directs sales planning in conjunction with the headquarter staff, which includes an analysis of competitive products and selling techniques, consumer research, marketing legislation, sales budgets, and quotas.

4. Administers sales budget preparation and evaluates performance against approved budget objectives.

5. Directs sales service activities, develops and maintains favorable relations with customers, and sees that satisfactory customer service is provided.

6. Directs and plans changes, with approval, in sales organization required for achievement of sales objectives. Ensures that all sales personnel are trained to perform their jobs effectively.

7. Supervises the development of estimates of sales and reviews and approves forecasts of sales by the field force.

8. Directs the reporting of and appraises the results of each authorized sales program against planned objectives and takes appropriate action.

9. Directs the constant appraisal of pricing, distribution, promotion, and other policies and procedures; recommends such changes as would improve effectiveness in obtaining the objectives of the company.

10. Sees that all orders and other customer communications are promptly and accurately handled. Ensures appropriate action on customer service problems.

11. As required, directs arrangements for participation in trade conventions.

12. Establishes and maintains top-level contact with the management of existing and potential customers.

13. Prepares, analyzes, and approves all expense budgets for sales personnel.

14. Responsible for ensuring that customers are current with 30-day terms policy.

15. Effectively manages the sales office and all allocations, center expenses, etc.

16. Responsible for management of allocations among districts and achieving planned sales.

Periodic Evaluation

Along with coping with the day-to-day demands of the job, some means must be devised to check all the facets of sales management execution for review and update. The following checklist was developed over the years by the Dartnell staff as a means to check the effectiveness of the operation. It would be worthwhile to run this list against current activities at least every six months or, better yet, on a quarterly basis.

EVALUATION CHECKLIST

Staff—Sales-Management Group

1. Does background and ability of all department heads fit 90 percent or more of the requirements set by job specifications?

2. Are all department heads working together in reasonable harmony?

3. Is each department head training a possible successor?

4. Is turnover of trainees, assistants, or other employees excessive in any one department? In the management staff as a whole?

5. Does one executive have full responsibility for forward planning from the sales and comprehensive policy position?

6. What is the degree of coordination between sales policies and advertising and production policies?

7. Are members of the sales-management group selected solely on merit and accomplishment?

8. Is each member of the group able to understand current competitive threats?

9. Does each member of the group recognize current and future potentials for enlarging markets and shares of markets?

10. Does executive compensation plan provide incentives to spur accomplishment of top-management objectives?

11. Is top sales executive (or company officer responsible for sales) aware of and able to use motivation devices appropriate to the people he or she directs and the conditions under which they work?

12. Are changes in, or additions to, the sales-management staff planned to strengthen or improve it during the next year or two?

    (If necessary, insert additional factors considered vital to the effective and progressive operation of this phase of your business.)

Staff—Sales Operating Group

1. Is field manpower adequate in number?

2. Is field manpower adequate in quality?

3. What is being done to improve effectiveness of first-line salespeople?

4. Does each territory or division have a good sales-recruiting program?

5. Does each territory or division have a good sales-selection program?

6. Is our sales training program adequate for current needs in each territory or division?

7. Is morale of the sales force at a satisfactory level in each territory or division?

8. If morale of salespeople is not satisfactory, do we know what to do to find and remedy factors which have a negative effect on productivity?

9. Are our channels of communication between the sales-management staff and field sales force adequate for today's conditions?

10. If channels of communication are adequate, are we using them with maximum effectiveness?

11. Have we recently checked into the effectiveness of the sales methods and techniques used by our salespeople in their daily selling contacts?

12. If these methods are considered satisfactory for today's requirements, what is planned ahead for improvement and application to conditions and problems we will be facing in the next two years?

13. Are the sales tools, manuals, exhibits, and similar equipment used by our sales force adequate for today's needs?

14. What is being planned for their improvement?

15. Do we explain to each salesperson how quotas are calculated and why they are important?

16. If we are doubtful about the accuracy or utility of our present quota system, what is being done about improving or replacing it?

17. Do our sales records, at the regional or divisional level nearest point of contact with the buyer, provide adequate control to assure that good accounts can't be lost before the danger of such loss is brought to the attention of the management people responsible for results?

18. Do we have some method for periodic merit review of field salespeople by their immediate supervisors?

19. If not, do we have factors in our compensation plan which provide incentives for steady and continuing improvement of sales performance?

20. If the answers to questions 18 and 19 are both "no,"—are our first-line sales supervisors able to constantly inspire salespeople to better efforts in the absence of these factors?

Policies

1. Are all major policies clearly stated, dated, and circulated to all those concerned?

2. Does a standard procedure exist for policy review?

3. Is it clearly understood which executives are responsible for establishing policy in given areas?

4. Are sales personnel in the field and on the first line of supervision consulted when decisions about policies are under consideration?

5. Do we have a clear-cut, comprehensive marketing policy for the company as a whole?

6. Does each unit or division within the company have a basic policy established for guidance and control?

7. Has our master marketing policy been stated in terms of what it means to our buyers and those who use or consume our product or service?

8. Do we have a well-understood pricing policy?

9. Does our pricing policy contain elements that enable us to make healthy adjustments, when necessary, within a framework consistent with the best long-term interests of all concerned?

10. Have we taken steps to "sell" our pricing policy to our own executives, sales supervisors, and salespeople?

11. Is the authority for making pricing decisions assigned to the executive responsible for the profit contribution of the product, service, or division?

12. Have we recently compared our pricing policies with those of our competitors and with those used by other companies of similar size and nature in other industries?

13. Are we constantly studying the pricing policies successfully used by leaders in all fields to determine which elements in them might find profitable application to our problems?

14. Have we allowed financial, production, or other executives to assume influence or power in making price policy?

15. Is it possible that these influences from other departments are leading to price policies which will have a negative effect on sales or profits?

16. Have we established some channels for wholesalers, dealers, or other links in the chain of distribution, to express their ideas to us about price and other policies?

17. Are we interested in what the end user or consumer thinks about our price policy?

18. Have we discussed our marketing and price policies with our public relations counsel?

19. If not, have we considered the public relations aspects of the impact of these policies? Since they have been established, have we reviewed possible changes in public opinion?

20. Has our marketing policy been "sold" internally to engineering, production, and all other personnel in terms of what it means to them?

21. Has our marketing policy been translated into quality and performance terms for use in stimulating production employees to improve quality and performance?

Programs—Marketing

1. Do we know where our company as a whole stands today in relation to our competitors?

2. Do we have similar information for each product, service, or division?

3. Have we established what our next goals should be?

4. Do we know how we are going to get there?

5. Have we recently tabulated our sales by product for as many years as data are available?

6. Have we compared these figures with total sales in the industry and with similar figures of our strongest competitors?

7. Have we made similar comparisons on a price-per-unit basis?

8. Have we plotted these elements on a graph to show the relationships between costs, volume, and price per unit?

9. Are we using the significance of such comparisons and relationships in our advance marketing planning?

10. Did we recently review our marketing program with a fair amount of objectivity?

11. Do we occasionally review marketing programs with the aid of qualified individuals who were not personally involved in the development of original plans?

12. Before deciding on marketing programs, do we double-check for possible information sources that may be influenced by a natural bias? (Such as market data furnished by media representatives who are more interested in selling space, programs, etc., than in supplying unvarnished facts that may not favor their special case.)

13. Have we checked our established and potential markets to find out if any shifts have occurred?

14. Have we analyzed any changes that seem likely to occur in the demand for our products by our principal customers or accounts?

15. Have we reappraised with care the adequacy of channels of distribution used in the past?

16. Do we know whether conditions have changed enough to warrant a revision of distribution channels?

17. Before making any changes, do we give careful consideration to factors that may show that unsatisfactory results may be due to poor utilization of a distribution channel, rather than to any fault or lack in the channel as such?

18. Have we checked our price structure to locate any special areas which price-conscious competitors could select as "soft-targets" to aim at?

19. Did we review our discount policies to see if they meet today's conditions with realism or are they merely a set of figures most people accept as a tradition?

20. Do we make it a regular practice to analyze accounts for the "profit contribution factor"?

21. Have we been making progress toward the improvement of "profit contribution factor"?

22. Did we set standards for controlling the costs of servicing accounts of various sizes?

23. Do we know if the use of such standards is bringing us a satisfactory increase in profits?

24. Are present facilities adequate to supply and service the preferred customers and prospects who are the targets of our marketing plan?

25. Have we made provision for adequate supervision of the sales force needed for the success of the marketing plan?

26. Are we planning to develop and improve these supervisors so that they will be well equipped to help their salespeople meet and beat the increasingly keen competition that is expected?

27. Are we planning to help our wholesalers, dealers, jobbers, etc., overcome the problems they expect to face in the next two years?

28. Did we check marketing-staff personnel to ensure timely availability of specialists and others with the skills needed to implement the marketing plan?

29. Did we review and evaluate the present mailing list of customers and prospects?

30. Did we set up a plan to add new names to the mailing list?

31. Do we have an effective direct-mail program?

32. Did we set up a plan for periodic review, correction, and improvement of catalogs, displays, presentations, samples, etc., to be used in selling?

33. Is one person in charge of the above activity?

34. Is our advertising agency making a first-rate contribution to our marketing program?

35. Have we given our agency an adequate description and explanation of our marketing program?

36. Have we established a centralized liaison link between our advertising agency and our top marketing executive?

37. If our advertising agency is primarily "media-minded," is the marketing function adequately represented by one or more marketing specialists in our own top executive positions?

38. If this is not the case, do we encourage our executives to consult with or retain the services of first-rate marketing counsel?

39. If we have reason to suspect that competitors (both within and from outside our own industry) are likely to make faster progress than we expect to make in the use of advanced marketing techniques, are we taking precautionary steps to ensure quick availability and utility of plans to take necessary countermeasures?

40. Have we established a policy for evaluating whether or not we should undertake a vigorous program for the development of new products?

41. If we are looking for new products, have we established a "yardstick" of important factors the new product or service must offer?

42. In evaluating new products, do we consider the possible profit contribution as an important factor?

43. Have we established "break-even" points for our present products or services?

44. Do we know, from our "break-even" information, at what point it pays us to invest additional sales-promotion dollars to "buy" unit volume calculated to produce a high (or above-average) profit return per dollar of sales volume?

45. Do we have some method of determining how a new product will change our "break-even" points?

46. Have we considered the possible advantages of seeking new products sold through different channels, or to markets that

stand a good chance of improving or remaining stable, if our present markets should suffer a setback?

47. If our present method of distribution relies heavily on the ability of others to establish our product or brand recognition with the eventual buyer or user, should we consider the possible advantages of doing more and better advertising and promotion work aimed directly at the buyer or user?

48. If the above is desirable but subject to limiting factors, have we considered the advantages to be gained from more careful selection of distributors, with renewed emphasis on their ability to meet our requirements for better recognition at the point of sale?

49. Have we recently reviewed the possible advantages to be gained by setting up more effective distributors by some program which would put them under more control in areas we know are vital?

50. Did we recently review our total distribution pattern to discover possible areas of duplication or neglect which were allowed to develop because of conditions which have since changed?

51. Have we given serious consideration to benefits to be derived from a continuing study of the actual results of our marketing program compared with the long-range intent of our marketing policies?

52. If the day-to-day operations of the sales force have developed resentments or antagonism toward the company on the part of some wholesalers, dealers, or users, are we aware of the nature and extent of these feelings?

53. Do we have a method for determining our cost of sales as a percent of sales?

54. Can we prepare a comparison schedule showing the trend in our cost of sales as a percent of sales compared to a similar trend of costs as experienced by our major competitors?

55. Is our cost-of-sales factor under control?

56. In the last two years, have we introduced new models, brought out new products, or given other evidence of ability to innovate or develop advanced ideas?

57. If we have been considered leaders in our line, is this leadership being threatened?

58. If we have been consistently gaining on the leaders in our line, have we maintained our rate of gain with some consistency?

59. If steady progress is our goal, have we taken steps to make all executives and employees aware of this?

Programs—Contact Selling

1. Is our recruiting program delivering an adequate supply of qualified candidates for contact-selling jobs?

2. Do we have a recruiting policy and a consistent program geared to current needs?

3. Have we given serious consideration to encouraging the development of and seeking out of those company employees who might be good prospects for contact-selling jobs?

4. Do we have a carefully planned and well-supervised sales selection procedure?

5. Does this procedure bring the supervisor, under whom the salesperson will work, into the interviewing and final selection steps?

6. Do we know our rate of turnover and reasons why those salespeople who leave us make the decision to do so?

7. Do we have a good idea of what this turnover rate is costing us?

8. Have we recently checked turnover rates to see if we are "in line" for our type of selling and to determine how those with better rates achieved them?

9. If some of our field supervisors have higher turnover rates than others, are we investigating causes?

10. Is our sales compensation plan in step with the times?

11. Does our sales compensation plan provide some form of incentive as a reward for better-than-average performance?

12. If not, are we able to make our salespeople feel that chances for advancement, prestige, or other nonfinancial rewards are worthy of serious study and work?

13. Are we avoiding the error of training salespeople and then losing them to our competitors?

14. Have we found a way to build for the future by developing people who eventually go into business for themselves either selling or using our products; or who are sought by our distributors as valuable employees?

15. Do we have some form of systematic merit review for our salespeople?

16. Do we have a system for finding out the vital statistics for territories and individual sales performance?

17. Does this system reveal for the individual salesperson the average number of calls required per sale by customer?

18. Does this system show, promptly, sales performance against quota?

19. Does this system allow periodic review of selling costs by territory, by salesperson; and if necessary by product, city, or type of customer?

20. Does our system show progress against plans for selling new products or setting up new accounts?

21. If we require salespeople to send in reports, do we have records of their receipt and provisions for acknowledgement?

22. Have we recently surveyed reports and other paperwork required from salespeople to see what can be eliminated or reduced to provide more time and attention for active selling?

23. Do we encourage our supervisors to work with their people in the field?

24. Do we provide inspirational and instructive opportunities to our salespeople so that those who want to improve skills and performance have guidance and encouragement?

25. Do we sometimes consult with our supervisors and ask them for ideas and suggestions; and by this means encourage them to do the same with their people?

26. Do we provide training and development opportunities for older or "advanced" salespeople as well as for beginners and newcomers?

27. Do we provide a sales manual that actually helps our salespeople?

28. Is our sales training based mostly on the real needs of our salespeople?

29. Do we have some effective method of evaluating the effectiveness of our sales training efforts?

30. Is each member of our sales force kept completely and promptly informed about every product improvement, price change, and other data?

31. Do we make every possible effort to personally sell each salesperson on our product?

32. Do we take special pains to put our salespeople on all mailing lists to receive material being sent to customers, stockholders, and employees?

33. Do we make an honest and consistent effort to get sales-people to feel that they are a part of the company as a whole and not just "outside people" with different interests?

34. Do we constantly encourage our salespeople by words and examples to make the best use of selling time?

35. Do we require our supervisors to be readily available to their people?

36. Do we encourage our supervisors to stay at least one step ahead of their people by being outstanding pace-setters and real leaders?

37. Do we set high yet obtainable standards for individual per-formance goals?

38. Are we sure our supervisors know how to assign people to the selling jobs for which they are best fitted?

39. Do our records, forms, systems, etc., lend themselves to the production of clearly understandable job assignments?

40. Have we provided our sales supervisors with systems and procedures that give them the means to hold good control over the activities of their people?

41. Is each supervisor held responsible for the results manage-ment has asked him or her to produce?

42. Does each supervisor hold his or her people responsible for the results they are assigned to produce?

43. Are supervisors trained to analyze and locate causes of trou-ble rather than to be content with constantly treating the symptoms?

44. Do we require a periodic check to see that each salesperson has all the necessary sales tools and aids required for his or her job?

45. Do we require a periodic check to see that all salespeople are using these tools and aids properly?

46. If a sales tool or aid can be proved unnecessary or inefficient, do we have a procedure for withdrawing or replacing it?

47. Are we always careful to avoid even the appearance of playing favorites?

48. Do our supervisors thoroughly understand the meaning of turnover and do we supply them with adequate information to direct salespeople's efforts where and when needed to have the best influence on turnover (if "turnover" is a factor in our operation)?

49. Have our salespeople been trained enough, or do they have ample experience, in the use of turnover pros and cons when speaking to customers and prospects?

50. Do we supply special visuals aids, surveys, reports, testimonials, and similar items designed to emphasize the plus benefits of turnover qualities associated with our products?

51. Have we established a good system for developing a steady flow of prospects for our salespeople?

52. Have we been able to train and develop our salespeople to find their own prospects?

53. Do we have some method of dividing leads, or names of prospects, fairly among all members of the sales force?

54. In the development of new business, do we have definite standards by which to qualify it and specific minimum order limits?

55. Are we constantly striving to train our salespeople to sell benefits rather than things?

56. Have we satisfied ourselves that those who train our salespeople have access to information they need to place heavy emphasis on benefits in ways that meet the needs of possible buyers?

57. Does our training program include attention to ways and means of handling the difficult buyer?

58. Do we also stress techniques of overcoming objections?

59. Do we have at least one tested and proved procedure recommended for closing the sale?

60. Do our salespeople understand, fully, the details of how delivery promises are made?

61. If such promises must be changed, do we have a way of notifying both salesperson and customer?

62. Have our salespeople been briefed on credit policies and practices?

63. Do our salespeople understand our guarantee and know how to explain it as a customer benefit?

64. Do our salespeople thoroughly understand service problems that may arise and are they in a position to help customers get assistance or action?

65. Do our salespeople know effective methods for handling customer complaints in accordance with company policies?

66. Whenever we establish a policy within our own department, do we make a habit of putting it in writing and circulating it to all concerned?

67. Do we make a steady effort to be impartial when setting up and assigning selling territories?

68. To keep this reputation for impartiality, do we do our best not to reduce a territory without an especially good reason?

69. If it should be necessary to take a good account out of a territory, do we make every possible effort to substitute an even better one in its place?

70. Do we have good reason to believe it would increase profits if we supply our customers with certain aids in using or reselling our product?

71. Does our sales force thoroughly understand the uses and benefits of our customer-aid materials?

72. Do we have some way of checking on the results obtained when salespeople are supposed to be giving special attention to customer aids?

73. Do we have a good method for reading all sales reports and sending prompt replies or acknowledgments back to the field?

74. Do we make a special effort to run sales meetings that hold interest, stimulate the individual, and deliver a desired result?

75. If we run contests, do we take special pains to base the awards on a fair relationship of "prize points" to dollars of sales revenue?

76. In running contests, are we careful to avoid the type where only a few top people win and all others get nothing?

77. When we participate in trade association or similar convention activities, do we look for opportunities to broaden the contacts and experience of the salespeople most likely to benefit from participation?

78. Have we found a way to make "exhibit duty" an honor and a challenge rather than a task to be ducked?

79. If packaging is important to our product, have we been doing a good job of improving the salesperson's ability to talk and think in packaging terms that will help his or her customers?

Organization

1. Is the sales and marketing function adequately represented in the top-management group?

2. Have we considered the advantages to be gained from inviting top executives from other departments to attend meetings and other activities which will increase their knowledge and understanding of sales and marketing?

3. Does an up-to-date organization chart exist for the sales department?

4. Does this chart clearly show line-and-staff relationships?

5. Does this chart show definite areas of responsibility and authority?

6. Have we recently given serious consideration as to whether or not our functional and geographic groupings of the organization are best designed to serve current and future requirements?

7. Where geographic groupings exist, are we sure they were determined on sound marketing principles?

8. Where functional groupings exist, are we sure they were determined on sound marketing principles?

9. If some of these groupings originated through the special abilities or influences of individuals, have we considered how new developments might make different groupings, based on sounder principles, safer and more advantageous?

10. Is each sales manager's sphere of operations set up so that the profitability factor for each division or product is accurately known at all times?

11. Have we recently studied what might be gained from organizing all activities related to one product or service under one executive who is then completely responsible for the profit contribution of his or her division?

12. If we are now operating under a division manager pattern, have we made a recent check to see if results are following according to plan?

13. In setting up our lines of organization, did we consider the effective "span of control" for each assignment?

14. In setting up our organization, did we give adequate consideration to principles of good communications between indi-

viduals? between departments inside the sales group? between headquarters and the field? between departments outside the sales group?

15. Have we analyzed the flow of reports in theory and checked this against practice?

16. If our organization chart is just an "interesting antique curiosity," are we taking steps to remedy the situation?

17. Do we have good reasons to believe a company policy manual would be worth preparing?

18. If we already have such a manual, is it up to date?

19. Is our organization manual clear enough to be fairly well understood by a new executive during his or her first day on the job?

20. Do we make regular checks to find out whether our organization structure is so rigid it acts as a hindrance to progress?

21. Do we make a periodic check to see if our sales activity is properly focused on new or allied products recently added to our line?

22. Each time we do the above, do we consider the advantages to be gained by setting up a separate sales division for those products or services?

Sales Management by Objectives

A method of sales management that has gained some popularity over the years is *sales management by objectives* (SMBO). It is based on the system of management by objectives, which can be described as:

A process by which the superior and subordinate managers of an organization identify jointly its common goals, define each individual's major area of responsibility in terms of results expected, and use these measures as guides for operating the unit and assessing the contribution of each of its members.

Larry Apley, long-time president of the American Management Association, defined management thusly: "It means getting results through other people." Building on this, Dr. George S. Odiorne, renowned expert on sales management by objectives, states: "If you apply this to your job it means that you hold your job because somebody assumed that you would be able to pick better people than yourself, train them, motivate them to their best efforts, and produce more results than you could ever do on your own."*

HOW MANAGING DIFFERS FROM SELLING

Dr. Odiorne submits that there are eight ways in which managing is different from selling. The manager:

1. Makes things happen by a variety of ways;

2. Gets things done through other people;

3. Uses some special tools and skills called organizing, planning, controlling, evaluating, directing and coordinating, and teaching others;

4. Is measured by the performance of his or her followers, not just personal efforts;

5. Decides what should happen and surrounds himself or herself with others who will do it;

6. Makes decisions best when the decisions are fact-based and related to achieving objectives;

7. Innovates and changes the character and direction of the business. He or she decides the *right things to do,* rather than merely *doing things right;*

8. Hires better people than himself or herself, finds the resources so they can do the job, provides training and help, evaluates results, and makes changes.

---

*George S. Odiorne, *Sales Management by Objectives* Chicago: (The Dartnell Corporation, 1982), pp. 2-3.

THE IDEAL SALES MANAGEMENT SYSTEM

While experience, intuition, and savvy are not obsolete, the following guidelines are suggested for use in working toward the ideal systematic approach to sales management by objectives.

1. Define the objectives for the sales organization, both long-run and short-run.

2. Define policies and sales plans that will make others more productive.

3. Provide the resources that will help the organization to focus attention upon its objectives.

4. Make sure that everyone in the sales organization from top to bottom is crystal clear on their objectives, including quotas and standards of performance.

5. Manage compensation and other rewards in such a way that people go in your direction because they want to go.

6. Think about strategies (multi-year objectives), as well as immediate sales operations.

7. Think in terms of multi-year spans of time, as well as the immediate quotas and targets for the month ahead.

8. Relate to the outside world and to those social, economic, and political influences which can have a long-run impact on your business.

9. Allocate your resources in ways that will produce the highest yield.

10. Manage change, both in response to pressures, and in anticipation of things that will be needed but aren't yet present.

11. Teach management to your subordinate managers. You know that the rate at which your organization grows is in direct proportion to the rate at which your people grow, not only in selling but in managing sales.

12. Interpret your organization to top management, and top management to your organization.

13. Constantly appraise and evaluate your organization, making adaptive moves to keep it going toward its goals.

14. Provide the selection guidelines for bringing new people aboard and adequate training programs to bring them up to your standards. Use systems to motivate them to go in the right direction, remain with you, persist in their efforts, and constantly grow in professional competence.

THE MANAGEMENT CYCLE

Figure 1, page 56, shows how management by objective works in sequence. Start at step 1 in this cyclical system.

Dr. Odiorne suggests that the following regular, basic objectives are those with which sales managers are most commonly concerned:

1. Dollar volume per month

2. Gross profit as percent of sales month

3. Dollar output per line per month

4. Dollar output per person per month

5. Gross profit percent per line per month

6. Gross profit percent per person per month

7. Advertising as percent of sales per month

8. Dollar volume of returned goods per month

9. Number of complaints per month

10. Number of new accounts per month

11. Dollar amount of training expenses

12. Lost accounts per month

Figure 1. Management Cycle

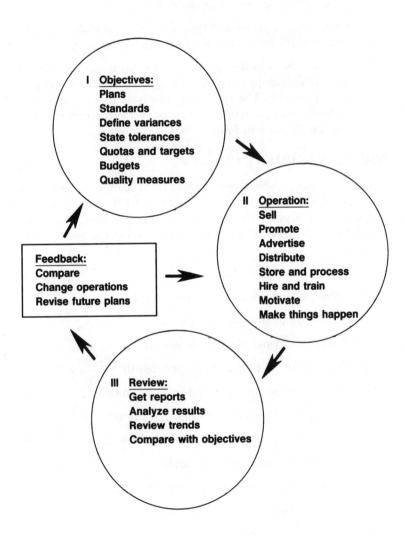

The Need for a Broad Viewpoint

The role of the sales executive in today's fast-changing and highly sophisticated marketplace is far different from what it was just a few years ago. He or she still must be able to motivate a sales staff, develop marketing programs, and forecast market trends, but he or she now must have much broader concepts in order to properly implement those functions. No longer is it possible to merely dip into the old bag of tried-and-true sales tactics. The customer has become too smart for that.

Today's successful sales manager must be attuned to the wave of changes in the marketplace and therefore must make a concerted effort not become the victim of executive isolation. Somehow, some way, the successful executive must find a way to sense the wants and desires of those for whom he or she must provide products or services.

All of us in marketing need wide-angle binoculars, not microscopes. All of us need a way to anticipate winds of consumer changes. Those who are able to sense or feel what might occur tomorrow will take command, and those people will be the ones who have broken the bondage of executive isolation.

Enjoy those in your peer group, but always remember that they are not typical of the vast majority of those you must deal with in the highly competitive and fast-moving sales arena. Gain and maintain a broad outlook and you soon will find that anticipating changes will become much easier.

Personal Professional Development

Many organizations provide the means for reviewing and improving sales management and marketing skills. For instance, many and varied seminars are offered by:

- American Management Association
  135 West 50th Street
  New York, New York 10020

- University of Chicago
  Office of Continuing Education
  5855 S. Kimbark Avenue
  Chicago, Illinois 60637

- University of Wisconsin
  Management Institute
  432 North Lake Street
  Madison, Wisconsin 53706

Many other universities and private seminar companies also offer a wide range of programs.

The Graduate School of Sales Management and Marketing sponsored by Syracuse University in cooperation with Sales & Marketing Executives-International (SME-I) offers a two-year (two weeks a year) program in June of each year. Details can be obtained from:

- Sales & Marketing Executives-International
  Statler Office Tower, Suite 446
  Cleveland, Ohio 44115

The American Marketing Association offers an annual Strategic Marketing Conference and an annual School of Sales Management plus numerous regional conferences and seminars. Contact:

- American Marketing Association
  250 South Wacker Drive
  Chicago, Illinois 60606-5819

Sales and Marketing Management and the American Management Association sponsor an annual marketing conference. Contact AMA or:

- Sales and Marketing Management
  633 Third Avenue
  New York, New York 10017

The Conference Board, 845 Third Avenue, New York, New York 10022, holds an annual marketing conference in either late October or early November in New York City.

The designations of Certified Sales Executive (CSE) and Certified Marketing Executive (CME) can be earned through the Professional Certification Program of the Accreditation Institute of Sales & Marketing Executives-International. Contact SME-I at the aforementioned address.

A Final Word

The sales manager has been aptly called "the person with three hats." He or she is responsible for showing a healthy profit on sales through marketing and sales management expertise. The sales manager is responsible to the sales force for representing their interests to management, and is responsible to the company's customers for maintaining the best possible customer relations. No managerial activity demands a broader range of skills and ability.

The traditional transition to a sales manager position has been from the ranks of the field sales force. This is a feasible path because the job requires a basic, thorough understanding and knowledge of the selling process. However, he or she goes from the world of "quota" to a world of "profit" and "cost." This requires the development of new skills, attitudes, and knowledge. It is marketing management's responsibility to provide for adequate managerial training to make the transition effective and successful.

Chapter 3

Compensation of Sales Executives And Sales Staff

Like other executives in a company, the sales executive's total compensation for a given year usually includes a base salary and bonus, plus supplemental income in the form of a stock option, profit-sharing, retirement plan, and enhanced insurance programs. Additionally, executive perquisites, such as expense accounts, company car, company-paid memberships in clubs and associations, extensive medical exams, and legal counseling are offered.

What the program, or package, consists of varies with size of company, the company's financial resources, the company's philosophy and the company's objectives and goals. The chairman of an eastern durable goods manufacturer expressed this view: "In addition to providing a good environment, we offer a competitive salary range; an incentive plan based on current performance that rewards the outstanding individual but takes full account of basic stockholder interest; a long-term stock option program; and a retirement plan that offers security to the sales executive and his or her family after retirement age."

Another view offered by the president of an electronics firm differs a bit: "The only valid rule I've found is that the real key executives are *less* interested in salary and bonus than in an opportunity to grow, financially and in job stature, as the company grows. Job security is also low on the list. The executive worth his or her pay realizes that his or her job is only as secure as he or she makes it."

Thus, while there can be differences in detail, motivation and performance are the usual bases for executive compensation plans, just as they are for salespeople.

Planning for Results

For the company to gain the greatest return on its compensation investment, it must have its objectives well in mind, and then design its compensation program to give emphasis to the attainment of those objectives, such as the following:

1. Production of maximum sales volume; for, as sales increase beyond the break-even point, profits climb rapidly

2. Production of maximum profits, which might be gained by selectivity in emphasis on product lines or on customer groups

3. Expense control, which will contribute to satisfactory profit attainment

4. Cash retainment for capital expansion, which might be achieved through maximum profits and through investment in facilities

5. Development and retention of a most efficient managerial group, which will assure the continuance of the prosperity of the company

6. Transition from centralized responsibility to decentralized management

What Management Expects

Perhaps, at a different level of analysis, we may gain an understanding of what management expects by reviewing some recent advertisements for sales executives, chosen at random from the New York *Times* and *The Wall Street Journal:*

NEWSPAPER ADS FOR
SALES AND MARKETING EXECUTIVES

National Sales Manager

Expansion minded, established manufacturer of 40 years in aerosol paints and related products is seeking an experienced, dynamic sales executive capable of accelerating our sales growth in consumer markets.

Thorough knowledge of consumer-oriented channels of distribution is essential. Knowledge of paint, chemicals, or related products will be helpful.

Position entails responsibility for establishing a new division; planning, strategies, programs, forecasts and budgets, developing and managing a new sales organization. It is a demanding position offering real opportunity.

National Sales Manager

We are a leading manufacturer operating as an autonomous subsidiary of a Fortune 500 company located in a medium size Midwestern city. Our products are sold primarily through industrial distributors.

We are seeking a degreed individual with a minimum of 5 years experience in sales and marketing management with the capacity to assume operational control of the company within a few years. The individual must possess strong leadership skills, financial acumen and expertise in industrial distribution, policy and procedure development, advertising, and marketing programs and strategies.

This position offers an excellent income program comprised of salary plus incentives, company car, and a complete fringe benefit package.

Vice-President—Sales

A leading publisher of el-hi materials is seeking an aggressive, dedicated individual with proven national sales management experience in the educational publishing field.

We publish quality supplementary texts which provide basic learning skills in the areas of regular and remedial el-hi education, special education, and adult basic education.

The successful candidate's responsibilities would include:

- Directing the sales efforts of a national sales organization consisting of a staff of four regional managers, 35–40 sales representatives, 4–6 adult ed specialists, and 6–10 per diem reps in targeted areas.

- Coordinating and directing the activities of an internal sales support staff consisting of customer service, telephone sales, and sales rep correspondents.

- Directing the activities of an internal promotion support group consisting of an advertising manager and his staff.

This executive position requires prior sales management experience at a national or substantial regional level. The company provides an attractive compensation package including a competitive base salary with substantial bonus income potential, an automobile, and excellent benefits. The position and the company are located in Austin, Texas, in the beautiful central Texas hill country. We invite you to explore this challenging opportunity by sending resume and compensation history to ....

Vice-President–Sales

Consumer durables company, subsidiary of a Fortune 500 company, is seeking a national sales executive to direct its field sales activity on a day-to-day basis. Gets the job done through regional sales managers and a force of commissioned sales representatives. Reports to vice-president of sales and marketing.

Successful candidate will come from a sales environment where a consumer product, or service, is sold directly to the customer. He or she must be a well-organized, sales-oriented leader with solid administrative skills and organizational ability.

Outstanding opportunity to work with an interesting, growing product line in a dynamic company. Desirable Midwestern city. Compensation over $60,000 plus excellent fringe benefits.

Sales and Marketing Manager

The Midwest's most dynamic plastic injection molder of dairy packaging, meat packaging, houseware products, and custom products, has an immediate opening for an individual to be responsible for researching, planning, developing, and directing formal sales and marketing programs for new and existing products that meet the growth and profit requirements of the organization; establishing and implementing formal sales forecasting procedures; assisting with customer service requirements; and creating and monitoring the performance of sales division budgets.

The position requires an individual with extensive sales and marketing experience managing company sales personnel, manufacturers' representatives and brokers; knowledge of plastic materials, including their functional characteristics; and knowledge of plastic technology, including injection molding, vacuum forming, structural foam and monaforming.

We offer an excellent complement of fully paid benefits, travel expenses, and incentives. If interested, please send resume in strict confidence to our corporate personnel office.

National Sales Manager

Billion-dollar diversified consumer packaged-goods manufacturer seeking to expand into hardware- and paint-sundries market with established and new-product lines.

We seek a national sales manager who is thoroughly experienced in hardware, sales, and sales administration. The individual will hire and develop a commissioned sales force, be based in our NYC headquarters, and probably will travel up to 50 percent of the time. This should prove to be an unusual opportunity for the qualified applicant seeking a challenge.

Vice-President—Marketing

A leading manufacturer of highly sophisticated thermoforming equipment, and a subsidiary of a major international corporation, is seeking candidates for the position of vice-president, marketing.

Reporting directly to the President, this senior staff position includes responsibility for direction of all marketing activities.

Applicants should have at least 8 years' experience in increasingly responsible marketing positions, preferably in the plastic processing equipment industry.

An education background which includes a BS/MBA combination is preferred.

A central Michigan location, close to fine recreational areas, offers an excellent environment for a family lifestyle.

Vice-President
Marketing and Sales

Securities broker-dealer, headquartered in southern California, wants a topflight marketing and sales leader. Will have responsibility for internal marketing staff and national sales organization. Securities experience required; insurance experience desired.

This is an outstanding opportunity with an industry leader and equal opportunity employer.

Marketing Manager

Our company is seeking an experienced person to head our marketing and sales effort. Must have at least five years' experience in sales, market research, data analysis, product and market expansion. A background in steel distribution or servicing the aircraft industry is preferred.

Sales and Marketing Vice-President

We are seeking a sales/marketing executive for one of our commercial refrigeration sales companies. The primary objective of the position is to plan and implement sales objectives in support of core business while also developing strategic business plans for growing a premium product brand name in other segments of the commercial refrigeration industry.

If you have at least 8 years of progressive sales management responsibility, including direction of: field sales team, internal sales administration, advertising, promotions, parts and service, and managing a multi-channeled distribution network in commercial refrigeration or food service/storage industries, then send a detailed resume outlining your work and salary history to:

National Sales Manager
Automotive Aftermarket

Our continuous expansion has created an excellent opportunity for a marketing professional within our Automotive Products Division. This person will be responsible for alternator and instrumentation sales management functions within the U.S. The individual we seek must have managed automotive aftermarket account sales in the alternator/instrumentaiton or related markets. Some technical experience and a college degree are preferred; management experience is essential.

Responsibilities will include:

- Management of a national aftermarket sales force, incentive programs, direction and career development.

- Forecasting aftermarket sales for alternator and instrumentation business.

- Development and implementation of customer strategies.

- Departmental budget responsibilities.

As a diversified and established leader within the electronics industry, we offer an attractive compensation program and an outstanding benefits package.

Motivating Factors

The need for money can be a primary force until the needs that money can buy are satisfied. After that satisfaction is fulfilled, money becomes something more—a tangible recognition for achievement. During the early 1980s, there seemed to be an undeclared race among CEOs of major corporations to see who would be the first to earn $1 million a year. Since then, the ante has risen considerably.

It is generally concluded that executives who want a larger proportion of their compensation in salary, for instance, are usually those whose present salaries are below average. They tend to be younger persons with fewer years with their companies.

Executives who are willing to accept greater incentive potential and less salary are those in fairly comfortable circumstances. They are able to take the risk of losing out on a bonus if that should happen. Age appears to be directly related to desire to postpone receipt of income.

It is interesting to note that except for lower-level supervisors, increased compensation in the form of longer vacations is least desired of all.

A University of Minnesota survey showed the following ranking of compensation preferences among executives:

1. Salary
2. Current individual incentives
3. Stock options
4. Current group incentives
5. Deferred individual incentives
6. Pensions
7. Insurance
8. Vacations

Natural competitiveness and the need for self-fulfillment are seen by corporate presidents as the motivations driving their executives, *Dun's Review* reported as a result of a study. Financial motives are generally agreed to be the most straightforward impetus, but a 300-president panel says that other ambitions and desires must be taken into account.

The presidents are almost evenly split between the competitive desire and the desire for self-fulfillment in naming the chief non-financial motive governing an executive's life. Some presidents say they hunt for "fighters," and believe that the competitive instinct is something inborn. Others think it is not only an inborn trait, but certain to "boil to the surface" in those with executive potential.

On the other hand, an equal number of presidents speak of the drive toward self-fulfillment. They seem to feel that "while top management can expect plenty of results from the 'tigers' it must generally devote more supervision to their work. By the same token, these panelists point out, the manager motivated by a desire to fulfill potential is less self-centered and, therefore, often more valuable to the company."

Compensating Marketing Executives

Executive performance and behavior is, to a large extent, controllable with a compensation plan. Different behavior and different levels of performance will result from different compensation plans. For this reason, if for no other, top-management leaders should keep in mind what it is they wish to do when they develop payment plans for their sales executives. Does the company wish to increase sales, gross margins, reduce inventories, increase its share of the market, improve its public image?

When employees are not properly motivated, their company gets short-changed by not getting the best efforts from its executives. At the same time, the executive gets short-changed because he or she could and should earn more if he or she were better measured and motivated.

It's one of the facts of business life that executive base pay usually lags behind company performance. Rewards for good performance in good years must wait until the next fiscal year begins before taking effect. Not so the bonus, however, which can be more closely and immediately related to the earnings statement. A raise in executive base pay means two things: 1) the executive has performed well in the year just ended and is suitably rewarded and 2) the company has hopes, and certainly a reasonable expectation, that he or she will continue to perform at the same level, with the same effect on the next profit report.

The General Sales Executive

As head of the sales or marketing department, the general manager has overall responsibility for all its activities and all the people in it. The activities vary, however, from company to company, depending on whether or not such functions as advertising, sales promotion, market research, product management, and the rest are under the charge of other executives.

Of the companies taking part in a Dartnell survey, advertising is the direct responsibility of the general sales manager in 34 percent, market research in 33 percent. Pricing of products or services is among this executive's functions in 32 percent of the companies surveyed.

What Do Sales Managers Earn?

Respondents to Dartnell's *24th Biennial Survey of Sales Force Compensation* reported that the national sales manager was paid a median average of $68,098 in total compensation. A breakdown of the contributing elements of salary and incentive pay are shown below in "full range," "range of the middle half," and "average of the middle half" categories. The "middle half" excludes the bottom 25 percent and top 25 percent of the full range of responses.

	Full Range	Range of the Middle Half	Average
Salary	$12,000-$150,000	$40,000-$70,000	$54,287
Incentive	2,000- 170,000	7,000- 20,625	13,645
Total Compensation	22,000- 220,000	51,304- 85,000	68,098

The regional sales manager earned a median average of $55,698 in total compensation. A similar breakdown is shown below.

	Full Range	Range of the Middle Half	Average
Salary	$ 7,000-$100,000	$35,000-$50,000	$42,800
Incentive	500- 210,000	7,000- 25,000	14,397
Total Compensation	15,400- 260,000	45,000- 70,000	55,698

The range of compensation in selected industries for both the national sales manager and the regional sales manager is shown in Tables 1 and 2, pages 70 and 71.

Sales' Share of the Sales Dollar

As an approach to establishing minimum and maximum salaries for the sales personnel, it is desirable to break down the sales dollar. What part of every sales dollar can a business afford to spend for sales administration, and how should that portion be divided by sales administrative functions? Opinions and practice on this point vary greatly, of course. They vary according to the type of business, the size of the sales operation, and the fairness of the management. They vary, too, according to the capacity of the individual at present holding these positions. But for the purpose of job evaluation, the ability or lack of ability of executives now holding these positions should be disregarded in setting minimum and maximum rates. In other words, there should be an established minimum and maximum for each sales job, and whether an incumbent executive is entitled to the minimum, the maximum, or a salary in between should be determined by his or her ability to get results.

On top of a base salary, provision should be made for some form of *contingent* compensation — compensation that is contingent upon an executive making certain things happen. In no case should the total compensation exceed the maximum that management has determined the business can afford to pay for that particular sales job. Such determinations should, of course, be dependent upon sales volume reaching the break-even point.

Table 1. National Sales Manager

	Average Annual Compensation Selected Industries			
Industry	Companies Reporting	Salary	Incentive	Total Compensation
Aerospace	2	$71,000	$ 2,000	$73,000
Automotive parts/Accessories	3	58,333	10,000	68,333
Auto and truck	2	53,000	10,000	63,000
Building materials	5	53,333	12,667	66,000
Chemicals	8	75,000	19,000	94,000
Computer products/Services	14	45,750	15,375	61,125
Electrical equipment/Supplies	6	55,750	9,500	65,250
Electronics	10	56,333	18,750	75,083
Fabricated metal products	15	51,749	16,679	68,428
Food products	8	57,500	9,800	67,300
General machinery	4	52,500	9,000	61,500
Healthcare products/Services	18	55,500	16,292	71,792
Instruments/Allied products	2	55,000	16,500	71,500
Office machinery/Equipment	2	57,500	20,000	77,500
Paper/Allied products	2	70,000	16,500	86,500
Printing	6	53,113	9,000	62,113
Publishing	4	42,152	12,000	54,152
Radio and television	3	42,233	27,333	69,666
Rubber, plastics, leather	3	60,333	20,000	80,333
Service industries	10	32,167	14,750	46,917
Textile and apparel	3	66,415	21,104	87,519
Tools and hardware	2	52,500	14,500	67,000

Table 2. Regional Sales Manager

Average Annual Compensation
Selected Industries

Industry	Companies Reporting	Salary	Incentive	Total Compensation
Appliances (household)	3	$46,000	$ 8,333	$ 54,333
Automotive parts/Accessories	3	61,000	80,667	141,667
Building materials	9	45,660	15,375	61,035
Chemicals	8	55,500	10,250	65,750
Computer products/Services	12	32,167	23,857	56,024
Electronics	8	40,000	10,180	50,180
Fabricated metal products	14	43,350	12,117	55,467
Food products	5	37,667	11,667	49,334
General machinery	5	48,667	30,000	78,667
Healthcare products/Services	22	46,227	14,000	60,227
Instruments/Allied products	4	36,500	21,500	58,000
Office machinery/Equipment	5	43,000	47,333	90,333
Petroleum/Petroleum products	4	43,500	4,250	47,750
Service industries	11	38,200	42,750	80,950
Transportation	7	45,500	10,500	56,000

Variations in What Constitutes Sales Expense

It is important to bear in mind that not all companies include the same items or functions as sales expense. This tendency to variation makes difficult a hard-and-fast breakdown of the selling dollar.

For example, one company may consider outgoing freight costs as a cost of distribution (selling expense), while another may classify freight as a production cost. These differences of classification arise because of the divergence of opinions as to where production stops and distribution begins.

Logic suggests that production should be considered finished and sales costs begun at the moment when the product is ready for shipment to customers or ready for placement in the finished inventory. But this does not completely solve the problem, since the question of warehousing and handling the finished product still may be charged to production by some companies and to sales by others.

One method of fixing the selling price, and working back from that to the compensation of the sales staff, is to call the production cost 33⅓ percent; the selling cost 33⅓ percent; the overhead and profit 33⅓ percent. This method is used in marketing specialties where the selling cost is about equal to the production cost of a product. In breaking down the one-third that is allocated for selling expense, which we will call 100 percent, the salesperson gets one-third, another third goes for his or her supervision (which in this case covers the compensation and operation of branch and division managers, as well as the general sales manager), and the remaining third is allocated for administrative expense, taxes, and profits.

Obviously, this method is not universally applicable, since the cost of distribution varies from low, in the distribution of basic materials, to very high, in such specialties as perfumes and cosmetics (where it may reach well above 50 cents of the sales dollar).

Influence of Sales Manager's Duties on Compensation

While the above methods of budgeting selling costs are followed by many concerns that start out from scratch, they are obviously theoretical. In actual practice, such a yardstick is seldom used. Compensation is based as nearly as possible upon a sales manager's contribution to the net earnings of the business, which in turn is determined by the nature of his or her duties.

There is a growing tendency, however, to consider the sales executive as a part of top management, rather than as a specialist. It is probable that in the future many sales executives now regarded as department managers will be elevated to the board of directors and given official status. As officials of the business they will automatically participate in the top-management bonus. Every activity of the business must be considered a part of the sales program, hence the need for dovetailing the sales executive into the overall management picture.

The highest salaries will be paid to sales executives who are primarily creative sales planners. Persons with necessary creative and analytical ability will be scarce. The successful sales director must understand not only the operation of a sales organization, but he or she must know marketing, sales research, advertising, public relations, and product engineering. Too many sales managers function only as "head salespeople." They concern themselves too much with driving a sales organization to the limit, along with producing a good volume of personal sales, and neglect to analyze the potential opportunity to develop new markets and improve selling techniques.

Incentive Compensation

Executive-compensation methods can be grouped into three general classifications. First, and of prime importance, is money.

The second classification of executive payment involves various deferred-compensation plans. Deferred compensation includes pension plans, profit-sharing plans, group life, accident and health insurance, and stock options, as well as pure deferred dollars.

The third classification of compensating executives might be termed "indirect fringe benefits." Examples of indirect fringe benefits are use of a company car, payment by the company of an employee's country club bills, payment of travel and entertainment expenses at conventions, and new carpeting in the office.

The Discretionary Bonus. A survey by the Controllers' Congress indicates that bonus plans have not changed substantially in the past decade. One of the most common methods, for example, is still the discretionary bonus, which is based upon the judgment of some higher officer or officers in the company.

There are several reservations about the judgment bonus. In the first place, it does not provide a specific method for informing the person receiving the bonus what he or she did to earn the bonus. Nor does it tell him or her what he or she should do better in order to increase his or her bonus next year.

The discretionary bonus is commonly found in organizations where top management has not prepared a well-defined operating plan. There are exceptions to this, of course, but lack of direction and discretionary bonuses tend to be found in the same company.

Aside from the judgment bonus, the most common basis of paying cash bonuses among retailers is a percentage of company profits. This method has merit, especially if management believes that a company with no profits should pay no bonuses. However, we question whether this is either completely rational or completely fair. Certainly, in compensating the chief executive officer, it makes sense. Perhaps it also makes sense in paying the top two or three executives. But what does this method of bonus payment do to motivate a merchandise manager of a women's apparel department who has increased sales and profits 20 percent in the department in a year when two new branches are opened and overall profits decline by 25 percent? Should he or she receive 25 percent less bonus in that year?

Bonuses based solely on sales can quite often discourage *profitable* performance.

Some companies, however, believe that profits are so elusive a short-term measure of managerial performance that over half their executives' bonuses are based upon nonmonetary factors. Here, for example, is a list of measures that determine the bonus payment of the top executive officers of the various divisions of a large diversified manufacturing and retailing company: dollar profits, adherence to the budget, return on investment, change in share of market, employee turnover, and percentage of pretax net to gross. It is complicated.

But in some situations, nonfinancial performance measures *should* outweigh the purely profit considerations.

Performance Bonuses. The most direct manner of motivating through compensation is by payment of a performance bonus. In a recent study of bonuses it was found that about two-thirds of the executives surveyed receive cash bonuses.

However, the sheer size of a bonus has only a limited relationship to its effectiveness as a motivating technique. In order to be an effective incentive device, the bonus must meet certain highly important conditions. *Otherwise, it will not really motivate.* In fact, the wrong kind of bonus plan can quite often have an effect opposite to that desired by the company.

To motivate properly with its bonus program, a company must do several things:

1. The company must identify, or decide upon, a set of specific short- and long-range goals, and these goals must be made explicit.

2. The company must identify the kinds of actions which are required on the part of its executives to assist in achieving these goals.

3. The company must design a bonus plan for a particular executive which will encourage him or her to take the right kind of actions, and discourage him or her from taking the wrong kinds of actions.

4. Finally, the company must convince the executive that the kinds of things he or she is required to do by the terms of the bonus arrangement are the best things to do from the standpoint of doing his or her job most effectively. In short, the plan must be "sold" to the executive.

Formula payments are usually based on the bonus fund being distributed on a set percentage basis among the executives, as shown in the following examples:

President	20%
Executive vice-president	15%
Vice-President, marketing	12%
Vice-President, manufacturing	10%
Vice-President, finance	10%
Managers of the —	
Marketing Division	15%
Manufacturing Division	10%
Finance Division	8%
	100%

Apportionment by Salary. With this method, the bonus fund is apportioned according to the relationship of the salary of each individual to the total salaries of the group. This presupposes that the salaries were equitably established in the first place. This system tends to compound any inequities that exist and does not give recognition to current outstanding contributions of individuals to the company's welfare.

A third method is to distribute 70 percent of the fund through one of the above formula methods, then to distribute the remaining 30 percent on a discretionary basis, the decisions being made by a finance committee or special bonus committee on advice received from individual executives concerning their subordinates. Usually the bonus committee does not participate in the bonus fund, and the bonus of the president is fixed by the board of directors.

Commission Payments. Like a bonus, commission payments are usually paid from net profits. But commission payments usually are attuned to the actions of an individual rather than to that of the group as a whole. A marketing executive or sales manager might receive a certain percentage of the profits of his or her individual division, department, district, or branch, or he or she may receive a percentage of the total sales volume.

The use of a percentage-of-sales basis is not always looked upon with favor, as it ignores the cost-control element of management and puts the entire emphasis on sales. The executive, if he or she has any control over prices, could easily sell the company into bankruptcy; or, if he or she does not apply expense controls, he or she could readily promote the company into a loss position. Since most executives have some say in pricing and a great deal of say in expense control, net profits are usually used as the base, with or without a minimum net profit earned before commissions are applied.

Frequently companies are combination systems, with half of the extra compensation opportunity represented by results of the executive's operation in his or her assigned area and the other half through participation in the company's executive bonus plan. In this way the executive who receives recognition in proportion to his or her individual effort is encouraged to cooperate with other executives toward the company's overall benefit.

Profit Sharing. One of the most frequent forms of profit-sharing involves paying a certain percentage of profits into a fund that is invested in stock of the company or of other companies. The earnings are distributed to the executives in accordance with their bonus or salary payment contributions.

Stock Bonuses. Similar to the cash bonus plans, stock bonuses pay in company stock rather than in cash. The stock payments can be made in a number of ways, depending on the funds of the company and the needs of the executives. The stock can be distributed at once or delayed until retirement. If paid immediately, the value of the stock is subject to normal income tax; if paid on retirement, it is subject to the income tax rate applicable at that time and is not considered capital gain. If current or deferred stock receipts are large, the executive might be short of cash to pay his or her income tax on the stock's market value. To assist, some companies divide the bonus between stock and cash in order to provide the necessary cash to pay the tax on the stock.

Stock distribution in any form is usually good, but it must be remembered that when given away as treasury stock, it dilutes the stockholders' equities. To overcome this, many companies buy the needed stock on open market and do not use treasury stock.

When payment of stock is deferred, the companies usually pay the dividends currently to the recipients.

Deferred Compensation. For higher paid and older executives, deferred compensation is becoming increasingly popular. A person younger than 50 usually prefers immediate payments rather than payments deferred until after retirement. To handle deferred payments, the company enters into a contract with the individual executive whereby, instead of receiving increases in salary or high bonuses, he or she will receive a sum equal to his or her present salary, or a percentage of it, for a 5-, 10-, or 15-year period after retirement, in return for which he or she agrees to act in a consultant capacity for the company and to refrain from going into competition with it.

The company benefits in offering its executives a plan advantageous to them. A hidden danger is that it may be committing itself to higher than desirable fixed expenses, should adversity occur. The executives benefit mainly in reduced income taxes over the remaining period with the company and for the period of the contract.

Stock Options. The popularity of stock options varies according to fluctuations in the economic cycle. When the trend is up, they are highly regarded as the stock grows in value due to improved business conditions and the extra effort of the executives. When the trend is down, the value of the stock may drop, even though the company is doing relatively well.

Stock option plans may be either "restricted" or "unrestricted"; the former is usually used. Under this plan the stockholders vote a certain block of stock that can be used for options.

Stock options were first introduced at top levels of management. They soon filtered down to lower executive ranks, sometimes all the way down.

Compensation experts say that this extension of options to larger numbers of company personnel removed the incentive value from them that was originally intended. Reason: The market value of the stock under option is closely related to the efforts and abilities of top management who make the decisions affecting the success of the company. This close relationship between executive ability and company profitability becomes more and more diluted the farther down we go through the executive ranks.

From the company's standpoint, of course, an executive is not expected to unload his or her stock at the earliest moment the law will allow. The options was given to him or her so that he or she might build up a proprietary interest in the company. More often than not, this happens. A Dartmouth College research team sampled 188 executives and found that about 40 percent of them still owned all the option stock they had purchased.

But plain facts are plain facts. Under the stress of financial necessity, many executives take their gain when they can get it, and when the cash is needed for other purposes. For these persons, the holding requirement represents an inconvenience, if not a hardship.

Retirement Payments. Whereas deferred-compensation contracts can be used for individual executives, retirement programs must include all employees. Although these programs are frequently very generous, expensive to maintain, and highly acceptable to the executives, their motivational value is limited. Lower-paid executives place more value on retirement programs than do higher-paid ones, the former not being in a position to build an estate to the same degree as can the latter group. Because of the uniform company-wide coverage of formal retirement plans, many companies augment them with a form of key-man insurance or other deferred compensation.

Family Benefits. This form of extra compensation may take the form of group insurance, key-man insurance, or a commitment on the part of the company to continue to pay the executive's salary at a reduced rate to his or her spouse or children if he or she dies. A stipulation may be that payment be made, provided the income of the survivors does not exceed a certain amount, or some other qualifications.

Family benefits are sometimes given in the form of educational awards, scholarships, or trips for members of the family.

Contingent Compensation. Profit sharing has been steadily increasing over the years. The need for all-out effort to get maximum production and employment has forced the wide use of sales incentives. So long as we operate under a profit-and-loss system, the appeal to gain will be required to make it tick. When you eliminate the opportunity a person has to make more money by doing more work, the whole profit system will collapse, and some other incentive will have to be devised.

The most widely used form of contingent compensation for sales executives, both general and division sales managers, is a percentage of sales after an established *break-even* volume has been reached. The complexity of the corporation tax structure has caused many companies that formerly operated profit-sharing plans to discontinue them. The reason is that it is often desirable to make adjustments in the profit-and-loss account that would work a hardship on sales executives compensated on a profit basis. For example, there are times when it is good business for a company to buy a competitor who is operating at a loss. In that case the current profits of the business might be materially reduced through no fault of those sharing in them. While in the long run, they too would gain with the stockholders by the transaction, they would gain only if they continued in the employment of the company. Then, also, under existing tax practice every opportunity is taken to charge off expenses against profits. So everything considered, it is to the advantage of both the sales executive and the company to base the bonus, if it can be fairly done, upon sales volume rather than profits.

New Approaches. Several new approaches have appeared in executive compensation plans. *Performance shares* are grants of stock units that are converted into actual stock if the company's three- to five-year performance objectives are attained.

Stock-appreciation rights are used as an add-on feature to nonqualified stock option plans. These rights entitle the executive, without exercising the option, to receive the appreciation in the market value of an option in cash, stock, or a combination of the two.

Phantom stocks are grants given to the executive in the form of stock units. The executive is paid the appreciation in the market value and the dividend equivalents on the units for the period from the grant to the date of vesting.

Evaluating Executive Compensation Systems

When evaluating the worth of any compensation plan, it should be borne in mind that the successful organization is an integration of separate but interrelated parts. For smooth operation, the interrelationship must be recognized. This means that overlywide separations, dollarwise or symbolwise, between groups must be avoided.

The compensation plan must be consistent and must treat all executives with equal consideration and with integrity. It must be *logical,* so that it can be put into practice, administered, understood, and talked about. It should not be a secret in the hands of only one or two people, or of such complexity that calculations are obscure. The executive should clearly understand what it was intended he or she should do, and what he or she did to earn the compensation received.

Today, adequate and proper compensation plans for sales executives are a "must" for two vital reasons:

1. A great scarcity of marketing talent makes it imperative that companies do not lose their executives. The high salaries paid competent sales executives proves the need.

2. Companies have large investments of time and money in their sales managers and executives; they cannot afford to jeopardize these investments.

Sales Staff Personnel

The performance of sales staff personnel is vital to the success of company operations. Guided by top management decisions and corporate policies, these persons must implement these guidelines through operating efficiencies and day-to-day decisions, some of which may be of great importance to the process of obtaining the best possible results in sales, costs, and profits.

Depending upon the organizational structure of a company, few or many sales staff personnel or specialists report to the sales manager.

Included in this managerial span can be the regional sales manager, the district sales manager, the sales promotion manager, manager of customer relations, product manager, and the market research manager.

Bonus, or incentive, compensation is just as important to them as it is to the sales manager. Most of these staff or supervisory positions carry expense responsibilities that can logically be tied into profit-based plans. Where one makes a direct or indirect contribution to sales, a reward in terms of achieving sales volume goals can also be applicable.

In all positions, incentive compensation beyond base salary is feasible, whether it be based on company or department profit, performance standards, sales volume attainment, or a combination of two or more of these measurements.

As a guide to the sales manager in managerial and compensation planning, implementation, and control, general descriptions of three key positions are presented. Compensation data for the regional sales manager were shown earlier in this chapter.

REGIONAL SALES MANAGER

The regional sales manager is responsible for the implementation and direction of the marketing/sales programs, policies, and procedures that will maximize sales at the highest returns on investments within a specific geographical area. He or she is responsible for the development of sales plans and forecasts that will contribute his or her appropriate share to the overall growth criteria of the company, and for the measurement of the overall effectiveness of the sales organization in his or her area. He or she directs the activities of the district sales managers. He or she is knowledgeable of competitors' developments, market trends, buyer habits, and related information, and regularly communicates this information, as well as his or her recommendations, to interested parties of the organization.

Alternate Titles: Branch manager, Sales manager

DISTRICT SALES MANAGER

The district sales manager is responsible for the implementation and direction of the marketing/sales programs, policies, and procedures that will maximize sales at the highest returns on investments within a geographical area of responsibility. He or she is responsible for the development of sales plans and forecasts that will contribute his or her appropriate share to the overall growth criteria of the company, and is responsible for the measurement of the overall effectiveness of the sales organization. He or she directs the activities of a group of field salespeople. He or she is knowledgeable on competitive developments, market trends, buyer habits, and related information, and regularly communicates this information, as well as his or her recommendations, to interested parties in the organization.

Alternate Titles: Area or zone manager

MANAGER OF CUSTOMER RELATIONS

The manager of customer relations administers sales service policy in a manner that maintains and promotes good customer relations. His or her unit serves as a liaison between the customers and the sales force and between the manufacturing and service facilities of the company, including the areas of returned goods, customer claims and complaints, and customer records control.

Alternate Title: Customer services manager

The Break-Even Point

The break-even point of the main area of responsibility in middle management can frequently be determined and used as an element in the extra-compensation program. The middle-management sales executive contributes to the general welfare of the company, so he or she can logically and profitably participate in any bonus fund assigned to the marketing division. He or she is usually included in retirement plans and can be allotted stock options, though in practice this is rare. Certainly he or she should receive appropriate status and other so-called intangible compensation.

Frequently, an element of the middle-management sales executive's extra compensation will be based on the results attained by the salespeople who report to him or her. For example, a manager may have eight salespeople in his or her branch, each with a quota of $200,000, or a total of $1,600,000. It may be that through no fault of the manager's, there is a high degree of salesperson turnover. His or her salary would then reflect the administration of the eight salespeople, plus the need for locating, hiring, and training one new person each year. Furthermore, rather than setting the quota of his or her branch at $1,600,000, it would be set at $1,500,000, which would give a little leeway and not penalize him or her too heavily when replacements occurred.

Thus his or her compensation program might include a base salary, an override on sales over $1,500,000, a bonus based on profits and expense control, and participation in the executives' bonus fund for the division. However, having more than two elements in the extra compensation plan might make the program too complex. It might, therefore, be better if only the elements most directly related to the manager's activities were adopted.

Compensation for Personal Production

A common weakness in compensation plans for field supervisors is that they put the supervisor in competition with the salesperson by paying partly on his or her own personal production and partly on the production of the persons under him or her. There may be times when this is the only feasible way to compensate supervisors. In the long run, however, it undermines the morale of the salespeople, works against the close cooperation which should exist between supervisor and salesperson, and usually results in an excessive turnover of salespeople. It is therefore bad practice, however expedient it may seem.

It is a time-tested principle of sales management that every 10 salespersons at work require a field leader, just as a file of soldiers, to be effective, requires a corporal to tell them what to do, and show them how to do it, and then see that they do it. It is possible, of course, to get along with fewer supervisors, and under some methods of selective selling one supervisor to 20 persons might be adequate. Remember, however, that you pay for adequate sales supervision one way or another. You pay for it in a profit on business you should have but are not getting if you have too few supervisors or if you have half-hearted field supervision. Therefore, it is good business to provide adequate supervision and to pay the best people you can find what they are worth.

Qualified Bonus Compensation Plan

A plan that requires the branch manager to qualify for over a given period of time before being allowed to participate in the distribution of a bonus awarded for the satisfactory operation of his or her office has proved a valuable aid in encouraging branch managers. One of the large store-equipment companies operates from a unified sales control through district managers who have under them territories that encompass several states. In strategic positions throughout the districts, branch offices have been established that are under the immediate supervision of a branch manager. Each branch manager is responsible for both the sales activities and the efficient operation of his or her office. Each manager is given a budgeted expense amount within which he or she is supposed to confine the expense of the operation.

The compensation of the branch manager is based on a straight salary arrangement. In addition, he or she is given an opportunity to augment personal earnings by effecting savings in the operation of the office, thereby possibly qualifying for the bonus paid as a reward for keeping the office on a profit basis. Under this arrangement any branch office may operate at a loss for two or three months or more, in succession, and during the time that the office fails to show a profit the branch manager does not share in the bonus that he or she might have enjoyed had the office been operated on a profitable basis. If any office has operated at a loss for three months in succession—that is, failed to reach its assigned sales quota or to keep its expenses within the figure established by the home office for that particular branch and during the fourth month shows a profit and makes its quota, the branch manager has then qualified for the bonus. Then, during the next three months the branch manager receives the bonus to which he or she is entitled. If, however, during any month after he or she has qualified, the office shows a loss, it is necessary to qualify again in order to be entitled to the bonus.

The compensation plan for regional managers of the Phillips-Van Heusen Corporation, makers of Van Heusen collars and shirts, has given consideration to the opening up of pioneer territories. The plan, with certain modifications, has been in use for a number of years. It was described by an officer of the company as follows:

"Our profit-sharing plan for regional managers is a very simple one. After a very close study of our field, we know just how much money it should cost us to market our various products. We set up a budget figure for each region to operate on. Out of that budget all expenses for the region must be met: office rent, salespeoples' drawings, traveling expenses, lost samples, etc. The manager's salary is also charged in here. If at the end of the year the manager has been able to save any money on this operation, we go fifty-fifty with him or her on any surplus he or she is able to build up, giving the manager his or her share in cash as soon as the year's books are closed.

"These budget figures, of course, vary according to the cost of doing business in the various territories, but in normal years with normal intelligence and sufficient aggressiveness, a region can operate within our budget figure. It is not a figure that is based on splitting hairs, but it is a perfectly fair, normal operating ratio. So far, this system has worked like a charm. Some of our people have drawn very handsome bonus checks.

"If there is a deficit on the region, we take into consideration the cause of the deficit, and if it is some unusual condition over which the manager has absolutely no control, the company meets him or her halfway and wipes out the deficit. If it is a deficit that has been caused by the manager but we still feel that the manager is a good person and worth saving, we charge that deficit against the region; it then must be wiped out before any profits can be shown.

"On the other hand, if it is a deficit against the region caused by incompetence on the part of the manager, we take appropriate action and give the manager the 'boot'."

IBM Rating Plan for Supervisors

The International Business Machines Corporation wanted to lay a foundation for a future sales compensation plan that would provide a reasonable salary to cover a person's living expenses and a commission contingent upon territorial and individual sales production. At one time, IBM operated its sales force on a straight commission basis, but special conditions made it necessary temporarily to revert to a straight salary plan. To provide data necessary for changing over to a salary and commission plan, a system of ratings was established on an experimental basis. Every 90 days, supervisors were required to evaluate the work of each person under their supervision, rating them on these 12 points:

1. Write-ups prepared covering detailed tabulating procedure in specific installations.

2. Time spent out of person's own territory.
   - Active time: in helping to close points not his or her own, in instructing at Endicott, in performing special assignments, in manning exhibits, etc.
   - Inactive time: specify cause, such as illness, other personal causes.

3. Suggestions made pertaining to sales, sales promotion, engineering, advertising, education, etc.

4. Contributions made to *Business Machines* magazine.

5. Speeches, of either business or nonbusiness nature, delivered to outside organizations.

6. Active participation in outside trade, accounting, or similar organizations, as member, officer, or director.

7. Trained new salespeople, systems service persons, or other IBM workers.

8. Recommended applicants for IBM employment.

9. Made concessions to customers: suspended rental—reason; other concessions—reasons.

10. Customers' attitude toward him or her.

11. Is this person ready for promotion? Why, or why not?

12. Remarks regarding other significant performances.

Chapter 4

Structuring the Sales Organization

The task of sales management is to attain its objectives by utilizing resources in the best calculated ways through a systematic plan of action, stated Herbert A. Simon in *Administrative Management* (Macmillan, Inc.). On "Creating a Management Framework"*, Simon wrote:

The role of organization in sales has been compared to that of the skeleton in the human body; it provides a framework within which normal functions may take place. There is, however, a degree of uniformity in the human skeleton that does not characterize the sales organization. Each firm has its own particular objectives and problems, and the structure of the sales organization reflects this diversity. Current trends in the direction of experimentation and innovation would seem to attest to efforts to adjust organization structures to changing conditions. An example is found in the case of a large firm, selling in both the industrial and consumer markets, that has recently reorganized by grouping related products into "profit centers." Each profit center is headed by a general manager who has under his or her direction a sales department with supporting staff services.

Whether the organization structure follows traditional lines or is in some way innovative, certain basic objectives remain to be accomplished. An effective organization plan defines lines of authority and fixes responsibility and accountability. The plan will, as a rule, establish line and staff positions in a manner to delineate the authority and responsibility of each. Effective organization is mindful of the necessity to have effective lines of communication, and will identify these lines. Basic to the success of the organization plan is the degree to which it contributes to solving the problems of coordination. When the plan of organization has been decided, it may be depicted in an organization chart. The organization structure is not static, but subject to modification as personnel and objectives change. It is perhaps safe to say that more effort is focused upon organization and reorganization of sales than on any other division of the firm. This is to be ex-

---

*Steuart Henderson Britt, Norman Guess, eds., *Marketing Manager's Handbook* (Chicago: The Dartnell Corp., 1983), 2d ed., pp. 139-140.

pected in view of the fact that it is the sales organization that must bridge the gap between the market and the productive capacity of the firm. As the market changes, the sales function accordingly adjusts its organization and manner of operation.

Meeting Changing Market Needs

A good example is the Signode Corporation, the world's largest manufacturer and distributor of strapping systems for use in packaging and material handling. As Paul J. Gerlach, vice-president of marketing, described it: "Seventy years ago, strapping was applied and sealed with simple hand tools. In the last decade, strapping systems grew more complex and customer needs become more sophisticated. This required reorganizing the sales structure by introducing a layer of power-equipment specialists assigned specifically to boosting power equipment. They became a resource for the sales representative and also performed training duties with the field sales force. In addition, an inside sales program was instituted to relieve sales representatives of that 15 percent of the business that came from a huge number of small purchasers."

Providing for Growth and Change

Business firms, small or large, usually begin with an anticipation of growth. As growth occurs it becomes necessary to modify the sales organization to meet increasing responsibilities. It is desirable, however, in planning the initial organization to look ahead as much as possible to future needs. As an example, effort should be made to avoid creating positions, or to avoid putting people into positions, where expansion or reorganization may create the appearance of demotion. Fortunately, the plan of organization common to many small firms lends itself well to expansion.

Figure 1, pages 92-93, contains charts which show some of the basic features in the organization of sales departments. The three examples are illustrative of the sales organization evolving from the simple to the more complex. Figure 1 (A) is a simple line organization with the sales manager reporting directly to the president of the firm. The sales manager in turn exercises direct control of the company sales reps. In Figure 1 (B), staff departments such as personnel, advertising, and market research have been added at a

Figure 1. Charts Showing Basic Features in Sales Organization.

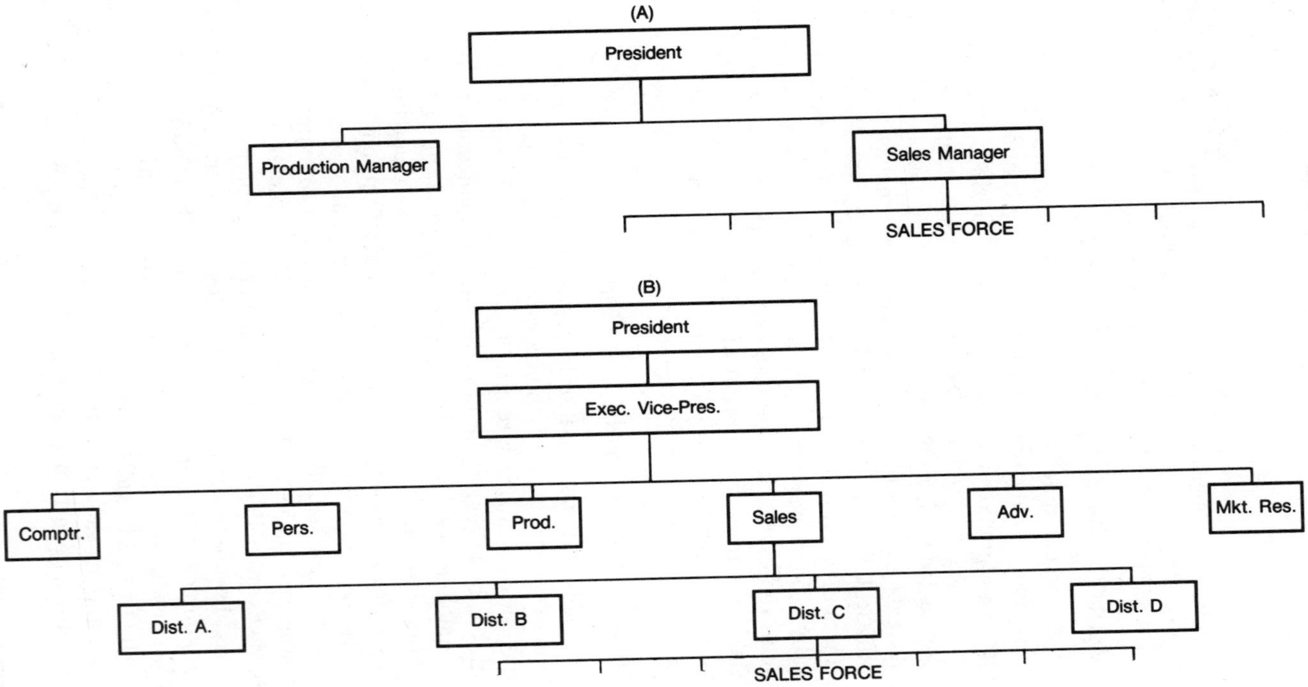

(A)

President

Production Manager

Sales Manager

SALES FORCE

(B)

President

Exec. Vice-Pres.

Comptr.

Pers.

Prod.

Sales

Adv.

Mkt. Res.

Dist. A.

Dist. B

Dist. C

Dist. D

SALES FORCE

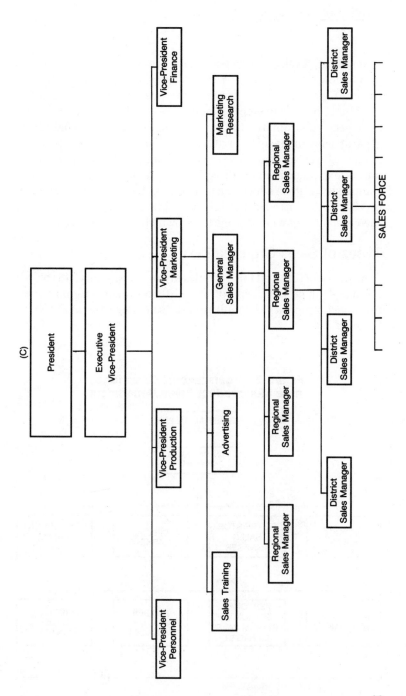

(C)

President

Executive Vice-President

Vice-President Personnel — Vice-President Production — Vice-President Marketing — Vice-President Finance

Sales Training — Advertising — General Sales Manager — Marketing Research

Regional Sales Manager — Regional Sales Manager — Regional Sales Manager — Regional Sales Manager

District Sales Manager — District Sales Manager — District Sales Manager — District Sales Manager

SALES FORCE

general staff level. Sales districts have been created with the salespeople now reporting to district managers. In Figure 1 (C), the position of vice-president of marketing has been created, and the staff functions of advertising, market research, and sales training have been subordinated to this position — along with that of the general sales manager. Territorial divisions now exist at the regional, as well as at the district, level. This type of organization may be expanded in many directions as the size of the firm and the complexity of its product line warrant. As the firm grows larger, a process of decentralization may take place, and each division of the company may emerge with its own sales organization.

Types of Sales Organizations

As the structure and form of sales organizations vary, it is worth taking a look at some examples of different organizational structures beginning with the multiproduct sales department shown in Figure 2, below.

Figure 2. Organizational Chart for a Large Multiproduct Sales Department

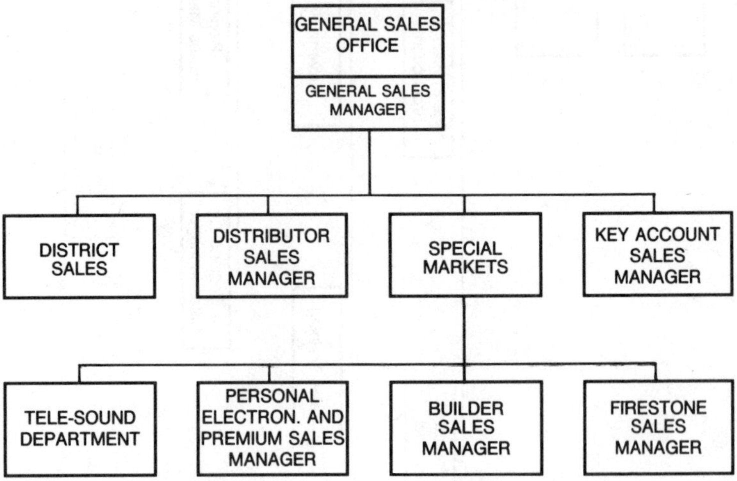

On the following pages, other examples are shown as follows:

Functional. In Figures 3 and 4 on pages 96 and 97, all the functional divisions are divided vertically, with the various levels of authority lined up horizontally. The lines of authority flow from the president through his or her functional managers; the other personnel are shown as staff.

Geographical Structure. Figure 5, page 98, illustrates a geographically structured, multiproduct company with all products sold by the same salesperson. The product managers of products A, B, C, and D are staff to the chief marketing executive. Their purpose is to investigate, plan, and record results of marketing their respective products. Members of the sales force sell all four lines of products; they report to branch managers who are assigned specific branch territories and who, in turn, report to one of the two district managers.

The advantages of such an organization lie principally in its simplicity and its economy of operation. Line authority and chain of command are direct; field services are not duplicated and decisions can be made at the level nearest the need.

The drawbacks start with the breadth of product knowledge that the sales force must attain to operate efficiently. Communications can become snarled as the four product managers vie with each other in trying to get equal field sales representation. One product line, although important to the company, may become neglected, due to the superior promotional effort by the manager of another product or because the first product is a little harder to sell and the salespeople shun it.

Functional activities vary considerably within companies. Many take on line characteristics, such as the sales manager of a product; others tend toward staff. Even with staff classification, a short line of authority exists from department manager to supervisors to clerks. Typical staff activities might include, but be not limited to, the following:

- Advertising
- Promotions

Figure 3. Chart of a Functional Sales Organization

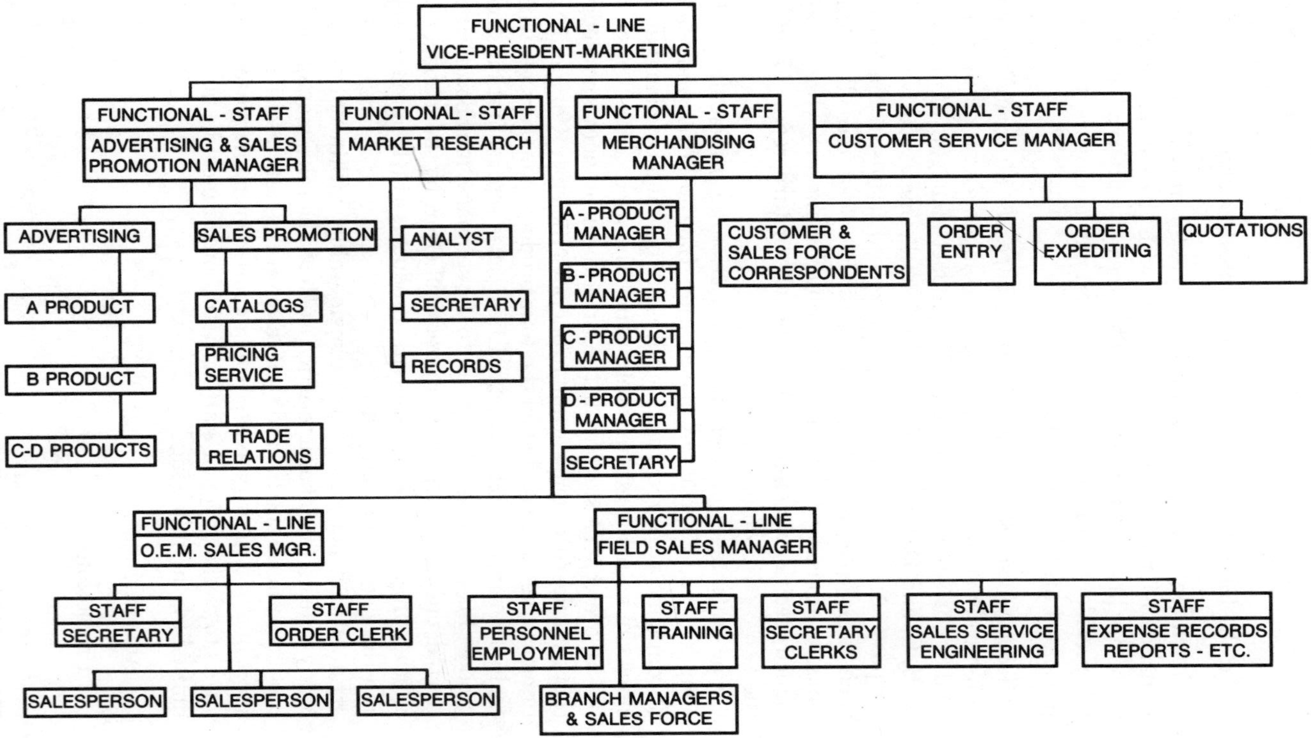

Figure 4. A Variation on the Functional Sales Organization Chart

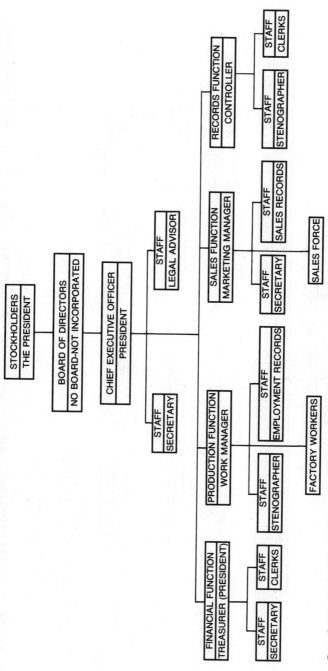

One form of modern sales organization is charted here. Note that the functional divisions are set up vertically, while the various levels of authority line up horizontally. The sales manager (or marketing manager) is on the second level of authority, lining up with the three other major executives.

Figure 5. Marketing Organization — Geographical Structure

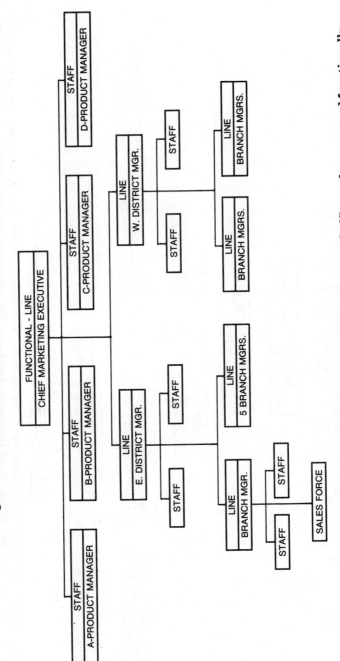

In this type of organization, most staff activities are located at the central office and are grouped functionally.

- Catalogs

- Pricing service

- Product research

- Market research

- Personnel employment

- Personnel training

- Customer correspondence

- Sales-personnel correspondence

- Sales service and engineering

- Quotations

- Order entry

- Order expediting

- Estimating costs

- Expense checking and recording

In a geographically structured company, most of these activities are located at the central office and are grouped functionally. For instance, advertising, promotions, catalogs, and pricing service may in themselves be under separate department heads who report to a director of advertising, who in turn reports to the chief marketing executive. These departments would serve all product groups, and each department might have a person assigned to only one or to two of the products.

Product-Structure. In the product-structured company illustrated in Figure 6, page 100, each product manager has more activities under his or her control and direction. Note that the staff of the chief marketing executive is small; each product sales manager has his or her own supporting staff and concentrates only on the products of his or her department. Since there are no branch managers in this example, an additional district manager would be needed to hold to 10 the number of salespeople reporting to each district manager.

Figure 6. Product-Structured Company

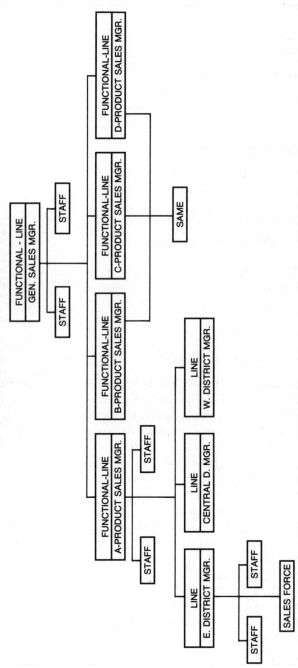

The staff and line personnel, shown on this chart, for Product Department A would be duplicated (with some variations) for each of the other product departments, B, C, and D. These have been omitted from the chart for reasons of space limitations. Thus, there would be four product sales managers, each staffed as needed and having separate sales forces. However, two or more product lines might, in some cases, be combined, such as B-C or B-D, under one product sales manager, and sold by one sales force.

100

The advantages of this system include the possibility of more specialization; the problems of communications are simplified, and customers can be more properly serviced. The disadvantages include considerable overlapping of territories and duplication of travel. It is conceivable that four product salespeople would call on the same customer, even on the same day. Customers have mixed feelings about this; some like to deal with the most knowledgeable salesperson available, while others resent having so much of their time taken up by one company. The company may lose, too, for a buyer might feel that, having bought all of his or her requirements for product A from the company, he or she would be justified in buying products, B, C, and D from other companies. The family concept of products is largely dissipated with the product organization.

Multi-Sales Force Organization

In many businesses, it is necessary to have more than one sales force to cover separate or specialized markets. Some companies make one line of products for industrial markets and another line for consumers. In others, it may be necessary to have different sales forces for different types of distribution or separate sales organizations geared toward specific types of industrial or commercial markets.

Examples of these are shown in Figures 7 and 8, pages 102 and 103.

Specific Assignments

In product-structured companies, specific assignment of major responsibilities is a requirement. Here's how such responsibilities generally are assigned.

1. *Product Research.* Product research will probably be under jurisdiction of product managers in a geographically structured company, and under the sales product manager in a product-structured company. Of course, if the company has a central research department, much of the actual research and development work will be done there.

Figure 7. Multi-Sales Force Marketing Organization*

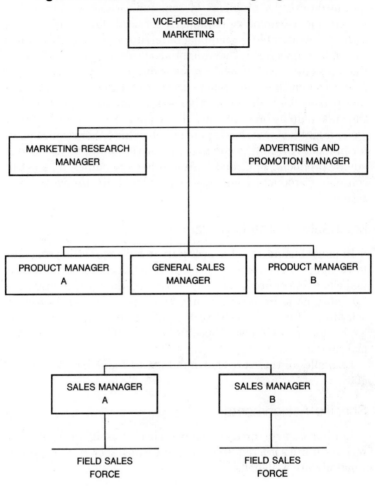

*Marketing Manager's Handbook, p. 132.

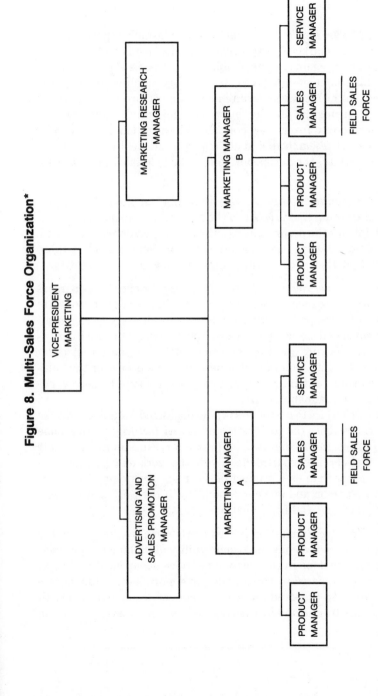

Figure 8. Multi-Sales Force Organization*

*Marketing Manager's Handbook, p. 133.

103

2. *Market Research.* Market research usually reports directly to the chief marketing executive. Research is his auditor of past performance against planned objectives; it is his eyes into the future, his source of objectivity. In a factory, quality control rarely reports to the factory superintendent, who is directly in charge of manufacturing the product, but to the chief production manager, who is removed from direct contact with the product. In like manner, market research should not report to the field sales manager, who supervises the salespeople, but to the field sales manager's superior.

3. *Personnel Administration.* Personnel employment and personnel training could report to the field sales manager, who is responsible for the performance of the selling personnel in the field. The field sales manager should have complete control of those hired, how they are trained, and what they do.

4. *Customer Service.* Customer correspondence, sales personnel correspondence, order entry, expediting, and quotations are frequently grouped together under a customer-service manager. This covers all clerical paperwork involved in order soliciting, receiving, checking, pricing, entering, and following up on order shipments. The handling of orders remains a part of the sales function until orders are ready in every respect to be turned over to production for manufacture.

Proper service to customers is not considered complete until the material reaches the customers and is satisfactorily in use. Some companies requiring two or more correspondents in their customer-service departments divide the work on a geographical basis rather than on a product basis. Thus a customer deals with one salesperson and one correspondent; if the work is well done, confidence and enduring relations result.

5. *Costing.* Estimating is frequently done by the production department, which has the responsibility of making the product. Or it may be done in the customer-service department from cost standards prepared by the production department. Actual quotations are then prepared in the customer-service department with deviations from standards authorized by a high-level marketing

person. It is wise for deviations to be made from known standards, rather than to use rough estimates made just to meet a market condition. Losses can thereby be minimized and the full value of special prices capitalized.

6. *Sales Services.* Sales service and engineering are frequently staff positions under the field sales manager. They are really tools for him to use in maintaining customer satisfaction. The personnel may be drawn from the production department, and the work offers excellent training experience for future salespeople.

7. *Advertising.* Advertising and sales promotion, in some companies, may be a staff function, but its efficiency, in practice, is determined by how closely it is intertwined with the sales department. In fact, in many organizations, it is an integral part of the sales department, with the advertising manager reporting to the sales manager.

Since the purpose of advertising is to increase sales, the advertising manager must be sales-oriented. He or she must be sales conscious, rather than simply being a channel for producing ads or promotional material. These activities may be left to specialists within the advertising department; the manager, however, should be a salesperson first and foremost, and all his or her decisions and efforts must be based on this premise.

8. *Expense Control.* Expense checking and recording are frequently done by the accounting department. Forms are prepared by this department along sound accounting lines. Salespersons' expenses are approved by the branch manager, or first principal level of authority over the salespeople; the approved expense reports are sent to the accounting department for auditing, recording, and payment. Monthly reports then are sent by this department to the field sales manager, who is responsible for economical field coverage.

The Company Sales Manual

Once the sales organization chart has been developed and approved, it should be included in the company sales manual along with policies and procedures.

However, to serve its purpose fully, the manual must be kept up to date through the issuance of new sections or pages as required.

Following is a comprehensive checklist of subjects that can be included in a company sales manual. The number of subjects actually covered will depend on a specific company's needs.

1. Advertising
2. Aftersale
3. Allowances
4. Application of salesmanship
5. Applications (uses) of product
6. Approach
7. Basic knowledge for selling product
8. Catalogs
9. Claims
10. Classes of trade
11. Close
12. Company, History of
13. Company outlook
14. Company policies
15. Conclusions
16. Correspondence with home office
17. Credit policies
18. Customers' buying motives
19. Dealer helps
20. Demonstrating
21. Design features
22. Dictionary of trade terms
23. Direct-mail literature
24. Discounts
25. Executives
26. Expenses
27. Field organization setup
28. Fundamentals of successful salesmanship
29. General instructions to sales personnel
30. General sales meetings
31. Helps for salespeople
32. Home office, Relations with
33. House literature
34. Information and duties of salespeople
35. Introduction
36. Invoicing
37. Lost orders
38. Management-employee relations
39. Manufacturing methods
40. Market study in graphic analysis
41. Merchandising
42. Miscellaneous selling suggestions
43. Missionary work
44. Objections, Handling
45. Organization chart
46. Organization, training, and supervision
47. Outselling competition
48. Personal development and personality
49. Planning and controlling work
50. Preapproach information
51. Presentation
52. Price lists
53. Product, Advantages of

54. Product, Classification of
55. Product, Companies using
56. Product, History of
57. Product, How to sell
58. Product, Market for
59. Product, Use of
60. Prospecting
61. Purpose of the manual
62. Quotations
63. Remittances, reports, and commissions
64. Report forms
65. Returned goods
66. Rural selling
67. Sales equipment
68. Sales techniques
69. Sales training, Field
70. Sales training, General
71. Sales training, Need and benefits of
72. Sales points
73. Sales policies
74. Self-analysis and self-improvement
75. Service and repair parts
76. Services offered
77. Shipping
78. Spoilage
79. Technical information
80. Territory analysis
81. Testimonial letters
82. Trade-ins
83. Typical installations
84. Visual selling

Marketing Functions by Organizational Assignment

Victor Buell* has presented the following review of the key marketing functions, including suggestions as to where the functions may be located in the organization. Although this was written in the mid-1960s, it is still relevant today.

Function	Where performed
1. Set policies and objectives	1. Corporate and marketing management
2. Identify markets for present and new products	2. Market research
3. Measure company's and competitors' standing in market	3. Market research
4. Forecast sales	4. Market research and sales
5. Recommend product and package specifications	5. Product manager, market research, marketing manager
6. Select channels of distribution	6. Sales, market research, marketing manager

*Victor Buell, *Marketing Management in Action* (New York: McGraw Hill Book Company, 1966).

Function	*Where performed*
7. Determine strategy and tactics	7. Marketing manager and department heads
8. Prepare short-range plans • Sales plans • Advertising and sales promotion plans • Product introductions	8. Marketing manager • Sales management • Advertising management • Product manager, advertising and sales
9. Prepare budgets	9. Marketing and department heads
10. Recommend and set prices • Administer prices	10. Marketing manager • Sales or product manager
11. Executive plans • Sales • Advertising and sales promotion • Introduce new products	11. Marketing department • Sales • Advertising and ad agency • Sales and advertising
12. Manpower training and development	12. Training development and all levels of supervision
13. Arrange for order processing, field inventories, and shipments	13. Marketing and traffic
14. Recommend credit and collection policies and procedures • Administer	14. Sales and marketing management finance • Finance and sales
15. Provide customer services	15. Customer services, technical services, sales
16. Establish and administer controls	16. All levels of supervision
17. Prepare long-range plans	17. Marketing manager and department heads

Conflicts with Non-Sales Functions

In most companies, the sales and marketing executive is faced with conflicts with other departments that do not necessarily have a customer-oriented point of view.

A number of these were noted by Philip Kotler of Northwestern University in an article in the *Harvard Business Review*. See Table 1, page 110.

All of these have an impact on marketing and sales strategies; much diplomacy and compromise must be observed in obtaining the company's basic goal of *customer satisfaction.*

Strengthening the Marketing Department

In reviewing and strengthening the organization of your marketing department, it would be well to keep in mind the following long-recognized and accepted principles:

1. There must be centralized control of all marketing activities within the area of responsibility, and proper authority must be delegated to attain the desired objectives. This means that all responsibility for the marketing of products should be centered in the top sales executive. Responsibility and authority for the various activities or phases of marketing should be delegated to managers, department heads, and successively lower supervisory levels, to assure satisfactory performance in every segment of the marketing organization.

2. Responsibility must be centered in an individual and not in a committee. A committee cannot be held responsible, it is too elusive. It operates too slowly and without sufficient definiteness. The purpose of a committee is that of discussion, whereby objectivity is brought to the fore. A strong executive uses his staff committees to talk out problems as the basis for his decisions; a weak executive hides behind the deliberations of his committees and follows their recommendations. To take a vote of a committee is dangerous; instead, management should give consideration to all pertinent, objective thinking and then make up its own mind for action.

Table 1. Organizational Conflicts

Other Departments	Their Emphasis	Emphasis of Marketing
Engineering	Long design lead time Functional features Few models with standard components	Short design lead time Sales features Many models with custom components
Purchasing	Standard parts Price of material Economical lot sizes Purchasing at infrequent intervals	Nonstandard parts Quality of material Large lot sizes to avoid stockouts Immediate purchasing for customer needs
Production	Long order lead times and inflexible production schedules Long runs with few models No model changes Standard orders Ease of fabrication Average quality control	Short order lead times and flexible scheduling to meet emergency needs Short runs with many models Frequent model changes Custom orders Aesthetic appearance Tight quality control
Inventory Management	Fast-moving items, narrow product line Economical levels of stock	Broad product line Large levels of stock
Finance	Strict rationales for spending Hard-and-fast budgets Pricing to cover costs	Intuitive arguments for spending Flexible budgets to meet changing needs Pricing to further market development
Accounting	Standard transactions Few reports	Special terms and discounts Many reports
Credit	Full financial disclosures by customers Low credit risks Tough credit terms Tough collection procedures	Minimum credit examination of customers Medium credit risks Easy credit terms Easy collection procedures

3. Delegated responsibility and authority must be commensurate. Responsibility without adequate authority is meaningless; authority without responsibility is foolhardy. They must be equal to obtain satisfactory performance.

4. All activities should be classified and grouped by functions, so that executives and supervisors may become specialists and experts in their fields. This may be accomplished by examining all activities and functions of the organization, then assigning related and homogeneous ones to respective positions. An organization chart, prepared in this theoretical manner without showing names of personnel, can later be adjusted to give recognition to personality traits and skills.

5. The number of subordinates reporting to any position should be limited. Care should be taken that no more responsibilities or subordinates are assigned to an executive than he can properly administer. A rule of thumb is no more than 8 or 10 subordinates, who, when added to contacts with his executive superior and contemporaries, keep an executive busy. This rule is flexible; in actual practice a great deal depends on the ability of the executive, and on maturity and abilities of his subordinates. Obviously, a district sales manager of an old, well-established district served by knowledgeable and seasoned salespeople, could satisfactorily handle more salespeople than could an equally capable manager in a newly opened district with unseasoned salespeople.

6. Direct responsibility must have full recognition in order that the organization may operate smoothly. There must be widespread understanding of duties, responsibilities, and authority of staff personnel.

7. There must be clear definition of the functions and activities assigned to respective divisions, departments, and sections. All personnel should have complete knowledge as to assignments of associated positions so there will be no conflict or overlapping of effort, and there can be full accountability.

8. All channels of communications must be adequate and open, with complete understanding of them by all personnel. These channels extend from the chief executive officer, functional divisions, staff positions, departments, and section leaders; equally important, they must lead upward from the most minor positions to the highest. It should be recognized and expected that channels of communication crisscross lines of direct authority, and only when it cannot be avoided should they follow formal lines of command.

9. The *principle of exception* should be adopted for guidance of all personnel. Under this principle, policies are set forth that cover the usual situations that are encountered at the various levels in the organization. Salespeople are expected to follow those policies that apply to their operations; when an exception is encountered, they refer the problem to their immediate superior. If it falls within his or her policy coverage, the superior handles it immediately; otherwise he or she refers it to the next highest level above. The purpose of this principle is to keep decision-making at the lowest possible level and close to the events that cause the decision to be made. The further up the ladder a decision is made, the more remote is the arbitrator from actual events; and the more biases may creep in to warp judgment. Personnel in the lower levels tend to shun authority and to look to their superiors for decisions.

Basic Considerations

It has been established that no one single formula will fit the structuring needs of every company. Many considerations should be taken into account, such as starting with the product or service and the consumer or end user. Is the consumer/end user best reached and served in the most direct and economical way through retail outlets, direct marketing, dealers' sales forces, distributors' sales forces, direct sales forces — whether general-line or specialized — manufacturers' representatives, key or national account salespeople, telemarketing, or are various combinations needed? And how much inside sales support is required?

Are there special requirements of each of the market segments you serve that warrant separate sales divisions for each? Many firms create separate sales divisions specializing in product lines or service categories.

What is the degree of personal selling influence required? Jerry Colletti, president of the Alexander Group, management consultants, cites examples of three degrees of personal selling influence which he designates as low, medium, and high. In the *low* category, he gives as examples the grocery products sales rep who calls on individual retail stores and the independent operator who represents nationally advertised products. The principal objective of the job is to maintain distribution, i.e., point-of-purchase displays and adequate levels of inventory. National advertising, trade promotions, and product appearance are quite important in stimulating sales demand and therefore more important than personal selling.

An example of *medium* degree of personal selling influence is a specialty chemicals sales rep who calls on engineers and purchasing agents in the paint, paper, and coating industries to present additive and process chemicals. Product literature, technical service support, and availability of service are *as important* as personal selling influence. In the *high* category, the example given is that of a computer-service sales rep who calls on business managers who have specific application needs that must be met with customized software. He or she must "design" the product, if you will, through the sales call process. Personal selling is the *most significant factor* in creating the sales.

WHAT IS THE IMPACT OF GOVERNMENT REGULATIONS ON YOUR BUSINESS?

Within recent years the Federal Trade Commission has intensified its concern with channels of distribution as employed by the business firm. The Commission, bolstered by court decisions, has caused certain restrictions to be placed on the efforts of sellers to control the activities of distributors. While the firm is still able to select the middlemen to handle its product, it is restrained in exercising control where title has passed to the middleman. Firms are restrained in granting territorial protection to distributors, and in the elimination of distributors or dealers who presently handle the product. One possible result of increasing regulation is to encourage greater vertical integration as the seller may move to take over the functions previously delegated to middlemen and thus move closer to the consumer. There may also be encouragement to replace the title-assuming middleman with agents who operate under the direct instructions of the seller. The decision of a seller to perform the wholesaling function, or to employ agents, will have the effect of modifying the sales organization.

WHAT ARE THE PREVAILING CUSTOMS?

The firm that enters a competitive market will find that certain methods, or patterns, of distribution are in existence. The extent to which the newcomer may deviate in methods may depend upon factors such as the maturity of the market. If retailers have been accustomed to buying nuts and bolts from wholesalers, it may not be easy to convert them to another method of buying; thus the newcomer may decide to market through wholesalers. Where it is deemed advisable to fall in with an existing pattern of distribution, there will be an obvious effect on the type of sales organization created.*

Characteristics of Good Organization

The following generalizations, as stated by William J. Stanton and Richard H. Buskirk in *Management of the Sales Force* (Richard D. Irwin, Inc.) characterize a good sales organization.

- Organizational structure should reflect a market orientation.

- Activities and not people should be organized.

- Responsibility and authority should be related properly.

- Span of executive control should be reasonable.

- Organization should be stable but flexible.

Marketing Manager's Handbook, p. 145.

• Activities should be balanced and coordinated.

In summary, a good sales organization defines lines of authority, establishes lines of communications, provides the framework for control, and provides for coordination of activities and for flexibility attuned to the changing marketplace.

Finally, the sales organization structure should recognize the significant roles of telemarketing and trade shows, which are having an increasing impact on sales and marketing success.

Chapter 5

Sales Job Classifications

A salesperson is a salesperson is a salesperson, to paraphrase Gertrude Stein. Not true. No two selling jobs are alike. The types of sales jobs and the requirements to fulfill vary as much as the colors of a rainbow. The detail salesperson calling on doctors in a missionary role is widely separated from the computer salesperson calling on the financial executive to sell a complex accounting and control system. The different marketplaces demand different selling approaches through varying distribution channels.

Variations in Sales Jobs

Obviously, the nature of the business and the distribution process will usually dictate the kind or type of salesperson and the sales mission involved. In many companies, more than one kind of salesperson is utilized.

There are at least 15 different kinds of salespeople engaged in distribution in the United States. First in order, beginning at the factory door, are the manufacturer's salespeople who call on the large distributors. There are usually only a few of these salespeople. For example, in marketing automobiles, 10 salespeople representing the home office, stationed in important distributing areas, may be responsible for marketing the entire output of the factory. They contact distributors and arrange for the actual distribution of cars in each district or zone. In smaller organizations this contact work is often done by the head of the business, or by the officers reporting to him. This is especially true when, as in the case of automobiles, the annual output of the factory is contracted for by distributors at the beginning of a "model year." These factory representatives must be capable of negotiating orders involving large amounts of money. They top the list when it comes to compensation. Thirteen other types of salespeople are as follows:

1. *Brokers' and Distributors' Sales Organizations.* Next in line, when the product is sold through established trade channels for resale to consumers or users, comes the distributor and his or her selling organization. Not all manufacturers or converters go through distributors. An increasingly large number sell direct to the wholesaler and even to the retailer. A few sell direct to the home. But when a distributor maintains an efficient selling organization it is often advantageous to utilize his or her services.

   In the food field, for example, distributors are called "brokers." They handle exclusive lines in a prescribed territory for a few manufacturers. They call on the wholesalers, institutions, chain stores, and other large-volume buyers and sell at a price that customers in this class would expect to pay the manufacturer if buying direct. Thus the service they render distribution enables a manufacturer to operate without a large sales organization to market his product. The broker or distributor, unlike the wholesaler or jobber who sells thousands of items, many of which are in competition with each other, concentrates on a relatively few *related* lines. Thus his salespeople are in a position to sell several lines with about the same expenditure of time and money as the factory man would have to spend just to sell *one* line. At least that is the theory.

   In actual practice, however, depending upon distributors with exclusive franchises to represent the company in a territory leaves much to be desired. The theoretical saving resulting from having one salesperson call, where several called before, is offset by the lack of control a manufacturer has over his distribution.

   While some manufacturers operating on a mass production basis have found it advantageous to market their products through distributors, there has been a tendency for producers to buy out distributors in order to secure better control of distribution and sales promotional activities. The difficulty of getting independent distributors to train their sales forces properly is another reason why some manufacturers are acquiring financial control of distributing organizations.

2. *Factors and Manufacturers' Representatives.* In the early days of the factory system as we know it today, it was customary for producers to give all their attention to manufacturing and procurement, and depend upon others to market their entire output. This procedure still is followed by some manufacturers in Great Britain. In this country there are still textile and paper mills in New England which operate on that basis. It is a hand-me-down from the days of the clipper ships, when great quantities of our manufacturers' goods were sold abroad by masters of trading ships, who in turn depended upon factors to finance and furnish them with cargoes. It is an easy way to distribute, but seldom the most effective and profitable way. Factors as a rule do little creative selling. A manufacturer depending upon this source of distribution has little or no control over his markets. Should a factor decide to change his source of supply, the manufacturer would be left high and dry without an immediate market.

In an effort to avoid that danger, and at the same time to get some measure of control over sales without diverting working capital to maintaining an expensive sales organization, many companies use manufacturers' representatives to market their product at home and abroad. The manufacturers' representative handles the product on an independent contractor basis. The factor, on the other hand, usually operates nationally or even internationally. The contract with the manufacturers' representative may or may not be exclusive. It may or may not restrict his or her area of operations. Usually it does not. The representative takes on the line, along with other lines and as many as he or she pleases, employs a sales force and sells the product wherever possible, but usually to an established clientele that looks to the representative for certain kinds of merchandise.

The manufacturers' rep offers many contacts and market knowledge. His or her territory is defined by the manufacturer. He or she doesn't have much, if any, power with respect to price and terms; orders are transmitted to the principal who fills and ships them. The subject of manufacturers' representatives is treated fully in chapter 7.

3. *Direct-Selling Factory Representatives.* These are salespeople selected, trained, and supervised by a general sales manager at the factory, with or without the help of district and crew supervisors in the field. They may be salaried or commission people, or both. But they are legally employees of the company, subject to company control and discipline, and operating under agreements which require that they devote their entire time to selling the company's products. In this respect they differ from the manufacturers' representative, who is an "independent contractor" *without* company employee status.

These factory representatives may travel out of the home office or out of a branch or they may be resident in their territory. They usually operate on a restricted territory basis. They may sell direct to dealers, to industrial plants and users, to offices and stores in the case of equipment salespeople, or door-to-door. They are usually creative salespeople, emphasizing what a product will do for the buyer rather than what it is. For that reason they are highly trained, and as a rule well paid. While salespeople of this type are expensive to employ, and frequently show a selling cost higher than what might otherwise be expected, the large volume of business they produce, as a result of intensive training and supervision, makes using them a most effective way to distribute in a competitive field. It is salespeople of this kind who largely have built our modern mass-production and mass-distribution system.

4. *The Special Representative.* There are situations in sales management that call for the use of a salesperson of special experience or ability. It is not always wise nor desirable to have these situations handled by a territorial or general salesperson. For example, in selling to the U.S. Government it is common practice to appoint a special representative to

handle this business. Selling to the government requires a knowledge of government buying methods not possessed by the average salesperson. Moreover the government buys, usually in Washington, for agencies scattered all over the country. To properly follow through on big deals, the special representative may have to go to cities which are within the territorial boundaries of another salesperson's area of operations. He or she therefore requires special status in the organization.

Thus addressing equipment for use by the Weather Bureau Service might be sold in Washington, but the order might depend upon first obtaining requisitions from a number of weather bureaus scattered over the country. It is desirable that one person make these contacts, rather than trusting them to the salesperson resident in each territory.

Sometimes company policy considers large buyers, such as Sears, Roebuck and Company, Inc., or The Great Atlantic & Pacific Tea Company, Inc., as house accounts. Because of the type of service required, they are often handled by a special representative who not only makes a business of knowing their business, but also is free to jump from one company plant to another if the need arises.

5. *The Sales Engineer.* Closely allied with the direct-selling factory representative is the factory representative employed by a manufacturer of a technical product to market it to technical users. These people must not only be good salespeople and capable of negotiating orders running into the thousands of dollars, but they must have a specialized technical or engineering knowledge besides. In the past the tendency was for manufacturers of engineering specialties and machinery to recruit such salespeople from engineering schools. This was on the assumption that to sell the product successfully the person must be an engineer first and a salesperson second. There has been a trend toward picking persons who were first of all good salespeople and then giving them a technical training or placing at their disposal the services of a trained engineer to assist them on important deals.

The sales engineer operates largely on his or her own and does not require, or should not require, the close supervision given general salespeople. He or she is not as easily controlled through a compensation plan, nor is he or she easily stimulated by contests and other promotional devices. The typical sales engineer doesn't feel he or she needs anything more than technical knowledge to make the grade. He or she is well paid and, once established in the job, stays put. The turnover among sales engineers is only a fraction of what it is among other kinds of salespeople.

6. *The Service Salesperson.* Like the sales engineer, the service salesperson sells a specialty, but instead of selling a product, he or she sells a made-to-order service, such as printing, insurance, securities, or even real estate. An understanding of the prospect's needs, plus a considerable amount of technical knowledge, is his or her distinguishing ability. Unlike the sales engineer, he or she has the problem of making the buyer want something for which no immediate need is felt, as in the case of a salesperson selling insurance. Some of the highest paid salespeople in America sell advertising, either for an advertising agency, a publisher, or a broadcasting station. This type of selling calls for a high order of intelligence and imagination, plus wide experience and knowledge of the application of the service to the buyer's business.

A different conception of the service salesperson is found in the office appliance, household appliance, and related industries. Service people, that is to say, mechanically trained people who are used to service the user's equipment, are often made responsible for the sale of supplies to customers. They receive a small commission on such business. As a rule they are not permitted to sell replacement equipment, which is the job of the regular salesperson in the territory, but they work closely with the territorial salesperson and are regarded as junior salespeople. Most of them ultimately are promoted to territorial salespeople if they show aptitude for creative selling.

Service salespeople of another kind are found in the shopping lines. They are used to sell "dealer help" advertising and display materials. They carry advertising materials in their cars and help dealers to arrange store and window displays. This is on the theory that dealers value most advertising materials in which they have a cash investment.

7. *The Specialty Salesperson.* This term, widely used in sales management, has come to mean any salesperson who specializes in selling a product or a service, as contrasted to a salesperson who sells a line of products. In merchandising, a specialty salesperson is considered to be a representative of the factory selling one special line, just as a specialty store has come to mean a store handling a specialty such as women's wear. There was an effort made some years back to call door-to-door canvassers "specialty salesmen"—in fact there is a magazine for such salesmen called *The Specialty Salesman.*

More correctly, however, a specialty salesperson is a salesperson concentrating on selling a specialty. A good illustration is the packing business where there are car route salespeople who sell practically everything sold through branch houses. Such a salesperson will sell meats, soaps, dairy products, lard, and similar products. But, in addition to these car route or general salespeople, it was the practice of the old Swift & Company (Esmark), for example, to have salespeople attached to each department who sold, exclusively, the products of that department. Thus there were, in addition to general salespeople, specialty salespeople selling soaps, fertilizers, margarine, and many other packing house by-products. These specialty salespeople called on institutions and large buyers of the specialty they sold. For example, soap salespeople got a large volume of business from hotels, which the general salespeople would probably never call upon.

The specialty salesperson, when the term is used in that sense, is important because he or she is a sort of salesperson-at-large for the company, and can develop business outside of the regular channels. By the same token he or she is usually a better salesperson than the general line person.

The very fact that he or she concentrates on selling one product, rather than a hundred or more, in itself assures a greater enthusiasm, a better knowledge of the buyer's problems and a larger measure of promotional salesmanship.

8. *The House-to-House Salesperson.* While it is true that every person who sells anything from door to door is broadly classified as a "canvasser," there are a number of hard-hitting sales organizations in this field that have made sales history. Notable among them is the Avon Company. It has built up a great national business through controlled door-to-door selling. Such sales operations are closely supervised by district and divisional sales managers. The salespeople are carefully selected, well trained, and work in a restricted sales territory.

9. *The Wholesale Salesperson.* These are the traditional American salespeople, once called "drummers." To these people, as much as any other group, must go the credit for the opening up of the West in a distribution sense. They are still one of the most important links in the distribution chain, since they make it possible for the merchant to buy most of his or her needs in small lots. If, as some persons advocate, the wholesaler were eliminated from the American system of distribution, the only way manufacturers could get the volume of orders needed for mass production would be to employ factory representatives to call on dealers directly. This, of course, would be very costly. A number of manufacturers who experimented with eliminating the wholesaler, learned, to their sorrow, that it did not pay.

10. *The Retailer Salesperson.* There are two kinds of retail salespeople: the inside, or store salesperson and the outside salesperson. Both are important factors in distribution, since they are the connecting link between the manufacturer and the consumer. Upon their knowledge of the merchandise or product they sell across the counter or in the farmyard depends, more than is generally appreciated, the movement of goods into the hands of the ultimate consum-

er. If dealers' retail salespeople know how to sell a product, reorders result. If they don't know how to sell it, or are indifferent about selling it, the merchandise will pile up on the top shelves and clog the channels of distribution.

11. *Detail Salespersons or Canvassers.* These salespeople as a rule do not take actual orders but are used to introduce products in a highly competitive territory. They are especially effective in marketing products through professional channels, as, for example, when calling on doctors to bring a product to their attention in the hope the doctor will in turn recommend it to his or her patients. The patients, in turn, will buy it from their druggist, the druggist will buy it from the wholesaler, and the wholesaler will buy it from the manufacturers.

Detail salespeople are also used in getting quick distribution for competitive products sold through wholesalers. When a manufacturer introduces such a product the wholesaler will invariably balk at stocking it "until there is a demand." So the manufacturer moves a crew of detail people into the territory. They call on merchants, usually in cooperation with the local newspaper in which advertising for the product is scheduled. The orders thus obtained are cleared through wholesale houses serving the territory, thus inducing them to stock the product. Such a procedure is, of course, costly and for that reason it is usually confined to quick-repeating products, such as coffee, breakfast food, soaps and cleaners, dentifrices, shaving soaps, etc. This type of selling serves as a training operation. Young salespeople who show aptitude are effectively screened out and promoted to better paying sales jobs or brought into the office as administrative assistants. College students frequently take such jobs during their vacations, both as a way of earning tuition money and to gain sales experience.

12. *Store Demonstrators.* These are employed by a manufacturer or a wholesaler to advertise and sell branded products. Orders taken by the demonstrator are filled from the stock of merchandise that the merchant buys in consideration of

the manufacturer assigning a demonstrator to the store. It is an effective way to get quick distribution for a new product that sells "on taste."

13. *Route Salespeople.* Some of the great businesses of this country, as, for example, The Great Atlantic & Pacific Tea Company, Inc., have been built by salespeople traveling routes. Basically these salespeople operate stores on wheels. Unlike the door-to-door salesperson, who seldom delivers what he or she sells because of antipeddler ordinances, the route salesperson makes his or her deliveries as he or she sells. Into this class of salespeople go laundry salespeople, bakery salespeople, towel supply salespeople, milk salespeople, and many others. Lately there has been a trend toward the unionization of such salespeople. There are many thousands of these route salespeople, calling on both homes and stores. As a group they play a very important role in distribution and present a fertile field for sales management. Good route salespeople, who really know their job and work at it, often make two or three times as much money as inside salespeople. A good example of route salesmanship is found in the farm agents used by The Standard Oil Company to market its products in rual territories.

National Account Manager

In addition to the sales jobs described, another one is relevant to today's selling environment—the national account manager. Some of the requirements of a corporation for consideration as a national account are:

- Size of purchase on a direct sale basis

- Centralized purchasing

- Prestige or reputation of account

- Strong financial position of the customer

Reaching corporate buyers requires a more sophisticated sales approach, incorporating company-wide application, planning, volume pricing, and service contracts. National account managers are equipped to identify company-wide sales opportunities and sell critically important national accounts.

Product Manager

"Product management job responsibilities vary widely by company and industry, among consumer and industrial products alike," stated Win Hamilton, vice-president and director of marketing, Refrigerated Products Division of Kraft Inc. in an article in *Business Marketing.* Duties range from an essentially sales services function to full profit responsibility for a product or group of products.

The product, or brand, manager must function well in five areas, according to Robert H. Randolph:*

- Product strategy
- Product planning, including goal-setting; sales and profit forecasts; promotional plans; selling plans; post-sale service plans, etc.
- Product development monitoring
- Product marketing
- Product business activities emphasizing the financial return on the product investment

---

Business Marketing, September, 1986.

Chapter 6

Defining the Sales Job

Companies expand and contract, functions and responsibilities are regrouped, products and markets change, and with them change the needs and requirements for successful selling policies and the sales function itself. The sales manager tries to develop the organization needed to meet the many challenges, the most important of which may be the efficient use of suitable personnel in the right jobs. Salespeople come and go; some are transferred to new territories; others move to new functions.

One of the most important documents and links in clear communications in a sales organization is the position description. It is essential to successful sales operations and provides a clear understanding of what the employer wants the employee to do. The nature of the job, the knowledge deemed essential, the exact duties and responsibilities, should be written out carefully and serve as a basis for the sales personnel program. The program should be, in fact, a blueprint for not only building, but also for activating salespeople and all other personnel in the sales department.

On the following pages are typical position descriptions for various personnel in the sales and marketing structure. They may be useful as a guide in preparing job descriptions in your organization. Since responsibilities and duties can change frequently, position descriptions should be reviewed annually for updating.

Typical Sales Position Descriptions

Title: Sales Representative

Organizational Relationships

Reports to: Branch manager

Primary Responsibilities

Responsible for soliciting orders, selling the company's products, and representing the company in accordance with its policies and in the area assigned; for maintaining an awareness of local competitive conditions, and for reporting them back promptly to management.

Duties

1. To maintain and increase the sales volume of assigned accounts or territories.

2. To aggressively solicit orders from present and prospective customers for the products assigned.

3. To provide useful and practical service to customers.

4. To aggressively seek new customers, and to formulate and follow plans for such action as directed by the branch manager.

5. To seek new uses and applications for company products with present and prospective customers.

6. To assist present and prospective customers in adopting company products to their own requirements and specifications.

7. To aggressively carry out merchandising programs as directed.

8. To authorize "return" goods in accordance with company policy.

9. To adjust customer complaints in accordance with company policy, and to advise management promptly of any situations beyond his or her scope of authority.

10. To comply with all company policies, instructions, and directives for the fulfillment of company objectives and for maximum profitable sales.

11. To be alert to competitive products and merchandising practices, and to keep management informed concerning them.

12. To prepare sales audits and analyses of present and prospective customers in accordance with company procedures and instructions.

13. To assist in developing sales forecasts, territory potentials, workload analyses, call programs, and routes.

14. To maintain up-to-date customer record books and other records in accordance with company instructions.

15. To prepare and submit call and expense reports as required.

16. To submit any special reports regarding the operation of the territory, acceptance of products, or competitive conditions as may be requested.

17. To recommend the addition of new products and the modification or deletion of present products to the line as appropriate.

18. To attend and participate in sales meetings, training programs, conventions, and trade shows as directed.

19. To maintain an awareness of likely candidates for the sales force and to call any such candidates to the attention of the branch manager.

20. To assist in the field training of any salesperson as requested.

21. To cooperate with all personnel in the branch, department, division, and other divisions on the execution of company programs.

22. To assume the obligations of good citizenship and to participate in worthwhile community activities as a public relations asset to the company.

Title: Sales Representative

Organizational Relationships

Reports to: Regional or District sales manager

Supervises: None

Primary Responsibilities

Responsible for providing sales coverage and developing best possible market penetration for all products to present and prospective accounts in his or her assigned territory in accordance with the company's policies and programs.

Duties

Company

1. To reflect both in personal demeanor and professional integrity the true image of the company to customers and prospects.

2. To maintain and increase sales volume with established accounts and to aggressively seek new customers by formulating and following planned sales strategies and company marketing programs to ensure optimum profitable sales penetration in the territory assigned.

3. To be sensitive to the current individual needs of customers and prospects, and to help them attain their goals through the proper utilization of the company's products and services.

4. To understand and administer customer service, in accordance with company policy, in a mutually beneficial manner, to ensure lasting goodwill between the customers and the company.

5. To seek new uses and applications for company products with present and prospective customers.

6. To assist present and prospective customers in adapting company products to their own requirements and specifications.

7. To aggressively carry out marketing programs as directed.

8. To authorize "return" goods in accordance with company policy.

9. To adjust customer complaints in accordance with company policy, and to advise management promptly of any situations beyond his or her scope of authority.

10. To comply with all company policies, instructions, and directives for the fulfillment of company objectives and for maximum profitable sales.

11. To be alert to competitive products and marketing practices, and to keep management informed concerning them.

12. To actively participate in the development of sales forecasts.

13. To maintain up-to-date customer and territory records in accordance with regional/district manager's instructions.

14. To prepare and submit call and expense reports as required.

15. To submit special reports regarding the operation of the territory, acceptance or rejection of products, and competitive conditions beneficial to other salespeople and company operations.

16. To recommend the addition of new products and the modification or deletion of present products to the line as appropriate.

17. To attend and participate in sales meetings, training programs, conventions, and trade shows as directed.

18. To attend and participate in allied trade meetings and organizational activities.

19. To actively participate in market or product test programs as directed.

20. To maintain an awareness of likely candidates for the sales force and to call any such to the attention of the regional manager.

21. To actively participate in territory and self-development programs.

22. To cooperate with all personnel in the region, department, division, and other divisions in the execution of programs and policies in order to achieve overall company objectives.

23. To assume the obligations of good citizenship and to participate in worthwhile community activities as a public relations asset to the company.

Customer

1. Analyzes customer's needs and formulates solutions by utilizing all resources made available by the company.

2. Offers service and looks for ways to help the customer do a better job.

3. Provides information to customers on new and current products, back orders, general order status, current pricing structure, company policy changes, and anticipates their future needs.

4. Achieves prompt, mutually satisfactory solutions to customer complaints.

5. Keeps promises and appointments. Exercises courtesy at all times.

6. Takes active part in customer sales meetings and trade shows.

Principal Working Relationships

1. Works with the sales administration manager in providing service to customer accounts.

2. Cooperates with market managers as directed by regional or district manager.

3. Cooperates with national accounts managers as directed by regional or district manager.

4. Cooperates with the company as directed by regional or district manager.

5. Cooperates with personnel as directed by regional or district manager.

Knowledge, Training, and Experience Recommended

1. Minimum five years field sales experience, or three years if related field.

2. Minimum two years college.

Title: **Sales Representative**

Organizational Relationships

Reports to: Regional sales manager

Supervises: None

Primary Responsibilities

The sales representative is the company's primary contact with accounts and prospects in a geographic sales territory. He or she is primarily responsible for promoting the sale of the division's consumer products through established customers in accordance with approved sales policies and programs. He or she initiates and maintains the continuing sales relationships with approved accounts, calling on them in a regular and consistent manner.

He or she is also responsible for achieving in his or her territory the sales and marketing objectives for all consumer product lines.

Duties

1. Contact all approved accounts and prospects in an established territory, or enumerated in a specific assignment, on a regular and clearly defined basis.

2. Sell and service existing accounts for all products in accordance with the company's established sales policies.

3. Develop accurate knowledge of the buying and selling methods and practices of each account in the territory in order to tailor individual sales approaches for each account.

4. Develop accurate knowledge and maintain appropriate records of competitive sales activity within the territory and with each account that would affect the division's sales efforts and policies.

5. Identify and approach each qualified prospective account in the territory to determine whether or not it would be a satisfactory outlet for the division's products.

6. Encourage wholesale and retail accounts to advertise and promote the division's products to increase the effectiveness of the company's advertising program at the local level. Work with account ad managers, sales promotion personnel, and merchandisers in setting up ads and promotions to take full advantage of the company ad allowances, seasonal specials, etc.

7. Assist each active account in the maintenance of optimum inventory levels of the division's products and the establishment of ordering points and order quantities that fit each account.

8. Take part in customer sales meetings, wherever possible and advisable, to increase the knowledge of sales personnel and to promote the display and sale of products.

9. Handle the quality problems that arise in the field with each distributor and retail chain in a fair and equitable manner to both the customer and the company.

10. Service selected retail accounts on a regular basis as directed by the regional manager, even though buying is handled in another territory.

11. Identify incentive merchandising prospects and develop into active accounts, calling upon the premium sales manager for assistance where necessary.

12. Maintain appropriate territorial records as required by sales management and submit required reports regarding conditions in the territory on a regular basis.

13. Take part in distributor trade shows where such attendance can result in further penetration of the market by the division.

14. Represent the company at national or regional trade shows as required and directed by the regional manager.

Working Relationships

1. Cooperate with home office sales personnel in developing special information on the territory, as directed by the regional manager or vice-president of sales.

2. Cooperate with the premium sales manager in developing prospective accounts and in servicing existing accounts, as directed by the regional manager.

Management Position Description

Title: Sales Engineer—Machinery

Organizational Relationships

Reports to: District manager

Department: Sales

Primary Responsibilities

Sells company's machine tools and related products.

Duties

1. Initiates machine and tooling proposals, follows up and closes the order.

2. Aids customer in writing orders.

3. Follows up sale of machines after delivery, reports problems quickly, mediates when necessary between company and customers.

4. Analyzes customer's machining methods and suggests improvements, where possible.

5. Helps solve machining problems. Advises machine repairs and safety rule observance where necessary.

6. Seeks out potential new customers and pursues all sales leads.

7. Obtains information regarding customer's present machining methods to assist proposal engineers.

8. Informs customers of new machine and attachment features and other technological improvements and of the advantages to the customer of using the company's products.

9. Keeps us with industry changes.

10. Prepares travel itinerary, call reports, call records, and expense accounts.

11. Reports on lost orders and reasons for competitive machine purchase and keeps district manager generally informed.

12. Helps advertising department in obtaining interesting customer case histories for company's ad program.

13. "Sells oneself" to the customer and potential customer.

14. Helps customers in writing purchase order justification for company products.

15. Encourages customer visits to company plant.

16. Entertains customers in a manner that will bring credit to the salesperson and the company.

17. Is knowledgeable about company's competition — their products, capabilities, strengths, and weaknesses.

Title: National Account Manager

Primary Responsibility

Manage an assigned sales territory, special assignment areas, and key accounts by developing and implementing strategies and objectives.

Duties

1. Generate profits through the sale of company services to all classes of customers as defined.

2. Identify and initiate contact with potential prospects in conjunction with customer sales and service representative.

3. Direct preparation of proposals, contracts, and supporting promotional activities.

4. Monitor industry and competitive market shifts and coordinate with market development manager.

5. Develop information for budget preparation.

6. Coordinate sales leads in secondary marketing areas.

7. Build consultative relationship within existing and new customer base.

8. Be responsible for accounts on corporate (in conjunction with home office staff), regional, and local levels.

9. Be responsible for state and local regulatory and fire officials within assigned areas and secondary marketing areas in conjunction with market development manager.

10. Troubleshoot field testing, contracts, and billing problems with customer.

11. Conduct field demonstrations of equipment (inside and out).

12. Participate in local, regional, and national trade shows, and regulatory meetings in conjunction with staff.

13. Join state and local petroleum marketing association, regulatory or fire association, and trade association as directed.

14. Be responsible for training and developing national sales representative, as directed by director of sales and marketing.

Title: Customer Sales and Service Representative

Primary Responsibility

Provide overall support to sales and marketing department.

Duties

1. Identify and initiate original contact with potential prospects. Conduct appropriate research on customers to identify qualified leads. Direct follow-up to appropriate salesperson.

2. Assist in preparation of proposals, contracts, and supporting promotional activities.

3. Coordinate yearly audits of customer contracts for renewals, price adjustments, and cancellations where applicable.

4. Coordinate activities between sales department and financial manager for credit approvals and problem accounts.

5. Interface with sales department to bring to a mutual satisfaction customer problems and complaints.

6. Interface with market development manager on customer surveys, market effectiveness, image awareness, and advertising.

7. Assist in coordinating all activities between marketing and sales.

8. Represent the company at trade shows and conventions.

9. Be responsible for setting up and coordinating trade shows, conventions, and meetings; negotiate rates and services with convention and agency establishments.

10. Research availability of facilities and maintain comprehensive files on hotels and other applicable services.

11. Assist in preparation of trade show, convention, and meeting budgets. Set up necessary controls for all associated cost.

12. Assist in personal contact with customers as directed.

Typical Sales/Marketing Management Position Descriptions

Title: Vice-President, Marketing

Organizational Relationships

Reports to: President

Supervises: Field sales manager
Merchandising manager
Customer service manager
Market research manager
Advertising and sales promotion manager

Primary Responsibilities

Responsible for the general direction of short-range and long-range planning relating to product development and marketing policies; for providing general consultation and advice on all aspects of the company's marketing program; and for the compilation and maintenance of current and complete information on the company's marketing activities and on industry development. Responsible for the general direction of distribution of the company's products in such a manner as to satisfy customer requirements; for building customer goodwill; for returning the required profit margins, and for providing sufficient volume to permit profitable use of the company's production facilities. Authority extends throughout the entire marketing division in all its varied activities, as required to fulfill the responsibilities assigned by the president of the company.

Duties

1. To exercise general supervision over all marketing activities of the company.

2. To supervise the building and maintenance of an aggressive, well-trained, adequately compensated, and well-integrated organization.

3. To maintain equitable compensation and personnel development schedules that will attract and hold competent personnel.

4. To maintain good morale and develop loyalty in the personnel of the marketing organization.

5. To supervise the development of plans for the solicitation of orders and distribution of company products to all worthwhile present and prospective customers.

6. To control selling costs and expenses, approve budgets of sales costs and expenses, and to strive to operate within approved budgets.

7. To approve traveling and selling expenses for all executives and managers in the marketing division, to review related monthly reports, and to institute remedial action when expense policies are violated.

8. To correspond with company personnel, and present and prospective customers, when required.

9. To guide personnel of the division in building goodwill with present and prospective customers.

10. To generally supervise the search for and the analysis of markets for company products.

11. To attain adequate profit margins and sales volumes as required to maintain profitable operations and to enhance the company's position and future growth in the industry.

12. To participate in marketing, distributor, and industry conferences and meetings as necessary to aid in product distribution.

13. To supervise the obtaining of data as to the sales plans, selling effort, markets, products, and prices of competitors to the extent that such data will be beneficial in determining satisfactory marketing policies, developing marketing plans, and assisting in programming manufacturing for the company.

14. To give general supervision and approval in the proper development and execution of advertising and sales promotion plans.

15. To serve on and constructively participate in such committee activities as may be assigned by the president of the company.

16. To supervise the preparation and interpretation of reports as to sales and markets, comparison of sales forecasts with actual sales, and the establishment of sales quotas, as may be needed for the guidance and use of company executives and sales-division personnel.

17. To participate in the review and approval of all requests for research and development projects concerned with new products or new models of old products, as they relate to development in the industry and to customer needs and usage.

18. To anticipate foreseeable marketing conditions and participate in the formation of company plans for future expansion or entrenchment programs.

19. To handle all marketing and distribution problems as assigned by the president and to be the president's advisor with respect to marketing management.

20. To cooperate with all other executives of the company and to require the cooperation of all marketing division personnel with other personnel throughout the company.

21. To assume the obligations of good citizenship and to participate in worthwhile community and national activities as may be required for sound public relations for the company.

Title: Sales Manager

Organizational Relationships

Reports to: Vice-President, marketing

Supervises: District sales manager
Sales training manager
Sales service manager
Sales statistics clerk

Primary Responsibilities

Responsible for all field sales activities; for the maintenance of an adequate field sales organization; for obtaining maximum sales volume; for hiring of all sales and other personnel in the department, utilizing the facilities of the company's general employment department; for the adequate training and retraining of sales personnel; for sales service and engineering functions; for the flowback of industry and marketing data from customers and on competitive conditions in the field; for maintaining an awareness for and acquaintanceship with those factors that influence sales opportunities and to plan astutely for their realization; for providing adequate forward stocks to assure proper sales and service.

Duties

1. To build, maintain, and direct an efficient, well-trained and effective field sales organization.

2. To develop and recommend to the vice president, marketing, for approval, policies and programs relating to:

- Size and type of sales organization
- Product lines
- Distribution channels
- Prices
- Sales objectives by product and geographical area
- Compensation levels
- Personnel development budgets
- Sales department budgets
- Advertising and sales promotion activities
- New product development and improvement of present products
- Credit policies
- Warehouse and deliveries

3. To establish and execute sales programs in accordance with approved policies.

4. To assign sales objectives to district, branch, and other sales territories; periodically to evaluate performance in their attainment; and to take necessary steps to bring results in line with objectives.

5. To organize, recommend to the proper executives, and administer procedures affecting sales, prices, terms, discounts, allowances on returned goods, sales service, and field engineering services.

6. To plan and conduct periodic sales meetings for the purpose of educating, training, and stimulating the sales organization.

7. To supervise the formation and maintenance of an adequate recruitment, hiring, training, and development program for sales personnel.

8. To approve travel and selling expenses of district and other departmental managers, to review related monthly reports, and to institute remedial action when expense policies are violated.

9. To keep management informed of significant sales developments affecting the company.

10. To prepare and recommend selling cost and expense budgets and to strive to operate within approved budgets.

11. To recommend the addition of new products to the line or the modification or elimination of existing items.

12. To achieve adequate profit margins and sales volumes as required to maintain profitable operations.

13. To assist in the preparation of advertising and promotion programs, and to supervise the execution of such programs by sales personnel.

14. To supervise the preparation and interpretation of reports as to sales and markets, and the comparison of sales forecasts with actual sales and sales quotas.

15. To correspond with other company personnel and customers as required.

16. To travel in the field, calling on present and prospective customers, consulting and supervising district managers, branch managers, and salespeople as the needs require. Calls on present and prospective customers are to be made in conjunction with the proper field representatives and for the purpose of assisting them by the field sales manager's executive prestige, and in no way should the effectiveness of the company's local representative be impaired.

17. To attend such industry conventions and to participate in industry activities as the vice president, marketing, may direct.

18. To participate in and contribute to such committee activities as the vice president, marketing, may direct.

19. To handle all sales distribution problems as assigned by the vice president, marketing, and to be his assistant and advisor in respect to sales coverage.

20. To interpret company policy in connection with questions arising in the field, and to consult with direct managers on matters beyond their authority and experience.

21. To motivate field salespeople through the district managers and branch managers so that they will attain maximum sales volume and product balance.

22. To inspect particularly the operations of district managers, district officers, branch managers, branch offices, and other field facilities to see that policies and instructions are properly executed and customers are properly served, and to take remedial action when required.

23. To cooperate with all executives and other managers in the company, and to require cooperation of all sales, sales training, and sales service personnel with other personnel in the company.

24. To assume the obligations of good citizenship and to participate in worthwhile community and national activities as may be required for sound public relations for the company.

Title: District Manager

Organizational Relationships

Reports to: Field sales manager

Supervises: Branch managers

Primary Responsibilities

Direct representative of management in the field sales organization.

Duties

The duties of a district manager may be summarized thus:

1. To direct and supervise the branch managers assigned to the district.

2. To see that all authorized policies, programs, and instructions issued from the general office are put into effect and carried out in all branches.

3. To review branch managers' reports, and to counsel, assist, and direct them as required.

4. To study market analysis figures furnished by the general office, and from them assist the branch managers in preparing sales coverage plans.

5. To review reports on sales activities and compare them with planned activities to assure close adherence to, improvements of, and maximal achievement of results.

6. To aid branch managers in controlling expenses; preparing budgets, call schedules, territory assignments and coverage; and in planning their work.

7. To aid branch managers in the planning of new distributor campaigns, and in the execution of such plans.

8. To make frequent and regular trips to the branches for inspection and counseling.

9. To accompany branch managers and salespeople when necessary in performing any of their duties, such as holding important sales meetings, making important distributor calls, and interpreting major policy decisions. In all contacts with distributors, it is very important that a district manager build the prestige and recognition of the branch manager and salespeople as the company's sales representatives in their territories.

10. To handle all necessary district sales correspondence.

11. To assist in the hiring of new sales personnel as may be requested by the field sales manager's office.

12. To plan and hold regularly scheduled district and branch conferences within the policy of the company.

13. To attend regularly scheduled district managers' conferences as called by the field sales manager, and to attend industry trade shows and conferences as directed by the field sales manager.

14. To perform required and necessary company entertainment duties with company distributors and prospective distributors.

15. To control expenses and costs within the district, approve expense reports of branch managers, and aid in the building of operating budgets and operating within them.

16. To assist branch managers in determining distributor and sales territory quotas, and in programming related sales effort.

17. To counsel with branch managers and recommend to the field sales manager compensation changes for branch personnel.

18. To fill out and mail promptly and completely all required reports.

19. To maintain awareness for and keep the general office advised of all competitive distribution trends, policies, new products, sales campaigns, prices, discounts, profit structures and "special deals" as these come to his attention.

20. To train and develop branch managers as possible candidates for the position of district manager.

21. To cooperate with all company executives and department heads for the maximum achievement of sales, profits, and satisfied customers.

22. To assume the obligations of good citizenship and to participate in worthwhile community activities as a public relations asset to the company.

Title: Branch Manager

Organizational Relationships

Reports to: District manager

Supervises: Salespeople
            Office and warehouse personnel

Primary Responsibilities

Responsible for maintenance and development of sales of company products in the areas assigned; for the development and maintenance of an effective, well-trained and efficient sales force to aggressively and profitably cover the areas assigned to them; for local interpretation of and compliance with company policy in the operation of the branch, and representation of the company to present and prospective customers.

Duties

The duties of a branch manager are summarized as follows:

1. To recruit and select capable branch salespeople. Hiring and severance of salespeople shall be on authority and approval of the district manager and field sales manager.

2. To train branch salespeople in the sale of company products, policies, and procedures of the company, following appropriate sales methods and techniques found to be in good practice, and as developed and outlined by the sales training manager.

3. To maintain an adequate sales force needed to cover the branch areas, to anticipate replacement needs sufficiently in advance so as to have a suitable candidate available for consideration or hire, and to maintain current files of pro-

spective candidates for sales positions. A branch manager may from time to time be requested to suggest the names of possible candidates for hire and assignment to other branches.

4. To assign sales force to territories, predetermined and balanced for sales opportunities, sales coverage demands within available time, and in line with the knowledge and skills of the sales force.

5. To recommend salary, position, and territory revisions.

6. To see that all company policies, programs, and instructions are put into effect and carried out in the branch assigned.

7. To review all salespeople's reports and schedules, and to counsel, advise, assist, and direct the salespeople in their activities.

8. To maintain an awareness of local market and competition conditions, of user preferences and desires, of industry trends, and to send such information promptly, with recommendations to management.

9. To periodically analyze, jointly with the salespeople, sales objectives for both present and prospective customers, sales and service activity demands, and programs for effective sales coverage.

10. To aid the salespeople in arranging for, planning, and conducting instructive and stimulating meetings with customer personnel.

11. To make frequent and regular field trips with the sales force for the purpose of inspecting activities, counseling with them, and generally supervising them.

12. To make field calls with the salespeople when advisable and thus to assist them by his or her managerial prestige. He or she is rarely to make calls alone on customers, as this tends to depreciate the authority and usefulness of the salespeople in the customers' eyes.

13. To review expense reports of the sales force and to take such steps as are advisable for controlling expenses within company policies.

14. To maintain and review records and reports of calls on customers and sales results obtained.

15. To handle correspondence with present and prospective customers, and with company personnel as needful.

16. To supervise the activities of the branch office personnel and the operations of the branch warehouse.

17. To plan and hold regularly scheduled sales meetings.

18. To attend regularly scheduled branch managers' meetings as called by management.

19. To attend such conventions and trade meetings as may be designated by management.

20. To maintain, completely and carefully, all records requested by management, and to fill out and mail promptly all reports requested.

21. To maintain an awareness for promotability of salespeople to more responsible territories or positions in the branch or in the company as a whole, and to assist in the development of those people for such advancement.

22. To cooperate with all company executives, department heads, and other personnel as may be required to assure increased sales volume and satisfied customers.

23. To assume the obligations of good citizenship and to participate in worthwhile community activities as a public relations asset to the company.

Title: Merchandising Manager

Organizational Relationships

> Reports to: Vice-President, marketing
> Supervises: Product managers

Primary Responsibilities

Responsible for the development of merchandising programs; for furnishing functional guidance to the field sales organization on all matters pertaining to the merchandising and sale of company products; for maintaining awareness of and for recommendations concerning competitive quality, customer utility, price position, and sales volume of company products; for keeping informed on competitors' products, determining their strong and weak points, and observing customer acceptance of company products relative to competition; for acting as liaison between sales, research, development engineering, and manufacturing departments relative to the design, salability, and utility of company products; for the study of pricing data and pricing policies, price lists, discounts, and gross margins in relation to competition and company needs; and for recommending changes in policy and practice, when required. Has no line authority over the field sales organization or other departments.

Duties

The duties of the merchandising manager may be summarized briefly as follows:

1. To advise and assist the vice president, marketing, in the development of policies and procedures pertaining to merchandising, pricing, advertising and promotion, packaging, and new product development.

2. To supervise the development of necessary sales tools, including literature or manuals, as may be required by the field force to sell the company's products.

3. To assist the sales training director in the development of training programs for the field sales personnel.

4. To work, and to cause the product managers to work, periodically with the field sales organization and customer personnel, through field calls, correspondence, or telephone, on current trends in industry, styling and customer acceptance. Field work should take at least 20 percent of his or her time.

5. To recommend, on the advice of the product managers, the addition of new products to the line or the modification or elimination of existing products or lines.

6. To supervise the preparation of and to recommend sales volume budgets for company products.

7. To supervise the product managers in their attention to sales volume, product acceptance, quality and utility of company products, and the competitive situation for these products in the market.

8. To supervise the accumulation of information concerning competitive products, features, specifications, prices, discounts, terms, merchandising policies and programs, distribution channels and outlets, and customer acceptance; to maintain or direct the maintenance of displays of competitive products for ready comparison with company products.

9. To supervise the review of reports from salespeople regarding product complaints and to take appropriate action.

10. To consult, and to cause the product managers to consult, with factory personnel and engineers on company products.

11. To attend industry conventions and marketing meetings as deemed advisable.

12. To review, and to cause the product managers to review, publications containing industry and trade news.

13. To review pertinent costs of sales and other reports and budgets related to company products.

14. To supervise the preparation of, and give assistance in, the execution of merchandising plans to stimulate sales.

15. To assist in establishing prices for each product line, using price structure forms and percentage "mark-ons" as approved by company policy. Prices and terms are approved by the vice president, marketing, and the treasurer, and copies are distributed to all principal executives. Once a price structure has been approved by management and the price published, changes may not be made without the formal approval of management.

16. To review sales quotas in cooperation with the vice president, marketing, field sales managers, and market research managers.

17. To assist in the preparation of bids and proposals.

18. To supervise and direct the activities of all personnel in the department.

19. To supervise the preparation of any regular or special reports that may be requested of the department from the vice president, marketing.

20. To recommend salary changes, promotions, demotions, or release of personnel under his or her control.

21. To cooperate with all personnel in the marketing and other divisions, and to cause the personnel of the department to cooperate with all other company personnel.

22. To assume the obligations of good citizenship and to participate in worthwhile community and national activities as may be required for sound public relations for the company.

Title: Market Research Manager

Organizational Relationships

Reports to: Vice-President, marketing
Supervises: Clerical and statistical staff

Primary Responsibilities

Responsible for the execution of economic studies that pertain to company's welfare and growth; for the interpretation of performance data as needed by management in establishing policies, directing marketing operations, and in correlating the planning of company activities; for maintaining data files and records available for company executive and management personnel; for conducting studies in cooperation with the merchandising manager, the product managers, and field sales organization personnel. No line authority over the field sales organization or other department.

Duties

1. To operate the market research department economically and effectively.

2. To consult with other company executives and personnel on performance, marketing, and sales problems.

3. To consult with marketing division personnel on methods best suited for use in dealing with specific statistical and research problems.

4. To study trade and government publications for indication of economic and industry trends and needs.

5. To direct correlation and other studies of company sales and production with available industry and economic data for the purpose of measuring company results, appraising foreseeable probabilities, and determining the company's position and progress.

6. To cooperate with the controller in preparing operating budgets.

7. To participate in industry and trade-association activities and studies on marketing and sales problems.

8. To receive sales, performance, and related reports, and to review and summarize them as required.

9. To prepare reports on sales, performance, products, markets, and economic conditions as requested.

10. To keep up-to-date files for reference as needed.

11. To assist in figuring commissions and bonuses as required.

12. To delegate work to other personnel as required and to supervise and direct their performance.

13. To cooperate with executives and departments as required to assure full use of available data, and to assist them in their problems of supervision, direction, and decision.

14. To assume the obligations of good citizenship and to participate in worthwhile community and national activities as may be required for sound public relations for the company.

Title: Market Development Manager

Primary Responsibility

Manage market activity, which includes market research, sales/contract proposals, contract negotiations, marketing strategy and advertising strategy.

Duties

1. Develop and assess new and existing business strategies and opportunities in existing and new technology. Identify, screen, and analyze all types of new business opportunities.

2. Work with appropriate ad agencies, public relations firms, etc., to enhance existing marketing plans and develop new strategies.

3. Assist in development and formulation of the overall sales/marketing plan, including long-range plan and annual budget.

4. Develop and maintain competitive price information affecting the company for use in analyzing, price changes, alternate strategies and developing marketing plans.

5. Monitor industry and competitive market shifts.

6. Provide sales department and appropriate management with technical product information, including existing technology, changes, or new developments.

7. Maintain technical library to include company and competitive products.

8. Conduct special studies of products, services, etc., in specific markets.

9. Provide sales assistance with key customers and trade associations.

10. Represent the company at trade shows, conventions, and meetings.

11. Monitor legislative and regulatory developments within U.S. and foreign markets. Conduct day-to-day liaison with executive and legislative branches of state and local regulatory branches.

12. Work cooperatively with trade associations and allied lobbying interests on matters of mutual concern.

Title: Customer Service Manager

Organizational Relationships

Reports to: Vice-President, marketing
Supervises: Sales correspondents
            Order clerks
            Expediting clerks
            Quotation clerks

Primary Responsibilities

Responsible for handling all correspondence with customers and salespeople dealing with inquiries and quotations, with routing and interpretation of regular and special orders, specifications, prices, shipping dates and other matters of similar nature. Also responsible for the maintenance of all records, files, preparation of reports that pertain to the department. Has no line authority over the field sales organization or other departments.

Duties

1. To supervise the activities of the customer service department.

2. To communicate with company customers and personnel, and others in regard to orders, prices, products, deliveries and other matters of similar nature as required.

3. To supervise and assist in expediting deliveries and in satisfying complaints as required for critical orders or special customer problems.

4. To act as liaison between customers and production on questions concerning orders placed, shipments, production schedules and inventories.

5. To direct the maintaining of records and the preparation of reports as required.

6. To assist in the preparation of production requirements based on sales and other pertinent data.

7. To review reports on shipments, inventories, and production and to assist in sales planning in collaboration with the vice president, marketing, market research manager, merchandising manager, field sales manager, and others designated.

8. To review the methods currently in use in the customer service department, and to make changes, improvements, and revisions as deemed advisable.

9. To delegate duties and work assignments to others in the department, to maintain and train adequate personnel to perform the functions of the department, and to assure good service and dispatch in handling customers' orders.

10. To cooperate with others in preparing the operating budget for the department, and to operate the department within the approved budget program.

11. To cooperate closely with product managers, sales managers, and others, and to handle special assignments as required to assure satisfactory order handling and deliveries.

12. To assume the obligations of good citizenship and to participate in worthwhile community and national activities as may be required for sound public relations for the company.

Chapter 7

Manufacturers' Sales Agents

A manufacturers' sales agent, also known as a manufacturers' representative or broker in some industries, is an independent salesperson representing manufacturers within a specified territory and is compensated on a commission basis. He or she is not an employee of the manufacturer represented. While an agent can be an individual proprietorship, many are members of sales agencies.

Sales agents are important as a marketing channel for manufacturers in a variety of businesses requiring specialized attention, as in the case of technical products, food products, engineering component systems, or institutional applications.

In some lines of business, manufacturers depend upon independent agents as their main channel of distribution. In other industries small companies have not reached the stage of developing their own sales organizations and they also operate through manufacturers' agents.

Usually a new company just starting in business employs agents as the quickest and most economical way to establish itself on a nationwide basis. Still other companies produce low-cost items, the total volume of which would not support the cost of field representatives. In all these cases manufacturers' sales agents can make definite and valuable contributions to the solution of the sales problems of their principals.

An agent does not take title to the goods, normally sells only a part of a manufacturer's products, and usually does not maintain an inventory. However, the trend over the last few years shows an increasing number of agents warehousing some inventory. In industries where replacement parts or odd sizes are a significant aspect of the customer's operation, agents have found that the added service of carrying emergency stocks enhances their position in the marketplace.

Control over prices, terms, credit, and other conditions of sales generally remains in the hands of the manufacturer. Because of the agent's expertness in a limited line of products, the manufacturers often seek his advice on these matters.

Increased Use of Manufacturers' Agents

Many companies are increasingly using manufacturers' agents as an alternative to hiring company salespeople. A major reason for this trend is the escalating cost of a company-paid direct salesperson. At least 50 percent of all manufacturers use sales agents, while the figure goes as high as 80 percent in the electronics field. Because agents are paid entirely by commission, they are generally more profit-oriented. Moreover, many agents have spent 20 years or more selling and building customer relationships in a single territory.

To determine whether using manufacturers' agents is a viable alternative, consider: How can agents help achieve the company's sales and marketing goals? To what extent does management wish to control the sales force? Can the firm offer agents sufficient support and technical training? How quickly must the market be penetrated?

When a decision is made to hire agents, gather information by interviewing candidate agencies. Determine how long the agency has been in business; the owner's background and expertise; the experience, responsibilities, and number of employees; the compatibility of the agent's other product lines; and the number of manufacturers the agency represents. Also consider the agency's gross sales; participation in trade shows; and methods of compensation.*

According to research by the Manufacturers' Agents National Association (MANA), there are a number of factors responsible for the trend to sales agents. First, agency selling does represent immediate market access. Agencies are in place and they are usually well-connected with the manufacturers' prospects and customers. Second, agencies do the job at no cost—until a sale is

---

*Manufacturers' Agents National Association.

made. This no-overhead benefit has hardly been wasted on recession-torn manufacturers. Third, agency calling has come of age. Some years ago, many agencies were one-man gangs covering more territory than they could handle. Agencies are now, for the most part, multi-person businesses covering tightly defined territories with highly qualified professionals.

Benefits of Agency Selling

Agency sales are attractive because they:

1. *Provide predictable sales costs.* The manufacturer and agent agree in advance on a set commission. Good times and bad, it remains the same for the life of the agreement; with the direct sales method, costs may go sky-high just when sales are floundering. Knowing the costs of sales up front—a percentage of the unit price—obviously eliminates many planning and pricing headaches.

2. *Lower sales costs.* Current estimates are that the average direct salesperson costs his or her company $60,000 to $70,000 per year. To a base pay of $40,000, add automobile, travel expenses, insurance benefits, stock and profit-sharing plans, sick leave, vacation and holiday pay and per diem expenses such as food, lodging, and customer entertainment. Covering these expenses currently requires a minimum of $10,000 to $15,000 per year.

   If this is disturbing, take a look at still another sales expense: payroll taxes. They will run between $17,000 and $18,000 over and above the salesperson's base salary and maintenance costs.

   Many newly formed manufacturers, with a minimum of financial resources and little or no market penetration, have relied upon the agent for market coverage.

3. *Reduce administrative overhead.* Internal costs of administrating the sales payroll and furnishing various backup services for direct salespeople is reduced when the switch is made to sales agents—and, of course, costs of administrative personnel will continue to rise.

4. *Eliminate the costs of training and turnover in sales person-nel.* The training period for the agent will be minimal and largely related to learning about your product. Whenever you hire a new direct salesperson you can estimate that he or she will miss thousands of dollars in sales that an estab-lished agent would have brought in. There is no way to re-cover these sales once they are lost. And, the manufacturer must pay the salesperson a salary plus expenses long before that individual is able to produce.

5. *Give immediate access to the market.* With the agent, manu-facturers have an experienced salesperson in the territory immediately. He or she will be very familiar with the area and have a number of good prospects ready to consider the new line.

   In the sales agent, the new manufacturer finds immediate geographical sales coverage. By employing an agent, the manufacturer can concentrate on production and product-line expansion, rather than incurring financial risk and ex-penses associated with establishing company sales offices.

6. *Provide a highly experienced more aggressive sales force.* Sur-veys show that today's agent is highly educated and trained and was a sales manager or a senior salesperson for a num-ber of years before going on to establish or work for an agen-cy. The agent has no base salary to rely on and can't afford to slack off at any time; the agent *must* sell to live, and he makes sales time count.

7. *Provide sales forecasting equal or superior to those of a direct sales force.* The volume of future sales is no less predictable with agents than with direct sales people; in fact, it may be better, since so many of today's agents use sales analysis and forecasting methods that are often more sophisticated than those of the manufacturers they represent.

8. *Provide a broader sales context for your product.* Because he or she sells several related items (none of them competitive with yours, of course) the agent calls on a wider variety of

prospects and customers and in so doing, often finds applications for products denied the single-line salesperson.

9. *Add marketing flexibility at less cost.* Sales agents can increase your volume by selling outside your present marketing territory—and you'll pay them only when they produce, by commission. Agents can also sell a new line without conflicting with your present sales organization. There are numerous ways that manufacturers' agents can fit into your marketing picture. Many companies use both direct salespeople and agents and find that the two sales forces are completely compatible.

10. *Increase sales.* Many manufacturers have switched from direct salespeople to agents and enjoyed increased sales. Further, it has been estimated that the individual agent sells approximately 70 percent more than the average company salesperson—due in large part, no doubt, to the agent's independent status and a greater need to succeed.

Selling through agencies is not for every manufacturer. But it is the most efficient method of moving goods and services known, and it currently produces an estimated $250 billion of the nation's gross national product. It may well be the method—used in whole or in part—to give your company the cost effectiveness and added sales impetus it needs.

Disadvantages of the Agent

Some of the major disadvantages of selling through agents or agencies are:

1. Lack of control, often considered to be the most limiting factor.

2. Lack of a full-time effort.

3. Limited direct factory contact with customers.

4. Some agencies are reluctant to provide service beyond selling. Service start-up and other services are frequently needed and must be supplied by the factory.

Manufacturers' agents usually think in terms of immediate sales. Many have little interest in building for the future, particularly if the company is likely to take its account away from them at some time in the future. They sell hardest those items that are easy for them to sell and on which they will obtain the greatest and quickest return.

A company buying their services may find its products offered as a secondary item or as an afterthought, the agent concentrating on his primary account. The agent is likely to ask himself, *"Why should I cut the selling time on my good accounts to promote a new one, particularly as my net sales commissions would remain exactly the same?"*

For example, suppose the agent spends 75 percent of his time on Company A's product and 25 percent on Company B's, and his income is $40,000 a year. Now Company B urges him to spend half his time on its product. If he does so, and his sales of B products rise while sales of A products fall, and his income still is $40,000, there is no incentive for him to change his work pattern and habits.

Since the main worry of some agents is that a company will take away its account and put in its own salesperson, they may try to guard against this by deliberately holding down their sales, so as not to build too attractive a "plum" for the company. Other agents are very secretive about their accounts, and discourage management visits to their areas. They refuse to furnish mailing lists, insist that all customer dealings go through them, and make use of every possible means to protect "their" accounts.

Because agents are independent operations, and therefore individualists in the first place, they are often slow to enter wholeheartedly into company programs. They frequently believe they know a better way, or "the program is a waste of my time." Customer audits, scheduled routes, daily reports, and campaign programs are difficult to install, unless such activities are clearly provided for in the agency agreement.

Manufacturers' agencies, being proprietorships, are subject to all the whims of the agent. The agent often may have his spouse, children, or other relatives working for him; they may be competent or they may not be. The agent may have a partnership or be incorporated, with the surviving partner or owners taking over on his death; and they may be far less capable than he. For these reasons, many companies include termination clauses in case of death or other important change in the operations of the agent.

It is difficult to divide or otherwise geographically change an agent's territory. He believes he has, and actually often does have, a vested interest in all the territory he covers for his combined sources. If one source should decide to transfer a portion of the territory to one of its company offices, the agent would experience a financial setback in trying to operate in that portion with his remaining line.

Commission rates are usually set for purchases in normal quantities. If a large user, such as an original equipment manufacturer (OEM) account becomes interested, the normal commission and even any agent commission might kill the deal. Therefore companies frequently retain the right to sell OEM accounts direct, or use graduated commission rates for increased volume orders.

Finally, an agent may obtain a line with the sole intention of sewing it up so someone else in his area cannot get it, or as a hedge for future promotion, should one of his current lines be lost or go sour. In the meantime the company loses representation and sales.

Territory to Serve

Agents' territories range in size from one city to several states. The sales territory is a geographical expression of a predetermined sales plan. Sales territories of manufacturers' agents are usually custom-made in conformance with the basic requirements of both agents and client. Such territories are almost always handled on an exclusive basis.

When the agent and the manufacturer begin to determine the extent of the area that he can properly cultivate, these fundamental factors should be considered: 1) The nature or type of product will have a substantial influence on the size of the agent's territory; products with a high turnover, many prospects, and repeat sales require a smaller area than products with a slow rate of consumption and few repeat sales; 2) class of customers selected will be determinant in the size of territory the agent serves; 3) density of the market is an important consideration in setting the boundaries of territory to be covered; 4) frequency of calls is related to buyer density, the class of customer, and type of product. Calls must be made frequently enough to meet competition and to satisfy the needs of the customer without at the same time incurring excessive selling costs.

Other fundamentals: The more service and non-selling activities required of the agent the more restricted will be the territory. The stage of market development of the product has considerable influence on the size of territory an agent is able to handle. The degree of competition, if vigorous, will require more frequent calls and restrict the territory an agent can adequately cover. Territories are often established on the basis of political boundaries, which are not necessarily adaptable to efficient marketing; trading areas often form the basis of better territorial boundaries. Other qualitative factors are the strength, size, and location of the agent's organization.

The Sales-Agency Agreement

Some of the provisions that should be included in the sales agreement are:

1. *Territory.* The exact territory to be covered should be delineated. If exclusive representation is to be given, this should be stated.

2. *Products.* The products to be sold by the agent should be designated clearly and it should be stated that the agent will refrain from representing or selling competing lines.

3. *Prices.* The manufacturer will set the prices at which products are to be sold. The agreement should specify what authority, if any, the agent has to change prices; what discounts are to be allowed, and under what circumstances they may be attained.

4. *Orders.* In some industries the contract provides that all orders are subject to the manufacturer's acceptance. This releases the manufacturer from any liability for errors or

other unacceptable factors that may appear in the order as submitted by the agent.

5. *Authority.* The general authority granted the agent by the manufacturer should be precisely described.

6. *Compensation.* The rate of commission and the dates or designation of time where such payments will be made, should be shown.

7. *Expenses.* If there is to be an expense allowance, the type, extent, and liability of the manufacturer should be clearly stated.

8. *Advertising.* Allocation of advertising expense should be designated and a description of the type and extent of such advertising should be given.

9. *House Accounts.* Client manufacturers sometimes retain house accounts. It is essential that the agent and manufacturer have a complete understanding from the outset of the relationship as to house accounts in the agent's given territory.

10. *Termination.* The agreement should stipulate methods for terminating the contract, extent of notice to be given by one party to the other, and the form in which the notice shall be submitted.

Figure 1, pages 168–170, shows a specimen Marketing Agency Agreement prepared by the Manufacturers' Agents National Association, P.O. Box 3467, Laguna Hills, California 92653. The MANA organization cautions that this specimen should not be used without consulting your attorney regarding state and local laws and conditions.

Now let's look at the aspects of proper agent selection, what information you should give to prospective agencies, what you should find out during the interview and what prospective agencies will be asking you. All of this helpful information is provided through the courtesy of MANA.

Figure 1. Marketing Agency Agreement

This Agreement is made on the date shown below by and between
_____ ("Principal") and _____ ("Agent").

1. **Exclusive Representative.** Principal grants to Agent the exclusive right (to the exclusion of Principal and all claiming under or through Principal), by acting as Principal's sales representative, to solicit orders for the Principal's goods, equipment and/or services_____

   _____ ("Product Description") within the following geographical area: _____ ("Territory").

2. **Sales Policies.** The prices, charges, and terms of sale of the Products ("Sales Policies") shall be established by Principal. The Sales Policies shall be those currently in effect and established from time to time by Principal in its price books, bulletins and other authorized releases. Written notice of each Sales Policy change shall be given by Principal to Agent at least 30 days in advance of such change.

3. **Orders and Collections.** Orders for Products solicited by Agent shall be forwarded to and subject to acceptance by Principal. The Principal agrees to refer to the Agent for attention all inquiries and to promptly furnish the Agent with copies of all correspondence and documentation between the Company and Customer. All invoices in connection with orders solicited by Agent shall be rendered by Principal, direct to the customer, and full responsibility for all collections and bad debts rests with Principal.

4. **Agent's Commissions.** The commissions payable by Principal to Agent on orders solicited within or delivered to the Territory shall be _____ ("Commission Rate"). Commissions shall be deemed earned by Agent upon acceptance or delivery of the order by Principal, whichever occurs first. Commissions earned by Agent shall be computed on the net amount of the invoice rendered for each order or part of an order, exclusive of freight and transportation costs (including insurance), normal and recurring bona fide trade discounts and any applicable sales or similar taxes. All commissions earned by Agent shall be due and payable to Agent on or before the twentieth (20th) date of the month immediately following the month during which the invoice applicable to an order is sent by Principal.

5. **Relationship Created.** Agent is not an employee of Principal for any purpose whatsoever, but is an independent contractor. Principal is interested only in the results obtained by Agent, who shall have sole control of the manner and means of performing

(continued)

168

Figure 1. Marketing Agency Agreement
(continued)

under this Agreement. Principal shall not have the right to require Agent to do anything that would jeopardize the relationship of independent contractor between Principal and Agent. All expenses and disbursements incurred by Agent in connection with this Agreement shall be borne wholly and completely by Agent. Agent does not have, nor shall he hold himself out as having, any right, power, or authority to create any contract or obligation, either express or implied, on behalf of, in the name of, or binding upon Principal, unless Principal shall consent thereto in writing. Agent shall have the right to appoint and shall be solely responsible for his own salespeople, employees, agents and representatives, who shall be at Agent's own risk, expense, and supervision and shall not have any claim against Principal for compensation or reimbursement. Agent shall not represent lines, products, and that which compete in any manner with the lines, products, and goods of principal during the existence of this contract relationship. Agent shall be responsible for filing the proper forms for his tax liabilities.

6. **Term.** This Agreement shall continue in full force and effect until the date ("Termination Date") set forth in a notice given by one party to the other indicating such party's election to terminate this Agreement, which Termination Date shall be at least one hundred twenty (120) days after the date notice of such election is given. Alternately, this Agreement may be terminated at any time by mutual written agreement between both parties hereto. If this Agreement shall terminate for any reason whatsoever, Agent shall be entitled to receive his full fees determined in accordance with provisions of Paragraph Four with respect to orders solicited prior to the effective date of such termination, regardless of when such orders are accepted by Principal (provided Agent can demonstrate such orders were solicited prior to the effective date of such termination) and regardless of when such shipments are made or invoices rendered.

7. **Hold Harmless.** Principal shall save Agent harmless from and against and indemnify Agent for all liability, loss, costs, expenses, or damages howsoever caused by reason of any Products (whether or not defective) or any act or omission of Principal, including, but not limited to, any injury (whether to body, property, or personal or business character or reputation) sustained by any person or to any person or to property, and for infringement of any patent rights or other rights of third parties, and for any violation of municipal, state, or federal laws or regulations governing the Products or their sale, which may result from the sale or distribution of

(continued)

Figure 1. Marketing Agency Agreement

(continued)

the Products by the Agent hereunder. This Agreement shall be subject to and shall be enforced and construed pursuant to the laws of the State ("Agent's State") where the Agent's principal office is located, as set forth below. Principal hereby appoints as its Agent for service for process in connection with any action brought by Agent against Principal hereunder the Secretary of State of Agent's state of residence at the time such action is brought. In the event of litigation, the prevailing party may recover court costs and reasonable attorney's fees.

8. **Notices.** Any notice, demand, or request required or permitted to be given hereunder shall be in writing and shall be deemed effective twenty-four (24) hours after having been deposited in the United States mail, postage pre-paid, registered, or certified, and addressed to the addressee at his, her, or its main office, as set forth below. Any party may change his or its address for purposes of this agreement by written notice given in accordance herewith.

9. **Severability.** If any part of this Agreement is held by a court of competent jurisdiction to be invalid, void, or unenforceable, the remainder of the provisions shall remain in full force and effect and shall in no way be affected, impaired, or invalidated.

10. **Entire Agreement.** This Agreement constitutes the sole and entire Agreement between Principal and Agent, and supersedes all prior and contemporaneous statements, promises, understandings, or agreements.

11. **Attorney's Fees.** If any legal action is necessary to enforce the terms of this agreement, the prevailing party shall be entitled to reasonable attorney's fees in addition to any other relief to which he may be entitled.

Date:_____

(Principal):_____

By:_____

Title:_____

Address of Principal's Main Office:_____

(Agent):_____

By:_____

Title:_____

Address of Agent's Main Office:_____

Proper Agent Selection

Good selection techniques are the foundation of a sound agent sales force, but it's obvious that selection itself is not a motivational tool. However, when the characteristics of a successful agent for your company are carefully spelled out, the chances are in your favor that the agents selected will be more responsive to both economic and noneconomic factors of motivation.

Remember, *when you recruit an agent, you are not looking for an employee—you're looking for a working partner.* Here are a few questions that will help you make the right choice and ensure that the agent will mesh well with your organization and will respond to your motivational efforts.

- Will your line be compatible with those already carried by the agent?

- Is the agent calling on the right people?

- Is the agent capable of supplying service if your product requires field assistance?

- Does the agent have the drive to do what you want him or her to do?

- Is the agent willing to expand if necessary? Or is your growth going to be limited by his or her definition of success?

- What does the agent think of you? Do you seem compatible?

There are, of course, many other questions that must be asked, but they relate more to the practical aspects of the business.

INFORMATION YOU SHOULD GIVE AND RECEIVE

Because the agency/manufacturer relationship is a close one, it is recommended that a letter to prospective agencies include these points in a profile of your company:

- A brief history of the company
- The mission of the company
- Plans for new products
- Plans for penetrating new markets
- A general financial picture of the company
- A brief background of key executives

In return, you should ask the agencies to provide brief answers to these questions:

- What did you do for the five years prior to forming your agency?
- Why did you decide to go into business for yourself?
- Who are your principals? How long have you had each, and may I have the opportunity of talking with them?
- What markets and territories do you cover, and how many people do you have working for you?
- How long have you been in business?
- What are your plans for your agency for the next five years?
- I have enclosed our product literature. Please give me your opinion of how successful you feel you could be with the products in your territory.

The Structure of the Interview

Now, let's look at some of the actual questions that should be covered. You will see that some of them are the same as those that were asked in the preliminary questionnaire. They are not included to trap anyone—they are included to move the action of the interview in a predictable and smooth way.

The following outline is all inclusive. You probably won't want to cover all the topics, simply because some of the points won't relate to your needs.

1. Agency size

   - How many field sales personnel does your agency have?

   - Do you use any outside personnel?

   - Is the owner actively involved as a salesperson?

   - What is the number of office personnel?

   - Describe your long range expansion plan.

   - Would you be willing to expand to accommodate a new account?

   - If so, how would you go about it?

2. Growth patterns

   - How long has the agency been established?

   - Describe your sales growth pattern during this period.

   - What is your present sales volume?

   - What is your sales volume per outside agent?

   - What are your sales objectives for next year?

3. Territory

   - Describe the territory covered by your agency.

   - Are you willing to expand the territory?

   - If so, how would you go about such an expansion?

4. Product line

   - How many lines do you represent?

   - Are your lines compatible with ours?

   - Do you feel that there would be any conflict of competition?

- Would you be willing to change from your present product market?

- If so, how would you handle the new product line?

- What do you consider the minimum sales volume necessary to handle our line?

5. Facilities and equipment

- Do you have warehouse facilities?

- If so, what size?

- What is your method of stock control?

- Do you have data processing equipment?

- If so, please describe.

- What type of communications equipment do you have? (i.e., TWX, Telex, WATS, FAX, etc.)

6. Company policies

- Describe your agency's program for sales staff compensation, benefit programs, and training.

- Do you have any special incentive or motivation programs?

- How do you monitor sales performance; sales volume; effectiveness; morale; reputation; reports?

- Would you and/or your sales staff attend factory seminars?

- If so, what expenses would you expect the manufacturer to pay?

- What is your policy regarding field visitation by factory personnel?

7. Customers

  • Describe the kind of customers you are currently contacting.

  • Are they compatible with our product line?

  • Who are your key accounts?

8. Principals

  • How many principals are you currently representing?

  • Do you have a line card?

  • Would you furnish us with a copy of your line card?

9. Marketing and sales promotion

  • Would you be willing to assist us in compiling market research information for use in establishing our sales goals?

  • Are you presently doing this for other principals?

  • Do you have a direct mail program?

  • If so, how many customers and prospects are on your list?

  • What type of mailings do you make?

  • What type of brochure or other literature do you use to describe your agency?

  • Do you participate in trade shows?

  • If so, will you attend out-of-town shows at our expense?

  • To what extent will you work with us on cooperative advertising?

10. Special services

  • Can your agency offer services such as writing quotes, making proposals, and helping with customer education?

  • Do you have a sales reporting system?

  • If so, are present records available?

- Do you consider your agency a sales and service organization?

- What do you consider your agency's major strengths?

11. References

- Banks

- Principals

- Customers

WHAT THE AGENCY MIGHT ASK

The interview is a two-sided affair. In addition to the information you will want from the agency, it, in turn, will probably ask many of the following questions during the interview.

1. What are the advantages and disadvantages of your product compared with those of your competitors?

2. How do you establish your prices? What are the policies on discounts, returns, and special products? How do your prices compare with those of your competitors?

3. What is your share of the national market? What is your share of market in the territory we will cover? What do you plan to do to increase this share of market?

4. How many actual customers do you estimate there are for your product in the territory? How do they buy? Is there regular repeat business once a sale is made? Who are the buying influences?

5. Describe the competitive situation in terms of: Number and strength of competitors, location, policies, strength in the territory, growth, and estimated profitability.

6. How good are the competitive salespeople? Are they company paid, or agents? Is there a high or low turnover rate?

7. Describe your present sales organization in terms of internal and external support services. How do you communi-

cate with your agencies, and do you do it on a regular basis? What are your sales objectives for the next year? The next five years?

8. How quickly can your production department deliver? Do you stock in sufficient depth to keep customers happy?

9. Describe your trade advertising program. Is it geared to producing inquiries? Are the inquiries pre-screened and sent to the field immediately? What are your policies on cooperative advertising?

10. What are the boundaries of the territory?

11. If you have house accounts, how are commissions to agencies handled?

12. Describe your field back-up policies.

13. What are your procedures for termination?

14. Are you prepared to invest in plant expansion?

15. Are commissions paid 30 days after shipment?

16. What are your provisions for paying commissions on business that exists in the territory?

17. Does your controller have a problem writing a big commission check? Do we both agree that the more I earn, the more you earn?

18. Are we getting together for the long pull?

19. How many representatives do you have, how long have they been with you, and may I talk with some of them?

Be prepared to answer these questions from agencies as you conduct your interviews. Remember that prospective agencies will be interviewing you at the same time you are interviewing them.

SOURCES FOR SALES AGENTS

In addition to advertisements in association newsletters and bulletins, national or regional trade journals, local newspapers and business magazines, and word-of-mouth from customers and associates, directories published by the following organizations can be helpful in locating candidates:

- Manufacturers' Agents National Association
  P.O. Box 3467
  Laguna Hills, California 92654
  (714) 859-4040

- *Verified Directory of Manufacturers' Representatives*
  Manufacturers' Agent Publishing Company
  663 Fifth Avenue
  New York, New York 10022

- *National Directory of Manufacturers' Representatives*
  McGraw-Hill Book Company
  1221 Avenue of the Americas
  New York, New York 10022

- United Association of Manufacturers' Representatives
  P.O. Box Drawer 6266
  Kansas City, Kansas 66106
  (913) 268-9466

Motivating Sales Agents

Because sales agents are independent entities, it is sometimes felt that they can motivate themselves. Nothing could be further from the truth. They are your "partners" and need all possible communications and feedback to let them know exactly how they are doing and to encourage them to do better.

Let's look at some forms of agent feedback, as suggested by MANA, that can serve motivational purposes.

1. *Reports.* Even something as simple as a commission statement can serve motivational purposes. Unfortunately, most accountants would never think to include a note of encouragement with a commission statement. They feel that their job is done when they do the computations and provide the print-out on time to the agents. But consider the impact if you arrange to have the statements sent to you first so that

you can send personal notes with each. When an agent does exceptionally well, a handwritten note from you will often mean as much as the added cash in the agent's pocket. And when an agent has a lean month, a word of encouragement can mean a lot, too.

2. *Meetings.* You have a lot of meetings at the plant that the agent never attends. The chances are, though, that a lot is said at these meetings that would be of interest to the agent and would provide him with information that not only can be helpful in technical and selling situations, but will let him know that you think he's important enough to be on the routing list. Even when you have meetings with individual agents, it's more than just courtesy to send a detailed conference report—it's sound motivation.

3. *Coaching Sessions.* When you spend time in the field with an agent doing coaching, the feedback from you after the session is often worth more than the pat on the back when you leave to return to headquarters. It's confirmation that what you said in person was truly meant, and it carries the force of being in print as a permanent record. Don't underestimate the power of words on paper. You can often talk with people forever and not convince them of something, but a follow-up in a letter is all that is needed to make the point.

4. *Newsletters.* You don't have to spend a bundle on a professionally prepared newsletter to do a solid motivational job with your agents. Even if it's typewritten on the company letterhead and duplicated on the office copier, it will have the effect of keeping the channels of communication open and letting the agents know that you are interested in them. To be most effective, this newsletter should be prepared exclusively for your agents. Even if you only have a few agents, it's still a good idea to do it. As mentioned earlier, recognition is an important factor, and when you mention an agent's success in a newsletter, you have said it to the universe—to all of the other agents. Sales letters to the

agency force can also serve as a great cross-reference as far as new and unique applications of your product are concerned. You'll find that the new application that the fellow in Buffalo has devised is of great interest to the guy in Dallas. It results in sales volume.

5. *Use the Telephone.* If you use the phone just to handle specific business problems or to complain, your agents will take to avoiding your calls. However, if you make frequent but random calls "just to talk," you will have built a solid communications bridge with each individual. Individual contact is the key to total motivation. When you do call, try to open the conversation with some form of compliment. Make the call seem as though you called specifically to tell the agent that you appreciate something he has done, even if it's a simple thing such as getting extra information on advertising inquiry cards that were sent back to the factory.

6. *Communicate with Everyone.* You should be on a first-name basis with everyone at each agency on your team, and all of the agents' personnel should know the headquarters staff. You can help get this into action by sending each agent a list of the names and direct dial phone numbers (if you have them) of all personnel in the plant.

Advertising to Back Up Agents

Failure to get distribution through manufacturers' sales agents can usually be traced to lack of advertising support. It has been proved times without number that salespeople who must sell a product not favorably known to the buyer soon become discouraged and stop trying to sell it. On the other hand, if the buyer has even a slight knowledge of the product from having seen it advertised somewhere, the sales job is simplified and the salesperson's task is lightened. Such advertising can be done at a relatively small cost in industrial or business papers slanted directly at specific groups of buyers or markets.

The function of advertising is definitely subordinate to personal selling among manufacturers' agents. Usually, the client assumes the major responsibility for the advertising and promotion. But the agent should be expected to provide close support for his manufacturers' advertising and promotional campaigns. In addition to handling tie-in promotional materials for clients, the agent frequently administers cooperative advertising programs.

In summary, the agent is an educator and problem solver as well as a salesperson, and is expected to perform many kinds of presale and postsale activities. These services are necessary and important if the agent expects to compete successfully for the buyers' favor among alternate suppliers.

Chapter 8

Telemarketing

Telemarketing is an invaluable sales tool for approximately 80,000 U.S. companies. According to the Direct Marketing Association, telemarketing is a $100 billion-a-year business, with annual expenditures for telemarketing now exceeding those for direct mail, and revenues from telemarketing increasing 25-35 percent annually. Telemarketing expands sales capabilities, cuts costs, and increases profits. By 1990, more than 265,000 companies are expected to use telemarketing.

The sales manager's interest in and involvement with the telemarketing activity concerns 1) overall sales for the company, and 2) the interaction between telemarketing and the field sales force.

The purpose of this chapter is to give the sales manager a broad overview and understanding of the telemarketing function. This can best be done by excerpting selected material from Peg Fisher's manual, *Successful Telemarketing,* published by Dartnell. The areas to be covered in this overview are: steps in the marketing/selling process, selecting telemarketing accounts, marketing strategies, direct mail support, internal support system, and job descriptions.

The trend toward telemarketing is in part because management has a better understanding today of what can't be accomplished by an outside sales staff. The hiring of more outside salespeople is one way around the problem. However, that's quite an expense to incur, especially if many of the accounts are small dollar-volume customers having limited sales potential or are geographically isolated accounts. What you really need for these types of customers is a more cost-effective way of keeping in touch, instead of expensive outside sales contact. In short, you need telemarketing.

Telemarketing is a "proactive" use of the telephone. Like outside sales, direct mail, and mass advertising methods, telemarketing is simply another method to reach out to customers and prospects with a sales and/or marketing objective.

Steps in the Marketing Process*

The process of marketing and selling can be defined as gathering information required to identify customer need, giving the customer information required to make a buying decision, and asking for the order. It's a simple three-step process. Or is it?

There are a number of steps that go into the process. Understanding the steps helps develop understanding of the knowledge and skills required by the telemarketing staff; management to identify which accounts will be telemarketing accounts; and helps determine specific sales and marketing strategies to assign to telemarketing. The main steps and a brief definition are provided here.

1. *Find and qualify prospects.* The objective of finding and qualifying prospects is to identify which prospects have the potential to use your company's products and services. To "qualify" a prospect implies two important steps:

   - Ask questions to determine need and sales potential.

   - Ask questions to determine if the prospect meets your company's requirements of a customer, e.g., credit.

2. *Qualify leads.* The process of qualifying leads can occur in prospect contacts and contacts with existing or inactive accounts.

   A lead can consist of a customer question, an inquiry about products or services, a comment about a problem. The qualification process consists of asking questions and giving information to help you determine the true nature of the customer's need. Once identified, it is possible to determine if your company's products and services meet the need.

---

*Peg Fisher, *Successful Telemarketing* (Chicago: The Dartnell Corporation, 1985), pp. 329-335.

3. *Gather information about prospects and customers and inactive accounts (market research).* The more you know, the better you can match products and services to account needs. Following are explanations of why it is important to gather specific kinds of account information:

   - *Type of business.* Different types of customers have different needs. The products and services used, for example, by a contractor can differ from a manufacturer or a municipal account or a small jobbing shop. Knowing the nature of a customer's business helps identify potential needs for products and services.

   - *Buying history.* Knowledge of a customer's past purchases helps to identify future needs for product. When this knowledge is coupled with an understanding of the type of business, it is possible to identify other products and services your company offers of use to the customer and to "target" these products as sales objectives.

   - *Names and titles of buyers and buying influences.* Some companies have more than one person responsible for purchasing, e.g., Sam buys product "X" and Bill buys product "Y" and Donna is responsible for all contract buying.

     When you know who buys what, you know who to sell what products and how to sell them.

     Larger companies often have a purchasing agent. This person is responsible for shopping suppliers for price and availability. Items purchased are often identified by someone referred to in sales terminology as the "buying influence." In order to sell your company or get your products specified, it may be necessary to contact the buying influence and sell this person on doing business with you.

   - *Buying criteria.* Buying criteria refers to the customer's standards used to determine how they work with their suppliers, as well as what criteria the supplier must meet to be on their approved list.

     Criteria can include supplier services, such as special

shipping/labeling/packaging of product, special timing on delivery to meet the customer's loading dock requirements, product testing and supplier certification, and no partial shipments or back orders.

You need to know if buying criteria exist. If yes, does your company meet the standard?

- *Buying cycles.* Different companies have different buying cycles or times when purchasing is done, e.g., monthly, weekly, or on an "as needed" basis.

  Some products can be on different cycles than others, e.g., expendable tooling might be purchased on an "as needed basis." New equipment purchases occur in the spring after the customer's annual budget meetings.

- *Use of name brands.* It is common for buyers to have certain name-brand preferences because of habit, or because the equipment they use specifies product-brand use. By knowing brand preferences, you can determine if your company has the brand or if you have a substitute brand that meets the preferred brand's specifications.

- *Use of competitive suppliers.* There can be many benefits derived from knowing your competition.

  1. You can identify your strengths compared to the competitor's weaknesses and use company features/ benefits statements that highlight your strengths.

  2. You have a good understanding of what you are up against in a competitive bid.

  3. You can stress your company's unique services as appropriate to the customer's needs.

4. *Present product/Company features and benefits.* Part of the selling process involves giving information to the customer that is required to make a buying decision. What the customer does not know exists, he or she cannot buy. Presenting company and product features and benefits helps develop awareness of what you have to offer, how you work with customers, and the benefits of doing business with you.

When talking with the customer about products, the use of product features and benefits demonstrates ability to talk the customer's language by being able to present information about products and product application in terms of customer needs.

5. *Company policies/Procedures explanations.* Each company is unique in its policies and procedures, i.e., its ways of operating with customers. The explanation of policies/procedures helps educate the customer about what to expect from you.

    Customers typically use many suppliers. Your objective is to create an acceptable "level of expectation" when doing business with your company. When an acceptable level of expectation is not met, the most common result is customer complaints. Or, the customer stops doing business with you altogether.

6. *Submit proposals, bids quotations.* Submittal may be a formal written document or a verbal quotation. The objective is to provide the customer with detailed and accurate information required to make a buying decision, to compare your bid with others, to clearly set out your price, terms, and conditions of sale, including discounts, as appropriate.

7. *Negotiate proposals, bids, quotations.* The objective of negotiating is to make certain the quotation is understood, answer questions and objections, provide required explanations, sell the features/benefits of the quotation and of doing business with you, and to reach agreement.

    When your quotation is being compared with another, the negotiating must encompass making sure the customer is comparing apples with apples—not with oranges. Remember: we might all like to have a Cadillac for the price of a Chevrolet, but in business, that's a good way to go out of business!

8. *Take/process orders.* The objective is to accurately handle customer orders in a timely manner in a way acceptable to the customer to help ensure repeat business.

During the taking of orders, the objective is to make appropriate suggestions and recommendations on add-on items, discount points, and product substitutions (if appropriate).

The order process includes having knowledge of your company's in-house order-processing requirements to prevent bottlenecks from occurring due to lack of proper documentation. This knowledge is also important for servicing the customer's need for expediting.

9. *Handle customer problems, e.g., billing, credit, product quality, delivery, shipping.* The professional and efficient handling of customer problems is the road to increased sales opportunities. The objective is to define the real problem and resolve it within your company's ground rules and to the customer's satisfaction.

   As appropriate, customer problems should be reported so the company can take steps to ensure they do not continue to happen.

Selecting Telemarketing Accounts*

This is really where everything begins. This is where the sales or marketing managers, outside sales staff, and data processing (DP) person responsible for programming (if you have one) sit down with your account lists and sales history/gross margin dollar history and begin making decisions.

The User Needs/Marketing Methods Identification information on the following pages should be discussed with the entire group of decision-makers. The basic decisions to be made are:

1. Which accounts will be outside sales accounts only? Why?

2. Which accounts will be shared accounts between outside sales and telemarketing.? Why?

3. Which accounts will be telemarketing only accounts? Why?

---

*Fisher, *Successful Telemarketing,* pp. 45-46.

4. Which accounts will receive only direct mailings and incoming customer calls handling? Why?

It is useful for this meeting to know your real cost of an outside sales call. Published figures indicate costs can be $200 and more. It is helpful to know the figure because this tells you which accounts you can't afford to call on in person even once. To do so costs you money.

Typically, the account selection meeting begins with gross generalizations and moves to specifics. For example, there may be general agreement that your company has a lot of "house accounts" or small dollar-volume customers with good gross margin that you want to assign to telemarketing. You may all also agree that telemarketing should contact inactive accounts for purposes of reactivation, and possibly do prospecting at some later time.

A few minutes' analysis of Table 1. User Needs/Marketing Methods Identification Chart, pages 189 and 190, quickly reveals potential telemarketing applications, as well as potential need for redefinition of the outside sales function. If your outside sales force functions with a route-sales/order-taking mentality, you have a basic problem to deal with along with the setting up of a telemarketing operation.

ONE IMPORTANT POINT*

The initial selection of telemarketing accounts is important for purposes of establishing guidelines within your company. But, remember—these guidelines may change, based upon results you achieve. For example:

- You may initially assign a group of inactive accounts along with small dollar-volume accounts. Results measures, however, may indicate telemarketing is much more profitable when you stick to existing accounts and prospecting. Thus, the original 100 inactive accounts might be pulled and replaced with other small dollar-volume "house accounts."

- Although you may initially think a certain block of assigned

---

*Fisher, *Successful Telemarketing,* p. 65.

Table 1. User Needs/Marketing Methods Identification Chart*

	Telemarketers (and back-up support staff)	Outside Sales
1. Immediate access to information and identification of ongoing changes in customer need		
• Order taking/processing	X	
• Inventory availability	X	
• Delivery schedules	X	
• Pricing and price negotiation	X	
• Products information and applications assistance	X	
• Cross-reference on competitive products	X	
• Add-on products, quantity discounts information, special promotions, new products introduction	X	
• Policies that have an impact on the user	X	
• Information about the company and services available	X	
• Ongoing information gathering about the customer for needs identification	X	
• Leads/problems information transfer to achieve required follow-up	X	
2. Problems resolution, i.e., technical applications problems-solving, billing/ shipping errors and return authorizations handling, repairs processing, and qualification of the need for outside sales problem-solving and defective product inspection	X	X

(continued)

*Fisher, *Successful Telemarketing*, pp. 98-99.

Table 1. User Needs/Marketing Methods Identification Chart*

(continued)

	Telemarketers (and back-up support staff)	Outside Sales
3. Literature/Samples mailings	X	
• Use of literature/samples during product introduction/demonstration		X
4. Sales contacts		
Product demonstration		X
Systems recommendations/product recommendations based on user situation/needs/problems		X
• User staff training on product use		X
• Product testing or assistance with test process		X
• Selected public relations contacts		X

*Fisher, *Successful Telemarketing*, pp. 33-34.

telemarketing accounts requires close coordination between outside sales and telemarketing, results may indicate this is not true. Buyer needs can, in fact, be handled 100 percent by telemarketing. Be prepared to reassign outside sales responsibilities.

The best way to approach the initial implementation stages of telemarketing is as a "test." Even when you have a viable operation up and running, you will continue testing new approaches.

Marketing Strategies*

A common cause of failure of telemarketing is the fact that management does not define a marketing strategy for the operation. Without a marketing strategy, it is not possible to identify staff support requirements, develop materials for staff use, train staff, or measure results.

The marketing strategy selected for telemarketing must be de-

*Fisher, *Successful Telemarketing*, pp. 79-88.

fined in conjunction with the company's overall marketing plan. It must take into account the following variables:

- Present customer base and their needs

- Prospective customers and their needs

- Products and services offered by the company and planned offerings

- Present way the company is organized to take products and services to the marketplace

- Future plans for taking products and services to the marketplace

- Costs of sales and any plans to reduce the sales expense ratio

Within the overall marketing plan for the company, there can be any number of marketing strategies selected for a telemarketing operation. Strategies selected can apply to all accounts or selected accounts or prospects. The overall objective of each strategy is to increase market share. The following are examples of types of strategies and specific objectives and approaches for each.

1. Truck route calls

    Objectives

    - To fill trucks and increase profitability

    - To prospect and reactivate along existing routes

    - To develop new and profitable truck routes

    Approach

    This is generally the simplest type of strategy. The telemarketer is directed to call all accounts along a specific route the day prior to delivery. The approach is: "Our truck will be in your area tomorrow. What are your last minute needs? I can add them to your order." *Specific* items and brand names should be recommended based upon customer purchasing history. This approach can be used with customers who have scheduled deliveries, as well as with inactives and prospects along the established route who do not.

2. New product/Service introductions

Objectives

- To achieve a quick and efficient way to introduce new products
- To qualify interest and need
- To send appropriate follow-up product literature
- To qualify need (as appropriate) for outside sales contact

Approach

Potential users of the new product should first be identified. Indiscriminate calling of all accounts may be inappropriate, depending upon product/service. Telemarketers must be trained to present product or service features and benefits, overcome potential customer objections, use sales collateral support material, qualify need for outside sales contact (depending upon the product/service), and discuss product substitution possibilities inherent in a new product.

Make certain new product introductions are coordinated with outside sales staff, should in-person contact be required.

This approach is appropriate with existing customers, inactives, and prospects.

3. Special promotions

Objectives

- To qualify account needs within terms and conditions of the promotion
- Quick and efficient account coverage on a promotion

- Qualify need for outside sales contacts (if appropriate to product or service)

- Timely mailings follow-up

Approach

Like new product introductions, potential users of specials should first be identified. Staff must be trained to discuss the features of the promotion, including terms and conditions.

- These types of calls are appropriate with existing customers, inactives, and prospects.

4. Advance bookings

Objectives

- To qualify interest and need

- To achieve better vendor prices based upon quantity purchases, or to take advantage of vendor prices dependent upon quantity

- To eliminate peaks/valleys in seasonal sales

Approach

Commodity line products are common advance-booking sales, although other products can be adapted to this concept. The concept is to contact appropriate buyers to identify estimated or actual future need for product. Then, contact vendors for price based upon purchasing in quantity and call back accounts to firm up price and availability. This process can also work in the reverse. Receiving a notice from a vendor about special pricing based upon achieving certain quantity purchases can prompt calls to customers to attempt to sell the quantity required to meet the discount.

5. Account reactivation

Objectives

- To reintroduce your company and the features/benefits of doing business with you

- To tap often unknown sales potential in this account group

- To sell the breadth of the product/services offering or selected offerings

Approach

The inactive account needs to first be defined, e.g., a customer who has not purchased product for a specified period, or a customer having total sales or gross profit last year of a defined dollar amount.

Some cautions: If management knows that accounts became inactive because of problems caused by the company, telemarketers should know what caused the problem and how to overcome objections to doing business with you.

Although this account base can be a good source of business, it can also include accounts that no longer exist, accounts having bad credit, or accounts having sales potential too low to be of interest to the company. The result of account contacts should be frequently reviewed to cull out nonproductive accounts or poor credit risks.

6. Prospecting

Objectives

- To increase market share in the existing territory or increase market share in new territories outside of your present geographical area

- To sell all or selected products and services

Approach

The approach to prospecting is similar to a "cold call" done in person. The objective is to give information to the prospect about your company and the features/benefits of doing business with you, as well as to gather information about the prospect to qualify need, interest, and credit information. Appropriate sales collateral materials and product literature mailings can either precede the call or be used as follow-up.

Prospecting calls can also be made to follow up on manufacturer's leads, and on prospect responses to distributor advertising campaigns and direct mail promotions.

Selection of the list of prospects can be as simple as consulting the Yellow Pages to researching various list sources, including:

- Dun & Bradstreet
- State or Municipal Regulatory Agencies for licensed practitioners, e.g., beauticians, electricians, plumbers
- Dodge Reports
- Chamber of Commerce
- Direct mail list houses

7. Account coverage

Objectives

- To incorporate all appropriate marketing strategies into the telemarketing position responsibility
- To increase account sales/service capability
- To increase account penetration through better coverage and frequent-need identification
- To coordiante efforts closely (as required) with outside sales
- To sell the breadth of the product/services offering

Approach

Assign a "mix" of existing customers, inactive accounts, and prospects to telemarketers and hold them responsible for sales/profits in the account base.

Have staff members become totally familiar with the customer's needs and the customer will develop a rapport and trusting relationship with staff members. Customers look to staff for ideas and recommendations.

Management responsibility

The key point to keep in mind is that whatever strategy or strategies are selected, it is management's responsibility to clearly define the telemarketer's role, as well as that of outside sales. Do not expect telemarketers to decide what products to offer as specials, which accounts to call for advance bookings, or what new products will be introduced and to whom.

No matter what the marketing strategy or account base selected for the strategy, management clearly has the responsibility to define:

- Who will make calls
- Who will be called about what and for what purpose
- Where the staff will be located
- How the function will be managed
- What internal systems are needed to support the function
- What direct mail and other sales support is needed and how it will be used
- How results will be measured
- How staff members will be compensated

Direct Mail Support*

There are significant differences between in-person sales and telemarketing. One major difference is the lack of visual feedback between the telemarketer and the customer, and the fact that the telemarketer cannot see the customer or his or her location. This lack of visual feedback dictates the need for special telemarketing job resources, including direct mail material.

Direct mail is used to enhance the results of a telemarketing function. Through appropriately directed mailings, the following telemarketing objectives are reinforced:

1. Establish and maintain company name visibility at the user location

2. Introduce and educate customers on the breadth and depth of the product line

3. Sell existing product(s)

4. Introduce and sell new products

5. Develop rapport between the telemarketer and the user

6. Provide technical data on products

7. Provide answers to questions on product applications

8. Introduce and sell services available from the company

Types of Recommended Direct Mail

The use of any given mailer must be determined based upon analysis of the account's needs and the classification of the account. Not all mailers are used with all account classifications.

1. *Company product and service listing (line card)*
   A company product and service listing should be used by telemarketers, outside sales, and route drivers. It should be a self-promotion piece that positions your company to the customer. Use it to identify the following types of information:

---

*Fisher, *Successful Telemarketing,* pp. 95-98.

- Types of products
- Types of services
- Manufacturers' lines
- Delivery
- Return/warranty information
- Telephone number
- Emergency telephone number
- Locations for pick-up

This can be a one-page card stock piece that is mailed to the customer for posting. It should display your company name and logo and—of course—the telephone number in large typeface.

2. *New customer information kit*
This type of material should be used by telemarketing and outside sales personnel. Along with the company product and service listing, it should house an introductory letter with names of the sales team, appropriate product catalogs, and company catalogs and brochures. When the kit is used by sales for prospecting, it should include a credit application form to be completed during the in-person call. Telemarketing sales staff can mail the kit to prospects and conduct follow-up calls to gather required credit information.

3. *Telemarketing brochure*
The telemarketing brochure should be developed prior to implementing your program. It makes an excellent follow-up mailer to telephone-account customers to reinforce the objectives of the operation and explain your goals of better service through the person assigned to the account. It should include a picture of the telemarketer and information on his or her background to develop credibility based upon experience, industry knowledge, special training, and background.

Figure 1, page 200, presents a format for use in developing a telephone sales brochure that is a two-fold mailer printed on 8½″ x 14″ paper.

A letter explaining the new telemarketing operation and how it is designed to benefit the customer is appropriate when signed by the company president. This letter should be sent immediately prior to program implementation. Make certain it is addressed to the buyer. If possible, it should also be sent to the buying influences within a customer account.

Internal Support System*

The point to keep in mind when establishing a telemarketing operation is that it will be different from what existed previously. It therefore must be coordinated with any existing systems for communicating in-house and for ensuring that telemarketers have the information available to do their job.
For example:

1. How will telemarketers be kept up-to-date on inventory information? Perhaps your office supervisor is the one who presently receives a copy of your inventory report. It does your telemarketers no good to know it is in his hands. They need it in their hands for immediate access to customer-required information.

2. How will telemarketers contact outside sales when in-person customer contact is required? How will telemarketers know what was accomplished during this contact, when the contact occurred, and what specific follow-up is needed from telemarketing?

TYPES OF INTERNAL SUPPORT SYSTEMS

When any new operation is installed within an organization, it is common to need to develop new internal systems to support the

*Fisher, *Successful Telemarketing,* pp. 105-114.

Figure 1. Telemarketing Brochure Example

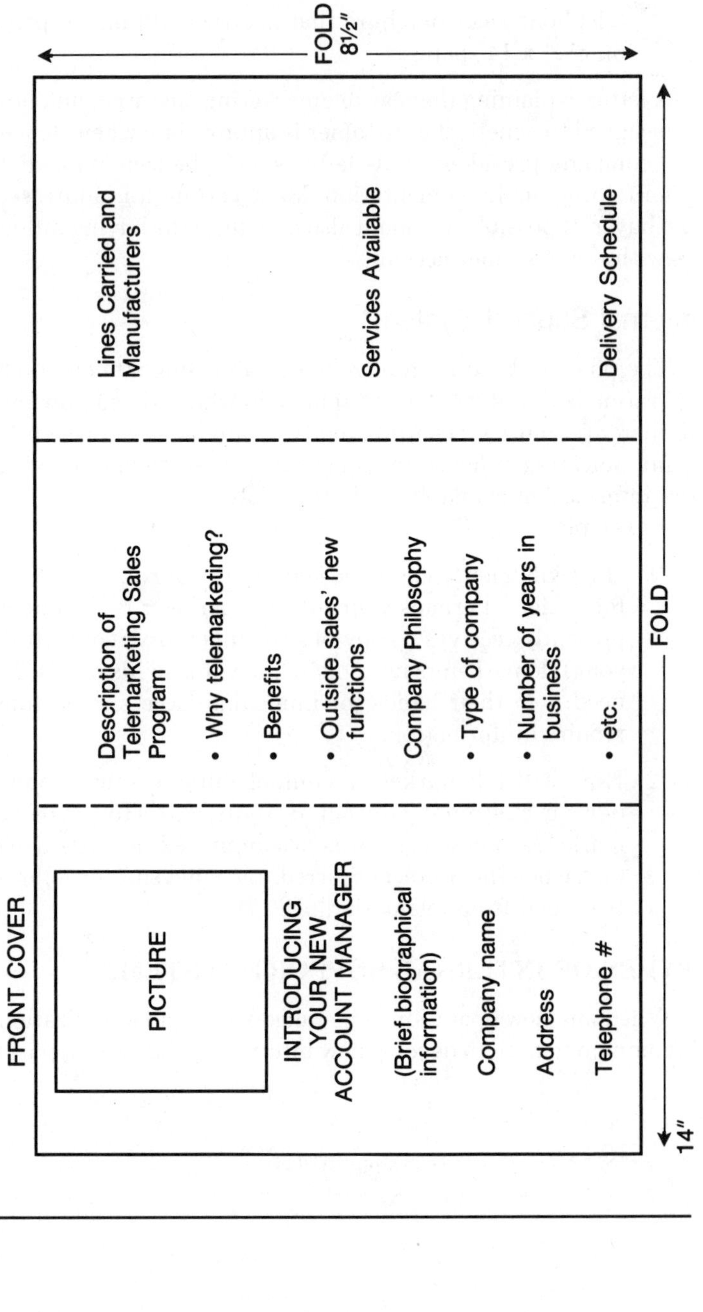

FRONT COVER

FOLD 8½"

FOLD

14"

PICTURE

INTRODUCING
YOUR NEW
ACCOUNT MANAGER

(Brief biographical information)

Company name

Address

Telephone #

Description of
Telemarketing Sales
Program

- Why telemarketing?

- Benefits

- Outside sales' new functions

Company Philosophy

- Type of company

- Number of years in business

- etc.

Lines Carried and
Manufacturers

Services Available

Delivery Schedule

function. The following are typical systems areas that may need to be revised or instituted to address the telemarketing operation.

1. Delivery information, including schedule changes

2. Inventory information that is real-time or close to it

3. Back-order status on customer orders

4. Customer credit status

5. "Slow pay" accounts; guidelines on how to handle

6. Pricing information

7. Discount schedules

8. Account information

9. Sales history data by account

10. New product information, applications training, product literature, specification sheets, price lists

11. Guidelines on the use of mailings

12. A lead system for transferring leads from and to outside sales

13. Schedules and other information on company-sponsored programs for customers, e.g., use of lab facilities, training clinics, product demonstration seminars, technical assistance training

14. Promotional materials

15. Telemarketer input to marketing strategies selection and design

16. Backup clerical support to take orders, handle mailings, perform administrative tasks

17. Updatings on company policies/procedures and any changes in the way business is conducted with customers

18. Cross-referenced information on competitive products

19. Competitive information

20. Attendance at sales meetings

21. Guidelines on authorization of returned goods

The point of having systems in place for keeping telemarketing management and staff in the mainstream of current information flow within the company is this: Any oversight can have a dramatic impact on your customer base in a short time. Consider this possibility: If one telemarketer is in contact with 40 accounts a day or 200 a week, what do you think might be the impact on these accounts if he or she wrongly positions a product? A company policy? A price? A promotion? A competitor? It won't take long before the entire assigned account base learns you have a "dumb bunny" on the telephone! The professional image of your firm is at stake in the marketplace!

Amazingly, so-called telemarketing operations are sometimes set up by company managers who never give a second thought to providing required information to the telemarketers. That so powerful a business tool can be arbitrarily assigned to untrained, unskilled, unprofessional, uninformed people is a bad reflection on top management.

This obvious error in reaching a conclusion is commonly found among managers who set up telemarketing functions. In essence, management takes the wings off of the telemarketing operation by not providing the information needed to do the job. Then, management accuses telemarketing of not working!

THE LEAD ALERT/CUSTOMER PROBLEM REPORT

One example of a required internal system is the lead alert/customer problem report. This is a form designed to ensure two-way communication between telemarketers and outside sales.

If telemarketer contact with a customer reveals the need for in-person product demonstration or on-site inspection of defective material, for example, a system must exist for:

1. Informing outside sales of the customer's need;

2. Getting information back to the telemarketer about the results of the in-person contact;

3. Tracking the level of lead/problem activity and timeliness of follow-up.

When this form is sent by the telemarketer, a notation is made and a date is set for follow-up with outside sales. The lead alert/customer problem report is directed to the appropriate outside salesperson. Figure 2, below, presents a format for accomplishing the transfer of information on leads and problems.

Figure 2. Lead Alert/Customer Problem Report Form

```
┌─────────────────────────────────────────────────────────────┐
│   LEAD ALERT/CUSTOMER      _____ Emergency           │
│      PROBLEM REPORT        _____ Date Requested      │
│   Customer: _____         │
│   Buyer's Name: _____         │
│   Phone: (    ) _____        │
│   Reason for Call: _____        │
│   _____       │
│   _____ TM/OS Initials: _____     │
│   ═════════════════════════════════════════════════════       │
│                                                               │
│   Contact Date: _____        │
│   Call Results/Solution to Problem: _____         │
│   _____       │
│   _____ TM/OS Initials: _____     │
│   Follow-up required by: _____         │
│   _____       │
│   _____       │
└─────────────────────────────────────────────────────────────┘
```

NOTE: This form is designed to achieve two-way communication. It can be initiated by telephone *or* by outside sales staff.

CODES:

TM = telemarketer
OS = outside sales

The Telemarketing Manager's Job*

The simplest way to start to define the ongoing management requirements of the position is to draw a parallel with the "known" management of outside sales staff. The outside sales staff manager's functions include:

1. Tactical planning and coordination of the outside sales effort

2. Identification of sales territories and staff assignment of accounts

3. Account analysis and sales strategy development, including identification of call frequency schedules, target sales potential, sales quotas

4. Tracking, analysis, and discussion of sales results with individual outside sales staff members

5. Reassignment of accounts based on sales results. For example, an account may be reclassified to "house account" status, be placed in someone else's territory, be assigned to top management, or have the call frequency schedule increased or cut back to allow time for contacting additional accounts

6. Staff coaching and counseling, including periodic travel with salespeople on joint calls to critique sales techniques, coach, counsel, make recommendations on account sales strategies, and demonstrate the use of new sales collateral or "how-tos" of selling products

7. Staff training, development, and performance evaluation

8. In-house liaison representing the outside sales operations in order to ensure required support, coordinate efforts between departments, and develop tools and programs for the outside sales staff

9. Establishment of ongoing lines of communication for purposes of staff problem identification and solution

*Fisher, *Successful Telemarketing,* pp. 126-128.

The essence of the outside sales management function is to direct the activities of the sales force to ensure that: 1) sales expense dollars are spent where there is the best opportunity to produce sales at a profit, and 2) that the type of sales activity reflects the company's overall marketing objective.

The outside sales management function is defined here because most managers understand at least something about it—even if they do not take the time to do it. The telemarketing manager job function has parallel responsibilities. Why is this true? Because the total company marketing effort encompasses outside sales, telemarketing, and mass marketing (direct mail, catalogs, brochures and trade show participation). As such, the telemarketing strategy is not separate from the outside sales or mass marketing strategy. These are simply different entities having the same objective: to generate sales and profits.

Telemarketing Manager Job Description

When telemarketing is viewed from the perspective outlined above, the function of the telemarketing manager can be defined as parallel to those of outside sales management. The job description might look like that shown in Figure 3, page 206.

Telemarketer Job Descriptions*

In order to accomplish the recruiting objective, as well as measure job performance once a candidate is on the job, management needs a defined, written job description for the telemarketing position. It is obvious that the job description can vary considerably from one company to the next. The job description is used during the interviewing process. It can help you to determine if a candidate who says he has prior telemarketing experience in actuality only took inbound calls from customers who placed orders and asked questions.

Remember—there is confusion abounding in the marketplace about the definition of telemarketing. A candidate may think you

---

*Fisher, *Successful Telemarketing*, pp. 144-147.

Figure 3. Telemarketing Manager Job Description

Title _____ Reports to: _____
Compensation Range: _____ Job Description Date: _____

Overall Responsibilities:
Responsible for directing the sales and service activities of the telemarketing staff to ensure that sales expense dollars are spent where there is the best opportunity to produce sales at a profit, and that the type of sales and service activity reflects the company's overall marketing objective; responsible for coordinating sales strategies, for day-to-day management, results measurement and analysis, staff training and performance evaluation, equipment evaluation and recommendations for new equipment requirements, operations budget control.

Specific Tasks:
_____ Tactical planning and coordination of telemarketing sales activity.
_____ Selection of telephone accounts and assignment to staff.
_____ Account analysis and sales strategy development, including identification of call frequency schedules, target sales potential, sales quotas.
_____ Track, analyze, and discuss sales results with staff.
_____ Reassign accounts based on sales results.
_____ Staff coaching and counseling including periodic monitoring of calls to analyze style, content and selling techniques, to make recommendations on account sales strategies, and to demonstrate sales techniques.
_____ Staff training, development, and performance evaluation.
_____ In-house liaison representing the telemarketing operation to ensure required support, coordinate efforts between departments, and develop required tools, programs, and call-scripts for the sales staff.
_____ Establish ongoing lines of communication for purposes of staff problem identification and resolution.

NOTE: Each of the above functions parallel functions included in the outside sales management job. Also included in the telemarketing manager position description can be the responsibility for supervising and analyzing the results of related customer-service activity. This, of course, depends upon how the telemarketing function is organized.

want a reactive customer service/order-taking person, when in fact you want someone interested and capable of (or willing to learn) proactive selling by telephone. Telemarketing is just like outside sales, except that it is accomplished by phone.

The job description can also help identify the job candidate with telemarketing experience in a boiler-room atmosphere. This is not to say that the person should not be hired for your position. It is, however, incumbent upon you to clearly define the differences and determine if the person has the knowledge, desire, and motivation to want to do this type of intelligent selling.

THE POSITION TITLE

It is highly recommended that you avoid the overworked misnomer so commonly used in business today: "inside sales." The traditional inside sales function is the order-taker/customer service/ sales support position that reacts to customer needs.

A more appropriate title for a telemarketing position with account coverage responsibility is telephone account manager, or account manager, telemarketing group.

Titles like solicitor and communicator are commonly associated with consumer selling and are otherwise both nondescriptive and negatively perceived.

SAMPLE JOB DESCRIPTIONS

Figures 4 and 5 on pages 208 and 209 show two totally different types of telemarketing job descriptions. The first job description is for a telemarketing account manager responsible for account coverage. The second describes an account manager responsible for lead qualification.

Figure 4. Account Coverage Job Description

Title _____ Reports to: _____
Compensation Range: _____ Job Description Date: _____
Overall Responsibilities:

Responsible for initiating and maintaining sales and service contacts with customers and for qualifying prospects for purposes of market maintenance and penetration.

The telemarketing function includes direct telephone selling and servicing of accounts, analyzing and qualifying customer information, implementing account sales strategies, pricing and preparing quotations, communicating appropriate information to management, maintaining related records and customer files.

Specific Tasks:

____ Conduct initial and follow-up telephone calls to accounts to build a relationship required to maintain the repeat business process.

____ Qualify accounts as to type and frequency of contact required to sell and service customer needs.

____ Establish and maintain callback-frequency schedules by account.

____ Gather and record customer information required to sell and service customers.

____ Compile quotations from standard price lists or other sources using established procedures. Maintain quote log and files.

____ Take and process orders; edit orders including price check, discount check, terms and conditions, and minimum-order quantities. Maintain open-order files and shipment documents by account.

____ Initiate correspondence as required, including memos to customers.

____ Select and mail appropriate materials. Maintain record of mailings.

____ Coordinate with management on implementation plans and results, including special promotional campaigns and overall telephone sales results.

____ Coordinate with traffic/shipping/warehouse departments on shipping schedules, carriers, pick-ups, inventory availability and lead times.

____ Qualify prospect calls as to type of account, needs, products used, sales potential. As appropriate, transfer leads using established procedures.

____ Review all mail orders from telephone accounts daily.

Figure 5. Lead Qualification Job Description

Title: _____ Reports to: _____

Compensation Range: _____ Job Description Date: _____

Overall Responsibilities:

Responsible for initiating telemarketing calls to leads generated via advertising in trade publications and incoming "800" number calls for purposes of:

1. Selling product
2. Generating marketing data about users/potential users of products
3. Transferring leads as appropriate to the sales engineer and sales manager

Specific Tasks:

1. Qualify leads using established guidelines.
2. Call leads within 10 working days of company mailing.
3. Handle up to 12 outbound telephone contacts per hour for up to four hours a day.
4. Complete the prospect profile record based upon contact results.
5. Mail follow-up literature to prospects as appropriate.
6. Complete the telemarketer summary-record on a daily basis and complete totals weekly for submittal to the sales manager.
7. As directed, meet with management to discuss call activity and results.
8. As required, process orders resulting from telemarketing calls, note trial offers on invoices indicating prepaid shipping costs, handle credit approval–form mailings and returns from telemarketer-generated customers.
9. Transfer appropriate leads and related records to the sales engineer and sales manager, using established guidelines.
10. Ongoing development of product and product applications knowledge through study of product materials and product-applications input from the sales engineer and sales manager.
11. Transfer completed prospect profile records to the marketing department for data analysis on a daily basis.

Chapter 9

Trade Shows

Trade shows are an important segment of the total sales effort and have become a multibillion-dollar industry. More than 7,800 trade shows are held annually with approximately 42 million attendees. Exhibitor budgets run about $9 billion annually.

Depending upon the size of company and staff available, the responsibility for planning and implementing the trade show function lies with the meeting planner, sales promotion department, the exhibit manager, an advertising agency serving the company, or the sales manager. While we will cover some of the major aspects of this sales-producing function in this chapter, a thorough and detailed treatment of the subject is contained in Robert Konikow's 250-page manual, *How to Participate Profitably in Trade Shows* (Chicago: The Dartnell Corporation, 1985).

What Are Trade Shows?

Trade shows, exhibitions, expositions, and trade fairs are all names for various forms and interpretations of the same animal.

In a presentation at Cornell University, Robert Black, founding publisher of *Tradeshow Week,* gave the following overview.*

> These events bring together in a single location, usually an exhibit hall and convention center or a hotel, a group of suppliers who set up physical exhibits of their products and services from a given industry or discipline.
>
> While many trade shows are parts of particular conventions and meetings, an increasing number are events in their own right with no formal convention or meeting connected with them.
>
> The size range of trade shows is enormous—from the 15 to 20 exhibits in connection with local or regional meetings to the industry gi-

---

*Published by Trade Show Bureau, P.O. Box 797, East Orleans, MA 02643.

ants with more than 800,000 net square feet of exhibit space, more than 1,000 exhibitors, and more than 100,000 attendees.

Although trade shows have been around from a long time, it is only since World War II that they have come into their own as significant factors in the promotion and marketing mix.

The proliferation of trade shows in both size and number has been driven by both the cost-effectiveness of the trade show medium and the diversification of technology and industry which has created hundreds of new disciplines and hundreds of thousands of new products.

The cost-effectiveness lies in the fact that a contact at an average trade show can cost between 25 percent and 35 percent of a sales call.*

Trade shows have been uniquely effective in new product introductions, establishing such products in the marketplace more quickly than the traditional sales and marketing tools of media advertising, direct mail, or sales calls. Companies participate in trade shows for a variety of reasons.

- Attracting and identifying new prospects
- Servicing current customers
- Introducing new products
- Enhancing corporate image
- Testing market response to new products
- Enhancing corporate morale
- Gathering competitive product information†

Trade shows vary widely in their functions and objectives: some concentrate on direct sales, particularly those serving consumer product areas, such as hardware, giftwares, consumer electronics, etc.

Some are basically educational, designed to introduce components that can be specified by engineers and designers in the development of products and systems. Such shows are numerous in the electronics components and similar technologies.

Other informational shows are in the medical, educational, and financial areas.

An increasingly significant aspect of the trade show industry is its "internationalism" in terms of both exhibitors and attendees. Many U.S. trade shows find a significant percentage of their total exhibitors to be manufacturers from Europe, Asia, and Latin America; an increasing number of U.S. shows now feature "pavilions" sponsored by the government export trade entities of various countries. Conversely, a growing number of U.S. companies participate in overseas trade shows, many times with the advice and assistance of our Department of Commerce.

Trade Show Bureau Research Report #2010, July 1986.
†*Assessing Trade Show Functions & Performance,* Roger A. Kiren and William A. Cron, Edwin L. Cox School of Business, Southern Methodist University, 1983.

Corporate Exhibit Management

The corporate exhibit management function includes budgeting the total trade show program; trade show evaluation and selection; exhibit design planning and supplier selection; analyzing show rules and industry practices; logistical and chronological planning; trade show services selection; planning collateral and show support materials; staffing, training, and on-floor scheduling of exhibit sales personnel; the installation and dismantling budget and plan; pre-show promotion; at-show sales lead recording; post-show sales lead follow-up; post-show reporting and evaluation.

The corporate exhibit management structure varies from the one-person department, in companies that participate in three or four shows a year, to major departments in companies that participate in from 25 to 200 shows a year. Regardless of size, the basic job functions of the exhibit manager remain the same. It is just as important for a small company to have a professional and structured approach to trade show participation as it is for an IBM or an AT&T. Job functions of the exhibit manager are as follows:

1. *Trade show selection and evaluation*

   - Information sources

   - Trade show "value" factors

   - Defining corporate objectives

   - Charting trade show benefits and establishing participation objectives

   - Analyzing and evaluating floor plans

   - Show management and association interface

   - International trade show analysis and evaluation

2. *Exhibit designer and producer selection and evaluation*

   - Information sources—the Exhibit Designers & Producers Association (ED & PA)—the range of ED & PA services

- Evaluating custom exhibits; modular exhibits; portable exhibits; rental exhibits
- Planning collateral exhibit services and materials

3. Show rules and industry practices
   - Evaluating specific show rules and regulations
   - Evaluating union rules and regulations
   - Evaluating convention center rules and regulations

4. *Budgeting trade show programs*
   - The primary cost checklist
   - Fixed costs and flexible costs
   - Exhibit building estimating
   - Installation and dismantling cost estimating
   - Special services cost estimating
   - Staff cost estimating
   - Housing, travel, and entertainment cost estimating
   - Collateral materials cost estimating

5. *Logistical and chronological planning*
   - Developing a master control chart
   - Developing a chronological planning chart
   - Developing a service contractor communications plan
   - Developing a red-flag control system
   - Meeting room evaluation
   - Security planning and evaluation
   - Food and beverage service standards and evaluation
   - Signage and traffic flow planning
   - Move-in/move-out logistical planning

- On-floor management and service contractor relations
- Union labor relations
- Convention center staff relations
- Budgeting in-hall operations

6. *Seminar and conference management*
   - Seminar and conference planning
   - Convention event planning
   - Association relations
   - Conference requirement evaluation
   - Food and beverage functions planning and evaluation
   - Speaker requirements
   - Registration and crowd control planning
   - Budgeting seminars and conferences

7. *Support and administrative services*
   - Housing planning and negotiation
   - Preregistration systems
   - Travel planning and negotiation
   - Convention bureau interface

8. Exhibitor directories
   - Publishing the show directory
   - On-floor information systems
   - Publication of papers or seminar proceedings
   - Post-show reporting and evaluation

9. *New business development*
   - Project conceptualizing
   - Trade show research and evaluation

- Association relations
- Market surveys and evaluations
- New show launch planning
- New business evaluation standards

10. *Show staffing, training, and information recording*
    - Estimating staff requirements
    - On-floor sales training
    - Establishing sales objectives
    - Sales lead recording and tracking systems
    - Post-show sales follow-up systems
    - Cost-per-sales-lead evaluation

11. *Installation and dismantling process*
    - Contractor service evaluation and selection
    - In-house planning
    - Show rules and regulations and union jurisdiction evaluation
    - Budgeting
    - Control planning
    - On-site services
    - Information resources

12. *Pre-Show promotion*
    - Targeting show objectives
    - Establishing media and direct mail pre-show promotion plan
    - Show and association management interface
    - Budgeting pre-show promotion

13. *Post-Show analysis*

- The post-show report
- Evaluating the cost per lead and cost per sales dollar
- Tracking post-show sales follow-ups

Trade Show Services

There are two primary businesses in the trade show services segment of the industry—exhibit designing and building and general trade show service contracting.

EXHIBIT DESIGNING AND BUILDING

The Functions

The exhibit designer and producer functions include sales and marketing; creative design and exhibit planning; exhibit building; installation and dismantling; exhibit storage; refurbishing and shipping; collateral customer services; estimating, pricing, and budgeting.

ED & PA services are unique and specialized. Exhibits must be designed to be dynamic visual traffic stoppers without overwhelming either the product or the corporate image. They must be creative, cost-effective, and fit the graphic image of the exhibiting company. It is one of the most challenging areas of creative commercial design.

Specialists have evolved to serve this particular need and there is a major industry group representing them, The Exhibit Designers & Producers Association.

Because exhibits are a visual medium, they represent a range from simple 10 x 10-foot displays to major area presentations.

The exhibit designer and producer can play an important role in the way a company uses the trade show medium. A classic example is the Pyne Corporation of New York and how, with the help of their exhibit designer and producer, this company used the trade show medium as a high priority tool to help them achieve spectacular growth. Pyne was established in 1965 to distribute Fuji medical X ray film and equipment in the United States. They entered their first trade show in 1965 with a 10 x 10-foot booth using modular construction with photographs and limited illuminations. By 1971 they had decided to use Greyhound Exhibitgroup Inc. in Los Angeles as their trade show designer and coordinator, moving up to a 10 x 20-foot display featuring illuminated headers and backwall panels.

By 1975 Pyne had expanded to a 10 x 30-foot exhibit with greater impact and more area for customer traffic flow. In 1978 the company increased again to a 20 x 30-foot island space, and Exhibitgroup expanded the design elements to include 12-foot-high header panels and some conference areas, while retaining the same graphic corporate image that had been established in previous exhibits.

In 1981 Pyne's exhibit space was expanded again to a 40 x 50-foot island space, and a theater was created for slide presentations. Illuminated light boxes projected to a height of 12 feet featuring Fuji film scenes from around the world. By 1985, the exhibit area was again increased to a 50 x 60-foot island space that featured two enclosed, air-conditioned conference rooms on whose outer walls were mounted light boxes featuring various Fuji products. The four corner areas provided carpeted platforms for actual product displays.

Needless to say, these successive expansions of trade show space over 20 years wouldn't have been planned unless sales and profits were also expanding to match. And they were. Pyne's sales each year regularly outstripped forecasts, and there were often two-year periods in which the most recent year doubled the previous year. This kind of performance is the sales manager's dream.

This brief overview provides an example of how an aggressive marketing organization, with the help of a creative exhibit designer and builder, moved its participation in trade shows from a minor to a decidedly major element in its total marketing program.

The specific job functions and executive responsibilities in the ED & PA business are:

1. *Sales and marketing*
   - Developing a sales and marketing plan
   - Defining the company's "market niche"
   - Particularizing the prospect universe
   - Establishing sales objectives
   - Creating sales and marketing materials
   - Budgeting the sales and marketing program

2. *Creative design*
   - Designing for objectives
   - Designing for corporate identity
   - Designing to budget
   - Designing with prebuilt modules
   - The designer/sales interface

3. *Exhibit building*
   - Materials and methods planning
   - Production planning and control
   - Labor skills and labor relations
   - Budgeting production and cost controls
   - Estimating

4. *Installation and dismantling*
   - Planning
   - Show rules and regulations
   - Convention center rules and regulations
   - Local union jurisdictions
   - Shipping alternatives

- Customer interface
- Estimating and budgeting services

5. *Pricing and budgeting*

   - Industry pricing standards
   - Industry cost and productivity standards
   - Cost control system
   - Estimating and pricing special services

THE GENERAL SERVICE CONTRACTOR

The second half of the trade show service segment of the industry is the general service contractor; such organizations provide the expertise, equipment, materials, and labor to move in, set up, and move out the show. As a rule, the general service contractor is appointed by show management and is the prime source of labor, equipment, and materials for the exhibitors.

Service contractor functions include warehousing and freight handling; labor planning and supervision; equipment and exhibit materials uncrating, set up, and recrating; logistical planning and control; furniture and floor covering rentals; on-floor management; floor plans and layouts; show management and exhibitor relations.

For large shows, many of these functions are highly complex, involving many skills and disciplines, the use of heavy equipment, and extremely complex logistical planning.

The industry organization is The Exposition Service Contractors Association. It has more than 100 member companies and has done an outstanding job in establishing ethical standards in the industry and sponsoring meetings at which the problems of the industry are addressed.

The specific job functions of service contractor executives are:

1. *Sales and marketing*

   - Developing a sales and marketing plan
   - Defining a "market niche"

- Particularizing the prospect universe
- Establishing sales objectives
- Creating sales and marketing materials
- Budgeting the sales and marketing program

2. *Labor planning and supervision*

- Union jurisdictions
- Labor rates and compensation packages
- Labor utilization planning
- Budgeting and billing labor
- In-house and on-call labor planning
- The management/customer/labor interface

3. *Warehousing and freight handling*

- Physical plant and equipment planning
- Economics of warehousing and freight handling
- Budgeting and billing warehouse and freight handling services

4. *Furniture and floor covering rentals*

- The economics of furniture and floor covering rentals
- Determining basic stock requirements
- Sources and costs
- Special equipment and materials
- Budgeting and billing furniture and floor covering rentals

5. *Optional services*

- Signage and sign shop operations
- Audio-visual equipment rentals
- Floral decorating services

- Cleaning services
- Electrical and utility services
- Security equipment rentals
- Modular exhibit rentals

6. *Floor plans and order forms*
   - Standard and special floor plans
   - Exhibitor service order forms
   - Order form control systems
   - Industry standards and customs

7. *Logistic planning*
   - Move-in, set-up, and move-out logistics
   - Crate storage and retrieval
   - Customer communications
   - Labor communications
   - On-floor services
   - Time-line planning

8. *On-floor management*
   - Determining labor and equipment needs
   - Labor and equipment assignments
   - Package service plans
   - Pre-show and at-show order processing
   - On-floor supervisory control
   - Pre-show management meeting
   - Pre-show exhibit hall meeting
   - Budgeting and billing on-floor services

Managing the Exhibit Function

One of the first tasks is to develop a budget by looking at the objectives to be attained by and then determining what must be spent to achieve those objectives. Here are some questions to be answered as guidelines to ascertaining costs:

- If you have an exciting new product to demonstrate, you will generate greater traffic, and you will need more space. On the other hand, if last year was your new product year, and this year you'll offer little that is new, will you need as much space?

- Does last year's schedule omit some shows that are held on alternate years, and that should be considered this year? Are some shows on your list not being held this year? Are there new shows that should be considered?

- Have you made changes in your marketing pattern that would affect your choice of shows? Are you entering any new markets? Are you dropping out of some?

Now you have a list of shows that are valid for your schedule, along with the number of square feet that seems reasonable for each. With the cost per square foot for each of these shows, you can develop the total cost for space. Other costs include exhibit construction, set-up and dismantling, transportation, special personnel, and booth manning.

You can approach a budget through a detailed analysis, item by item, of what you will have to spend at each show. A checklist like the following, which includes all the items connected with participation, is a good way to start. Some of them may not pertain to a specific show, and others may not, in your company, be under your control, but they are all possible costs, and should be considered as budget items.

1. Space Rental

2. Exhibit fabrication

   - Design/redesign

- Construction and/or refurbishing
- Insurance

3. Show costs
   - Drayage
   - Installation
   - Rental of rugs, floor coverings, drapes, furniture
   - Electrical
   - Plumbing
   - Flowers, plants
   - Refrigeration
   - Water
   - Gas, compressed air
   - Telephone
   - Cleaning
   - Photography
   - Dismantling
   - Shipping to show

4. Arrangements
   - Rooms for personnel
   - Suite entertainment
   - Food and beverage
   - Transportation for personnel to and from show city
   - Additional registration fees for personnel
   - Guest passes

5. Publicity, advertising, and promotion

6. Exhibit staff
   - Company personnel
   - Special personnel (models, demonstrators, etc.)
   - Guards
   - Transportation and travel
7. Company material
   - Equipment for display
   - Product for sampling or demonstration
   - Catalogs, brochures, etc.
   - Installation and dismantling of equipment
   - Shipping
   - Blazers, shop uniforms, etc., for booth personnel
   - Advertising specialties
8. Disposition
   - Reshipment
   - Handling costs
   - Exhibit revision
   - Storage
9. Other expenses

CHECK YOUR EXHIBIT PLANS

A checklist for making sure all arrangements and procedures are covered for exhibits can save considerable amounts of time and money. One company devised the following excellent checklist (Figure 1, pages 225 and 226), which you can adapt for your particular needs.

Figure 1. Exhibit Check Sheet

1. Has ample time been allowed for preparation of the event? ☐

2. Has a budget sheet been prepared covering all anticipated expenses? ☐

3. Has the objective(s) for the affair been clearly defined in writing? ☐

4. Has a theme been selected? ☐

5. Have committee meeting dates been established and all members notified? ☐

6. Have definite assignments been made to responsible individuals? ☐

7. Has a working calendar been prepared, so that agreed-upon completion dates can be checked off? ☐

8. Has a display firm been engaged? (Include details.) ☐

9. Has exhibit space been contracted for? ☐

10. Have several rough sketches of possible layouts for the booth and background been prepared and presented? ☐

11. Have specific products to be featured or displayed been decided on? ☐

12. Have all types of literature and handouts been ordered? ☐

13. Has a shipping material list been prepared and dates for shipment established? ☐

14. Have all utilities for the exhibit been checked for electric current characteristics, nearness of outlets, plumbing, etc.? ☐

15. Will extension cords be needed? ☐

16. Have all union regulations been checked? ☐

17. What furniture or seating will be necessary for the booth? ☐

18. Has a program been established for developing attendance? ☐

(continued)

Figure 1. Exhibit Check Sheet

(continued)

19. Have invitations and a follow-up phone call system been prepared to develop attendance? ☐

20. Have novelties, throw-aways, or interest-attracting devices been ordered? ☐

21. Has someone been designated to be at the exhibit site to check in and supervise unloading? ☐

22. Have all arrangements been coordinated with other company divisions? ☐

23. Have meeting and sleeping rooms been reserved? ☐

24. Have entertainment facilities been arranged? ☐

25. Has a manning schedule for the booth and the entertainment suite been prepared? ☐

26. Has a room for confidential discussions been reserved? ☐

27. Have plans been completed for a "dry run" of all personnel the night before opening day? (Purpose of the "dry run" is to familiarize everyone with procedures, time schedules, purpose, and names of firms and persons expected to attend.) ☐

28. Has a budget sheet been prepared and approved for the program? ☐

How to Exhibit at Trade Shows

Trade shows can provide a boost that helps in an overall marketing plan. Like other advertising and sales promotion media, trade shows have strengths and weaknesses that must be considered before attempting to exhibit at them.

In the following article from Dartnell's *Sales and Marketing Executive Report*, Robert B. Konikow, pubic relations counsel for The Trade Show Bureau, offers practical tips on how to get the most out of the medium and suggests sources of assistance in demonstrating products at trade shows.

Each of the various advertising media, like newspapers, magazines, radio, and television, has its strengths and advantages. So, naturally, has the trade show. It offers manufacturers:

- An opportunity for the seller and the buyer to meet face to face, where the products being shown can be demonstrated and handled;

- A pre-selected audience, with specified interests, at the show for the purpose of learning about new products;

- An opportunity to reach people who are ordinarily not accessible to sales representatives, and to uncover unknown buying interests;

- A place where buyers can do comparative shopping, can discuss their problems with many technical people, and thus a place where the buying process can be shortened.

Setting Objectives

A trade show offers the small manufacturer (who knows how to use it) an opportunity to achieve one or a number of objectives. One major user of trade shows has listed the following possibilities:

- To make sales;

- To maintain an image and continuing contact with customers;

- To create an image, initiate contact with potential customers, and qualify buyers;

- To introduce a new product;

- To demonstrate nonportable equipment;

- To offer an opportunity for customers to bring their technical problems and get solutions;

- To identify new applications for an existing or projected product by obtaining feedback from booth visitors;

- To build the morale of its local sales force and of dealers;

- To relate to competition;

- To conduct market research;

- To recruit personnel or attract new dealers;

- To demonstrate interest in and support of the sponsoring association or industry.

Before you get involved in a trade show, you should decide which of these objectives is the primary one that you should strive for. Unless you have a good idea of what you wish to achieve, you have no way of evaluating a particular show, no guidelines for deciding what you should show and how you should show it, and no way to determine afterwards whether or not your investment (which may be considerable) was worthwhile.

Picking a Show

There are more than 7,800 trade shows a year in the United States, which means that you should have little trouble in finding one that will deliver the kind of audience you want to reach.

Once you have found a show that sounds right, you must get more information about it. Start by writing show management for the literature it has prepared for prospective exhibitors. This is a selling document, designed to present the show in its strongest light, but it should give you a better idea of the nature of the audience the show attracts. You want to know more than how many attend; you also want to know where they come from, which industries they represent, and what their titles and their job responsibilities are. Most shows issue detailed breakdowns of attendance. If these reports are independently audited, they are somewhat more reliable, but you can usually depend on many show managements to issue accurate figures.

One of your better sources of information is the list of exhibitors at previous shows, whose names you may find in the promotional material, or which can be obtained from show management. But when you talk to earlier exhibitors, dig a little deeper than simply asking how useful they found the show. Your objectives are not necessarily the same as theirs, so you simply can't ask them what you should do. To get the answers you need, you have to probe a little deeper. Make sure you ask them about cost and any problems they encountered.

Determining How Much Space You'll Need

Once you have decided that a particular show will be the right one to help you reach your objectives, you must now decide how much space you need. The most common unit of space is a 10-foot by 10-foot booth, although some shows offer smaller units. There is sometimes a price differential depending on location. If space is available, you can get as many booths as you want. But how do you determine how much space you really need?

Here's one way of finding out, based on long trade show experience. Start by making an estimate of how many people visiting the show are logical prospects. You can base this on a study of the attendance reports, counting the number of visitors with meaningful titles, job responsibilities, and so on. You won't be able to reach all of them, but you should be able to get half of them to your booth.

Divide this number by the total number of hours the show will be open. This will give you the average number of visitors per hour. Now, how many people can a sales rep handle per hour? This varies according to the nature of your product, but a good starting figure is 15 per hour, so use it unless you have a better reading. Divide the hourly visitor rate by 15, and you'll get the average number of sales representatives you should have on hand to handle the number of people you expect.

Experience has shown that two people talking need about 50 square feet of space. With less space than this, the visitor gets a feeling of being crowded, and is unwilling to stop. If there is more space, he becomes unwilling to intrude, and hesitates to step into the display area. So multiply the number of sales reps you came out with by 50, and you'll get an approximation of how much clear space you should have to reach your objective. Add to that the space occupied by your demonstration equipment, furniture, and displays, and that's how much space you need. (In the standard 10 x 10-foot booth, two reps can usually work easily.) More than that is likely to be a waste of money; less, and you will probably reach fewer than your original audience estimate.

Designing Your Display

Designing an exhibit, like designing a house or designing an ad, is best done by professionals. You will find the help of such a professional invaluable; most will be glad to discuss your plans with you, even if you finally decide to do it yourself.

In planning the design of an exhibit, you must bear two factors in mind:

- You want to select, from all those attending, those who are good prospects for whatever you are showing. The most visible part of your display must act like a headline in a good ad—it must attract the attention of the right people in the few seconds it takes them to walk past your booth.

- You want to use the unique advantages of the medium, which means that you should show your product in action, fully and three-dimensionally, so your prospect can see and touch and handle it.

An exhibit booth is neither a warehouse nor a store window, although it has some of the characteristics of both. Like an ad, it needs something to catch the eye. This can be a picture or a headline, or better yet, something active and three-dimensional.

Once the interest of the visitor has been obtained, the exhibit must lead into a selling story. In an ad, this is the body copy; in an exhibit, it may be copy on the back wall, but it is more often a demonstration or the presentation of a sales representative.

Finally, there should be a call to action. An ad tries to get the reader to visit a store or send in a coupon. At an exhibit, you may want to close by making an appointment for a later sales call, get a name and address for a mailing list, or perhaps make an actual sale.

Each Show Has Rules

When you sign up for space at a trade show, your rental usually includes nothing more than a draped area and a sign with your name on it hung on the rear wall. You can use this space any way you want, subject to the show rules. Be sure to read these carefully, or get your exhibit designer to go over them with you. They tell you how high you can build your display; how much of the cubic footage of the display area you can use; how to order electricity, lights, furniture, etc.; and what you can and cannot do. The exhibitor's manual also tells you when you can get into the exhibit hall and when you have to get out. It includes order blanks for labor and equipment.

Follow these instructions to the last detail. You can get yourself and even the whole show in great trouble if you try to take shortcuts. Most trade show operations are covered by union and management rules, which occasionally make little sense to a newcomer, but which have grown up as the result of many years' experience in putting together the complex structure of trade shows. In addition, the rules vary from city to city, so each show must be approached on the basis of its own rules.

But It's Your Exhibit

The kind of exhibit that you end up with depends, to a large extent, on the kind of message you are trying to put across, its complexity, the nature of your audience, and your budget. Some exhibitors do very well with little more than a table or two on which to lay out goods or conduct a simple demonstration. Others need elaborate structures, custom designed and built, which may include a theater or conference rooms.

Between these two extremes, you can get simple custom-made displays; or you may purchase or rent modular units, semipermanent structures to which you apply your own graphics. Modular units come in both plastic and cardboard, and each has advantages and disadvantages that only you can weigh for your particular needs.

There are also kits of rods and panels, held together by joining members, that can hold shelves and graphics. These can be bought directly from manufacturers, as well as through local exhibit designer/

producers, who may recommend them when they feel that the combination of your objectives and your budget indicate this kind of standard unit. If you are just beginning an exhibit program or will exhibit only occasionally, you might consider renting your exhibits from a display house or exhibit service contractor.

Building Traffic to Your Booth

When you take space at a trade show, for the three or more days of that show, you have a place of business, a place where you can meet and talk to customers and prospects. Like any other place of business, it will be busier if you encourage people to come specifically to see you and do not rely on accidental passersby.

Promotional Material

The first thing to do is simply to let people know that you'll be at the show. Many show managements prepare promotional material, like posters for your show windows, stickers to add to your correspondence, insignia to drop into your magazine ads, admission tickets to the show for special customers, and so on. The very fact that you're participating in a show can build your image in your customers' eyes, even if they don't go to the show and see you.

Special Prices

May exhibitors offer special prices on merchandise bought at the show. Make your special prices known in advance, and they will help to build traffic. Special prices are especially effective if your products are not expensive and do not require a large commitment.

Advertising Specialties

Some companies use advertising specialties, often called giveaways, to increase the impact of their participation. Specialties are too often passed out indiscriminately; they add to the cost of participating in a show, but contribute little to sales. The best specialty appeals almost exclusively to potential users of your products, the sort of item that the recipient will keep for a long time. Be sure to check show rules; not all shows permit distribution of these items.

Targeted Special Giveaways

One effective way to use specialties is to help bring specific people to a booth. You can make up a list of the names and addresses of some very important prospects whom you are eager to lure to your booth. Then send each of them something like one of a pair of handsome cufflinks or earrings, perhaps designed around your trademark, if you have one. Your covering letter would promise the other of the pair when the recipient visits you at the show. If you have selected both your list and the specialty item carefully, you can expect a high proportion of responses. A good specialty advertising counselor can help you develop a creative promotion.

New Product Introduction

A trade show is an excellent place to introduce a new product. People come to trade shows to learn what is new. If you can get the word out, you should develop a valuable list of booth visitors.

Tell people, especially your old customers and good prospects, that you will have something new at the show, and give them an idea of what it is. See that advance announcements are sent out to the publications that cover your industry. Most of them run booth previews and follow-up articles on important shows. Since many need their material eight to 10 weeks before a show, it is worth the special effort to decide early what you will be showing. At the show, leave press releases in the show pressroom, and have an extra supply in the booth for those editors who stop by to chat.

People in Your Booth

The effectiveness of your booth depends to a great degree on the effectiveness of the people you have working in it. It is a different and sometimes bewildering place for most sales representatives, who are more used to visiting prospects one at a time in their offices, not having prospects come up and ask for information.

Booth personnel must be friendly, must be able to tell good prospects from curiosity-seekers, and must be able to move quickly toward advancing the sale. You must let your people know what your objectives are, so that they can work toward reaching your goals, whether it is setting up appointments, getting literature into the right hands, giving a demonstration, or making a sale.

Working a trade show booth is hard work, and you cannot expect people to keep at it steadily all day long. Develop a schedule of duty hours, so that everybody has some time to unwind and recuperate.

But when your people are on duty, they should be fully on duty. That means: being up front, ready to welcome visitors, not talking in a corner with others on the staff and not sitting down except when a visitor prefers to sit and talk.

Follow-up and Evaluation

We started out by saying that you should always have an objective before you enter a show. Whenever possible, this objective should be stated numerically—so many appointments, so many new names for your mailing list, so many orders, so many new wholesalers.

After the show, look at the results. Did you reach the numbers you have aimed for? Did you stay within your budget? If you didn't, where did you go wrong? Was it the wrong show? Was your exhibit adequate? Did you have too much space? Too little? Were your people functioning adequately?

It is only by looking at these factors that you can improve your record. You will learn from experience only if you study your experience systematically. Those who use shows correctly have found that it is a productive, economical medium.

(Sales and Marketing Executive Report, August 24, 1983, The Dartnell Corporation, Chicago.)

More Exhibit Tips

Suzette Cavanaugh, marketing manager of H. Salt Company (a division of Heublein), is a firm believer in making a trade show profitable on the balance sheet. She follows these seven basic guidelines to make sure her trade show dollar goes the farthest.

1. *Show your product.* Far too often a prospect is allowed to pause at a booth, look at the product, pick up some literature and walk away. Was this a "hot" prospect? You'll never know.

2. *Make your product the focal point of the exhibit.* Your exhibit visitor is interested in *products,* not company image or elaborate "look at me" displays.

3. *Make your exhibit understandable.* Don't make your visitors have to guess what your product is and what it does.

4. *Keep your exhibit simple.* Bright, flashing lights, loud whistles and gaudy costumes take attention away from your product. Work to create an atmosphere conducive to selling, not competitive with it.

5. *Show as many products as you can.* Show visitors are there to see *products,* not photographs of products. Cover all bases and show your complete line if possible.

6. *Use demonstrations.* What better place to show your product in action? Good demonstrations attract immediate attention and hold interest.

7. *Put your product to use.* If your product has multiple applications, make sure your visitors know about them.

The Art of Boothmanship

The personal behavior of the people in your booth is a key to the success of your exhibit, and therefore it should be a matter for your concern. Manning a booth is a great endeavor, and to handle it properly, with the minimum of personal friction, set up a set of rules and enforce them strictly but fairly.

While on duty, booth personnel should constantly realize that their attitude and behavior are an essential part of building their company's image. Boothmanship has been summarized in many ways, one of which is shown in the following list, as developed by Barton Lewy, The Display House, Philadelphia. However, boothmanship may also be summarized in a single sentence: Behave in a way that encourages visitors and demonstrates a friendly attitude.

1. Don'ts
   - Drink
   - Smoke
   - Sit (except with a prospect)
   - Gab with cohorts
   - Wander away
   - Ignore a visitor
   - Be rude
   - Be overly aggressive
   - Fake it
   - Wear yourself out at night

- Underestimate your visitors
- Leave questions or problems unanswered

2. Do's

- Know yourself
- Know your product or service
- Know your prospects' needs
- Relate your product to needs of prospect
- Know your competition
- Be there
- Be ready to talk (and demonstrate)
- Be carefully groomed
- Work hard
- Be enthusiastic
- Be confident
- Be on the level
- Know the show
- Keep your booth clean, neat, and attractive
- Know your way around your booth
- Work with all prospects, even those not from your territory
- Be nice to "lookers"
- Be able to talk costs
- Meet frequently, critique and revise your activities
- Plan ahead

3. How to do it

   - Rehearse
   - Prepromote
   - Greet visitors
   - Open with attention-getting statement
   - Establish your identity
   - Learn your visitors' identity (accurately)
   - Call him or her by name
   - Determine his or her problem
   - "Involve" your visitor
   - Show proof
   - Anticipate objections
   - Used case histories
   - Keep some strong points in reserve and follow up fast and lovingly

4. Know what your visitors want

   - Alert booth personnel
   - Fewer sex symbols
   - Technically qualified personnel
   - Less high pressure
   - More information
   - Better literature
   - "What's new"

The Big Payoff

Edward A. Chapman, district manager of exhibits planning, AT&T Information Systems, has an answer when asked how he evaluates the success of trade shows. In an article in *Sales & Marketing Management,* he said: "Through sales leads." He says he doesn't need to get 100 percent response on the leads sent out to the field sales force in order to make a judgment. By the time 25 percent of them have been returned, he can evaluate one show versus another.

A well-structured lead card can be the key to trade show return on investment. In the same article (see below), a generic form that can be used as a guide and modified to coordinate with a company's specific procedure is described. The form was designed by Kitzing Incorporated, a Chicago-based trade show marketing agency.

Kitzing's form (Figure 2, page 238), is intended to be used both during the show, when prospects are being identified and qualified, and afterward, during the all-important follow-up. The form is scored vertically so it can be folded to fit into a jacket pocket. At-show data are recorded on one side, post-show data on the other.

At-show data begin with the prospect's name, the date, and information on company affiliation. The salesperson then lists the product in which the prospect is interested, the application (the use to which the product would be put), and what product, if any, he or she is now using for that application. Next is the buying timeframe—if, for example, the need is immediate or will not be crucial for a number of weeks or months—and how much money has been allocated for the purchase. If the person supplying this information is not the sole buyer or buying influence, space is also provided to include the names and titles of others involved in the decision-making process.

Next the salesperson indicates whether the prospect wants to see someone at the show or would prefer to receive literature later on.

The boxes on the form are a critical part of it: this is where the first qualifying process is done. The salesperson should indicate whether the prospect is, in his opinion, "hot," a potential customer, or, perhaps, a student or literature collector. For a super-hot lead, one that's A +, the salesperson might stick a fluorescent "hot dot" on the form to help the person sorting the leads spot it more quickly.

The next line would, of course, contain the name of the specific trade show. It could either be printed on the form or, if a company wishes to use the same form for more than one show, written in at the time the form is being filled out. The name of the show must be included to help management track sales to their source and thereby evaluate participation in a specific show.

All that's left is for the salesperson to sign the card and add any comments. The salesperson's name is necessary so that he can be con-

Figure 2. Kitzing's Form

XYZ SHOW CHICAGO JULY 12 to 14 1986
DISTRIBUTION/TRACKING
☐ MAIL ON _____ BY _____ DATE _____
ENCLOSURES _____

CONTACT NAME _____
DATE _____
COMPANY NAME _____
DIVISION _____
ADDRESS _____
CITY, STATE _____ ZIP _____
TELEPHONE ( ) _____ - _____

☐ TLPH ON _____ BY _____ DATE _____
COMMENTS _____

PRODUCT INTEREST
A _____
B _____
C _____
D _____
APPLICATION _____

☐ FIELD MANAGER _____ DATE _____
SALESPERSON _____
FIELD CALL DATE _____
FEED BACK DEADLINE _____
COMMENTS _____

FIELD CALL DATE _____
COMMENTS _____

PRODUCT NOW IN USE _____

COMMENTS _____

FIELD CALL DATE _____
COMMENTS _____

BUYING TIME FRAME _____

BUDGET ALLOCATED _____
OTHER BUYING INFLUENCES
NAME _____
TITLE _____
NAME _____
TITLE _____

FIELD CALL DATE _____
COMMENTS _____

OUTCOME REPORT
☐ SALE MADE DATE _____
DOLLAR VALUE _____

REQUESTS PERSONAL CALL ☐ DATE _____
REQUESTS LITERATURE ☐
Ⓐ Ⓑ Ⓒ Ⓓ Ⓔ
ABC MANUFACTURING COMPANY
XYZ SHOW CHICAGO JULY 12 to 14 1986
RECORDED BY _____
COMMENTS _____

☐ DEAD DATE _____
REASON _____
COMMENTS _____

DISTRIBUTION OF COPIES
HOME OFFICE   2   FIELD MANAGER   3
  (ORIG. TO TS FILE)   (TICKLER FILE 2)
  (TICKLER FILE 1)   ONE INTERIM REPORT
MAIL FULFILLMENT   1   ONE FINAL REPORT
TELEMARKETING   1   (SALESPERSON 1)
                          RETURN TO FIELD MGR.

Exhibit designer/producer: Kitzing Inc.

Customizing a basic lead card can result in stronger sales.

tacted if there are any questions that arise while the follow-up is being conducted.

The procedure for the other side of the card varies. The cards could be further qualified and sorted at the show itself, if, for example, there is a sales executive in attendance who wants to review all leads. This also allows for on-the-spot follow-up with the salesperson who filled out the cards. Or cards could be returned immediately to the home office. There, someone can sort them according to those who require mail or telephone follow-up, and forward the ones that require a personal sales call to the appropriate field manager.

The first section of the distribution/tracking side is used to record what material is sent, by whom, and when. Whether the mailing is handled internally or by an outside fulfillment house, the material must be sent while the show is still fresh in people's minds. Moreover, a cover letter should accompany the material, mentioning the show, thanking the prospect for his interest in the products, and perhaps including a reply card to enable the prospect to request a telephone or in-person contact.

If the prospect is contacted by phone, the person making the call should record the subject and date of the call and all relevant comments about the conversation in the next section. Thus, if a sale is not made, the notes may help reveal the reason why and may also be used for future contacts.

If the lead is to be followed up with a sales call, copies of the card should go to the sales manager, the field salesperson, and a tickler file as necessary. The sales manager can use his copy to keep track of the call or calls made by the field salesperson and the results. The form shown allows space for tracking four field sales calls.

Finally, there's the outcome report, which indicates that the sale was made and either records its dollar value or that the account is considered dead and the reasons why.

The generic form shown suggests patterns of distribution of copies to the home office and field staff. Of course, these numbers, like the other parts of the form, will vary by company. As Kitzing account executive Christopher Kappes points out, "There is no lead form that fits everyone's needs and wants, like stretch socks."

But with a card like this one as a sample, a sales manager can develop a lead card that does fit his needs exactly. And if the card is properly designed and carefully filled out at the show, "The field salesperson has everything he needs to go in and make a call," says Fred Kitzing. "He goes in prepared."

AT&T's Chapman points out that use of a lead card also helps management convince reluctant salespeople of the importance of exhibiting effectively at trade shows. "The perception of being helpful to the field is critical," Chapman says, "and that's what a sales lead does for you."

As a result of using lead cards, you can not only excite your sales force about its capabilities and potential, but qualify leads faster and more easily than before. And all this is done with an eye toward that ever-present goal: making sales.

Why Trade Shows are Popular

A study conducted by the Trade Show Bureau gives rather convincing evidence why trade shows pay off.

The report, based on 1,521 responses, showed these results:

- Fifty-four percent of the respondents said no call was needed to close a trade show lead

- Number of calls needed to close a trade show lead are:

  1 call—16 percent

  2 calls—10 percent

  3 calls—6 percent

  4 or more calls—4 percent

  Unknown—10 percent

Since only 0.8 sales calls are needed to close the average trade show lead, the average cost to close a trade show lead is $67.88 for the cost of generating the lead, plus eight-tenths of the cost of a single sales call of $178.00. This amounts to a total average cost of $210.28, compared with $907.80 to close the average industrial sale.

Chapter 10

Sales Promotion

The sales promotion function in any given company can be the direct responsibility of the marketing executive, the sales manager, the merchandising manager, or the advertising executive.

The sales manager is vitally concerned with this function as it interacts with the field sales force and the various channels of distribution, be it wholesaler, distributor, dealer, or retail outlet. It is an important function in both industrial and consumer markets. Many of the basic concepts included in this chapter are derived from Dartnell's *Sales Promotion Handbook.**

What Is Sales Promotion?

The role of sales promotion was the subject of a survey conducted by Professor Albert W. Frey, the results of which were analyzed in a booklet published by the Amos Tuck School of Business Administration of Dartmouth College. Although published some years ago, the report contains comments and observations which effectively apply with equal force today.

The survey was based on a questionnaire sent to 652 persons: 197 sales promotion managers in companies with separate advertising managers, 130 sales-promotion managers in companies with no advertising managers and 325 combined advertising and sales promotion managers. Fifty-three in the first group, 40 in the second, and 139 in the third responded.

Respondents' companies included producers of consumer goods (about 39 percent), industrial goods (about 27 percent), and both (about 34 percent). The answers showed no significant differences in practice or viewpoint between the two types of manufacturers.

Sales Promotion Handbook, 7th ed., rev., Ovid Riso, ed. (Chicago, The Dartnell Corporation, 1979).

The first point to become clear was that a great majority of the companies covered do distinguish between advertising and sales promotion. Of the 232 respondents, 180 (77 percent) said their firms distinguish formally; 32 (14 percent) indicated their companies do not distinguish formally, but they themselves do informally; one said his company "doesn't distinguish, but—."

Of the companies that distinguish formally, 100 (57 percent of those for which respondents gave this information) have separate sales promotion budgets. Sixty-six (37 percent) provide for sales promotion in their advertising budgets, seven (4 percent) in salespeople's activities budgets and three (2 percent) in other budgets.

In defining sales promotion, some of the comments received were:

"Neither advertising agencies nor sales departments have a full understanding of what is involved."

"A sales-promotion manager's responsibilities are to do the thinking to negotiate the marketing program, which the sales manager is too busy to do and the advertising manager doesn't know how to do."

"It must by its nature be close to both advertising and selling, but neither ad agencies nor sales departments have a full understanding of what is involved."

"Sales promotion is the other half of the job begun by national advertising, which, by itself, cannot complete the sale—at least in our business."

"Sales promotion should always be treated as a separate function—no matter how interrelated and connected to advertising it becomes—because it's so important to support sales on a broad front; the whole idea of sales promotion is conducive to the broader thinking and action that modern merchandising requires."

"In the soft-goods industries, sales promotion activities are more important than national advertising, which serves nevertheless to give stature and focus to the sales promotion at the retail level. The best national advertising campaign fails without intensive sales promotion at store level in our industry. A sound budget in soft goods provides more money for local sales promotion than for national advertising. It is costing industry millions of dollars because its sales promotion effort is weak as a result of lack of interest on the part of agencies and failure of management to do the job if the agency neglects doing it."

How Do Advertising and Sales Promotion Differ?

In brief, an overwhelming majority seemed to feel that advertising and sales promotion differ in many ways.

Advertising consists in 1) choosing the media through which a company will transmit its message to consumers and the trade, 2) buying space or time in those media and 3) composing and presenting the message. The media typically are owned and controlled by others, who sell their space and time at established rates.

Sales promotion, on the other hand, "educates" and arouses the enthusiasm of salespeople, middlemen, consumers, and perhaps others through a variety of materials, tools, and devices *that the company itself controls.*

Every marketing program, of course, has two other major components: merchandising and personal selling. The first deals with the company's products, prices, and service, the second with the sales force and individual customers.

The four are not equally essential. While few firms could exist without personal selling or merchandising, and many could not without advertising, most could survive without sales promotion, and not a few do. But sales promotion buttresses and strengthens a marketing operation, thereby magnifying a company's profits and success.

The reason is that, while merchandising can produce and present an attractive product, and while personal selling and advertising can effectively inform and persuade dealers and the public about it, only sales promotion can add an *extra* element of persuasion and *engender enthusiasm.* As one respondent put it:

"Sales promotion is the catalyst of business, big or small. It is the agent that gives direction to an advertising campaign, drive to a dealer organization, and enthusiasm to a sales force. Its addition to a company can speed up sales in a specific area or throughout the country. ... The efforts of sales promotion thrive on one ingredient—enthusiasm. ... Any sales organization feels the impact of promotional efforts. The spread of enthusiasm is a powerful weapon that can carry the sales force forward each year in its sales at an ever-increasing pace."

Unlike personal selling, which typically is directed at individuals, sales promotion is beamed at groups; but unlike advertising, which aims at masses of people, sales promotion aims at comparatively small, well-defined groups. While advertising, then, is "constant for the long pull," sales promotion seeks specific immediate objectives; it represents a rifle, rather than a shotgun, approach. Therefore it operates largely in periodic pushes, for any of which every individual among its targets—salespeople, distributor, dealer—may be specifically identified.

A sales promotion manager must also be intimately familiar with the situations in which his creative efforts will work. Said one respondent:

A good sales promotion person needs field selling experience and a full knowledge of dealers' problems, as well as the salespeople's, in order to prepare practical promotional aids that will help the sale. Advertising can bring them in, but promotion does the 'on-the-spot' selling. An advertising person only needs to know copy, media, distribution, layout, art work, and agency functions; he or she does not have to be a field person."

Sales Promotion in Detail

The merchandising manager ensures that the company's product and service are sound; the sales promotion manager, starting where the merchandising manager left off, finds ways to make them more attractive and exciting. The advertising manager prepares an interesting, imaginative advertising campaign; sales promotion may give it an *extra* measure of interest and imagination.

But the bulk of the sales promotion effort, we have seen, is beamed at company salespeople and middlemen. Therefore the sales promotion manager works *especially* with the sales manager.

The salesperson's basic education about product, price, company policies and how to sell is a sales department function—but sales promotion personnel, equipped and trained to do more than sell, create and provide visual aids that sharpen the teaching. The sales department can devise sales contests, manuals, portfolios and other equipment—but sales promotion can create better ones. The sales department can run conventions and meetings, but sales promotion people, trained in ways to hold and move audiences—and adept at "thinking up" new ways—can make them more stimulating and educative.

The increased sales force enthusiasm that sales promotion thus engenders is inevitably reflected not only in increased sales to distributors but also in greater distributor enthusiasm. But sales promotion is not content only to influence distributors so indirectly. It also wins their attention, interest, and cooperation through skillfully prepared direct mail, catalogs, house organs, product information sheets and service bulletins, through trade shows and exhibits, through merchandised advertisements, through contests and premiums for distributors' salespeople and through films and other visual aids company salespeople will use at meetings of the distributor sales force.

The increased enthusiasm of distributors and their salespeople, in turn, is reflected in greater sales to dealers and greater dealer enthusiasm—but dealers are also targets of *direct* sales promotion activity. In so far as this seeks merely increased enthusiasm, its techniques are much like those it uses on the distributor level. But it seeks also to help the dealer sell, and to do this it gives him window and interior display material, advertising mats, radio copy, TV films, direct mail, demonstrations, and educational material for his salespeople.

And increased dealer enthusiasm inevitably influences consumers—but sales promotion goes directly to the consumer, too. Typical tools include premiums, samples, coupons, contests and, for the industrial market, catalogs and technical bulletins. Some companies channel some of their consumer-beamed sales promotion material through distributors and dealers, and unquestionably the customer enthusiasm that results warms the distributors and dealers as well.

Sales Promotion Defined

Assuming the trend will continue—and reason and results to date indicate it will—we now find sales promotion not nearly as hard to define as it once was. This definition probably reflects today's majority opinion; it almost certainly reflects tomorrow's.

Sales promotion is that component of the marketing mix that continually creates and applies materials and techniques that, reinforcing and supplementing the materials and techniques provided by the other components, *increase* the capacity and desire of salespeople, distributors, and dealers to sell a company's product and make consumers *eager* to buy it.

In its broadest sense, sales promotion includes all those functions which have to do with the marketing of a product or the promotion of a service—personal selling, advertising, displays, exhibitions, and all other activities designed to increase sales and expand the market.

In point of fact, sales promotion differs from advertising only in terminology; advertising is a form of sales promotion and sales promotion is a form of advertising. Yet there is a convenience in making a distinction even where no great difference exists, in that sales promotion is a somewhat broader term.

The advertising manager of a large manufacturing company defined these terms as follows:

"Sales promotion moves the product toward the buyer, while advertising moves the buyer toward the product."

An executive of a retail chain-store organization has called sales promotion "merchandising the advertising."

It is significant of the difficulties of definition to note that some companies use the title manager of advertising and sales promotion, while others reverse the words to read manager of sales promotion and advertising.

The Committee on Definitions of the American Marketing Association offers the following definition of sales promotion:

1. In a specific sense, those sales activities that supplement both personal selling and advertising and coordinate them and help to make them effective, such as displays, shows

and expositions, demonstrations, and other nonrecurrent selling efforts not in the ordinary routine.

2. In a general sense, sales promotion includes personal selling, advertising, and supplementary selling activities.

This definition, while good, puts emphasis on sales promotion as a nonrecurrent selling effort. Most sales managers agree that the great weakness of sales promotion in business today is the "campaign" psychology which surrounds it. Sales promotion is no different from any other form of selling; it requires a continuing effort, for it has been amply demonstrated that "shot in the arm" techniques leave much to be desired. Then, too, the illustrations used in the definition belittle the function. There is a too-evident desire to subordinate sales promotion to advertising, when the trend is the other way, and advertising is being subordinated to sales promotion. While it is true that advertising usually involves a larger expenditure of money, modern usage of the term tends to regard trade, consumer, and industrial advertising as a part of the overall sales promotional program. For regardless of whether sales promotion is to be the tail that wags advertising, or advertising the tail that wags sales promotion, prevailing practice combines the two functions, at least so far as production is concerned.

Sales Penetration

As the tempo of competitive selling increases, the need of covering all factors in the sale grows apace. Consumer advertising can and usually does do an important market-conditioning job, thus making it easier for the salespeople and the dealer (if distribution is through that channel) to sell the product. But the influence of advertising is limited. Not all the people you hope to influence read advertisements, listen to the radio, or watch television. They may not even observe outdoor bulletins. Yet in many instances it is most important to the eventual success of a distribution program to make sure that every buying factor is covered, and that the more important factors *thoroughly covered.*

This is a "sharpshooting" undertaking that can usually be best done by sales promotional techniques, including selective direct mail advertising, trade shows, demonstrations, and service promotions. It is especially important in negotiated selling, but it becomes essential in all types of selling when there is keen competition for the customer's dollar. For example, in selling a product not presently carried by department stores, it is necessary to get the story across to: 1) The store owner or manager; 2) the section merchandising man; 3) the department buyer and (perhaps) the manager of store promotions. Since it is improbable these executives will act until they observe some evidence of consumer demand, local advertising, either direct or through the store, may be required. It could be, as some advertising agents like to think, that high-powered general advertising will give a manufacturer all the penetration needed, but with advertising costs where they are, it is too expensive for most marketing operations.

One company's program serves to illustrate the importance which some sales executives attach to promotional penetration: "We have more than doubled our advertising in trade publications, to at least partially sell the dealer before the salesperson calls. We are currently using two weeklies, one bimonthly, and two monthly trade papers, which are the five with the largest circulations, and, we think, with the most constant readership.

"We have stepped up the tempo of our direct-mail campaign to dealers. We now have a weekly mailing to 22,000 dealers, consisting of solicitations for business on unadvertised items, institutional copy, and reprints of all our trade-paper ads.

"We have more than doubled the number of point-of-sale pieces developed, and more than doubled the quantity prepared of each. They are all distributed to our dealers free of charge. We have quadrupled the amount of printed material that we supply to our dealers without charge, to be used as envelope stuffers, or for distribution in the stores."

The promotion program of a leading television manufacturer likewise concentrates on dealer penetration: "At the dealer level," an official of that company said, "we are putting into effect a merchandising type of advertising, which is the type of selling copy producing greater volume sales during the current buying season, as well as in preparation of proportionately greater sales in the new year to follow. This, also, is further supplemented by additional effort now being made in the development of a dealer 'awareness' in the effective use of window displays, local representation in community publications, participation in all advertising of a pamphlet nature edited by social clubs and other organizations, etc.

"In addition to these items, a great deal of emphasis is being placed upon the development of a stronger and more loyal dealer organization, which is prompted by a greater interest in the coordination of all affairs pertaining to the distributor-dealer chain of relationship. Further, we are conducting a greater number of the type of dealer meetings that provides each attending member with the most current and advanced sales analysis, sales promotion, and sales administrative programs, which are interpreted as accurately as possible as they pertain to the tangible problems of our retail outlets."

Surveys Should be Planned

It is to the credit of sales promotion and advertising people that they are placing more dependence on hard facts, and less on hunches, in planning promotions. But, as in most selling methods, there is a danger that too much reliance may be placed on inconclusive or inadequate surveys. Just as a little knowledge can be a dangerous thing, so too small a sample can be equally dangerous when it comes to making a survey. In that connection a sales promotion executive with General Motors Corporation offers the following suggestions regarding direct-mail surveys:

Never try to appraise the results of a survey without first studying the questionnaire, with special reference to such points as the following:

1. Was the questionnaire skillfully developed?

2. Were the questions easy to understand—with a minimum chance of being misunderstood?

3. Are the questions properly arranged? Consider not only the construction and arrangement of each individual question, but:

4. Is the sequence or continuity such as to avoid confusion and facilitate the respondent's "flow of thought"?

5. Are questions or similar items asked the same way? This is especially important as regards any series of items where the answers are to be compared on a relative basis.

6. Do the questions cover the subject adequately?

7. Do they afford the opportunity for the respondent to give any kind of answer that may reflect his individual reaction?

8. Does the questionnaire provide for all the data that will be needed for an adequate statistical breakdown?

9. Does it invite the respondent to qualify his or her answers with remarks and comments? This can be extremely helpful in enabling the researcher to properly interpret the statistical findings. (See item 25.)

10. Is the questionnaire short enough to ensure high returns?

11. Is it attractive and inviting or does it look as though it were developed by a bureaucratic statistician?

12. Do you think that you yourself would have bothered to fill it out?
    And here's another practical method of appraisal:

13. How does the quality and attractiveness of the questionnaire stack up against the *finished report or formal presentations of the results?*

    All too frequently there's a tendency to skimp on the questionnaire itself—then "shoot the works" and spend any amount of time and money on dolling up the report. (Attractive presentations are important, but it's even more important to have an attractive questionnaire!)

Samples:

14. How was the questionnaire distributed and to whom?

15. Was it directed to the particular group or groups of people best qualified to give the answers?

16. Was the sample adequate as to size?

This depends primarily on the degree to which the data are to be broken down or cross-indexed. The finer the breakdown, the greater the number of samples required.

17. Was the sampling scientifically controlled so as to properly reckon with territorial locations? Makes of cars? Ages of cars? New car buyers versus used car buyers?

This does not necessarily mean that the mailings (or the returns) shall be in exact proportion to the characteristics of the market. Frequently it is more logical to take care of this by "weighting" the data incident to the statistical complications. But it is important that the incoming questionnaires be properly identified as to the classifications that need to be reckoned with.

Reports:

18. Does the report include all the essential information that is needed for proper understanding and interpretation of the results?

19. Were the statistical procedures sound?

20. Were the returns properly "weighted" so as to compensate for distortions in the distribution of the sample?

21. Are the questions as quoted in the report exactly the same as they appeared in the questionnaire?

22. Are the statistical column headings consistent with the real meaning of the figures?

23. Are the data intelligently and effectively presented—in a manner that is conducive to proper interpretation and practical action?

24. Are any of the findings out of line with what you *positively know to be the facts?*

25. How does the report stack up as regards what we might call "internal consistency"? (In other words, do its various parts hang together and tend to support one another, or is it contradictory in any respect?)

Sponsors:

And last, but not least, here's a general question that it's always well to bear in mind:

Did the agency responsible for the survey have an "axe to grind?"

But that's not quite the right way to express it. Nobody makes a survey without having some reason for making it and the fact that these people had an "axe to grind" should not within itself be taken as a negative factor.

But in appraising the results it's always well to consider the following:

26. Just what *kind* of axe did they have to grind? Then scrutinize the results in the light thereof.

Coordinating Sales Promotion

Another important recent development in sales promotion is the way it is being geared into other marketing activities to produce a balanced sales program. This is particularly true of sales research. The approved formula for successful business management is to find out what the customer wants to buy and sell it to him or her, rather than try to sell what you want to make. This philosophy is demonstrated in the customer research activities of the General Motors Corporation. The surveys that this department of GM is continually making to determine customer preferences not only provide all divisions of the corporation with data useful in designing new models, but provide a solid foundation upon which the company bases its sales promotional activities.

Similarly, consumer testing of new products is depended upon by some sales managers to give them the best "angle" to use in planning the promotional effort. It is a well-established fact in sales management that the first step to the order should be to find out *why* old customers bought the product and how it is used. Very often we find, to our amazement, that the real reasons people buy are quite different from those we think caused them to buy, or even reasons the salespeople give for their buying. For example, for years cash registers were sold as "thief catchers." An analysis of buying reasons showed that an overlooked factor in selling a merchant a cash register was that it removed the temptation any employee might have to pilfer from the cash drawer. Coordinating sales promotion with advertising is not an easy problem for the sales executive. In many companies the two functions are successfully combined and are the joint responsibility of one executive who thus serves as the director of advertising and sales promotion for the business. This often works out quite well, especially in cases where the sales promotional effort consists mainly of printed literature and dealer helps. Joint administration is almost universal in the case of companies whose advertising is confined to specialized rather than general media, as for instance companies making engineering specialties. In the case of a company doing extensive consumer advertising, as well as an aggressive job of promoting its products, it is extremely difficult to separate sales promotion from advertising because the overlapping functions and responsibility involved eventually cause difficulty.

One solution is to have a sales promotional section in each sales division of the business that is responsible for recognizing the need for a certain kind of promotional activity, and able to "put it over" when crystallized. The unit promotion person, upon approval of the division sales manager, gets all the facts and background material needed to develop the project. The advertising department then creates all the required promotional material, working in close cooperation with the divisional sales promotion unit. When the materials are ready they are turned over to the sales promotion manager of the unit and that executive, along with the division sales organization, is then responsible for the successful conduct of the campaign in the field. This division of responsibility, for example, was practiced with satisfactory results by Armstrong Cork Company and others operating on a product divisional plan. Some companies followed the same procedure in the case of geographical sales divisions. Westinghouse Electric Corp. for example, operated a sales promotional unit in each major territory of its wholesale division. In this case, however, the principal job of the divisional promotion unit was to carry through a national program developed in Mansfield.

Gearing Sales Promotion to Personal Selling

Integrating the sales promotion program with personal selling begins with "selling" the sales organization (including the dealers' salespeople in the case of companies selling through established trade channels) on the company, its policies, and its products. This may or may not include formal sales training. Usually it does, although in some large organizations this function is performed by a sales personnel officer. However, there is a growing tendency to bracket sales training with sales promotion, since modern selling is becoming more and more promotional in its concept. This is especially true in training dealers and their sales personnel. Most sales promotion programs depend upon the wholehearted cooperation of the field organization to "put them over." The sales promotion department therefore has a direct interest in training all those responsible for selling the product to the customer or at the point of sale. For example, in the marketing of Hoover cleaners, where a large sales force selling direct to the home was required, the recruiting, selection, and training of these salespeople was a very important responsibility of the sales promotion manager. It was, in fact, the crux of the whole Hoover promotion program.

Modern practice therefore contemplates the sales promotion job as having three steps: 1) planning, 2) production, and 3) execution. It is extremely important that any sales promotion undertaking, if it is to attain a full measure of success with a minimum of cost, be painstakingly coordinated with the company's sales research operation to assure wise planning; the company's advertising department and advertising counsel, to assure economical and skilled production of sales promotion materials; and finally with sales field operations to make sure that after the plan is conceived and the required materials produced, it will be followed through intelligently and enthusiastically by the sales force.

Local Promotion Programs

In many industries, and particularly when products are sold through distributors, local promotion programs are required. The salesperson should be provided a "shopping bag" full of promotion material—advertising cuts, displays, direct mail pieces, etc.—that allows him or her to assist distributors in their own promotion, be it open houses, local trade shows, or direct mail programs. The salesperson should be trained and then given an individual budget and a great deal of latitude. Because the salesperson knows the customers' strengths or deficiencies and local objectives, he or she can tailor a program that meets the distributors' needs.

Twelve Tips for Top Promotions

In a talk to the Association of National Advertisers, Carmela Cicero Maresca, vice-president of Ogilvy & Mather Promotions, cited these principles to help create promotion campaigns and reduce risk of failure.

1. Add value to the basic product, don't discount it.

2. Brand your promotions. Make them exclusive to you.

3. Focus on the future. Look for repeat business.

4. Give your promotion a theme to help reinforce your advertising.

5. Make your promotions targeted and quantifiable.

6. Look for ways to reward your best (most frequent) customers.

7. Look for cross-promotional opportunities where you come out on top.

8. Look for ways to make your customers feel good about you.

9. Present your promotions in a first-class way. It's worth the extra expense.

10. Make the promotion exciting and rewarding for the sales staff.

11. Make promotions fun and easy to execute.

12. Test! Test! Test!

Premiums and Trade Deals

The three factors in a successful premium program are the objectives, the offer itself, and the sales program or campaign behind it.

A list of sales objectives most frequently achieved by the use of premiums, as compiled from questionnaires received from manufacturers and wholesalers in a study by Dr. Arnold Corbin of New York University, included:

- Introducing a new product

- Getting new customers for existing products

- Achieving regular or more frequent use

- Building goodwill with the trade

- Offsetting competitor's activity

- Beating a slump in sales (seasonal or otherwise)

- Increasing the size of orders

- Stimulating the sales force to achieve present objectives

- Improving shelf position

- Making it easier to get orders, retailer displays, newspaper features, and other promotional support

- Checking on radio and TV results

Premium Services and Sales Aids

A growing number of major manufacturers are entering the premium field by offering their own products for use as incentives and stimulating interest through incentive-planning guides, merchandising books, and promotional aids.

For example, the Owens-Illinois (Libbey Glassware Products) Premium Merchandising Plan Book outlines 20 purposes for which premiums are used, lists the steps to take in developing promotional programs, and shows how 25 companies in various industries have used Libbey products.

Store Demonstrations

In the marketing of foods and household specialties such as vacuum cleaners and microwave ovens, much importance is attached to store demonstrations.

Manufacturers have broken through entrenched competition by following this practice. In some instances they are willing to pay the dealers, especially department stores, liberally for the use of space. They also stand all expenses of demonstrators, materials, and local advertising. But in most lines the manufacturer makes the dealer share the expense, usually on a fifty-fifty basis, and here again care must be used to see that such store demonstrations are done in such a way that no discrimination is shown. The same service must be made available to all customers buying an equal volume of goods.

Use of Premiums to Build Mailing Lists

A concern that used a key container as a premium to a large dealers' list had an interesting experience. First of all the company wrote a letter to half the list advising the dealers that if they would send the names and addresses of 10 jobbers' salespeople they would receive the key case free. Results from this mailing were disappointing, although a number of names were obtained.

The offer was then reversed. Each dealer was sent a key container with a letter from the manufacturers asking the dealer to accept the key case with his compliments. The letter also mentioned that the manufacturer would like to send one of these containers to every jobber's salesperson who called on that dealer, if the dealer would provide their names.

The response to this appeal was considerably better. It accomplished the strategic effect of putting the dealer under obligation to reply. The manufacturer then approached the jobbers' salespeople, whose names were sent in by the dealers, in the same way. He told them he wanted to send every member of their sales force a key container just like the ones he was sending them, if the salespeople would provide the names of as many of their fellow salespeople as they knew.

In this way, at an amazingly small outlay, the manufacturer build up a most complete list of jobbers' salespeople in a field where it is supposed to be impossible to get such a list.

Use of Coupons

At a seminar conducted by *Advertising Age,* Paul Runyon, director of client services of Flair Communications Agency, Inc., made some useful distinctions among the several ways in which coupons are used by advertisers. He pointed out that:

"Direct mail coupons have a high redemption rate, rapid impact, nonduplicated coverage and relatively high cost control with high executional demands (post office problems);

"In-pack, on-pack coupons have a 20 percent redemption, excellent selectivity, duplicated coverage. Despite low merchandisability, coupons can be used to develop loyalty among current users, insulate against competitive introductions, and offer trade features simultaneously.

"Newspaper coupons have moderate cost, great merchandisability, rapid impact, specific geographic interest, and are 'something that the trade understands.'"

Popularity of Discount Coupons

Another form of promotion that has become very popular is the use of discount coupons, probably because they are easier to handle and because consumers know exactly how much they are worth.

The coupons are used to promote or introduce a vast array of items ranging from soap powder and mouthwash to cereals and salad dressing. Consumers redeem them at grocery stores for credit. The store owner relays the coupons to the manufacturer, who then reimburses the retailer for the amount of the coupon plus an amount to cover handling costs.

According to Grocery Manufacturers of America, over $200 million a year is redeemed through coupons. Although most of the larger companies in the grocery field issue coupons, there is a difference of opinion among marketing people as to their effectiveness. Coupons do move products, some experts say, but they undermine brand loyalty by appealing solely to the pocketbook. Quite often the coupons are simply turned in for cash and the merchandise is not sold at all.

Supporters of coupons declare that they do more for a good product and do it faster, better, and at less cost than any other medium.

To begin a coupon program, a company decides first on the products to be involved, the size of the discount, and the territory to be covered. Salespeople are then notified of the proposed move. They, in turn, seek cooperation at the retail level. Such cooperation might include large orders during the coupons' effective period and prime display position in stores. Much of this is now arranged by food brokers.

Rebates

The use of a rebate program is prevalent in all types of consumer goods, from automobiles to television sets to personal computers to household appliances. The product is advertised at a given price with a rebate amount listed. The customer receives a rebate form, upon purchase, which is then sent to the manufacturer to claim a rebate of the stated amount.

Award-Winning Premium Programs

At the National Premium Sales Executives meeting in Chicago in 1986, six companies won awards for their outstanding premium programs. Their efforts are worth citing as examples of thought-provoking, stimulating ideas for producing successful programs.

1. *Arby's.* In a seasonal effort to promote sales for their restaurant franchises, Arby's joined with Libbey Glass to offer consumers premium holiday stemware as a self-liquidating direct premium. The program brought a 19.4 percent sales increase for the Arby's franchise.

   Arby's developed the program and tested the stemware with favorable results before offering it to franchise outlets. By offering a quality premium at a low cost, Arby's hoped to increase sales volume during the holiday season.

   With the purchase of an Arby's large or medium soft

drink during the promotion, a customer could purchase a holly-decorated stemmed glass for 89 cents.

Seasonal point-of-purchase display kits, store decoration kits, ad slicks, and TV and radio spots were made available to Arby's franchises to support the campaign. A coupon-book program was initiated during the Holly Stemware program to encourage revisits after the holiday season, and a ceramic candle-holder offer was made as an extension of the stemware offer.

"Arby's made one sale of glassware for every three customers, compared with previous Arby's glassware offer figures of one glassware sale for every five customers," Andrew Dyakon of Arby's noted. Two and one-half million glasses were sold during the promotion.

Eighty percent of Arby's 1,400 units used the promotion and reported a 19.4 percent weekly sales increase from $20,424 to $24,390. Melinda Ennis, director of sales promotion, noted that, "Arby's increased sales and profits, increased customer-visit frequency, increased trial-visits by non- or infrequent customers, and reinforced Arby's image of value through the Holly Stemware offer."

2. *Armstrong World Industries, Inc.* A leading manufacturer of flooring products, Armstrong teamed with New York Steak to provide flooring product dealers with incentives to buy their Designer Solarian roll flooring and Glazecraft vinyl tile. The program exceeded Armstrong's sales objectives.

Armstrong used a "Steak Your Claim to Armstrong" theme to give dealers a chance to earn gourmet food items from the New York Steak food line by purchasing full rolls of Solarian or 20 cartons of Glazecraft. Special assortments, offering six items from the food line, were offered to buyers of six rolls or 120 cartons of flooring product.

The Glazecraft Days promotion, a two-day push to promote sales of Glazecraft, featured direct sales efforts by Armstrong and wholesaler personnel who encouraged retailers to call a toll-free number for Glazecraft information.

DAC Associates, the Jay Group's telemarketing arm, handled the calls.

Armstrong salespeople were also rewarded with steak knife sets for exceeding their quota of calls, and steak awards for making their quota of Glazecraft orders. A steak party package was awarded to the wholesaler office generating the highest percentage of call quota in each of the 18 sales districts.

Overall, during Glazecraft Days, Armstrong received 217 percent of its quota of calls and 154 percent of its sales quota.

Armstrong substantially beat their sales goals for the Steak Your Claim promotion, according to Laurence A. Lehmann of Armstrong World Industries. "Enough flooring product was sold during the promotion to stretch a tile line from Washington, D.C., to the Statue of Liberty," Mr. Lehmann noted.

More than 5,000 incentive units were distributed during "Steak Your Claim." After the successful campaign, New York Steak awarded a live steer to Armstrong and others who participated in the promotion.

3. *Campbell Soup Company.* In an effort to promote faster stock turns for Franco-American SpaghettiOs, Campbell developed a direct premium mail-in campaign offering Binney & Smith Crayola crayons to consumers for purchases of SpaghettiOs. The program exceeded marketing expectations, according to Terrence J. Atkins of Campbell Soup.

SpaghettiOs and Crayola crayons share identical demographic markets; children between two and 12 years of age in families earning at least $25,000 annually. Both products are top-selling brands in their categories.

Campbell's made the offer with an ad run nationally in a free-standing insert with a circulation of 46 million. Consumers were offered a free 14-piece Crayola sample pack for eight proofs of purchase of any of the four SpaghettiOs varieties. Only the form on the ad could be used for ordering, and the offer was limited to one sample-pack per family. Fulfillment Systems Inc. handled the sample-pack mailings.

A brochure resembling a Crayola box was used to sell the program to the trade. For each display of 10 cases or more, Campbell's provided stores with a special near-pack sample display of 100 Crayola crayon four-packs. To provide immediate gratification, consumers received a free Crayola four-pack for every two cans of SpaghettiOs purchased.

Response from dealers to the in-store direct premium offer was 50 percent greater than originally projected. Usage of Campbell's retail displays with the Crayola near-packs was up 18 percent over previous experience.

At the close of the program, 300,000 four-packs and 250,000 sample packs had been distributed. SpaghettiOs' deal case volume rose 10 percent over the same period during the previous year.

4. *Ligget & Myers Tobacco Co.* L & M developed a free mail-in premium program using their generic-brand trademark to promote consumer loyalty for their 294 varieties of cigarettes that are sold under 41 generic and private labels. The program helped Liggett & Myers face heavy competition in the generic cigarette market.

The Quality Seal, a "Q" label on top of every cigarette pack, was designed as a unifying quality message for L & M's generic and private-brand products. During the premium offer, consumers could save the seals from the cigarette packs to earn incentive awards.

Consumers could earn a lady's eelskin French clutch purse by collecting 70 Quality Seals, a man's eelskin bi-fold wallet for 55 seals and a brass cigarette case for 25 seals. Consumers could pick up a saver-card to collect seals and a reply envelope from in-store displays and easel cards.

Liggett & Myers launched the campaign with a co-op advertising offer to more than 2,900 chain and wholesale accounts. More than 800 accounts participated in the co-op plan.

Seventy-five thousand out of 150,000 retailers selling generic cigarettes of any kind offered the premiums to their customers. Stores displayed any of six point-of-sale promotion pieces that were set up by Liggett & Myers' sales force. One hundred thirty-eight thousand premium requests—approximately 2.5 percent of the five million saver-cards printed—were received, more than doubling the number of redemptions expected. The purse was the most requested item.

Liggett & Myers held 56 percent of the generic market with its 'Q-Seal' products before the promotion, and their share jumped to 64 percent of the market during the six-month premium offer.

5. *Sunkist Soft Drinks.* In an effort to place display racks in stores throughout the country, Sunkist teamed with Citadel Industries to provide a sales incentive program for independent bottlers who handle the placements. The program generated a tremendous increase in rack placements.

Sunkist is the leading producer of orange soft drinks, claiming about 35 percent of the total orange soft drink market. Diet Sunkist, originally introduced in 1981, was reintroduced to the market during the incentive campaign.

Sunkist's 1985 campaign used a "Win—Place—Show" theme that exorted salespeople to win awards by placing display racks and showing both Sunkist and new diet Sunkist to the consumer.

When a bottler placed a rack or dump, Sunkist awarded them $4 in prize certificates that could be exchanged immediately for merchandise awards or saved to earn more valuable prizes. Sunkist worked with Citadel Industries to provide a wide variety of quality prizes from Citadel's plateau catalog, including items with the Sunkist logo, such as rafts and miniature cars.

About 50 percent of the bottlers distributing Sunkist participated. Close to 3,000 bottler salespeople sold racks and earned awards.

Sunkist awarded their efforts with $50,000 worth of incentives. Ninety percent of these items came from the Citadel catalog, while Sunkist items accounted for the rest. Fifteen thousand racks were sold during the five-month promotion, a 3,000 percent increase in retail display usage, according to Cuyler Caldwell of Sunkist Soft Drinks. On average, 25 cases of Sunkist products were sold from each rack. Most racks were filled three or four times during the program.

"The displays, which usually remain in place for one or two weeks, remained in place for six weeks in most stores," Mr. Caldwell reported.

6. *Uniroyal and PMH/Caramanning.* These companies worked together to provide a sales incentive program to move top-of-the-line Royal Seal automobile tires out of inventories to make room for new stock. The program moved 300,000 tires.

Uniroyal timed its "Triple Play" sales incentive promotion to occur during the 1985 baseball pennant race and beyond. Dealer principals, distributor salespeople and dealer salespeople were targeted by the promotion.

When a dealer salesperson sold four Royal Seal tires, or when a distributor salesperson or dealer principal sold eight Royal Seals, they received an instant-winner ruboff card. Seven thousand four hundred card recipients received winning rub-off cards and claimed awards from a six-level catalog provided by PMH/Caramanning.

Special awards were given to the 100 top sellers in four regions, and to 10 top-sellers nationally. By correctly answering six true-false training questions on each card, participants were eligible for Uniroyal's monthly Grand Slam training drawing, which offered a travel incentive and 54 awards of incentive items from the merchandising catalog.

To spur early sales, Uniroyal gave distributors and dealer salespeople a chance to earn additional incentive prizes for sales during the campaign's first two months. New dealers were recruited during the promotion with a bonus of five rub-off cards and the offer of a Royal Seal Demonstration Display unit for a minimum initial order of 30 tires.

Monthly reports to distributors and an eight-issue newsletter entitled *Sporting News* were used to promote interest in the campaign and encourage continued participation.

At the distribution level, 7,967 winners were awarded; 275 training-question sweepstakes awards were presented. William B. Scott of Uniroyal, concluded: "Uniroyal achieved its goal of moving 300,000 tires, markedly improved the quality of salesmanship in the field, and picked up new dealers for the Royal Seal line."

Premium Dictionary

The following defines the various types of premiums in use today.

- Account-opener. A direct premium offered by a bank or savings and loan association to a depositor opening a new account.

- Advance Premium. One given to a new customer on condition that it be earned by later purchases—a technique originated by home-service route firms.

- Advertising specialty. Close cousin to a premium—a useful item bearing an advertising imprint and given freely with no strings attached.

- Banded premium. A form of direct premium—a factory-pack attached to a product package by a band of paper, tape, or plastic film—and on-pack premium.

- Bounce-back. An additional offer mailed with a self-liquidator. Several items may be offered, frequently related to the first.

- Business gift. A gift to a customer, stockholder, employee, or other business friend—most often at Christmas—as an expression of appreciation.

- Combination sale. A tie-in of a premium with a purchase at a combination price; sometimes self-liquidating; often an on-pack.

- Container premium. A type of factory-packed direct premium —a reusable container that serves as a product package; all or part of the extra cost may be added to the price to make the promotion self-liquidating.

- Contest. A competition based on skill in which prizes are offered. Proof of purchase is usually required with entry. (Compare *Sweepstakes.*)

- Continuity program. A self-liquidating (or profit-making) plan offering a set of related items—one a week for six to 15 weeks—most often in supermarkets. Term may also apply to Coupon Plan.

- Coupon plan. A continuous program offering a variety of premiums for coupons, labels, or other tokens from one or more products.

- Credit-card offer. A direct mailing to a credit-card holder of a merchandise offering (originally a self-liquidating premium device), often using premiums or sweepstakes to close a sale or a trial-offer acceptance.

- Dealer premium (or dealer incentive). One given to a retailer with a specified purchase of one or more products—or for coupons or purchase credits accumulated over a period of time.

- Direct premium. The simplest kind—an item given free with a purchase at the time of the purchase. Includes on-packs, in-packs, and container premiums, as well as those given separately.

- Display premium. A form of dealer incentive that is part of a point-of-purchase display—may be a sample of a consumer premium or a functional element of the display itself.

- Door-opener. A relatively inexpensive premium given by a door-to-door salesperson to induce a prospect to listen to a sales presentation.

- Factory-pack. A direct premium attached to a product— includes in-packs, on-packs, and container premiums.

- Free. A magic word with some strings attached. Its use is not so severely restricted as it once was—but it's still wise to be sure it really is free if the advertising says it is. Conditions on which the "free" offer is made should be clearly stated.

- Give-away. A low-cost item handed out fairly freely—akin to an advertising specialty or a traffic-builder. Now also sometimes used as a term for any direct premium.

- Hostess gift. The party plan's way of compensating a woman for the use of her home to conduct a demonstration party. She usually gets value in proportion to sales and party bookings written at her party.

- Incentive. A reward offered for desired performance; now often used as a synonym for "premium."

- In-pack. A direct premium enclosed inside a product package.

- Loader. An obsolete term (also "dealer loader") for a dealer premium given with a specified product purchase. In disfavor because of obvious negative connotation; "dealer premium" or "dealer incentive" has replaced it.

- Lottery. A plan (generally illegal in sales promotion) that awards a prize on the basis of chance and requires consideration to enter. Becomes a legal sweepstakes when consideration is removed, or a contest when chance is eliminated.

- Mail-in. Any premium offered upon mail request—either a self-liquidator or a free offer for multiple proof-of-purchase tokens.

- On-pack. A direct premium attached to the exterior of a product package—or, sometimes, riding with it in a special sleeve, carton, or film wrap.

- Package enclosure. An in-pack premium.

- Part-cash redemption. An option often included in coupon plans, permitting the consumer to get premiums faster by redeeming fewer coupons with a cash amount that may be self-liquidating.

- Premium. An article of merchandise offered as an incentive to the performance of a specified service.

- Preselected winner. A winner determined by chance based on a number or game piece selected in advance—a plan that may be held to be a deceptive practice unless a drawing is also used to award unclaimed prizes.

- Prize. Reward given to winner in a contest, sweepstakes, or lottery; also sometimes refers to salespeople's incentive award.

- Proof of purchase. A boxtop, label, trademark, coupon, or other token from a product, that qualifies a consumer to receive a premium.

- Purchase-privilege offer. A term little used today, once commonly applied to food-store promotions akin to the tape-redemption or continuity programs; often used trade cards.

- Referral premium. One offered to a satisfied customer who refers the seller to a friend who purchases a product. Also "use-the-user plan."

- Sales contest. A sales-incentive program. The word "contest" is used less today than previously, since direct competition among salespeople is no longer the rule.

- Sales incentive. An award to a salesperson for performance-exceeding a quota, signing new accounts, reopening accounts, selling specified product or other stated objectives of the company.

- Self-liquidator. A consumer premium offered (usually by mail) for proof of purchase and a cash amount sufficient to cover the merchandise cost plus handling and postage. May refer to any promotion in which the recipient pays the premium cost.

- Specialty advertising. See *Advertising Specialty.*

- Sweepstakes. A promotion which awards substantial prizes on the basis of a chance drawing. Similar to a contest, but without the element of skill—and usually, for legal reasons, without "consideration."

- Tape plan. More formally, "cash-register-tape redemption plan." A continuity promotion by supermarkets, offering a variety of premiums in return for register tapes representing specified purchases—and, most often, cash amounts sufficient to make the promotion self-liquidating or profitable.

- Trade card. An old plan, now little used, in which a retailer punches the amount of consumer purchases into a card until they reach a total qualifying the customer to buy a premium at a self-liquidating price.

- Trading stamp. A gummed stamp given by a retailer, usually for each 10 cents of purchase, to be pasted in a "saver book" to accumulate 1200 or 1500, then redeemable for premiums presented in the stamp-company catalog.

- Traffic-builder. A relatively low-cost premium offered free as an inducement to visit a store for a demonstration.

- Travel incentive. A trip—group or individual—offered to salespeople or dealers. Often tied in with sales meetings at resort areas.

- Use-the-user plan. See "Referral Premium."

Courtesy of National Premium Sales Executives Inc.

Chapter 11

Direct Marketing

"Direct marketing traces its origins to direct mail and mail order—time-tested ways to sell a wide variety of products and services and which had been applied particularly in such fields as catalogs, magazine circulation, and book and record clubs," said Robert F. DeLay, president of the Direct Marketing Association, (DMA) in the preface to the book, *The Direct Marketing Handbook.**

DeLay also commented that direct marketing has broadened from the traditional products and service areas and now is being applied for marketing purposes by nearly every type of firm selling to consumer or business customers. In addition, direct marketing has found substantial applications in fund raising, the political process, the arts, education, and organizations advocating social change.

While the function of direct marketing is usually the responsibility of the marketing or advertising executives, often with the involvement of an outside direct marketing agency, the sales manager in smaller companies could be directly involved. Therefore, the sales manager should be familiar with this activity as it contributes to the overall sales effort.

Some years ago the Direct Marketing Association prepared two lists that provide guides to help analyze how direct mail can best serve a company's needs.

Direct Mail Functions

The first guide is a list of the six basic functions of direct mail:

1. *Creating more effective personal sales contacts.* This in-

---

*The Direct Marketing Handbook, ed. Edward L. Nash (New York: McGraw-Hill Inc., 1984).

cludes direct mail advertising that creates a specific opportunity for salespeople to call by getting inquiries or leads for personal follow-up. It also means paving the way for salespeople by lessening resistance, arousing interest, and educating and informing the prospect before intended sales calls, but without trying to get back an order or response from the prospect through the mail.

2. *Bringing the prospect to you.* This applies particularly to the retail field and to service businesses (like banks) that do not have sales forces. It has other applications, such as getting customers or prospects to visit new plants or special displays.

3. *Delivering background, sales, or public relations messages to customers, prospects, employees, or other special groups.* This includes mailings that are designed as pure advertising. It also covers any prestige reminder or goodwill advertising, employee relations, or anything to influence selective groups along certain lines of thought or action, but without direct response being sought by mail or without any direct personal follow-up intended.

4. *Taking actual orders through the mail.* This function is direct mail selling or mail order selling, where every step in the sales process, from the initial contact to the final sale, is done exclusively by mail. This applies to publications and news services as well as to selling merchandise by mail. It also applies to raising funds by charitable and educational organizations.

5. *Securing action from the prospect by mail.* This covers any promotion intended to secure response or action by mail, but not designed to secure an order or result in a personal contact between the prospect and the advertiser. Included in this category would be getting entries in a competition or securing requests for general information literature.

6. *Conducting research and market surveys.* This covers every phase of research, investigation, and fact-finding by mail.

49 Ways to Use Direct Mail

For many years, the basic check list of direct mail uses has been DMA's "49 ways" chart. While many committees have sought to expand this list, nobody has yet come up with a more efficient check list. DMA suggests you use this list to analyze your own direct mail program in three steps:

1. Check the ways you are *now* using direct mail.

2. Mark the ways you are *not* now using direct mail but that could be profitable possibilities.

3. Double-check those direct mail applications you are now using that could be altered, improved, or increased for greater results, effectiveness, and efficiency.

IN YOUR OWN ORGANIZATION

1. *Building morale of employees.* A bulletin or house magazine published regularly, carrying announcements of company policy, stimulating ambition, encouraging thrift, and promoting safety and efficiency, will make for greater loyalty among employees.

2. *Securing data from employees.* Letters or questionnaires occasionally directed to employees help cement a common interest in the organization and bring back practical ideas and much useful data.

3. *Stimulating salespeople to greater efforts.* Interesting sales magazines, bulletins, or letters help in unifying a scattered selling organization, in speeding up sales, and in making better salespeople by carrying success stories and sound ideas that have made sales.

4. *Paving the way for salespeople.* Forceful and intelligent direct mail that is both persistent and continuous will create a field of prospective buyers who are live and ready to be sold.

5. *Securing inquiries for the sales force.* Direct mail can bring

back actual inquiries from interested prospective customers—qualified prospects your salespeople can call upon and sell.

6. *Teaching salespeople "How to Sell".* A sales manual, or a series of messages, will help educate and stimulate the sales force to close more and bigger sales.

7. *Selling stockholders and others interested in your company.* Enclosures with dividend checks and in pay envelopes, as well as other messages, will sell stockholders and employees on making a greater use of company products and services, and in suggesting their use to others.

8. *Keeping contact with customers between sales calls.* Messages to customers between salespeople's visits will help secure for your firm the maximum amount of business from each customer.

9. *Further selling prospective customers after a demonstration or salesperson's call.* Direct mail emphasizing the superiorities of your product or service will help clinch sales and make it more difficult for competition to gain a foothold.

10. *Acknowledging orders or payments.* An interesting letter, folder, or mailing card is a simple gesture that will cement a closer friendship between you and your customers.

11. *Welcoming new customers.* A letter welcoming new customers can go a long way toward keeping them sold on your company, products, and services.

12. *Collecting accounts.* A series of diplomatic collection letters will bring and keep accounts up to date, leave the recipients in a friendly frame of mind, and hold them as customers.

BUILDING NEW BUSINESS

13. *Securing new dealers.* Direct mail offers many concerns unlimited possibilities in lining up and selling new dealers.

14. *Securing direct orders.* Many organizations have built ex-

tremely profitable businesses through orders secured only with the help of direct mail. Many concerns not presently selling direct by mail can and should do so.

15. *Strengthening weak territories.* Direct mail will provide intensified local sales stimulation wherever you may wish to apply it.

16. *Winning back inactive customers.* A series of direct mail messages to "lost" customers often revives many of them.

17. *Developing sales in areas not covered by salespeople.* Communities unapproachable because of distance, bad transportation schedules, or poor roads, offer the alert organization vast possibilities to increase sales by direct mail.

18. *Developing sales among specified groups.* With direct mail you can direct your selling messages specifically to those you wish to sell, in the language they will understand, and in a form that will stimulate action.

19. *Following inquiries received from direct advertising or other forms of advertising.* A series of messages outlining the "reasons why" your product or service should be bought, will help you cash in on inquiries whose initial interest was aroused by other media—publications, radio, television, etc.

20. *Driving home sales arguments.* Several mailings, each planned to stress one or more selling points, will progressively educate your prospective customer on the many reasons why he or she should buy your product or service, and from you.

21. *Selling other items in line.* Mailing pieces, package inserts, or "hand-out" folders will educate your customers on products and services other than those they are buying.

22. *Getting product prescribed or specified.* Professionals, such as physicians and dentists, will prescribe a product for their patients if they are correctly educated on its merits and what it will accomplish. Likewise, consumers and dealers will ask for a product by name if they are thoroughly famil-

iar with it. Direct advertising can be profitably used for this purpose.

23. *Selling new type of buyer.* Perhaps there are new outlets through which your product or service might be sold. Direct mail is a powerful tool in the development of new sales channels.

ASSISTING PRESENT DEALERS

24. *Bringing buyer to showroom.* Invitations through letter or printed announcements will bring prospective customers to your showroom or factory.

25. *Helping present dealer sell more.* Assisting your dealer with direct mail and with point-of-purchase helps will sell your product or service faster and step up turnover. The right kind of helps will win hearty dealer cooperation.

26. *Merchandising your plans to dealer.* Direct mail can forcefully present and explain your merchandising plans to the dealer—and show how to put your promotion ideas and material to work as sales-builders.

27. *Educating dealers on superiorities of your product or service.* Memories are short when it comes to remembering the other fellow's product or service and its superiorities, especially when you keep telling your dealers the benefits and advantages of your own.

28. *Educating retail clerks in the selling of a product.* Clerks are the neck of the retail selling bottle. If they believe in a company and a product, their influence is a powerful aid to sales. If indifferent, they lose their sales-making effectiveness. Direct mail that is friendly, understanding, helpful, and stimulating will enlist their cooperation and increase the sales curve.

29. *Securing information from dealers or dealers' clerks.* Letters, printed messages, a bulletin, or a house magazine will bring back helpful data from the individuals who actually sell your product or your service—information you can pass along to other dealers or sales clerks to help them sell more.

30. *Referring inquiries from consumer advertising to local dealers.* The manufacturer can use direct mail to refer an inquirer to his or her local dealer for prompt attention. At the same time, the dealer can be alerted with the details of the prospect's inquiry.

THE CONSUMER

31. *Creating a need or a demand for a product.* Direct mail, consistently used, will stimulate the demand for your product or service, and will remind the customer to ask for it by name.

32. *Increasing consumption of a product among present users.* Package inserts, booklets, etc., can be used to educate customers to the full use of the products they buy, especially new benefits and advantages.

33. *Bringing customers into a store to buy.* This applies to retailers. Personal, friendly, cordial, and interesting direct mail messages, telling about the merchandise you have, and creating the desire to own that merchandise, will bring back *past* customers, stimulate *present* patrons, and lure *new* people for you.

34. *Opening new charge accounts.* This also applies to retailers. There are many people in every community who pay their bills promptly and do the bulk of their buying where they have accounts. A careful compilation of such a list and a well-planned direct mail program inviting them to open charge accounts will bring new customers to your store.

35. *Capitalizing on special events.* Direct mail helps retailers to capitalize on such events as marriages, births, graduations, promotions, etc. Likewise, letters can be sent to select lists featuring private sales. Other lists and formats can cover general sales.

OTHER USES

36. *Building goodwill.* The possibilities of building goodwill and solidifying friendships through direct advertising are unlimited. It's the little handshake through the mail that cements business relationships and holds your customers. Certain "reminder" forms also can help build goodwill.

37. *Capitalizing on other advertising.* Direct advertising is the salesmate of all other media. As the "workhorse" among advertising and promotion media, it helps the sponsor capitalize on his investment in all visual and audio advertising—especially when initial interest can be given a lift and converted into action and sales.

38. *As a "leader" or "hook" in other forms of advertising.* Publication space, as well as radio and television commercials, is often too limited to tell enough of the story about a product or service to make a sale. Direct mail provides the "leader" or "hook"—in the form of booklets, folders, catalogs, and instruction manuals—that other advertising media can feature, to stimulate action as well as to satisfy the inquirer with the full story of product and service.

39. *Breaking down resistance to a product or a service.* Direct mail helps to overcome resistance in the minds of prospective customers.

40. *Stimulating interest in forthcoming events.* A special "week" or "day" devoted to the greater use of a product; an anniversary, a new line launched by a dealer, special "openings," and scores of other happenings can all be promoted by direct mail to produce sales.

41. *Distribution of samples.* There are thousands of logical prospects who could be converted into users of your product if you proved to them its merits. Direct mail can help you do this by letting prospects convince themselves by actual test, provided your product lends itself to sampling by mail.

42. *Announcing a new product, new policy, or new addition.* There is no quicker way to make announcements to specific

individuals or groups, to create interest and stimulate sales, than through the personal, action-producing medium of direct mail.

43. *Announcing a new address or change in telephone number.* When these important changes are made, a letter or printed announcement sent through the mail has a personal appeal that will register your message better than any other form of advertising.

44. *Keeping a concern or product "in mind".* Direct advertising includes many forms of "remember" advertising—blotters, calendars, novelties. Regular mailings help keep you in the minds of customers and prospects.

45. *Research for new ideas and suggestions.* Direct advertising research is a powerful force in building sales. Direct mail can be used to find market facts, cut sales fumbling, and chart direct, profitable trails to sales. It furnishes all the important tools for sales research, to discover what, where, how, and to whom to sell—and at what price.

46. *Correcting present mailing lists.* Householders have an average annual change of 22 percent; merchants of 23 percent; agents of 29 percent; and advertising people of 37 percent. Keeping a mailing list up to date is a most important detail. Direct mail can be employed to keep your list accurate, by occasionally asking your customer if his or her name and address are correct ... or if there are others you should be reaching in your customer's organization.

47. *Securing names for lists.* Direct mail can help you build mailing lists by securing names of customers and prospects from many sources, such as direct from distributors, salespeople, clerks, stockholders, employees; from people who have access to the names of individuals in specific groups; from recommendation of customers and friends; from special mail surveys, questionnaires, etc.

48. *Protecting patents or special processes.* Shouting forth the ownership of such patents or processes by direct advertising

can leave no question in the minds of your customers, present or prospective, as to who owns such a product or process. At the same time, it gives you greater protection from possible infringers.

49. *Raising funds.* Direct advertising affords an effective, economical method of raising funds for worthy causes.

The Seven Rules of Success in Direct Mail

The late Ed Mayer was regarded by many as an outstanding leader in direct mail. His seven rules for success have stood the test of time and are just as pertinent today as twenty years ago. Here they are:

1. *What is the objective?* What are you trying to sell? The more specific you are, the more effective your return.

2. *Address correctly—to the right list.* Sending mailers to anyone at random is self-defeating. The more specific the list, the greater the result. If you want to promote your nursery school, you don't send the literature to senior citizens. Conversely, if your book is *How to Enjoy Retirement,* you don't send it to newlyweds.

   If your mailing is on a regular basis, have your list "cleaned" with correct addresses every few months. A simple "address correction requested" on the bottom of your mailer will bring it back to you if the address has changed.

3. *Tell readers the benefits.* Use the word "you" in your copy. Tell the reader in the headline and/or first paragraph the most important benefit they will receive. Back this up with proofs, endorsement, and what happens if they don't act ... now!

4. *Make the layout and copy fit.* Selling high-priced merchandise should have a different "look" than selling low-priced items. The Cadillac brochure looks entirely different from the insert from the nearby drug chain in your daily paper. Your mailer should "look" like the item it is selling.

5. *Make it easy for the customer to act.* Each mailer should call for an action of some kind: inquiry, purchase, visit to your store; or your visit to them. One way is to *set a deadline.*

6. *Repeat your story.* Yes, you told your story in the headline. Yes, you repeated it in the first paragraph. Now, once again, at the end, repeat it with feeling.

7. *Research your direct mail.* What were the results of your last mailer? The last three? What pulls best? Keep accurate records. Test one technique, then another. Your percentage of return will increase as you find out what works best for you.

Sales Brochures—15 Pitfalls to Avoid

Next time you plan to create a sales brochure, consider the following "commandments" carefully—*and don't follow them!* That's the advice of Joseph J. O'Donnell, Jr., director of communications, Transport International Pool, Bala Cynwyd, Pennsylvania, as reported in Dartnell's *Sales and Marketing Executive Report.* [*]

1. Try to make the brochure be all things to all possible—even remotely potential—publics.

2. Ask your salespeople what they want—instead of what kind of problems they're having.

3. Decide exactly how much you are going to spend on the brochure even before calling in a supplier to discuss the project.

4. Consider the total cost of the brochure project in complete isolation from either the selling price of the product or the amount of profit one sale produces.

5. Let your engineering or engineering design people do all the drawings. Make certain every intricate valve, circuit, or other detail is depicted, regardless of how miniscule it might be in proportion to the total drawing.

---

[*]November 2, 1983, Vol. VI, Number 22, p. 8.

6. Don't leave even one square inch of "white (or breathing) space" on any page. (After all, you're paying for every bit of the paper, aren't you?)

7. Never offer a free sample, trial, or test of your product in the brochure.

8. If photographs are necessary for the brochure, always take them yourself or have somebody in your company who's "good with a camera" take them. Never consider that a professional photographer be used.

9. Don't use picture captions; let photos and art speak for themselves.

10. Always choose one of the more stylized type faces for the copy in your brochure. Never consider a plain style of serif type.

11. Talk first in the brochure about your product's features: size, dimensions, colors, power requirements, wavelengths used, number of circuits, buttons, etc. Always let the prospect determine the relevance of these features.

12. Within the brochure, let your presentation jump around a lot; don't follow any logical sequence since it might bore your reader into "understanding" and "knowing" what your product's all about before finishing the brochure.

13. Get three or four printing quotes and go with the cheapest vendor every time.

14. When setting print quantity, don't plan out exactly how you're going to distribute the brochure.

15. Once the brochure has been printed, do not issue a press release about it, lest a competitor finds out about it and writes for one.

If you really want to communicate, try to avoid all of these "commandments" like the plague. Remember that in a competitive environment, any brochure that takes the tactic of presenting its contents from the marketing (i.e., the prospect's customer's) viewpoint stands a better chance of communicating than one that doesn't.

Direct Mail Practices and Trends

Dartnell's *Sales and Marketing Executive Report* reported on a survey of interest to all direct mail practitioners.

More than 1,000 member companies of the Direct Marketing Association responded in 1986 to a 30-minute mail questionnaire concerning current marketing practices and trends. Conducted by the Direct Marketing Association's Marketing Council, in cooperation with DMA's Research department, the survey covered 12 subject areas including database usage, media usage, industry growth, strategies, and diversification.

Fifty percent of the respondents were vice-presidents or presidents.

Following are highlights of the survey.

- Three major trends, not yet peaked, are: 1) retailers selling through catalogs (66.5 percent), 2) catalogers opening retail stores (62.3 percent), 3) direct marketers entering other direct marketing product areas (62 percent).

- Direct marketers enjoy a sophisticated understanding of the uses and values of databases, but that knowledge is not currently matched by usage levels (69 percent think they are behind, or at best, just keeping up). The projected future trend is toward more sophisticated use.

- Greatest future growth is expected in the areas of financial services, telecommunications, computer hardware/software, and health care.

- Respondents indicate that usage of almost all media is expected to decline from current levels, which could result in an even shallower name pool.

- The four most important industry problems cited are: 1) finding new lists, 2) decreasing response percentages, 3) the cost of acquiring new names, 4) increasing the number of new mail order customers.

- The use of frequent buyer programs is accelerating.

- The majority of respondents have run image ads, and 69 percent expect to in the future.

- Sixty-nine percent believe that agencies will continue to diversify by acquiring related direct response service businesses.

- Global marketing trends are considered to be good for the direct marketing industry: imported product ideas, joint ventures with foreign companies, and selling products through direct marketing techniques outside the U.S.

PART 3

Sales Planning and Control

Chapter 12

Market Planning and Markets

Sales planning and subsequent control of the activities that affect the end sales result is a process involving many functions covered in this and subsequent chapters.

Where does it begin? William J. Stanton and Richard H. Buskirk, in their book, *Management of the Sales Force,** state: "Planning sales force activity begins with a consideration of market and sales potentials, because the basic concepts developed in analyzing potential markets are used throughout the planning process. All budgets fundamentally are dependent on the sales forecast, which in turn should not be developed without an analysis of the market potentials of the products or services to be sold. Sales quotas and sales territories are dependent upon market analysis and planning."

Another view is expressed by T. Edward Ormsby, vice-president of sales, Wrangler Womenswear, Blue Bell, Inc. He said: "Sales planning is the key ingredient to the success of any organizational plan. The keys to successful planning and execution are:

- Invite participation from all who must carry out the sales plan—all subordinates down to the territory (salesperson) level.

- Integrate advertising, sales promotion, and selling actions.

- Communicate the plan to all who are responsible for executing it."

A look at the marketing planning process is in order, followed by some market considerations.

---

*William J. Stanton and Richard H. Buskirk, *Management of the Sales Force* (Homewood, Illinois: Richard D. Irwin, Inc., 1987), 7th ed.

Marketing Planning

A marketing plan typically strives to answer three questions, all directed at the company's goal of obtaining customers:

1. Where are we now?
2. Where do we want to go?
3. How can we get there?

As a measure of market performance and as a guide to the attainment of future growth, most companies develop a comprehensive annual marketing plan. In fact, many companies establish a five-year program that is reviewed or modified each year, according to present performance and new projections for the future.

A review of several marketing plan seminars conducted by the American Management Association reveals that, based on the subjects discussed plus additions from other sources, a planning program covers the following ground:

1. Introduction

   • The annual marketing plan—its relationship to corporate plans and to long-term market plans

   • Purposes of the plan

   • Organizing for marketing planning

   • Involvement with other departments

2. Identification of problems and opportunities

   • Data gathering

   • Areas to be analyzed

   • Product planning and management

   • Markets—size, scope and share

   • Distribution channels

   • Competition

   • Advertising and promotion

   • Technological changes

- Economy—industry and national
- Pricing
- Legal aspects
- International markets
- Methods of analysis

3. Establishment of objectives
   - Review of previous-year results
   - Annual objectives within the long-term plan
   - Primary objectives regarding:
   - Sales and share of market
   - Profits
   - Turnover
   - Return on investment
   - Development of overall marketing strategies

4. Action programs
   - Integrating corporate effort
   - Establishing priorities and schedules
   - Control procedures
   - Manpower development

5. Financial considerations
   - Forecasts
   - Budgets
   - Resource allocations
   - Profit projections

6. Implementation

- Establishment of controls
- Coordinating the effort
- Review periods
- Modifications

Elements of a Long-Range Plan

While a sound plan for expanding any business must include many factors, present-day conditions place particular emphasis on distribution. As a result, the sales phases of the plan need painstaking consideration.

During the past several years, Dartnell has carefully observed the trend of sales management. Members of the staff have enjoyed close relations with many sales leaders in all lines of business. The following conclusions have been reached as to what a sound customer-relations policy for the average business should encompass:

PRINCIPLE NO. 1

Your long-range sales policy should speed the movement of goods and services into the hands of those who can use or sell them at a profit.

This means you should predetermine those customers who are able to use your products, the quantities in which they can use them, and then eliminate, so far as possible, those functions which add to the cost of distributing to those customers. It means putting "profit" ahead of "coverage" as a main consideration in sales planning, administration, and concentration of sales effort.

PRINCIPLE NO. 2

Your long-range sales policy should provide for selling and moving goods and services in economic quantities, at economically sound prices, through the most economically sound channels of distribution.

One of the most important jobs of sales management is to determine how much is needed to sell any given customer to earn a profit on his purchases. Millions of distribution dollars have been wasted because too many customers had the turnover craze and bought in such small quantities that there was no profit to the supplier, and the purchaser penalized himself by carrying inadequate stocks.

Another great loss results from too careless a selection, or no selection at all, of distribution outlets. Too many companies undercut established markets by selling mass distributors at stripped cost prices. Such a policy is unsound.

PRINCIPLE NO. 3

Your long-range policy should include the training of every salesperson, distributor, wholesaler, dealer, and consumer to sell and buy in economical quantities.

This is fundamental in any program aimed at the reduction of prices to the consumer. It makes no difference whether a buyer buys too much or too little; if the quantity is uneconomical, costs are needlessly increased and waste results.

The control of this waste calls for intensive buyer and seller education. It cannot be done overnight. But provision should be made in sales planning for more of this all-important work. We must lay aside any ideas we have about selling buyers all we can get them to order and pay for, and sell them economical quantities determined by dealer and consumer studies.

PRINCIPLE NO. 4

Your long-range sales policy should seek to determine, by trustworthy means, the customer structure of each customer's business. This determines his chances for survival.

It is reasonable to assume that the establishments that will survive highly competitive selling will be those that had the foresight to build a solid customer structure. The manufacturer's sales policy should be aimed at educating customers and their customers in turn, in order to build the same kind of foundation for lasting relationships.

PRINCIPLE NO. 5

Your long-range sales policy should determine the sales objective, measure the sales power needed to reach that objective, and then seek to apply the needed sales power to attain the objective at an economical cost.
This means more than just establishing the potential sales expectancy from a territory. It means first of all determining a break-even point in sales production. It means the intelligent allocation of that volume among all sales-production factors, with a corresponding allocation of the sales effort.

And more than anything else it means focusing the sales effort upon the main objectives by the use of scientific controls and proper budgeting of expense and with the least possible dissipation of effort on sideshows and frills. In short, it means doing a superlative job of planning; of doing the first things first, of planning the work and then working the plan.

In developing distribution for most products in the general classification of consumer goods, the distributor and dealer require the most important considerations of sales management.

"Dealer coverage" means sales-territory coverage; sales volume falls or rises in proportion to the number of good dealers selling the product. They are on the firing line confronting the consumer.

Product Life Cycle

At some point in the planning stage, an important consideration should be given to an analysis of the life cycle of products. One management expert states that life cycle analysis is utilized in three ways:

1. Prognostication of new products

2. Monitoring existing products

3. As an element in an effectively integrated product management system.

Recognizing the stage a product has reached will set the direction and the emphasis of the selling effort, advertising, and sales promotion.

Four stages in a product's life cycle are:

1. Development stage

   - New product/new market
   - Demand exists or must be created
   - Competition depends on type of product
   - Duration of cycle variable, dependent on market (size, activity, acceptance), pricing, competition, marketing effort, and strategies
   - Marketing effort intense

2. Growth stage

   - Market/product usage/acceptance/sales expand
   - Profits begin
   - Competitive activity accelerates
   - New competition enters market
   - Marketing activity to be reviewed
   - Pricing to be reviewed
   - Technical acceptance verified
   - Marketing effort remains high

3. Maturity stage

   - Growth levels off
   - Market/product usage/acceptance/sales stabilize
   - Product modification begins
   - Product distribution may alter
   - Product packaging may alter
   - Competitive activity stabilizes
   - A holding pattern evolves

- Product future to be reviewed
- Profit squeeze is on
- Marketing effort levels off

4. Obsolescent stage
   - Market/product usage/sales decline
   - Marketing effort declines or terminates
   - Profit often on decline
   - Withdrawal consideration finalized
   - Competitive activity usually declines, unless competitors step up activity to force others out and preserve market for themselves

The product life cycle analysis can be applied to major or minor market segments within markets, as similar stages of introduction, growth, maturation, and deterioration can be encountered.

Demographic and Socioeconomic Changes In the Marketplace

In an insightful feature in *Sales and Marketing Management's* Survey of Buying Power, Richard Kern, editorial director of S&MM Surveys, documented many changes that will radically alter the face of the average American consumer.

As Kern states: "The shift underway in this country's demographic and economic composition is already creating some unique challenges that require a careful reevaluation of the kinds of goods and services we bring to the marketplace, and also of the methods used to sell them.

"Any discussion of the future demographic makeup of America must begin with the baby boom of post-World War II. The roughly 75 million people born between 1946 and 1964 currently account for more than one-third of the nation's population, and while they have always provided marketers with a neat age package, they also represent a continuously changing focus in terms of income and lifestyle because of their sheer numbers and scope as a group.

Whatever happens demographically and socioeconomically in this country is very directly tied to this generation and the clout it represents."

Following are statistics that can be used as guidelines for marketers in looking at markets now and in the future.

Median Age. The aging of the baby boom is having its most visible effect on the nation's median age, now charted at 31.0 years (1986). By the year 2000, all members of the baby boom generation will be over age 35, lifting the median age in this country to 36.3 years, a figure that's expected to increase to over 40 by the year 2030.

Population Size and Growth. The annual rate of population growth—currently charted by the Census Bureau at less than one percent—is at its lowest rate since the 1930s, and it is expected that such rates will continue well into the next century, with growth slipping below one-half of one percent by the year 2000. As the baby boomers move into old age and, by their sheer numbers alone, contribute to the rise in the death rate, immigrants will have to move in and take up the slack, providing the only real growth in the U.S. population, which is expected to increase to approximately 268 million by the year 2000. (Later in this chapter we will look at the increasing Hispanic and Asian markets.)

The Dependency Ratio. There will be a dramatic shift in the overall ratio of dependents (children and elderly) to the working-age population. The Census Bureau reports that the child portion of this dependency ratio will continue to decline from its high point in 1965 (when the ratio was 65.7 children per 100 working-age people) to 40.7 by the year 2000. The elderly dependency ratio, now at an all-time high of around 19.4, will continue to rise through the next century, reaching a projected figure of 21.1 elderly dependents per 100 working-age people by the year 2000, and nearly doubling that figure by the year 2050. The implication here is very simple: there will be fewer children to support on the one hand, and more elderly dependents on the other. This will require new and different ways of dealing with elderly dependents through government, public, and private programs.

The "Graying of America" Market. We are living in an "aging" nation, a trend that will continue well into the next century. The term "elderly," as it is used by the Census Bureau, currently covers anyone and everyone over the age of 65. However, there are at least three markedly different groups within this segment, groups so different in age, lifestyle, and income, that we must necessarily develop some new terminology to deal with this highly fragmented and rapidly growing market.

For this group as a whole, the growth projections are quite impressive. In 1980, those aged 65 and over numbered roughly 25.7 million, or 11.3 percent of all Americans, and by the year 2000, the 65 and over population will increase to 34.9 million, a gain of just more than 9 million people in 20 years.

The Demographic Institute reports that the most rapidly growing type of elderly consumer unit should be women living alone, increasing 29 percent during the decade. The number of elderly men living alone will increase only 14 percent during the eighties. Families headed by the elderly will increase 16 percent.

Forget the image of retirement as the desperate years. An article in *Insight* indicates that people older than 65 constitute the nation's second-richest age group and are increasingly able to maintain preretirement standards of living. Only those Americans in the next-oldest age bracket, from 55 to 64, are better off. The assets of the aged are now nearly twice the median for the nation: The median net worth of their households in 1984 was $60,266, while the median for all Americans was $32,677. An indication that this market is worth pursuing is the Federal Reserve Board's Survey of Consumer Finances, which some years ago pinpointed the sources of wealth for the elderly at that time: More than half had savings accounts, with a median value of $2,400. Certificates of deposit were held by 37 percent of elderly families, with a median value of $20,000. Stock holdings by 21 percent of the elderly had a median value of $10,000, while money market accounts, held by 18 percent, had a median value of $11,000.

Race Distribution. Aside from noting the gains recorded in recent years by the Hispanic and Asian populations in the U.S., projections for individual racial and ethnic groups are not broken out in current Census Bureau statistics. However, the Hispanic and Asian markets will be discussed separately later in this chapter. As far as overall growth figures are concerned, these groups, lumped together under the Black-and-other category, show continued expansion during the next 100 years, growing to around 45.3 million by the year 2000, comprising 16.9 percent of the total projected population of 267.9 million. In 1980, this segment comprised just 14.1 percent of the entire population, with projections for the years 2030 and 2080 showing them reaching 20.7 percent and 25.5 percent respectively.

Reflecting the growth in racial and ethnic segments apart from the Black population, the Bureau reported that Blacks will constitute an increasingly smaller portion of this category as a whole, declining from 89.7 percent in 1970 to 78.9 percent by the year 2000, and further declining to 70.4 percent by 2080. This will occur, according to the Bureau, "in spite of the fact that Black fertility is assumed to be considerably above that of other races." The relatively high net immigration rates of other races is a contributing factor to this decline.

The white population, for its part, will experience a considerably slower rate of growth, increasing by just 13.8 percent between 1980 and 2000, while the Black-and-other-races segment grows by 41.3 percent. This will contribute to a more racially and ethnically mixed U.S. population by the turn of the century, a point that should be of particular interest to marketers who sell to any of these individual groups.

Manufacturing versus Services. Kern states that because of the volatile nature of the American economy, economic projections are not as easy to come by as demographic data. Nevertheless, he addressed America's changing economic focus as follows: The miles of press that have been generated concerning the metamorphosis of the nation's economy from manufacturing to services can be boiled down to one simple statement: America's economy *is* changing. In fact, this is not such a new phenomenon, since employment in service-producing industries has exceeded that of manufacturing for more than 40 years now.

In his book *Beyond Industrialization,* author Ronald Shelp cites data from the Bureau of Labor Statistics estimating that by 1990, a full 75 percent of the U.S. workforce will be employed in service industries. This is not to say that America's manufacturing sector will soon become extinct, but that the growth in Third World economies, based for the most part on cheap labor, will continue to displace capital-intensive industries here at home, creating the necessity for more high-tech and service industry expansion to take up the slack. In its *1986 U.S. Industrial Outlook,* the Commerce Department provides the following assessment of the current—and future—situation: "Domestically, gains in the high-tech sectors have exceeded losses in the smokestack industries by a comfortable margin. High-tech industries continue to expand, with employment growing steadily. In contrast, serious structural and regional unemployment still exists in the smokestack sectors and may continue for several years."

This current obsession with a service-based economy has some people rightfully concerned that America might turn its back on heavy manufacturing, embracing services as a quick-fix solution to the larger problem—a shift in the world's economic focus. The plain truth is, America is no longer the center of cheap labor and raw materials it was at the turn of the century. The maturation of this nation's economy, from agricultural giant to industrial giant, is now entering a new phase in which heavy manufacturing takes a back seat to "clean" industries and services.

This doesn't necessarily mean that we are going to become a nation of paper pushers and burger baggers, and it would be a mistake to assume that manufacturing in this country is dead or even dying. The backlash of this current obsession with services has already produced a careful reevaluation of the kinds of manufacturing best suited to take advantage of the changes in the domestic economy. For example, in California, a state noted primarily for its agricultural and high-tech output, marketing plans for the future now include heavy emphasis on the development of manufacturing industries such as steel fabrication and automaking. Christy Campbell Walters, director of the California Commerce Department, shares the state's philosophy on the future of heavy industry: "If you look back about 100 years," she says, "less than 50 percent of all jobs were agriculture-related. Now it's down to less than two percent, but we've been able to produce more and more, particularly in California, and that's what has made us grow. Manufacturing is going to see that same kind of decline in employment, but with an increase in productivity much the same as agriculture has experienced, and that is where it would be misleading to think that we can ignore manufacturing."

Kinds of Markets

A market is usually identified with a generic class of products. These are *product-markets,* meaning customers who in the past have purchased these products. For the sake of convenience, these individuals are classified into groups, all of which have similar characteristics. The use of product identification for a market carries with it the assumption that those persons who *will* buy a product in the future will be very much like those who have purchased it in the past. This assumption is usually valid, because purchasers are likely to repurchase the same product in the future if their wants or needs have been satisfied.

Once the market has been identified by *product class, subclass,* or *brand,* purchasers may be described according to: 1) size of the market; 2) geographical locations of purchasers; 3) demographic descriptions of purchases; 4) social-psychological characteristics; 5) reasons why products are purchased; 6) who makes the actual purchases and who influences the purchaser; 7) when purchases are made, and 8) how purchasing is done. Even more descriptive classifications could be added, such as methods of distribution, effects of pricing changes, or results of sales promotion.

Another concept is that markets be identified by consumer needs rather than by product classes. Theodore Levitt, writing in the *Harvard Business Review,* argues that a market is composed of persons who have various needs and wants. Ideally, when such needs or wants are recognized by the manufacturer, a special product is made and sold to fulfill them.

Sometimes markets are defined in terms of geographical places. One hears of the Los Angeles market or the Dallas market or the suburban market.

But manufacturers may be misled into thinking that their competition consists only of manufacturers of their class of product, when in reality their market is composed of all manufacturers who meet a special consumer need; i.e., the competitors of airlines are not just other airlines, but *all transportation companies.*

Metropolitan Statistical Areas

One of the ways in which marketers divide and plan their markets is through the concept of Standard Metropolitan Statistical Areas. These have been developed by the government and are determined by the Bureau of Census to meet the need for the presentation of general-purpose statistics about metropolitan areas. This statistical concept is based upon a body of published objective criteria.

A standard metropolitan statistical area always includes a city (cities) of specified population, which constitutes the central city and the county (counties) in which it is located. A Standard Metropolitan Statistical Area also sometimes includes contiguous counties. Such an area may even cross state lines. (See Table 1, page 300, for metro market projections through 1990.)

The basic criteria for such an area must include at least (a) one city with 50,000 or more inhabitants or (b) a city with at least 25,000 inhabitants that, together with those contiguous places having population densities of at least 1,000 persons per square mile, has a combined population of 50,000 and constitutes, for general, economic, and social purposes, a single community, provided that the county or counties in which the city and contiguous places are located has a total population of at least 75,000. There are other specific criteria and for the serious researcher it is recommended that you obtain the latest edition of *Standard Metropolitan Statistical Areas,* which is available from the Superintendent of Documents, U.S. Government Printing Office.

The Youth Market

Teen spending hit $65 billion in 1985, according to a recent study, and $35 billion of that amount is family income spent on household items.

The rest, averaging $80 per month for America's 29 million teenagers, is their own money, spent on clothing, cosmetics, toiletries, and other discretionary items, according to the study by Teen-Age Research Unltd. (TRU), Lake Forest, Illinois.

Over half (52 percent) of American teenage girls do the weekly

Table 1. Metro Market Outlook Through 1990

Category	1990 Projection	% Change 1985-90
POPULATION (Thous.)		
U.S. Total	**253,027.0**	**5.06%**
Metro	193,575.5	5.29
Nonmetro	59,451.5	4.32
HOUSEHOLDS (Thous.)		
U.S. Total	**94,773.8**	**7.20%**
Metro	73,011.1	7.51
Nonmetro	21,762.7	6.18
EFFECTIVE BUYING INCOME (EBI) ($000)		
U.S. Total	**$4,226,154,002**	**50.92%**
Metro	3,450,966,907	51.52
Nonmetro	775,187,195	48.28
AVERAGE HOUSEHOLD EBI		
U.S. Average	**$44,592**	**40.78%**
Metro	47,266	40.94
Nonmetro	N.A.	N.A.
TOTAL RETAIL SALES ($000)		
U.S. Average	**$2,086,383,490**	**49.53%**
Metro	1,707,373,364	50.29
Nonmetro	379,010,126	46.21
PER HOUSEHOLD RETAIL SALES		
U.S. Average	**$22,014**	**39.49%**
Metro	23,385	39.79
Nonmetro	N.A.	N.A.
BUYING POWER INDEX (BPI)		
U.S. Total	**100.0000**	—
Metro	80.6799	+ 0.40%
Nonmetro	19.3201	− 1.66

Notes: **N.A.**—Not Applicable. The **Buying Power Index (BPI)** is a weighted index that combines population, Effective Buying Income, and retail sales, expressing it as a percentage, which indicates a market's ability to buy. All BPI figures are expressed as a percentage of the U.S. total (100.0000). **Effective Buying Income (EBI)** and **Retail sales** projections are expressed in current dollars. The 1990 projections apply to the 317 S&MM metro markets as currently defined by the Office of Management and Budget, Washington, DC.
Source: Sales and Marketing Management's *1986 Survey of Buying Power—Part II*
©1986 by Sales and Marketing Management

family grocery shopping, and 25 percent choose the brands themselves.

The increased financial responsibility of today's teens is also reflected in the fact that 74 percent have savings accounts and almost 17 percent have checking accounts. In addition, 12 percent have access to credit cards.

Electronics is one of the most popular categories of discretionary items for teens, with 48 percent renting videotapes, and 71.2 percent owning portable radio-cassette players. Teen ownership of computers has risen 50 percent since 1984. Other big-ticket items popular among teens are bicycles, with 71.4 percent ownership and wristwatches, bought by 68.8 percent of teens.

Clothing is another area heavily influenced by teens. Since they no longer are wearing designer jeans and athletic wear, sales have dipped. Influenced by Madonna and Cyndi Lauper, teenage girls have taken to buying uncoordinated pieces and combining them in a hodgepodge effect. "This designerless look may be a rebellion against conventional fashion modes, but with sustained use, it could become the norm," said Grady Hauser, TRU's vice president of marketing.

The study also found that girls become less interested in clothing in their later teens.

The "youth market" has received increased attention in recent years by manufacturers, their advertising agencies, and trade publications, because of the buying habits of consumers under 25 years of age.

In a speech at the annual meeting of the southwest council of the American Association of Advertising Agencies, Robert M. Stelzer maintained that there is no one youth market. "It's four distinctly different markets—children, teens, collegians, and young adults," he said. "Each group must be reached by its own media, influenced by its own motivations, and sold through its own appeals.

"There is one exciting common denominator for young people from 5 to 25. That's their willingness to accept new ideas and try new products. They're eager to spend money, and they have it to spend."

Stelzer went on to say that the biggest mistake advertisers make "is trying to *talk like teens* to teens. Today, teenagers are more discriminating in their buying than were their parents, demand better quality and value, and want what's in style for them. What they want most, of course, is to be accepted by their peers."

Sampling is more effective than any other audience-measuring surveys for the teenage market, including Nielsen, ARB, or Hooper [now Starch/INRA/Hooper, Inc.] said Gordon McLendon, president of McLendon Corp. "I urge you to sample teenagers individually and by panel. Even a simple telephone or random sample will be more effective then the above-mentioned surveys can possibly be," he said.

While popular belief has the young-adult group spending as wildly as "the dances it gyrates to," this is a misleading view, argues market researcher Daniel Yankelovich. He said the young-adult market consists of four groups: young married couples, unmarried couples, unmarried college students, and unmarried noncollege youngsters. The young marrieds, he holds, find themselves hard-pressed financially, hence tend to be more practical in their shopping than middle-aged adults. "A young woman buying a washing machine will tend to pick the strongest work-horse machine she can find, with great emphasis on trouble-free operation," he says. "The reason: she can't afford service calls."

The college market differs from the other segments, Yankelovich feels, because of its geographical concentration; the separate and distinct campus culture with its own fads, fashions, and values, and the presence of young adults with their own set of values and points of view.

The findings in a study conducted by Paul Gilkinson, College of Business Administration of Bradley University, reported in the *Journal of Retailing,* reveal significant changes in the buying frames of reference of teenagers over the past couple of decades. For example, parents have declined in importance as a source of influence on teenagers' buying decisions in most of the product lines researched. On the other hand, friends of the teenagers have increased in influence. With the up-to-date knowledge of the teenager's own conscious feelings about the buying of goods and services, as provided by this research study, the researcher, merchant, or parent possesses valuable marketing information. This information certainly can and should prepare these observers of teenagers better to understand the tendencies of human buying behavior during the teenage years.

A survey sent to 100,000 teenage girls from Donnelley Marketing's Teen Life list found that 86.4 percent of the 12- to 19-year olds ordered items through the mail in the last 12 months.

They were asked, "Which items have you, yourself, purchased in the mail in the last 12 months?" They responded this way: 52.2 percent bought magazines, 41.8 percent catalogs, 31.9 percent records, 26.9 percent cosmetics, 19 percent gifts, 18.7 percent books, 16.3 percent jewelry, 15.7 percent T-shirts/sweatshirts, 13.5 percent posters, 12 percent swimsuits, 24.7 percent other, and 13.6 percent never order through the mail.

Other questions pertinent to direct marketers included those about coupons. Teenagers get their coupons from magazines, 32.4 percent; Sunday newspapers, 22 percent; daily newspapers, 18 percent; and by mail, 16 percent. In answer to the question, "Do you often use coupons for products for yourself?", 90 percent answered yes and more than 25 percent said they redeem at least four coupons when shopping. Some use up to five per shopping trip. Coupon use in 1986 surpassed that of 1985.

The survey was done "to get an idea of consumer buying habits of teenage girls," said Susan Lester, a Donnelley spokesperson. "We found they use coupons and don't always shop for themselves. They often shop for the family because both parents are working, so they make brand choices early and stay loyal. The group is more important than most think."

The Hispanic Market

The U.S. Department of Commerce, Bureau of Census, gives the following synopsis of the Hispanic market:

- The market consists of 17.6 million people, of whom 10.4 million are of Mexican descent, 2.4 million of Puerto Rican descent, 1 million of Cuban descent, and 3.7 million of other Hispanic origins.
- Hispanics comprise 7.2 percent of the total U.S. population.
- From 1980 to 1985 the Hispanic population grew 20 percent as opposed to 3.3 percent for the general population.

- Hispanic median income now is $19,900 per household.

- Total aggregate household income for the U.S. Hispanic market approximates $124 billion.

- It is estimated that purchasing power of Hispanics could reach $172 billion by 1990.

The Census Bureau report said the 1982 total U.S. population of 232.1 million people is expected to grow by 15 percent by the year 2000, an increase of slightly more than 36 million people. Of that increase, Hispanics would account for 9 million people; white non-Hispanics, 15 million; Blacks, 8 million; and other races, 3.7 million.

As shown in Table 2, below, only 15 states had more than 100,000 Hispanics in 1980, the latest census figures. More than 90 percent of the nation's Hispanic population lived in those 15 states.

Table 2. The Top Fifteen

	1980			1970		
	rank	number	percent distribution	rank	number	percent distribution
United States ..	—	14,608,673	100.0%	—	9,072,602	100.0%
California	1	4,544,331	31.1	1	2,369,292	26.1
Texas	2	2,985,824	20.4	2	1,840,648	20.3
New York	3	1,659,300	11.4	3	1,351,982	14.9
Florida	4	858,158	5.9	4	405,036	4.5
Illinois	5	635,602	4.4	5	393,204	4.3
New Jersey	6	491,883	3.4	7	288,488	3.2
New Mexico . . .	7	477,222	3.3	6	308,340	3.4
Arizona	8	440,701	3.0	8	264,770	2.9
Colorado	9	339,717	2.3	9	225,506	2.5
Michigan	10	162,440	1.1	10	151,070	1.7
Pennsylvania . . .	11	153,961	1.1	13	108,893	1.2
Massachusetts .	12	141,043	1.0	15	66,146	0.7
Connecticut	13	124,499	0.9	16	65,458	0.7
Washington	14	120,016	0.8	19	57,358	0.6
Ohio	15	119,883	0.8	11	129,995	1.4
Total	—	13,254,580	90.7	—	8,026,186	88.5

Source: U.S. Census Bureau

The Asian American Market

The Census Bureau lumps nine diverse groups together as Asians and Pacific Islanders. The total population of 3.5 million Asians, based on 1980 census figures, breaks down in this manner:

- 806,000 Chinese
- 775,000 Filipinos
- 701,000 Japanese
- 362,000 Asian Indians
- 355,000 Koreans
- 262,000 Vietnamese
- 167,000 Hawaiians
- 42,000 Samoans
- 32,000 Guamanians

While Asians were the fastest growing racial group in this country during the 1970s, Leon F. Bouvier, vice-president, Population Reference Bureau, Washington, D.C., projects a growth of 58 percent to 5.9 million in the 1980s, and another 38 percent in the 1990s to 8.1 million.

Asians are concentrated in five states: California, Hawaii, New York, Illinois, and Washington, which are home to about 75 percent of all Asian Americans. In his book, *The American People,* Bryant Robey observes that as a market, the Asian Americans are a cut above the usual image of a minority. They have higher incomes and more education than white Americans. Proportionately, more Asians are managers and professionals, a higher share of Asian women are in the labor force, and Asians are more likely to live in families.

In a special report in *Advertising Age,* Ruben Lopez, marketing director for special projects, Metropolitan Life Insurance Company, states: "The U.S. Asian market is much more complex than the Hispanic market. There are more languages, more cultures, more subtleties to deal with." However, they are better educated and have more disposable income than recently arrived Hispanics, Mr. Lopez says. U.S. Asians had a 1980 median family income of $23,000, compared with a total U.S. figure of $20,000. And some 32 percent of Asian adults are college educated, compared with 17 percent of white adults.

Mr. Lopez concluded: "We use the Hispanic market as a prototype for our efforts in the Asian market. A lot of what we learned in the Hispanic market can be applied to the Asian market."

To conclude the discussion on ethnic markets, Leon F. Bouvier observed: "By the year 2000, one in four Americans will be Black, Hispanic, or Asian."

The Agricultural Market

The farms in America today range from the great corporate-owned farms to the single family units of under 500 acres. Altogether, they form a good industrial market for manufacturers of farm machinery, equipment, and tools; for building equipment and automotive supplies; for containers; for agricultural chemicals, such as fertilizers, lime, insect sprays, etc., and the variety of other farming aids used in the process of raising a crop. A glance through any of the major farm journals' advertising sections indicates the many types of equipment and supplies needed for the successful operation of a farm.

It is interesting to note that farming receives special attention from the U.S. Government through several departments, with county agents throughout the country; through cooperation with local banks that help to finance agricultural operations; and through the distribution of useful and instructive publications for specific problems encountered by the average farmer.

The farm is an industrial market. It will continue to grow as the needs of the United States and the world continue to expand at a great rate.

Many manufacturers of products used primarily in industrial operations have adapted them to the requirements of the agricultural field. In addition, many manufacturers are serving the farm market without knowing too much about it. But a visit to a modern farm reveals the widespread use of mechanical and electrical products.

WHERE THE FARMS ARE

The United States has nearly 2.3 billion acres of land. More than 63 percent (1,438 million acres) is nonfederally owned rural land, and one-third (760 million acres) is federally owned. About 3 percent (61 million acres) is in urban and built-up areas.

Of the nonfederal rural land, 438 million acres is cropland, 482 million acres is grassland, and 462 million acres is forest land. Land used for farmsteads, farm roads, rural nonfarm residences, investment tracts, in coastal dunes, marshes, strip mines, and other miscellaneous uses amounts to 56 million acres.

The ten major farming regions in the United States differ in soils, slope of land, climate, distance to market, and in storage and marketing facilities. Together, they give a glimpse of the agricultural face of the nation.

The Northeastern States—from Maine to Maryland—and the Lake States—those bordering on the Great Lakes, from New York to Minnesota—are the nation's principal milk-producing areas. Climate and soil in these states are suited to raising grains and forage for cattle and for providing pasture land for grazing. Broiler farming is important in Maine and from New Jersey to Maryland.

The Appalachian Region—Virginia, West Virginia to North Carolina, Kentucky, and Tennessee—is the major tobacco-producing region of the nation. Peanuts, cattle and dairy production are also important.

Farther south along the Atlantic coast is the Southeast Region. Beef and broilers are important livestock products. Vegetables, such as sweet potatoes, are grown in this area, along with peanuts. And, of course, there are the big citrus groves and winter vegetable production in Florida.

In the Delta States—Mississippi, Louisiana, and Arkansas—the principal cash crops are soybeans and cotton. Rice and sugarcane are also grown.

The Corn Belt, extending from Ohio to Nebraska, is a region with rich soil, good climate, and sufficient rainfall for excellent farming. Corn, beef cattle, and hogs are the major outputs of farms here. Other feed grains, soybeans, and wheat are also important.

Agriculture in the Northern and Southern Plains, which extend north and south from Canada to Mexico and from the Corn Belt into the Mountain States, is restricted by low rainfall and, in the northern part, by cold winters and short growing seasons. Nearly three-fifths of the nation's winter and spring wheat is produced in the region. Other small grains, grain sorghum, hay, forage crops, and pastures form the basis for cattle and dairy production. Cotton is produced in the southern part.

The Mountain States—from Idaho and Montana to New Mexico and Arizona—provide a still different terrain. Vast areas of this region are suited to raising cattle and sheep. Wheat is important in the northern parts. Irrigation in the valleys provides water for such crops as hay, sugarbeets, potatoes, fruits, and vegetables.

The Pacific Region includes the three Pacific Coast States. Farmers in the northern area specialize in raising wheat and fruits; vegetables and fruit and cotton are important in the southern part. Cattle are raised throughout the entire region.

Along with the influence of mechanization, good roads, the automobile, and higher prices for farm products and farm lands, improved communications have added to the importance of the farm market.

At the time of this edition, this market had become sorely depressed from its previous peak years in the 1970s. It is hoped that, in time, farming will regain its role as one of the nation's biggest businesses, buyer and supplier, furnishing vital products to the nation and the world.

The Government/Defense Market

It is difficult to think of any commodity, product, or service that is not purchased by some branch of the government. For instance, the products that the General Services Administration buys include paper, chemicals, lumber, small hand tools, office equipment, automobiles, computers, and machine tools, to name a few.

The National Aeronautics and Space Administration buys such things as general supplies, parts, engineering consulting, and spacecraft and communication equipment. The Department of Transportation uses petroleum products, fire-fighting equipment, and marine navigation equipment.

The Defense Department buys food, basic materials, petroleum products, shoes, clothing, operational vehicles, aircraft and ships, computers, weapons, and radar and sonar equipment; and this listing is only a start.

Because of the wide diversity of standard commercial products used by the government, just about every manufacturer has an opportunity to sell to the government, if he chooses. It is the specialized and high-tech products and services, covered by detailed government specifications, that differ.

Government procurement is governed by the Federal Procurement Regulations. Department of Defense procurement is governed by the Armed Services Procurement Regulations (ASPR). Space procurement is governed by the National Aeronautics and Space Administration Procurement Regulations.

The United States Department of Defense is the largest single customer of American business. It is served by a multitude of large and small manufacturing companies and service organizations, which supply the three and one-half million items used.

There is nothing particularly new or different in selling to the various Department of Defense organizations. The basic principles followed in selling within the commercial field apply in dealing with the Department of Defense. Two principles that are especially appropriate are:

Learn the customer's needs as well as his or her buying policies and practices.

Follow leads on where buying is done and search out selling opportunities in all segments of the defense organization.

One of the first things that should be done is to submit completed copies of the Bidder's Mailing List Application and the Supplement, available at all defense procurement offices. The principal offices are listed in Part II of the defense department publication "Selling to the Military," along with indications of the types of commodities and services they buy.

Specifications for items used by the military are generally available at the procurement offices responsible for the items.

Each procurement office that has a firm on its bidders' lists will forward "Invitations for Bids" or "Requests for Proposals" as requirements develop.

The *Commerce Business Daily,* published by the Department of Commerce, is a valuable source of information to businesspeople in identifying products and services that individual procurement offices currently plan to buy. This publication provides the following information:

Current Defense Department proposed procurements estimated to exceed $10,000, and civilian agency procurements expected to exceed $5,000; recent contract awards, which provide leads to subcontracting opportunities: surplus sales information and other information helpful to businesspeople who seek to participate in federal procurement activities.

The daily may be purchased on annual subscription through the superintendent of Documents, Government Printing Office, Washington, D.C. 20402.

Offices in the Washington, D.C. area that can provide information and guidance on federal procurement activities include:

U.S. Department of Defense
The Pentagon
Washington, D.C. 20301-1115
202-545-6700

General Services Administration
General Services Building
18th and F Streets, N.W.
Washington, D.C. 20405
202-655-4000

Small Business Administration
Imperial Building
1441 L Street, N.W.
Washington, D.C. 20416
202-653-7561

Federal Trade Commission
Procurement and Contracts Branch
6th & Pennsylvania Avenue, N.W.
Washington, D.C. 20580
202-523-3598

National Aeronautic and
Space Administration
400 Maryland, S.W.
Washington, D.C. 20546
202-453-8400

MILITARY EXCHANGE SERVICES

Procurement of resale merchandise for post and base exchanges in the Continental United States is accomplished by five exchange regions located in Fort Sam Houston, Texas; Cameron Station, Virginia; San Francisco, California; Charlestown, Indiana; and Montgomery, Alabama. Each exchange region buys for approximately 25 installation exchanges physically located in the region's general geographical area.

Procurement of resale merchandise of United States origin for overseas exchanges, including the Alaskan Exchange System and the Hawaii Regional Exchange, is made by the buyers at Army/Air Force Exchange Service Headquarters, Dallas, Texas 75222.

NAVY EXCHANGES

There are two basic methods of doing business with Navy exchanges—directly with each exchange, or through the Navy Resale System Office (NRSO), Brooklyn, New York, or the NRSO Branch Office. Oakland, California. All exchange equipment is centrally procured or approved for local procurement by NRSO.

For further information, companies may contact the Navy Resale System Office, 29th Street and Third Avenue, Brooklyn, New York 11232; the NRSO West Coast Branch Office, Building 310, Naval Supply Center, Oakland, California 94625; or the Navy exchanges located at various Naval installations.

Vendors desiring to sell to United States Marine Corps exchanges should contact the Marine Corps Exchange Service, Code COE, Headquarters, United States Marine Corp, Washington, D.C. 20380.

HOW THE MILITARY SPENDS

Unlike the private business sector of the economy, the scale and composition of military purchases are determined by the decisions of the federal budget process rather than in response to market trends. The authorization of military-spending programs results from the interaction of many competing demands and requirements—not only of the various military services but of the numerous nondefense programs and of taxpayer groups. Moreover, the federal budget is not determined in isolation but in relation to domestic political and economic conditions, as well as to the expected state of international tensions.

In the period since the Korean Conflict, the Air Force has supplanted the Army as the largest military customer. This shift is evidence of the increased emphasis being placed on strategic-weapon systems rather than tactical warfare programs involving masses of people and conventional land equipment.

The procurement function may be relatively concentrated in one central agency, as in the Air Force with its Systems Command for major products and the Army with its new Material Development and Logistic Command, or split up among the service's technical system commands, as in the Navy. Extreme decentralization gives appropriate officials in individual service bases and installations authorization to handle their own procurement of special services and goods.

The various military agencies financing research and development activities report that they receive many more proposals than they can accept. For example, virtually all basic proposals submitted to the Office of Naval Research (ONR) are unsolicited. The three major criteria used by ONR in evaluating research proposals are:

1. *The scientific merit of the proposal.* This evaluation is performed against the background of the importance of the scientific field, the importance of the specific area within the field, and the probable degree to which more knowledge will be accumulated. In essence, is the proposal likely to produce significant new scientific knowledge?

2. *The relevance to the military mission.* The knowledge to be gained from the research is evaluated from the viewpoint of how it will contribute to the long-range technical development and future evolution of the service financing the project. In the case of ONR, that would be the Navy Department.

3. *The competence of the investigator.* The investigator's background, experience, and general knowledge of the field are carefully reviewed.

TYPICAL GOVERNMENT CONTRACTS

A relatively unique aspect of the market for military products is that the price of major weapons systems frequently is set in negotiation with military-procurement officers rather than in response to impersonal market forces. Some explanation of the nature of price formation in the military market may be desirable.

The four major types of contracts used for military procurement are 1) cost with no fee, 2) cost with fixed fee, 3) incentive, and 4) firm fixed price. Contrary to some popular misconceptions, contracts for cost plus a percentage of cost do not exist. They are not allowed by the congressional statute governing military procurement.

Under incentive contracts, the producer is given an incentive to cut costs because he shares with the government a portion of the cost reduction. This type of contract operates as follows: Target costs and profits are established early in the program. Upon completion of production, actual costs are compared with target costs. In the case where the actual costs are lower than the target cost, the actual profit is higher than the target profit by a stated percentage of the cost reduction. Conversely, where the actual costs are higher than the target cost, the actual profit is lower than the target profit by a stated percentage of the cost overrun.

Recent statements by government officials indicate that increasing use will be made of incentive-type contracts, even in development and research.

Under the firm-fixed-price contract, supplies are furnished at a specified price with no provision for adjustment.

COST NOT NECESSARILY MOST IMPORTANT

Cost is only one of a number of factors considered in awarding contracts for military weapons systems, and there are many other factors on which rival potential suppliers compete. The previous performance of the company may be an extremely useful indicator of its effectiveness on a future contract.

Following is a list of the factors considered in contracts for a missile program. The relative weight given to each factor is shown. The low importance of cost is clearly shown. It should be borne in mind that previous actual low-cost experience may carry greater weight than optimistic estimates of future low costs on a cost-plus type of contract.

Factor	Points
• Understanding the scope of work	80
• Management control in government practices	80
• Management availability and capability..........	100

Factor	Points
• Management philosophy and organizational experience	100
• Resources, skills, and manpower available	100
• Weapons system knowledge and experience	80
• Prior experience and performance on like-type projects	80
• Labor relations and understanding of human factors	80
• Quality-control organization and follow-up	100
• Acceptance of the conditions of contract	70
• Acceptance of statement of work	50
• Cost and fee	80
Total	1,000

Companies are not automatically placed or kept on bidders lists. The request is initially screened to establish and identify the company's capability, as well as the items for which it is qualified. Moreover, a company that has not responded to several consecutive solicitations may be dropped from a bidders list unless it notifies the purchasing office that it desires to remain on the bidders list for future solicitations. Companies not on formal bidders lists may request a copy of the bid invitation or request for proposal.

For the producer of component parts of military weapons systems, the customer may generally be the industrial company that is the prime contractor (or associate contractor), rather than the military service itself. Each of the major military producers maintains procurement or material department that is charged to deal with current and potential subcontractors or sub-subcontractors. Again, the prospective seller needs to become aware of the emerging needs of the contractor as they develop.

The announcement of the award of a new major aircraft or missile contract is often interpreted by the uninitiated as a signal for would-be suppliers to contact the winning prime contractor. Generally, this is too late a stage in the procurement process. In the preparation of its proposal, the winning contractor usually has worked with and received assistance from the companies that will become its subcontractors and suppliers.

Market Segmentation

Marketing is the focusing of strategic planning and resources toward the satisfaction of customer needs, against competitive thrusts, at a profit. Customers and markets are constantly changing. Market segmentation is a strategic weapon for keeping up with fast-changing market situations.

In a presentation to an Association of National Advertisers Conference, James D. Culley, senior marketing specialist, Du Pont Company, described Du Pont's five-step process, which can serve as a guide to companies of all sizes. Here is a digest of his remarks:

Segmentation is critical in order to get a focus on strategic business opportunities. A given product and the way it's offered may not match the value structures of all potential customers. For example, the product may lack certain properties, the terms of sale may not be satisfactory, or traditional relationships between buyer and seller may not be to our advantage. If we eliminate prospects where opportunity is lacking and concentrate our finite resources on prospects where we do have an opportunity, we focus on those that are strategically important to the business. And our marketing programs can be on target the first time we launch them.

A second reason for segmenting markets is to provide a competitive advantage. As we practice segmentation, we develop a deeper, better understanding of the market and our customers which allows us to respond faster and more accurately to opportunities. Our communications, our selling strategies, our channel relationships and our research programs all become rifle shots rather than shotgun, maybe-we'll-get-them reactions to market change.

Du Pont's definition of a market segment is "a group of customers anywhere along the distribution chain who have common needs and values—who will respond similarly to our offering and who are large enough to be strategically important to our business."

Note the key elements of that definition:

• Common needs and values.

- Respond similarly to our offering.

- Important strategically.

In other words, individual market segments are precisely defined targets of importance. To exploit those opportunities segmentation offers, a sound marketing program generally follows five steps.

1. *Grouping customers based on differences or similarities.* The key task is finding people who are the same within groups but different from those in other groups. Here are some of the more common ways to segment business-to-business markets:

   - Demographic, such as by standard industrial clasification code, industry type, sales volume, etc.

   - Geographic, by state, region, country, etc.

   - Industry specific, such as soil type, crops, diseases, for agriculture.

   - Psychographic, such as lifestyle, or social and cultural values, etc.

   - Customer behavior with the product, its end use, function, purchase situation or type, desired benefits and features, usage rates, etc.

   - Any of those in combination.

In selecting the most appropriate way to segment a particular market, it is rarely clear at the start which approach will give the best insight into the market. Therefore, a great deal of judgment is required. And it may help to try several ways at the same time.

2. *Describing the groups or segments identified.* The description of each segment should indicate how one differs from the others, in terms that are important to the business.

   Early involvement by all marketing functions, including communications and sales professionals, is very important at this stage to determine precisely who constitutes the audience. For example, who are the decision-makers, and the influencers; which media reach them? The main focus of activity in step two is on developing an in-depth understanding of each segment.

3. *Selecting target segments.* The criterion the planning team uses to select segments reflects what is strategically important to sustain or enlarge the business. Because it's unlikely that two competitors in the same market will view the segments the same way, the segmentation plan should be considered of strategic importance and be carefully guarded.

   Marketing communications, for instance, can provide insights about communicating with candidate segments. Can they be reached efficiently with mass communications, direct mail, etc.? Can sales and the company's marketing information system identify the key purchase influencers in the segment? Given the company's resources, what leverage does it have in the segment and how can it exploit a competitive advantage?

4. *Developing the competitive positioning of the offering to each segment.* The final two steps in the segmenting process essentially define how we create and sustain competitive advantage and provide the strategy that the business expects to pursue for each segment during the next several years.

   Step four assesses our strengths and weaknesses compared with those of the competition, in each segment. For example, how do competitors promote themselves? How much do they spend on applications engineering, communications, distribution, sales territory coverage, after-sales service and support, etc.?

5. *Shaping the total offering to achieve competitive advantage.* This step provides the direction that the business will pursue in each segment. An implementation plan should be created for each selected segment, spelling out how the business intends to achieve or exploit its advantage. Within a particular segment, product management, sales, and communications need to be coordinated for maximum effect.

From a communications standpoint, for instance, the plan must provide measurement and monitoring activities, communications objectives for each segment, a prioritizing of segments, and basic tactical considerations such as media, frequency, cost to reach the segment, etc.

Segmentation of some sort is a tool we all have used implicitly by the very act of planning. But it is now more important than ever to follow the five steps that make up the formal segmentation process.

The Industrial Outlook

According to the Bureau of Labor Statistics, the service-producing industries should account for about 75 percent of the nation's job growth between 1982 and 1995, a gain of nearly 20 million jobs. In contrast, the goods-producing industries are expected to gain only 6 million jobs. Take a look at the outlook by industries, Table 3, below, which varies dramatically.

Table 3. Employment by Industry: 1982-1995

	1982	1995
Goods-producing Industries	27.1	33.0
Agriculture	3.2	3.0
Mining	1.1	1.2
Construction	3.9	5.8
Manufacturing	18.8	23.1
Service-producing Industries	66.5	86.2
Transportation, communications, and public utilities	5.7	6.9
Wholesale and retail trade	20.6	26.8
Finance, insurance, and real estate	5.4	7.2
Other services (including health, education, legal, and business)	27.5	37.2
Government	7.5	8.0
Total Employment	93.6	119.2

(in millions)

Projections of employment by industry from *Occupational Projections and Training Data,* 1984 edition, Bureau of Labor Statistics, Bulletin 2206, available from the Government Printing Office, Washington, D.C. 20402.

SERVICE-PRODUCING INDUSTRIES

Transportation, Communications, and Public Utilities. Communications will be the fastest growing segment of this industry because of rising demand for telecommunications services.
Wholesale and Retail Trade. Employment in these industries will rise faster than average, despite self-service merchandising and computerized inventory systems. The fastest growing sector will be retail trade, with employment in eating and drinking places, department stores, grocery stores, and new car dealerships increasing the most.
Finance, Insurance, and Real Estate. The demand for credit and other financial services is expected to boost employment in this sector, but automatic teller machines and computerized banking and stock transactions will cause output to grow faster than employment.
Other Services. These industries, which include hotels, repair shops, hospitals, engineering firms, schools, and nonprofit organizations, will provide the most new jobs in the next decade. Business services, personnel supply, the commercial cleaning will be the fastest growing. While efforts to control health costs could lower the projected employment gains in health services, large gains are projected for engineering, legal, social, and accounting services.
Government. Growth should be sluggish in this sector because of the public's desire to limit government spending.
Agriculture. Farm productivity is expected to continue to rise even as employment declines.
Mining. Employment gains in mining will slow dramatically because of improved mining technology.
Construction. Employment in construction will continue to rise because of business expansion and the maintenance of existing buildings.
Manufacturing. Foreign competition, productivity improvements, and technological change will limit job gains in manufacturing. Employment growth in durable goods will be twice as fast as in nondurable goods because consumers will spend a smaller share of their rising incomes on staples such as food and clothing.

Chapter 13

Sales Research

Long-term marketing success is built on accurate market estimates and forecasts. And marketing and sales research is management's best way of guarding against costly guesswork that often hampers the development of potentially successful products. Certain buying motives are dominant in purchasing, and the salesperson should seek to learn, and to appeal to, these motives. These patterns preceded the work of the psychologists in the management field who, with the help of a few psychiatrists, sociologists, semanticists, and others concerned with the workings of the human mind, formulated motivation research. This they described as "the use of social-science techniques to discover and to evaluate the fundamental motivating forces or drives that impel human behavior in the marketplace."

In recent years, some of the large companies, such as those in the automobile industry, adopted this clinical approach to isolate the particular buying motives that applied to their products. Through motivation research, these companies determined that certain colors stimulated women in their purchases while others left them unresponsive; that often men who bought sports cars were trying to satisfy an unrecognized desire for raciness; and that those who bought black limousines wished to gain dignified respectability.

While the findings of motivation research in many cases have undoubtedly been entirely sound psychologically, the attempt to project them into every type of sales situation has led to a sort of "complicated oversimplification," which some sales and marketing executives have found difficult to accept.

Furthermore, the cost of nationwide surveys has been beyond the reach of some of the smaller corporations. An executive of a small company, which makes an accessory purchased by fleet owners for the comfort of their truck drivers, believed that his product was purchased as much for prestige as for comfort, and that if he could pinpoint the primary buying motive, he could better promote his product. He considered having a motivation research study made; but, after investigation, he decided the cost was prohibitive. He reported:

"I could use the money more effectively in improving the comfort qualities of my product, and then letting those qualities speak for themselves to the user. These are sound buying motives that you can put your teeth in; prestige will take care of itself if the user tells friends about satisfaction with the product."

To sum up, an understanding of why buyers buy is vital both in selling and in designing to sell; it is only the dangers inherent in the projective techniques of motivation research that have led to the rejection, in some quarters, of this type of market research. Perhaps the answer is in the factor of overconfidence: used as one of many possible tools in market research, motivation studies can be helpful and useful; used as the be-all-and-end-all of market analysis, this tool may lead to multimillion-dollar fiascos.

The marketing concept in American business has grown increasingly sophisticated and complex. In essence, its basic principles, as stated in an annual report of General Mills, are 1) find out what the consumer wants and needs; 2) develop or improve products or services that answer those wants and needs better than ever before; 3) find ways to induce the consumer to choose your product and to keep on choosing it.

Today nearly all progressive companies have research operations under way. These divide themselves into: (a) product research; (b) market research; (c) methods research; (d) consumer testing; and (e) record analysis. Some of these companies find it profitable to employ outside management-consulting organizations to do this work; others have set up special departments that operate in conjunction with a planning committee. All are finding out a great many things that management might have suspected, but never did very much about.

Major manufacturers have learned that product improvement and development of new products can lead to increased profits. That's why research and development funds constitute the largest appropriation in many corporations' annual budgets. Some companies estimate that 80 percent of their business today comes from products that weren't on the market 10 years ago.

The Benefits of Research

Sales managers who have invested in market research have found the benefits compare favorably with those obtained from laboratory or engineering research activities. A report of their findings to the American Management Association is summed up as follows:

1. An organization is enabled to build its marketing structure on facts, thus eliminating much of the inefficiency and waste incurred by distributive efforts based wholly on past experience, intuition, and pure chance.

2. Marketing executives and sales personnel, as well as employees in general, are more confident of the soundness of operations and activities that rest on the bedrock of a desirable and acceptable product or service, a favorable competitive position, and tested channels of distribution.

3. Major operating executives in the organization develop an understanding and appreciation of the product or service and of market methods in general, giving them a good reason to become "sales minded."

4. The findings of marketing research indicate the direction that technical research should take by providing concrete data on customer preference relating to composition, design, or other attributes of the product or service.

5. Marketing research fosters goodwill, both in the consumer market and in the industrial market. As the activities become more firmly rooted in scientific methodology and professional viewpoint, a cooperative spirit is introduced between producer and consumer, between producers of complementary products, between producer and wholesaler, etc. The result is improved marketing methods for entire industries.

Modern management must increase the precision of its decisions; it must come to rely more and more on judgments made in the light of adequate facts, or it will find itself outmaneuvered by competition. This process requires a highly objective attitude. Vigor and decisiveness alone are not enough. They all still vital, of course, but they must be supplemented by an eagerness to get facts and a willingness to use them objectively. Unless and until that state of mind exists, there is little reason for management to spend money on sales research.

An objective attitude may, and in fact should, be a critical and skeptical one. Uncritical acceptance of any set of statistics is not objectivity. One of the big problems of management is how to distinguish between competent and dependable research and those statistics that, as the quip has it, "tread a path of mathematical logic between an unwarranted assumption and a pre-conceived conclusion."

In the office of one successful marketing expert there appears this bit of business wisdom:

"Find out what people *like* and do *more* of it. Find out what people *don't like* and do *less* of it."

Business is keenly aware of this situation, and a number of companies are setting up "proving grounds" for testing customer opinion and customer reactions.

Developing the Market Research Function

A large, broad-based company with continuing research needs develops its own research department with experienced personnel and can afford to have outside specialized research services as well.

Companies planning to conduct their own research must soon decide whether the research function should be limited to special objectives or widened to include other purposes, such as new-product testing. For companies establishing research departments for the first time, a good view of the problems and functions involved is afforded by the outline on the following page.

1. *What a company should expect from marketing research*

   - Definition and scope of the function
   - Types of work most frequently requested of market research in a variety of companies
   - How much money for market research?
   - Using professional agencies versus developing inside staff

2. *The market research manager*

   - What personal qualifications are required for performance of market research work?
   - Recruitment sources for qualified personnel
   - Integrating the market research personality into the company

3. *Defining and organizing the market research contribution to market planning and problem solving*

   - Orienting research to the kinds of management decisions that must be made in your company
   - Planning the research program
   - Problem definition: line management's role and the research role

4. *Research methodology—tools and techniques*

   - Research on markets
   - Research on products and services
   - Research on sales methods
   - Sales forecasting

5. *The research report to management.* Ensuring usable findings and practical recommendations.

6. *Enlarging the marketing research function.* Combining with product planning, market development, business research, etc.

The Development of Motivation Research

There are motivational aspects in every purchase—the desire to gain comfort, economy, convenience, savings of effort, prestige, and other benefits. Skillful salespeople have long appealed to these desires, changing their approach and emphasis as conditions demanded. Promotional programs have been attuned to them, trying to match the motives of buyers in the markets at which they were aimed.

Sources of Market Information

As part of the annual marketing plan, the Goodyear Tire and Rubber Company lists the following as sources of market information:

1. Outside the company

   - Customers (most important source)
   - Competitive literature
   - Suppliers
   - Trade magazines
   - Trade associations
   - Professional organizations

2. Government

   - Census data
   - Patent reviews
   - Federal publications

3. Inside the company

   - Market research reports
   - Sales call reports (data keyed to develop market information)
   - Orders

- Complaints
- Informed persons
- Past year's customer correspondence
- Sales meeting summaries
- Technical reports

Richard Kern, editorial director of *Sales & Marketing Management Surveys,* reported on a study published by *Money* magazine called "Americans and Their Money," which revealed some interesting demographic facts. As Kern commented:

This survey, now in its fourth year, shows us what Americans do with their hard-earned money and how they feel about what happens to it once it has left their pockets. Questions on financial planning, money management, savings and investments, real estate, and even the federal deficit were put to a representative sample of 2,555 Americans; two-thirds were men, one-third were women.

Section 9 of the survey, American versus Imported Products, asks respondents the following question: "If you were in the market to buy various products, would you prefer to buy American-made products or imported products?" Surprisingly, respondents indicated that they preferred American-made apparel (66 percent) and automobiles (69 percent), although in the category of entertainment equipment, only 38 percent voted American.

As to whether their preference for domestic products has increased over the last three years, the greatest percentage of respondents (45 percent) said that they are buying more American-made products now than they were in 1983. Only 16 percent indicated that they were buying more imported products, and the remaining 39 percent reported no change in preference either way.

In all five income groups surveyed, the categories of apparel and automobiles charted heavily American in terms of preference, even for those respondents with household incomes of $50,000 or more. This is particularly interesting, given our natural equation of wealth with foreign cars and European designer clothing. The same holds true for the four age-group breakouts, where apparel and autos recorded even larger margins of preference (60 percent or above) in the American-made column.

The one exception to this resounding support of American-made goods was in the category of entertainment equipment. Here, the income and age-group breakouts showed a different picture altogether.

In the three middle-income groups, covering the range between $15,000 and $49,999, the split between preference for American or imported goods was nearly even. On either end of the income spectrum, however, opposing preferences emerged, showing a 45 percent pro-American score for those with incomes under $15,000, while respondents with incomes over $50,000 preferred imported products in 44 percent of the cases. Age-groups showed a similar pattern, although the split here was more black and white. Those under age 50 showed a slightly greater preference for imported entertainment equipment, while respondents over age 50 indicated a much heavier preference for American-made products.

For marketers, these breakouts are particularly interesting, since they show who is buying imported and who is buying domestic. Now that we know this, it becomes a simple matter to isolate the age and income groups that are more prone to buying imported goods.

In the same issue, S&MM's *1986 Survey of Buying Power Data Service* revealed the information shown in Table 1, below, of what Americans spend on merchandise and in what store groups.

Table 1. Store Groups and Merchandise Lines: How Much do Americans Spend?

Store Group Category	Total Sales ($000)	Merchandise Line Category	Total Sales ($000)
Supermarkets	$271,073,696	Groceries & other foods	$239,564,770
Department stores	$135,903,334	TV, VCR, & tapes	$ 10,322,941
Apparel & accessories	$ 71,818,974	Audio equip., musical instruments, & supplies	$ 16,763,426
Automotive dealers	$304,006,652	Men's & boys' clothing	$ 38,901,289
Drugstores	$ 47,734,704	Women's & girls' clothing	$ 75,586,797

Source: **S&MM's** *1986 Survey of Buying Power Data Service.*
© Sales and Marketing Management

A survey of America's food-buying habits was made by The Marlboro Group, Marlboro Marketing, Inc., 500 Tenth Avenue, New York, NY 10018.

Some of the conclusions provide interesting marketing insights to the consumer market and dispel some mass-marketing myths.

For instance, the notion that the West is always the innovator in every new lifestyle trend no longer appears accurate. While western supermarket shoppers lead the country in buying foods designed specifically for microwave ovens and buying generic/ store brands, they are behind shoppers in the rest of the country in purchasing trendy new gourmet foods, bulk foods, salad bar items and deli/carryout foods. Midwestern shoppers, long perceived as "set in their ways," are actually more venturesome in their buying patterns than easterners, buying more salad bar and generic items. They also purchase more foods designed for use in microwave ovens.

Other unexpected results include the following:

- Middle-income shoppers ($15,000–$25,000) are far more likely to buy generic or store-label products than the very poor ($7,500 or less).

- Modest-income families ($7,500–$15,000) are the most likely to purchase delicatessen foods; 40 percent of this group regularly purchase expensive gourmet and specialty items. (Only 36 percent of the more prosperous $15,000–$25,000 group did so.)

- Stores in lower income areas do far better with salad bar items than those in affluent areas.

- The pre-baby-boom generation is the most venturesome of all subgroups. People in this category—not the much-publicized baby boomers—lead in five of the six food categories covered in the study (bulk foods for use in microwave ovens, deli/ carryout foods, salad bar items, generic foods, and gourmet items).

According to the Howard Marlboro Group, the "bottom line" of the study can be summed up as follows: "The neat U.S. mass-marketing system, which worked for decades, is showing still more signs of rusting out completely. It is becoming trickier and more difficult to predict consumer likes/dislikes on the basis of membership in large demographic groups.

The breakdown of the mass-marketing system means it is no longer possible to reach consumers in huge, costly megablocks as before. As the population continues to fragment into an even greater number of boxes, consumer behavior defies easy prediction. This creates the need for a new kind of block-by-block micro marketing. It also makes advertising choices more difficult and more expensive for manufacturers.

Westinghouse Territorial Blueprint

Westinghouse Electric Corporation makes, periodically, a blueprint of each sales territory that it uses advantageously. Westinghouse normally sells the bulk of its products through wholesalers, distributors, or other sales outlets. In order to determine accurately the sales value of these distributors, it is necessary to work through them to obtain the information needed about the customers.

The information is compiled to include complete customer information. In addition to the customer's name, address, and annual purchases, the card gives his (a) industry classification; (b) location of buying control; (c) billings of Westinghouse products through local jobbers and also direct; (d) number of calls scheduled for salespeople; (e) number of calls made by salespeople.

By analyzing these cards either by territory, by industrial classification, by jobber, or by salesperson, information of vital importance may be quickly obtained. Here are a few points upon which light is thrown:

- Customer assignment to salesperson.
- Which salespersons are overloaded or underloaded.
- Whether additional or less manpower is needed.
- Whether a salesperson is devoting his or her time to customers from whom sales effort will yield a maximum return.
- Sales performance of an individual salesperson.

Obviously, a detailed territorial study of this sort requires considerable time. It is also expensive. But it is possible to get the cooperation of distributors, and the study provides data of tremendous value in sales planning.

"Careful selection of customers and proper allocation of marketing effort would reduce delivered costs and enable expanded sales volume to take place through reduced prices," said Donald R. S. Cowan, in an address to the Association of National Advertisers.

"The study of the best outlets for particular products would eliminate some costly, haphazard selling. Consideration of whether a product should be marketed by itself or as one of a group is also important in endeavoring to reduce marketing costs. Reduced marketing costs are just as important as reduced factory costs in making possible lower prices and expanded sales volumes.

"It should be borne in mind that the great masses of people are in the low-income brackets, and if the prices of luxury goods now sold mainly to the small high-income market can be reduced, their sales volume to the huge mass market can be multiplied many times. Similarly, the marginal buyers of industrial goods can be induced to buy larger quantities. Analysis of selling and advertising methods may enable the choice of those that will accomplish a given task with least expense." Every progressive company does a certain amount of research work, if only to study the reports of salespeople. But it should be organized.

Testing New Products

In recent years some companies have tested proposed products by trade clinics to determine accurately which qualities the consumer prefers; what price will give the largest sales volume; and what name and package are most likely to "click." This method of pre-determining salability will be even more widely used in the future than in the past. However, to be worthwhile, such tests must be representative of the whole market, and not merely a section or a portion of the market.

Another drawback is that a use test does not tell much about sales possibilities. Many an intrinsically worthy product fails to achieve recognition merely because it is hard to sell, or because it does not have "shelf appeal" or because the price (at least at first) seems high. Use tests do not always reveal these obstacles.

As an alternative, actual sales tests might seem to be the answer. Properly conducted, they can be of great help. This means that they must be carried on under conditions as nearly normal as possible—which rules out tests in stores in the manufacturer's home town, for example.

A New-Product Policy

Experience shows clearly that, to be successful, a new product must fit into the existing company. In developing a sound policy, the human and physical assets and liabilities of the company should be listed and studied.

A partial checklist of important areas is given below. It suggests the kinds of topics that are significant in deciding what kinds of products can be logically considered. Lack of strength in a given area is not necessarily a criticism of current operation. It is rather a reason for avoiding products which depend for success on strength in that particular area.

1. Desires of stockholders and directors

2. Management abilities, interests, and experience

3. Technical skills

4. Types of current production operations

5. Quality and availability of labor

6. Sales and distribution arrangements and background

7. Plant location with respect to markets

8. Reputation with consumers

9. Product philosophy (specialty or mass production, high or low price ranges, and so on)

10. Financial condition

11. Raw materials—availability, cost, location

12. Transportation

13. Site utilization

14. Special competitive factors

Through a searching, objective study based on this sort of checklist you can uncover a number of limitations on the kinds of new products that you should consider at all. For example, a company with an outstanding reputation for high-quality specialties would be ill-advised to get into the mass production of a cheap item. A well-established and successful sales organization suggests that new products be suited to this strong resource.

Sometimes, a study will suggest that a company should put its present operations in order before considering any new activities at all. Diversification is not a substitute for good day-to-day management of the existing business.

Increasing Market Share

Intergraph Corporation, marketer of CAD/CAM (computer-aided design and manufacturing) systems bucked an industry's recession-caused slowdown and increased sales and earnings. George C. Steinke, vice-president of product marketing, said the key was the formation of a group of application managers specializing in such sectors as plant design, architecture, mapping, and electronics. "We decided to approach our markets on an application, rather than on an industry, basis, because you have to address the individual's job," he commented. "If you meet his needs with a highly technological set of hardware and software, it's relatively easy, later on, to sell a particular industry. The application managers figure out the requirements of the marketplace, what must be done to meet those needs, and to articulate those activities to product development people. Working with sales personnel, the managers go on customer calls to provide advice on specific applications and explaining how Intergraph's software will answer client needs.

Van de Kamp's Frozen Foods Division of General Host saw an opportunity to gain the number one spot in Mexican frozen foods. Dan Barnett, marketing vice-president, reported that there was room for another category of Mexican food: restaurant-quality frozen entrees that the affluent segment of the population would be willing to pay for.

The payoff was the direct result of careful marketing and planning. Van de Kamp spotted two trends: an average annual growth rate for Mexican restaurants of 26 percent over the past five years, and the rapid rise in the number of affluent one- and two-person households. As a result, the company test marketed four frozen products, and the results were so impressive that 70 food brokers, covering 80 percent of the country, took on the line, and three more items were added.

And while we're at it, an article in *Advertising Age* demonstrates how *not* to increase market share in the Hispanic market. It was reported that some companies tend to trip over their tongues when they jump into the Hispanic market. Direct translations of general market themes into Spanish may be not only meaningless, but ludicrous. The following examples were quoted in the article:

- Chicken magnate Frank Perdue's slogan, "It takes a tough man to make a tender chicken," was directly translated and read, "It takes a sexually excited man to make a chick affectionate."

- Budweiser ended up being "the queen of beers," while another brand was "filling; less delicious."

- A candy marketer wanted to print a statement on its package, bragging about its 50 years in the business. When a tilde did not appear over the appropriate "n," the package claimed it contained 50 anuses.

- One food company's burrito became *burrada,* a colloquialism for "big mistake."

Getting Customer Reactions

There are many ways of submitting samples to consumers for tests. Obviously, the methods used must be adapted to the particular item in question. In any case, it should be remembered:

1. That no one type of test will give all the answers.

2. That it is desirable to test only one variable at a time; hence a series of lesser experiments is preferable to one far-flung effort.

3. That conditions of the test should be as natural as possible, and that respondents should be judged by their acts, rather than by their opinions.

4. That questions having to do with price are likely to elicit unreliable replies.

5. Provide for a control group. Group A cannot be judged except in comparison with some other group (group B). Moreover, in order to compare group A with group B it may be necessary to compare each of them with a third group (group C).
6. Submit alternative choices rather than a single choice. When asked about a single product, with no alternative choice, reactions all tend to be favorable.
7. In testing a new product, pair it with the nearest comparable, best-known and most successful competitive product.

Preparation of samples for pretests must be done with the utmost care. It is not enough merely to describe the new product and ask the test consumer whether he or she would like it. Such hypothetical judgments are unreliable. The product should be actually made up and packaged so that the consumer can see it and try it out under realistic conditions. If the inherent quality of the product is to be tested, the package should be unbranded, carrying merely an identification label and a guaranty of purity, so that questions of brand prestige will be eliminated.

Market Research in Small Cities

In a market research program covering small cities the manufacturer should first select the cities, according to studies of buying power, retail outlets available, type of stores, and trading area. This can be done through a study of marketing statistics, available from the U.S. Department of Commerce and business publications.

A number of manufacturers have found it profitable to close many small, weak accounts, where proper merchandising effort is lacking. They have found it far more profitable to select one strong dealer, and help that dealer, than to have three weak dealers, none of whom buy enough to make the salesperson's visit profitable.

For most manufacturers, to profitably sell in small towns means that there must first be a basic list of desirable towns, and then a similarly basic list of desirable dealers.

From this list, distribution is obtained through the dealers who will agree to live up to certain requirements. Each manufacturer must know that it is possible for the dealer to meet the requirements to which he or she is held. This knowledge usually comes only after careful tests under controlled conditions, or from long experience.

Every town offers special possibilities to certain manufacturers. A school town, with several thousand students, offers a market for special types of merchandise. A railroad-stop town means sales of certain kinds of work clothing. A farm town that has no industry to speak of means sales of certain types of clothing, as well as farm implements and supplies.

Similarity in size does not always mean similarity in buying taste and sales possibilities. Schools, industries, mines, railroad activities, tourist trade, farm conditions, proximity to larger cities, weather, and many other factors create many differences in sales possibilities; these factors all need to be known and recorded on sales records of manufacturers who want their product sold in highest possible volume.

Retail Development Center

Some years ago, Armstrong Cork Company developed a Retail Development Center with five objectives in mind:

1. To observe the changing retail environment as it relates to the needs of the retailer and the consumer;

2. To analyze the merchandising implications of those changes on the distribution of Armstrong products;

3. To create merchandising elements and programs that meet the changing needs of retailers and consumers;

4. To test new merchandising concepts with both retailers and consumers in a shopping environment;

5. To make sure the fruits of the efforts reached the retail floor.

Marketing research was involved in all steps, especially observing, analyzing, and testing. Subjects of particular interest were packaging, displays, point-of-purchase materials, sample presentations, integration of samples with the stock of merchandise, signage, communications, relationship to adjacent displays, and advertising and promotion.

Focus group interviews were used to probe consumer wants, needs, problems, communications, and expectations. Retailers and wholesalers were interviewed during visits to the center.

A member of the Marketing Research Group and/or the Retail Development Service visits one or more store locations to observe, photograph, and discuss merchandising assistance and Armstrong displays with company field people and store personnel. The field information and the store requirements are studied and reviewed, and recommendations are fed back to the stores.

This research brought the company and the Market Research Group closer to distributors and retailers and helped all parties to do their jobs more effectively.

Advertising the New Product

No one knows how many thousands of new items and millions of dollars go into test marketing each year, but two things are certain: New-product test marketing is basic to the food business, and no one has come up with the best way of doing it. Manufacturers might spend as much as a quarter-million dollars in testing one item, may saturate a test market with newspaper, regional magazine, radio, and television advertising, flood the mails with samples and coupons, and offer retailers substantial discounts to stock the product and extra allowances for choice display space.

Supermarket executives, well aware that new products often carry a higher price tag than the old (aerosols and frozen foods, for example), grudgingly go along with the manufacturers, hoping to make enough extra profit on the introductory discounts to make up for the extra time and handling. To a chain-store buyer, the most important single factor in a manufacturer's new-product test-marketing program is the advertising campaign.

For new-product introductions, television is usually ranked as the most effective medium, followed by newspaper advertising with coupons, coupon mailing, sampling, and newspaper advertising without coupons. Regional and local editions of national magazines are relatively new and not yet widely accepted as test-marketing media. But their greater use seems likely, for many test markets extend beyond the coverage of the central city's newspapers and radio and TV stations, and the chains want advertising in all the communities in which they stock the new product.

Heavy advertising is basic to traditional test marketing, in which a new product is introduced on a grand scale with discounts to grocers and consumers and, hopefully, distribution in every store in the test area. But test marketing is also done more quietly and selectively, especially through food brokers. And market research firms now work in conjunction with the manufacturers' salespeople or, in many instances, handling everything—warehousing, distribution, auditing, and cleanup—except the advertising.

Many chains question the value of heavy advertising in test marketing. "Almost any item will move if advertised enough," said the chief grocery buyer for a four-store cooperative trading group. "It is better to use normal advertising and promotion and a market-survey firm." A merchandising vice-president for a nationwide chain of more than 100 stores agrees: "You can get a customer to try anything if you make the offer attractive enough. This is why Kellogg's freeze-dried fruit cereals did so well in test marketing and fell flat afterwards. Advertising should not be so extensive that it distorts the results."

To reduce distortions, manufacturers are turning to market-research firms. Methods vary among the firms, and may consist of any combination of consumer diaries, in-store audits, and consumer interviews. For example, one of the largest field-survey firms in the East first makes a two- or three-month survey of a product category in selected stores to determine shares of market and sales trends. It then introduces the new product on consignment, handling all warehousing, delivery, in-store stocking, displaying, pricing, point-of-purchase promotion, and take-back. Monthly or weekly audits are made during the test period—which may range between 6 and 24 months—and auditing continues for a time after the product is withdrawn.

Some Doubts about Test Marketing

Test marketing is not bringing the right products to the right people fast enough. It now takes about two years and at least $500,000 to test a new consumer product to the point where it is ready for national distribution. The things that can happen in two years are many and forceful. Consumers change their buying habits, competitors introduce similar, or better, products; and packaging advances can affect retailing practices.

Yet the idea persists that test marketing is conducted in a vacuum. There is the erroneous idea that findings gleaned today in one, or more test markets are indicative of what will happen to a product in national distribution two years from now. There are just too many variables for that to be true.

In a growing number of companies and agencies, the whole concept of test marketing and new-product introductions is undergoing a shakedown. The reason is that, in some cases, marketing generalists, using experience and intuition, have introduced products cheaply, quickly, and successfully with a minimum of advice from researchers. And there have been too many cases where complex testing procedures have not only slowed down new-product introductions but have also produced inaccurate indications.

"Test marketing historically has not proved to be a dependable ally of the advertising or agency innovator. The tests have usually been difficult to arrange, costly to execute, and suffer the added penalty of tipping off competition to the innovator's advance plans. More damaging has been their proclivity to produce equivocal or uncertain results."

That observation came from Frank Stanton, formerly senior vice-president and director of information management, Benton & Bowles, an agency specializing in new-product introductions.

In a similar vein, J. K. Duncan told an American Marketing Association audience in Chicago that:

"Test marketing these days is passé. It takes too long, costs too much money, and delivers too little in the way of information. More often than not, what is referred to today as 'test marketing' is really the regional rollout of a product that the company is pretty sure will make the grade."

The chief executive of a large container-manufacturing company stated:

"When we put a product into test markets, we are aware that there can be pitfalls in this approach. Some of the so-called typical markets—South Bend and Indianapolis are among them—have been so overworked as test markets that they are now, in fact, atypical.

"When people become too sophisticated about the test-marketing techniques, they just aren't very reliable indicators any more—they are more like the test marketers themselves. And we take into account, too, the possibility that the competition occasionally might step in and buy up the product just to confuse the results. On the whole, though, we set a good deal of store in test marketing as a helpful indication."

Suggestions for Surveys

The value of any consumer survey is in proportion to the honesty with which it was made. The bad odor sometimes attached to surveys can be traced to an experience the sales manager had with some survey designed to prove a point rather than to chart a condition. The following suggestions may prove helpful in conducting a consumer market study or survey:

1. *Start off with a "know-nothing" attitude.* This will give you a clear, fresh approach; such an approach is necessary in order to avoid perverted results.

2. *Conduct survey to learn—not prove.* If the basic idea behind your survey is to produce sales material, it is best that you forget the whole thing. You will get plenty of good sales material as a by-product of an objective survey.

3. *Avoid preconceived ideas of results.* If you already know the answers, why make the survey? No honest survey will perfectly follow the pattern you *think* it will take, so don't warp the results by striving to have them parallel your unwarranted conclusions.

4. *Strive for absolute accuracy.* You won't achieve it—no one ever did—but the only way to approach perfection is to make perfection your aim.

5. *Apply stiff accuracy tests to both desirable and undesirable results.* It is just as easy to go wrong in one direction as another, so either test everything from all angles or let the chips fall where they may.

6. *Don't hide unpleasant results—tell the whole truth.* It is surprising how much will be added to the believability of your report if you include those few embarrassing results.

7. *Use a scientifically accurate sample—there's no safety in numbers.* Certainly, get an ample number of reports, but most important, the people interviewed must be typically representative of the whole.

8. *Include questions to check against known facts.* This is the best method of testing the accuracy of your sample. When your survey results on these questions parallel recognized statistics such as U.S. Census figures, you may be sure your sample is both adequate and accurate.

9. *Avoid complicated, unexplainable methods.* If the basic problem behind your survey is so complex that a complicated method is necessary, call in an outside organization to do the job.

10. *Explain method fully in all published reports.* Make certain that you cover the five "Ws"—who, what, when, where, and why. Who made the survey, what it's about, when it was made, where it was made, and why it was made. These five things are just as important as your general statements of *how* it was made.

11. *Point out any weaknesses or limitations in your method.* There is no perfect method, so be sure you enumerate those imperfections. The recipient is just as likely to jump to conclusions as you, so prevent such suicidal leaps by plainly stating all limitations.

12. *State sources clearly for all outside information used.* Some answers can be better qualified if correlated with outside statistical material. Label every item of this type so it won't be confused with survey results.

13. *Don't extend results to market size unless you definitely state the size of your sample.* Preferably, don't extend results at all, but if you do, make certain that everyone understands how much you have extended them.

14. *Don't try to learn too much from too few reports.* Circumstances can affect individual answers, so protect yourself by avoiding conclusions from too few reports. The law of averages cannot function if cramped in space and numbers.

15. *Avoid basing percentages or extensions on small numbers.* An absolute minimum in this respect is 100 reports, because, on anything less, one report will make a difference of more than 1 percent.

16. *Keep your sales story divorced from your statistical report.* The recipient is certain to be more interested in your statistics than in your sales story. Cash in on this interest by serving him a pure diet, ungarnished by selling material.

17. *Keep report brief, with more details available on request.* An immense mass of complicated statistics cannot be digested at one sitting, so breeze through it and leave those detailed cross-checks for a future call back. You are most certain to be invited to return.

Use and Misuse of Questionnaires

It is increasingly difficult to get people to answer questionnaires. Whereas 30 to 40 percent was once considered a good return from questionnaires, the average return has now sunk to below 10 percent, according to one direct-mail expert.

To get the best returns on questionnaires there should be some definite gain to the person who must fill it out. This should be set forth in the first paragraph of the letter. It may be an offer to send a summary of the returns that would be of value to him or her; it may be a booklet or a key ring or some other useful personal item. One company reports excellent returns by enclosing a useful booklet and stating in the letter that it was being sent in advance, since filling out the blank would take two or three minutes of the recipient's time.

Another sales organization, which continually checks user attitudes, reports exceptionally good returns from questionnaires used to "open up" a new mailing list. In fact, this company has adopted the rule of always conditioning a new mailing list, or a new group of names, with a questionnaire mailing asking questions designed to accomplish a double purpose:

1. Condition the person for the sales effort to follow.

2. Obtain group reactions to the company's present policies, sales methods, and services.

An eastern publishing company that makes an extensive use of questionnaires in its editorial work reports that it never asks a reader to answer more than 10 questions at one time. The editorial director of these papers, who is very close to his readers, contends that detailed and exhaustive questionnaires used by market-research people usually go directly into the wastepaper basket.

It is this editor's experience that most people will take a minute or two to jot down answers to a few carefully selected questions if properly and courteously approached. However, he also warns that the questions should be set up so that accurate answers will be obtained and not just "yes" or "no," which do not provide any shade of opinion.

Another market-research expert reports good returns when the questions are printed on the back of the letter of transmittal, thus saving paper and getting the proposition before the executive in a more concise manner.

A manufacturer of supplies sold to banks uses a questionnaire to determine when the bank will be in the market for certain products. This proved a hard nut to crack. The answer was obtained by using a personalized form letter. After 10 days, if the letter was not answered, a copy was attached to another questionnaire and used as a followup. A very brief note, asking for the courtesy of a reply and attached to the copy, did the trick.

A company selling a line of merchandise through dealers had occasion to ask them some questions concerning dealer store layout and the type of sales helps they could use.

The first test of the questionnaire was disappointing. The "sample poll" was inadequate to form accurate conclusions. So another test was made with a partially filled out questionnaire. The dealer's name, annual purchases for three years back, credit key, and the name of the salesperson who called on him or her were typed on each questionnaire before it was sent out, instead of after it was received as had been the plan.

A brief letter of transmittal explained that in order to provide the type of sales promotional material dealers could most effectively use, certain information was required by the sales promotion department. Would the dealer please cooperate by completing the enclosed, partially filled out questionnaire, after checking it carefully to make sure that the names and addresses were correct?

The average dealer does not have an accurate picture of how much business he gives any particular source of supply over a three-year period, so his interest is aroused. An objection to the plan is that the dealer may think he or she is giving the company too much business, but this company has not found this to be true. On the contrary, many comments were received from dealers stating they were surprised to see that the orders they had been giving the company showed a falling off, but they would try to increase them next year.

Follow-up Pays

In his book, *A Procedure for Securing Returns to Mail Questionnaires,* Stanley S. Robin describes a program to secure returns to mail questionnaires that are comparable in quantity to returns obtained by interviews. The steps include:

1. A prequestionnaire letter, intended to pave the way for a sympathetic reception of the questionnaire.

2. The questionnaire itself, a cover letter, and a stamped, self-addressed envelope.

3. First follow-up letter, reminding the subject of lack of response and mentioning that a stamped envelope was supplied.

4. Second follow-up letter, along with another copy of the questionnaire and another stamped envelope.

5. Third follow-up letter, again emphasizing the stamped envelopes sent previously, and inviting the respondent to get in touch with the investigator for another questionnaire if needed.

The results of such a thorough procedure are impressive. Out of nine cases, four had 90 percent or greater response, four more had 80 percent or greater response, and the remaining one had 66 percent response rate.

Effective Use of an Account Audit

Here are some facts brought to light by one company as a result of an account audit. It provided information that the management was able to use effectively in recasting sales territories when salespeople were released from service:

1. Between one-third and one-half of the customers sold in the usual way by competing wholesalers are unprofitable.

2. These unprofitable customers buy only from 5 percent to 15 percent of the individual jobber's volume.

3. The wider margin of gross profit on sales to these customers, arising from higher prices on the small quantities purchased, is not sufficient to cover out-of-pocket expenses.

4. The high rate of expense of serving them is due to the disparity between the volume obtained from large and small buyers and the various kinds of effort expended upon them. Large customers often buy 20 times the volume of small customers, but require only two or three times as many interviews, telephone calls, deliveries, and the like.

5. A shift in effort from unprofitable to profitable types of customers may increase the typical jobber's net profits as much as $10,000 annually, if properly carried out.

6. Such a shift in effort must be made according to the needs of each sales territory, because unprofitable customers range from 5 percent to 70 percent of the total customers on different routes.

7. By a simple extension of the method, the comparative selling expenses for different products may be obtained, sometimes revealing that certain products cost three times as much to distribute as others in the same line and yield much smaller profits, notwithstanding greater markups.

In food wholesaling, such audits led to the establishment of cash-and-carry depots, where small retailers could share in part of the savings achieved by eliminating deliveries, billing, etc.

In a changing world it is essential to get these new viewpoints, as they often provide the peg on which an important shift in policy may be hung.

Attitude Studies and How to Make Them

Another type of research that can profitably be conducted is "opinion checks" to determine negative situations in the current operations of a business. These may have to do with a wide range of activities, any or all of which might have a bearing on the sales operations of the company.

Appraisals of the attitudes of customers, dealers, salespeople, or employees require intelligent interpretation and for that reason the work should be assigned to someone of experience. It cannot be done effectively by the run-of-paper research worker. In the first place, he or she lacks the background for skillful interviewing; in the second place, he or she lacks the judgment necessary to properly weigh information obtained from the persons questioned.

Most companies using attitude studies to help formulate sales policies emphasize the importance of the indirect approach. The most successful method is to employ an executive who has a flair for interviewing.

A skillful interviewer will quickly determine whether a person is sincere or not, and be guided accordingly in making his report. He or she should also have enough experience in business to recognize persons whose opinions and suggestions are valuable and those who are not sound thinkers. Very often the best suggestions and the most important opinions come from relatively young people who have a fresh point of view toward so-called traditional policies.

Practical Uses of Sales Research

In outlining the practical uses of an advanced type of sales research, A. C. Nielsen, a national authority, speaking before the Association of National Advertisers, urged members to be armed with a reliable means of 1) detecting each change promptly; 2) determining its importance, its direction, and its rate of change; 3) determining the best means of altering marketing methods, tactics, and policies to meet changed conditions; 4) determining, promptly and accurately, whether each alteration actually does meet the new conditions successfully.

Fourteen practical uses for this type of sales research were outlined, as quoted below. The "index" referred to is the Nielsen Food and Drug Index. These 14 uses, presented in brief from the experiences of nearly 100 national advertisers, offer a guide for many companies planning to take advantage of changing conditions:

1. Ensuring profitable distribution of advertising and merchandising effort by territories, city-sizes, store-sizes, consumer income levels, etc. This is possible because the *index* reveals the total available market (all brands combined) in each subdivision of the national market, and shows your competitive strength in each subdivision.

2. Ensuring profitable seasonal distribution of advertising and merchandising effort. This follows from the fact that the index reveals the true seasonal fluctuations in sales (all brands combined) at the point of consumption. For many products, the *consumer* seasonal curve differs widely from the *factory* seasonal curve.

3. Getting deals properly sized, priced, timed, and distributed. A vast amount of light has been shed on this complex subject, because the index has revealed the true effect (i.e., the consumer sales increases) resulting from dealer loading operations conducted by hundreds of manufacturers.

4. Detecting profitable or unprofitable advertising appeals, media, or methods. The true effect (on consumers) of every advertising campaign is recorded accurately by the *index.*

5. Detecting profitable or unprofitable merchandising methods, by showing the consumer sales trend following deals, combination offers, premium offers, couponing, sampling, display work, price changes, package changes, etc.

6. Evaluating the effectiveness of the advertising and promotional methods being used either nationally or on a regional basis.

7. Providing advance warning of your sales declines or of sales gains by your advertised competitors or by unadvertised brands. Consumer sales usually show a decline or a gain many months before the change is revealed conclusively by factory sales records. Time is vital in such cases.

8. Revealing weak spots, either nationally or in any subdivision of the market, e.g., weaknesses in competitive sales position, distribution, inventories, stock-turn, out-of-stock percentages, prices, gross profit, displays, special sales, etc. If, following the detection of any weak spot, an effort is made to improve the situation, the *index* reveals, promptly and accurately, the *result* of the effort.

9. Revealing need for a change in product, for a new product, or for a new size or type of package. Any trend away from your *type* of product is detected instantly. And if you decide to add a new type to your own line, the *index* shows which markets will prove most receptive, what package sizes and types are most popular, how to price the product for maximum profit, etc.

10. Detecting gains or losses in dealer goodwill, by revealing changes in the amount of display and special sales given to your brand.

11. Determining the most profitable consumer price level. This is done by the use of complex cross-analyses revealing the extent to which your competitive sales position in any group of stores is affected by differences in the ratio of your price to competitors' prices.

12. Furnishing a sound basis for setting territorial quotas and measuring quota attainment. The *index* shows how much business is actually being done in each territory (by all brands combined), thus eliminating the use of quotas based on telephones, bank deposits, and other factors whose relationship to the total *consumer* sales of any type of goods cannot be determined by analyzing the *factory* sales of any single manufacturer.

13. Predetermining the result of any proposed expenditure. This is done by testing the proposed plan in a "laboratory" consisting of 10 cities in one or more specially selected territories. We test not only advertising copy but also advertising quantity, media, displays, deals, sales coverage, detailing, sampling, couponing, price changes, package changes, cooperative advertising, etc. While this complex subject cannot be treated in detail here, it should be stated that many common "fetishes" of advertising and merchandising are being exploded by the hundreds of test campaigns being conducted.

14. Launching a new product. Certain enterprising manufacturers have used the *index* to decide whether to enter a new field and then, after deciding to launch the new product, they have used the *index* as a means of directing their efforts into the most profitable channels.

Making the Research Appropriation Pay

A criticism of sales research as conducted by many companies is that too much information thus obtained gathers dust on some top shelf. Seldom are data put to work making money for the business. Sometimes a research department is set up to meet a specific need, and then after that job has been completed, the research personnel scurry around to find something else to do. Or to go to the other extreme, let's take a department already in operation; every executive suddenly becomes alerted to the need of getting "facts" about this, that, or the other operation to support his or her own opinions or a position previously taken with a superior. On this point an official of Lever Brothers told Dartnell:

"Two things are necessary to prevent misuse of research. The first is to require that a research project either contribute meaningfully to a specific 'action decision' or, at the very least, provide information regarding an area about which little or nothing is known. The second requirement is that all concerned should be committed *in advance of the research* to agreement on exactly what minimum findings will support a proposed decision.

"Actually, certain advances in market research in the past several years have tended to make its techniques inherently more actionable, and less prone to misuse. Modern research and information-handling techniques, including computerization, have enabled marketing research to reduce the time it takes to secure and report information, thereby increasing the likelihood that the information will be available in time to be acted on.

"In addition, techniques have been developed to measure the probability of future consumer behavior. This enables market research to predict earlier and with greater accuracy what will happen in the marketplace—and why—and will increasingly minimize the necessity of conducting expensive and time-consuming test marketing to evaluate proposed new products, advertising campaigns, and the like."

Analyzing Marketing Costs

Marketing cost analysis is a key to locating unprofitable sales and to determining the losses for which disproportionate spreading of marketing effort is responsible. In a simple form, it can be made from five basic company records: 1) names and locations of customers, 2) types of businesses of customers, 3) number of each customer's orders in a given period, 4) total sales to each customer in the same period, and 5) total sales and gross profits on each product in your line. Most plants will not find it hard to get this information.

A brief description of some of the more advanced marketing cost analysis methods follows. Although a complete, detailed discussion of the procedure involved would be too lengthy and technical here, two basic principles may be readily summarized.

1. *Classifying Costs.* The marketing expenses of a business, which are usually entered in the accounting records on a "natural" expense basis, are reclassified into "functional" cost groups. This brings together all the direct and indirect costs associated with each marketing activity performed by that company. For example, in a natural classification, all expenditures for supplies are grouped together; but with a functional breakdown, the costs of supplies are segregated according to the activity that used them, such as advertising, shipping, and so on.

2. *Allocating Costs.* These functional cost groups are then allocated to territories, to products, to customers, and to any other desired segments of sales. Allocations are based either on known facts or on the product and customer characteristics that control the size of these costs.

    Having your records set up to yield a functional classification for your firm's marketing costs is an indispensable step. It has a number of advantages even though you make no further analysis. Remember, of course, that your functional breakdown of marketing costs should parallel the actual organization of your business and the responsibilities for expenditure. Once you get this done, your classification itself will help in controlling marketing expenses just by revealing how money is being spent.

A Dangerous Numbers Game

Any discussion of market research must conclude with a word of caution. With so many schools of thought about the methods and techniques employed, questions are bound to arise about their relative merits.

Numbers are important in all marketing research. But without proper evaluation numbers can be dangerous, observed a senior vice-president of Kenyon & Eckhardt, New York, in an address before the American Association of Advertising Agencies:

"There are booby traps involved in the numbers game," he said. "Far too many people believe numbers express reality, when in fact, they represent abstractions from reality to a high degree. It's important to remember that they are only shorthand descriptions of pieces of the truth, no more than that."

The booby trap in the numbers game is to assume that:

- Bigger numbers are always better.

- More numbers are always better.

- Negative numbers are always bad.

- Numerical differences are always meaningful.

- Any number is better than no number.

- Assigning a number to a guess somehow makes it a reality, not a hypothesis.

- The number descriptions we have today describe the future.

Addressing the American Marketing Association, David C. Wright, as director of corporate development, United States Gypsum Company, said:

"We have made such great strides in developing and refining the techniques of market research that many companies today are running the risk of permitting market-research methods to become so rarefied that they lose touch with their basic purposes. No matter how sophisticated the techniques and how accomplished the practitioners, market research cannot make its full contribution to the success of the company unless it is conducted with a continuing awareness of the principles that make it effective.

"These principles may seem obvious—and, indeed, they should be—but the fact is that a preoccupation with questionnaires, statistical techniques, and other tools of analysis often cause marketing researchers to lose sight of the fundamental purposes of their efforts."

Checklist for Sales Researchers

Numerous special surveys and similar market investigations have been made by individual publishing organizations and advertising agencies to present to advertisers a cross section of the market these publishers serve. Some of these are quite valuable in the projecting of a sales program. Others are too limited in their scope to reflect a typical situation, and some are downright deceptive. It is possible to make a survey prove anything. It is just a matter of picking the right people or establishments to survey, and framing the questions so that the desired answers will be obtained. Therefore it is now common practice to double-check information obtained through surveys. One example is the kitchen cabinets test where interviewers actually check products in consumers' kitchen cabinets to determine what products they buy.

To assist sales managers in appraising the true value of sales research and surveys, particularly those made with the idea of selling something, the American Association of Advertising Agencies has prepared and published the following tests:

1. *Who made the survey?* Complete information should be given regarding the names of the organizations or individuals who conducted the survey, made the tabulations, and interviewed the results, together with their qualifications and the extent of their interest, if any, in the findings.

2. *Does the title indicate exactly the scope of the survey?* No report should bear a title that suggests more than results justify.

3. *Does the report contain all pertinent data as to how, when, and where the survey was made?* The following information should be furnished:

   • Reason for making the study.

   • Who financed it?

   • Exact period of time covered in collection of data.

   • Date of issuance or publication.

   • Definition of terms used.

   • Copies of questionnaires and instructions.

   • How field work was conducted and supervised.

   • List of localities where information was gathered, together with number of calls in each locality, and how calls were divided among different sections and different strata of the population.

   • Actual data, as well as percentages and averages.

   • Explanation of bases on which percentages are figured.

   • Sources of collateral data.

   • Description of statistical methods used, together with reasons.

4. *Is the sample ample?* Lack of adequate sample is one of the commonest weaknesses in market research. There is no rule that can be laid down to cover all cases. In the first place, it must be shown that a true cross section has been selected. Then it must be proved that the size of the sample is adequate—

   • By showing that when results are divided into groups, such as the first 200 or 300, the second 200 or 300, etc., a point has been reached where results are not materially changed by the addition of more instances, or

   • By checks against known facts, or

- By other acceptable statistical proof.

5. *Have data collected in one city or section been used to draw conclusions for the country as a whole?* This is a question of the adequacy of the sample. If results obtained in a limited area are projected to cover the entire population, justification for doing so should be established by reasonable evidence.

6. *Are percentages figured for groups or classes that contain too small a number of instances?* It often happens that although there may be enough data to furnish an adequate total, breakdowns into income groups, geographical sections, or other forms of groupings, leave too few instances in individual classes to justify figuring of percentages. In other words, the sample becomes too small when broken into parts. When such breakdowns are used, actual figures should be furnished.

7. *Are percentages of increase figured on ample bases?* Percentages of increase are frequently figured on such small numbers as to be entirely misleading. This is a common error in the case of sales of new products, circulation, and advertising increases, etc. Actual figures should be used in such cases.

8. *Was information obtained by mailed questionnaires?* Information obtained by mail usually does not represent a true cross section of the market or of the population. When data have been obtained in this way, proof should be furnished that the questions are of such a nature, and that sufficient safeguards have been set up to ensure representative replies.

9. *Is casual relationship attributed to one single factor, when other contributing factors are present?* It must either be proved that all other factors are held constant, or allowance must be made for the other variable factors.

10. *If questionnaires were used, were questions of such a nature as to give fair and adequate answers?* Care must be taken in

interpreting the answers to questions that are too general, that suggest answers, or that are subject to biased replies.

11. *Was information gathered of such a nature that the memories of the people interviewed might have resulted in inaccuracies?* When any of the so-called "recall" or "recognition" methods are used, the results should be looked upon primarily as a measure of the impressions of the people interviewed, rather than as a measure of facts, unless it can be proved that such impressions correspond with such facts.

12. *Can type of information obtained (either by interview or by mail) be relied on as accurate?* Questions involving income, personal expenditures, personal pride or prejudice, reading habits, education, etc., often do not yield correct answers.

13. *Have any original or unique statistical devices been employed?* When devices are used for which there is no well-established, published authority, adequate explanation of the method should be presented, and proof must be furnished that the method is valid.

14. *Are charts misleading?* In graphic presentations, the titles must be clear, scales must not be exaggerated, the vertical scales should start with zero (except in special cases, as in index numbers that fluctuate over and under 100), curves must be clearly labeled (or easily compared with distinct legends), and simplicity should be the main objective.

Sampling the Market

Researchers have many more classifications of samples than we have room to discuss here, but a few of the most important are worth mentioning. They are described by Craig S. Rice, market research expert, as follows.

"The simple, random sample is a little like drawing names from a hat. In this method, every member of the universe has an equal opportunity of selection. One way is to select every 10th name, for example, from a list of 'the universe.' This kind of sample has two important advantages; the error is the smallest and can be accurately calculated. The degree of risk can be determined. The disadvantage is that the method requires the most time and effort (hence, money) to execute.

"The cluster sample is an economy measure whereby the sample is randomly selected in groups. For example, if every 10th person in a town were to be sampled, the interviewer would have to travel extensively, boosting cost. However, if a number of blocks were selected at random and each resident of each block interviewed, travel time and costs would be reduced. The cluster sample is not as accurate as the random sample, but it is much less expensive.

"The stratified sample is specifically designed to match known facts about the universe. For example, if the universe contains one-third urban families, one-third rural, and one-third suburban, the sample would be selected in that way. In this way, some expense is saved. However, each member of the universe does not have an equal chance of selection, unless the selection is random within each stratum. Normally, this is not a random sample and it can have considerable error that cannot be accurately calculated.

"The convenience sample is, basically, just about what it sounds like. The sample is selected among those most readily available. They may be all about the same age, location, and income. Consequently, this sample can generate the largest error of all, the error size cannot be calculated, and these errors can lead to serious investment loss.

"From a practical standpoint, the sample should be as random as the budget will permit. In cutting corners, one should recognize that it is almost impossible to find a truly 'typical' person and few researchers know just what such a person would be like. Even successful executives mistakenly believe themselves to be typical of the general population in preferences for product, advertisements, etc.

"True random samples are very rare. Nonrandom samples, if selected with good judgment, are better than swivel-chair guessing. Even fairly crude research can obtain important data. A random sample is not even necessary if the attribute to be measured is randomly distributed.

"The sample size is the second factor affecting sample accuracy. Increasing the size of a random sample will increase the accuracy, but not proportionately. Doubling the sample will not halve the error! We can calculate error for each sample size. However, as the sample increases, it also becomes more expensive, even though it is somewhat more accurate. The key question is, 'How accurate must we be?' or, 'How large an error can we risk?' We must keep in mind the cost of a wrong fact and a campaign failure. On minor decisions, often we can take a chance on data that has a wide range of error.

"A handy little formula has been used to calculate the error for any given sample size. The size of the error is called 'sigma,' or 's.' This error is equal to the square root of an even split in answers obtained from the sample (50 percent in favor, 50 percent against). This calculation is divided by the size of the sample, or as shown in this figure:

$$\text{sigma} = \frac{\overline{\sqrt{PQ}}}{n}$$

"P and Q represent the 50-50 split and 'n' is the sample size. Using this formula, for example, we can see that a random sample of 100 will have an error of 5 percent, which is read plus or minus 5 percent. A sample of 300 has an error of about 2.9 percent (tripling the sample does not quite reduce the error to one half).

"One additional factor tells the degree of confidence that we might place in this estimate. The factor is called 'The Confidence Interval,' or C.I. It is a statement of how many times out of a hundred our estimate is probably correct. For example, if we use just one confidence interval, we are probably right 95 percent of the time. The C.I. is simply the number of sigmas that we use. If we want to work to one C.I. (and be 68 percent certain), we use one sigma. If we wanted two C.I.s (or 95 percent certainty) we would use two sigmas."

(Note: This is a highly simplified, rule-of-thumb formula. It will have accuracy only under ideal circumstances, such as a pure random sample, etc. Otherwise, it has definite limitations and good judgment is essential.)

Geomapping

Automated cartography on microcomputers is rapidly increasing as a way for making market decisions, reports *Marketing Communications*. The basic ingredients of automated mapping are a personal computer, an output device, boundary files that provide delineations of geographic sectors, data files that supply information such as consumer demographics and product performance, and mapping software that merges both the boundary and data to produce a map. Merging enables the user to overlay various data sets to form a clear picture of business trends. For instance, a marketer can identify target markets by one or many demographic variables, add on an overlay of current market penetration, and then correlate the present level of penetration with the market's potential.

The software's flexibility, therefore, permits a quantifiable assessment of performance versus potential and evaluation of the allocation of limited resources. This procedure can provide answers to some of the vital questions a marketer must ask: Has the sales force been deployed effectively? Are the promotional dollars flowing into a given area warranted? Did a specific promotion or advertising campaign improve product demand? Is a high potential area being ignored? Is too much attention being given to a low growth area?

Utilizing the Sales Force

The sales force can play an important role in market research in identifying and analyzing new trends, distribution patterns, competitive studies, new market potentials, and so on. It is most helpful when examining new markets to determine how customers buy, what they buy, and where they buy it. Organizing a task force of field sales personnel for such tasks and demanding a complete professional report serves two purposes. First and foremost, it gives you the information you want. Secondly, it is a motivator of people, as it is a public recognition of these individuals. It gives them a chance, during the study period, to meet with senior marketing and sales management and to learn how management thinks. From management's viewpoint, it allows you to observe your salespeople in a new planning and thinking role and to evaluate them for future management positions.

If, as a result of that study, your company enters a new market, introduces a new product, or makes any decision, the members of that task force will get great benefit and satisfaction in knowing they played an important part.

Salespeople are in a key position to furnish "intelligence," because they must be familiar with competitors' product strengths and weaknesses, number of salespeople in a territory, and location of offices and factories.

Sales force call reports can provide an excellent source of sales research data, but the salespeople must be alerted as to what to look for and report on.

Other "inside" valuable resources are account executives who call on company accounts, product specialists who are often in contact with customers during product development, service representatives who make daily contact with both customers and end-users, marketing specialists who obtain information on specific markets in order to help satisfy customers' needs and wants, and engineers in the field who are in a position to evaluate the products of both the company and its competitors.

To gain the greatest cooperation from the sales force in information-gathering projects, many companies either furnish salespeople with tape recorders for recording reports between sales calls or have them telephone their reports into the office for a staff person to prepare written reports.

Getting the Lowdown on Competitors

Matthew Lesko, former head of Washington Researchers, put together the following guidelines on how to get information on competitors, as reported in Dartnell's *Sales & Marketing Executive Report:*

Compiling information on a specific company can be very similar to detective work for the researcher. It is very unlikely that you will find a large amount of information in any one place. It is more likely that you will slowly uncover bits and pieces of information from many sources, and as you get deeper into the research you will see that these pieces will gradually fit together to produce a complete picture of the company in question. What follows is a description of information sources that are most likely to be helpful for compiling a profile on almost any company.

1. *The library.* This is a good place to start. The librarians at the business division or reference section of your local public or university library should prove to be very helpful. You will want to perform a current literature search by using current indexes such as Business Periodical Index, F & S Index, and the *Wall Street Journal Index.* Also check to see what information is available in the standard reference publications on corporations produced by such organizations as Standard and Poor's and Dun and Bradstreet. You will also want to investigate Dun and Bradstreet's credit reporting service. Your librarian may have other suggestions.

2. *The company in question.* Call the company itself and ask for sales literature. This should be done early in your search. The information you receive is usually very helpful in identifying the company's clients or other individuals who may be helpful as your work progresses. Once you are along in your research, it is a very useful exercise to ask questions point blank to the executives of the company you are examining. You never know; you may reach someone at a soft moment.

   You also want to try to talk with individuals within different functional divisions of the organization, and with persons at various levels. Throughout your research, periodically call the company switchboard and ask to talk with either customer services representatives, salespeople, the production manager, or even the president.

3. *The federal government.*
   a) *Regulatory Agencies.* If the company is one of approximately 10,000 corporations publicly traded in the United States, you are in luck. The public document room of the Securities and Exchange Commission (SEC) contains masses of useful information. A telephone call to the

SEC's Public Reference Room (202-523-5360) will tell you if your company is required to file any documents.

However, since only approximately 10,000 of the nation's corporations are required to file with the SEC, you may not find this source productive. Remember that throughout the federal government there are countless offices that regulate and investigate the activities of specific industries.

All these offices produce documentation on the work they perform; this documentation is available to the public. A copy of the latest edition of the *U.S. Government Manual* is helpful in identifying specific offices that may help you.

> b) *Federal contracts.* If the company performs any work for the federal government, much of the contract is public information. Contact the procurement offices of those government departments and agencies that you know or suspect may be purchasing the company's goods or services.

> c) *Capitol Hill.* The committees and sub-committees very often investigate the activities of specific industries and companies. There are also many occasions when business executives testify at hearings held by these committees. You can call Capitol Hill to see if there is a committee interested in the industry or the company you are researching, or you can consult the *Congressional Information Index* at your local library. This publication provides an indexing service to hearings and other publications from Capitol Hill.

4. *State sources.* Every corporation doing business within a state must file disclosure information that is available to the public. In addition to articles of incorporation, in nearly every state the company must also file an annual report. The amount of detail contained in an annual report varies from state to state. Under the Uniform Commercial Code, the company must also disclose if any of the assets are offered as collateral on a promissory note. Corporations whose stock is publicly traded only within one state are not

required to file with the Federal Securities and Exchange Commission, but they are required to file with the state securities office in the state where they are located. The place to start for information on any of these three areas is the Secretary of State's office.

5. *Industry observers.* Individuals who spend their careers observing the industry in which the company in question operates, can offer unique insight into how the company compares with its competitors. These observers can be trade association executives, trade periodical editors, or one of the industry analysts at the U.S. Dept. of Commerce. Your local library can show you reference publications identifying the appropriate associations or publications. The Office of the Ombudsman at the U.S. Dept. of Commerce can connect you with one of its industry analysts.

6. *Local organizations.* Once you have identified the hometown of the company, you should contact the local chamber of commerce. If possible, you should talk to its research department and to one of the chamber executives. A very important local source that is often overlooked is the local newspaper. Talk to an editor or reporter of the financial section.

7. *Customers and suppliers.* The names of such organizations may be difficult to obtain and the degree of difficulty will vary with the industry in question. A list of customers may be in the company's literature. The industry observers may be helpful here in suggesting whom to contact. Also, once you obtain one name, that company may be able to provide you with several others. Using this method, your list can quickly grow. You should always remember to follow the chain of distribution. Just because a manufacturer sells exclusively to retailers, it is still likely that large distributors of similar products may also know something about the company.

8. *Competitors.* These are probably among the best sources of information on a company. Their survival often depends upon how much they know. Here, too, as in contacting the company itself, you should call several departments within the organization. A copy of Thomas' Register at your local library or a relevant trade periodical should provide you with a list of competitors.

9. *Makers of complementary or alternative products.* You can be sure that the manufacturers of hot dog buns know about those companies that manufacture hot dogs, and that margarine manufacturers know about butter manufacturers. These organizations can be identified by using the same methodology presented under competitors.

10. *International.* If the company you are interested in is based overseas, the U.S. Dept. of Commerce, through its World Traders Data Report Service, can provide you with a profile of almost any company for a modest charge. It is a good starting point.

The sources of information presented above are by no means the only bases to touch when trying to find company information. These sources will provide you with a good start. From here, the researcher must use creativity along with a winning personality. The creativity must lead to sources of information no one else has thought of before; a winning personality is needed to ensure that your sources are cooperative. There are two additional points a researcher must always remember when investigating a company:

1. Each important fact must be verified by at least one individual independent source.

2. Every source contacted has the potential of providing you with at least three additional sources of information. If an information source cannot provide you with relevant material on a company, don't forget to ask for other possible sources of information.

How to Monitor Those Market Developments

Perhaps the best way to sum up most of this chapter is to draw on an article in *Successful Salesmanship* (published in Johannesburg, South Africa), extracted from Robin Hood's book, *Ad Valorem,* which shows businesses how to draw on their in-house resources in order to monitor what is going on in the marketplace.

"Market research is a management tool. The higher you go in the hierarchy of industrial companies, the more revered it becomes. And the farther you go down the line, the more it's disregarded and often disdained. Yet all research is simply a business of asking questions, either to find answers to what you don't *know* about something; or to confirm what you *believe* is so when you're not absolutely sure about it.

"The first questions to ask are those you ask yourself. Do I *need* to know the answer? Do I *need* to confirm a belief? When I have the answer, or the confirmation, is the resulting judgment or decision sufficiently critical to the forthcoming conduct of my business to warrant the cost of a research study? In short, will it pay off?

"Before you embark on a professional investigation, you must be convinced that it is necessary and that it will supply the data you seek—because formal research is costly. And it's probable that do-it-yourself persons will only consider using it when a large number of people have to be interviewed in order to obtain a valid cross section or sample.

"The next question to ask is how to obtain information by using the company's staff. There are two ways: 1) internal, or *desk research,* and 2) external, or *field research.*

"Desk research will embrace:

- Sales analysis from company records—by volume, region, type, and size of customer; customer historic performance; nature of product take-off; cost of making sales; assessment of representatives' effectiveness; market profitability; measurement of market-share (if industry total sales are available); and so forth.

- Other data, from government, industry, and other available statistics; evaluation of industry trends; assessment of company performance relative to the economic activity of specific markets; analysis of the market potential for new products.

"Field research will cover:

- *Product.* Applications; customer attitudes; adaptions of improvements made by customers; performance of competitive products; market reaction to product range rationalization; assessing acceptability of, and potential for, proposed new products; relationship of existing products to technological developments in specific industrial sectors.

- *Service.* Customer attitudes and suggestions for improvement or additional facilities; competitive strengths and weaknesses.

- *Market.* Short, medium, and longer-term climate; effects of mergers, takeovers, and diversification activities; identification and assessment of levels of importance of recommenders, influencers, and decision-makers in the purchasing progression.

"Desk research, particularly sales analysis, should be a continuous process dedicated to the provision, interpretation, and application of the data disclosed.

"Field research comes in three categories:

1. *The day-to-day gathering of any useful information by all staff in contact with customers.* This includes the reporting of rumors for evaluation by management and possible further investigation.

2. *A specific instruction to the company's representatives to seek intelligence of a given nature.* This instruction may be isolated or may form part of a monthly information-gathering program designed, over a period of time, to cover the overall situation in the marketplace.

3. *A formal survey, of one kind or another.* Use of a written questionnaire to supply answers to questions or confirma-

tion of beliefs, relative to product, service, or market. These surveys may be undertaken by sales staff or by management, depending on their geographical scope and on the extent of probing necessary to uncover the data required.

"Many companies will engage, as a regular practice, in the basic activities described in the first two categories. Conversely, too few employ formal research methods to guide them in the direction they're proposing to travel. Yet there is nothing esoteric in the technique, unlike that applied to the highly specialized field of consumer research. Planning and conducting a field survey will develop along these lines:

1. *State research objectives clearly.* Limit these strictly to essentials—preferably one only. A thirst for peripheral knowledge leads to lengthy, tiresome questionnaires that irritate respondents and encourage misleading answers.

2. *Define respondent groups.* Interviews will normally be sought with a single information source—influencers, recommenders, or decision makers. If the primary objective is to discover who these are—either by name in individual companies or by title across the board—the respondents will often be determined according to size of company: presidents in smaller ones and managers in bigger organizations. Respondent groups will otherwise be described by industrial category or by whatever classification is relevant.

3. *Prepare a provisional questionnaire.* Draft questions designed to reveal desired answers. Examine questions carefully and objectively to eliminate ambiguities. Ensure that none is included which does not bear directly on survey objectives. Questions will generally be phrased to yield:

   • Yes, no, or other categorical answer.

   • A positioning on a continuum, or scale of values, which may be verbal or numerical.

   • A verbatim playback of respondents' experience or opinions, which need recording as longhand notes. (These may be amplified by the interviewer by dictation on a portable recorder.)

Try a questionnaire on a small sample of typical respondents to iron out bugs and establish that the data required are coming to light in a usable form. Time these interviews so that respondents to the survey proper may be informed of the likely length of proposed meetings. (Resistance may be met if these require more than 30 minutes.)

Questionnaire forms should always begin with a statement of survey objectives and how the company expects to use information gathered for the benefit of the respondent group. This statement will be memorized by interviewers and delivered in a normal conversational manner. Provision will be made, of course, for name of respondent, title, company and its classification, and interview date.

4. *Arrange interviews.* These may be solicited from a list of all companies in the industrial category as defined. The survey would then be described as embracing the population, or universe, of that category. If this is too large for practical purposes, a sample of the population may be covered. This must be big enough to be representative of the whole and should be subdivided into appropriate sub-samples, such as small, medium, and large companies; and geographical representation. As a rule, interviews will be sought by phone, with the solicitor stating the survey objectives and length of time normally needed to complete the questionnaire.

If information is wanted from any companies who may be able to give it, but who have not been identified by name or industry category, representatives could be allocated a particular industrial area to canvass. The technique is to call on every likely-looking company in the area, explain to the receptionist why the call is being made, and ask if a suitable person is free to be interviewed. If not, ask whether an appointment may be made for an interview at another time. This kind of open-ended survey continues until sufficient data have been accumulated, or until, after repeated calling, no new data have been disclosed.

5. *Analyze and interpret survey data.*

6. *Apply the information yielded, as appropriate.*

7. *Write to all individuals interviewed.* Thank them for help given and describe briefly the outcome of the survey, especially as this may benefit the respondent group. *Never* use these letters to solicit the respondents' customer unless the door was left open for this when interviewing. Contact subsequently may be renewed, at which time the survey can be mentioned and a meeting requested in the ordinary course of business.

"These brief observations on the role of market research, and its application, are designed to encourage do-it-yourself companies to consider its use."

Chapter 14

Market Data Sources

The next step in the development of a successful sales campaign is how to obtain the basic market information. Where can you obtain it and how reliable is it?

In the preceding chapter, we discussed market analysis, along with consumer research, motivation research, and the determination of consumer preferences, as a means of obtaining quality control in product design. In this chapter, we shall discuss market analysis for quantitative determination. Assuming that the product is in marketable shape, where can it be sold and in what quantities?

This knowledge is necessary on a regional and geographical area basis, as well as on an economic and population-stratification basis. Products that can be sold on the Atlantic coast may have limited demand on the Pacific coast; some may be in demand in the South but not in the North or even in the Midstates. Nationality and ethnic groups also vary greatly.

Not only must the segmented and overall quantities of the product demand be known, but also the growth pattern and probable future trend in demand must be understood. With this knowledge, production requirements can be estimated, cash flow and capital investment demands can be foreseen, sales coverage and personnel requirements can be anticipated, and territories and compensation programs laid out.

Fortunately, there is a wealth of statistical data available as to past demand and flow of products, and on those economic and geographical factors that contribute to such movements. Some of the important sources for these data are listed in this chapter, together with the major classifications of data included.

TYPES OF MARKETING DATA

Marketing data fall into two broad classification groups:

1. *Primary,* which originate from company records, field sales reports and direct interviews with consumers, buyers, dealers, and wholesalers.

2. *Secondary,* which, after being collected, are published for use by others. By far the most prolific dispenser of secondary data is the U.S. Government. It collects a wealth of statistics that, while sometimes late in distribution, are inexpensive, easy to obtain, and often exceedingly useful.

Government Data

These publications are obtained from the Superintendent of Documents, U.S. Government Printing Office, Washington, D.C. 20402.

Population Statistics. These data are from the Decennial Census of the population of the United States, made by the Bureau of the Census. They include statistics on the number of inhabitants for states, counties, other civil divisions (townships, incorporated and unincorporated cities and towns, wards of cities) and for urbanized areas. They also cover such characteristics of the population, by the above geographical and political areas, as race and color, age, nativity, citizenship, country of birth, marital status, household and family units, education, employment status, occupation and industry classification, and income.

These data have been collected, in expanded form, since 1790. Thus they provide valuable information on both current conditions and on trends in population growth and characteristic changes.

A sales executive wishing, for example, to plan ahead for possible sales in a regional market composed of young-married, native-white, college-educated persons in a medium-income bracket could use such data to advantage.

Census of Housing. These data are based upon tabulations from the Decennial Census on Housing. They include such occupancy characteristics for states, standard metropolitan areas, cities, and urbanized areas as: occupancy and tenure, race and color of occupants, population per occupied dwelling unit, number of persons per room. There are data on such structural characteristics as numbers of rooms per housing unit, type of structure and year built; on such plumbing facilities as water supply, toilets, and baths; on equipment and fuels used, such as electric lighting, radio, television, refrigerators, kitchen sinks, and heating and cooling fuels. There are statistics on contract monthly rent, gross monthly rent, value of housing units, and mortgage status.

Thus, a sales executive wishing, for example, to determine the saturation status and the replacement market for kitchen cabinets or carpeting in a certain area can readily do so with these data.

Census of Manufacturers. These data are collected by the Bureau of the Census from manufacturers, trade associations, and government agencies. This census has been made periodically since 1809, and contains a wealth of information on many aspects of our manufacturing economy. Data by geographical area and for many individual industries are available on number of employees, production, related work man-hours, cost and quantity of materials consumed in production, value of shipments made by individual and class of products, value added in manufacture, inventories, expenditures for plant and equipment, fuels consumed, electric energy and water used, horsepower of equipment, selected metalworking operations and equipment employed, distribution of manufacturers' shipments, plant specialization, data on individual groups of companies, and indexes of physical volume of production for many individual and groups of industries.

Products and services needed by manufacturers can be pinpointed with this data and segmentation by type of industry can be strategically accomplished.

Census of Business. The data presented in these reports cover the retail, wholesale, and selected service trades. They are collected by the Bureau of the Census from mail canvasses of business establishments and records of the Internal Revenue Service and the Bureau of Old Age and Survivors' Insurance. There are data on the number of establishments, sales, payrolls, and number of paid employees for many types of businesses, such as food stores, eating and drinking places, general merchandise groups, apparel and accessories stores, furniture and appliance stores, automotive dealers and accessories, lumber and building-material dealers, drugstores, and other retail outlets.

A manufacturer of food preparation products could gain information as to the geographical markets for his products by referring to the statistics on eating places or drinking places. A publisher of books could find equally valuable information on relative sales of bookstores in selected geographical areas.

Data covering the *wholesale trade* include the number of establishments by type of operation and commodity lines, inventories at the year end, operating expenses, payrolls, number of employees, single-unit or multiple-unit operation, credit sales, receivables, bad-debt losses, warehouse space, bulk-storage capacity of petroleum, bulk plants and terminals, sales by merchandise agents and brokers, and bin space of grain elevators.

For *selected services,* data cover the number of establishments (by annual receipts groups), receipts, payrolls, and number of employees and proprietors. Those selected include (but are not limited to) such personal services as barber and beauty shops, funeral homes, photograph studios, laundries, and Turkish baths. They include such business services as advertising agencies, credit agencies, news syndicates, duplicating services, detective agencies, sign-painting shops, automobile-repair garages, parking lots, watch and clock repair, blacksmiths, and bicycle shops. Many types of amusement services are included, such as movie theaters, poolrooms, bowling alleys, race tracks, baseball fields, golf courses, swimming pools, and dance halls; also hotels (year-round and seasonal), motels, trailer parks, and recreation camps.

Censuses are taken as follows:

- *Population and housing censuses.* Every 10th year ending in "0"—for example, 1980 and 1990.

- *Government census.* Every fifth year ending in "2" or "7"—for example, 1982 and 1987.

- *Business, manufacturers, and mineral industries censuses.* Every fifth year ending in "2" or "7"—i.e., 1982 and 1987.

- *Agriculture census.* Usually every fifth year ending in "4" or "9"—for example, 1984 and 1989.

Thus, a sales executive could obtain data that would assist him in estimating the market for air hoses used by service garages, for diving boards used at swimming pools, self-propelled caddy cars used on golf courses, or popcorn sold in movie theaters.

United States Census of Agriculture. This census has been taken periodically since 1840. The current data include information for states and counties as to the number of farms, acreage, value, use, color, and tenure of operator, class of work power and specified equipment, labor force and expenditures, wage rates, livestock and poultry, nursery, greenhouses, forest products, and specified crops harvested.

Should a manufacturer of grain storage silos or of tractors wish to appraise the potentiality of new markets or their growth trends, he could readily do so by reference to these statistics.

County and City Data Book. Published by the Bureau of the Census, U.S. Department of Commerce.

Mineral Yearbook. Published by the U.S. Bureau of Mines.

Statistical Abstract of the United States. All the above referred data and a great deal more are conveniently summarized in this publication. Convenient as a reference source for these data, the abstract offers a guide to other statistical publications and sources for more detailed information when needed.

Federal Reserve Bulletins. Current monthly data of significance relating to financial and business developments in the United States are contained in this publication, including department-store sales, consumer-credit estimates, production indexes for an extensive list of industries, construction activities, wholesale and consumer prices for many products, interest, rates, security prices, and real-estate credit.

From these data, a sales executive can quickly trace the trends in the production of paper and paper products, in tobacco products, or in construction.

Survey of Current Business. This is a monthly publication issued by the U.S. Department of Commerce. It contains current business statistics of the nature outlined in various census reports and other surveys. Included are many phases of the national income and production, such as personal income, new plant and equipment expenditures, farm income and marketing, industrial production for a broad list of specified industries, wholesale and consumer prices for numerous products, construction expenditures for various classifications of buildings, retail trade, employment and earnings, transportation and equipment, and security prices.

These data are broad in scope, currently maintained, and extend far enough back to provide meaningful trend analyses. This publication is a useful tool for the analytically minded sales executive.

For information on other government publications, reference should be made to the following:

Monthly Catalog of U.S. Public Documents. A list of current printed material of the federal government, classified by various departments.

Government Reports Announcements and Index. National Technical Information Service. Technical and research literature that, in general, is not covered in the Monthly Catalog.

Commerce Publications Update. A biweekly listing of latest titles from the U.S. Department of Commerce.

Government Periodicals and Subscription Services.

In preparation for a National Marketing Conference in Washington, attended by company presidents, marketing executives, and government officials, the Business and Defense Services Administration of the U.S. Department of Commerce prepared a list of publications of interest to the marketing community. It included:

- *Business Conditions Digest*

- *Business Statistics* (included in above *Survey of Current Business*)

- *Bureau of Census Catalog*

- *Census of Business 1982* (write GPO* for list)

---

*Government Printing Office

- *Census of Housing 1980* (write GPO for list)
- *Census of Manufacturers 1982* (write GPO for list)
- *Census of Population 1980* (write GPO for list)
- *Census Publications from GPO*
- *Census of Transportation* (write GPO for list)
- *Commerce Business Daily*
- *Business America*
- *County Business Patterns* (53 reports)
- *Current Population Reports*
- *Current Retail Trade Reports* (write GPO for list)
- *Franchise Opportunities Handbook*
- *Monthly Catalog of U.S. Government Publications*
- *Monthly Product Announcement*
- *Monthly Wholesale Trade Report: Sales and Inventories*
- *Patents, General Information Concerning*
- *Pocket Data Book, U.S.A.*
- *Statistical Abstract of the United States* (issued annually)

Other Sources of Statistical Information

Besides the federal government, many states collect information in great detail. They list manufacturers in urban and rural civil areas, showing the types of products manufactured, the number of male and female employees, average yearly sales, and other pertinent data. Chambers of Commerce are also important sources of local information, including local weather conditions, availability of water, taxes, transport, and labor markets.

Many magazines, radio broadcasting and television stations, and newspapers issue periodic reports based on consumer panels and individual surveys. Consumer analyses are published yearly by all major media in principal American cities.

Such data cover the buying habits and the overall use of many types of products in selected markets, as well as the leading brands in consumer preference. Included are items such as baby foods, baking mixes, baked beans, breakfast foods, dog foods, frozen food, juices, pie-crust mix, waxed paper, and many others. There are data on the brand preference of soaps, laundry starch, steel wool, and waxes; on alcoholic beverages, beer, ginger ale, nail polish, electric shavers, toothpaste; on clothes dryers, dishwashers, electric mangles, sewing machines, television receivers; on antifreeze, brassieres, cigars, hosiery, and tires.

From these data, a sales executive can appraise the value of individual markets for instant coffee versus packaged coffee; for safety razors versus electric razors; for gas ranges versus electric ranges; and so on.

Trade associations are prolific collectors and distributors of information concerning the operations of their industries. These data often include operating expenses and sales force compensation policies, as well as production or sales. Although individual companies contribute to the collection of these data, some of the contributors do not use them to their full advantage.

For example, a manufacturer of work gloves had sent elaborate sales reports each month for years to his trade association, and had religiously examined the returned reports received. However, he had not maintained any continuous time records of his position in the industry and was amazed to find, when they were presented to him, that although his sales had grown steadily for the past five years, he had actually been losing his industry position. A manufacturer of packaged peanut-butter sandwiches was similarly chagrined when he was presented with time records of his sales as compared with those of his industry.

Other sources of useful market data include:

- *Advertising Age:* 740 N. Rush St., Chicago, Illinois 60611

- *Automobile Registrations:* Reuben H. Donnelley Corporation, 2000 Clearwater Dr., Oak Brook, Illinois 60521

- *Bacon's Clipping Bureau:* 14 E. Jackson Blvd., Chicago, Illinois 60604

- *New Car Registrations:* Reuben H. Donnelley Corporation

- *Construction Contracts Awarded:* F. W. Dodge Corporation, 1221 Avenue of the Americas, New York 10020

Sales and Marketing Management, 633 Third Avenue, New York, New York 10017, publishes the following surveys:

- *Survey of U.S. Industrial & Commercial Buying Power.* Includes U.S. totals for four-digit Standard Industrial Code (SIC) industries and state & county SIC totals.

- *Survey of Buyer Power Part I.*

- *Survey of Buying Power Part II.* Includes an annual survey of newspaper and TV markets.

- *Survey of Test Markets.* A sample is shown at the end of this chapter.

- *Survey of Selling Costs.* Includes metro sales costs, compensation, sales meetings and sales training, and sales support and incentives.

- *Survey of Buying Power Data Service.*

- *The Computer in Sales & Marketing.* An annual directory of personal computer-based sales and marketing applications software.

Additional sources are listed in the Principal Business Directories listing in the Ready-Reference section at the end of this Handbook.

There are also a number of companies that conduct ongoing market research programs for their clients, such as A. C. Nielsen Co., Northbrook, Illinois, and Starch/INRA/Hooper, Inc., Mamaroneck, New York.

Although the greatest portion of the findings of these companies are private, they also occasionally publish some public information.

Maps also are useful in planning marketing campaigns. Following are two major sources for map material:

1. Rand McNally Marketing Aids
   Rand McNally & Company, P.O. Box 7600, Chicago, Illinois 60680.

   - *Commercial Reference Map and Guide*

   - *Zip Coded Atlas*

   - *Green Guide: U.S. Places with Over 100 People*

   - *Yellow Guide: United States Counties*

   - *Sales and Marketing Atlas*

   - *MarketMap—U.S.*

   - *Color MarketMaps II—U.S.*

   - *MarketMaps—State*

   - *MarketMaps—Regional*

   - *Sectional Sales Control Maps*

   - *Zip Code Map of the U.S.*

   - *Thematic Maps*

   - *State Wall Maps*

   - *Cosmopolitan Series Wall Maps*

   - *Cosmopolitan Map Merchandisers*

   - *International Travel Planner and Appointment Book*

   - *Executive Travel Planner and Appointment Book*

   - *Pocket Travel Planner and Appointment Book*

   - *Travel Planner and Appointment Book*

   - *Road Atlas*

   - *Gift Edition Road Atlas*

- *Deluxe Road Atlas*
- *Business Traveler's Road Atlas*
- *Business Traveler's City Guide*
- *Compact Road Atlas*
- *Motor Carriers' Road Atlas*
- *Deluxe Motor Carriers' Road Atlas*

2. American Map Company, 46–35 54th Road, Maspeth, New York 11378

- *Business Control Atlas*
- *Cleartype Outline Maps with populations*
- *Cleartype Market, Media, Mail, Road and Rail Maps*
- *Sectional Maps*
- *Cleartype-Colorprint Sales Maps*
- *Travel Maps*

DUN'S MARKETING SERVICES (A DIVISION OF DUN AND BRADSTREET)

The major product line of Dun's Marketing Services are computer services, market research, and business directories, which utilize certain parts of the information contained in Business Information Reports as their basic ingredient. Information extracted from reports is stored in a computer data bank that contains information of approximately 4.2 million business establishments and is believed to be the largest computerized source of business information in the world.

The objective of Dun's Marketing Services is to supply products and services that bring buyer and seller together more economically. Specific services include *Management Information Products* (MIP), which is a computer-generated marketing service used to determine and classify markets; *Customer Analysis Service,* a system which combines a company's internal sales activity data with external marketplace data to determine detailed information on that company's marketing efforts and performance; *Vendor Analysis Service,* a service to corporate financial and executive office management, enabling them to analyze purchasing and expenditures in an aggregate form. Direct Response Products (DRP) provides the marketing information output on various mailing labels or magnetic tape.

Dun's Marketing Services publishes three marketing directories: *Million Dollar Directory, Middle Market Directory,* and *Metalworking Directory.*

In addition, Dun's Marketing Services is the prime selling vehicle for five international marketing directories: *Principal International Businesses, Canadian Key Business Directory, Guide to Key British Enterprises, The Australian Key Business Directory,* and the *Guide to Irish Manufacturers.*

Practical Use of Marketing Data

Examples of the use of marketing data may suggest possibilities for preliminary research probing by sales executives. More exhaustive and detailed studies should be conducted by trained statisticians and marketing professionals.

A manufacturer of electric-line power connectors, clamps, fittings, and accessories used in the transmission and distribution of electric energy by utilities, telephone companies, and industrial plants was able to appraise the market potential and his industry position by reference to dollar shipment of pole and transmission hardware as reported by the U.S. Department of Commerce, corrected for price inflation by use of price indexes for nonferrous metals and for finished hardware. Although these indexes were not fully applicable, they did represent the cost of nonferrous metals and labor involved in manufacture. By applying them, an indication was obtained of physical volume. From Dun and Bradstreet reports, analysis was also made of competitive sales.

Capital expenditures by the electrical industry in transmission and distribution facilities, for a seven-year period; the number of meters installed each year during that period; a projection of these data by McGraw-Hill's *Electrical Industry Statistics* and the companies' sales for the preceding eight years were studied and compared. This analysis indicated that the connector industry had not grown over the period under study and would probably remain somewhat level in the foreseeable future. On the other hand, the company had enjoyed good growth, which was considerably better than that of the industry. With this knowledge, the company was in a position to make sound plans for the future.

By referring to information on water systems (jet, nonjet, and submersible pumps) published by the U.S. Department of Commerce in *Facts for Industry,* a manufacturer of domestic water pumps found that there had been little increase in the number of units sold by the industry during the previous nine years; in fact, there had been a decline for three years. The company, on the other hand, had improved its position slightly each year. This meant that although the number of units it had sold each year had declined in recent years, the trend had been less severe than for the industry as a whole. Future planning for sales was predicated on this knowledge.

A national distributor of residential heating equipment was interested in determining the marketing potentials and trends of air and water heating systems. From the *American Gas Association Directory,* he obtained information as to the number of manufacturers of steam boilers, of central gas furnaces, and of unit heaters. From *Facts for Industry,* information was obtained on unit production of boilers and radiation (radiators, convectors and baseboards, both cast iron and nonferrous); from the Department of Commerce and the National Warm Air Heating and Air Conditioning Association, data on unit production of warm air furnaces were obtained. These data permitted the company to compare trends of the two types of systems and of its percentage of the volume sold.

Data on one-family and multifamily, nonframe dwelling units, by geographical areas of the country, were obtained from the U.S. Department of Labor statistics. This permitted the company to measure the relative importance of the different areas and its penetration into those markets. As a result of this study, the company dropped its line of hot-water systems.

A manufacturer interested in the sale of camp trailers wished to appraise the growth possibilities of his market. From reports by the U.S. Department of Agriculture Forestry Service, he obtained information as to the number of people visiting national forests for the primary purpose of camping during each of the previous 10 years. From reports by the U.S. Department of the Interior National Park Service, he obtained similar information as to the national and state parks. These data showed a 200 percent increase in visits per year over the period. Camper days at state parks showed the national distribution of interest, California having the highest percentage (23.1 percent of national), Michigan (14.2 percent), and New York (14.1 percent). From these data, he established sales objectives and determined distribution policies.

At a number of universities across the United States, data archives and data libraries are already operating, collecting statistics from the federal government, from survey organizations, private sources, state governments, and academic institutions. Currently, most of their requests come from users within the academic community, although a few, like Columbia University's Center for the Social Sciences, are doing data searches for private-sector organizations and corporations.

An example of what data archives can produce is shown in Table 1, page 383, the Oakland, California, Sampler, developed in *Sales & Marketing Management's Survey of Buying Power.*

Census of Governments

In the 1987 Census of Governments conducted by the Commerce Department's Census Bureau, these are a few of the multitude of questions asked: How many governments are there in the U.S.? How many state and local officials are directly elected? How many are women? Blacks? Hispanics? The tabulation of race and sex is a first.

The Bureau will scan more than 82,000 local governments and all states, school districts, and special districts.

The first government census was taken in 1840. Results of the last one were published in 14 reports. Most of the data are received

Table 1. Oakland, California, Sampler

1984 Population: 1,875,800
Median age: 32.2 yrs.
% of population age 25-34: 19.4%
Total households: 726,300
Total Effective Buying Income (EBI): $25,682,910,000
Median Household EBI: $32,005
% of households with EBIs in excess of $50,000: 22.5%
Total retail sales: $11,587,461,000
General merchandise sales: $1,490,948,000
Food store sales: $2,373,522,000
Automotive dealer sales: $2,519,355,000
Total shipments, all manufacturing industries: $14,776.5 Mil.
Total manufacturing establishments: 873
Major industry shipments/receipts:
  Metals cans (SIC 3411)—$390.2 Mil.
  Internal combustion engines (SIC 3519)—$359.5 Mil.
  Cane-sugar refining (SIC 2062)—$611.4 Mil.
  Petroleum refining (SIC 2911)—$4,609.2 Mil.
  Nuclear power (SIC 4912)—$943.0 Mil.
Projected population, 1989: 1,995,500
Projected total households, 1989: 789,500
Projected average household EBI, 1989: $35,361
Oakland newspaper market coverage:
  726,300 households (35.1% household coverage)
Oakland (San Francisco) TV market coverage:
  2,080.6 households
  (Population age 2-11, 653,800)
Average daily lodging cost: $60.35
Average daily meal costs: $30.65
Cost of two drinks: $4.00
Taxi, airport to downtown: $14.00
Distance and travel time, airport to downtown:
  11 miles, 10-15 minutes

Sources: S&MM's *1985 Survey of Buying Power, Parts I & II; 1985 Survey of Industrial & Commercial Buying Power; 1985 Survey of Selling Costs.*
©Sales & Marketing Management

by mail, but much information comes from state sources, published records, and field representatives.

State and local governments are important elements of the economy. In fiscal year 1982–83, says the Census Bureau, they spent $567 billion, or 12.4 percent of the gross national product.

Special districts are the fastest growing segment of government. In 1982 they totaled 28,000, representing a 10-percent gain between that year and 1977. Special districts manage activities such as flood control, public housing, hospitals, or fire protection.

Results of the 1987 census are available in two volumes: *Governmental Organization* and *Popularly Elected Officials*.

The Nation's Most Popular Test Markets

Listed here are the nation's most often used test markets, established by studies by *S&MM* and revised every year. *S&MM* defines a standard market as one where companies sell the product through normal distribution channels and monitor the results, often by using an auditing service.

Akron
Albany-Schenectady-Troy
Albuquerque
Ann Arbor
Atlanta
Augusta, GA
Austin
Bakersfield
Baltimore-Washington, DC
Bangor
Baton Rouge
Beaumont-Port Arthur-
    Orange, TX
Binghamton, NY
Birmingham-Anniston
Boise
Boston
Buffalo

Canton
Cedar Rapids-Waterloo
Charleston, SC
Charleston, WV
Charlotte
Chattanooga
Chicago
Cincinnati
Cleveland
Colorado Springs
Columbia, SC
Columbus, GA
Columbus, OH
Corpus Christi
Dallas-Forth Worth
Dayton
Denver-Boulder
Des Moines

Detroit
Duluth-Superior
El Paso
Erie, PA
Eugene, OR
Evansville
Flint
Fort Smith, AR
Fort Wayne
Fresno
Grand Rapids-Kalamazoo-
  Battle Creek
Green Bay-Appleton, WI
Greensboro-Winston-Salem-
  High Point
Greenville-Spartanburg-
  Asheville
Harrisburg
Hartford
Houston
Huntsville
Indianapolis
Jacksonville, FL
Kansas City, MO
Knoxville
Lansing
Las Vegas
Lexington, KY
Lincoln, NB
Little Rock
Los Angeles
Louisville
Lubbock, TX
Macon, GA
Madison
Manchester, NH
Memphis

Miami-Fort Lauderdale
Milwaukee
Minneapolis-St. Paul
Mobile
Modesto
Montgomery
Nashville
New Haven
New Orleans
Newport News
New York
Oklahoma City
Omaha-Council Bluffs
Orlando-Daytona Beach
Pensacola
Peoria
Philadelphia
Phoenix
Pittsburgh
Portland, ME
Portland, OR
Poughkeepsie
Providence
Quad Cities: Rock Island &
  Moline, IL; Davenport &
  Bettendorf, IA
  (Davenport-Rock Island-
  Moline metro market)
Raleigh-Durham
Reading, PA
Reno-Carson City
Roanoke-Lynchburg
Rochester, NY
Rockford
Sacramento-Stockton
Salem, OR
Salinas-Monterey

Salt Lake City
St. Louis
San Antonio
San Diego
San Francisco-Oakland
Savannah
Seattle-Tacoma
Shreveport
Sioux Falls, SD
South Bend-Elkhart
Spokane
Springfield, MA
Springfield, MO

Springfield-Decatur-
  Champaign, IL
Syracuse
Tallahassee
Tampa-St. Petersburg
Toledo
Topeka
Tucson
Tulsa
West Palm Beach
Wichita-Hutchinson
Youngstown

Chapter 15

Sales Forecasting

A fundamental step in all sales planning activities is making the sales forecast. Predictions of future revenues are key to intelligent business planning. From a marketing standpoint, sales forecasting is an attempt to predict sales conditions and situations from one to five years in the future. In discussing the subject in his column "Marketing Management Viewpoint," Dale J. Thomas states:

"The marketing and product manager involved in forecasting must always remember one thing. The forecasts which he or she develops have significant impact upon virtually every department and activity in his or her company. This places upon that manager a gigantic responsibility to ensure that the forecasts provided are made only after thorough and thoughtful deliberation and calculation.

"There are three common steps in the preparation of a forecast: 1) information gathering, 2) analysis and projection, and 3) application. Typical of the information gathered for forecasting are past sales records, data concerning changes in business conditions and changes in competition, and changes in internal factors, such as product line and sales force. Some more experienced marketing managers will occasionally include reports of government published indexes to add further sophistication to their data base.

"Once the analysis and basic projections are completed, the marketing manager must finally apply those projections to his or her own specific circumstance (products); the result is a forecast. This process constitutes the third step in forecasting-application."

The Importance to Company Planning

The sales forecast is the key to all planning and budgeting activities in the company, and it can be the basic tool for planning all of the next year's activities. The functional areas of the business include:

- Production scheduling
- Inventory control
- Sales quotas
- Goals for incentive compensation
- Cash flow planning
- Earnings forecast
- Advertising and promotion plans
- Product planning
- Personnel requirements and territory layout

Sales Forecasting Periods

A survey of companies indicated that forecasts are prepared primarily on an annual basis, followed by quarterly and semiannual time periods. The sales forecasting period usually coincides with the company's fiscal period because of the dependency on it by other company planning functions.

However, while forecasts are made on an annual basis, they are subject to periodic review during the year and adjusted to fit the existing or changing conditions as the year progresses.

Types of Forecasts

The sales forecast can take many forms. While "total dollar sales" is the most widely used for general company planning, additional breakdowns can be made quite easily through computer data processing equipment. These may be used for setting salespeople's goals and compensation rewards and as a refined aid in production, capital and personnel needs. Here are some of the breakdowns that can be made for more intelligent, finite planning:

- Total dollar sales
- By geographic area or territory
- Product units
- By major product lines
- Special forecasts for new product introductions
- By channel of distribution
- Special forecasts for contests or promotions

Factors Affecting Sales Volume

To reduce the "crystal-balling" element in forecasting, many factors must be considered in order to obtain the most accurate forecast possible.

1. Internal, or company conditions, such as product life cycle, price adjustments—either up or down—change of distribution channels, product line or product changes, size of field force, promotion/advertising expenditures, changes in telemarketing and/or trade show activities.

2. Industry activity, such as what the competition is doing in terms of price, product, advertising, strength of field force; new competitors entering the market affecting market share.

3. General business conditions and government regulation activity.

Limitations on Growth

While in some instances, the sales *potential* may be the same as the sales *forecast,* there are several reasons why the forecast can be less than the potential. From a practical point of view, a number of limitations, in addition to the capacity of the market, can restrict the sales growth of a company. They include:

- Decision not to sell beyond a given geographic area
- Desire to limit expansion

- Limit on expanding manufacturing capacity and overhead

- Lack of qualified sales and sales management personnel

- Threat of competitive reaction

- Decision not to utilize additional sales and distribution channels

- Legal restrictions

- Conservation of cash for acquisition expansion

All of these possible factors, where applicable, will have an effect on the final forecast of sales and should be given proper consideration.

Forecasting Methods

A Dartnell survey revealed that there are innumerable approaches to sales forecasting, ranging from intensive statistical analysis to subjective opinion. Let's review and comment on the most commonly used methods.

Jury of Executive Opinion. This is the oldest and simplest technique. It works best when there are few executives involved. In essence, this method utilizes the opinions of top executives, combining and averaging their views. It is felt this results in a more sound forecast of sales than a single estimator could make. These rule-of-thumb estimators can arrive at their opinions on the basis of fact, observation, and intuition.

The persons in this group usually include the president, sales manager, marketing executive (with input from the market research group), financial officer, advertising manager, and the production executive. The president makes a final estimate based on opinions expressed, or he or she may average the estimates for a representative forecast.

A disadvantage of this method is that, because the results are based on personal opinions, a personal bias could be injected by participants with no sales or marketing backgrounds. Therefore, it is important, if not vital, that members of the jury have access to sales statistics, economic forecasts, and marketing and sales reports before rendering opinions.

Sales Force Composite. This method is a process for obtaining the combined views of the field sales force as to the future sales outlook in their territories. This is the most commonly used method, because companies feel that a salesperson, who is in closer contact with the market than anyone else in the company, is better able to judge what is likely to take place in his or her area of sales activity. It is generally felt that the broad base formed by many individual estimates results in a more accurate overall forecast.

Individual sales projections, by customers and products, are made on special forms provided by the home office and are usually based on historical records of each salesperson. The regional, district, and/or general sales executive adjusts these individual forecasts, based on experience and knowledge of the salesperson and on the broad economic and company picture.

A big plus for using this method lies in the fact that it places most of the responsibility of forecasting in the hands of those who must meet the established goals, so that each salesperson sharing in the responsibility of implementing the sales program takes part in its development.

A disadvantage most often cited is the contention that if the forecast is used as a basis for subsequent quotas, a salesperson will tend to understate the sales projection. This is where the experience and judgment of the salesperson's superior(s) comes into play to make any calculated adjustments. Some companies control this possible problem by offering a bonus if sales efforts come within five percent of forecast. Another control method is to set territory advertising and sales promotion expenditures on the basis of a salesperson's forecast and, if the forecast is too low, the salesperson's promotional support and income would be cut for the year.

The Delphi Technique. This method was developed by the Rand Corporation. Instead of a group meeting, each executive involved makes an anonymous forecast and sends it to the leader of the group. The forecasts are combined, averaged, and a median forecast is returned to the members of the group. Each member makes a second forecast and the process is repeated until a consensus is reached.

The advantage of interfacing with other members in a group meeting is lost in this approach and the final result is a composite of figures not broken down by products, customers, and territories. Obtaining these breakdowns requires additional time and effort by sales staff members. It is important that, as in the case of the jury of executive opinion, each participant has access to the same sales statistics, economic forecasts, and marketing and sales reports before making his or her forecast.

Customer Survey. This method basically involves asking key customers, on a personal basis, of their buying intentions for the coming year. It is important to note that this technique should be limited to well-identified buyers, preferably the top 20 percent of customers, who can be relied on to give honest and accurate responses. This method serves as an excellent supplement to other forecasting methods.

Other Methods

In addition to the methods described, there are others that are helpful in supplementing or reinforcing the basic method used.

- *Industry survey* involves making a forecast of the probable future year's sales of the industry. Then an estimate is made of the percentage of sales the company could capture.

- The *product line analysis* is a forecast developed by combining the results of independent forecasts of sales of various product lines by government sources, trade associations, trade publications, etc.

- *Trend analysis* is a method of forecasting by studying the basic factors underlying fluctuations in sales. The pattern of sales of any company is largely the result of three basic influences: long-term growth trends, cyclical business fluctuations, and seasonal variations.

Cyclical Trends

Like the best-laid plans of mice and men, the best-planned long-range forecasting can be thrown out of kilter by events such as war, rumors of wars, and recessions. What, then, is the best method for establishing cyclical trends?

One method is by plotting unit sales on a time chart and then drawing an "average" line through the dots; this at least gives a rough comparison.

Seasonal trends can be indicated by totaling sales for individual months, over a period of 5 or 10 years; then taking the percentage of distribution for the 12 months.

Cyclical trends can be indicated by fitting curved lines to the dots obtained on the sales-time chart; a refinement can be achieved by using a moving average line developed by statistical methods.

The U.S. Department of Commerce offers a monthly report, prepared primarily for specialists in business-cycle analysis. This report, entitled "Business Cycle Developments," contains basic economic-time series organized in a convenient form for short-term economic analysis and interpretation. It supplements other reports of the Department of Commerce that provide data for analyzing current business conditions.

The presentation and classification of series in this report follow the business-indicator approach. The classification of series is that designated by the National Bureau of Economic Research, which, for many years, has had the leadership in this field of investigation.

Unique features of the report are the arrangement of economic indicators according to their usual timing relations during the course of the business cycle; a cross-classification of these indicators by nine economic processes: employment and unemployment; production, income, consumption, and trade; fixed capital investment; inventories and inventory investment; prices, costs, and profits; money and credit; foreign trade and payments; federal government activities; and the inclusion of special analytical measures and historical cyclical comparisons that help in evaluating the current stage of the business cycle. These measures are made possible by processing on computers.

About 90 principal indicators and over 300 of their components are used for the different measures shown. The movements of the series are shown against the background of the expansions and contractions of the general business cycle, so that "leads" and "lags" can readily be detected and unusual cyclical developments spotted. Almost all the basic data are available in published reports. The chief merits of this report are the speed with which the data for indicators are collected, assembled, and published, and the arrangement of the series for business-cycle studies. Composite monthly indexes of leading, coinciding, and lagging indicators provide convenient summaries of the data.

As an example, here is a report of how principal business indicators might look. Those indicators regarded as especially reliable are distinguished by asterisks (*).

Thirty-six leading indicators

1. Average workweek of production workers, manufacturing*

2. Nonagricultural placements*

3. Accession rate, manufacturing

4. Initial claims for unemployment insurance, state programs

5. Layoff rate, manufacturing

6. Index of net business formation*

7. Number of new-business incorporations

8. New orders, durable-goods industries*

9. Construction contracts, total value

10. Contracts and orders for plant and equipment*

11. Newly approved capital appropriations, 1,000 manufacturing corporations

12. New orders, machinery and equipment industries

13. Construction contracts awarded for commercial and industrial buildings, floor space

14. New private nonfarm housing units started

15. Index of private housing units authorized by local building permits*

16. Change in business inventories, all industries

17. Change in book value, manufacturing and trade inventories*

18. Purchased materials, percent reporting higher inventories

19. Change in book value, manufacturers' inventories of materials and supplies

20. Buying policy, material, percent reporting commitments 60 days or longer

21. Vendor performance, percent reporting slower deliveries

22. Change in manufacturers' unfilled orders, durable-goods industries

23. Industrial-materials prices*

24. Stock prices, 500 common stocks*

25. Corporate profits after taxes*

26. Ratio, profits to income originating, all industries

27. Profits per dollar of sales, corporate, manufacturing

28. Ratio, price to unit labor cost, manufacturing*

29. Change in money supply and time deposits

30. Change in money supply

31. Total private borrowing

32. Change in consumer installment debt*

33. Change in bank loans to businesses

34. Change in mortgage debt

35. Liabilities of business failures

36. Delinquency rate, installment loans

Twenty-five roughly coincident indicators

1. Nonagricultural job openings, number pending

2. Index of help-wanted advertising in newspapers

3. Man-hours in nonfarm establishments

4. Employees in nonagricultural establishments*

5. Total nonagricultural employment

6. Unemployment rate, total*

7. Insured unemployment rate

8. Unemployment rate for married males

9. GNP in current dollars

10. GNP in constant dollars*

11. Industrial production*

12. Personal income*

13. Labor income in mining, manufacturing, and construction

14. Final sales

15. Manufacturing and trade sales*

16. Sales of retail stores*

17. Manufacturers' unfilled orders, durable-goods industries

18. Backlog of capital appropriations, manufacturing

19. Wholesale prices, excluding farm products and foods

20. Wholesale price index, manufactured goods

21. Treasury-bill rate

22. Treasury-bond yields

23. Corporate-bond yields

24. Municipal-bond yields

25. Free reserves

Eleven lagging indicators

1. Unemployment rate, persons unemployed 15 or more weeks*

2. Business expenditures, new plant and equipment*

3. Machinery and equipment sales and business-construction expenditures

4. Book value, manufacturing and trade inventories*

5. Book value of manufacturers' inventories, finished goods

6. Labor cost per dollar of real corporate GNP

7. Labor cost per unit of output, manufacturing*

8. Consumer installment debt

9. Commercial and industrial loans outstanding*

10. Bank rates on short-term business loans*

11. Mortgage yields, residential

In addition to these series, classified according to their timing, other U.S. series with business-cycle significance, analytical measures, and international comparisons are included in the report.

The Future Science of Forecasting

The fundamental marketing problem constantly facing a manufacturer is that of accurately estimating future sales. In all manufacturing and distribution organizations, every effort, every plan, every idea, eventually comes to focus on this all-important problem, beside which all others are secondary!

In production, the path from the drawing board to the finished product is well charted and planned in advance. Every stage is a definite one, and all are based on *precision*. The engineers and production people use every possible device, mechanical or electrical, to measure, test, and control the design, engineering, and manufacture of their product in advance.

With the finished product, however, we move over to the sphere of marketing. Here we lose the vital element of precision. The sales department, which originally told the factory the total number of products to manufacture, was guided chiefly by its experience of the previous year, plus reports from, or conversations with, individuals in its distribution channels!

The results are sometimes disastrous. Either the factory makes too many units, or, *equally as bad,* not enough. When the distribution people overestimate the market, the result is excessive inventory, price-cutting, additional advertising costs, or outright loss. When the distribution people underestimate the market, potential sales and profits are lost forever.

Obviously, present methods of estimating markets to determine future sales result in high manufacturing costs and lower profits. While industry worries about pricing and packaging, warehousing, and dealer coverage, the main task of developing a practical method of predicting future sales with greater accuracy goes largely unattended.

Regardless of price, package design, number of retailers, efficiency of the sales organization, or anything else, each season the manufacturer must decide how many product units to make. This depends on one thing and one thing only: "How many will we sell?"

The curious thing is that we have had before us, for a long time, two excellent examples pointing to a possible solution of the problem. Magazines and book clubs know *in advance* exactly how many customers they have for their product each and every month. They accomplish this through the simple but all-important expedient of offering buyers a reward for telling them in advance that they intend to buy the product.

The customer who subscribes to a magazine for a year receives a better price than if he buys a newsstand copy each month after publication. The customer who becomes a member of a book club agrees to purchase four books the first year and receives a better price plus a premium of two books for merely signing up. In each case, the publisher or the book club knows in advance exactly how many copies are presold!

There is our missing element of precision, so fundamental in production and so sadly lacking in distribution.

Costs of Distribution

Once you get control of distribution costs, you are on your way to higher profits, because there are many ways that you can use cost control in making marketing decisions.

Finding the costs of distributing your products can be almost as complex as running the business itself. Yet unless you bring distribution costs under control, you sacrifice profitability.

"Classic cost analysis," said Albert Bergfeld, former president of Case and Company, consultants, "makes the distinction between *fixed* costs—which go on day after day regardless of sales or production volume—and *variable* costs, which vary with activity, whether by volume of production sales or the activity of a particular department."

Modern cost analysis takes the process a step further, by breaking fixed costs into components that Case and Company refers to as "constant costs" and "programmed costs."

"In the distribution function, programmed costs include the cost of new-product development, advertising and promotion, and the amount you must pay salespeople to open new accounts."

Programmed costs are taken on to influence volume, sales revenue, and profits.

Programmed costs can be further separated to show, for example, expenditures made to increase the sale of a particular product. These specific programmed costs should be considered as an offset to revenues from that product.

"Generally speaking, distribution activities are programmed more than are production activities," said Bergfeld. "For example, whether to take on an advertising campaign for one of your products is a management decision that comes up every year. You can raise the advertising appropriation, lower it, or even eliminate it entirely."

Distribution-cost analysis can also help you pick the geographical areas where you want to concentrate your marketing effort.

Variable costs include sales commissions, transportation charges, running cost of trucks, order entry, billing, and many credit and collection expenses. These are more easily assigned to product line and product than are specific programmed costs.

Taking a tip from the production side of business, some cost-conscious managers are considering imaginative adaptations of the engineering-developed "value analysis" technique as a means of uncovering some of their true costs of doing business.

The objective is to relate each specific cost to the function, service, or operation purchased by that cost—to make certain that every element of cost (labor, material, supplies, styling, and services) contributes proportionately.

Then imaginative thinking is used to develop a better or less costly means of obtaining the function; and, finally, the most promising alternative is adopted.

A Final Viewpoint

A composite look at the forecasting function was summed up by a corporate vice-president of marketing: "Meaningful forecasts can only be developed by looking at the many segments of your business and the economic influence on each—rather than examining each geographical area as represented by a salesperson.

"Ideally, forecasts should use a three dimensional matrix to break the business into forecasting cubes: first, a breakdown by product lines, and then identification by each channel of sale. This is extremely important where different sales channels are used, as each probably represents varying price levels, stocking requirements, promotional expenses, and other factors.

"Finally, it should be further broken down into major market segments. Each significant cube can then be individually reviewed and a reasonable forecast developed. Though any segment may be wrong, the sum of these segment forecasts can be quite accurate.

"On the other end of the product spectrum, when forecasting

large, engineered machinery, the salesperson's input is extremely important relative to identifying projections. Purchases of this type of equipment may take six months to a year to negotiate. But again, marketing management should listen to the murmurs of the 'grass roots,' but set forecasts by use of independent economic tools.

"Is asking for forecasts from the sales force reasonable? Yes, but its primary purpose is to establish a base for the individual salesperson's quotas and territorial plans, and not to set national forecasts.

"The quality of a marketing forecast is directly proportional to its use. If manufacturing builds products and maintains inventories so as to meet the forecast, the accuracy of the forecast will improve dramatically; the marketing management knows it suffers the consequences of less-than-expected performance. However, if manufacturing builds to its own schedules and ignores the marketing forecast, or uses it for excuses, forecast quality will deteriorate rapidly, as it quickly becomes apparent that the forecasting time is a wasted effort."

Chapter 16

Sales Budgeting

Budgets are far more than columns of figures, computer print-outs, and monthly reviews. They are reflections of underlying sales and management objectives, always subject, of course, to financial considerations, with company-wide impact. The ultimate result lies in the bottom line: *profit.*

Clarence E. Eldridge, who served as vice-president of marketing for the General Foods Corporation and as executive vice-president of the Campbell Soup Company, was commissioned to do a series of essays on budgeting for the Association of National Advertisers. Here is a digest of his main theme.

Management is called upon to make no decisions that are more important, or that can more significantly affect the health, growth, and profitability of the business than those involving the marketing budget. In many companies the cost of marketing is the largest controllable expense; in some companies the cost of marketing the product is even greater than the cost of producing it—including raw materials, labor, and packaging costs.

Questions to Answer

Of prime importance, of course, is the total amount of the budget. How much money is needed to achieve the agreed-upon marketing objectives? How much is affordable, consistent with the agreed-upon profit objectives? What compromise is permissible between need and affordability, without unduly jeopardizing either the marketing or the profit objectives?

Of almost equal importance are questions such as these: How should the budget be allocated among the several functions of marketing, such as advertising, selling, promotion, and market research? How should the money be divided among individual products or groups of products? How should it be divided among established and new products? How should it be apportioned geographically?

Finding a foolproof method of determining the marketing budget is not easy, particularly one that gives due consideration to the need for sales volume, the financial and profit needs of the business for the immediate future, and the longer-range health of the business. Perhaps such a method cannot be found, and if so, the more or less fatalistic approach to the subject, which is now so typical, eventually may prove to be justified.

At present there are two principal ways—each of which has many variants—by which the amount of the marketing budget is determined. Which of the two ways is used in any given situation depends largely on the relative influence on top management of the company controller, as compared with that the marketing vice-president.

The methods are different, and they both are wrong. The one is wrong because it fails to ascribe to marketing activities (including advertising) any productive role or to recognize any relationship between marketing expenditures and sales results. The other is wrong because it assumes, without adequate proof or evidence, that there is a predictable correlation between expenditures and results and that the correlation can be reduced to a mathematical exactness.

Probably no marketing company, certainly no sophisticated one, uses either of these methods to the exclusion of the other. Most companies try to balance the two—evaluating need against affordability, sales volume against profitability.

The budget is an indispensable tool of management. It represents, in fact, a profit plan for the period in question, whether it be a year, a quarter, or a month. The estimates of sales volume should be as realistic as possible, if anything underestimating—rather than overestimating—sales. Product costs can, in most instances, be predicted with almost mathematical accuracy, and marketing expenditures are also subject to absolute and precise determination. Thus, two of the factors that affect profits can be predicted with absolute accuracy. The only unpredictable factor is the sales volume.

Goals of Budgeting

Budgeting or, as its practitioners prefer to call it, financial planning for the future, involves both short-range and long-range goals and methods. Originally they were used mostly as an expenditure-limiting device. But, in recent years, they have developed as a basis for planning the business. "To be effective," said a vice-president of marketing, "the planning activity must be a continuous process that makes corrections and adjustments in response to changes in the business situation."

Some of the purposes of sales budgets are:

1. To bring into clear focus sales opportunities, sales objectives, and sales quotas for minimum satisfactory performance

2. To budget reasonable expense investment to attain those objectives

3. To help stimulate cooperative effort among participants

4. To encourage broad overall coverage of product lines, balance between sales effort, sales expense, and planned results

5. To offer a means for evaluating planning and effort

6. To stimulate maximum attainment through emphasis on profitable lines of products, profitable marketing areas, and profitable present customers and prospective customers

To attain these objectives and the satisfactory use of budgets, suitable responsibility and authority must be established. Each department head and manager must be charged with responsibility for the areas that he or she administers. There must be a suitable accounting system established to accurately identify sales by sales territories, by product lines, and by customer groups, and to properly allocate costs of production, services, and selling and promotional activities to those areas.

No budget can be meaningful unless the source of information is reliable and accurately maintained. This involves such factors as:

1. Classification of ledger accounts

2. Perpetual inventory records

3. Clearly understood and easily used recording and reporting forms

4. Cooperation and thoroughness on the part of personnel

Then there must be a well-devised program to distribute reports of results on a regular basis, either weekly or monthly.

No sales executive should be asked to participate in budget formation or control in areas beyond his responsibility and authority. It is foolish to expect a sales executive to meet a profit budget when production costs are rising. However, given standard production costs, he or she should be expected to meet a net-profit budget. Budget periods usually extend for a year, but some companies budget for 5 or 10 years or even longer.

Determining and Controlling the Budget

Sales budgets, generally speaking, are based on company experience, competition, and economic conditions. The processes for determining the budget, however, must be considered.

Some companies depend on fixed guidelines, such as a percentage of increase over the previous year's performance. The planned introduction of new products will play an important role in budgeting, and this is a factor in what is generally known as the "task" method. Finally, some budgets are purely arbitrary and subjective in nature.

Whichever method is used, results are the one and only objective; the budget must be subject to continuous control. In large corporations, monthly reports issued to all executives in the sales organization show "actual" versus "budget" for the period and for the year-to-date. They form the basis for review and control.

It is interesting to note that in the "fixed guidelines" process, the overall budget total is *broken down* into allocations for each product line or division; in the "task" method, the budget is *built up* according to the requirements of each product classification to arrive at the total figure.

It is important that the sales executive be alert in guarding his or her budget against inroads from charges or expenses that belong in other departments, such as engineering or service, but that are improperly charged against his budget. Detailed budget reviews are essential.

Forecasting the Budget

In most companies the budget for all functions and departments, including sales, is scheduled on a monthly basis. That is no longer enough. Today, with computer capability and the increased emphasis on costs and profits, management must have a more immediate picture of the motion and direction of its organization. The fast-changing marketplace no longer allows leisurely budget analysis.

A plastics company, for example, has adopted the practice of having its financial analysts interview division heads and department managers about the middle of each month to obtain forecasts of monthly budget performance. This procedure allows managements to maneuver overall company costs and to avoid possible damage caused by the failure of any number of departments to meet their individual budgets. Another company also utilizes a monthly system for revising the budget. This is called goal estimating. Through new estimates prepared on the 12th working day of each month, the control-budget figures are updated for the rest of the year.

Field Sales Budgeting

Deciding how much to spend on field sales activities is one of the sales manager's toughest tasks, as these expenditures constitute the greatest portion of the sales budget.

There are no hard and fast rules that apply to all companies because of the variation of the personal selling influence with different products, markets, and distribution channels.

In an article in *Business Horizons,* Hans B. Thorelli and Douglas J. Dalrumple commented that perhaps the simplest budgeting approach is to take the previous year's expenditures and make adjustments for inflation and changing conditions. The obvious problem with this method is that it fails to consider customer needs, sales potential, or company resources. The authors covered two other approaches in depth, which are digested here.

Percentage-of-sales approach bases the sales budget on what the sales manager believes to be a reasonable percentage of planned sales. The percentage is usually derived from industry standards, such as "x" percent for salary and incentive compensation and "x" percent for travel and entertainment. A source for industry standards is featured in the annual late February issue of *Sales & Marketing Management.*

A *workload approach* is based on decisions regarding the frequency and length of calls needed to sell existing and potential customers. The total number of salespeople required can be estimated with this approach.

There is some conflict between the two methods. A sales manager may compromise and settle on a figure somewhere between what he or she can "afford" and the larger figure of the workload approach.

Defining Expenses

In considering the break-even point, there should be a clear definition and understanding of the difference between variable and fixed expenses. While these differ somewhat in various types of sales work, they can generally be listed somewhat as follows:

Fixed expenses	Variable expenses
Rent	Incentive pay (bonus and
Salaries	commission)
Insurance	Postage
Taxes (some)	Shipping costs
Essential travel	Taxes (some)
Fixed entertainment	Optional travel
costs	Optional entertainment costs
Depreciation	Advertising
Maintenance	Packaging
Auto leasing	Promotion

In other words, fixed expenses are those which remain constant, regardless of the fluctuation of sales volume, while variable expenses can be controlled according to planned determinations after considering sales volume. Rent will be the same, whether sales are good or bad; but the advertising appropriation can be cut or boosted, according to what the figures show on the profit and loss statement.

Uses of a Break-Even Chart

There are many specific uses to which a break-even chart can be put by management. Some of the more significant ones are the following.

1. *Budgetary control.* It helps to indicate what changes, if any, you need to bring expenses into line with income.

2. *Improvement and balancing of sales.* It acts as a warning signal to alert you to potential trouble in your sales program. If your sales relative to other things are not as high as you think they should be, this fact will obviously show up on the chart. Then it may be time to reevaluate your sales techniques.

3. *Investigation and credit control.* It provides answers to specific questions such as the following: 1) How much of the present sales volume can the company lose before profits disappear? 2) How much will profits increase with an increase in volume?

4. *Determination of price policy.* It visualizes the probable effects on profits of price changes in combination with other changes. For example: 1) What changes may be expected in profits with changes in price, assuming all other factors remain constant? 2) If prices are reduced, what is the most practical combination of volume and cost changes to expect and what is the net effect of the combination of changes on profits? 3) Similarly, if prices are increased, what combination of changes and what effect on profits may reasonably be expected?

5. *Discussion of wages.* It assists management by: 1) quickly reflecting the probable influence on profits of proposed wage changes (assuming no change in employee efficiency), and 2) providing visual aid in determining possible economies and efficiencies that might protect the profit position of the company.

6. *Appraisal of merchandising policies.* It will enable critical examination of the "merchandise mix." A break-even chart for each line is a valuable help in visualizing which products should be pushed and which may be allowed to coast or possibly be eliminated.

7. *Assessment of further capitalization and expansion decisions.* It provides a visual means of appraising in advance the wisdom of making capital expenditures that may change cost structure of the business.

How to Construct a Break-Even Chart

Break-even charts are useful. A simple one is shown in Figure 1, page 410.

The break-even chart helps to keep management on the alert to find ways and means of improving its margin of safety. If all efforts to reduce the break-even point fail, the chart serves as a constant reminder to management that it is operating on a thin margin of safety. Under such conditions, all decisions must be weighed in the light of their effect upon that margin. As a result, programs may be undertaken to stabilize the margin and to protect it in the event of a business recession.

Fixed expenses increase with increased sales volume but not in direct ratio to it. Examples would include such things as opening new territories, adding salespeople to the sales force, and increasing expense allowances. These expenses, once approved, would be fixed for the time being, although sales volume would not increase proportionately.

In this respect sales travel and basic advertising would be fixed, because even if sales dropped drastically the company would still

Figure 1. Sample Break-Even Chart

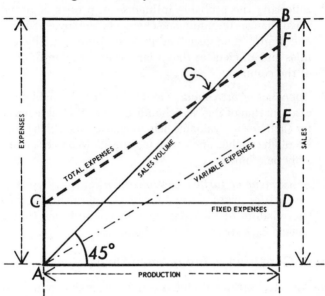

Line A-B indicates the sales-volume line, C-D the fixed-expense line, A-E the variable-expense line, C-F the total-expense line. (A-E being moved up to start at Point C) and G, the break-even point.

The two vertical lines represent expenses (left) and sales (right) in dollars, and the horizontal line (bottom) represents production in units or in percentage of capacity. Where the total expense line, C-F, crosses the sales volume line, A-B, is the break-even point. Sales volume less than the amount indicated would generate a loss; volume above this point would generate a profit.

The break-even point can be lowered by lowering either or both fixed and/or variable expenses. If, to obtain added sales volume, the rate of increase in variable expenses rose rapidly, the added volume might generate a loss instead of a profit. The same is true if the fixed expenses were raised. Frequently, profit can be built up faster through the lowering of fixed and variable expenses than by increasing sales volume.

have its salespeople out covering their territories, assisted by advertising and promotional activities.

A marketing executive should take the stepped-up fixed expenses into consideration and indicate them on his or her break-even chart, probably by adjusting the fixed-expense line at increased volume increments. All of his or her expenses should be carefully listed, indicating those that are fixed, those that are stepped-up-fixed, and those that are variable. This will permit the creation of a meaningful budget.

Chapter 17

Sales Quotas

The word "quota" is the clarion call to sales action for the salesperson. For the sales manager, quotas are a key measure in the planning, control, and evaluation of sales activity to increase the marketing efficiency of the company.

Dartnell Survey

As the costs of a typical sales call and other sales management overhead continue to mount, sales managers are increasing their control over the productivity of the individual salesperson, as revealed in a study by the Dartnell Management Research Institute.

The definitive survey involved 55 companies, all employing their own salespeople, of which 7 employed 10 salespeople or less, 12 from 11–25 salespeople, 9 between 26 and 50 salespeople, and 26 firms employed more than 50 salespeople.

In the important area of setting sales quotas, most companies based them on dollar volume (40 percent), the potential of the territory (24 percent), and unit volume (19 percent). Minor factors were the number of new accounts opened (5 percent), calls made (3 percent), and services rendered (2 percent). Major responsibility for setting quotas was divided among top management and sales force (53 percent). In 33 percent of the cases, top management alone set quotas. Others who shared responsibility were the market research department (7 percent) and the sales force itself (5 percent).

A majority of the companies (80 percent) attempted to achieve balanced-line selling when they carried a varied product line. Various methods were used: 14 percent relied on commission variations while 11 percent used a quota system.

The methods used to determine the amount of time to be devoted to each account were usually based on potential (24 percent).

Other factors were also significant. They included the individual salesperson's discretion, the size of the account, population, market trends, the cost-revenue ratio, the grade of the account, present dollar volume, the dealer volume and importance, and the percentage ratio.

One of the respondents offered the following comments on his company program: "Quotas must be challenging, obtainable, and rewardable. They must be fair to the salesperson, to sales management, and to the company, and must support the overall company goals and objectives.

"The salesperson and the sales manager must work together in establishing the quota. By so doing, the salesperson will be totally committed to it. In a sales management-by-objectives fashion, a bottom-up and top-down forecast is developed that finalizes a quota for each salesperson during a face-to-face meeting with the sales manager. During the latter part of the year, the salesperson completes a territory summary report that lists all accounts over a minimum level and showing current year's estimated sales, next year's potential sales, and call requirements.

"The summary becomes a part of the sales planning and reporting system as it relates to the overall sales coverage plan. It also requires the salesperson to make a detailed account-by-account analysis, which is the basis for establishing account sales objectives along with strategic plans and strategies for their achievement. Additionally, the salesperson, working with the regional manager, develops an annual call-planning guide as a basis for a monthly call-planning work sheet and for a weekly itinerary plan and contact report.

"When the final quota is settled upon, other rewardable non-sales objectives, such as product mix, prospecting, and management training are agreed upon. The participating salesperson is often more demanding on himself or herself than is management. This can be a strong self-motivating force.

"The salesperson receives a 100 percent bonus if quota is achieved. The salesperson receives a base salary for obtaining 85 percent of the established quota and then can earn up to the full bonus (20 percent of the base salary) by achieving the last 15 percent of his or her quota. This is the regular bonus for attaining the sales quota and represents 80 percent of his or her total bonus. The remaining 20 percent can be earned through the completion of various non-sales quotas, which are not standard but tailored to each salesperson to encourage growth. Up to 25 percent additional bonus can be earned by exceeding quota by 25 percent. Sales management quotas are established in a similar fashion, with such bonuses divided into sales attainment, cost control, and management action."

Forms for Auditing and Evaluating

The best approach calls for an analysis of the sales opportunities and work demands for each present and prospective account. It also calls for the establishment of call schedules and realistic sales goals. Two forms used by the Univex Manufacturing Company—a customer-prospect audit form and a workload evaluation form—are shown in Figure 1, pages 416 and 417, and Figure 2, page 418.

Customer-Prospect Audit Form. In this form, all customers and prospective customers are listed in the first column. If there is more than one important person to be called on regularly, but at different intervals, their names are included, as shown for the Carlisle Company.

The meaning of the letters "P," "S," and "G" are defined on the form. (It is important that all forms be self-explanatory, so that a salesperson required to use them can refresh his or her memory regarding their use. "P" stands for potential, the customer's total purchases from all sources in the product area being considered. "S" stands for the company's past year's sales to the customer. "G" stands for the salesperson and the manager's planned sales goal for the coming year.

Scheduled calls are then entered, based upon last year's call activity tempered by the coming year's planned activity. For Martin Company, 12 calls (once a month) have been planned; for the Carlisle Company, 55 calls have been planned. Note that the salesperson would probably visit the Carlisle Company twice a month; he or she would call on Braun and Morrison on each visit, on

Marzano every fourth visit, and would be sure to see Minor, the president, once during the year.

Inventory checks should be made for the Martin Company once during the year, and for the Carlisle Company twice a year. Both the Willard Company and the Carlisle Company have salespeople who call on dealers; it is well for salespeople to spend time with these men in the field, calling with them on their customers; time must be reserved for this activity.

The Workload Evaluation. This is merely a summation of the data recorded. Note that the full potential of the territory is $1,300,000 for the company, its past sales have been $190,000, and it has set its sights for $220,000. There are 150 customers out of the 175 listed who are expected to buy product A.

There have been 1,280 calls scheduled. It takes about a half a day for an inventory, and since the company has set 8 calls per day as an acceptable average, the 25 inventories scheduled are equivalent to 100 calls; the 70 days of dealer work are equivalent to 560 calls. There must always be some time reserved for unscheduled promotional or exploratory work to replace customers lost through normal attrition or if the territory is to grow in volume; 80 calls, or about 5 percent, have been allocated for this work.

A work year has been assumed as 50 weeks (allowing 2 weeks' vacation) with 10 days deducted for holidays, meetings, and sickness. With a 5-day week, this equals 240 days a year. With 8 calls a day, the normal workload year would be 1,920 calls. Because of the variation in work habits of salespeople and the need to get a territory started even if it isn't up to full coverage efficiency, the minimum acceptable call load schedule has been shown as 1,760 and the maximum 2,400. If the call load should drop below 1,760, the best part of the territory should be absorbed by an adjoining territory or it should be covered by a manufacturers' agent who has other lines. If the workload exceeds 2,400 calls, the territory should be reduced to assure planned coverage.

A further provision of a minimum sales goal of $150,000 has been shown. Here it is assumed that on sales less than that amount, the company will sustain a loss. However, if management feels that, within a reasonable time, the volume can be brought to

Figure 1. Customer-Prospect Audit Form

UNIVEX MANUFACTURING COMPANY
CUSTOMER-PROSPECT-AUDIT

Salesperson_____ Sheet____ of____   Territory_____ Date_____

Names of Companies, important persons in the companies to be seen individually, and cities to be listed below.		Product Line A	Product Line B	Product Line C	Miscellaneous	Total	Scheduled Calls	Inventories	Dealer Work Persons	Dealer Work Days
		SALES OBJECTIVES (Dollars)					WORK SCHEDULE (Per Year)			
Martin Company 528 First St.-St. Charles	P	5000	2000	—	1000	8000	12	1	—	—
	S	500	100	—	100	700				
	G	1000	500	—	200	1700				
Willard, Inc. 2802 Oak St.-Aurora	P	4000	6000	3000	1000	14000	12	—	4	8
	S	1000	—	2000	500	3500				
	G	1500	500	2000	500	4500				
Carlisle Company 1650 Park Rd.-Mokena	P	10000	8000	6000	3000	27000		2	6	10
	S	6000	8000	—	1500	15500				
	G	8000	8000	2000	2000	20000				
M.C. Braun, P.A. J.C. Morrison, maintenance	P						24	55		
	S						24			
	G									
A.D. Marzano, engineer R.A. Minor, president	P						6			
	S						1			
	G									

(continued)

Figure 1. Customer-Prospect Audit Form (continued)

UNIVEX MANUFACTURING COMPANY
CUSTOMER-PROSPECT-AUDIT

Salesperson_____ Sheet_____ of_____   Territory_____ Date_____

Names of Companies, important persons in the companies to be seen individually, and cities to be listed below.		SALES OBJECTIVES (Dollars)					WORK SCHEDULE (Per Year)			
		Product Line A	Product Line B	Product Line C	Miscellaneous	Total	Scheduled Calls	Inventories	Dealer Work Persons	Days
Styleright Company Elgin	P	500	300	—	500	1300	—	—	—	—
	S	100	50	—	100	25				
	G	—	—	—	—	—				
Amex Corporation Springfield	P	2000	5000	3000	1000	1100	12	—	—	—
	S	—	—	—	—	—				
	G	500	500	300	200	1500				

INSTRUCTIONS: All customers and all worthwhile prospective customers are to be listed. "P" refers to potential, the full value of items handled by the company and purchased from all sources, or the firm's reasonable sales possibilities. "S" refers to the company's sales to the firm during the past 12 months. "G" refers to the sales goal over the coming 12 months. Only dollar sales are to be shown. Individual persons who are to be called on separately are to be listed, and their scheduled calls shown. Prospects are to be scheduled for regular promotional calls. This form is to be filled out jointly by the salesperson and his manager. 1 copy for salesperson, 1 copy for manager, 1 copy for general office.

417

Figure 2. Work Load Evaluation Form

Univex Manufacturing Company
Work Load Evaluation Summary

Salesperson_____ Date_____

SALES GOALS				
PRODUCT LINES	POTENTIAL	CURRENT SALES	SALES GOAL	NUMBER OF CUSTOMERS
A	$ 350,000	$ 65,000	$ 75,000	150
B	250,000	40,000	50,000	175
C	500,000	75,000	85,000	175
Misc.	200,000	10,000	10,000	175
TOTAL	$1,300,000	$190,000	$220,000	175

ACTUAL WORK LOAD			
TYPE OF WORK	AMOUNT SCHEDULED	CALL EQUIVALENT†	ADJUSTED CALLS‡
Calls*	1280		1280
Inventories	25	4	100
Days of Dealer Work	70	8	560
Promotional Work Not Scheduled*			80
			2020

*Customers, prospects and promotional

†It is assumed that the company's call objective is 8 per day. To take an average inventory takes a half a day, equivalent to 4 calls.

‡A typical work year is 240 days. This is based on 50 5-day work weeks, less 10 days for holidays, conventions, and sickness. With the company's objective of 8 calls per day, a typical work year would include 1,920 calls.

Some allowance should be made for promotional and exploratory calls to replace normal attrition of established accounts and for growth.

Territories with sales goals of less than 150,000 and scheduled adjusted calls less than 1,760 should be increased. Territories with scheduled adjusted calls in excess of 2,400 should be reduced to assure planned coverage and effective sales work.

well above $150,000, it might open the territory, considering the expense a capital investment.

By this method or similar means, sales opportunities, market coverage, anticipated profit position, workload, and manpower may all be brought into balance.

Some Questions about Quotas

Marketing managers are far from agreeing on how to set up and administer a quota system, and a few still hold against quotas altogether, according to Leslie Rich, as quoted in *Dun's Review*. Some of the questions frequently asked are:

- How, in the first place, do you arrive at a fair quota for any individual?

- Should a salesperson's quota be higher than you actually expect him to produce? If so, how much higher?

- How can you keep quotas from interfering with the development and service calls so neccesary to most companies?

- Should quotas be set in product units or dollars, according to profits?

- Should quotas be the same for everybody, or different according to territory potential, experience, and ability?

- What relation should quotas have to salary?

- How can you "sell" salespeople on quotas?

- What do you do when a salesperson fails to meet his or her quota?

Many concerns find that in order to give every salesperson a chance to make a showing it is necessary to take into consideration the salesperson operating that territory. A nationally known company gives equal consideration to the salesperson's past record, his or her ability, and conditions and possibilities in his or her territory. This encourages the salesperson who does not stand at the top of the list in volume and gives that individual an equal chance to beat quota. Each person is given a quota of 1,000 points for the year, which represents a certain amount in dollars and cents. While the total number of points is the same for every salesperson, the values of the points vary. The value of one point is arrived at by dividing 1,000 into the sales figure set for the year for each salesperson.

A sales manager of the Maytag Company pointed out that all other reports common in marketing come "after the fact." Only quotas can be used for planning.

In the plumbing and heating division of American Standard Inc., for example, quotas have been tied directly to a budget based on yearly market forecasts. As outlined in *Dun's Review,* the 10-person market research department begins to assemble data in October for each of the 13 geographical sales districts. The analysts talk to company people in each district, go over economic bulletins from local banks and building and loan associations, and compare this with national predictions on housing. They try to judge the type of building planned (multiple or single dwelling, for example), the possibility of American Standard penetration into competitive markets, and the historic comparison of one region's housing with the nation as a whole.

"From all this, we make our considered guess on next year's sales for each of our 20 major products in each district," said the division manager of market research. "And 'guess' is the correct word."

However, after years of refinement, this department now regularly comes within a few percentage points of actual sales each year.

In most companies, the following factors are considered in establishing or revising quotas:

- The amount of last year's sales

- The trend in the territory over the past several years

- Economic trends (regional or national)

- Movement of current or potential customers into or out of the territory

- Competitive conditions

- Customers' buying habits

- The company's advertising programs

- New product introductions

Some companies request each salesperson to make an analysis of his or her major accounts and potential customers and then reconcile them with management estimates in order to arrive at equitable totals.

Practical Values of Quotas

The two basic uses of quotas are, first, to provide standards of measurement of each individual salesperson's performance and, secondly, to provide the basic data for company sales forecasting and financial control.

In an address delivered at a Midwest Marketing Conference, a marketing executive outlined the purposes and practical values of sales quotas, as follows:

The quota is the lifeblood of a business and serves both as a goal and as a means of measuring the performance of a company in relation to that goal. It is also a basis for setting sales and operations budgets. For a salesperson, it stands as a method of measuring performance and qualifying for advancement. It is a common objective both for the salesperson and the company.

In order properly to analyze a salesperson's quota, consideration must be given to three other types of quotas upon which the individual salesperson's quota is usually based. The first is the long-range quota that sets the stage for projected corporate planning. The second is the national yearly quota, the 12-month objective, which is a stepping stone that leads to ultimate growth potential established by the long-range forecast. The third type is the regional quota, which is a breakdown of the national quota.

From all these come the individual salesperson's quota, which is generally a breakdown of the regional quota.

There are factors that apply to quotas that need not always be considered in setting national or regional quotas, which are broader, and which do not always reflect the market-by-market considerations that must influence salespeople's quotas.

Sales force quotas, in general, are more easily determined and controlled in the "institutional" types of business—drugs, opticals, books. These businesses do not suffer from, or profit by, the peaks and valleys that are found in the more volatile types of business, such as clothing, tires, and liquor. Quotas present a greater problem in these volatile businesses where sales often depend upon seasons, weather, fashions, or other hard-to-predict factors.

Regardless of whether yours is a volatile or an institutional type business, there are some fundamentals we should consider when establishing equitable quotas for salespeople:

1. A company should determine what share of the industry it wants, both nationally and in each market area. This, of course, requires a knowledge of what the total industry is doing, along with projections of expected growth. Usually, these data are available from either industry associations or trade magazines. We use figures supplied by the Air Conditioning and Refrigeration Institute, from the buying-power-index issue of *Sales & Marketing Management* magazine, and from the National Electrical Manufacturers' Association. We then adjust these data variously, by climatic conditions, so that they will better apply to air conditioning and heating markets, using both industry and buying-power figures.

2. A knowledge of what a company's historical position has been in each market is also an important factor. We cannot afford not to learn from history; a company must build upon the foundations laid in the past. In other words, consider your heritage, your status, your reputation, and your image in the marketplace.

   How well an area has been managed is an important factor to consider when setting an equitable quota for a salesperson. Poor management, even in a prime market, may force you to set lower quotas than penetration and industry sales figures might indicate. The comparison of such figures also gives you an insight into whether your present management is strong or weak in any given area.

In short, it is vital that you know what your product's and company's reputation is in each market, and such knowledge should be reflected in each salesperson's quota. It is this factor which has the greatest influence on whether the salesperson's quota is equitable. A company may nationally enjoy a high percentage of industry volume, but, for any number of reasons, be relatively weak in some salesperson's territory. We would not be fair to those salespeople to expect them to bring our penetration up to national levels overnight.

3. Consider the national economic outlook—where the experts think the economy is going and how your industry's predictions fit in. For example, a predicted increase in personal income might be offset by industry statistics showing that your product is reaching a saturation point. Of course, new product introductions, a planned product diversification, or other such factors must be considered and should be reflected in the quota.

4. The salesperson's quota should be attainable. Setting unrealistic quotas that cannot be met only results in a morale problem and serves no useful purpose. Too often, management is guilty of fooling itself in putting down figures that are no more than wishful thinking.

The questions now arise as to how do you determine, after having considered these factors, whether or not your quotas were correctly set. As a general rule you have set equitable quotas for salespeople if your weaker salespeople fail to attain them and if your better salespeople either reach them or slightly exceed them.

If a quota is properly and fairly established, it should be the best single measuring stick you can use to evaluate a salesperson. Of course, this general rule may not apply in any given case, because of peculiar or extenuating circumstances.

Another rule of thumb is that in the more volatile industries your sales force quotas should be at least 10 percent higher than the previous year's performance. The more institutional business may look for more modest increases in the 3 to 5 percent area. This general rule must also be tempered by consideration of local conditions.

It is the responsibility of management or the home-office marketing group to set these quotas and to administer them. It is not usually wise to let field sales representatives have too big a part to play in the establishment of quotas. You need the marketing information from them, as well as records of past performance. However, if given too much authority, you may find that they will endeavor to set higher-than-attainable quotas, particularly if by doing so they can command a higher income. Or, they may desire larger quotas because they will bring with them increased budgets.

Also upon management's shoulders is the responsibility of following up quota performance. It is, I think, apparent that once-a-year checks will not suffice. We find that monthly checks on performance-to-quota permit us to keep our fingers on the pulse of a salesperson's progress. Such checks bring to light any problem areas so that we can give them our immediate attention. Markets making outstanding progress are also checked and the reasons for this success are quickly dispatched to other areas for their consideration.

At first glance, it would seem that money is the primary motive for a salesperson to attain quota. Perhaps it is, but this basic motive can be supplemented with sales programs and contests. We have found success with both types. Sales programs and promotions that help salespeople and retailers to sell to the ultimate consumer have proved their worth.

We run from two to six contests a year, usually for our salespeople or sales outlets. We've had success when the awards have been exciting and when the contest goals have been within the reach of all. Normally, for contests that constitute an addition to a salesperson's income (either with cash or merchandise), special contest quotas are established. Thus, we begin to pay off when more-than-the-normal quota results are attained. Ideally, a contest should motivate salespeople to do more than the yearly quota as prorated over the contest period and, by doing so, give you a sales reserve and frequently bolster sales in product areas that are showing a weakness.

Special quotas should be set for contests, and should be estimated at a higher level of performance. The basic regional quota, as we have said, should be set fairly and realistically. You should expect it to be met in most cases. Therefore, you should not have to reward a person for doing what is basically his or her job. The contest gives him or her a reward for above-average performance.

Thus, contests are means of getting extra business. We do not recommend *counting* on contests to help attain the basic yearly quota. This basic quota, as we have said, should be established as an attainable goal without the assistance of contests or special promotions other than the promotional tools or sales programs you may normally provide.

Salaries, commissions, bonuses, and contest prizes may be the keys to quota attainment, but let us not forget one final ingredient—accomplishment.

Salespeople—the hundreds of good ones that we know—are somewhat like professional athletes who, although they perform for financial rewards, play the game to win because they want to win and because they want to better their previous records. This internal feeling of accomplishment is perhaps one of the greatest rewards in life. We are all motivated by our salaries, but we would not have progressed if this were our sole motivation. Just as a batter may try to break 300 for the sake of accomplishment, so too, will a good salesperson work the extra hours to meet or exceed a quota. Although financial gain is a motive, let us not forget a person's inborn desire to excel.

A salesperson's quota that is equitable for him or her and for the company provides the best basis for a salesperson's earnings, as well as the best measuring stick to qualify him or her for advancement. As such, it provides management with an essential tool for continued growth and sets up for the salesperson an attainable goal that he or she can achieve with justifiable pride. See Figure 3, page 426, for an example of a working quota. Figure 4, page 427, shows the relationship between gross dollar sales and the number of sales calls made in a year on a particular account.

Figure 3. Working Quota

DEALER		BINDERS	FLOPPY DISKS	PHONE INDEXES	CALCU-LATORS
Ward's Office Supply Ames, Iowa	Estimate	100	25	50	50
	Your Personal Sales				
Weaver Stationer Newton, Iowa	Estimate		Will not handle again		
	Your Personal Sales				
Doyle's Dubuque, Iowa	Estimate	75	50	75	
	Your Personal Sales				
Fisher & Marshall Davenport, Iowa	Estimate	310		15	5
	Your Personal Sales				
Estelle's Shop Muscatine, Iowa	Estimate		NO GOOD		
	Your Personal Sales				
	Total	485	75	140	55

By listing all accounts in a territory and then having each individual salesperson estimate what he or she feels each account should buy during the year, and by then averaging these estimates with potential quota, a satisfactory working quota can be established.

Quota Incentives for Distributors

A major corporation in the appliance industry offered its distributors extra discounts as a reward for meeting or exceeding quotas. In a general announcement to all distributors, it outlined the plan as follows:

Starting with this convention, October 1, through September of next year, distributors will be eligible for a special quota fund.

Figure 4. Yearly Sales Calls and Gross Dollar Sales

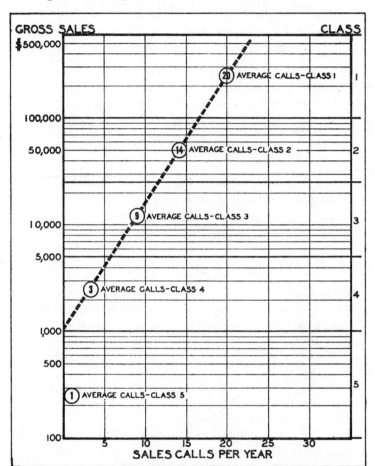

Plotted here is the number of sales calls per year in relation to gross dollar sales for a chemical-products company. To plot the sales cost in relation to customer size (Class), the mean customer size of each class has to be determined. The average call frequency of the class was plotted in relation to the average dollar size of the class. The straight-line relationship on the semilog graph represents an exponential function.

1. If a distributor makes quota in October (four-week month) he or she will receive 1 percent on all his October sales.

2. The distributor who repeats in November (four-week month) will receive 1½ percent on all November sales.

3. If the distributor again repeats in December (five-week month) by doing 100 percent or more of his quota, he or she will receive 2 percent on all his December sales.

4. The distributor will continue to receive 2 percent for each consecutive month in which he or she makes quota until October 1 of next year.

5. If a distributor misses quota in any one month, the procedure is repeated beginning with "1."

6. All credits will be issued automatically and in accordance with weekly sales reports.

The Use of Quotas in Incentive Trips

Contests and prize trips as a means of stimulating distributors and dealers to meet their quotas are used widely. Many companies offer their dealers free trips to their annual conventions as a reward for meeting their quotas. Some companies provide incentive trips to such places as Bermuda, Puerto Rico, and Acapulco, Mexico.

A kitchen appliance manufacturer took 450 distributors and their dealers to Bermuda. This was followed by other trips to Puerto Rico, Holland, and Italy.

The manufacturer paid for half the cost of the trip; the distributor paid the other half. When a dealer, plumber, or builder purchases a product he or she receives points toward a potential trip. The points were awarded during an 11-month period.

The Primary Purpose of Sales Quotas

Sales quotas provide standards whereby sales volume responsibilities may be distributed, and achievements measured and motivated. Quotas may be based on any of the following factors:

- Dollar volume

- Unit volume

- Calls made

- New accounts opened

- Demonstrations made

- Services rendered

Or they may be based on a combination of these.
Sales quotas also may apply to such concepts as the following:

- Geographical areas

- Organizational departments

- Product lines

- Market classifications

When attuned to volume responsibilities distribution, the setting of quota is:

- From top management down

- From the field sales force up

- A combination of both

Many companies establish quotas by first estimating their total sales for the coming year and then apportioning them to the respective sales divisions, districts, branches, and sales territories. Various means are used in the apportioning process:

- Past sales

- Theoretical potentiality

- A combination of past sales and assumed potential

- A good guess

Past sales are certainly an important element, but this as a basis may compound past inequities. Salesperson A might have sales of $300,000 or 1 percent of the firm's total; Salesperson B, $500,000 or 2 percent. Should the company anticipate an increase of 10 percent, A's quota would be increased 10 percent to $330,000, while B's quota would go to $550,000. However, A might be having an exceedingly difficult time even in getting the current $300,000 because of limited sales opportunities or severe competition; while B, with sales of $500,000, may merely be skimming the cream from what could be a much more lucrative territory. Then too, A may be headed into a bonanza with a surging economy in his or her territory, whereas B might be headed for trouble through some event such as the death of an important customer.

For these reasons, an increasing number of companies are making valiant efforts to measure the potential of their respective sales areas as one basis for distribution of sales responsibility. There are many indexes that can be used. One basis is population, wherein the company divides company sales by population figures. This unit is then extended to all the territories, as a measure of past sales opportunities. These estimates are then increased proportionately to reach in total the company's anticipated sales.

Another method is to proportion the total sales of the industry by population figures or other indexes, then apply the resulting unit to the population indexes for the individual areas.

This gives their theoretical full potential, which must be reduced by the ratio of the company's anticipated sales to the industry's total sales. The first method is attuned to company average sales; the second method has little reference to company sales.

A third method is to divide the sales of the best territories by population figures or other indexes, then apply this unit to the population of the poorer territories as a measure of what they should have done.

Population figures can be very misleading because of inequalities in buying power, tastes, and types of customers in the various geographical, race, nationality, and environmental sections of the nation.

Other indexes, such as those suggested in Chapter 14, Market Data Sources, should also be considered.

Another difficulty arises in using dollar sales rather than physical unit sales. Dollar sales are subject to changes due to price increases or decreases, national economic inflation or deflation. If dollar figures are used, they should be reduced to constant dollars, by dividing sales for each year by cost of living or other indexes.

Probably one of the greatest handicaps to basing quotas on management estimates of total sales is the likelihood that salespeople can't or won't perform as management expects them to perform. If management sets its production schedules and operating budgets on such anticipated sales figures and the salespeople fall down, management is in for trouble and the company is in for losses.

Using Estimates of Salespeople

Many companies have their salespeople anticipate their sales for the coming year, adjusting these estimates by branch manager and district manager judgment, totaling the results, and calling the final figure the company's sales goal for the year.

To sharpen the salespeople's estimates, management instructs the sales force to call on all their customers and discuss with them their anticipated activities and demands.

However, salespeople usually dislike this assignment, as they fear they may antagonize their customers. Customers frequently feel that the salesperson is being nosy, and they become cagey and give answers best suited to their own ends. There is a strong possibility that haphazard estimates will be made, hardly reliable enough for company programming.

Then, too, salespeople are, as a class, inclined to be optimistic. If no penalty results from wrong estimates, they will be inclined to place them too high. Or some will place them too low, so that they can make a good showing. In either case, the salespeople are usually not very objective unless held under tight rein.

Defining Quota Terms

Quota, sales goals, and incentive base are three terms frequently used synonymously. However, they have different connotations.

A *quota* is a standard established to measure achievement and used in organizing, programming, budgeting, and controlling company activities. It is carefully, conservatively, and cautiously planned.

A *sales goal* contains more wishful thinking; it is something hoped for and worth striving for, but company budgets (financing, production, and profits) are not geared to it. They are geared to the quota.

An *incentive base* is a measure of minimum satisfactory achievement, often apportioned to the company's quota but more often set a little lower, to provide incentive compensation payments in recognition of achievements above the satisfactory level.

A Combination of Methods

Probably the safest method to follow in setting quotas is to work from both ends, from the top down and from the territories up, and then compromise to reach the final figure.

As management prepares its figures based on economic and market studies, the branch managers conduct customer audits with their individual salespeople. Every attempt is made by the branch managers to obtain realistic sales goals, colored by the characteristics of the salespeople and their individual customers. The sales goals of all the territories are totaled and compared with management's initial quota; if these are reasonably close, management's quota stands.

Working from both ends is a practical method. For unless the branch managers and salespeople can sell the quota on paper, they can hardly be expected to sell it in fact. If top management's initial quota is higher than the field force honestly feels it can produce, management's quota had best be lowered, or new plans projected by the force that will make achievement realistic. Conversely, if the estimate of the field force is high, its program should be searchingly examined; if it still looks reasonable, top management should raise its sights, if practicable.

Scheduling Sales Calls

It is the responsibility of sales executives to direct the planning of where the company's salespeople go in their sales work, when and with what frequency they make their calls, and what they do when they get there. This may be symbolized by W-W-W: Where, When, and What.

Where to Call. Applying the philosophy that markets and sales territories are the property of the company and not of the salespeople, it behooves sales executives to see that all present and prospective customers are analyzed for sales opportunities and that the salespeople be required to service them well.

In proper sequence, one might say a company should first obtain a suitable product; then a suitable sales force; and last, but far from least, determine where the sales force should go and direct its activities.

Too frequently, salespeople are assigned to territories with no other instructions than to cover them as they deem fit; sometimes prospect cards or customers' names are given to them, but too often they must dig this information out for themselves. Naturally, some salespeople adopt a course best suited to themselves with little regard or thought as to what is best for the company.

Sales calls should be made where the greatest sales opportunities exist; it is wiser to pass by a poor prospect and call on a prospect with greater potential, even though more travel time might be consumed, than it is to call on everyone, determinedly and blindly.

An individual salesperson, when trained and aggressively working, can make, on an average, only a certain number of calls a day, be that 3 or 5 or 15 or more. His or her time is not elastic; it is fixed in respect to amount. Therefore, it is necessary that policies be adopted that outline how he or she should expend his or her time. He or she is like an army officer with a given number of soldiers to direct; some need to be sent to cover this objective, others sent to cover other objectives. In like manner, the salesperson, with a given number of calls available, should be guided and instructed as to how he or she should deploy them and on whom they should be expended.

When to call. All customers or prospects do not demand the same degree of attention or service. With a prospect, exploratory calls may need to be made only once in six months, while, with a very active and important account, calls may need to be made daily.

Seasonal patterns or buying traditions also enter the picture. Christmas goods are sold early in a year for fall delivery; therefore many calls must be made in the spring during the buying period, but few need be made around Christmas during the retail sales period.

Seasonal patterns also prevail for farm products. In the construction industry, the call activity is increased when contractors are bidding on projects; during the actual building period, calls may become fewer and take on the aspect of service calls.

Besides the different call-demand characteristics of products, industries and markets, there are differences in the requirements of individual buyers or of personnel in a customer's organization. Some buyers rely heavily on the salespeople with whom they do business; they may open their requisition files to them and expect the salespeople to pick out those that apply to their materials and to enter buying orders for them. Or, as with the retail trade, buyers may expect salespeople to call daily (as with bread) or weekly (canned goods), check inventories, replace stales, and reorder stock. Frequently the buyer merely signs the purchase orders, depending on the salesperson not to understock or overstock him.

Customer Audits

It is important that customer audits be conducted regularly at scheduled times, possibly once or twice a year, and jointly by the salespeople and their immediate managers. The sales manager should feel responsible for getting the salespeople to cover their territories wisely; therefore, he or she must participate in planning the sales strategy. Furthermore, salespeople are inclined to hold their goals low so as to make a good showing. Sales managers need to act as a counter-balance, to keep quotas as high as reasonable in order to provide meaningful challenges.

Whether in a small, moderately-sized, or large company, it becomes quite a problem for the chief executive to see that widely separated or even functionally separated executives adhere to company programs simultaneously; and that, where there is repetition of the same operation, each recurrence be similar, no matter how long the time interval between them; or that programmed actions take place in proper sequence.

Chapter 18

Sales Territory Planning And Control

Share-of-market is one of the standards by which a company determines the effectiveness of its marketing efforts. In this regard, the sales manager has two primary field responsibilities; developing sales territories in terms of planning, and assisting his or her salespeople to more effectively manage their territories for sales and profit.

Where Do You Start?

Let's begin by defining what a territory is. Charles C. Schlom, sales management consultant, offers these definitions:

- A sales territory can be thought of as a franchise from which must come sufficient dollars to be profitable to management, who underwrites it, and to the salesperson responsible for working it.

- A sales territory is usually thought of as a geographic area containing customers and prospects. But it is primarily one segment of a company's total market.

The next step is to analyze each individual sales territory according to its actual potential.

For example, if electrical power is introduced into a region where none existed before, the potential sales for all kinds of electrically-operated equipment will be greatly improved and the percentage increase in this territory should be much greater in relation to other sales districts. Similarly the addition of new distributors or the assignment of extra salespeople to a territory have a decided influence on the sales to be expected from that particular area.

At one time sales territories followed geographical boundaries or traditional routes. Then sales managers realized that in order to be sure they were getting a full share of the existing business from each territory, more precise information was needed. The question, for example, of which territories should receive intensive sales cultivation and which should be treated as fringe territories can hardly be answered without reliable data on each sales unit. The question of reducing territories, always a headache in sales management, cannot be properly considered unless the sales executive has fairly dependable facts on the territory. Moreover, such information is necessary to "sell" the salesperson on taking a smaller territory. Where to direct the advertising and sales promotion effort with the best chances of success can likewise only be properly determined in the light of market data. Today especially, when sales planning is in terms of selective selling rather than seeking all-over coverage, it is most important that each market be carefully studied, appraised, and classified as to its sales potential.

How are sales territories drawn? A Dartnell survey disclosed that the most common method is by county lines or other geographical marks (46 percent). Trading areas (20 percent) were the next most popular. Key cities were used by 14 percent. However, 17 percent of the companies used their own methods to establish territories, using zip codes, Nielsen areas, key account assignments, work loads, etc.

Analyses of individual prospects within a territory were the favorite (28 percent) way to establish the potential of a sales territory. Using a population count also was important (24 percent), as were comparative economic consumption rates (13 percent). Less used were the "smokestack count" (3 percent) and average disposable income within the territory (6 percent).

The County as a Unit of Measurement

Marketers differ in their opinion as to what is the best unit to use in measuring markets. Some favor setting up areas determined by the nature of the business and establishing a sales potential for each area. A notable and widely used plan that became a classic was developed by Pacific Mills. The country was broken down into small territorial units; population by income groups was then determined for each unit. The units were gathered into sales territories and the unit potentials added together to get the territory potential. In establishing the potential, known per-capita purchases of the products were used. This per-capita purchase figure was adjusted according to income groups, since it was found there was a definite relationship, for example, between a man's income and the number and quality of shirts he was apt to buy. This method, however, can be used only for consumer products on which the government or other agency had made studies to determine per-capita purchases.

Most companies that distribute nationally find the county unit most convenient for measuring sales potential. This method is not without its drawbacks, not the least of which is the 10-year lapse between taking the U.S. Census. Then, too, it is not always possible to secure the variety of information needed to establish county potential. But at least when you know the approximate potential in each county, it is a simple matter to combine the counties into sales territories and establish reasonably accurate territorial potential.

Trading-Area Units

Some marketing organizations, notable publishers selling circulation in concentrated areas, outdoor advertising companies, and TV and radio stations, contend that the county is of questionable value as a sales unit because of the inaccessibility of many counties. They contend, with some logic, that if your salespeople or distributors are unable to maintain sales contact with any given county, that county, however much potential it may have, is of little or no sales worth.

In a talk before a trade association recently, a marketing executive of a highly successful nationally operating company explained how these trading-area potentials were determined:

"For more than 25 years we have been developing the trading-area system of sales control. In brief this is what we have done. We have studied every town in the country—65,000 of them—and, by a long process of elimination, have reduced the ordinary map of the United States, with all its confusion of political boundaries, its details of mountains, rivers, and deserts, into a simplified "Marketing Map of the United States," which shows the normal flow of trade in this country and the shortest route to the national market.

"We have developed and drawn the boundaries for the principal trading areas in the United States. We have been guided by buying habits that pay no attention whatever to political boundary lines. We have used 33 factors to make sure we are right. These 33 factors, which determine the principal trading centers and their consumer areas, cover such subjects as physical characteristics; people and homes, transportation, communication, and distribution machinery; valuation of products and sources of personal income; volume of business, wealth, and standards of living.

"In developing the trading-area system of sales potentials, we have broken down the national market as a landscape engineer would break down 7 meadows into a fine golf course. We have laid out 613 selling holes, called consumer-trading areas.

"The factor of concentration is very important. Selective marketing means concentration. For example, every sales manager should know that most of the business in any town is transacted by a few dealers. He or she should know that the best 25 percent of his or her dealers will account for 75 percent of the volume total. So it should not surprise the manager that of 65,000 towns, the key cities, or principal trading centers of the United States account for more than 70 percent of the total annual retail business in this country.

"To search out these important markets, we have analyzed every city. We surveyed the wholesale and retail advantages, the ratings of the stores, and their variety in each community. After this was done, comparative values were made of all places in each section, resulting in the choice of the most dominating commercial center for each area.

"Sometimes a city with a smaller population than another has been selected as the key point of a trading area. This is because an impartial examination of all 33 major factors has ultimately resulted in its selection despite its smaller population.

"When we have completely analyzed each of the 33 factors, we are ready to determine the extent of the key city influence. We trace the railroad lines, the roads, and visualize the flow of trade throughout the section. We trace the buying habits, customs, and trade tendencies in each section. Then we interlock the small pieces of the trade pattern until we have a section that rightly fits against another section—just like a jigsaw puzzle.

"The trading-area system offers sales managers the following opportunities for closer sales control:

1. Establishing your sales control by consumer "trading-area units" in contrast to political lines.

2. Revising your sales districts and assigning logical territories of these control units to salespeople.

3. Selecting the principal trading centers in each territory that should receive the greatest amount of sales and advertising energy.

4. Concentrating the time of salespeople in these key cities to obtain greatest results from their time, expense, and selling ability.

5. Checking the sales performance either by months, quarters, or half-year periods against sales potentials.

6. Deciding whether present retail distribution is adequate or justified. This may mean too many or too few retailers in certain markets.

7. Determining the sales potential within each trading-area unit and comparing it with sales performance.

8. Paralleling all your advertising efforts with sales efforts in the most profitable consumer-trading area."

A marketing executive who inherited an old-fashioned marketing setup and turned it into a scientific operation, based on trading areas instead of geographical territories, commented:

"There can be no question but that trading areas are more meaningful than county lines. Just one example of many I might mention is St. Louis, Missouri. Much of the marketing area for this city lies across the Mississippi River, in Illinois.

"However, this does not mean that county-based geographical

territories should be ignored. In many instances, trading areas can be built up, using counties as building units. Of the thousands of counties in the United States, about 75 percent of the national business is concentrated in approximately 25 percent of the counties. It is important, therefore, to study county population and other sales statistics when building trading-area sales territories."

Visualizing Market Potential

The well-managed business establishment, marketing its products on a national or seminational scale, not only has figures to show where the best sales opportunities lie in every state in which it does business, but it maintains map records on which these data are projected and pictured. Much of the value of sales or marketing facts is lost to a business through the failure of management to utilize them properly after they have been compiled. For the purpose of graphic presentation of market data, it is recommended that outline state maps showing each county in the state, but with no other distracting information, be used. Such maps may be obtained from any sales equipment supplier.

A sales manager, to do an effective job, must chart the operations of his or her salespeople just as a military leader must visualize the movement of troops. To do this requires that sales figures be plotted against sales opportunities in such a way that lost opportunities or neglected markets will be flagged. Here again the outline county map and figures on sales by counties are recommended. Territories can be marked out on the map and colored crayons used to indicate the potential sales for each territory, as determined by county quotas, actual sales for the preceding year, the peak sales, and current sales expectancy. This same picture may also be obtained through the use of tacks and similar devices in a map mounted on a soft board.

It is significant that, after experimenting with elaborate market studies, many concerns are coming back to modified population figures as a basis for gauging sales potential. No matter what line you are in, in the long run you will find it is the number of people in a county, multiplied by their per-capita buying power, that most influences their sales. But, of course, if the product is sold through dealers a great deal depends on the number of stores in the county selling your product. For example, Lake County, Illinois (which lies next to Cook), has a high buying power per capita and a large population. While the residents of that county formerly shopped in Chicago frequently, suburban malls and shopping centers in the suburbs of both Cook and Lake counties are drawing more of the shoppers.

By a test of some kind, determine just what proportion of the per capita income is being spent for your product or service. Probably you already have data on this point. But even though you are selling roadgraders or computers it is important to have a per capita basis for working out quota figures. With this information available, it is an easy matter to figure the exact business that you should get each year out of a given county. When you have worked out these figures, post them on the proper county, leaving room to note beneath them actual yearly sales that show you how far short of the mark you are falling. At the end of a year or two it is possible to combine these figures and thus arrive at what you will find to be a very practical and effective sales potential for each territory. These figures also are available in laying out subterritories, or assigning territories to agents or exclusive dealers, jobbers, and other distributors.

Locating Branch Offices and Sales Agencies

Many companies have not paid any great attention to the efficient location of warehouses, branch offices, or jobber connections. As a result, countless orders are being lost through the inability of manufacturers and jobbers to give the prompt service that present merchandising conditions demand.

An outline state map usually is used to decide where to locate jobbers so as to assure the manufacturer of the best distribution facilities in each state. The salesperson serving a certain territory is stationed at a point located on the map with a ringed dot. Stocks are carried by local distributors at various cities in each state. These cities are indicated on the map by dots, and territories are assigned on county lines according to accessibility from cities indicated. Territorial boundaries can be outlined by red lines. Either the quota for a particular subterritory or the number of dealers being served by a jobber or whatever information is essential in a particular line of business can be shown by placing the proper figures below the names of the cities.

Trading area maps are usually worth studying with some care. There must be sound reasons for every curve and every indentation. This long arm that projects to the north may indicate a prosperous valley, a good road, or unusually convenient transportation facilities. It may measure also the relative success of your promotional activities.

If you are located in one of the larger cities, it is not safe to assume that you draw trade from the entire city. If you have mapped your local or immediate trading area carefully, you may observe from its outlines that you are getting no business to speak of from certain residential districts to which you have always assumed you made a strong appeal. On the other hand, you may discover that much of your trade comes from districts populated by people whom you had ignored in your merchandising plans or who, for some other reason, have been overlooked. Then, too, the location of paved roads may easily carry your trading territory 50 miles along that highway, whereas it would extend only a few miles if such roads did not exist.

How to Estimate Total Sales in Territory

Having defined your trading area and analyzed it with some care, your next step is to estimate its share of the country's total sales. This can be done in two simple ways; and it is well to use both in order to be able to check one with the other.

The first method is based upon the population of your trading area, which usually can be calculated with little difficulty. Divide your estimate of the total population of your trading area by the average number of persons in a family at the present time in order to get the number of families. Now, estimate the proportions that should be classed, respectively, as rural and as urban (bearing in mind that people living in towns or cities of 2,500 or more are classed as urban, and those living in smaller towns or villages or in the country, as rural); figure out the number of families in each of these two groups. The Census Bureau publications contain data on number of families in major areas in the country. If you now multiply the number of rural families by the average for the entire United States, and the number of urban families by the urban average, and add the resulting figures, you will have a rough, yet helpful, estimate.

To check this estimate based upon population alone, consult one of the many excellent national surveys (you probably can secure one from your advertising department), from which you can estimate the approximate percentage of national buying power represented by your trading area. For our purpose it will be safe to assume that sales of your product in your territory should bear about the same ratio to total national sales as the ratio between the buying power credited to your trading area and national buying power.

It may be necessary, however, to make allowances for the effects of current economic forces. If your trading area should be suffering from unusual depression or other conditions unfavorable to retail trade, your estimate should be reduced accordingly. On the other hand, if conditions are unusually good, you should increase your estimate.

Take into account the habits of the community. If it is largely industrial, families are doubtless moving in and out rapidly; if it is principally farming territory, moves are likely to be relatively infrequent, though the farming population is on the decrease.

The type of population is also a factor to be considered; different races and nationalities not only have different tastes in home furnishings, but also occupy different economic levels.

Metropolitan Market Data

In laying out a sales plan aimed at a group of metropolitan markets rather than at a definite marketing area or geographical trading unit, the best source for market information is usually the local newspaper; the next best bet is the Chamber of Commerce.

Other dependable sources of information concerning the relative condition of business in different cities are the United Business Service and Babson's Reports, Inc., both of Boston. Babson publishes, in connection with its service, a map showing which territories are the most active from a sales standpoint each month. Other reliable indexes of this kind are the summary of debits to individual accounts (check transactions) as reported by the Federal Reserve banks, and other government statistics.

Many manufacturers are making wide use of the syndicated services offered by A. C. Nielsen Company of Northbrook, Illinois. Nielsen, in addition to national reports, provides "breakouts" of major markets such as Chicago, New York, Los Angeles, etc. Nielsen has a nationwide staff of field auditors checking grocery, drug, camera, and appliance stores in order to determine the sales of entire market groups (e.g., cake mixes, detergents, cold tablets, etc.), as well as the individual brands within each product group. The raw data, developed by means of store audits, are projected to regional, as well as national, totals. In addition to showing sales and sales share, the report also provides data relative to distribution, inventories, out-of-stock, prices, special factory packs, and so forth. Nielsen service is provided on a continuous basis so that marketing trends of all types can be evaluated as they occur.

Census of Distribution Data

Among the many useful data available for market analysis purposes is the Census of Distribution made by the Department of Commerce, Bureau of the Census, Washington. The following suggestions for the use of these data in sales planning and market determination are offered:

How to Determine Distribution. Base your distribution on the number of retail stores, in any given kind of business, that carry your kind of goods.

Learn What Other Stores Might Carry Your Products. By a comparison of the breakdown of sales by commodities in the retail reports, you can learn whether there are other kinds of stores with which your sales department is not familiar, and that might be induced to carry your products.

Map the Wholesale Resources in Your Proposed Territory. By a study of the wholesale census reports, you can discover how many wholesale merchants, brokers, jobbers, and other types of whole-

salers there are in any particular section of the country who distribute your kind of goods. To the manufacturer or primary producer, the wholesale statistics enable the producer to follow the
principle of selective distribution. By study of the wholesale reports, he or she can determine roughly where his wholesale market
lies and the extent of market. He or she will find the basic facts to
enable selection of brokers or selling agents in territories where
they will serve his or her interests most efficiently. The manufacturer or primary producer can select wholesale merchants or jobbers on a scientific basis and discover the location and relative
strength of chain warehouses. It is also possible to see how widely
other manufacturers have established wholesale branch houses.
Information is given for 92 commodities that shows the volume of
commodity sales by different trades and by all of the various types
of wholesale middlemen operating in those trades. These factors
are of inestimable value in formulating an intelligent selective
program.

How to Measure Your Potential Market. The retail census reports contain schedules showing the commodities sold by each
kind of retail store, as well as the percentage of sales of each commodity in relation to the total sales of that kind of store. A given
commodity is often found in many kinds of stores. To measure
your potential market, compile the total sales of all the stores of
each kind that sell your products, and apply thereto the percentage
that represents the sale of your classification of goods. This can be
done for any city, county, state, or combination of states.

Adapt Your Sales Policies to the Requirements of Retailers.
Many ambitious sales campaigns are failures because they were
not checked in advance by experienced distribution experts to ensure that they would be acceptable to retailers. Producers should
understand the problems that retailers face. In the absence of a retail consultant, manufacturers may, by a careful study of the retail
census reports, gain a sympathetic understanding of the many
problems faced by retailers. This understanding applies particularly to such factors as operating expenses, customers' returns and
allowances, extent and character of competition, credit that must
be extended to customers, and the availability of wholesale distributors.

How to Determine Price Policies. You know that the potential market is greater when the price is lower; however, the producer's price cannot disregard the conditions under which the article is finally retailed. Certain retail prices are not popular with the public, and of course increase sales resistance. On account of this the retailer many times may be forced to adopt too high or too low retail prices, because the producer did not follow through to the consumer in planning his price policies. A study of the retail and the wholesale census reports will allow the producer to set margins between his price and the planned retail price that make due allowance for distribution costs. If you plan to distribute through any of the several types of wholesale channels, this method is particularly applicable.

Establishing Workloads

Basic to establishing profitable territories is the necessity of establishing the number of accounts to assign to each salesperson and desired call patterns.

It is a widely accepted practice to classify customers into three categories, A, B, and C, depending upon their value and potential. While it is obviously impossible to determine exactly what constitutes profitability for every type of business, there are several guidelines.

Key accounts consist of those customers whose value is so high that losing just one could be a major disaster in the territory and for the company. Their actual or potential value in terms of volume and profit are great indeed. Though few in number, it is not unusual to find the top 10-or-more customers worth almost as much as all others combined.

Because key accounts demand high standards of performance from the salesperson, the number he or she can effectively handle is limited—probably to no more than 20 or so—unless calling on them is his or her only assignment.

Regular accounts constitute the bulk of customers in any territory. While their level of purchases falls below those of key accounts, their present or future worth warrants a regular sales program.

This reservoir of buying power is a tremendous asset. Not only are such accounts usually loyal and not overly demanding but they are also essential to sales success in the territory.

Unprofitable accounts are those representing an actual loss when the true worth of serving them is calculated. Within this category are the marginal operators, new firms struggling to get underway, customers tied in closely with competitors, and those whose potential exceeds their present purchases.

Depending upon the results of analysis and objectives to be achieved in the territory, you may want your salespeople to:

- Continue calling on such accounts because of future possibilities for sales growth

- Maintain the account because little or no selling effort is involved

- Convert the account to different sales, service, and distribution coverage through agents, brokers, distributors

- Cover by direct mail or through telemarketing

- Maintain present call schedules on these accounts until more productive replacements can be found

Not all accounts will fit neatly into precisely defined categories. Some, pending further analysis and evaluation, may not be clearly defined as to potential. Others, because of unique or special requirements, may need additional investigation. A few, because of location or other circumstances, may require in-depth research before any concrete decisions are reached. The point to remember is that the number of unclassified accounts should be kept to a minimum, and should be assigned a category as soon as identified.

The number of times an account in each category should be called upon depends upon the nature of the account. Should all customers in category A be called on once a month or do some need more frequent attention? In category B, can all customers be called upon once a month? twice a month? Can the accounts in category C be adequately taken care of with calls every two months? As individual Class C customers start to increase in sales volume and profitability, it may be necessary to move them up into category B, which might require an adjustment in the territory with the increased workload.

Sales call patterns are the result of the number of calls to be made in a day and the frequency of visits to each account. Both factors are affected by time and distance in traveling, the complexity of the product or service being sold, and the characteristics of the customer. A recent Dartnell survey reported that the national average of the number of sales calls made per day was slightly over 7. On the basis of about 240 working days a year, approximately 1,680 calls can be made a year. Making your own calculation and factoring in the categories of customers and number in each with prescribed call frequency will give some definition to the sales workloads.

The Territory Audit

One of the big problems of the sales manager is keeping on top of what is going on in the individual accounts and prospective accounts in his or her sales area. A Dartnell report investigated this problem. Here is a digest of the recommendations.

The territory audit correlates the manager's supervision of his or her people with the job of getting the most business possible from customers, clients, and prospects.

While it is true that most territories are described by geographic lines, many sales organizations are set up by categories of customers and prospects calling for specialized coverage. In these latter industries there may be two or more separate sales "territories" that overlap or are superimposed in the same geographic area.

The territory audit is a useful tool by which the sales manager can do a more effective job of supervising the activities of his or her salespeople and of developing their personal potential.

The procedure also has a training aspect. By going through the territory-audit routine, a great many things can be pointed out to the salesperson during the audit which, under ordinary circumstances, might never come to the surface.

PRELIMINARY ARRANGEMENTS

Where is the audit to be conducted? Who is to be involved? This might include someone from the advertising department, accounting department, etc. What will be the timetable?

Where outside departments are involved, a specific timetable and agenda should be set up and appointments made with the other people in advance of the session, so that the salesperson's time away from his or her territory can be reduced to a minimum. Of course, a timetable of this sort is not necessary when only manager and salesperson are involved.

Since this "audit" procedure involves more than ordinary digging into the background, information, and progress of each account, some salespeople may feel that this is an invasion of their authority, or shows a lack of confidence of the superior in his or her subordinates. If there is any suspicion on the part of the sales manager that such a feeling may exist in the mind of the salesperson, it would be well to stress that this is not the case.

A good sales manager, once the lines and limitations of authority have been established and mutually understood, will make no decisions which his or her subordinate should make except as a training procedure. Subsequent decisions on the same matter should be tossed back to the subordinate to make him or her stand on his or her own feet. Only thus can he or she grow and develop.

Prior to the interview or audit with the salesperson, the sales manager must determine what information is needed about each account in order to give the salesperson the most effective supervisory guidance.

Here is a list of possible points regarding which the sales manager would like broader information, or which he or she wishes to discuss with the salesperson.

- Official business style of the firm.

- Names of the heads of the business and a short estimate of the foibles, capabilities, and the "degree of influence" of each. Same information about the actual buyer.

- Who are "centers of influence" who affect, even remotely, the purchase of our kind of product?

- General characteristics of the executives in the account: Are they forward-looking and progressive or reactionary? Is their management sound, mediocre, or poor?

- Are their business facilities adequate with regard to buildings, equipment, machines, trucks, etc.?

- How much of our type of product do they use?

- What percentage of such material do they buy from us?

- Can we get a bigger share? Why or why not?

- Do we have any items to which they have not been introduced? If they have seen and have not bought, why? What can we do about it?

- How can or should we improve our service to, and relations with, this account?

- How correct is our call frequency? Are we wasting time and money by calling too frequently? Would additional calls generate enough extra volume to justify the expense?

- What is the economic climate in this particular market or industry, and what steps should we take to exploit or minimize it?

- What are our credit arrangements with this account and would a revision result in more business?

After each individual customer has been covered, each prospect should be investigated in the same manner, with individual plans for action to be taken with each.

SUMMARY FOR TERRITORY

When each customer's status and potential have been explored, and plans for approach to prospects have been developed, it is usually useful to build a summary of general activity for the territory as a whole. This should include such data as the following:

- Present gross sales for territory

- Potential of territory (our total sales plus total sales of our kind of product by competition)

- Our present penetration (percent of potential we enjoy)

- Long-range objectives for territory (possibly three to five years)

- Short-range objectives (next few months, but not more than one year)

- Matters requiring immediate attention, including opportunities or special events to be exploited, as well as situations to be improved or corrected

FREQUENCY OF AUDIT

Admittedly, the territory audit is no small task, nor is it easy to do. Obviously it cannot be done so often as to require a burdensome amount of time. In most industries and companies, an annual audit is adequate.

Timing must be determined by each manager to fit his or her own needs. It is hardly ever practical to take on all salespeople in rotation, day after day. It is more practical to spread these interviews through the year, possibly one salesperson every month or two. The real test is the thoroughness of the job.

Unless yours is an unusual organization, the chances are that even the more experienced salespeople have had very little instruction in planning their time or the sequential order of coverage of their territories. Accordingly, some sales managers feel that the territory audit is not quite complete without constructing, jointly with the salesperson, a basic but tentative plan for coverage of the territory, including the geographical progression best suited to cover the territory and the approximate time to be spent in each market.

Such a time-management discussion can be most valuable. Both parties to the "audit" should make notes on the agreed coverage and include the geographical sequence and estimated needed time at each location. After such a plan has been worked out with a salesperson a few times, he or she will become adept at weighing the job to be done in each market and organizing his or her time accordingly.

The manager can also use the customer and territorial summary as a yardstick in measuring performance, as well as in assessing areas where the salesperson needs help. Not the least of the benefits to the sales manager is the eventuality that he or she can use this "audit" information to show that he or she is on top of the job as a planner, coordinator, controller, and developer of people.

The audit, or analysis, should also permit you to:

- Determine possibilities for achieving additional volume on products presently sold in the territory;

- Define opportunities for stimulating sales to new groups of accounts or to middlemen;

- Detect problems or dangers that would have remained concealed or unknown unless an analysis had been made;

- Detail any unusual differences between the territory audited and others within the district or company, and determine the reasons why.

Take the Pulse in Each Territory

In his manual, *How to Plan and Manage Sales Territories Effectively,** Charles C. Schlom suggests an evaluation process, presented here in the following digested outline.

1. Exercise your manager's prerogative by periodically evaluating each salesperson's territorial responsibilities, including:

   - Accounts worth more calls or less calls.

   - Accounts to whom company wants to sell and how much.

---

*Charles C. Schlom, *How to Plan and Manage Sales Territories Effectively* (Chicago: The Dartnell Corporation, 1974).

- Re-checking for accuracy the number of account categories in the territory.

- Efficiency with which salesperson handles work loads, travel time, calls, etc.

- The percent each territory has of the company volume—enough or too much.

2. After each territory has been analyzed and evaluated, summarize to obtain the same information for the district as a whole.

3. You can then more effectively direct each of your salespeople to:

   - Check objectives developed for their territories.

     · Are they still realistic, achievable?

     · Which ones are being achieved on schedule? Which ones are not?

     · What changes or revisions will be necessary to keep objectives on target?

     · What additional steps will be required of the manager? salespeople in other territories? members of company management? other departments?

     · What new objectives are needed?

   - Consult records, reports, correspondence, personal observations in the field, customer contacts, etc.

     · What accounts will require greater frequency of contact? which ones less?

     · Are call costs, time expenditures, etc., worth it? What changes are needed now? later?

     · What additional services should be provided? within what limits?

   - Review their modes of travel.

· Check maps to hold down excessive travel.

· The car is usually the most suitable, but not always. Stress that urgency of a call or importance of an account takes precedence over distance or expenses of travel.

• Evaluate prospecting procedures used by each of your salespeople.

· Do they have specific criteria for qualifying prospects?

· How are prospects located, identified, evaluated? What changes may be necessary in these procedures?

· What sources yield best results? How effectively are they being utilized?

· Do salespeople's records, files, maps, etc., provide means for noting pertinent facts observed and obtained about prospects?

• Examine expenses in relation to sales.

· What are the major costs incurred in the territories?

· What are salespeople now spending for transportation, hotel/motel accommodations, meals, entertainment, etc.?

· What costs should be cut?

· Where should more be spent to stimulate sales?

· How does each salesperson's coverage of his or her territory affect sales and sales expense?

• Compare overall performance against plans.

· Coverage plans do not automatically come to fruition.

· Periodically compare each salesperson's planned performance against actual performance.

· Find out if each salesperson has been able to raise the

number of calls on prospects with genuine potential on a predetermined basis.

- · Has number of selling interviews been increased?
- · Has each salesperson been able to increase the number of customers seen because of better coverage patterns and routing routines used?
- · Have the salespeople been able to raise the dollar value of their selling time?

4. Devise daily/weekly schedules and priorities.

- • Before implementing their plans and activities, you, as the manager, want each of your salespeople to ask themselves:
  - · What results do I need today? tomorrow? next week? six months hence?
  - · What do my customers expect from me and from the company I represent?
  - · What does my manager require of me so that company goals and objectives can be realized?

- • This approach will help each of your salespeople:
  - · Focus in on the priorities.
  - · Maintain working communications between yourself and the company.
  - · Determine major job responsibilities.
  - · Estimate time required for handling the really important jobs.
  - · Correctly structure time outlays.
  - · Prepare for emergencies.

- • To encourage your salespeople to do more of what is important in their territories, get them to:

· Schedule around key events. Note what they are. Group sales calls and selling activities.

· Organize activities. Keep related tasks together. Indicate activities that will depend upon the activities and/or actions of others.

· Prepare an informal schedule. Estimate the time each activity will take. Set deadlines. Cut out overlapping or redundant activities.

· Periodically evaluate schedule.

Here are some final thoughts on helps you can provide your salespeople to more efficiently manage their sales territories.

1. Require that long-range strategies be worked out for each account. This includes:

• A statement of objectives;

• Selling tactics to be employed;

• Number of calls to be made;

• Specific objective for each call.

2. Each call should result in a step closer toward the long-range objective, which is getting a stated share of the account's business. Supervise continually! You cannot allow your salespeople's plans to remain merely good intentions. Work with them systemically. Keep in close touch between contacts via the phone or correspondence. See to it that each salesperson carries out his or her plans so that:

• The sales value of each customer can be realized.

• The best possible coverage patterns can also be used as guides in scheduling calls.

• Each salesperson knows who to see and where and when to see them.

• Each salesperson's personal and territorial objectives are accomplished.

Chapter 19

Computers in Sales Management

Peter F. Drucker, management guru, described the computer as a logic machine. He said that all it can do is add and subtract. All operations of mathematics and logic are extensions of addition and subtraction; the computer can perform all mathematical and logical operations by just adding and subtracting very fast, very many times. It can store information capable of being handled through addition and subtraction, theoretically without limits.

Now some 20 years later, that "logic machine" has revolutionized the way American business is conducted. Three basic characteristics of the computer are its accurate memory, its endurance, and its speed. Computers are helping marketers in several standard data processing activities: billing and invoicing, accounting, and other record-keeping activities. The greatest benefits to marketing and sales management, however, come from computer analysis of product and line sales, profitability, pricing, distribution, forecasting, budgets, and sales force performance. Computerized linkage between company and customer, company and salesperson, company and distributor, and dealer and distributor and customer is becoming quite common.

Use of Computers in Sales

A survey of suppliers of computer hardware and software showed a growing list of the ways the computer is used in sales, and the list continues to grow each day. Here is a representative sample:

- Entering orders
- Checking order status
- Checking inventory
- Developing sales quotas

- Preparing sales forecasts
- Planning and scheduling
- Managing territories
- Managing accounts
- Reporting expenses
- Sales call reports
- Itineraries
- Analyzing customer requirements
- Preparing bids and proposals
- Sales inquiries and leads
- Developing competitive information
- Pricing
- Qualifying prospects
- Customer mailing lists

Computer Development

Computers have been getting smaller and cheaper at a great rate, while at the same time retaining the capacity to meet the requirements of average-size business organizations. The minicomputer has, in turn, led to the microcomputer, which is revolutionizing the retail industry, for instance, in the form of electronic cash registers. "The minicomputer industry is a mere 25 years old," reported *Business Week*, "but in that time, its products have gained dramatically in power and capability while prices were dropping from $50,000 to as little as $2,000. The market is growing at something like 50 percent a year ... while prices are declining at 15 percent a year." In the meantime, microcomputers are taking over the function of electro-mechanical components, creating new products with expanded capabilities, and bringing computer technology within reach of smaller businesses.

The development of on-line systems has been further segregated into two major segments: 1) the true on-line system wherein the computer is at the control of distant terminal operators on a continuous, second-by-second basis. Input, processing and output are instantaneous; 2) the "remote batch" system, wherein data are gathered by the computer from on-line terminals, after which the processing of the data is carried on by "off-line" methods under control of the computer room operating personnel. The final output is often sent back over the phone lines to other terminal sites later in the same day or on a subsequent day.

The Computer and Marketing Decisions

Direct access to a constantly updated computer can enable management to make marketing decisions immediately—in response to a dynamic environment.

The Research Institute of America predicted that:

"In the immediate future, some computers will not only decide when and how much, but also *who* gets the order. Data on suppliers' performance and other factors are programmed into the computer and, when an item is needed, the machine supplies the best probable sources. At some future date, bids themselves may be fed into the machine for a purchasing *decision.* All the human buyers have to do is decide which suppliers to ask for bids and which products and services to program into the computer."

At a meeting of the American Management Association, in discussing the subject of marketing and the computer, an economist said the computer can enable marketing strategists to learn quickly and thoroughly why the successes of the past were successes and why failures were failures. He also said they are now experimenting with computer analysis that employs a key concept (analyzing past strategies as if they were experiments), the building of a simulation model, and the use of the model to generate "go" decisions.

Benefits of Computers

What benefits has the computer brought about? By helping business make the most efficient, fullest use of available resources, computers and information processing systems are in effect enabling businesspeople to eliminate waste, increase productivity, cut expenses, and thereby offer customers a wider variety of products and services at the lowest possible price.

An outstanding example of wider services as a result of the computer has been the use of real-time computer systems in air transportation. Airlines book and maintain control of millions of reservations and, in addition, even reserve a steak for a passenger's meal aloft. Through computers, airline reservations clerks in many different cities are able to simultaneously check into seat availability for hundreds of flights and to book them as far as a year in advance. Through data communications, clerks obtain responses to inquiries in seconds. Large-scale systems used by major airlines today are capable of storing complete information on any individual passenger, including name, address, telephone number, and meal preference. Computers may also book a rented car or reserve a room at the passenger's destination.

Test Market Selection

Thousands of areas in the United States have similar interests and buying habits. The computer helps the sales executive to find out where they are. By tabulating and evaluating stored reports of past buying performance, the computer can produce a selective listing of areas that may be grouped into a test market.

Campaign Analysis

The results of a sales or promotional campaign can be registered on a day-to-day basis. The computer stores data on buying, product ordering and reordering, promotion costs and, in the publication field, new subscriptions and renewals.

Small Firms Can Use Computers

A combination of data-processing techniques, including the use of an electronic accounting machine, data-communications equipment, and a service-bureau computer, enabled a firm to save $600 a month in clerical costs (a significant savings over former manual methods) while providing valuable management information that was previously unavailable to the firm.

This on-line service approach to data processing is designed to allow a small industrial supplier to gain benefits usually realized only by much larger firms. This same firm employs 135 people to handle, control, and sell approximately 57,000 items. It has automated accounts receivable, payroll, accounts payable, and order-processing applications.

Moreover, by making use of the services of a local service bureau, this firm was able to obtain sales and cost-analysis information that would have been impossible to attain by manual or semi-automated methods. The direct on-line system using one or more terminals is the natural choice for heavy and consistent users of data base information.

Service Bureaus

The business of a service bureau is to process your data and produce the reports you require. It either has its own computer or leases time on someone else's computer and usually has trained programmers and computer operators on its staff. The types of service offered vary from city to city, and the number of service bureaus available also varies, depending on the size of the business population in the area.

In a typical arrangement with a service bureau, source documents are delivered or mailed to the service bureau on an established schedule. The service-bureau staff enters the transactions onto tapes or disks to be used as input to the computer. The computer then processes the input and prints the reports according to programs written earlier by the service-bureau staff.

Some small businesses use a service bureau for only one function of the business—for instance, inventory control. Keeping track of inventories is one of the most successful business applications of EDP.

Problem-Solving by Simulation

Simulation is a decision-aiding tool that provides the executive with a method of evaluating various business plans without taking the risks represented by each. As stated by IBM, "Ideas are expressed as assumptions or alternatives introduced into a simulated system having the same variables, constraints and goals as the real system the executive works with. He then observes the behavior of the simulated system and reviews the consequences of alternate approaches before making the final decision."

The key element in simulation is the model, of which there are three basic types: the physical, the analytical and the descriptive. The physical, traditional, model is exemplified by the scale model of a manufacturing plant, for instance, or, in the case of certain products, the preliminary "mock-up." Analytical models are mathematical expressions of characteristics, usually given in sets of equations. Models of systems described in words require a minimum of time, costs and skills.

Computer-based simulation models enable the executive to learn in advance how his organization may be expected to respond to demands under a variety of conditions. Simulation may be used to answer such questions as: What happens if we change existing procedures? Add a new department to handle special orders? Reduce the number of distribution points?

In Cambridge, Mass., Keydata Corporation has pioneered a commercial computer time-sharing service, an information-processing utility that provides data-processing service in much the same way that public utilities provide gas and electricity to their consuming public. Each Keydata subscriber has direct access to the central computer system and pays only for his shared time on the large-scale computer. Thus, computer-generated business graphics enable managers to review and evaluate highly complex statistical data in an efficient, comprehensive manner.

Computer Programs in Action

Because computers are becoming ever more essential in sales and marketing, *Sales & Marketing Management* increased its coverage of computers with an every-issue newsletter devoted to their increasing role. Following is a digest of practical applications reported over the past few years:

- Estimatic Corporation, which provides information services to the construction industry, got around the "telephone tag" problem by hooking its seven people into a computer-based electronic mail set-up (Telemail, marketed by GTE). Each salesperson is assigned an electronic mail box, which he or she queries over the phone line via a Vector Graphics small computer. The computer retrieves all of the messages waiting for the salesperson.

- Hewlett-Packard uses its in-house electronic mail set-up, HP mail, to boost sales rep productivity. If sales reps use HP mail instead of the phone on 90 messages a month, they gain 6.5 hours of selling time, or enough time for at least one or two more sales calls.

- Mitchell Management Systems reported that their sales and marketing management integrated software boosted their close ratio from the 10 percent range to the 20 percent range. It provided sales reps with 40 percent to 50 percent more selling time by eliminating considerable paperwork and administrative chores.

- Black & Decker outfitted 250 sales representatives and field managers with hand-held terminals. The previous order entry cycle of four to six days was reduced to a maximum of 24 hours. An electronic mail system slashed long-distance phone bills by 30–40 percent by eliminating "telephone tag."

- Merrell Dow Pharmaceuticals used a personal computer-based mapping software (Maps III) to realign sales territories. The personal computer does the arithmetic for a territory in a matter of seconds and it creates a map of realigned boundaries in two minutes.

- Haworth, Inc. installed a computerized sales forecasting program that allows 4 regional and 17 divisional managers to develop sales goals customized to their own selling environments; used in tandem with a corporate sales forecast, the program becomes the cornerstone of the quota-setting process.

• Monsanto Polymer Products updates its salespeople daily on their accounts, products, and performance with the Online Automated Commercial Information System for precall planning.

• Savin Corporation uses Thoughtware Trigger software to maintain weekly and monthly summaries of each sales representative's activities, including appointments made, cold calls, demonstrations, orders, and revenue. It also provides the relationship between appointments, demonstrations, and orders.

• Benjamin Moore & Company devised a computerized color-matching system to be sold to its paint dealers to give them a competitive edge.

• IBM equipped thousands of field service representatives with specially developed hand-held terminals. The reps use the terminals to receive and send messages, communicate with each other, access data bases for solutions to customer problems, and receive automatic reminders of planned activities.

• Softsel Computer Products built a direct access, order-entry system for dealers, using a personal computer with a modem or a terminal.

• At Rockwell International's heavy vehicle components division, sale representatives were given personal computers to help sell automatic slack adjustors.

• The Direct Marketing Group gave its 25 sales representatives personal computers to provide them with the capability of showing clients, on the spot, the impact of any changes on their scheduled use of media during the coming months.

Sales and Marketing Software

An annual directory of personal computer-based sales and marketing applications software is published by *Sales & Marketing Management,* 633 Third Avenue, New York, New York 10017. The directory lists in sequence:

- Vendor's name and address
- Title of software package
- Specific application
- Minimum internal memory required
- Purchase price
- Computer model or operating system with which the application is used

The listing is representative of what is available. The software packages cover a wide range of applications, such as:

- Account Managing
- Advertising Planning
- Budgeting
- Compensation
- Direct Marketing
- Expenses Reporting
- Inquiry/Order
- Lead Tracking
- Mapping
- Marketing Management
- Marketing Research
- Product Management
- Sales Analysis
- Sales Forecasting
- Sales Management
- Sales Planning
- Sales Presentations
- Telemarketing
- Territory Management
- Word Processing

Representative entries in the "Sales Management" category are shown in Table 1, page 467.

The American Marketing Association, 250 S. Wacker Drive,

Table 1. Sales Management Software Applications

Vendor	Software	Applications	MIM*	Price	Hardware
Applied Software Technology	VersaForm XL	Sales management, sales analysis, order entry	512K	$159	IBM PC-XT, -AT and compatibles
Chang Laboratories	Fileplan	Sales database management, quota/goal commission tracking, expense reports	256K	$199.95	Any PC or compatible with 2 drives
Computer Associates	SuperCalc 3, Release 2.1	Spreadsheet with integrated graphics and data management	96K	$395	IBM PCs and compatibles; AT&T 6300
	SuperCalc 4	Report generation	256K	$495	IBM PC-XT, -AT; AT&T 6300
Envoy Systems	SalesMate	Integrated package of seven modules: Sales Inquiry, Sales Order, Sales File, Sales Aid, Sales Mail, Sales Plan, and Sales Desk	256K	$300-$700	IBM PC-XT, -AT: Data General DG-One model Ii; GRiD; Hewlett-Packard Portable Plus
ETS Systems	Star-Trak	Sales tracking and sales management system	256K	$6,000	IBM PC-XT and compatibles
Executive Data Systems	The Prospector	Sales management database	128K	$300	MS-DOS; PC-DOS
GRiD Systems	Management Tools	Integrated package with word processing, database, spreadsheet, and graphics and record playback	512K	$790	IBM PC-XT; GRiD Compass, GRiDCase
	Task	Customizes sales applications	512K	$50	IBM PC-XT; GRiD Compass, GRiDCase
InterActive Systems	OMNITRAC	Sales lead management, sales forecasting, market management	512K	$395	PC-DOS, VMS, Unix Key Systems
	Prospecting	Sales and marketing support	256K	$395-$595	IBM PCs and compatibles, Network Novell

*MIM—Minimal internal memory required

Source: Sales & Marketing Management magazine.

Chicago, Illinois 60606, publishes a similar directory of software for marketing and market research. The listing includes:

- Vendor's name and address
- Product name
- Application
- Industry or activity served
- Hardware and/or operating system required, and minimum memory required
- Price

Portable (Laptop) Personal Computers

Sales forces continue to be "automated" at a rapidly increasing rate. The job of selling is becoming more analytical and professional as a result of the use of portable (laptop) computers. Some of the reasons given for the popularity of these computers are a shortening of the order-shipment cycle, the value in increasing inventory turnover, and faster and better customer service.

Thayer C. Taylor of *S&MM* reports the largest installation to date of sales-oriented, full-function portable personal computers: Chrysler recently spent $5 million outfitting 600 district managers with laptops. Before making a call on a dealer, the district sales manager can receive the following:

- Number of orders the dealer has in the pipeline, the dealer's allocation, and what was produced for him;
- The dealer's performance in market penetration versus other dealers in his market and versus all-U.S. average;
- Measurements such as the dealer's "satisfaction" score in consumer surveys and whether he is delivering cars in the proper condition to buyers;
- How the dealer's facility is rated and whether anything has to be done to improve it;

- Financial data on the dealer's results for the current month and year-to-date.

By the end of this decade, one of every three laptop personal computers shipped will be destined for a salesperson, versus one in six currently, according to a study of the portable computer market by International Data Corporation. While total sales of laptops will soar 146 percent to 420,000 units in the 1984–1990 time frame covered by the study, shipments to the sales force automation segment will skyrocket 4,633 percent to 142,000 units. Steve Bosley, author of the report, said a lot of big companies have perceived sales force automation to be very cost-effective.

Making the Transition

Going from manual to computerized operations is no easy task. It requires a great deal of thought and planning. In choosing a system, you have to clearly define your needs. Few software and hardware dealers care to match a complete package to your requirements. An article in *Marketing News* suggests you ask the following questions of your potential suppliers in order to get a reliable system compatible to your needs.

- What can your software do?

- How is your software better than other packages currently on the market?

- Who developed the software and what experience does the developer have?

- What other companies are using the software?

- How do lease and purchase costs compare?

- What hardware is compatible?

- What software maintenance and updates will be available?

These questions plus others pertaining to your specific needs should guide you to the best possible system for your requirements.

Chapter 20

New Product Considerations

Markets are constantly changing; they expand and contract, are affected by cycles and seasons, and by changes in people's habits and desires. Technology is constantly changing; new materials and processes make today's method of making things obsolete; new products replace old products.

Today's successful product has a limited life span; we know that every product goes through successive stages in its life, just as a human being does. Eventually the product will come to the end of its lifeline. At this point, the alert company will have anticipated the change and have another product ready to fill the gap.

What Is a New Product?

The classic definition is "a commercial product that has never before been offered in the marketplace." In practice and for the sake of practicality, however, the term "new product" has broader connotations and can represent any of the following:

- A product that is new to the company but not to the marketplace
- A product that has a different physical form and appearance than it had formerly
- A product that has a different size than it had formerly
- An improved version of a product that is in existence
- A truly new product, by the classic definition

Selection and Development

Few companies can survive without new products. Hence most firms are constantly searching for, screening, analyzing, testing, commercializing, and ultimately abandoning products. As Figure 1, page 471, shows, the mortality at each stage of the product development cycle is very high.

Sources. The sources of product ideas vary widely. Chlorodent toothpaste was brought to Lever Bros. by a pair of J. Walter Thompson ad agency vice-presidents. Lustre Creme shampoo was developed in the laboratory by Colgate-Palmolive. Minute Rice came to General Foods from a member of the Afghanistan royal family. Krilium soil conditioner was developed in the laboratory by Monsanto. The transistor was invented by the Bell Laboratories. The Waring blender was the invention of an orchestra leader. Amdahl's products were initially envisioned by an IBM employee, Gene Amdahl.

Most new products originate within or close to the firm. Many companies are indifferent or outright hostile to outside inventors. This attitude usually results from the fear of lawsuits or humorous experiences with crackpot inventors.

Figure 1.*

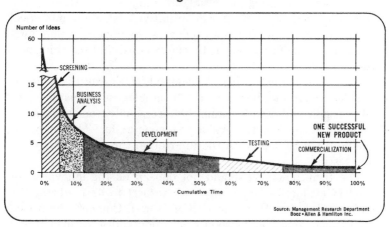

Marketing Manager's Handbook, Steuart Henderson Britt and Norman F. Guess, eds. Dartnell Corp. 1983, Chicago, Illinois, p. 642.

Although there is no specific company policy that assures the flow of product innovations, the technically progressive firm should be aware of its sources of ideas. These are suggested by Table 1, page 473.

Screening and Selection. Often firms flounder in their effort to develop new products, not because of the lack of candidates, but because of the lack of objective criteria. Formal criteria should be developed, and endorsed by senior management, for the initial screening and the final selection of new products. The new-product screening criteria—often called a "model"—must be specified in accordance with the interests, capabilities, and willingness to assume risk of the individual firm. However, the model should account for—and be approved by—all major operating departments, not just marketing. Product decisions are generally shared with all line departments, especially during the selection stage. The standards for final selection would normally be more rigorous than those used during the initial screening process. Although the screening model provides for quantitative evaluation, numerical evaluation of a potential new product is less important than forcing all potential new products through a consistent screening process.

Development and Testing. A General Electric executive said his firm learned from experience that "technology is intimately related to people and usually cannot be successfully transferred as an impersonal commodity of value in its own right." The innovator should often be kept with the innovation through development and testing.

The firm, however, should not depend on the innovator for product evaluation, especially with respect to its marketability and profitability. Here the Bell & Howell Company approach seems most sensible. As soon as a product idea survives initial screening, a marketing person is teamed with the innovator and a market evaluation is begun. At any time the marketer is convinced there is not a sufficient market to profitably support the product, the product idea is abandoned.

The testing program consists of product testing in the laboratory or field. Often it will also include market testing. This involves

Table 1. Checklist of Major Sources for New-Product Ideas*

---

1. Company staff, records, experience

Research & engineering staffs	Employee suggestions
Sales staff	Customer suggestions, inquiries, & complaints
Market research department	
Sales reports & other records	

2. Distributors

Brokers	Wholesalers or jobbers
Factory distributors (Manufacturers' agents)	Retailers

3. Competitors

Customers of competitors	Exhibits & trade shows
Competitors' products	Foreign products
Mail-order catalogs	

4. Miscellaneous

Inventors	Industrial consultants
Patent attorneys & brokers	Management engineers
Firms going out of business	Product engineers
Manufacturers of parts & accessories	Marketing research agencies
Suggestions from the public (or industry) as a result of advertising	Advertising agencies
	Trade associations of executives & laboratory personal
University & institute laboratories	Trade-magazine writers & editors
Commercial laboratories	

Source: U.S. Department of Commerce, *Developing and Selling New Products* (Washington, D.C.: U.S. Government Printing Office).

---

*Marketing Manager's Handbook, p. 643.

the use of the product by prospective buyers, as was the case with Chrysler's experimental turbine-powered car. Or it involves pilot production, followed by promotion and sale in a local test market. An example of this is the test marketing of king-size Coca Cola in Dallas, prior to its introduction in the national market. If the product fails in the test market, it is abandoned.

Commercialization. If the product survives all the previous steps and is selected for commercialization (about one product idea out of 58) the firm has the following options: 1) internal manufacture and marketing, 2) joint venture, 3) licensing, 4) sale, or 5) a combination of these alternatives.

The first option generally offers the greatest profit, but the largest risk. The second takes advantage of another firm's capabilities, either in marketing or production, and lessens the risk. The third and fourth minimize risk, but also profit. They are very difficult options to pursue if the product is not fully developed and proven in the marketplace.

Abandonment. Product life-spans vary from a few hours (an example being a single-performance theatrical or sport event) to an indefinite period. Electricity illustrates the latter. As the railroads discovered, there is a real danger in assuming that the demand for the firm's products or services will last forever. The market should be under constant surveillance—a job for market research—and management should be prepared to abandon the product when it is no longer profitable. Profit, for purposes of this decision, should reflect opportunity costs.

Designing to Sell

After the technical features and services of a new product have been approved, the sales and marketing executives are called in to voice their opinions and views of the style and design of package, container, labels, etc.

The design of a product is of primary importance to its success in the market; improvement of design in an established product is an assured way to increase sales. The strategy is at its best in the packaged-goods field. In the automotive field, new-model designs play an important part in the whole sales strategy. New-car models form the peg on which an intensive and expensive annual advertising and publicity campaign is hung. They create the interest that brings potential customers into the showroom and trade shows. They make people who ordinarily might drive their automobiles several years trade them in for "new models" every two or three years. Were it not for the "annual model" and the frequent change in design of automobiles, it would be impossible for the industry to make and sell millions of cars a year.

A sound business must be built on a sound product or service, one with merits that satisfy user needs. If the product or service is without merit, few people will buy it. If it does not satisfy a need, few people will buy it. This need may be psychological or physical; it may involve a desire for recognition, for security, for pleasure, for alleviation of labor, or any other of the many so-called buying motives. But whatever its character, the product or service must be of a nature to provide satisfaction to the purchaser.

For years it was the tendency of companies to manufacture products they liked best to manufacture, products that were the easiest, the cheapest, the least complex. Industry is strewn with the corpses of such companies, those that never quite understood that the tastes and needs of the world were changing and passing them by. Others awoke from their dreams, and at great cost and with tremendous effort returned to the practice of serving their customers. Ford with its Model T has long been the classic example of a sleeping giant that awoke; Ford with its Edsel will go down in history as a giant company that for a moment slumbered again; Ford with its Mustang marked the rebirth of a creative and adventuresome spirit within the company.

Elements of Industrial Design

Art BecVar, manager of Industrial Design Operation, stresses that:

"Customers are satisfied by well-designed products that are reinforced by the real quality of the parts the customer uses—not flimsy gadgets or trim—but solid parts.

"A washer, for example, should look sturdy, dependable, and well-made. Our job is to put it into a package that reflects these qualities."

General Electric's industrial design team puts great emphasis on human factors to meet the physical requirements and convenience of people. These factors include accessibility, size and dimensions, reach, line of sight, safety, lighting, control locations, and cleanability.

"The trend is away from gaudy-looking products to more functional designs with primary emphasis on safety," BecVar points out. "From the design standpoint, the human factors that make products easier and safer to use are receiving increasing emphasis.

"Today's consumers are much more discriminating in product selection and design features. How controls feel, read, and work are important considerations. Many people think that quality among major brands is comparable. Consequently, the human factors and useful features become more important."

Styling a product so that it will fit into the home environment is another design criterion. Unlike furniture, which is made in a specific style, such as French Provincial, appliances must be styled to integrate into any decor.

"Washers, for example, always were installed in basements," BecVar points out. "But many women now prefer them on the first floor. The change of location means washers have to be attractive and appropriate for the family and utility rooms and for the bathroom.

"The kitchen is no longer just a work area, but an integral part of the home. It is now subject to the same care in color selection and decorating as the rest of the house.

"The effects of color and form in other home furnishings tend to interrelate to the design of the kitchen, laundry, and air conditioning equipment. Design elements in our products help contribute to making the kitchen and laundry areas attractive and safe to work in."

BecVar sees the changes taking place in life styles and social habits as having a catalytic effect on appliance features and appearance.

"Waste, pollution, consumerism, retail distribution and urbanization will all have a significant impact, too, providing both constraints and opportunities."

Vernon P. Johnson, general director, styling and design, of Reynolds Aluminum, in a statement to Dartnell, writes:

"As I see it today, the designer's challenge is to cope with federal and industry regulations in location and size of copy, in finding space for the nutritional clause on small packages and labels, in converting familiar graphic layouts to include the Universal Pricing Code configuration, child-safe packaging, stress on recycling and biodegradable materials, and other components that usurp valuable space for the standard 'impact, identification, and information' elements.

"The thoughtful designer must consider all these things as he or she develops the initial concept, or else the primary effect is considerably weakened by additions, revisions, and subsequent committee-action adjustments. He or she must now, more than ever before, present an honest and forthright story in structure and graphics in order to reach the consumer who is a conscientious but increasingly confused buyer at the point of purchase.

"Over the years successful package design has been composed of honest communication through manipulation of elements that display well and offer handling and convenience information; but more than this, the good design effectively communicates the product, brand, and end-use advantages succinctly and in good taste. This objective hasn't changed, but imposed controls and sociologically-related demands have made it difficult to employ these design fundamentals with continuity.

"The designer must be alert to the regulations and other contributors to impaired display factors. With current knowledge of design hurdles, his or her role can be invaluable by including these things at the outset of planning in order that costly and time-consuming revisions can be held to a minimum as the work progresses. The finalized design should meet all requirements as it goes into production."

Principles of Good Design

Simplicity in design is essential, whether it has to do with a grain, a building, a display, a product, a store front, or anything else. Industrial design has been defined by Walter Dorwin Teague, a prominent American designer, as the external organization of product to reflect their internal efficiency for mass production and mass sales. The two go hand in hand. Good design is aimed at a specific objective, such as to influence acceptance at the point of sale, to stimulate "impulse" buying, to permit the effective use of less costly materials (such as plastics), or to build a desired impression in the public mind. The test of good design is not how "pretty" a product looks, but how effectively it attains its major objective. Too many designs miss the mark because they attempt to do too many things.

Function and Design

"Form follows function," a fundamental first voiced by famed architect Louis Sullivan, is a rule of good design that applies to all products, whether objects of impulse buying or studied purchases of lasting value, necessity, or long-felt want.

A grinding machine developed into an example of functional excellence because it enabled the operator to man all controls from one station. Originally, controls were on all four sides of the machine. The setup time was reduced, and the new organization of controls provided safety to the operator. Incidentally, the operator was proud of the new machine and its efficiency and production accordingly, increased capacity.

The recording companies are sensitive to the importance of package design. Their consensus is that, "it's what's in the grooves that counts, but intriguing packaging sure helps." Acy Lehman, former RCA art director, states that "packaging is the young people's art form. Young people want art they can identify with. I sometimes think that the kids would rather have bad art than good." But this sort of thing, according to *Graphic Arts,* "will always be exciting because it's personal, fast-moving, and free. Anything goes (on a record package) except pornography."

Paper products mirror the American housewife's growing affluence and changing life style. The metamorphosis of toilet tissue is a good example. Originally a white, single-ply roll, toilet tissue is now found on the average supermarket shelves in 60 varieties: double ply, colored, patterned, in multipacks, and even scented.

Steps in Designing to Sell

Having selected the designer, the next step is to provide him or her with the information on the sales objectives sought. Take a hypothetical product—say a fountain pen. How does the designer go about his task? Usually the first thing to do is to make a survey. He or she will check with users and those who merchandise the product to determine consumer preferences that should be recognized. Then historical files and patent records are searched to learn what "not to do" and that is important. Materials from which the product can be made are carefully studied. Then says Walter Dorwin Teague:

"A look at the production line may lend inspiration. Perhaps time and motion studies alone might cut down production costs. We ask questions, analyze every possibility. A designer must *contribute* something to the product; reduce production steps or cost; and improve the sales appeal.

"Any radical departure in design must have well-founded compensation factors that require studied sales promotion. Progress is spattered with the skeletons of questionable designs. It might be said that design should follow evolution, not revolution.

"A succession of sketches, renderings, conferences, and engineering drawings pass to management. The sales executive who knows the market potential expresses judgment. Visual or working models may be ordered and tested on school children and adults and at stores. Improvements will be incorporated in the designs and production when started.

"Next, the pen must be well-packaged for display. A strong appeal to the eye bolsters sales by giving new breadth to advertising and promotion. Color is very important psychologically. It has attention-dominance, atmosphere, and distinction. Whatever the product, color can be useful as a means of company identification. It can 'trademark' retail chain stores or a company's offices and products. The industrial designer can use color to establish and maintain a consistent theme in product and architectural work. We have all seen examples of design identification in standardized filling stations, reception rooms, trucks, letterheads, employee uniforms, and so on."

Replacement Programming

The development of a new product is a tedious, exacting, long-drawn-out and time-consuming pioneering process. It is surprising that so many manufacturers do not appreciate the length of time involved, and try to enter the market with half-perfected products.

A manufacturer of electrical equipment spent considerable time developing a variable-speed electric drill. The laboratory model had been brought to a point of performance satisfactory to the company's manager of research and development. He had placed about one hundred hand-made samples with potential users to test. No adverse comments had been received, and those comments offered were all favorable. The company was on the verge of placing extensive orders for production equipment when an outside consulting firm was requested to conduct a field investigation for the purpose of confirming the conclusions of the company's engineers.

All the plants that had been supplied with drills for test were visited, only to find that many of the drills had failed early and had been discarded. Since the manufacturer had not followed up on their use, the testing companies had assumed that the manufacturer knew about the inferior condition of the product and so had not notified the manufacturer. Revised samples were prepared and distributed for use under controlled conditions. Most of these eventually failed. How tragic it would have been had the manufacturer gone into production as originally intended!

Another company planned to market insulated aluminum wire for use in the manufacture of motors, transformers, and other electrical apparatus. It had perfected and patented a new process for covering wire; there was a shortage of copper wire; the company's engineers and salespeople had canvassed potential customers and had found the response encouraging; it had approached an investment house that was about ready to make it a sizable loan. At the request of the investment house, a field study was undertaken to verify the company's findings. The same respondents were called on and the same favorable responses received, but with reservations, which had not been pursued by the company. Yes, the manufacturers would use aluminum wire, *provided copper remained in short supply and the price remained high.* In addition, extensive redesign of the motors would be required that would take many months, even years, when proper field testing was included. The project was dropped.

This company had placed too much confidence in the market reports of its own engineers and salespeople; the former had been carried away by the attractiveness of their idea; the latter are inherently optimistic about the salability of anything new.

Under the extreme pressure of competition, many people in a firm get into the mood for taking a chance. Customers push the salespeople; salespeople push the sales manager; the sales manager pushes the director of marketing; the president pushes both the sales department and the research and development manager. The little danger signals that arise are overlooked or ignored, and a new, inadequately designed product hits the market, at which point money is lost, customers are lost, and time is lost.

To safeguard against these dangers, many companies establish strongly organized product-planning departments charged with the responsibility of screening all new ideas presented and of following them through set steps of product development to completion, including:

- Screening and evaluation

- Formal approval and assignment of projects for research and development

- Laboratory development of the design needed

- Field tests of the laboratory model

- Refinements resulting from the field tests of the laboratory model

- Preparation of production prototypes

- Technical and marketing field tests of the production prototypes

- Refinements resulting from the field tests of the prototypes

- Production of products for distribution
- Continued field tests and refinement of the production model

The greatest shakeout of new ideas comes in the screening and evaluation period. Here the mortality rate is amazing. A Bell & Howell executive has estimated that each year his company considers about 200 new product ideas. About one-fourth—or 50— receive research assignment; about half of this group—25— eventually are considered marketable products; but the company, for various reasons, actually markets only 12 of them, 10 of which may prove successful. Thus, out of the original 200 ideas considered, only 10, or 5 percent, are successfully marketed.

Another large company has estimated that out of 100 new product ideas considered, only 1.8 percent emerge as successful new products.

Screening Procedures

Some companies have established screening procedures, which include:

- Determination and formal application of evaluation criteria
- Appraisal, in writing, of all ideas submitted
- Preliminary market studies
- Advance profit assumption and similar financial safeguards

If an idea for a new product passes these preliminary tests, detailed financial analyses are made, which include:

- Estimates of possible sales-volume achievement
- Probable price levels for various sales-volume attainment
- Break-even points in manufacture
- Return on capital and marketing investments
- Cash flow and financial requirements

In the marketing aspects of these analyses, consideration is given to the company's overall and long-term objectives; to whether the product is being aimed defensively to *maintain* market position or offensively to *broaden* its market position. If the latter, it is kept in mind that all consumer demands in the markets to be invaded are currently being satisfied to a high degree of acceptance; therefore, the problem is to determine what competitive products can be replaced and how to go about doing it.

Time was when a company would have a half-dozen package designs made up by an artist, and then call in a few of the women from the office to decide which one they liked best. Today, scientific equipment is available for measuring the attention-getting values of signs, displays, package designs, and so on. One such type of equipment, designed by a Chicago firm specializing in visual communication, is described by an executive of that firm:

"The equipment consists of a helmet to which are attached a pair of dark glasses and a small spotlight. The woman doing the appraising sits in a dark room, with the package or display on a slanting shelf in front of her. As she turns her head to examine the item, the photographic light track shows what most attracted the subject's attention, what was skipped, and what was merely glanced at. At the same time, a tape recording is made of the person's comments—giving clues as to whether pauses, for example, are caused by interest or by confusion."

Other types of visual equipment are available for checking consumer reactions to colors, type sizes and type faces, length of line in printed material, and other items of visual communication related to product design and packaging.

Sales managers long have known that redesigning the labels on a product can materially increase its sales. An attractive, well-designed label helps greatly to win attention, which is the first step in making any sale. Labels not only cause the product to stand out on the dealer's shelf, but they add to its advertising possibilities. The more strength a label has, the more eye appeal it has. A good label should be simple. It should have the least "copy" consistent with good advertising and a color scheme that can be easily and inexpensively reproduced in advertising literature, as well as in outdoor bulletins and magazine ads. It should have bold, easy-to-read lettering. Top-quality art work is required. The dollars spent in designing a family of labels will work to the advantage of the seller for years to come, and pay dividends out of all proportion to the money invested.

Needless to say, today's label designers must work with one eye on the ever-changing but vitally important U.S. and state government regulations. This is an area in which the sales manager should be an expert. It should not be left to the purchasing agent or advertising manager.

Federal Regulations

A federal packaging law now regulates most product labeling. The principal requirement is that the quantity declaration on packages under 4 pounds or 1 gallon must be stated not only in terms of whole units and fractions, but also in total ounces. Thus, a bottle or can containing 3 pints of liquid must state "1 qt., 16 fl. oz." and also "40 fl. oz." This is a minor label-design problem.

Industry reaction to the law as a whole is summed up by a spokesman for General Foods: "The law seems to us in the food industry to be sound legislation. It preserves for private enterprise the vital right of self-regulation and—what is most important— the essential opportunity to innovate and offer consumers valuable new products and packages."

The main provisions of the federal packaging bill are as follows:

1. The Food and Drug Administration (FDA), for food, drugs, and cosmetics and the Federal Trade Commission (FTC), for all other consumer goods, are empowered to issue regulations requiring consumer-goods producers to put on every product package a statement of contents both in ounces and, if applicable, in full pounds, pints, or quarts, plus fractions thereof. This rule would apply only to packages weighing less than four pounds or smaller than one gallon.

2. The FDA and FTC are further empowered to regulate what size packages can be described by such terms as "small,"

"medium," and "large," and to regulate (but not outlaw) the use of such promotional labels as "cents-off" and "economy size." Food processors who specify the number of servings in the package will be required to state the quantity of these servings. Also, the bill bans slack filling that is "not necessitated by product protection or automatic machine packaging."

3. The Secretary of Commerce is authorized to call on manufacturers and distributors to develop voluntary standards whenever he or she decides an "undue proliferation (of package sizes)" is making it hard for consumers to make intelligent choices.

All manufacturers of packaged products in any form face a host of government regulations and requirements with which sales managers, new product managers, and packaging designers should be acquainted. For instance:

All aspirin-containing products shipped into retail outlets must be packaged in federally approved, child-resistant containers. There is an exception: Manufacturers will be permitted to market one package size that does not comply with the Poison Prevention Packaging Act (PPPA), but it must be clearly labeled: "This package for households without young children."

An excellent source for this information is a *Compilation of Selected Public Health Laws, Volume II,* printed by the United States Government.

Included are the Federal Food, Drug and Cosmetic Act; Federal Hazardous Substances Act; Poison Prevention Packaging Act; Tea Importation Act; Filled Milk Act; Imported Milk Act; Caustic Poison Act; Flammable Fabrics Act; Clean Air Act; Solid Waste Disposal Act; National Material Policy; Occupational Safety and Health Act; and the Lead-Based Paint Poisoning Prevention Act.

The concept of minimum weight is relatively new. It is designed to replace existing practices of labeling the contents of a package in terms of "average weight." Under current practices, some deviation in the weight of the contents of a package is permitted, so long as the average weight of all the packages in a lot conforms with the declaration that appears on the label.

Milan Smith, former executive vice-president of the National Canners Association (now known as the National Food Processors Association), claims that the minimum-weight requirement fails to "give reasonable consideration to utilization of high-speed lines, running as many as 1,000 containers per minute." These, he says, have brought economies to consumers.

Nabisco's vice-president of communications, protested that a minimum-weight proposal would force food companies either to pack more in a box or reduce the stated contents on the label. "Either case increases the cost of doing business," he says, "which, of course, is passed on to the consumer."

Other regulations were forthcoming from FDA dealing with mandatory labeling for drugs and cosmetics under the law. FTC also is responsible for regulations for other household products such as detergents and paper goods.

But the regulations covering the mandatory sections of the law are only part of the picture. The federal agencies also enforce the second half of the law—the so-called "optional provisions," designed to cope with such problems as "giant family size," "5 cents off" and the proliferation of package sizes.

As a mater of policy, the law declares: "Informed consumers are essential to the fair and efficient functioning of a free-market economy. Packages and their labels should enable consumers to obtain accurate information as to the quality of the contents and should facilitate value comparisons."

Part of the problem lies in enforcement of the law. Authority is split among the Commerce Secretary, the Federal Trade Commission, and the Food and Drug Administration. To compound the confusion, the measure gives the Commerce Department no real power of enforcement.

Through the National Bureau of Standards, the Secretary of Commerce is empowered to determine when, in a specific commodity, there is "undue proliferation" of package sizes or weights that might confuse consumers. If the Secretary makes such a finding, he or she must ask the industry involved to propose a voluntary standard that would remedy the situation.

If, after a year, the Commerce Secretary finds the industry has failed to come up with a viable standard, or if it has developed a standard but fails to conform to it, he or she then must ask Congress for regulatory authority to deal with the matter.

The FTC is authorized to handle regulations covering packaging and labeling of all consumer goods except foods, drugs, cosmetics, and medical devices, for which FDA is responsible.

Deeper Aspects of Packaging

Mitsubishi International Foods Division asked 18 food brokers what they thought of the company's new package design for its 3 Diamond brand of canned pineapples. Twelve brokers replied that they thought it would help them to sign up new accounts for the Chicago company's line of canned fruits, vegetables, and sea foods. The company also stated that since the new label went on supermarket shelves, sales increased by 20 percent over a period of nine months.

Designing a package to sell goes deeper than eye appeal. There is, for example, the problem of conserving shelf space if the product is sold through self-service stores. A number of companies found that using a square package rather than the conventional round package helped sales. It reduced the size of shipping cartons, facilitated stacking on the shelf, and brought the full label into view instead of just a part of it. Dairies found that square bottles, in place of the conventional round bottles for milk and cream, enabled them to load more bottles into a truck and lengthen routes; and that they packed tightly into refrigerators, leaving more room for other things.

Lipsticks sold more readily when designed so that they could be used as a pencil and carried without muss in a woman's pocketbook.

Display values naturally play an important part in designing any product to sell. There is a vogue of display cards, for counter or show-window use, which are cut out so that the actual product can be placed in the card, instead of merely illustrating it. This device has great attention value, but the product should be designed for the purpose. By a slight change in design, and the use of this display device, a food product's sales were increased by 25 percent.

In the same way, sales have been increased by designing a package so that it would have a second use after the product itself was consumed. A manufacturer of food specialties hit the jackpot with a container that would do double duty as a storage jar. It had a big opening so the housewife could put leftovers in it. Sales of cheese spreads increased when packaged in decorated glass containers that could be used afterwards for serving short drinks. Another popular container can be used, after being emptied, as a flowerpot; still another becomes a kitchen canister.

It was not too long ago that effective packaging was looked upon largely as a means of protecting the product during shipment. But, in the past 10 years significant changes have occurred, resulting from a multiplicity of products on the market and from increased selling and production costs.

Out of these changes has grown a broader and more realistic concept of what effective packaging is—and a new opportunity to reduce the costs of selling and production while adding merchandising impact at point of sale.

Today, effective packaging is generally recognized as a total of six broad areas: consumer use, merchandising, physical distribution, production, product development, and planning.

The "Silent Sell"

Elinor Selame, executive vice-president, Selame Design Associates, Newton, Massachusetts, speaking at an American Management Association seminar titled "How to Sell the Mass Merchandiser" said:

"In creating package designs for the mass market, it is important to keep the design as simple as possible. Find the one most important message, present it boldly with *very few* other competing graphic elements, and visualize your results as the product will appear in mass display. Does it have strong shelf impact? Will a busy consumer be able to spot your product quickly and quickly understand its benefits?"

Addressing a meeting of advertising executives, Russell A. Sandgren, of Sandgren & Murtha Inc., design and marketing consultants, said:

"The package identifies the product—no matter where you see it, under what circumstances you see it, or when you see it. A package is the product's personality, its reality. It has the basic obligation to position the brand in the marketplace, and keep working for that same brand—not just at the supermarket, but in the home.

"In the supermarket, the product is at least 4 feet away, and often it's 12 feet away. Here the consumer hasn't any time to fool around and, in fact, usually has an average of three to four seconds to make up his or her mind about any one product among the more than 50,000 items available.

"Packaging also has the further responsibility of providing factual information. Contents. Legal requirements. Ingredients. Recipes. Instructions. Name and address of manufacturer. It occasionally bears news of contests, sweepstakes, prizes, and premiums.

"In some cases, the package inspires the ad. In a recent product campaign, a design element was transplanted from the original package and incorporated in the advertising, the promotion materials, point-of-sale displays, price sheets, and other collateral materials. It was a perfect example of the synergistic theory behind many brand, marketing, and total communications programs. In this case, it provided a powerful product launching."

Humor is often appropriate in advertising, Sandgren noted, but most packages have a life expectancy of two to three years, and humor goes stale with prolonged exposure. Warnings were also sounded against the temptation to tamper with a successful, accepted package simply to be different or faddish, or to go after a specific market segment.

One company, he noted, changed its packaging to complement a TV commercial series and then canceled the commercials shortly after the new package was introduced.

Again and again, Sandgren concluded, it has been found that the package *is* the product.

Packaging redesigns, which are far more numerous than new-product packaging programs, are critical, and far more so than the development of packages for new products. A package for a new product can be changed a number of times in test markets before it is finalized.

Joseph M. Murtha, president, Sandren & Murtha, Inc., New York, writing in a trade magazine, said:

"A redesign can threaten all the equities and investments behind a brand and the disastrous errors, which start with a lack of clearly defined marketing objectives, established criteria, careful analysis, or consideration of possible sensitivity to package change in the product category, come to light only in the test-market situation."

It has been estimated that over 50 percent of all package redesigns never get to market. With shelf environment and competitive packaging constantly undergoing change, the decision to do nothing can result in heavy sales erosion. On the other hand, the decision not to proceed can sometimes save a product from critical losses.

Experience has taught that some products can weather packaging changes better than others. Even slight redesign should be approached very cautiously in circumstances like these:

- If the product category is declining at a steady rate (especially dangerous in a regional market).

- If the product is not capturing new users.

- If the consumer is of low income, education, and employment level (brand loyalty is higher in these groups and a package change may weaken loyalty).

- If the product category has not undergone packaging changes for several years.

- If there has not been much new product activity in the category being considered.

- If the product is in a "high anxiety" category. (Hair coloring products and certain drugs, for example, have a higher anxiety level than soap or cereal. In this connection it is, of course, dangerous to generalize, since any brand has unique characteristics and the pace of product introduction and supporting communications can serve to alter such "anxiety levels.")

When Not to Change

Sometimes it is better not to make any change in design. Here are some points to be considered:

- *Beware of the new brand manager's desire to innovate.* When a new brand manager appears, the prevailing calm begins to stir with intellectual probes, intoxicating ideas, stimulating thinking, and often, the brand manager's natural desire to innovate and push toward new sales goals. But, in order to reach them, he or she may feel the need to make a recognizable change in the marketing of the product and finds it easiest to do so by focusing on its packaging.

- *Don't change to imitate your competition.* When a direct competitor changes his product, it is always unsettling, especially when the change is as dramatic as packaging changes often are. When your competition makes such a move, you must assume that it's a carefully reasoned one, but it may not be a wise one.

- *Don't change for innovation alone.* New concepts in physical packaging are exciting, sometimes to the point where one can lose sight of the ultimate sales goal and the most direct way of reaching it.

- *Don't change for design values alone.* A poor-looking package might strike the proper note with certain types of audience. Because of its unappealing design, it may clearly say "I'm a bargain" to the price-conscious customer.

- *Don't change when product-package identification is strong.* Some products are so strongly identified in the consumer mind with a specific physical package that change endangers sales.

- *Avoid change that may hurt the branding.* When a product's brand identification is strong, any change must be approached with great care and the brand itself must be treated with something close to reverence. All effort must be directed toward preserving the equities of that brand and its appearance.

The chief executive of a major corporation said in a presentation to a marketing conference:

"In recent years there has been a good deal of talk about how package and product in the end become one. I think some validity has to be given to that point of view, especially now when so often the package won't sell a poor product—certainly not more than once, anyway.

"But from our point of view, the other side of the coin is more important: The individual who sells a quality product has a very valuable franchise from the consumer, and that is one thing that must not be jeopardized.

"We've got to make a package that will preserve the integrity and quality of the product; we've got to provide the same degree of protection the seller has always had, and we've got to make absolutely sure that the product gets to the consumer in the pristine form that the manufacturer insists on. We can make all kinds of improvements for this customer, but never anything that threatens in any way the quality of what is being sold. We would do everyone—including ourselves—a great disservice if we took that kind of a risk."

Packages and Product Failures

Package designers isolated from the marketplace are partly to blame for the high annual rate of new-product failure, according to Richard C. Christian, chairman of Marsteller Inc.

"One of your packaging designers comes up with an idea for a new package," he told members of the Packaging Institute. "It is novel. Nobody has ever done anything quite like it. You tend to react to the novelty of the idea, not its real or potential usefulness.

"It is not unusual to carry such an idea all the way to completion, then hand the product to the sales force and tell them to find somebody to sell it to."

The agency executive also said: "Most of your packaging design people are busily engaged in trying to find new and ingenious ways to use up more of the products you produce—paper, aluminum, glass, etc."

He urged that a way be found "to bridge the gap between your customers and your package design people." He added: "There's nothing sacred about an idea; if it has no practical application, there is no reason to preserve it or reward its author.

"When it comes to measuring the success of any idea— evaluating a package's total contribution to profits, reputation, and growth potential, the customer's success is the only key."

Self-Service Store Requirements

The trend toward self-service retailing makes the matter of packaging highly important. Since this type of store seldom permits a manufacturer to set up displays in the store, or put up advertising signs, the package and the label must carry the biggest part of the point-of-purchase advertising load. A survey of supermarket and discount-house merchandisers made by the Research Institute of America indicates that the four main factors in designing a package to sell itself on retail counters and display racks are:

1. *Simple design, keyed to the character of the product.* As competition increases, there's a premium on a package that will *stand out* and catch the customer's eye. Obviously, consumer tastes differ, and different products require different package treatment, but as a general guide, note that supermarkets find their best sellers among bright clear reds, yellows, and blues, contrasted with black or white. Off-shades, dark colors, and pastels don't usually attract the mass display. In most cases, retailers prefer clear, large lettering and a striking and uncluttered layout. Colored reproductions of contents and transparent wraps have been particularly successful in food stores. Retailers report that they get attention, put across the idea of quality, and identify the product quickly with the customer.

2. *Strong brand identity is growing in importance.* In case after case, sales have increased when packages were redesigned with an easily recognizable name, distinctive lettering, and an eye-catching trademark or symbol. If a clever selling message can be incorporated in the package, so much the better.

A distinctive trademark pays extra dividends when a manufacturer adds new lines in new packages. If the company symbol isn't sufficiently distinctive, family identity is lost and with it potential sales. Separate grades and types of products in a given line must, of course, be distinguished; but the identification should be worked out within the framework of the general family design.

Illustration: This is an old principle but its importance has received new proof in recent self-service experience. For instance, when Ralson Purina Co. added a line of farm sanitation products to its cereal and feed business, it created a little outline character called "Sanitation Sam." He's shown on the label doing whatever the contents indicate (scrubbing, spraying, etc.). Another idea that's gaining acceptance is the use of basic catch phrases from the manufacturer's advertising campaign.

3. *Full, brief information about the product.* What is it? How much does the package hold? How is it used? What does it cost? Retailer surveys show that if the label doesn't answer these questions quickly and completely, the dealer, as well as the consumer, will turn thumbs down. Informative labeling is increasingly necessary as a sales aid and servicing feature for all types of merchandising today.

Retailers prefer packages that have a "price spot"—a space in which the price can be marked. A *Sales & Marketing Management* survey proves the influence of price figures. Forty-three percent of the shoppers queried said they were frequently led into unplanned buying when price was shown. Other tests show sales drop sharply when price is removed.

The importance of pretesting any package change at the point of purchase is highlighted by the experience of a packer of dried food products. In an attempt to stem a decline in sales, the company decided to change from cellophane bags to a paperboard container. The new design was tested by means of consumer interviews. Eighty percent of the respondents said they preferred the new design, and the company invested in new packaging machinery and new cartons. *But* when the paperboard container was put in the stores, it stayed on the shelf while the cellophane bags moved out. Whatever was wrong, the trouble could have been avoided by testing under actual selling conditions.

4. *Convenience in handling and use.* The size of your package may or may not be a sales factor, but retailers have voiced complaints that should be noted by manufacturers. Some packages are too large to be handled easily; some are so small that they don't *look* like value. The whole problem of optimum size and weight and number of sizes should be checked at regular intervals, so that changes in retail merchandising and consumer preferences can be reflected.

Using Market Research

Market research is used throughout the product-planning program on a continuous basis. Some companies find it profitable to employ outside management consultants to assist them. Marketing executives who have invested in market research have found benefits as summed up in the following report by the American Management Association:

1. An organization is enabled to build its marketing structure on facts, thus eliminating much of the inefficiency and waste incurred by distributive efforts based wholly on past experience, intuition, and pure chance.

2. Marketing executives and sales personnel, as well as employees generally, are more confident of the soundness of operations and activities that rest on the bedrock of a desirable and acceptable product or service, a favorable competitive position, and tested channels of distribution.

3. Major operating executives in the organization develop an understanding and appreciation of the product or service and of marketing methods in general, giving them a good reason to become "sales minded."

4. The findings of marketing research indicate the direction that technical research should take by providing concrete data on customer preference relating to composition, design, or other attributes of the product or service.

5. Marketing research fosters goodwill, both in the consumer market and in the industrial market. As the activities become more firmly rooted in scientific methodology and professional viewpoint, a cooperative spirit is introduced—between producer and consumer, between producers of complementary products, between producer and wholesaler, etc.—resulting in improved marketing methods for entire industries.

Modern management must increase the precision of its decisions; it must come to rely more and more on judgments made in the light of adequate facts, or it will find itself outmaneuvered by competition. This process requires a highly objective attitude. We have passed out of the period when vigor and decisiveness alone are enough. They are still vital, of course, but to meet today's conditions, they must be supplemented by an eagerness to get the facts and a willingness to use them objectively. Unless and until that state of mind exists, there is little reason for management to spend money on sales research.

An objective attitude may, and in fact should, be a critical and skeptical one. Uncritical acceptance of any set of statistics is not objective. One of the big problems of management is how to distinguish between competent and dependable research and those statistics which "tread a path of mathematical logic between an unwarranted assumption and a preconceived conclusion."

Launching the New Product

The product concept has been accepted and approved. Prototypes have been developed and tested with all the technical specifications spelled out. Marketing strategies have been mapped out; the market niche, size, and distribution channels have been determined. Pricing and terms have been calculated. Production is geared up to handle the anticipated sales volume. Now, how do you roll it out to the market successfully? Here are several suggestions:

- Educate and train the inside sales support group, and advertising and sales promotion people on the use and operation of the product.

- Give telemarketing personnel a thorough training and education, including features, advantages, and benefits of the product. Supply them with lists of prospects.

- Train the field sales personnel along the same lines. Many companies time new product introduction with annual sales meetings. The excitement and stimulation of the unveiling of a new product in a group setting will ensure more rapid sales results. Make sure that technical and production personnel are on hand for the training process.

- If the product is subject to maintenance and repair, make sure the field service personnel are adequately trained. Make sure maintenance contracts and replacement parts are available.

- Highlight the new product at scheduled trade shows with appropriate fanfare.

- Time a direct mail campaign with the scheduled launch date. Have national and/or regional advertising, including radio and TV, ready to break at scheduled times.

- Supply the field sales personnel with adequate stocks of promotional literature and order forms.

- Publicity should include product news releases with photographs, as well as marketing news releases for trade publications and press conferences.

The investment and calculated risk involved in new products is great enough to demand that you give it your best shot.

Sales Policies

Chapter 21

Price Policies

There are three kinds of price-making. These are market pricing, administered or business-controlled pricing, and government-controlled pricing. Market pricing exists whenever the seller has no control over the price he receives in the marketplace and when price is determined solely by the free play of the forces of supply and demand. Administered or business-controlled pricing exists when prices are established by business firms at their own discretion. The seller sets the price and the buyers buy or do not buy as they wish. Government-controlled pricing exists when the prices of goods and services produced by private business are set by government.

Pricing a line of products in a complex and competitive market is not so simple. In fact, it presents one of the most difficult problems in sales management. If the price is set too low the business cannot long remain solvent. If set too high, the product may be priced out of its markets, cutting sales volume below the break-even point. Therefore, setting prices is a compromise between what the producer would like to get and what the buyer is willing to pay. The sound approach is from the viewpoint of the buyer.

Pricing Is Complex

Many general managers are unhappy with their pricing efforts. They feel sure they are leaving money on the table in some cases and missing volume in others. They also have a nagging feeling that there must be some strategic pricing moves they can make to get overall industry prices up and thereby improve their profits. But they are not certain of the legal limits and they are often afraid to raise prices for fear of losing volume.

Pricing is one of the most complex and least understood aspects of industrial marketing. James Naut, in a Conference Board Report, put his finger on the problem when he said:

"Pricing is a subtle art. Too often it has consisted of black magic—a mixture made up of one-third facts, one-third myths and delusions, and one-third economic theories that are out of phase with reality. If we are smart, we will work to eliminate the black magic and make pricing decisions based on facts."

In that spirit, we will not dwell on the theoretical aspects of pricing, e.g., price/demand curves, learning curves, penetration versus skim pricing, and marginal pricing. These elements are discussed in any marketing text. We will instead highlight the practical aspects and discuss actual techniques that managers have used to improve their pricing.

The first question often asked is, "How can I determine whether I have a pricing problem and thus take remedial action?" We have found that the use of the following simple checklist of ten questions can assist management in understanding the presence and magnitude of a potential pricing problem:

1. Are prices falling in real terms, yet share is constant or declining?

2. Do you have the feeling you are leaving money on the table, but cannot substantiate it with hard data?

3. Are your salespeople always claiming your prices are 3 to 5 percent high, yet your share is holding steady or rising?

4. Are pricing approval levels acting more as a volume discount mechanism than a control mechanism?

5. Do pricing approval levels reflect real profit levels?

6. Do your prices reflect customer-specific costs (e.g., transportation, setup, or design costs)?

7. Do margins (after customer-specific costs) vary widely by customer?

8. Can you define/describe your competitors' pricing strategies/rules?

9. Can you predict how and when competitors will react to your price moves?

10. Do you have a planned method of communicating price moves to 1) customers, 2) competitors (legally, of course), and 3) sales force?

Answering these questions requires detailed understanding of the company's pricing system (i.e., how prices are derived and administered, competitive price level over time, and price/cost relationships by product and customer). If one cannot answer these questions favorably or precisely, there probable is potential for price improvement.

To capitalize on this potential, one must know why there is a problem. Here a distinction must be made between *strategic* pricing and *tactical* pricing. Strategic pricing is principally the pricing image a company establishes for itself, "conventional warfare" pricing. Most industrial managers do a respectable job of strategic pricing, mainly because they are forced to by the marketplace. On the other hand, tactical pricing can be defined as the day-to-day management of the pricing process or "guerilla warfare" pricing. We have found that the tactical area is often overlooked by management. Yet, because so much industrial pricing is negotiated, guerrilla-warfare pricing most often affords management the greatest pricing opportunity.

Industrial Versus Consumer Pricing

Price is used far less as a competitive weapon in industrial marketing than it is in consumer marketing. The factors of importance to the industrial buyer are delivery, service, and general capability and reliability of the seller, as well as price. Buyers tend to place a great deal of emphasis on evaluating suppliers. They look at quality of both product and of the application engineering, customer service, and the capability of the supplier to work cooperatively with the buyer to maximize his or her satisfaction. Factors other than price are growing in importance, while price tends to decline in relative significance.

Criteria for Pricing Decisions

In determining how price decisions relate to profitability planning, it is recognized that individual industry conditions and company objectives can have a controlling influence on the goals of a particular pricing action. The most important factors include:

- Gross margin objectives
- Return-on-investment goals
- Buyer reaction to a proposed price
- Expected volume at an alternative price
- Probable competitive reaction
- Newness of product and degree of competition

Reasons for Changing Price

While every sales manager wishes for product price stability over lengthy periods of time, several factors mitigate against this utopian state. When a survey of companies was made regarding the primary reason for changing prices on existing products, the following were named most often:

- Change in cost element
- Competitive price change
- Periodic review
- Pressure from customers
- Increased competition as product loses its newness

It is worthwhile to note that price changes on existing products are made more quickly than are price determinations on new products. Under some market conditions, same-day or even same-hour decisions are made, while under other circumstances no penalty would result from a delay of months. Most commonly, revision of prices on existing products is made on a yearly basis, with a substantial number of companies making changes on a semiannual basis.

Pricing Variations

Different segments of the marketplace or ordering procedures dictate the need for variations in prices, terms, or discounts. Companies will structure price variations on the following bases:

- Quantity ordered for delivery at one time
- Channel of distribution
- Quantity ordered over a period of time (e.g., yearly volume)
- Type of customer (direct, chain store, etc.)
- Geographical location of customer
- Services required

Four types of control information are generally used for establishing price variations: 1) information from the field or competitive moves; 2) break-even and profit contribution by varying product volume levels; 3) formal statements showing relative profitability by type of product; and 4) regular reports of the relative costs of distribution for different products.

Other factors of lesser importance are regular reports on profitability by channel of distribution and type of customer or level of investment by product type. Most companies utilize the type of product and profit information that is readily available through existing sales reports and accounting records.

Research Methods Used

Various techniques are used in developing factual data for pricing decisions. Five of the most commonly used are:

- Analysis of competitive price/volume relationships
- Profitability model constructed from a sales forecast
- Test marketing or other sales experimentation
- Surveys of dealers or other trade sources
- Survey of ultimate users

Other possible sources are the data of manufacturing and selling costs.

Ratio of Fixed and Variable Costs

When a company is faced with a competitive move that suggests a price drop to hold market share, it must ask: "What additional volume must be gained to have the company remain at the same profit level?"

Figure 1, page 506 was designed to show a series of curves demonstrating added volume necessary to maintain profits at different ratios of fixed to variable costs. As is apparent with the pattern of the curves, the higher the variable costs in relationship to fixed costs, the greater the need for additional volume to compensate for price decreases.

Various Pricing Techniques

A pricing strategy that works successfully for a producer employing production-line techniques will not work for all. Some products, such as cement, must be priced according to the market or to the going price in various localities. It is not a question of selling at a price that assures a fair profit; it is a question of producing to a selling price as low or lower than that charged by competitors. The same is true in marketing fresh meat. The large packers are content to show a profit of 2 cents on each dollar of sales. Since they are in competition with local butchers, their competition actually sets the price for them. Because of this problem, the tendency in low-profit industries is for members of an industry to work together as closely as practical in setting prices, without exposing themselves to a charge of illegally fixing prices.

Pricing parts and materials sold to converters affords more leeway, since competition is not so keen and a producer is usually able to get a price above his competitors *if he can prove value.* It is at that point that salesmanship enters the picture. It is the general practice in such cases to add enough to the cost to do a constructive sales job, not only so far as the producer's own salespeople are concerned, but to provide for adequate advertising and sales promotion. In fact, the pricing formula usually allows about as much

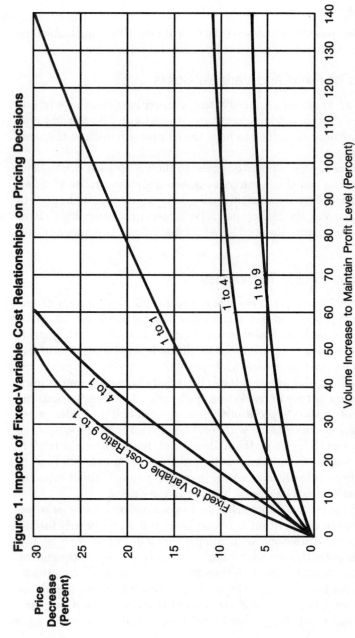

Figure 1. Impact of Fixed-Variable Cost Relationships on Pricing Decisions

Price Decrease (Percent) [y-axis]

Volume Increase to Maintain Profit Level (Percent) [x-axis]

Fixed to Variable Cost Ratio 9 to 1

4 to 1

1 to 1

1 to 4

1 to 9

This fixed and variable cost relationship is of particular significance to high variable cost nonmanufacturing types of businesses. All jobbers and distributors would fall in this category.

for marketing the product as for the cost of producing it. A commonly used method is to set the price at a figure that will allow one-third for production, one-third for selling, and one-third for administrative expense and profit. The aim is to arrive at a price that will yield 10 percent on sales. In good years the profit may exceed that goal; in poor years it falls below the mark. But over the years it should, if a business is to prosper and grow, average close to ten percent.

Still different pricing strategy is required when the product is sold for resale. In merchandising practice prices are set backwards—that is to say, a producer starts with the price at which he determines the product can best be sold over the retail counter. This is his or her catalog or list price. By a system of discounts from that price the producer arrives at a selling price to distributors that permits a fair profit over and above the cost of production, marketing, and administration. It also provides flexibility, since the price can be changed to different classifications of buyers by simply adjusting the discount.

The Pricing Pattern

The sound course to follow in pricing—and this applies especially during a period of changes in the general price index—is to establish a pricing pattern flexible enough to meet any condition, and yet rigid enough to provide an adequate profit at varying levels of sales production. Dr. Joel Dean, former professor of business economics at Columbia University, offers the following suggestions for establishing such a pricing pattern:

1. Alertness and flexibility should be the keynote of your pricing activity. Things are moving fast and prediction of the economic future cannot always pan out. Hence, policies must be continually reviewed and revised. A normal lifetime of price-setting decisions is being concentrated in a few months.

2. A philosophy of pricing is indispensable today. A patchwork of price decisions cannot successfully meet a continuously changing situation. You should formulate a pricing strategy

in terms of your long-range objectives and the efficient ways of attaining them. Surprisingly few companies have really done so.

3. Undertake basic research that will lay a sound foundation for more scientific pricing in the future. Price policy is probably the least scientific sector of marketing policy. Though techniques and tools for practical pricing research have definitely proved their usefulness, they are still in an early stage of development. In many instances price rises have not exceeded the increases in unit costs and price changes have lagged behind cost changes.

4. Adjust your costs to current and prospective price levels.

5. Adjust your income statement to fit economic realities. Otherwise the whole set of profit guides becomes distorted.

6. Align your prices with competitive and substitute bench marks to get the kind of buyers' action and market-share results that will attain your company's long-range objectives.

7. Put your price-differential house in order now. In many companies the structure of geographical, quantity, functional, and product-line price differentials have grown haphazardly.

8. Actively recognize the role of public relations in determining your pricing policies. Pricing is a public responsibility, particularly for firms that are pivotal in our economy.

The "Value Added" Pattern

A specific example of pricing policy in a diversified-product company was offered by the manager of marketing development for a metal products company:

An organization of the size and magnitude of Williams Metals, Inc., with its great diversification of products, develops a pricing procedure geared to profits. In developing a pricing structure of the various products, factors considered include the amount of the product that will be sold, relationships to material cost, manufacturing expense, overhead, and the cost of all other supporting elements in the manufacturing and marketing phases.

Products that are novel require a different pricing treatment because they are distinctive. The distinctiveness of a proprietary product may maintain its exclusiveness for a time due to patent positions or manufacturing technologies. Products not restricted by these conditions will be readily adopted by competitors who will attempt to take away your market by bringing out substitutes. The speed at which these products lose their uniqueness depends on many factors. Among them are the investment required by competitors to manufacture and market such a product, the strength of patent protection, and the aggressiveness of competitors.

Manufacturing experience and actual cost analysis are acceptable guidelines for pricing existing products. One may consider pricing policies successful when they achieve the following objectives: producing profits and maintaining market position in face of strong competition.

The strategy in pricing a product or products relates to a choice between "penetration" and "skimming" pricing. There are many intermediate positions depending upon a broad range of circumstances.

Our company, with its broad range of product lines, avoids adherence to a specific pattern of pricing and treats each product line individually because of the many variable factors related to the "create, make, and market system." The basis of our computation of pricing for profit is an adaption of the "value added" formula. "Value added" is the difference between the basic material cost and the selling price.

The Sales Manager's Role

The prime responsibility of the sales executive in pricing is to know, or be able to find out, what the customer will buy, and in what quantities he will buy at varying price ranges. Since the ultimate consumer actually dictates the price of most products, the sales manager should be in a position to advise top management as to the sales and advertising effort required to move a given volume within a certain time into the market.

At this point, it may be well to differentiate between *markup* and *markon*. Markon is the amount of profit added to the full cost of an item, while markup is the profit expressed in terms of a percentage of the sale price.

Another term of importance in price discussion is *price line.* Successful companies are careful to retain their price lines— $9.95, $29.95, $39.95, etc.—for years. While costs may vary, the selling price of a price-lined item remains fixed, and profits may shrink or rise in proportion. If the profit grows too small, the seller may jump the price to the next price line, or he may change the specifications of the product to reduce its cost. This practice is found particularly with consumer goods at the retail level but not at the manufacturers' and distributors' level.

No one has yet come up with a convincing explanation of why there is less resistance to buying a product priced at $19.95 than at $20.00; it's just one of the facts of life, which, for want of a better term, is called "psychological."

A price may be hopelessly high or low in terms of accounting formulas and still be psychologically correct for maximum sales. The comment following is by the vice-president in charge of research of one of the great mail-order chains. Note that three of the six factors in this company's price policy are psychological.

1. *The type of clientele* to which the store caters. X department store regularly gets 45 percent on an article for which Y can get only 38 percent. People who shop at the Y store are very price-conscious and are satisfied with the barren interior, the poor delivery system, and the cheap wrappings.

2. *Price line.* As merchandise increases in price, higher markups are taken. The customers for a pair of $60 shoes are less concerned with price than the customers for a $20 pair.

3. *Tradition.* For several reasons some types of merchandise get a higher markup than others. For example, piece goods and white goods are always sharply marked, while some jewelry gets a high markup.

4. *Cost of selling.* There are two factors involved in this point: class of salesmanship and hazards of merchandise. When an article requires knowledge of the merchandise and selling ability in the clerk, this higher cost of sales must be recognized and absorbed in the markup. As for hazards, anything with style is vulnerable to quick changes in public taste; a dress, which can become old-fashioned overnight, has to have a higher markup than a keg of nails. Any goods that are fragile, soilable, or perishable must absorb these risks. Mirrors, for instance, get at least a 50 percent markup.

5. *Turnover rate.* Since all merchandise must absorb its share of the overhead, an item with monthly turnover needs less of a markup than one which has an annual turnover rate of four or five because the unit overhead cost is lower.

6. *Location.* Percentage of markup differs from city to city. For instance, the average markup in Evanston, Illinois, is much higher than in Centralia, Illinois.

Psychological factors are involved in industrial pricing as well as in the pricing of consumer goods. A generator manufacturer said: "Two- and three-kilowatt generators can be manufactured and sold for the same amount, but the profit is better on the three-kilowatt unit because our customers expect the two-kilowatt unit to be cheaper."

Influence of Turnover on Profits

The rate of turnover is the most important factor in business. Offer any merchant two units of merchandise, one he or she can sell at a profit of 10 percent on his or her investment and the other at a profit of 15 percent, and the merchant will invariably take the 15 percent article. The merchant gives but little consideration to the fact that it may be possible to sell three of the 10 percent items while selling one 15 percent article, and in doing so make a gross profit of 30 percent, as against 15 percent on the long profit article.

Computed in terms of annual income, a merchant making

$30,000 a year with a stock investment of $10,000 would double his or her income with the same investment by turning over the stock twice as often.

Merchants should realize that, by handling slow-moving merchandise, they have to take losses in the shape of investment, interest, markdowns, salaries and wages, shelf or storage room rental, plus the prestige and reputation that are lost through handling unknown brands.

Pricing by Customer

The prices and discounts you set should be arranged to make all customers contribute equally to your profits. Since distribution represents the larger part of costs for many products, pricing by customer demands knowledge and control of distribution costs.

The Robinson-Patman Act states that price differences must be specifically traceable to the differing volume or character of your transactions with customers that compete with each other. What it amounts to is marking up the cost of each transaction by the *same percentage* for each customer.

Some customers require costly packaging. Others require special delivery or special facilities for displaying their goods. These can best be handled as extras or rebates, since their specific costs are fairly readily determined and directly assignable to particular customers as they occur.

The Philosophy of Price-Cutting

Consideration should be given here to price cutting as a way to increase sales, to move seasonal stock, to reduce inventory, etc. Cuts in price may also take the form of loss leaders or price leaders—an attractive price is intended to increase store traffic and to carry over to favorably influence buyers to purchase other products. It has been found that loss leaders attract so much store traffic, which leads to the sale of other goods at list price, that the loss is more than made up; to get this same promotional value through advertisements or other promotions would be far more costly.

However, when cutting prices, it must be realized that competitors will follow suit immediately with price cuts on the same product or on substitute products. Price wars can become dangerous experiences, and it then may become difficult to raise prices back to normal.

On the other hand, not to meet a cut price is equally dangerous; a competing product may attain recognition or customers may be lost. Price cutting is, therefore, a very serious matter. A company should engage in it with its eyes open and with the pros and cons all carefully considered beforehand. (See Figure 2, page 514.)

To Sum Up

All the factors bearing on the price decision are seemingly endless: costs, product, product life cycle, services, distribution channels, credit, demand, market share, competition, economic situation, etc. Costs and sales results are historical, while pricing is for the future. You can utilize mathematical models and sophisticated approaches but, when you come down to it, price is the result of a discretionary value judgment of a manager after he or she has considered and evaluated all possible factors.

Federal Trade Commission Guides Against Deceptive Pricing*

These guides are designed to highlight problems in the field of price advertising that have proved to be especially troublesome to business people who in good faith desire to avoid deception of the consuming public. Since the guides are not intended to serve as comprehensive or precise statements of law, but rather as practical aids to the honest businessperson who seeks to conform to the requirements of fair and legitimate merchandising, they will be of no assistance to the unscrupulous few whose aim is to walk the line between legal and illegal conduct. They are to be considered as

---

*Inquiries concerning these guides and requests for copies should be addressed to the Bureau of Industry Guidance, Federal Trade Commission, Washington, D.C. 20580.

Figure 2. You Must Sell More to Break Even

To find the percentage of increase in unit sales you will need to earn the same gross profits when you cut a price, look in the column headed present gross profit.

If You Cut Your Price	And Your Present Gross Profit is							
	5%	10%	15%	20%	25%	30%	35%	40%
1%	25.0%	11.1%	7.1%	5.3%	4.2%	3.4%	2.9%	2.6%
2	66.6	25.0	15.4	11.1	8.7	7.1	6.1	5.3
3	150.0	42.8	25.0	17.6	13.6	11.1	9.4	8.1
4	400.0	66.6	36.4	25.0	19.0	15.4	12.9	11.1
5	—	100.0	50.0	33.3	25.0	20.0	16.7	14.3
6	—	150.0	66.7	42.9	31.6	25.0	20.7	17.6
7	—	233.3	87.5	53.8	38.9	30.4	25.0	21.2
8	—	400.0	114.3	66.7	47.1	36.4	29.6	25.0
9	—	1000.0	150.0	81.8	56.3	42.9	34.6	29.0
10	—	—	200.0	100.0	66.7	50.0	40.0	33.3
11	—	—	275.0	122.2	78.6	57.9	45.8	37.9
12	—	—	400.0	150.0	92.3	66.7	52.2	42.9
13	—	—	650.0	185.7	108.3	76.5	59.1	48.1
14	—	—	1400.0	233.3	127.3	87.5	66.7	53.8
15	—	—	—	300.0	150.0	100.0	75.0	60.0
16	—	—	—	400.0	177.8	114.3	84.2	66.7
17	—	—	—	566.7	212.5	130.8	94.4	73.9
18	—	—	—	900.0	257.1	150.0	105.9	81.8
19	—	—	—	1900.0	316.7	172.7	118.8	90.5
20	—	—	—	—	400.0	200.0	133.3	100.0
21	—	—	—	—	525.0	233.3	150.0	110.5
22	—	—	—	—	733.3	275.0	169.2	122.2
23	—	—	—	—	1115.0	328.6	191.7	135.3
24	—	—	—	—	2400.0	400.0	218.2	150.0
25	—	—	—	—	—	500.0	250.0	166.7

Example: Your present gross margin is 25 percent and you cut your selling price 10 percent. Locate 10 percent in the left-hand column. Now follow across the column headed 25 percent. You find you will need to sell 66.7 percent MORE units to earn the same margin dollars as at the previous price.

This "Look Before You Cut Prices!" table has been used by a manufacturer to discourage price-cutters.

guides, and not as fixed rules of "do's" and "don'ts," or detailed statements of the Commission's enforcement policies. The fundamental spirit of the guides will govern their application.

The basic objective of these guides is to enable the businessperson to advertise goods honestly, and to avoid offering the consumer non-existent bargains or bargains that will be misunderstood. Price advertising is particularly effective because of the universal appeal of bargains to consumers. Truthful price advertising, offering real bargains, is a benefit to all. But the advertiser must shun sales "gimmicks" that lure consumers into a mistaken belief that they are getting more for their money than they are.

GUIDE I. FORMER PRICE COMPARISONS

One of the most commonly used forms of bargain advertising is to offer a reduction from the advertiser's own former price for an article. If the former price is the actual, *bona fide* price at which the article was offered to the public on a regular basis for a reasonably substantial period of time, it provides a legitimate basis for the advertising of a price comparison. Where the former price is genuine, the bargain being advertised is a true one. If, on the other hand, the former price being advertised is not *bona fide* but fictitious—as, for example, where an artificial, inflated price was established for the purpose of enabling the subsequent offer of a large reduction—the "bargain" being advertised is a false one; the purchaser is not receiving the unusual value he or she expects. In such a case, the "reduced" price is, in reality, probably just the seller's regular price.

A former price is not necessarily fictitious merely because no sales at the advertised price were made. The advertiser should be especially careful, however, in such a case, that the price is one at which the product was openly and actively offered for sale, for a reasonably substantial period of time, in the recent, regular course of business and not for the purpose of establishing a fictitious higher price on which a deceptive comparison might be based. The advertiser should scrupulously avoid any implication that a former price is a selling, not an asking, price (as, for example, by use of such language as, "Formerly sold at $_____"), unless substantial sales at that price were actually made.

The following is an example of a price comparison based on a fictitious former price. John Doe is a retailer of Brand X fountain pens, which cost him $5 each. His usual markup is 50 percent over cost, for a regular retail price of $7.50. In order subsequently to offer an unusual "bargain," Doe begins offering Brand X at $10 per pen. He realizes that he will be able to sell few, if any, pens at this inflated price. But he doesn't care, for he maintains that price for only a few days. Then he "cuts" the price to its usual level, $7.50, and advertises: "Terrific Bargain: X Pens, Were $10, Now Only $7.50!" This is obviously a false claim. The advertised "bargain" is not genuine.

Other illustrations of fictitious price comparisons could be given. An advertiser might use a price at which the article was never offered, which was not used in the regular course of business, or which was not used in the recent past but at some remote period in the past, without making disclosure of that fact; the advertiser might use a price that was not openly offered to the public, or that was not maintained for a reasonable length of time, but was immediately reduced.

If the former price is set forth in the advertisement, whether accompanied or not by descriptive terminology such as "Regularly," "Usually," "Formerly," etc., the advertiser should make certain that the former price is not a fictitious one. If the former price, or the amount of percentage of reduction, is not stated in the advertisement (as when the ad merely states, "Sale"), the advertiser must take care that the amount of reduction is not so insignificant as to be meaningless. It should be sufficiently large that the consumer, if he or she knew what the reduction was, would believe that a genuine bargain or saving was being offered. An advertiser who claims that an item has been "Reduced to $9.99," when the former price was $10.00, is misleading the consumer, who will understand the claim to mean that a much greater, and not merely nominal, reduction was being offered.

GUIDE II. RETAIL PRICE COMPARISONS AND COMPARABLE VALUE COMPARISONS

Another commonly used form of bargain advertising is to offer goods at prices lower than those being charged by others for the same merchandise in the advertiser's trade area. This may be done either on a temporary or a permanent basis, but in either case the advertised higher price must be based upon fact, and not be fictitious or misleading. Whenever an advertiser represents that he or she is selling below the prices being charged elsewhere in the area for a particular article, he should be reasonably certain that the higher price advertised does not appreciably exceed the price at which substantial sales of the article are being made. A consumer should consider the reduction to be a genuine bargain or saving. Expressed another way, if a number of the principal retail outlets in the area are regularly selling Brand X fountain pens at $10, it is not dishonest for retailer Doe to advertise: "Brand X Pens, Price Elsewhere $10, Our Price $7.50."

The following example, however, illustrates a misleading use of this advertising technique. Retailer Doe advertises Brand X pens as having a "Retail Value $15.00, My Price $7.50," when the fact is that only a few small suburban outlets in the area charge $15. All of the larger outlets located in and around the main shopping areas charge $7.50, or slightly more or less. The advertisement here would be deceptive, since the price charged by the small suburban outlets would have no real significance to Doe's customers, to whom the advertisement of "Retail Value $15.00" would suggest a prevailing, and not merely an isolated, price in the area in which they shop.

A closely related form of bargain advertising is to offer a reduction from the prices being charged, either by the advertiser or by others in the advertiser's trade area, for other merchandise of like grade and quality. Such advertising can serve a useful and legitimate purpose when it is made clear to the consumer that a comparison is being made with other merchandise that is, in fact, of essentially similar quality and obtainable in the area. The advertiser should, however, be reasonably certain that the price advertised as being the price of comparable merchandise does not exceed the price at which such merchandise is being offered by representative retail outlets in the area. For example, retailer Doe advertises Brand X pen as having "Comparable Value $15.00." Unless a reasonable number of the principal outlets in the area are offering Brand Y, an essentially similar pen, for that price, this advertisement would be deceptive.

GUIDE III. ADVERTISING RETAIL PRICES WHICH HAVE BEEN ESTABLISHED OR SUGGESTED BY MANUFACTURERS (OR OTHER NON-RETAIL DISTRIBUTORS)

Many members of the purchasing public believe that a manufacturer's list price, or suggested retail price, is the price at which an article is generally sold. Therefore, if a reduction from this price is advertised, many people will believe that they are being offered a genuine bargain. To the extent that list or suggested retail prices do not in fact correspond to prices at which a substantial number of sales of the article in question are made, the advertisement of a reduction may mislead the consumer.

There are many methods by which manufacturers' suggested retail or list prices are advertised: large scale (often nationwide) mass-media advertising by the manufacturer; pre-ticketing by the manufacturer; direct mail advertising; distribution of promotional material or price lists designed for display to the public. The mechanics used are not of the essence. These guides are concerned with *any* means employed for placing such prices before the consuming public.

There would be little problem of deception in this area if all products were invariably sold at the retail price set by the manufacturer. However, the widespread failure to observe manufacturers' suggested or list prices, and the advent of retail discounting on a wide scale, have seriously undermined the dependability of list prices as indicators of the exact prices at which articles are in fact generally sold at retail. Changing competitive conditions have created a more acute problem of deception than may have existed previously. Today only in rare cases are *all* sales of an article at the manufacturer's suggested retail or list price.

However, this does not mean that all list prices are fictitious and all offers of reductions from list deceptive. Typically, a list price is a price at which articles are sold, if not everywhere, then at least in the principal retail outlets that do not conduct their business on a discount basis. It will not be deemed fictitious if it is the price at which substantial sales are made in the advertiser's trade area. Conversely, if the list price is significantly in excess of the highest price at which substantial sales in the trade area are made, there is a clear and serious danger of the consumer being misled by an advertised reduction from the price.

This general principle applies whether the advertiser is a national or regional manufacturer (or other non-retail distributor), a mail-order or catalog distributor who deals directly with the consuming public, or a local retailer. But certain differences in the responsibility of these various types of businesspeople should be noted. A retailer competing in a local area has at least a general knowledge of the prices being charged in the area. Therefore, before advertising a manufacturer's list price as a basis for comparison with his or her own lower price, the retailer should ascertain whether the list price is in fact the price regularly charged by principal outlets in the area.

In other words, a retailer who advertises a manufacturer's or distributor's suggested retail price should be careful to avoid creating a false impression that a reduction is being offered from the price at which the product is generally sold in the trade area. If a number of the principal retail outlets in the area are regularly engaged in making sales at the manufacturer's suggested price, that price may be used in advertising by one who is selling at a lower price. If, however, the list price is being followed only by, for example, small suburban stores, house-to-house canvassers, and credit houses—accounting for only an insubstantial volume of sales in the area—advertising of the list price would be deceptive.

On the other hand, a manufacturer or other distributor with a business on a large regional or national scale cannot be required to police or investigate in detail the prevailing prices of his or her articles throughout so large a trade area. If he or she advertises or disseminates a list or pre-ticketed price in good faith (i.e., as an honest estimate of the actual retail price) that does not appreciably exceed the highest price at which substantial sales are made in trade area, the manufacturer or distributor will not be chargeable with having engaged in a deceptive practice. Consider the following example:

Manufacturer Roe, who makes Brand X pens and sells them throughout the United States, advertises this pen in a national magazine as having a "Suggested Retail Price $10," a price determined on the basis of a market survey. In a substantial number of representative communities, the principal retail outlets are selling the product at this price in the regular course of business and in substantial volume. Roe would not be considered to have advertised a fictitious "suggested retail price." If retailer Doe does business in one of these communities, he would not be guilty of a deceptive practice by advertising, "Brand X Pens, Manufacturer's Suggested Retail Price, $10.00, Our Price, $7.50."

It bears repeating that the manufacturer, distributor, or retailer must in every case act honestly and in good faith in advertising a list price, and not with the intention of establishing a basis, or creating an instrumentality, for a deceptive comparison in any local or other trade area. For instance, a manufacturer may not affix price tickets containing inflated prices as an accommodation to particular retailers who intend to use such prices as the basis for advertising fictitious price reductions.

GUIDE IV. BARGAIN OFFERS BASED UPON THE PURCHASE OF OTHER MERCHANDISE

Frequently, advertisers choose to offer bargains in the form of additional merchandise to be given a customer on the condition that he or she purchase a particular article at the price usually offered by the advertiser. The forms which such offers may take are numerous and varied, yet all have essentially the same purpose and effect. Representative of the language frequently employed in such offers are "Free," "Buy One - Get One Free," "2-For 1 Sale," "Half Price Sale," "1¢ Sale," "50 Percent Off," etc. Literally, of course, the seller is not offering anything free (i.e., an unconditional gift), or 1/2 free, or for only 1¢, when he or she makes such an offer, since the purchaser is required to purchase an article in order to receive the "free" or "1¢" item. It is important, therefore, that where such a form of offer is used, care be taken not to mislead the consumer.

Where the seller, in making such an offer, increases the regular price of the article required to be bought, or decreases the quantity and quality of that article, or otherwise attaches strings (other than the basic condition that the article be purchased in order for the purchaser to be entitled to the "free" or "1¢" additional merchandise) to the offer, the consumer may be deceived.

Accordingly, whenever a "free," "2-for-1," "half price sale," "1¢ sale," "50 percent off" or similar type of offer is made, all the terms and conditions of the offer should be made clear at the outset.

GUIDE V. MISCELLANEOUS PRICE COMPARISONS

The practices covered in the provisions set forth above represent the most frequently employed forms of bargain advertising. However, there are many variations which appear from time to time and which are, in the main, controlled by the same general principles. For example, retailers should not advertise a retail price as a wholesale price. They should not represent that they are selling at factory prices when they are not selling at the prices paid by those purchasing directly from the manufacturer. They should not offer seconds or imperfect or irregular merchandise at a reduced price without disclosing that the higher comparative price refers to the price of the merchandise if perfect. They should not offer an advance sale under circumstances where they do not in good faith expect to increase the price at a later date, or make a "limited" offer which, in fact, is not limited. In all of these situations, as well as in others too numerous to mention, advertisers should make certain that the bargain offer is genuine and truthful. Doing so will serve their own interest as well as that of the public.

These guides were adopted December 20, 1963 and supersede the Guides Against Deceptive Pricing adopted October 2, 1958.

Chapter 22

Terms of Sale and Discounts

The businessperson has a fairly free hand in establishing prices for his or her products, so long as this is not done in collusion with others for the purpose of restraining competition.

It is in the area of setting terms of sale and establishing discount policies that the sales manager must be alert for an innocently-inspired violation of the provisions of the Robinson-Patman Act and the regulations of the Federal Trade Commission.

The sales manager must remember that whatever terms of sale and discounts offered, these must be available to *all* customers who comply with qualifying requirements for the terms and discounts. Thus, if one wholesaler is allowed a large discount for an extremely large order, the same discount must be made available to any other customer willing to purchase a like quantity of goods. Furthermore, the manager must offer the same terms of sale. He or she cannot allow one customer a 2 percent discount if the invoice is paid within 10 days and insist upon the full price from another who pays within 10 days of delivery.

Payment Requirements

Terms establish the conditions under which invoices must be paid. They may be classed as ordinary, extra, or dating ahead terms.

- *Ordinary Terms*

    1. *Net.* Terms such as net/30 means that payment of the face value of the invoice must be made within 30 days or within the number of days stated.

    2. *Open Account.* Such terms usually imply payment within one week or 10 days or whatever period is agreed upon by the buyer and seller.

3. *FOB* (free on board). Normally, this term means that the item sold is placed free on board a truck, railway car, or aircraft. Where overseas shipment is involved, the term FAS (free alongside ship), is often used. In both cases, the buyer takes over all transportation costs. In the absence of any contractual terms to indicate a different agreement, the buyer bears the risk of loss when merchandise is shipped FOB. Qualifications are often added; for example, FOB destination, FOB factory, or FAS New York.

4. *COD* (cash on delivery). This is used quite frequently, either at the buyer's or seller's request. Under such terms, the seller assumes freight charges both ways if the purchaser refuses to accept shipment unless the merchandise can be sold to another customer in the vicinity.

5. *SDBL* (sight draft—bill of lading). Before shipment will be made, the buyer is required to make immediate payment on a "sight draft," which is attached to an advance bill of lading.

In all the above terms, with the exception of "net," a cash discount may or may not be given. Net terms, as the name implies, carry no cash discount.

• Extra or Dating Ahead Terms

1. *EOM or MOM* (end of the month or middle of the month). These terms indicate that the credit period starts either on the last day of the month in which the goods are shipped, or on the 15th. For both terms, the purpose is greater convenience for both buyers and sellers. Buyers can make many purchases during a month, pay bills monthly with a single check, and still take advantage of the regular discount. Sellers can cut accounting and billing costs because there are fewer settlements of accounts.

Using EOM terms, for example, you make purchases on August 1, 9, 17, and 25. But all these orders are invoiced to you as of September 1. With terms of 2/10, net 30, you could take your prompt payment discount up to September 10; the full amount would not be due until September 30.

Using MOM terms, you make purchases on September 1, 5, 7, 9, and 12. But all these orders are invoiced to you as of September 15. If you buy on September 16, 20, 22, 26, and 29, those orders are billed as of October 1.

2. *Proximo* (specified date in the coming month). Terms 2/10 proximo require payment on the 10th of the month following purchase to secure the 2 percent discount. Actually such terms are the equivalent of 2/10 EOM.

3. *ROG or AOG* (receipt of goods; arrival of goods). Under these terms, the discount period is based on the date on which the purchaser receives the goods. For example, merchandise with a 2/10, n/30, ROG dating received September 15 must be paid for by September 25 if the discount is to be taken.

ROG terms are employed to meet objections of distant purchasers who would be at a disadvantage if terms were based on "date of invoice." A supplier located in the East with customers throughout the nation must, of necessity, employ ROG terms if he or she is to meet competition from the customers' local suppliers.

The buyer gets the benefits of ROG terms only when the bill is discounted. If he does not pay the bill in time to take the discount, the net period is measured from the date of the invoice.

4. *"Extra" Terms.* Where these terms apply, the discount can be taken until the expiration of the "extra" period. Thus, in the wholesale drygoods trade, you find terms such as 2/10–60 (2 percent 10 days, 60 days extra). These terms allow the buyer a 2 percent discount if he or she pays the bill within 70 days of the invoice date. Another term is 3/10, 2/10–60, which allows a 3 percent discount if payment is made within 10 days, but only 2 percent if payment is made after the 10th day.

Close examination of the term 3/10, 2/10–60 reveals

that the actual prompt payment discount is only 1 percent, to be taken when the bill is paid within 10 days. The other 2 percent should really be considered a "trade" discount.

Quantity Discounts

The time-honored practice of allowing larger discounts in consideration of larger orders, as has been stated, is sanctioned by the Federal Trade Commission, provided discounts represent actual cost savings, or the buyer renders special services as a consideration. The Robinson-Patman Act also allows different quantity discounts to different customers *if the customers are not in competition with one another.* A sale of merchandise to isolated customers, at larger discounts, for example, is not considered discriminatory, if both customers do an intrastate business and are located in different states. In the same way wholesalers do not compete (in theory) with retailers, so a seller would be in the clear if he gave the wholesaler a larger discount than he gave a retailer in the same territory, even though the retailer claimed to be in competition with the wholesaler on industrial and other accounts. But broadly speaking the test of legality of quantity discounts is the savings the seller is able to pass on to the buyer by selling in larger quantities.

Functional or Trade Discounts

Whereas quantity discounts are extended to all firms in the same distribution level (horizontally applied), functional or trade discounts are extended to firms in different distribution levels (vertically applied). The accompanying Discount and Markup Chart—A-From List (Table 1, page 526) illustrates this. Note that the consumer is normally expected to pay the list price of $1. However, at times he may purchase in such quantities as to justify a 10 percent discount. His normal buying quantity is shown on the solid line.

The retailer is expected to buy normally in lots of 1,000 units or more and to receive a 38 percent discount from list, outlined by the

Table 1. Discount and Markup Chart

A—FROM LIST

CONSUMER

Quantity	Discount	Net Price
1-99	—	$1.00 List
100+	10%	.90

RETAILER

Quantity	1-99	100-999	1000+	Extra
Discount	20%	30%	38%	38-5%
Net Price	.80	.70	.62	.589

MARKUP

Retailer	20%	30%	38%	
(Wholesaler)	(12%)	(-)	(Loss)	
Retailer	11%	22%	31%	
(Wholesaler)	(19%)	(7%)	(Loss)	
(Wholesaler)	(31%)	(21%)	(11%)	
(Wholesaler)	(47%)	(28%)	(19%)	(15.1%)

WHOLESALER

Quantity	Discount	Net Price
1-99	30%	.70
100-999	35%	.65
1000-4999	45%	.55
5000+	50%	.50

B—FROM FUNCTIONAL LISTS

Quantity	CONSUMER — List $1.00		RETAILER — List 80c ($1.00 less 20%)		WHOLESALER — List 70c ($1.00 less 30%)	
	Discount	Net Price	Discount	Net Price	Discount	Net Price
1-99	—	$1.00	—	$.80	—	$.70
100-999	10%	.90	12.5%	.70	7.1%	.65
1000-4999			22.5%-	.62	21.4%	.55
5000+			22.5-5%	.589	28.6%	.50

solid line. If he or she sells to the consumer at list price, the retail markup is 38 percent; if the retailer sells at 10 percent less list, the markup is 31 percent. However, at times the retailer may buy smaller quantities, as for instance 50 units. In this case, the retail discount is 20 percent; and if the retailer sells to the consumer at list less 10 percent the markup is only 11 percent.

In the example, the wholesaler normally buys in lots exceeding 5,000 units on which he or she receives a 50 percent discount. If the wholesaler sells to the retailer in normal quantities of 1,000 or more units, the wholesaler receives a markup of 19 percent. If he should extend the retailer an extra 5 percent (list-38 percent-5 percent) the retailer would pay 59 cents and the wholesaler would realize a markup of 15.1 percent.

In lots of 2,000 units, the consumer would receive a discount of 10 percent from list; the retailer 38 percent, and the wholesaler 45 percent.

Functional List Discounts

Another way to handle functional or trade discounts is shown on the same chart under "B-From Functional Lists." Here the consumer quantity discount of 10 percent has been taken from a base of $1. The retailer's quantity discount for normal purchases exceeding 1,000 units has been taken from a base of 80 cents ($1 less 20 percent discount). The base used for the wholesaler is 70 cents ($1 less 30 percent). The resulting markups remain the same as shown in Part "A."

This method of discounting requires the printing of three price lists. These are quite frequently printed in three different identifying colors. When quoting a wholesaler, the manufacturer sends all three lists. The wholesaler sends the retailer the retail and consumer lists, etc.

Some manufacturers issue only one price sheet with quantity discounts shown, and rely upon the quantities purchased to classify the buyers into their respective functional groups.

The Effective Total Discount

As discussed by R. R. Gist and W. D. Poole in Dartnell's *Marketing Manager's Handbook,* prices are often quoted as a chain or series of discounts. This "chain" is deducted from a specified "list" price. It is often helpful to be able to appraise these chain discounts in terms of the effective total discounts they embody. An effective total discount is what the chain would be if quoted as a single discount from list price. A simple example will illustrate this idea: Assume that competing suppliers offer discounts from the same list price of a) 30, 10, 5, and 2 and b) 35, 5, 5, 2. Which of these chains represents the largest effective total discount, and what is the effective total discount for both of the offers?

The chain discount from source a) taking all discounts results in a payment of 58.653 percent of list price. The effective total discount of that chain is, then, 41.347 percent. Note that the effective total discount is not simply the sum of the elements in the chain. The effective total discount is defined as one minus the product of the complement of each of the elements in the chain. Our 41.347 percent is derived as follows:

$$1 - (.7 \times .9 \times .95 \times .98) = 41.347 \text{ percent}$$

Note that the .7, .9, .95, and .98 in the statement above correspond to the four elements in the chain discount—they are simply complements. Note also that in calculating the effective total discount of a chain, it makes no difference in which order the elements in the chain are considered. This is not to say that the order of the discounts is inconsequential when determining the amount of a specific discount—such as the quantity discount, the promotional discount, and so forth. If the amount of a specific discount element is sought, then one must take the discounts in order. What is the effective total discount corresponding to our second chain? It is, again, defined as $1 - (.65 \times .95 \times .95 \times .98)$. This second source then offers an effective total discount of 42.60385 percent off list price.

"Early Order" Discounts

Encouraging buyers to place quantity orders by placing them in a definite yearly purchase classification and giving them a special discount if they order 40 percent in the early portion of the season, has proved successful in many cases where volume is especially important. It can be justified under the Robinson-Patman Act from a cost standpoint. A rubber company used the following plan:

Dealers who buy out of stock and whose annual purchases are over $10,000 receive a discount of 15 percent on their early orders and 10 percent on their fill-in orders. Dealers who buy between $8,000 and $10,000 receive 12½ percent early-order discount and 10 percent on fill-in orders. Dealers who buy from $5,000 to $8,000 receive 10 percent early-order discount and 8 percent on fill-in. Dealers who buy from $2,500 to $5,000 receive 8 percent early-order discount and 5 percent fill-in. Dealers who buy from $1,000 to $2,500 receive a volume rebate at the end of the year of 2½ percent.

Those dealers who receive an early-order discount receive this only when they place a substantial early order of at least 40 percent of the volume classification in which they fall.

Our policy of protecting buyers against price decline applies only to those buyers whose resale price is controlled in any way by our actions. This means that price protection with us is limited only to jobbers who follow our printed prices to retailers.

Our merchandise is very seasonal and therefore we guarantee full price protection on all deliveries of rubber footwear that we make between April 1 and December 1, but in our entire history there has never been a change of price in this period. Therefore, the above statement that our guarantee applies only to jobbers is correct.

In addition to this price guarantee applying to retailers and jobbers, we protect our jobbers against a decline in price after December 1 and up to our initial announcement of prices for the succeeding season, covering all goods that they have on hand that were delivered after December 1, plus all goods they have on hand delivered between April and December 1 up to a total equal to 20 percent of our deliveries to them from April 1 to December 1.

Cash Discounts

Strictly speaking, the cash discount is a financial discount and not sales expense. The Federal Trade Commission recognizes this difference between cash and trade discounts. In actual practice, however, buyers add discounts together and treat them as a trade discount, according to whether or not it is their practice to discount their bills.

Even the most casual inquiry into this matter of cash discount reveals a woeful lack of general understanding among buyers that 2 percent 10 days, net 30 days, is equivalent to 36 percent per annum on their money. There is an equally deplorable lack of understanding on the part of sellers who endeavor to use a slightly increased cash discount as a sales lever, that 3 percent 10 days, net 30 days, is equivalent to 54 percent per annum on the money. In this connection Table 2, below, may be useful.

The cash discount is what a seller is willing to give customers for paying their bill 20 days before the expiration of the full 30-day period. A 2 percent cash discount thus gives the buyer an inducement of 36 percent a year, since there are 18 periods of 20 days each, which might be anticipated by the buyer if he were having shipments made throughout the year.

Table 2. Cash Discount Table

```
 ½% 10 days—net 30 days =  9% per annum
 1 % 10 days—net 30 days = 18% per annum
 1½% 10 days—net 30 days = 27% per annum
 2 % 30 days—net  4 mos. =  8% per annum
 2 % 10 days—net 60 days = 14% per annum
 2 % 30 days—net 60 days = 24% per annum
 2 % 10 days—net 30 days = 36% per annum
 3 % 10 days—net  4 mos. = 10% per annum
 3 % 30 days—net 60 days = 36% per annum
 3 % 10 days—net 30 days = 54% per annum
```

Unearned Discounts

Some customers deduct the cash discount even though the discount has passed. This amounts to the customer dictating his own terms of payment. If customers are allowed to dictate the terms of sale, it amounts to allowing them to dictate the price at which they will buy. This, of course, is contrary to the Robinson-Patman Act, which requires that no advantages in price or terms be granted one customer that are not allowed all customers under similar conditions.

The usual practice when a customer takes an unearned discount is to return the check, thus leaving the account open and the buyer's credit impaired. However, it is not legally necessary that the check be returned. It can be accepted in part payment of the account. If that policy is followed, care must be used to see that endorsement of the check does not constitute receipt in full for the items covered. But no matter how the unearned discount is handled, it invariably leads to unpleasantness, especially with well-rated customers. For that reason some sales managers prefer to accept the loss and allow the discount, rather than make an issue out of the incident. But once the customer "gets away" with taking an unearned discount, he may soon take other advantages. A courteous, but firm policy is best in the long run, explaining to the customer that it would be unfair to those who pay promptly to get the discount.

Advertising Allowances

The advertising allowance is used mainly by manufacturers of branded products, either as a means of introducing a new product or getting added dealer "push" behind an old product. Properly used, it is an excellent method of stimulating sales.

Many manufacturers have found it profitable to offer an advertising allowance to encourage local retailers to do more advertising, to take advantage of local advertising rates that might not be available to a national manufacturer, and to benefit by the retailer's knowledge of local conditions. When applying this allowance, manufacturers usually insist that a tear sheet of the advertisement accompany the retailer's request for allowance. Otherwise the retailer might take the allowance and add it to his or her profits, a practice considered unfair under the Robinson-Patman Act.

In some industries advertising allowances are based on a detailed program formally distributed as the company's "cooperative advertising policy." The rules and regulations under which the allowances are made to distributors or dealers are spelled out to avoid possible misunderstandings and to ensure compliance with the terms of the policy. Usually the conditions are these:

1. A percentage of the value of each shipment made is reserved in a distributor's individual account. This percentage varies from 1 to 2½ percent depending on the profitability to the company of each model in the line.

2. Advertising claims submitted by distributors, together with evidence of the advertising, are then credited at the rate of 50 percent of the amount actually spent by the distributor.

3. If the advertising originated initially with a dealer, the procedure is for the distributor to credit *the dealer* with 50 percent of the total amount expended. Thus, the division of the total expense becomes dealer 50 percent, distributor 25 percent, manufacturer 25 percent.

4. Credits from the manufacturer must not exceed the amount in each distributor's fund at any given time.

Freight Allowances

The practice of absorbing the freight into prices was held to be discriminatory (except in unusual cases) by the U.S. Supreme Court in the Big Steel basing-point case. This decision empowered the Federal Trade Commission to step in whenever any seller featured "delivered" prices and to determine if the method of selling was not in restraint of trade. Since that decision, many manufacturers have changed over to an FOB-factory basis of pricing.

However, there are ways of granting certain customers an allowance to cover all or part of the freight that are within the law. Pooling shipments to customers in a certain city to get the benefit of the carload rate is one way.

One eastern concern sends a salesman to work the Middle West. In two or three weeks he accumulated about 200 dealers. He then makes the entire shipment in one car, delivering the car to a public warehouse in Chicago. The warehouse notifies the respective purchasers that their shipments are in and they send their trucks to pick them up. By giving the customers the advantage of this freight saving, it is possible for this company to undersell competitors, without in any way cutting profits, and without cutting prices. This same concern has interested several other manufacturers in using the same warehouse, and they pool their Chicago shipments.

Freight is not as inflexible an item of cost as generally supposed. In many cases eastern concerns compete in San Francisco with California manufacturers on a prepaid freight basis. This they are able to do by warehousing their stocks on the coast.

Chapter 23

Consignment and Installment Selling

Selling goods on consignment is on the decline as it is looked upon as simply a method of "loading up the dealer" to keep out competition.

The policy may be useful in the introductions of new lines or new products, but otherwise it has many disadvantages and pitfalls.

It is obvious that such a sales method is costly, and many consider it to be unsound because it makes a banker out of a manufacturer. It takes away the incentive a dealer needs to push a product in which his or her own money is invested, and makes it easy for the distributor to carry a larger stock than necessary.

Well-financed and well-established dealers usually frown on consignment selling. They feel this practice encourages fly-by-night and under-financed companies to enter their markets. They prefer to own their stocks and set their own selling policies.

On the other hand, some manufacturers favor consignment selling because it permits placement of adequate stocks in desired locations, particularly with under-financed distributors or retail outlets; it makes the selling job considerably easier, since the buyer is relieved of financing problems; and it permits the manufacturer to have more accurate knowledge of point-of-sale demand, since complete records and reports must be regularly prepared. One substitute for consigned stock is the use of public warehouses. In this way the manufacturer retains control of the stock and maintains complete records.

Legal Pitfalls

Setting aside the uneconomic principles involved in consignment selling, the practice has numerous disadvantages not apparent at first glance. Many of these are legal difficulties. For this reason, a manufacturer should carefully study the laws of the individual states before taking any concrete steps to enter a new consignment market. The legal technicalities that differentiate conditional sales, absolute sales, bailments, and agency contracts are subtle but important, and should lead the manufacturer to consult legal counsel before acting.

Installment Selling

It is generally agreed that installment selling is a method that discounts future selling, and in the event of a recession could cause considerable difficulty for both manufacturers and retailers. The argument in its favor is that it stimulates sales and consequently low-cost mass production. It is, however, inflationary. For that reason, and because of the danger of a backing up of merchandise in a period of wide unemployment, many sales managers contend that installment selling should be avoided wherever possible, even though it appears to be an effective way of meeting competition.

The Westinghouse "Equity" Plan

In a buyers' market it is important that a manufacturer help dealers to finance customer paper without paying the high rates demanded by concerns specializing in that type of financing. Westinghouse recommended to its dealers that they work, when possible, with local banks. To help the dealer make the most advantageous arrangement with his banker, Westinghouse developed what it calls an "equity plan." The dealer agreed to operate on the recommendations of the supplier—namely 10 percent down payment, initial financing period 90 days, and the usual 30-day extension privileges. The operation of the plan was as follows:

1. The dealer signs an application for floor-plan accommodations, if such form is required by bank.

2. The dealer submits a financial statement to the bank on whatever form the bank requires. The bank then passes on dealer's credit and usually notifies dealer and distributor of the amount of credit approved.

3. The dealer should sign a signature authorization form. The use of this form and procedure is optional for both dealer and bank. Many will want to use it, however, because it saves considerable time and effort in the future. The wording of such form is as follows:

"For the convenience of the undersigned in making such arrangements as may be necessary for you to finance undersigned's purchase of merchandise under the terms of the Westinghouse Equity Plan—Wholesale Repurchase Agreement—undersigned hereby requests and authorizes you, through your designated employees, to execute, on behalf of undersigned, such trust receipts or other title retention instruments as you may require in connection with such financing, together with such accompanying notes or drafts as are customary, and including such affidavits or other documents as may be necessary for the filing or recording of such documents. You are to advise undersigned of the execution of any documents pursuant to this authorization. Your authority, hereunder, shall continue until you are notified otherwise in writing."

4. When the dealer places an order for merchandise, either the distributor's representative or bank obtains a down payment of not less than 10 percent of the net wholesale invoice, plus transportation or other charges not already included in such invoice. Financing charges should be prepaid by the dealer.

5. The distributor ships the merchandise to his dealer and presents invoice to the bank. Bank should promptly remit the amount due. Country banks may prefer to have their city correspondent bank handle remittances for them when such city correspondent bank is located in the same city as the distributor.

6. The bank executes the Wholesale Repurchase Agreement in duplicate, dating it, in Article 16, the same as the first floor-plan title-retention instrument received from a Westinghouse dealer to whom bank extends floor-plan

credit under this agreement. No additional repurchase agreement is required to cover subsequent Westinghouse dealers to whom bank extends floor-plan accommodations. Upon receipt, Westinghouse will sign and return one copy to the bank for its files. Eligible Westinghouse distributors and merchandise are listed and attached to the agreement. Banks having one or more branches need execute only one agreement, following the identical procedure outlined above.

To sum up, there are certain salient points to consider in consignment selling: The most vital point is, of course, the state in which the dealer does business, since the goods will be in the dealer's possession and the manufacturer's rights will be governed by the laws of the state in which the goods have been attached.

Retail Installment Selling

A number of practical considerations enter into the practice of retail installment selling. Among them are the gross profit (before expenses) that you make on the sale, your ability to get cash from other sources at a cost lower than the discount charged, the extent of your other expenses, and the volume of your installment sales compared to your cash sales.

You will probably sell your installment accounts either to a sales finance company or to a commercial bank. Usually their discount rates are competitive, and both give you and your installment customers similar services.

Installment paper is sold in three different ways: nonrecourse, recourse, and repurchase.

Under the *nonrecourse* plan of purchase, you are not responsible if your customer fails to pay. The financial institution that bought the paper stands the loss. In repossession, the financial institution is fully responsible. It retakes, reconditions, and resells the item and collects any balance the customer owes.

Often whether a retailer can afford to sell on installment credit depends on whether he can find a buyer for these accounts on a nonrecourse basis at an acceptable discount rate.

Under the *recourse* plan of repurchase, you are liable for any balance due in case your customer does not pay. You have to do your own repossessing, reconditioning, and reselling.

Under the *repurchase* plan, you are required to buy back the property for the unpaid balance after the financial institution has retaken it from your customer. Here you share the burden with the institution.

Expenses and Income

What are some of the expenses connected with installment selling? Among them are:

1. Salaries for people to run your credit operations;

2. Expenses of office space, supplies, and utilities (you may not have to rent additional space, but you will have to consider the sales you might have made in the space devoted to credit operations);

3. Collection and repossession expenses;

4. Interest on money borrowed to carry on your business.

The longer the contracts, the larger the amount of money you will have to tie up in receivables to do a given amount of installment business. You will also have the advertising bill for announcing and promoting the plan.

If you are selling on cash and on open charge and add installment credit, you will have the problem of separating expenses connected with installment selling from those resulting from open charge accounts. This lets you know whether each credit plan is paying its own way.

You offset such expenses by selling more. Gross income on installment sales should pay for the program.

Customers help cut the expenses by paying a service charge for the privilege of buying on installment. This charge varies with different stores. To find out what is enough for you, you will need an accurate cost study of your expenses in serving installment customers.

How Many Dollars?

Installment payments for any given month are equal to the total of new installment business written in previous months (not including the given month) divided by the contract period.

Installment receivables for a given month are equal to installment receivables of the previous month, plus the new installment business written during the given month, minus installment payments received during the given month. In Table 1, below, the receivables increase by smaller and smaller amounts each month. They reach a peak of $33,390 in the sixth month and remain unchanged thereafter.

With a smaller down payment, your maximum dollars tied up in receivables would increase. However, if you used a contract for three months instead of six months, your number of dollars tied up in receivables would decrease.

Table 1. Maximum Dollar Amount Tied Up in Installment Receivables

Month	New Business Written	Installment Payments	Month-end Receivables
1.	$9,540*	—	$ 9,540
2.	9,540	$1,590	17,490
3.	9,540	3,180	23,850
4.	9,540	4,770	28,620
5.	9,540	6,360	31,800
6.	9,540	7,950	33,390†
7.	9,540	9,540	33,390
8.	9,540	9,540	33,390
9.	9,540	9,540	33,390
10.	9,540	9,540	33,390
11.	9,540	9,540	33,390
12.	9,540	9,540	33,390

*Equals installment sales of $10,000 minus down payment of $1,000 plus the service charges of $540 based upon the beginning unpaid balances.
†Peak.

Given certain conditions, what would be the maximum number of dollars you could have tied up in installment receivables? Suppose you hope to sell $10,000 of merchandise a month, or $120,000 annually, on installment terms. Suppose also that your contracts call for a 10 percent down payment, six months to pay, and a service charge of 1 percent per month. The maximum dollar amount you would have tied up in installment receivables is seen in Table 1 on the previous page.

Federal Trade Commission Guides to Retail Credit Transactions

These guides relate to retail credit transactions in the District of Columbia and to transactions in interstate commerce.

GUIDE I. DISCLOSURE IN ADVERTISING AND PRICE TAGGING

No retailer of any article of merchandise should represent a) a price in connection with a specified weekly or monthly credit payment or installment, when the aggregate of such credit payments or installments is in excess of the represented price; b) a specified, weekly, monthly, or other periodic credit payment or installment, unless in immediate conjunction with each such representation there is clear disclosure of either the total number of payments required for payment in full or the total amount of the payments for which the purchaser will be indebted.

GUIDE II. DISCLOSURE OF COSTS PRIOR TO CONSUMMATION OF CREDIT

In a retail credit transaction no seller should fail, before consummation of the credit sale, to furnish the buyer with an itemization in writing separately stating each of the following: a) the cash price of the article, b) the amount of any sales, excise, or other tax to be paid by the purchaser, c) the amounts to be credited as downpayment and/or trade-in, if any, d) the unpaid cash balance owed by the buyer to the seller, e) each finance, credit, service, or carrying charge to be paid by the purchaser (including any amount covering insurance premiums, service-contract charge and a specification of any other charges, separately stated, which are capable of determination at the point of sale), f) the amount and the total number of each weekly or monthly installment payment, g) the total amount for which the purchaser will be indebted, *and* h) the total credit transaction price (item [g] plus [c] above).

Failure to separately disclose such amounts may have the capacity and tendency to deceive the purchaser as to the nature of his or her costs in the transaction and may be an unfair method of competition since it does not enable the consumer to make meaningful price and credit comparisons between competitive products.

GUIDE III. DISCLOSURE OF NEGOTIATION TO THIRD PARTY

No seller of any article of merchandise at retail should fail, before consummation of the credit sale, to disclose orally and in writing with such conspicuousness and clarity as likely to be observed and read by the purchaser, that the conditional sale contract and promissory note or other instrument executed by the purchaser may at the option of the seller be negotiated or assigned to a finance company or other third party.

GUIDE IV. DISCLOSURE OF BUYER'S CLAIM TO THIRD PARTY

No seller in a retail credit transaction as defined herein should assist, sell, or otherwise transfer to a finance company or other third person a retail installment contract or other credit instrument after the seller has been notified, either orally or in writing, of any claim or defense respecting the seller's performance, unless the seller makes written disclosure to the transferee of the existence of the buyer's claim or defense.

GUIDE V. MERCHANDISE AS SECURITY FOR OTHER TRANSACTIONS

No seller or other party in a retail credit transaction as defined herein should designate merchandise which is the subject of one retail installment contract as security for the buyer's performance under any other retail installment contract.

GUIDE VI. PASSAGE OF TITLE TO BUYER

No seller or other party in a retail credit transaction as defined herein should refuse or fail to pass title to the buyer or merchandise purchased under a retail installment contract when the full time price of that merchandise has been paid.

GUIDE VII. PRORATING PAYMENTS

No seller or other party should prorate a buyer's installment payment among several retail credit installment contracts unless:

1. The buyer is notified in writing that such action is being taken, and

2. The ratio between the amount of the consolidated payment prorated to any one of the contracts and the total amount of the payment is the same as the ratio between the total amount originally due under that contract and the sum of the total amounts originally due on all contracts whose payments have been consolidated.

Chapter 24

Exclusive Distribution Outlets

Some companies depend on wide distribution, through every type of dealer, while other organizations prefer limited, exclusive outlets. Why is this? Part of the reason involves the nature of the product. Another consideration is that each policy has its advantages and disadvantages.

A dealer won't spend money to promote the sale of a product if he or she is not sure of getting the reorders. On the other hand, if he or she can be shown that any money spent in building up a demand for a certain product means increased business, and that such business will not go to competitors, he or she will get behind the product and push it. The exclusive-agency arrangement is one that protects the dealer and thus encourages him or her to push your product energetically.

The outstanding advantages of the exclusive, or selected agency are:

1. Its superiority as a means of increasing the reputation of the goods, and the prestige of the manufacturer. Seldom or never is this system of much value to the manufacturer of goods that are unidentified as to origin by means of trademarks or trade names. To the manufacturer of trademarked goods, however, it is worth the possible sacrifice of a few sales to ensure the standing of these goods in the public mind through adequate presentation of their merits.

2. Dealers who are protected in the enjoyment of exclusive privileges are more apt to make an effort to push a particular line and give it special prominence in display. Special advertising cooperation can be given to exclusive dealers as needed without incurring the ill will of their competitors. It is also much easier to secure advertising cooperation on the part of the dealers. The manufacturer can also exercise a direct influence to improve the dealer's selling efforts.

3. Credit risks are obviously reduced when salespeople are calling upon a limited number of dealers who have been selected in advance or already passed upon by the house. Credit is one of the main considerations in appointing a dealer, and closer supervision by the company helps to keep the dealer's credit good.

4. Salespeople can cover more territory more efficiently when calling on exclusive agencies.

5. When dealers are protected, there is less likelihood of their engaging in unfair price-cutting because they are not subjected to cut price competition on the same product. Comparatively few dealers are price-cutters from deliberate policy, but are forced to cut to meet competition. It is not difficult to eliminate the deliberate cutters from consideration as agents, which generally takes care of the problem. It goes without saying that the fear of losing an exclusive agency will often deter a dealer who might otherwise cut prices.

In that connection it will be necessary to determine what your relationship with customers, especially dealers and distributors, will be. Is it best to sell through exclusive agencies, one in each community, or through the dual-agency plan whereby several outlets in each community work together under factory supervision? How should those exclusive dealerships be set up? Should the stock be sold outright or placed with the dealer on a consignment basis? How can resale prices be protected? What provision should there be in the agreement to assure whole-hearted sales support for the line? What about advertising and sales-promotion expense? What part, if any, should the dealer assume? These and other questions are vital to the success of any plan for selling to selected accounts.

In this chapter we are concerned only with independents. We are not taking into consideration such elements as company-owned stores (SSMC Inc.) or chain stores.

The Dual-Agency Plan

A product that is featured by only one or perhaps two stores in a trading center does not assume great importance in the minds of the consumers. But when it is featured on all sides, it assumes a prominence that is difficult to secure otherwise. Advertising alone sometimes will accomplish wonders, but it cannot often give the prestige that is secured by adequate distribution.

This is why most manufacturers of convenience goods who rely upon selected outlets have largely abandoned the exclusive agent for what are generally referred to as dual agencies. Instead of the single agent, who enjoys the complete suppression of local competition, these manufacturers employ two or more agencies. These are strategically located to serve the public to the best possible advantage, and at the same time to supplement the efforts of one another in giving the product prominence. This is the policy followed by many of the most successful sorts, which will generally all do better than any one of them could do alone. The benefits of such a policy to the manufacturer are fairly obvious. It increases sales materially, as well as the prestige of the goods in the community. It also increases the effectiveness of advertising, both that which is run over the names of the dealers and that in national media.

Sometimes concerns hesitate to employ selected distributors through fear that, in case it is later necessary to make changes, they will offend their most valuable customers and cause them to "throw out the line." Experience seems to show, however, that there is very little substance to that fear. At least there is little danger if the original agreement is drawn properly and the situation handled with tact and restraint. In most cases, the dealer who is large enough to warrant selection as an exclusive agent is intelligent enough to grasp a sound argument. Very few concerns report any serious difficulty in this connection. In those cases where trouble is experienced it is likely to be due to the fact that rash promises were made in the first place, or that the situation was handled in too arbitrary a manner. An occasional dealer may throw out a profitable line in order to spite the manufacturer, or out of belief that the manufacturer cannot get along without it. In the majority of cases, however, the dealers are likely to come back later or when it is clearly demonstrated that they are losing money by the action.

Dangers in Exclusive Agreements

Section 3 of the Clayton Antitrust Act reads in part as follows:

"That it shall be unlawful for any person engaged in commerce, in the course of such commerce, to lease or make a sale or contract for sale of goods, wares, merchandise, machinery, supplies, or other commodities, whether patented or unpatented, for use, consumption, or resale within the United States ... or fix a price charged therefor, or discount from, or rebate upon, such price, on the condition, agreement, or understanding that the lessee or purchaser thereof shall not use or deal in the goods, wares, merchandise, machinery, supplies, or other commodity of a competitor or competitors of the lessor or seller, where the effect of such lease, sale, or contract for sale or such condition, agreement, or understanding may be to substantially lessen competition or tend to create a monopoly in any line of commerce."

It is clear that this covers only those forms of exclusive agency agreements whereby, in return for exclusive territory, the agency or dealer agrees not to handle competing products. It does not apply to the more common practice of leaving the dealer free to handle competing products, but making the franchise of sufficient value to induce him or her to concentrate primarily on pushing the goods. Furthermore, the addition of the concluding clause makes it unnecessary for the manufacturer of trademarked goods, under ordinary circumstances, to worry about the legality of his exclusive-agency arrangements.

To the great majority of business people, the likelihood of any difficulty arising from the above conditions may seem to be very remote. It is only fair to emphasize once more, however, that the enforcement of this section of the Clayton Act is entrusted to the Federal Trade Commission, and a complaint from any individual may inspire an investigation by that body. It is advisable to obtain competent legal counsel before putting into effect specific contracts for exclusive representation.

Formal Contracts Needed

Formal contracts, covering the operation of exclusive agents in detail, are usually necessary under the following conditions:

1. When it is the agent's duty to establish contract relations with his or her customers by which the company's rights are affected. This applies broadly to such commodities as office and store appliances, machinery, musical instruments, household appliances sold on partial payments, building, equipment sold to contractors, heating and lighting equipment, etc. In such cases the agent is acting as the direct representative of the company; the agent's acts must be definitely controlled and his or her authority definitely limited.

2. When the agent is entrusted with the job of hiring salespeople, who act as representatives of the company, but who are not directly under the company's control. The same considerations apply here.

3. When the agent acts as licensee under patents. This does not apply to all commodities that are covered by patent, but only where the patent license is made the basis of representation. In such cases it is necessary to have a definite expression of the company's intention, as well as to control the acts of the agent.

There are also numerous cases where agents render special service in installing equipment, or keep it in working order, either at the company's expense or their own. Under such conditions, when the goodwill of the company largely depends upon the proper installation or operation of the product, many concerns feel that formal contracts are essential. It is necessary, in other words, to specify definitely and in detail just what the duties of the agent are, and what free service the customer should have.

Aside from the foregoing, however, there seems to be a marked tendency to avoid tying the hands of either party with formal contracts, and to rely upon a general understanding as to terms and conditions. This leaves the company free to make changes promptly when changing local conditions warrant.

Chapter 25

Selective Selling

Greater customer sales analysis, sophisticated credit management, media market studies and segmentation of computerized mailing lists have given the concept of "selective selling" new value. What is meant by selective selling? Simply that one customer is *not* just as good as another. Tiffany's, while willing to sell to anyone who can pay the price, creates an affluent clientele by the quality and price level of its luxurious merchandise, by the good taste of the store surroundings and the way in which the goods are displayed, and even the manner of the clerks. On the other hand, because those with affluent tastes are not always affluent with money, Tiffany's has developed good judgment in rating customers on their ability to pay.

The discount stores practice selective selling when they attract customers looking for price rather than quality into their stores by giving them a "low price" atmosphere—plain tables piled high with inexpensive wares, sold on a strictly cash and self-service basis. Their goal is high volume on a low profit margin, with quick turnover of cash.

Whether your product is sold to the ultimate consumer, as in house-to-house selling, or to distributors or wholesalers for resale, you will need a policy to guide you in the selection of your customers. This calls for consideration of the following points:

1. The degree of selectivity in choosing customers

2. The degree of exclusive arrangements with selectively chosen customers

3. The degree to which credit is to be offered

4. The extent of consignment selling, if any

5. The offering of national or private brands, or possibly both

6. Cancellation of orders and acceptance of returned goods

7. The degree to which service and technical advice should be extended

Selective selling can be extremely important in many industries. When any product is sold through distributors and dealers on a nationwide basis, adequate "dealer coverage" determines the degree of success in sales. However, it is commonplace in the appliance industry to say that 25 percent of the dealers do 75 percent of the business. In addition to having enough dealers in order to make it convenient for customers to buy, it's equally important to have the right kind of dealers. This is why in the large cities well-known department stores and chain stores are eagerly sought after by manufacturers.

Naturally the choice will be affected by the nature of the industry and the type of product involved. The next step is to determine whether to sell through distributors or directly to dealers. Still, that does not cover the entire situation. Licensing independent organizations (franchising) and selling to national accounts afford additional channels of distribution.

In recent years, many companies have realized the necessity of making the sales force conscious of its role in profit making.

As a senior marketing executive of a major appliance manufacturer said, "Traditionally, sales managers have been concerned only with sales volume and market share. However, the type of customers sought, the amount of credit extended, and the inventory required to service customers all have a profound effect on return on investment." To make clear the connection between sales decisions and profits, his company developed a three-phase course for all its managers, which culminated in a computerized game that compressed a year's business activity into three days. Those participating get the feel of running a complex organization in a realistic setting.

As the executive explained at a marketing-strategy conference of the Sales Executives Club of New York, the program included a week-long course on management aimed at mastering the principles of hiring, motivating, and appraising personnel.

Factors to Consider

Some of the factors to consider when selecting prospects or customers are:

1. Credit status

2. Stature in the market

3. Purchase requirements (potential)

4. Growth possibilities

5. Competitive status in relation to other outlets

6. Location for customer convenience in the shopping area

7. Location for efficient routing of company salespeople

8. Type of goods offered—staple or specialty

9. Relationship with competing manufacturers

Obviously, it is of little value to spend time selling a customer who does not pay his or her bills, or to expect large orders if the customer is not properly financed. Policies and procedures for extending and handling credit, as well as the role that salespeople can play in assisting in the proper function of credits in marketing, are discussed elsewhere in this Handbook.

The most respected retail outlet, or industrial customer in the market environment, should be given first consideration. The prestige of this customer will greatly assist in obtaining other customers. However, sometimes unfavorable considerations may be found in other factors, that will mitigate against too close an alliance with the prestige customer.

When going out after orders, it is usually preferable to fish in the larger pools rather than in the smaller ones. A call resulting in a $1,000 order frequently costs no more to make than one producing a $100 order. Furthermore, if a salesperson is averaging $100 a call from a customer, and that amount represents the customer's maximum buying power, there is probably little value in the salesperson stepping up his or her sales effort with that customer;

whereas, if the customer has a $1,000 potential, the salesperson can well invest more selling time.

Conversely, even through a customer currently has only $100 per order buying power, he or she might be young, imaginative, energetic, and on the upgrade. Selling time invested with him or her should bear attractive returns and he or she should be selected for the long pull.

Location Is Important

Sometimes local competitive rivalry makes it almost impossible for a salesperson to sell another outlet in the same locality. If a choice has to be made, it is better to select the firm that will give the best representation.

When selling a consumer product, it is well to choose an outlet that is convenient for the ultimate consumers to visit. Frequently you may find it necessary to have many outlets, particularly if your product is an impulse item. If style goods or an appliance, it is preferable to choose outlets that are located near other outlets handling similar items. Better to choose a growing outlet with current low sales in a well-patronized shopping center than a larger one off the beaten path; the latter may often be on the way down. Distributors or industrial goods outlets may not need to be so well located, but even with these, convenient location in a marketing area is preferable.

When routing salespeople, it is important that crisscrossing, backtracking, and long dead-end runs be eliminated as much as possible. The face-to-face sales time of salespeople is absolute and not expandable. Time must be conserved and used judiciously. Customers should be carefully selected, with return per call given careful consideration.

It is possible that in every respect a prospective customer might be attractive, but through the years has become so closely tied to a competing manufacturer that to disrupt the relationship would be too difficult. Or the owner of the store might have a son or daughter working for a competitor and nepotism might be too strong to combat.

By-Products of Sales and Cost Analysis

The owner of the Timms Supply Company, Spokane, Washington stated that local suppliers should have in their records a complete "picture" of each account on their books.

At his own firm, cost analysis of every account has resulted in more effective management control, greater operating efficiency, and "a better job done for each customer."

Among the by-products of sales analysis, he said, the distributor would have practical knowledge of what products customers bought, in what quantities, the gross profit realized, and the net profit for each account.

Armed with these figures, Timms Supply's own salespeople are able to evaluate products by customers and potential by customer, and can plan their time and efforts for the greatest return. They also are able to determine quickly where improvements can be made, and when less time and fewer special services should be given.

How Gormaly Meter Makes Sales Audits

Gormaly Meter Manufacturing Company, manufacturer of water meters, conducts customer audits for all its sales territories. The form it uses is in Figure 1, page 553. Note the instructions at the bottom of the form, whereby the salesperson and his or her district manager are requested to review all municipalities in the territory, both customers and prospects; those of a worthwhile nature are listed on the form. All persons who might be involved in preparing specifications, giving authority to purchase, issuing orders, and even repairing or maintaining meters are shown. It is essential that no important person be overlooked and that the salesperson reserve all necessary time for calling on each individual.

Then in the fourth column, the essential number of units that might be purchased from all sources during the ensuing 12 months is inserted. These estimates may not be very accurate the first time they are made, but as time passes they can be revised. In any case, a good, conscientious, objectively considered estimate is much better than no estimate at all. Also, while some will be too

Figure 1.
GORMALY METER MFG. COMPANY
CUSTOMER-PROSPECT AUDIT

Sales Representative_____ Territory_____ Date_____ Sheet_____ of____

| City | Persons To See | Position | Meters | Yearly Sales | | Calls Per Yr. |
				Current	Goal	

INSTRUCTIONS: All municipalities, both customers and prospects, of a worthwhile nature are to be listed. All persons with their titles to be seen regularly are to be shown; this includes engineers, purchasing agents, elected personnel (mayors, etc.), repair and maintenance people. Insert the estimated number of meters, dollar sales (drop cents) for the current year, the sales goal for the coming year and the expected number of calls to be made on each individual. It is not anticipated that the same number of calls will be made during the year on all persons; the purchasing agent and maintenance department may be seen on each visit, the engineers and elected personnel only once a year. All cities will not be visited on each trip, some may be seen on alternate trips. This form is to be filled in jointly by the salespeople and their district managers.

low and others too high, they should average out quite accurately. Such estimates of potential are exceedingly important in planning sales strategy.

In the next two columns are inserted figures on past sales, which act as benchmarks of what might be done against potential, and what can be reasonably expected as goals for future effort. The goals should not be set so low as to offer no challenge nor so high as not to be attainable. They should be reasonable; the salesperson and his or her district manager should both be satisfied that they are fair.

The last column is for entering the anticipated number of calls that should be made during the year on all individuals listed. It is not expected that the same number of calls will need be made on all individuals listed for a company; the purchasing agent probably should be seen on each call, the maintenance person or engineer might be seen every other call, and the head of the firm only once a year to maintain rapport. Also, all companies need not be seen with the same frequency; a large one demanding a lot of attention may need to be called on once a week, or even daily, while a smaller one may need to be seen only once a month or even only once every three months.

The scheduled number of calls should merely be considered an optimum objective. If conditions change, as may occur when a customer gets ready to place a large order, calls should be stepped up as required; when the period of intense activity ends, the salesperson should drop back to his or her original schedule.

Chapter 26

National Versus Private Brands

Manufacturers have the option of producing a national-brand product, the merchandising and advertising of which they can fully control, or produce "private label" merchandise for suppliers.

Many manufacturers do both. The makers of a nationally famous cleansing powder also produce cleansing powders for chain department, variety, and food stores under many private labels. Sears, Roebuck and Company has many private brand products made by manufacturers of national advertised brands.

Actually, both kinds of merchandise probably are needed to provide the merchandise mix demanded by today's large and diversified markets.

The basic brand classifications are:

1. A company sells only brands owned by a producer. These are referred to as "national" or "manufacturer's" brands.

2. A company sells only brands owned by a distributor or mass retailer. These are known as "private" or "distributors'" brands.

3. A mixed-brand policy, where both manufacturers' and distributors' brands are sold.

Some of the factors which affect brand policy are the level of prosperity in the economy, the product's life cycle, and *consumer reaction to price and quality.*

Advantages of National Brands

A safe rule in establishing a policy on branding is to use a national brand if the product lends itself to national distribution and national advertising. For one thing the manufacturer of a national brand is in a better trading and operating position. Any goodwill created for the brand or company, accrues to the manufacturer. There are instances where brand names have been sold for millions of dollars. It is more costly to build national distribution for a product, but the market thus established cannot easily be taken over by a competitor. Once people accept a national brand and get the habit of asking for it at their local dealer's store, the dealer will hesitate a long time before deciding not to stock it. So long as the quality of the product is maintained, and national advertising is adequate, you are assured of satisfactory sales volume.

Advantages of Private Brands

Producers usually adopt the policy of making goods to be sold under a distributor's private brand when their competition sells well-entrenched national brands. Rather than make the investment in national advertising and store-to-store selling required to put another national brand on the market, the manufacturer will go to a sectional distributor and arrange to furnish large quantities of the product, bearing the distributor's own private brand, at an attractive price. The manufacturer may or may not allow the distributor an additional sum to be spent for advertising in territories within the distributor's trading zone. The manufacturer may prefer to take the need of introductory advertising into consideration when setting the price, leaving it to the distributor to decide what to do about advertising. The distributor may wish to put demonstrators in key stores, sample, or do something other than space advertising.

But, as so often happens, these arrangements are only secure so long as a manufacturer can produce the goods for the distributor at a price lower than "just as good" merchandise available from a competitor. In fact, it is the history of private brands that in a buyers' market, distributors show no compunction in switching producers when they can find somebody to make approximately the same product for a few cents less. The fear that this might happen hangs over all the transactions between the producer and distributor. It places the manufacturer in a tight position, where he must either cut his already small profit or sacrifice volume. There are a few distributors, but not many, smart enough to realize the importance of protecting their sources of supply and who do not constantly try to hammer suppliers down on price. In the long run manufacturers who depend upon making products for large distributors to be sold under brand names owned by the distributors, usually become a department in the distributor's business and find themselves working for the equivalent of a small salary. They end up being the owner of a run-down plant with nothing in the way of goodwill to sell.

The Combination Policy

Sometimes makers of nationally advertised products, in order to spread their overhead over a larger volume, accept large private-brand orders from large retailers, mail-order houses, co-ops, and other mass producers on what they call a "run-on" basis. While the product supplied on such deals may be equal in most respects to the product carrying the national brand, it is usually slightly different. Such orders, of course, are filled at a price far below what a distributor would pay for the national brand, since no selling expense is involved. Even though much of the manufacturer's overhead expense has been absorbed in the production of the national brands, there is still a chance for making a fair profit even at a lower price.

While straddling the issue in this way seems attractive, it has its drawbacks. In the first place, it requires a large outlay of capital to create national acceptance for a product under the maker's brand. This must be done before production can reach a point where a manufacturer can shade the price sufficiently to interest the mass distributor, and at the same time make a worthwhile profit. In the second place, it soon leaks out—sometimes with the help of the mass distributor who starts a whispering campaign—that the product listed at a greatly reduced price in the catalog is identically the same product as others pay a fancy price for at their local dealer's. The difference, of course, is that the mail-order house doesn't have to pad the price for advertising! All of which doesn't make the independent dealer who handles the nationally advertised product too happy.

Why Some Retailers Favor Advertised Brands

While a few large merchants, like Marshall Field & Company in Chicago, have established sufficient public acceptance for anything they place upon their counters, smaller retailers favor advertised brands even though the profit per sale may be a little less. There are several reasons why this is so. In the first place, well-advertised national brands usually turn over quickly. It takes less time to sell them. Merchants have learned the hard way that profits come from turnovers and not leftovers. In the second place, a store that features well-known advertised products builds a local reputation for handling quality products. That prestige attracts and holds customers.

Changing Customer Concepts

But there are rumblings of change all over the country among retailers of all types and sizes. They are saying that uniform supermarkets, with standard stock and traditional "catch-all" merchandising, are becoming outdated. Customer loyalty is dwindling. Retailers are becoming increasingly aware that each store unit must tailor its assortment of goods and its merchandising and promotional strategies to appeal to the shopping habits and preferences of the particular families living in the community it serves. Retailers have to know how their customers shop, how they differ from one another—what it takes to please young married couples, or suburban white collar families, or lower-income working-class households—or whatever other type family lives near their stores. Private brands are one element in this problem, but an important one.

Private brands represent an increasing trend. Dr. Arnold J. Corbin, in *New Trends in American Marketing,* points out that retailers generally find they can promote their own brands within the stores more profitably because they make a wider percentage of profit, even though they sell them at lower prices to their customers. They also have the advantage of being able to display their own brands at eye-level. Although retailer brands are a growing trend, there have been some limitations. There are some chains that have found they are not large enough to do a good job on their own brands. They have found they cannot obtain the rate of turnover fast enough to generate an adequate return on their investment. Even when private-brand percentage margins are greater, if you cannot get as many unit sales within a given period of time as you can with a manufacturer's well-known brand, you are likely then to prefer the manufacturer's brand. However, many retailers believe that by promoting manufacturers' brands they are not building store loyalty; any retailer can carry such brands, but with their own private brands they build loyalty to their own stores.

Chapter 27

How Credit Helps Sales

The credit manager plays a key role in attaining the goals set by top management. In robust and growing companies, there is an understanding of the manner in which his or her performance affects sales and even the very survival of the company.

Working with the Credit Manager

Some executives believe the sales department has no concern with credits or collections. Its job is to get the order. When the order is on the books, it is the job of the credit department to get the money. Back of this thinking is the fear that salespeople cannot do their best work if they are burdened with credit responsibility in any form. The people who hold this view also feel that the qualities which make a good salesperson usually do not make a good credit person.

There may be cases where this is good reasoning. By and large, however, close cooperation between credit and sales pays off. Salespeople waste much time calling on customers they *think* are good credit risks, only to have the order turned down by the credit department when checked against credit reference books and other data available to the credit manager. When the credit manager works closely with the sales manager, it is possible to rate in advance the prospective customers upon whom the salesperson will call. This is known as selective selling. It is widely used today. Before a salesperson starts out on a trip the credit department provides him or her with the credit status of each dealer in his or her territory. From these data the salesperson determines how much time to give different accounts.

Even though salespeople may not be responsible for collections, sales managers know that a salesperson can sell more to a customer who is paid up than to a customer who is behind in payments. Thus it is said: "Closed collections make for more sales." So it is the practice to periodically furnish salespeople, calling on established trade, information useful to them in contacting accounts. See Figure 1, page 562, for an example of a typical credit-reporting form. Figure 2, page 563, shows a form used by salespeople to evaluate dealer credit rating.

Today's marketing manager, with a broad range of responsibility keyed to achieving return on investment, should have greater jurisdiction over credit policies, believes Dr. Michael Schiff, former chairman of the accounting and taxation departments of New York University's graduate school of business.

Schiff noted in a talk before a management seminar in Buffalo that the "measure of effectiveness of business management should be return on investment, and not merely sales volume produced, or profit as a percentage of sales." For this reason, he told about 200 western New York executives, "credit should be a marketing function." Credit policy should not be an all-finance decision handled in the treasurer's office, but should be more closely allied to the responsibility of marketing managers.

In order that salespeople may be provided with data they need to concentrate on potentially strong accounts, the credit department should develop background information not only on the desirable accounts, but also on the less desirable accounts. This will permit a salesperson in the field to know why the credit department regards the account as "less desirable." He or she is then in a position to make a field check. If the salesperson's findings are at variance with the credit department's information this can be reported to management. This is important, since most credit-reporting services fail to take into consideration important factors affecting the sales value of an account. Such factors may include the competitive position of the account in the community, or the certain know-how a dealer may have that would be of considerable importance as far as his or her ability to succeed is concerned.

It is becoming more and more the practice of companies that sell selectively to hold meetings periodically with representatives of both the credit and the sales departments. At these meetings, both sides discuss accounts and compare notes. Whether an account should be placed upon the desirable or the less desirable list is de-

Figure 1.

CREDIT LIMIT APPROVAL		

LOCATION OF ACTIVITY | **ACCOUNT TYPE**

ACCOUNT NAME | **ADDRESS** | **CITY AND STATE**

D & B RATING | **YEAR STARTED** | ☐ CORPORATION ☐ PARTNERSHIP ☐ PROPRIETORSHIP | **GUARANTEE OR SURETY, IF ANY**

SOLD SINCE | **PAYMENT RECORD** | **ESTIMATE OF PURCHASES — IF NEW ACCOUNT OR IF INCREASE IS EXPECTED**

CREDIT LIMITS AND TERMS	PRESENT		REQUESTED		APPROVED	
	LINE	TERMS	LINE	TERMS	LINE	TERMS
GENERAL FLOOR PLAN						
EXTRA A/C FLOOR PLAN						
OPEN ACCOUNT						
RADIO PROGRAMS						
OTHER						
TOTAL						

CREDIT EXPERIENCE—OTHER SUPPLIERS

NAME	HOW LONG SOLD	HIGHEST RECENT CREDIT (LAST 6 MONTHS)	TOTAL AMOUNT OWING	TOTAL AMOUNT PAST DUE	TERMS OF SALE	MANNER OF PAYMENTS			
						ANTICI-PATES	DIS-COUNTS	PAYS WHEN DUE	DAYS SLOW

FINANCIAL STATEMENT DATED | **TYPE AND SOURCE**

FINANCIAL REVIEW

AMOUNT				RATIO		
	19	19	19		19	19	19
NET WORKING CAPITAL				NET WORKING CAPITAL			
TANGIBLE NET WORTH				QUICK ASSET			
TOTAL SALES				T.N.W. TO T.L.			
EARNINGS AFTER TAXES				EARNINGS AS % OF SALES			

CREDIT COMMENTS — SPECIAL CONDITIONS OR CIRCUMSTANCES (USE REVERSE SIDE IF NECESSARY)

ACTIVITY CREDIT MANAGER | DATE | **MANAGER OF DISTRIBUTION FINANCING DEPT.** | DATE

ASSISTANT TREASURER | DATE | **FILE ENCLOSURES**
☐ F.S.   ☐ D & B REPORT   ☐ TRADE CLEARANCE

CORPORATE CONTROLLER | DATE | ☐ BANK REFERENCE   ☐ OTHER

REMARKS

Form used by top corporation as credit record for customers.

Figure 2. Customer Credit Report

Name of Dealer_____ Address_____

	Please check	Less Than 2 Years	☐
Kind of business_____	how long	2 to 5 Years	☐
	established	Over 5 Years	☐

Your estimate of the value of stock_____

	Good	☐
Appearance of store	Fair	☐
	Poor	☐

Name of dealer's bank_____ Address_____

Please list names of factories or wholesalers from whom dealer principally buys

Name_____ Address_____
Name_____ Address_____
Name_____ Address_____
Name_____ Address_____

Other   {   Article_____ Name of manufacturer_____
Products
Sold   Article_____ Name of manufacturer_____

Will our finance plans be used?_____ Did you explain our plan?_____

Name of other finance plans used, or does

dealer carry own paper?_____		Good	☐
_____ Please give your opinion of		Fair	☐
financial condition of locality		Poor	☐

Remarks:_____
_____
_____
_____
_____
_____
_____

_____19		
Date	Sales Representative	Territory
	PLEASE ANSWER FULLY	

One of several forms used by a salesperson to evaluate dealer credit rating.

termined by these joint committees rather than by one or the other of the two departments acting alone. By that method of appraisal both points of view are considered and much of the friction that so often develops between the two departments is eliminated. Johns-Manville Corporation, for example, thinks of the credit department as the "business-extension department" and calls credit people "financial consultants."

Keeping Credit Informed

Obtaining the cooperation of the credit department can be facilitated by having a duplicate of the salesperson's route sheet sent regularly to the collection department. A well-known paint manufacturer has a duplicate of each route sheet sent to the credit person immediately upon its receipt by the sales department. The credit person then goes over the accounts in various towns on which the salesperson is to call and sends to the salesperson statements of any accounts which are slow. This gives the salesperson all necessary particulars before he or she sells in the town.

Another point in correlating collection and sales work is to make it a rule not to send dunning letters to any customer without first consulting the sales department. If the person who is responsible for sales has an opportunity to check the collection effort, he or she will endeavor to secure the money in such a way that the door will be left open for future orders.

The importance of consistent effort in the collection of insurance premiums is evident when it is understood that in the insurance business the company cannot take credit in its annual statement for any outstanding premiums over 90 days old. They have to be carried as a liability, so that insurance sales organizations make every effort to transform outstanding premiums into collected items.

Using Credit as a Sales Tool

In his book on credit as a sales tool, Joseph L. Wood, former credit manager for Johns-Manville, has listed the observations gained in a working lifetime of successful credit management. Here are his conclusions:

- Credit is not primarily a financial device; it is a sales technique.

- The sole purpose of industrial enterprise is not merely sales, but the earning of profit.

- The credit department is your full partner. It utilizes the art of credit to increase sales.

- Consult your credit manager for help in making important decisions.

- Be observant of the progress or lack of progress of your customers and maintain a flow of information to your credit manager.

- Make friends with the bankers in each town in your territory and keep regular contact with them for helpful information.

- Be familiar with the various types of credit safeguards and understand how, in some cases, they help you make sales that could not otherwise be made.

- Requests for financial statements and other credit safeguards help, not hinder, you.

- Help your credit manager in collections. You'll be helping yourself. Try to find the reason why the customer has not paid on time and, if possible, offer sound suggestions for correction. If they prove successful, you will have cemented your good relationship with your customer.

- Keep the line of communications open both between yourself and the credit manager and between the customer and the credit manager.

- Understand cash discount and be adroit in maintaining its principles.

- Know the techniques of securing additional sales through secured credit.

- Learn the sales channels and approach in selling the manufacturer.

- Master the sales and credit aspects in selling the contractor.

- Realize the importance of insurance and, particularly, the *assurance* provided by the intensive training of qualified persons for the eventual assumption of top-management responsibility.

- Finally, keep constantly in mind that you, the credit manager, and every member of your company have one responsibility and one aim—the success of the business through the earning of profit.

While the sales manager is not expected to be a credit expert, it is in the best interests of your company that he or she be at least acquainted with the procedures involved, especially in the granting of credit. There are some indicators, or indexes, with which every sales executive should be familiar.

Credit Control Indexes

Perhaps the best known indexes used in measuring the effectiveness of credit are the rejection percentage and the percentage of change in credit-sales volume. Along with the rejection percentage, you may keep figures on the number of accounts added, the number closed, and the net gain or loss in number of accounts. In addition to the change in credit-sales volume, you can follow such closely related indexes as the ratio of credit sales to total sales volume, the change in the amount of accounts receivable outstanding, the ratio of inactive accounts to total accounts, and the turnover of customers. These ratios have been profiled by the Small Business Administration.

1. *Rejection percentage.* The rejection percentage is computed by dividing the number of applications for credit declined (for lack of proper requirements or for other reasons) by the total number of applications received. Thus, if 150 applications or first orders are received during a given period and 15 are declined, the rejection percentage would be 0.10 or 10 percent.

   If you discover that your rejection percentage is becoming extremely high, you may rightly inquire whether your credit-granting policy is so strict that it is preventing you from enjoying a much greater sales volume. If the percentage seems to be getting excessively low, you should check to see whether this is causing abnormal collection expenses and bad-debt losses.

2. *Trend in number of accounts.* You should be interested also in the actual number of applications accepted and the net increase or decrease in the number of accounts on your books. In progressive firms, figures are calculated monthly (and often daily) for the number of new accounts added, the number of accounts closed, and the net gain or loss in number of accounts.

These three figures may be expressed only as percentages of the number of accounts on your books at the beginning of a period. The figures or percentages may be compared with those for the previous period and also with those for the same period in the previous year.

3. *Change in credit sales volume.* Of perhaps even greater interest are measures of increase or decrease in credit-sales volume. To show the percentage of change in credit sales from one period to another, divide the difference between the figures for the two periods by the amount of credit sales for the less recent period.

For example, if your credit sales were $100,000 for last month and $125,000 for the preceding month, divide the difference ($25,000) by the sales for the less recent period ($125,000), giving a percentage of 0.20 or 20 percent.

4. *Ratio of credit-sales volume to total sales.* To find this ratio, divide the figures representing the sales made on credit by total sales for the month, or other period. Thus, if your total sales for the past month were $62,000 and $34,100 of this volume was made on credit terms, divide the credit sales of $34,100 by the total sales figure of $62,000, yielding 0.55 or 55 percent.

Your ratio of credit sales to total sales may change with seasonal conditions during the year, or in response to the introduction of new credit plans, different policies, or because of other factors. In short, do not arbitrarily assume that a decline in the ratio is always due to inefficiency in credit granting. By the same token, a rise in the ratio may not always result from credit-sales-promotion efforts alone.

5. *Change in accounts receivable outstanding.* Important, and closely connected with indexes of changes in your firm's credit-sales volume, are measures of your accounts receivable outstanding. In progressive firms, the amount of accounts receivable outstanding (the total amount of money owed to the firm by its customers) is calculated daily. The increase or decrease from the preceding period, or from the same period of the preceding year, is then expressed in percentages.

   The dollar figures obtained in these calculations disclose a very important fact, namely, the extent to which your money is tied up in financing customers. Comparative percentage figures reveal the trend.

   To find the percentage change in your receivables from one period to another, divide the difference between the amounts outstanding in the two periods by the amount outstanding in the less recent period. For example, if your accounts receivable outstanding amounted to $100,000 at the end of last month and are $120,000 at the end of this month, divide the difference of $20,000 by the outstandings for the less recent period ($100,000), giving a percentage figure of 0.20 or 20 percent.

6. *Ratio of inactive accounts to total accounts.* You will find that monthly figures on the number of accounts becoming inactive are important in controlling the correct and full use of accounts. These figures help in maintaining and increasing credit-sales volume.

   You find the percentage of inactivity—that is, the proportion of customers not buying on their accounts during the month—by dividing the number of accounts not making any purchases during the month by the total number of accounts on the books at the beginning of the month.

7. *Ratio of turnover of customers.* This ratio expresses the proportion of customers you lost during a given period, usually a year. To obtain this figure, divide the number of accounts removed from your books during the year by the total number of accounts on your books at the beginning of the year.

Changes in this turnover ratio indicate the degree to which you are succeeding or failing in your efforts to keep customers after you have once placed them on your books.

Credit Cards

The use of credit cards in making retail purchases, obtaining airline tickets, rental cars, hotel reservations, gasoline, telephone calls, etc., has become universal. Additionally, many department and chain stores issue charge plates. They have been a boon to merchandisers inasmuch, for a prearranged fee, the responsibility for collecting for goods or services purchased is assumed by another agency. On the other hand, the use of credit cards has, ever since their inception, contributed to the very high level of consumer debt.

The Truth in Lending Law

The purpose of the Truth in Lending Law that went into effect July 1, 1969, is to let consumers know exactly what their credit charge is, and to let them make comparisons more readily of the charges from different credit sources. The law therefore requires creditors to state such charges in a uniform way.

The law makes it easier to know two of the most important things about the cost of credit. One is the finance charge—the amount of money we pay to obtain credit. The other is the annual percentage rate, which provides a way of comparing credit costs regardless of the dollar amount of those costs or the length of time over which we make payments. Both the finance charge and the annual percentage rate must be displayed prominently on the forms and statements used by a creditor to make the required disclosures.

Some creditors levy a service charge or a carrying charge or some other charge instead of interest, or perhaps they may add these charges to the interest. Under the Truth in Lending Law they must now total all such charges, including the interest, and call the sum the finance charge. Then they must list the annual percentage rate of the total charge for credit.

The law, and the regulations issued by the Board of Governors of the Federal Reserve System to carry it out, contain many other detailed provisions. Businesspeople extending credit should familiarize themselves with all of these, to make sure they are complying with the law.

The nine agencies involved in truth in lending laws and regulations, and the businesses they cover, are listed below. The law provides criminal penalties for willful violators.

- Retail department stores, consumer finance companies, and all other creditors not otherwise listed.
  Division of Consumer Credit
  Federal Trade Commission
  Washington, D.C. 20580

- National banks
  Comptroller of the Currency
  United States Treasury Department
  Washington., D.C. 20220

- State chartered banks that are members of the Federal Reserve System
  Federal reserve bank serving the area in which the state member bank is located

- State chartered nonmember banks that are insured by the Federal Deposit Insurance Corporation
  Federal Deposit Insurance Corporation regional director for the region in which the non-member insured bank is located

- Savings institutions insured by the Federal Savings and Loan Insurance Corporation and members of the Federal Home Loan Bank System (except for savings banks insured by Federal Deposit Insurance Corporation)

- Federal credit unions
  Regional Office of the Bureau of Federal Credit Unions, serving the area in which the federal credit union is located

- Airlines and other creditors subject to the Civil Aeronautics Board
  Director, Bureau of Enforcement
  Civil Aeronautics Board
  1828 Connecticut Avenue, N.W.
  Washington, D.C. 20428

- Creditors subject to Interstate Commerce Commission Office of Proceedings
  Interstate Commerce Commission
  Washington, D.C. 20523

  Board of Governors of the Federal Reserve System
  Washington, D.C. 20551

Chapter **28**

Cancellations and Returned Goods

A constant increase in sales is the goal of every sales manager, but in the final analysis, profits depend on costs. For instance, sales can easily be increased by reducing prices, but what is the resulting effect on profit margins? Every effort should be made to keep costs under control in every aspect of sales operations. Cancellations and returned goods are areas that can significantly and adversely affect costs and profits if not properly controlled.

In spite of every effort to eliminate waste, the problem of handling returned goods and permitting cancellation of orders continues to perplex business management. Increasingly concerned with the need of turning capital quickly, the buyer is growing more and more averse to buying anything beyond his or her immediate requirements. The buyer is prone to unload back on the manufacturer whatever the manufacturer unloads on him or her. Competitive conditions make it easy to do this, and the buyer utilizes this advantage to the fullest.

The Returned Goods Problem

No business need have a high percentage of cancellations, or more than 2 percent of its total billing returned, if it is willing temporarily to lose some business. The returned-goods problem is nine-tenths psychological. It exists for a number of reasons:

1. Management considers it a necessary evil.

2. Salespeople oversell to bolster their orders.

3. Salespeople are permitted to encourage customers to overbuy, with a promise to "fix it up" later.

4. Salespeople are not taught to sell in such a way as to make an order stick.

5. Salespeople are not made to understand that cancellations and returned goods are a reflection on their sales ability.

6. Prices decline, but provisions have not been made to handle the situation.

7. Competitors come in with lower prices and the customer had not been properly sold.

8. Buyers change their minds after the salesperson leaves them. This may be due to high-pressure salesmanship without adequate product value.

9. The product might be of low quality or defective.

10. There may have been delays in shipment which caused the buyer to no longer need the goods, or to no longer need them in the quantity ordered.

11. The buyer may have overestimated his or her requirements, or market needs may have changed after order was placed.

A check of the work of individual salespeople in a number of different concerns, both manufacturers and jobbers, shows that a liberal returned-goods policy not only does not help sales but, on the contrary, mitigates against a larger volume. Invariably the salespeople who produce the most business have a lower percentage of returned goods and cancellations, whereas the salespeople who produce the smaller volume of business invariably have the highest percentage of returned goods and cancellations. Good salespeople do not need a lax returned-goods policy to lean upon, and such a policy only serves to bolster up the weak salespeople without in any way increasing the productiveness of the stronger ones.

A salesperson selling oil pumps "slopped over" the sale by attempting to get the contract signed without the buyer reading it, and then "forgetting" to leave a duplicate copy of the order with the customer. Salespeople are prone to do this when the order form is complex, fearing that the various legal clauses in the contract will cause the customer to hesitate and ask questions, thereby getting off the main track. Order forms should be as simple as possible and free from legal verbiage.

Importance of Clean Orders

Among the losses that result from canceled orders the following might be mentioned:

1. The wasted cost of making the sale

2. The cost of the office paperwork involved

3. The cost of handling and shipping the order

4. The unnecessary capital tied up in expanded inventory

5. Wear and tear on the goods, which may need to be repaired or refinished, or which possibly may no longer be salable

6. The possible disappointment of some other customer who has not received an order because the goods were sent elsewhere

How to Avoid Canceled Orders

Among the practices of companies that have been successful in reducing order cancellations, the following points are considered of importance:

1. Establishing conditions for accepting cancellations, and clearly stating them on the order form

2. Establishment of procedures to correct any losses due to faulty material, delayed shipments, or other causes under the manufacturer's control

3. Establishment of procedures for conditions beyond the control of the manufacturer

4. Establishment of charges to cover costs involved in cancellations

5. Establishment of routines that give salespeople complete facts on delivery and other details, so they will not give incorrect information to their customers

6. Careful analysis of all cancellations and returned goods, so that identifiable causes can be corrected

One large wholesale house tightened up its returned-goods policy and reported the following results:

"We were very lenient with customers who returned goods at first, cheerfully accepting losses, thinking that gradually the situation would clarify, and that the goodwill of the jobber would reimburse us in future profitable business. Strange as it may seem, the jobbers with whom we were most lenient failed to become good customers, and those with whom we adopted a sterner policy buckled down to learn the "game," instructed their sales forces, and are now doing a very fine business in many cases without any worry to us, the manufacturers.

"Our tightening-up policy began with letters of protest to the jobbers, explaining to them why they were failing, and how serious the matter was from the manufacturer's standpoint. This helped with a certain percentage, but others still insisted on sending goods in on slight pretext or no pretext at all, charges collect, and often in damaged condition. Finally we adopted the policy of receiving no merchandise unless permission to return had first been secured from the service department. Goods arriving were refused and a postal notice mailed to the consignor stating the case, informing him that the shipment was being held by the transportation company, and that we would not pick it up unless sent in for repairs, and unless the jobber agreed to stand charges incurred, and agreed to the return of the shipment after inspection or repairs.

"This policy brought protests, of course, but after the customer understood our sincerity and earnest desire to be fair, usually he or she would consent to our terms. Sometimes customers would tell us that they were through with us, but fortunately by the time this policy was put into effect the trade had begun to appreciate the profit possibilities of the line and was not anxious to give it up.

"The result has been an almost complete stoppage of unjustified losses, a more wholesome relationship between the factory and the jobber, and development of sounder channels of distribution."

Legal Status of Association Agreements

While many returned goods and cancellation problems have been sidetracked through the operation of codes, it should be remembered that the antitrust laws are still in effect and that the courts have held, and will probably hold again, that uniform trade practices constitute restraint of trade if adopted by a group of companies in an industry.

Chapter 29

Customer Service Policies

Lee A. Iacocca, chairman and CEO of the Chrysler Corporation, has established his company as one of the most successful in the automobile industry. One of the foremost reasons is his dedication to customer satisfaction. This was first evident back when he was president of Ford Motor Company. At that time, he wrote, in a statement to Dartnell:

> The circumstances and atmosphere in which business is conducted today are of course a lot different than they were even a few years ago. But the name of the game hasn't changed at all—it's still customer satisfaction.
>
> On the face of it the winning combination is a good product or service backed up by good customer handling. But that's an oversimplification.
>
> We'll never achieve 100 percent perfection in what we offer the public. Even our space vehicles have their malfunctions, let alone products that are made by the millions. But the public and our customers understand this. I don't think customer satisfaction demands perfection, but it does require that the quality of a product or service match what the customer expects.
>
> The buyer of inexpensive merchandise in the discount store can be just as well satisfied with his or her purchase as the shopper in the exclusive stores on Fifth Avenue. Why? Certainly not because the quality of the merchandise is the same, but because the expectations of the discount store shopper are different from those of the Fifth Avenue customer.
>
> On this basis, customer complaints aren't entirely the result of mistakes in product design or lapses in production quality control. The gap between reality and expectations is in part, at least, the responsibility of the marketing and sales side—those who create the expectations.
>
> Furthermore, customer dissatisfaction may be the smallest consequence of creating unjustified expectations.
>
> The Federal Trade Commission, among other government agencies, has felt the lash of consumer advocates and the changing times and is cracking down on practices that never before stirred up more than a raised eyebrow, if that.

It seems to me that the signs are unmistakable both in the marketplace and in the halls of government. American business is on notice not only to provide better quality in its goods and services, but also to use greater candor and preciseness in marketing them.

The apparent lack of confidence in American business these days is quite properly a matter of worry and concern for those of us who believe in private enterprise and the free marketplace. But in my view it would be the biggest mistake we could make to assume that our troubles were created by our critics as part of a nefarious scheme to scuttle our capitalist system.

No, I'm convinced that our problems and our opportunities lie with our customers themselves and their simple wish to get their money's worth—to have their expectations met. That's a job for all of us.

Customer service is the most serious internal problem facing industry today. No matter how big or small the company, how great its reputation or how widely accepted its products, it will, eventually, rise or fall according to the soundness of its customer-service policies.

Arjay Miller, former president of Ford Motor Company, addressing the National Automobile Dealers Association said: "Customer service ranks right beside traffic safety, air pollution, and highway congestion in terms of public interest." He continued:

> Nothing will so much affect the future of the franchise system as our ability—and particularly your ability—to meet the car owner's demand for better automotive service. No law, and no change in factory-dealer cost reimbursement, can offer a real solution. The real solution can only be in more effective dealer-factory cooperation in identifying, evaluating, and responding to what the customer expects from us.

While the actual supervision of servicing is not generally a function of the sales manager, yet coordination between the service department, or outside servicing sources, is an important selling responsibility. It goes almost without saying that poor servicing policies or practices can undo all the favorable efforts of salespeople to obtain customer acceptance for their products.

Furthermore, a surprisingly large number of sales executives fail to take full advantage of the profit potentials of servicing. In many lines, service items, parts, and supplies may contribute as much as 50 percent or more profit beyond that realized in the original sale.

An Approach to Consumer Problems

The director of consumer affairs—or someone with an equivalent title—is rapidly becoming a fixture of U.S. corporate management. The formation of a national association of consumer affairs officers indicates how far the trend already has gone.

As editorialized in *Business Week,* this is all to the good. It indicates a growing awareness of the strength of the consumer and a willingness to listen to customer complaints. It gives the frustrated consumer an opportunity to register a protest with management instead of going to Congress or to the regulatory agencies.

To operate effectively, the consumer affairs director must function as part of management, not as a glorified receptionist outside the executive suite. He or she must be able to analyze the sources of trouble and devise ways to correct them. Above all, he or she must be listened to at every level of the company.

It can be done, as the experience of many companies—General Electric, Sears, Motorola—demonstrates.

The Consumer Wave

A senior vice-president of General Electric Company saw the wave of consumerism as a potential sales benefit.

"People simply want to know how the product works and what's in it, a better explanation of its features, a clearer understanding of the warranty and terms of purchase. The prudent manufacturer provides dealer support, so that they in turn can present a complete product-and-service story—and back it up.

"But there can't be a double standard for consumerism. Dealers can't apply consumerism one way for manufacturers to rectify those inadequacies. We encourage everyone to support a single, universal standard for consumerism."

Variable Factors in Servicing Practices

Analysis of the practices of several hundred companies reveals the following considerations to be of concern to those who determine service policies:

1. Service is rendered to assist the wholesaler and retailer in the profitable completion of their functions, and the consumer in his or her satisfactory use of the product.

2. Through service, a manufacturer can gain highly valuable knowledge about a product in use. Careful records should therefore be kept so that product weaknesses can be quickly corrected.

3. A manufacturer must either provide service or train others to supply it.

4. The manufacturer who has others do the servicing must educate or train them. This training may be conducted at the factory or by using traveling training schools. Usually the wholesalers or retail outlet people pay their own traveling expenses and the manufacturer provides the trainers, props, and supplies. Some companies give certificates to trainees on completion of the training.

5. For many consumer items, the service is supplied in the form of tags, instruction sheets or labels. Collarbands on shirts may state "Do not starch;" with some synthetic fabrics, tags stating how to wash are attached; a simple appliance may have a user's service manual or instruction sheet included in the package.

6. For industrial goods, more servicing is usually required. This may start with a study of installation problems to assure proper installation. Also periodic inspection or maintenance after installation may be necessary to assure proper operations. These services may be charged for as an extra or included in the contract price.

7. Manufacturers may license outside shops to do maintenance and repair work on their products. For example, automobile-jack manufacturers contract with shops that do not sell jacks, but merely repair them. The manufacturers protect themselves by selling their parts only to these licensed shops. Or manufacturers may maintain their own local repair shops, as with hearing aids or electric razors.

8. On repairs or replacement of inferior parts, manufacturers may:

- Provide this service for a stated period of time and include labor, material and transportation;

- Limit it to material only.

To control service, many manufacturers provide warranty cards with their product. This is customary with appliances. The ultimate user is expected to fill in the card, showing the dealer's name, address, date of purchase, and any other pertinent data that the company desires to obtain. From these cards, valuable marketing statistics can be obtained. The trouble is, many people hold the cards for a period of time, thinking they thereby extend the length of warranty.

Some manufacturers maintain highly trained "preventive maintenance" service departments, and contract for such service. Notable among them are computer, typewriter, and other office-equipment manufacturers.

Service—a Tool for Selling

Jim and Tom Anthony have been in the retail appliance-electronics business in Inglewood, California, for several decades. When asked how their Anthony Bros. store became one of the leading independents in the metropolitan Los Angeles area, they cited service.

"It's not only vital to fulfilling the contract with a customer when he buys from us, it's our bridge to this customer's next purchase," said Jim Anthony, who is in charge of service. "If we do a good job servicing an appliance or electronics product—whether he's bought from us before or not—we're more than halfway toward establishing ourselves as a good place to do business."

The Anthony brothers firmly believe that service is a tool for selling. Salespeople are instructed to refer to the store's complete service facilities during their sales presentations.

"We also try to make certain that everyone who works in this store remembers that service means sales," pointed out Jim

Anthony. "Repair people on house-service calls are in a perfect position to spot a homeowner's need for a new appliance or television set. We pay them 2 percent of the gross for any business that results from a lead they direct our way."

Led by the high-tech companies, firms selling products that need repair, replacement, and/or maintenance, place a major emphasis on well-rounded training programs for their field service representatives. They realize there is more to the field service function than putting "nuts and bolts" together. A field service representative or technician who can't deal effectively with people can create dissatisfied customers, which often leads to high rates of equipment cancellation, excessive requests for time-consuming service calls, and lack of faith in the company's new products, and loss of profits.

These companies also realize that the field service rep can have closer contact with the customer than anyone else in the company. Therefore, the rep is in a position to recommend replacement or new equipment, supplies, and maintenance contracts. The trend is to teach field service reps "people skills" and to expose them to the rudiments of the basic selling skills.

Chapter 30

Sales Management and the Law

There are a number of laws designed to protect the public from monopolistic power in the market and from unbridled competition that gives rise to misleading and deceptive practices in selling and advertising.

To enforce these laws, the main agencies involved are the Federal Trade Commission, the Food and Drug Administration, and the Federal Communications Commission.

Major legal complications in which management may become involved usually are the result of violations of government rules and regulations, competitive situations, or of consumer actions. Violations can result in heavy penalties, especially in antitrust actions.

Product safety and truth in advertising have come under greatly increased scrutiny from the Food and Drug Administration and the Federal Trade Commission.

There are six acts of Congress bearing on the regulation of interstate commerce. Each must be considered in establishing a sales policy or in making sales decisions. These are as follows:

1. *The Federal Trade Commission Act* gave the commission power to act as business police against illegitimate competitive methods.

2. *The Wheeler-Lea Act,* amending the Federal Trade Commission Act, eliminates the necessity for the Federal Trade Commission to prove injury to competition before a complaint can be made and, for the first time, establishes a fine and imprisonment as possible penalties for violating the prohibitions of the law.

3. *The Robinson-Patman Act* prevents unfair price discrimination between competitive purchasers of the same merchandise.

4. *The Sherman Antitrust Act* is the first of the antitrust laws to outlaw contracts, combinations, and conspiracies in restraint of trade.

5. *The Clayton Antitrust Act* prohibits *competitive practices leading* to monopoly. This law was designed to supplement the Sherman Antitrust Act, which merely forbade *monopoly*—not the *practices* that created it.

6. *The Fair Labeling and Packaging Act* is aimed at correcting abuses tending to mislead or confuse the consumer, such as variations in sizes, quantities, contents.

Trade Practices Considered Unfair

Competition is one of the hallmarks of the U.S. business scene. Any firm must compete successfully if it is to exist and prosper. But competition does not mean "anything goes." There are legal safeguards against unfair competition and discrimination. These safeguards apply to large and small concerns alike.

Valuable protection against unfair competition is provided by the Federal Trade Commission (FTC). The FTC administers the Federal Trade Commission Act, the Clayton Act as amended by the Robinson-Patman Act, and six other related statutes. Its main objective is to protect and promote competitive business and to protect the interests of the purchasing public. Among the rights the FTC seeks to preserve are the right to buy as cheaply as competitors, freedom to buy only items and quantities needed, and freedom to sell goods in an open market. In addition, the FTC guards against such unfair competitive methods as rigging prices and markets, illegal price discrimination, granting or receiving discriminatory promotional allowances, false disparagement of competitors, pirating employees, offering fake buying advantages, and using false and misleading advertising.

The commission bases its official legal actions on the facts of each individual case. Its formal procedure involves investigation, complaint, hearings, and if warranted, an order "to cease and desist." Such orders by the commission are subject to review in the courts. In addition, there is a consultation program designed to aid businesspeople in understanding the requirements of the law and in complying voluntarily with them. This program involves industrywide trade-practice conferences, and the advisory and assistance work of the Division of Small Business.

Location of Federal Trade Commission Offices

The locations of FTC headquarters and regional offices are:

• Headquarters
Federal Trade Commission
Division of Credit Practices
6th & Pennsylvania Avenue, N.W.
Washington, D.C. 20580
(202) 724-1139

• Regional Offices

1718 Peachtree Street, N.W.
ATLANTA, Georgia 30367
(404) 881-4836

150 Causeway Street
BOSTON, Massachusetts 02114
(617) 223-6621

55 East Monroe Street
CHICAGO, Illinois 60603
(312) 353-4423

118 St. Clair Avenue
CLEVELAND, Ohio 44141
(216) 522-4207

1405 Curtis Street
DENVER, Colorado 80202
(303) 844-2271

11000 Wilshire Boulevard
LOS ANGELES, California 90024
(213) 209-7575

26 Federal Plaza
NEW YORK, New York 10278
(212) 264-1207

450 Golden Gate Avenue
SAN FRANCISCO, California 94102
(415) 556-1270

8303 Elmbrook Drive
DALLAS, Texas 75247
(214) 767-7050

915 Second Avenue
SEATTLE, Washington 98174
(206) 442-4656

Numerous specific practices that tend to injure competition are prohibited by the laws enforced by the Commission. These include (but are not limited to) the following techniques.

- *Granting discriminatory allowances.* Granting allowances for advertising, or furnishing services or facilities such as demonstrators, to one or more customers competing in the distribution of similar products, when such allowances or services or facilities are not made available on proportionally equal terms to all competing customers of a supplier.

- *Manipulating prices.* Agreements or combinations for the purpose and with the effect of raising, depressing, fixing, pegging, or stabilizing the price of commodity.

- *Rigging production and markets.* Agreements or combinations that restrict production, divide territories, establish a so-called "protected market," or divide customers among competitors.

- *Inducing discriminatory allowances.* A purchaser's knowingly inducing or receiving payments for advertising allowances from a supplier when such payment is not affirmatively offered or otherwise made available on proportionally equal terms to all other customers competing in the distribution of that supplier's products.

- *Using bait advertising.* Engaging in promotional campaigns that offer at an unusually low price certain items in which the public is interested, and which the dealer has no intention of selling but advertises merely to attract potential customers for more expensive merchandise of the same type.

- *Bribing patronage.* Bribing buyers, purchasing agents, or other employees of customers and prospective customers in order to obtain or hold patronage.

- *Spying trade secrets.* Procuring the technical or trade secrets of competitors by espionage, by bribing their employees, or by similar illicit means.

- *Pirating employees.* Inducing employees of competitors to violate their contracts and enticing them to leave their jobs with the intention and effect of hampering or embarrassing competitors in the operation of their businesses.

- *Disparaging competitors.* Making false and disparaging statements regarding competitors' products and businesses.

- *Selling used items as new.* Selling for new, items that actually are rebuilt, second-hand, renovated or old products, or are made in whole or in part from used or second-hand materials, by representing such articles as new, or by failing to reveal that they are not new, or that they contain second-hand or used materials.

- *Cornering competitors' merchandise.* Buying up competitors' merchandise for the purpose of hampering them and stiffling or eliminating competition.

- *Merchandising by lot or chance.* Selling or distributing punchboards or other lottery devices for use in the sale of merchandise by lot or chance, or using merchandising schemes based on lot or chance.

- *Offering fake buying advantages.* Creating the impression that customers are being offered an opportunity to make purchases under unusually favorable conditions when such is not the case.

- *Using misleading names.* Using misleading trade, company, or product names.

- *Employing deception.* Employing any other false or misleading representation that deceives or has the capacity to deceive or mislead.

Fair Labeling and Packaging

Congress enacted the Fair Labeling and Packaging Law (public law 89-755) in 1966. This went into effect on July 1, 1967.

The responsibility for administering the law has been divided among the Food and Drug Administration, the Federal Trade Commission, and the Department of Commerce. This has led to some confusion and overlapping of responsibilities.

In essence, the Food and Drug Administration supervises products and distribution practices in the food, drug, and cosmetics industries. The Federal Trade Commission is responsible for all other household package goods, such as detergents and paper products.

The FDA and the FTC issue regulations specifying the typographical arrangements on the basic information panel on all packages.

The Department of Commerce administers that section of the law which provides for the use of voluntary standards to reduce the proliferation of unnecessary package sizes.

The job of "selling" industry on the use of voluntary standards has been assigned to the deputy director of the Institute for Applied Technology in the National Bureau of Standards.

The act makes provision for both mandatory regulation and regulation by administration discretion. As part of the mandatory requirements, packages must bear labels specifying:

1. Identification of the commodity.

2. Name and place of business of the manufacturer or distributor.

3. Net quantity of contents (in terms of weight, measure, or numerical count). The statement of quantity must appear in a uniform location upon the principal display panel of the label.

4. If the package weighs less than four pounds (or one gallon if liquid measure), its weight shall be expressed in both ounces (specified as avoirdupois or fluid ounces) and in pounds, with any remainder in terms of ounces or common or decimal fractions of the pound. Liquid measure shall be shown in the largest whole unit (quarts or pints as appropriate), with any remainder in terms of liquid ounces or common or decimal fractions of the pint or quart. The law also makes specific provision for packages whose contents are commonly specified in length or area, and for random-weight packages.

5. Statements about number of servings must include net weight, measure, or numerical count of each serving.

Government Clearances

Promotional material of some new products may require advance government approval. In the drug industry, for instance, not only are new drug products subject to approval, but labels must be approved and all marketing or promotional materials must "follow" the labels. Similarly, labels and promotional materials for alcohol must be approved in advance. It is well known, of course, that promotion and publicity for all new securities require clearance by the SEC.

Loose Lips Sink Sales Ships

When operating in a competitive marketplace and in the heat of getting the sale, some salespersons can, inadvertently or otherwise, make illegal statements or claims to a customer that could later lead to legal action and the ensuing costs, loss of customers, and damage to the reputations of both the salesperson and his or her company.

Misrepresentation and breach of warranty are two legal causes for action which can occur when either false statements or exaggeration of the capabilities of products or services are made.

In an article in *Sales & Marketing Management,* Steven Mitchell Sack, a New York City practicing attorney, offered these suggestions for salespeople in order to avoid lawsuits.

1. Understand the distinction between general statements of praise and statements of fact made during the sales pitch (and the legal consequences).

2. Thoroughly educate all customers before making a sale. Salespeople should tell as much about the specific qualities of the product as possible. The reason is that when a salesperson makes statements about a product in a field in which his or her company is considered to have extensive experience, the law makes it difficult for the salesperson to defend himself or herself by claiming it was just sales talk.

3. Be accurate when describing a product's capabilities. Avoid

making speculative claims, particularly with respect to predictions concerning what a product will do.

4. Know the technical specifications of the product. Review all promotional literature to be sure that there are no exaggerated claims. Keep abreast of all design changes as well.

5. Avoid making exaggerated claims about product safety. The law usually takes a dim view of such affirmative claims, and these remarks can be interpreted as warranties that lead to liability.

6. Be familiar with federal and state laws regarding warranties and guarantees.

7. Be well versed in the capabilities and characteristics of your products and services.

8. Keep current with all design changes and revisions in your product's operating manual.

9. Avoid offering opinions when the customer asks what results a product or service will accomplish unless the company has tested the product and has statistical evidence.

10. Never overstep authority, especially when discussing prices or company policy. Remember, a salesperson's statements can bind the company.

One final point from Mr. Sack: It's generally easy for customers to recover damages on the grounds of misrepresentation and breach of warranty. In many states, this holds even when a salesperson's statement is made innocently. So tell your salespeople to stick to the facts!

For further information on how to comply with warranty law, you may wish to obtain a copy of *Warranties: Making Business Sense Out of Warranty Law*. Produced by the Federal Trade Commission, this pamphlet is available from the Superintendent of Documents, Washington, D.C.

Chapter 31

Trademarks and Trade Names

What's in a name? Or a trademark? This question, often frivolously asked, is not so frivolous in business; the legal right to a trademark or tradename can have serious consequences. One indication of the importance of trademark protection is that a branch of the legal profession specializes in this field.

Trademarks are, for many companies, their most important, vital assets. A plant might burn down, or some other catastrophe might occur, but the continuation of a company's business is assured by virtue of its possession of a well-known established trademark. A forum conducted by the U.S. Trademark Association brought out these points.

A trademark is essentially a symbol of identification. It identifies a product with a given source. That source may not be known as such to the consumer. That is, the consumer may not know the name of the company that makes the item, but the trademark enables the purchaser to recognize a familiar item, either on the basis of a previous satisfactory use of it, or on the basis of a conviction or a persuasion to purchase inspired by advertising and promotion.

A trademark is not a trade name. A trade name identifies a company. A trademark identifies a product.

A trademark is not to be confused with a copyright, nor is it to be confused with a patent. Both of these are, in essence, government monopolies for a limited period of time. The patent pertains to an invention of a new product or of a new process, and it is granted and extended to you by the government. It does not exist until the government creates it for you, and it exists only for a limited period of time—17 years.

Copyright, on the other hand, pertains to the creation of usually what is termed a work of art. You will recognize it immediately when we speak in terms of a musical composition or a literary piece.

"Use" Is Key Word for Trademarks

It is important to keep in mind that no one gives you a trademark as the government might, for example, with a patent. You create your own rights in a trademark, and a trademark also can be eternal. Those rights will be viable so long as you continue to use the mark. That word "use" is the essential word in the field of trademarks.

Your rights in the mark automatically begin with use. You don't need the government to tell you that you have a trademark. It begins from the day you first use the mark. Ultimately you may obtain registration of it, but that simply confers upon you certain procedural advantages. Essentially, the fundamental rights you have are created merely by your use of it, and they will subsist just as long as you continue to use it.

The most important thing about a trademark, whether it be a word, a symbol, a device, or a combination thereof, is that the mark is distinctive enough that it can be protected not only on the goods on which the mark is used, but also relative to those goods that are related or close to the goods specifically identified by the mark.

If you have a distinctive mark, you are able to effectively enforce your rights in court to prevent infringement. You also are able to obtain a federal registration, if you have use of the mark in interstate commerce, and thereby enjoy the benefits the registration gives you. It is very important to have a mark that is readily available for expansion of use to other products, as you expand your business or come out with new products and services.

Kinds of Trademarks

There are four categories of trademarks: a coined mark, an arbitrary mark, a descriptive mark, and a suggestive mark.

The *coined mark* constitutes a word that is invented and not in the language prior to its adoption.

The classic example of a coined trademark is Kodak.

Other examples of coined words are Colgate's trademark Ultra

Brite for toothpaste and General Foods' trademark Sanka for decaffeinated coffee.

An *arbitrary mark* is a word that is already in the language, but, when applied to a certain product, does not describe the product in any way.

Examples of this are Tornado electrical equipment, True for cigarettes, Arm & Hammer for baking soda.

The next type of mark is a *suggestive mark*. This suggests to some degree what the product is, or what it does, or what the use of the product is. There is a fine line between whether a mark is suggestive or descriptive.

An example of a suggestive mark is the Head and Shoulders trademark for hair shampoo. Another is Close-Up, trademark for a toothpaste.

These marks can also be very strong protection, depending upon the reputation they have acquired.

Then you get into the area of *descriptive marks*. These are the marks that give company lawyers headaches.

The marketing and advertising people naturally like a mark that describes a product and that tells the consumer what it is. There is nothing wrong with this, as long as the owner realizes that there are substantial pitfalls in adopting a mark that describes; once such a mark is used, others can come along and use the same or similar words in its apt descriptive sense.

Examples of descriptive marks include SugarTwin for sweeteners, and Instant Breakfast for breakfast food.

A descriptive mark is a mark that describes the product, whereas a suggestive mark is a mark that suggests something about the product but does not actually describe it.

The difference between descriptive and suggestive is more a difference in kind than a difference in degree.

A descriptive mark is one that tells you something about the product. It may be geographically descriptive, or descriptive of its qualities. As an example, Diehard was held descriptive for a line of batteries. So was Accent for food flavoring.

It is not the generic name of the product—that is something else again. A generic term is the common descriptive name of the goods and may never be a trademark. For example, Intensive Care is a trademark (albeit descriptive) but "hand lotion" is a generic term. It describes a quality or something about the origin.

Are Trademarks a Monopoly?

A trademark does not ever constitute a "monopoly." A trademark provides the exclusive right to use the mark on the goods. Sometimes trademarks identify products that are substantial market leaders; the trademark enables consumers to continue to select these brands over others. That's not, however, a monopoly. In reality, trademarks create fair competition in the marketplace where consumers can select the particular product (brand) they prefer from among others in the product category. Trademarks may establish and encourage brand loyalty.

Trademarks and Advertising

It is primarily the trademark that makes it possible to employ national advertising profitably as a selling auxiliary, and trademarks are widely featured in advertising. For this reason it is often assumed that the trademark is an advertising device, intended to recommend the goods or call attention to their quality or utility. Keep in mind that trade characters, slogans, and logotypes may be trademarks.

A clear distinction may be made between the function of advertising, which is to describe and recommend the goods, and the function of the trademark, which is to indicate their origin. A trademark may acquire a certain advertising value, but such value is purely incidental and inferential. Unless it clearly indicates the source or origin—and not the character or quality—of the goods, it is not an *exclusive* mark of identification, and the "monopoly" in its use cannot be protected. This is because any producer or seller of similar goods has an equal right to describe his or her product and to indicate its quality, utility, features, or general desirability.

It is essential that you have notices of registration in your advertisements, but if you are in an area where there is a likelihood that the trade press or fashion writers are going to misuse your mark, you probably are taking a step toward preventing that if, when you use your mark, you use it to tell the world, including the editor and the writer, that it is a trademark.

You do not have to use an ® if the mark is registered, but it is advisable because, for one thing, it means something to the public. The consumer may not have any idea of what the ® means on a product, but generally knows it is a badge of ownership.

The Exercise of Diligence

Essentially, it is advertising that creates the meaning for a trademark in the first place, and advertising may change that meaning into a generic term or preserve the validity of the trademark, depending on how it is used. Sydney A. Diamond, when he was a member of the New York Bar, stated in *Advertising Age* that sometimes the brand becomes so firmly established by advertising that the public starts to misuse the trademark as if it were a generic term for the product itself. Judge Learned Hand warned of the peril in a famous trademark opinion: "Its very success may prove its failure." If caught in time, this trend can be averted, and even reversed, by advertising directed to the specific objective of education for proper trademark use.

To take a specific example: When American Cyanamid acquired Formica Corp. in 1956, it inherited a problem that tends to affect products in dominant market positions. Formica was so well known that many consumers were unaware of any other name for laminated plastic. This led to substitutions at the retail level and a drop in market share. Cyanamid instituted a corrective program that included a series of educational advertisements designed to strengthen Formica as a trademark.

Another use for the name theme is to explain that a manufacturer's trademark applies to a family of products, not merely one item. An individual product name, therefore, must accompany the trademark for complete information, and the resulting combination of generic term with trademark is just about the best possible way of preserving the manufacturer's legal rights.

The predecessor company of Chesebrough-Pond's once used a similar approach in an advertisement headed, "What's Their

Whole Name?" which showed photographs of famous persons with their first names followed by blank spaces for middle and last names. The body copy read:

"Vaseline, the registered trademark owned by Chesebrough-Pond's Inc., is not a complete name for any one product, but rather it is the brand word for the whole family of products made by that company.

"It should never be used alone, but always with the name of the product it designates, viz.: 'Vaseline' petroleum jelly, 'Vaseline' hair tonic, 'Vaseline' lip ice pomade, etc. We'd appreciate it if you'd keep this in mind. Many thanks!"

The care a company must take to protect the proper usage of its trademark is indicated by the following letter from Friden, Inc., to a leading business publication:

"We are faced with the continuing problem that incorrect use of a trademark may lead to its loss.

"We would appreciate your assistance in preventing future misuse of our trademark Justowriter automatic composing machine, which appeared in *Sales & Marketing Management.* In this case it emerged as Adjuster Writer, which is fairly imaginative but incorrect."

Essentials of a Trademark

Trademark rights are acquired only through actual use of the mark as attached to the goods, or in direct association with the goods, in bona fide commercial transactions. No right is created by the mere adoption or invention of a trademark. The right begins when goods bearing the mark are actually placed on the market, and the extent of the rights is proportional to actual use in the market.

A trademark must be distinctive, so far as the kind or class of goods on which it is used is concerned. It must not be identical with or similar to any other trademark used on goods of "the same descriptive properties." Goods are of the same descriptive properties when they are so closely related or generally competitive as to make confusion likely in the public mind. Thus, automobiles are held to be of the same descriptive properties as automobile tires or accessories. This, however, does not prevent the use of the same trademark on totally unrelated products, such as automobiles and pianos, for example, or baking powder and plows.

The Selection of a Trademark

Since it is difficult and expensive to make any change in a trademark after it is adopted and put into use, it is important to give careful attention to the matter of selection. Much expensive litigation may be avoided if due care and study are given to this phase of the problem in advance. The courts may be relied upon to protect trademark rights; but they can only protect such rights as actually exist *as a matter of fact* at the time the action is brought. They cannot correct past errors of judgment, and little or no weight can be given to motives and intentions.

First of all, it must be borne clearly in mind that the name or mark selected must be one that the public can use to identify the goods. The public must understand it as meaning goods from a single source or origin, and it should not be possible for this meaning to be confused. The public bestows its own meanings upon the names it uses in trade, just as it does upon any other words in the language, and the public use of a term cannot be restrained or restricted. Also, the name selected must be one that can be monopolized and used exclusively for the purpose of identification, without interfering with the rights of others.

Thus there are certain groups or classes of words that can be eliminated at the start as not suitable for the purpose. Obviously it is necessary to avoid imitating or duplicating any trademark that is already in use in connection with goods under the same classification. If there is any doubt on this score, an attorney experienced in trademark law should be retained to search the U.S. Patent Office records. Other general classes of names it is well to avoid are the following:

1. Descriptive terms, which include all words indicative of the kind or quality or utility of the product and laudatory adjectives intended to recommend or advertise the quality of the goods (Wonderful Automobile). Such terms are not regis-

terable, and a monopoly in them cannot be sustained, since any maker of similar goods may also rightfully use them.

2. Geographical names are equally open to objection as non-registrable.

3. Family names. Though there are a great many well-known family name trademarks (Heinz, Mennen, Smith Brothers, Colgate, etc.), a name of this character is apt to prove troublesome, since others entitled to the same name have the right to use it in connection with their products. The L. E. Waterman Pen Co., for example, was in litigation for many years with a concern making A. A. Waterman pens, carrying the case eventually to the Supreme Court without obtaining adequate relief.

The Trademark Act provides that a mark which is "primarily merely a surname" cannot be registered under normal circumstances. This is based partly on the theory that nobody should be able to take a family name out of circulation by registering it as a trademark, until such time as the purchasing public reacts to it as a trademark, rather than as just a surname, as the result of extensive and exclusive use. Of course, a family name frequently acquires this special kind of status when the product to which it is attached achieves commercial success. Ford, Kellogg, and Wrigley are three well-known examples.

A trademark must be considered in its entirety, not dissected into separate parts. If it is a combination of various elements, it nevertheless makes its impression on the public as a combination, and that is the way in which its registrability should be tested.

Aside from the foregoing, there obviously remains a very wide field from which a choice may be made. A common dictionary word may be chosen that is purely fanciful, as "Ivory" is for soap, "Carnation" for condensed milk, "Cream of Wheat" for farina. Or a purely arbitrary word may be preferred, such as "Star" or "Anchor" or "7-20-4." The main point is to select a name that is easy to recognize, to pronounce, and which is so obviously fanciful or arbitrary that there is no possible confusion as to its significance as a mark of identification.

Coined Words as Trademarks

Many believe that the best trademark is the coined word: Kodak, Vaseline, Kleenex.

Such manufactured words have, as a matter of fact, made up the bulk of the applications for registration in the Trademark Office. There is, of course, no technical objection to them, but they have certain disadvantages when used as trademarks, aside from the fact that it is difficult to invent a new word that is entirely distinctive and easy to recognize and pronounce. Radio and television advertising have given added importance to easily remembered names.

For one thing, the adoption of a coined word implies that the public must be taught the meaning of an entirely new term, which in itself is something of a task. For another thing, there is the likelihood that the public will see fit to bestow a meaning of its own upon the mark—to use it in short as a convenient generic term for a certain kind of variety of product. The more widely such marks are advertised, the greater is the possibility of such misconception. Typical instances are "Kodak," which is widely used as synonymous with "camera." "B.V.D." was popularly understood for years as referring merely to a certain athletic style of underwear, making substitution an extremely simple process, and leading to a large crop of vexatious and expensive lawsuits. "Celluloid" is a perfectly valid technical trademark, which only one producer can lawfully use *as a trademark;* that is, as "attached to the goods." But the popular use of the term as referring to a certain substance has been so widespread that any manufacturer of that substance may lawfully sell it as celluloid. Technically, the original proprietor is protected, but practically he is not, since the public use of the term is paramount.

Hence the coined word may quite possibly become a liability, especially where the public does not deal directly with the owner of the trademark, but with irresponsible vendors who may or may not be scrupulous. So far as the right to exclusive use is concerned, the common dictionary word (like "Ivory" or "Carnation," for example) is of equal value, and there is far less likelihood of confusion or misconception as to its significance.

Trademarks on Patented Products

When a product is manufactured under the protection of a patent monopoly, special attention should be given to the trademark problem in order to avoid loss of goodwill when the patent expires. The patent monopoly consists in the right to exclude others from making, using, or selling the product in question for a limited term. At the end of the term, right to make, use, and sell passes to the public, and with it there necessarily passes the right to *describe* the product in terms that ordinarily will be understood. This is inevitable, since the right to make would be of small value without the right to tell what is made. On the other hand, the monopoly of the descriptive phraseology by the original patentee would practically mean indefinite extension of the monopoly.

Hence, if the name that is used as a trademark during the life of the patent is the *only name the public understands* as descriptive of the product, it will pass to the public when the patent expires. A specific example of that is "Aspirin," which the courts decided is the only name the general public understands as referring to a particular chemical compound of acetylsalicylic acid. "Linoleum" is another name originally used as a technical trademark, but now employed generally as an ordinary descriptive term referring to a certain kind of material. The Supreme Court in the famous sewing machine case refused to enjoin a competing manufacturer from using the name "Singer" in connection with machines made under the specifications of Singer patents that had expired. Singer, however, later regained the exclusive right to use its name as a trademark.

No general rule of procedure will apply to all cases. The only safe plan is to obtain competent legal advice, as far as possible in advance of the expiration date of the patent. The common error is to delay action until the patent is about to expire, and then adopt some expedient that may actually confuse the situation rather than clarify it. Where patent rights are involved in conjunction with trademarks, competent advice at the start will save many times its cost in ultimate loss of goodwill and unnecessary litigation.

Registration of Trademarks

There was no federal legislation in effect on trademarks until 1870. That year Congress passed an act codifying some of the principles of law which had been applied by common law and in equity courts at the time.

The first federal trademark legislation came under review by the Supreme Court in 1879. The court, while invalidating an enactment because it failed to find constitutional authority to support it, nevertheless recognized and stated the principle that:

"The right to adopt and use a symbol or a device to distinguish the goods or property made or sold by the person whose mark it is, to the exclusion of the use of that symbol by all other persons, has been long recognized by the common law and the chancery courts of England and of this country, and by the statutes of some of the States. It is a property right for which damages may be recovered in an action at law, and the violation of which will be enjoined by a court of equity, with compensation for past infringement. This property and the exclusive right to its use were not created by the Act of Congress, and do not now depend upon that Act for their enforcement. The whole system of trademark property and the civil remedies for its protection existed long anterior to the Act of Congress, and remain in full force since its passage."

Broadly speaking, therefore, it may be asserted that our law has always recognized the fundamental basis on which trademark protection rests, namely, the principle that business integrity is to be preserved in order that the individual may be protected in his or her business reputation, and the public may be protected against interlopers who seek to reap where they have not sown. In a word, it has always been the objective of trademark law, both on common-law principle and by statute, to compel fair play and common honesty in business.

As the Supreme Court said in the case to which reference has been made, this principle exists and is protected quite independently of federal legislation.

The advantage of federal legislation on the subject was recognized by Congress. After the invalidation of the first Trademark Act a new law was enacted in the year 1881.

That act remained without substantial change until 1905, when the whole subject was reviewed and the act of that year, having the objective of extending the scope of protection of trademark owners, became effective.

From time to time the 1905 act was amended, but with the exception of an act passed in 1920, the amendatory acts dealt mainly with procedural matters.

The act of 1920 broadened the scope of subject matter entitled to registration primarily for the purpose of affording protection to American citizens under foreign trademark legislation.

While there was no substantive change in the protection afforded by federal legislation, judicial interpretation developed many uncertainties as to the rights and remedies of trademark owners. A large number of the decisions dealt with principles commonly referred to as unfair competition, and based on encroachments upon business reputation that were independent of technical infringement of registered trademarks. There was a gradual growth of the scope of protection of business outside of the preview of the Trademark Act, and it was recognized by the Supreme Court and other federal tribunals that the essential element in trademark cases was the same as in unfair competition cases unaccompanied by trademark infringement, and that the common law of trademarks was but a part of the broader law of unfair competition. This principle was enunciated by the Supreme Court very clearly in the often-quoted *Hanover Milling Co.* case reported in 240 U.S. 403.

Newer Legislation

Largely because of the uncertainties arising from varying judicial interpretations, and because of the growth of the law of unfair competition, agitation for new legislation arose both from within and without Congress. This finally resulted in the enactment of our current law, which was approved July 5, 1946, effective July 5, 1947.

The basic purposes of the 1946 legislation (the Lanham Act) were well stated in a report of the Senate Committee preceding the passage of the act. This report said:

"The purpose underlying any trademark statute is twofold. One is to protect the public so it may be confident that, in purchasing a product bearing a particular trademark that it favorably knows, it will get the product that it asks for and wants to get. Secondly, where the owner of a trademark has spent energy, time, and money in presenting the product to the public, he is protected in his investment from its misappropriation by pirates and cheats. This is a well-established rule of law protecting both the public and the trademark owner."

In 1946 act embraces an extension of the nature of trade indicia, which is subject to federal registration, beyond technical trademarks applied directly to merchandise. This extension of federal recognition of the symbols of goodwill is designed to include prohibition of the use of deceptive and misleading trade indicia that heretofore was cognizable only under the doctrine of unfair competition. The purpose of the new act specifically includes protection against unfair competition and the provisions of the act are designed to prevent fraud and deception by any unfair use of reproductions, copies, counterfeits, or colorable imitations, whereby merchandise or services are distinguished in the course of commerce, whether the indicia be technical trademarks directly applied to the goods, as was the case under prior statutory provision, or whether it is used in other ways in connection with the offer to the public of products or services. The act, therefore, includes not only remedies for technical trademark infringement but also for service marks used in the sale or advertising of services; certification marks, which are marks used in connection with products or services by others than the owner of the mark whereby the origin or certain characteristics of the goods or services are certified; and collective marks, which are marks used by cooperative associations or other groups.

Another important step toward more liberal protection of trademarks may be found in that provision of the Lanham Act that recognizes use of the mark either on goods themselves or on any displays associated therewith as statutory basis for trademark protection. Under the old act, a trademark was protected by statute only if and when it was actually affixed to the merchandise itself or its container.

No mark can be registered that contains immoral or scandalous matter. It must not include any simulation of the flag or other insignia of the United States, or any state or municipality, or any foreign nation, or any emblem of any philanthropical or fraternal society. Registration is prohibited of any name, emblem, etc., adopted by any institution, organization, club, or society incorporated prior to use by the applicant. Portraits of living individuals are not registrable except upon written consent, and no portrait of a deceased president may be registered during the life of his widow, except by her written consent. No mark which is identical with that used by another on the same class of goods, or which so nearly resembles it as to be likely to cause confusion, can be registered. A mark consisting merely of the name of the applicant can be registered only when it is written distinctively (as a signature, for example) or printed. The Trademark Counterfeiting Act of 1984 imposes criminal penalties for counterfeiting trademarks.

The Lanham Act

Under the Lanham Act (1946), which combines and augments the acts of February 20, 1905, and March 19, 1920, the procedures in registering and using trademarks and servicemarks were modernized and liberalized. The new law for example:

1. Gives the owner an "incontestable right" to his trademark if it is consistently used for five years after registration under the act—and *provided the owner is vigilant*

2. Consolidates all previous trademark legislation and codifies the accumulation of 40 years of legal interpretations and statutes

3. Protects trademark holders from interference by state legislatures

4. Assures carrying out U.S. commitments under international trademark agreements

5. Provides "broader protection" against unfair competition and infringement

While retaining the old law's prohibition against trademarks that are immoral or scandalous, or those using the seal or insignia of the United States or of any state or municipality, the new legislation adds another forbidden category—marks that "disparage or falsely suggest" a connection with persons living or dead, institutions, beliefs or national symbols, so as to "bring them into contempt or disrepute."

The Lanham Act is more lenient than the old act toward the use of trademarks involving the names of places or persons. Under the old law, the registration of the trademark "Kem" for plastic playing cards was denied because there is a Russian river with this name. The fact that there was a U.S. Senator by the same name, James P. Kem (R., Mo.), would also rule out registration under the old law. But the Lanham Act would permit "Kem" to be registered as a trademark since it is not "primarily" the name of a river or a person, such as "Rhine" or "Smith" would be.

The U.S. Commissioner of Patents and Trademarks termed "extremely fortunate" the Lanham Act's elimination of the "mere existence" of a surname or corporation name as grounds for rejecting a trademark. Take the almost perfect trademark of Noxon. (It can be spelled forward or backward and read upside down.) Under the old law, it would have been rejected because the Patent and Trademark Office staff—avid readers of metropolitan telephone directories—would have found Mrs. Lillian Noxon listed in a directory.

Since the same directory listed a Mrs. Helen Kodak, the office would have had to reject a trademark application for a well-known camera.

The new law also permits the registration of trademarks that have acquired "secondary meaning." For instance, "Philadelphia Cream Cheese" now signifies a certain type of product. Under the old law, this term could not have been registered unless it was exclusively used by the same trader back in 1895—10 years prior to the 1905 Act. The new law rules that "Philadelphia" as it is used here has a "secondary meaning" beyond that of naming a city. Therefore, it may be registered.

Advantages of Registration

Registration does not grant any rights to exclusive use of the trademark that do not actually exist as a matter of fact; such rights are acquired through use, and not through compliance with statutory requirements. The acceptance or rejection of an application by the Patent and Trademark Office has no affect upon trademark rights *per se*, as the office passes only upon the right to register and not upon the right to exclusive use. Registration is, however, of the highest importance as evidence of the existence of common-law rights, and the owner of a registered mark is in a position of material advantage with respect to the protection of his or her rights.

Registration is a public record. It also certifies that all prior registrations have been officially examined, and that the registrant is the only known user of the mark in question. Furthermore, it is legal notice of priority, effective with respect to all users of identical or similar marks on the same class of goods.

Federal court jurisdiction is generally advantageous, both with respect to increasing the damages that may be assessed for infringement, and the power of the federal courts to order the seizure and destruction of infringing labels, etc.

Registered trademarks may be filed with the Treasury Department, and the importation of foreign goods bearing infringing marks may be stopped at ports of entry.

Registration in the Patent and Trademark Office is needed as a prerequisite to registration abroad. Most countries will not register a trademark owned by an alien unless it is registered in the country of origin. Registration abroad is of high importance, since in many instances the *first registrant* is held to be the legal owner of the mark, irrespective of use. This is true in particular of Latin American countries. Any local resident, a selling agent for example, may register an American-owned trademark in his or her own name, and place himself or herself in a position to make terms with the original user.

Only registered marks are protected under the federal counterfeiting law.

Finally, registration is of great value since it is held to be "coterminous with the territory of the United States." The owner of an unregistered mark ordinarily can establish rights only throughout the territory where it is actually used. These rights do not extend beyond the actual market in which goodwill has been built for the mark. If a competitor later adopts the same mark in other territory, and registers it, he or she immediately acquires rights throughout the United States *except* the first user's local territory. Thus the first user is practically confined to the local market, and cannot extend the use of his or her mark into additional territory.

Hence, in general, it is advisable to promptly register any trademark used in interstate commerce. Neglect of this is far too common, many executives being inclined to regard registration as a formality of slight importance in comparison with more pressing merchandising problems. Even today, there are occasional applications for registration under the "10-year clause," indicating marks in use since 1895 without registration. Registration is so simple and inexpensive that there is no good excuse for neglecting it.

There are many strong, valid trademarks that are used by major companies that are *not* registered in the Patent and Trademark Office, yet they can enjoy most of the benefits and protection as if they were registered.

The advantage of having a registration is that it is notice throughout the 50 states that this is your claim of trademark rights. Also, it creates a presumption of exclusive rights to use the mark. It becomes particularly advantageous when you get involved in litigation and you want to establish your priority rights and exclusive rights to the mark.

You can take the certificate of registration and introduce it into evidence without going through the effort of getting sales figures, invoices, and copies of labels.

Valuation and Purchase of Trademarks

A trademark that is widely known is obviously an asset of great value, and sometimes may be the principal asset of a business. Since it represents exclusively the goodwill of the business, however, it is inseparable from all the other assets of the business, and cannot be sold or transferred except in conjunction with them. In any purchase of "trademark rights," it is, therefore, important to make certain that title is also acquired to all the other assets of the business in connection with which the mark has been used. Adequate protection in the courts is difficult, and often impossible, to obtain unless the exclusive right to use the trademark includes the exclusive right to manufacture *all of the products* to which the same mark was formerly applied.

When a trademark is acquired through purchase of the assets of a business, it is, however, necessary to appraise its value separately. This value is clearly the value of the goodwill, since possession of the trademark implies possession of the goodwill. The generally recognized formula for an appraisal of goodwill as an asset is in terms of potential earning power, the basis being the average of the annual net profits over a term of years. A trademark in continuous use in connection with a going business may normally be assumed to be worth at least five times the average annual net profits. This is, of course, merely a basis for negotiations, and special circumstances may increase or decrease the figure that is finally agreed upon.

A mark that has been in continuous use in the same business over a long period of years is worth more than a trademark representing the same potential earning power that was more recently established.

A trademark that has been extensively advertised has a greater potential value than a mark advertised less extensively, or only occasionally.

In general, the potential earning power of a trademark increases in proportion to the number of actual customers to whom it is known. On an actuarial basis, goodwill divided among a million customers will die out much more slowly than when there are only a few hundred or a few thousand. Thus trademarks for articles in common daily use among the mass of consumers have a higher potential value proportionately, than those used in connection with products having a more limited sale.

For example, the name Maxwell House Coffee was sold at one time for $5 million. The Postum Company paid the Calumet Baking Powder Company $33 million for the Calumet name. The goodwill, and the trademarks of the old *New York World* were sold to Scripps-Howard for $5 million after the paper had been out of publication almost a year! And when Chrysler bought out Dodge in 1926 for $146 million, the purchasers appraised the value of the Dodge name alone as worth $79,341,318.22. Since in nearly every instance names and identifying indicia, the prices paid for them illustrate the balance sheet value of goodwill and the importance of properly protecting it.

Infringement of Trademarks

Trademark infringement in general consists of the copying or simulation of the mark by competitors. The test of infringement is not, however, the degree of similarity between the marks, but the question of fact as to whether customers are *likely* to be misled or deceived. Where the ordinary customer mistakes one mark for another, so that he unintentionally buys one producer's goods while thinking he is buying another's, there is infringement. Where evidence can be brought to show such actual or probable deception of the public, the courts will protect the owner of the original mark by enjoining further use of the offending mark and awarding damages. (See Figure 1, page 610.)

When such a situation arises, prompt legal action should be taken, even though the infringer may be operating in limited territory and for the time being doing slight damage. This is important not only because the damage done by an infringer may increase with great rapidity, but also because delay in taking action may reduce or even perhaps destroy the right to protection. Exclusive rights to a trademark cannot be maintained if its use by others is allowed, and to secure relief in the equity courts one must show at least reasonable vigilance in the protection of one's rights. The only safe remedy to infringement is the legal remedy, and it should be applied as soon as evidence can be secured.

The first invoice showing a shipment of the goods should be carefully preserved. In addition, appropriate copies of the original records, if possible, of the invoices and order to the printer for the first label—any evidence that tends to show when you first went into business on the product—should be kept (and *not* in the regu-

Figure 1. Trademarks in Conflict

In cases involving registration in the U.S. Patent and Trademark Office, a conflict was found between the following marks:

BIG MAC (toy trucks)	BIG MAC (hamburgers)
TIME OUT (Farah—men's slacks)	TIME OUT (Blue Bell—men's slacks)
ROLLS-ROYCE (radio tubes)	ROLLS-ROYCE (automobile)
ULTRA-DENT (denture cleanser tablets)	ULTRA-BRITE (toothpaste)
TECTRON (semi-conductors)	TEXTRON (corporate identity)
MOUNTAIN KING (artificial Christmas trees)	ALPINE KING (artificial Christmas trees)
COMCET (corporate identity)	COMSAT (corporate identity)
TORNADO (electrical appliances)	TORNADO (electrical equipment)
TYLENOL (nonaspirin analgesic)	EXTRANOL (nonaspirin analgesic)
SPRAY 'N VAC (rug cleaner)	WOOLITE SPRAY & VACUUM (rug cleaner)
THE UNCOLA (soft drink)	NO-CAL (soft drink)
ARM & HAMMER (baking soda)	ARM IN ARM (aerosol deodorant)
BREATH SAVERS (breath mint)	BREATH PLEASERS (breath mint)
AMP, INC. (corporate name)	AMP ELECTRIC COMPANY (corporate name)
"Where there's life—there's bugs" (slogan)	"Where there's life—there's Bud" (slogan)

lar corporate records, which are going to be cleaned out from time to time).

If there is an inside legal department, the records should be kept there, or if the company has outside trademark counsel, it probably should entrust the records to counsel's care.

You may get into litigation 20 or 25 years after the adoption of the mark. If that happens, you may have a great deal of difficulty if you can't find the original records.

International Trademark Problems

The registration of trademarks on a worldwide basis is a serious consideration for companies with international activities on a wide scale. It may be a costly process, but corporations with licensees, subsidiaries, or distributors in foreign markets take every precaution to safeguard their trademarks, at least in principal markets.

In Monaco, an expatriate by the name of Aries had run into the local registrar's office and claimed rights in a series of something like 300 trademarks, most of them owned by United States companies, and a number of them by European companies, and practically all of them extremely valuable and important trademarks. This incident raises the question of the international considerations in the adoption, use, and protection of a trademark.

In the majority of foreign countries, rights are obtained in a trademark by the mere fact of registration. You do not have to establish that you have used the mark in order to acquire rights in that country, as opposed to the United States, where you have to use the mark first in order to have your rights accrue.

When Tidewater Oil started to export to South America, it found it was blocked in practically every country, because somebody had already tied up the Tidewater trademark.

There is quite a problem for a company that intends to use the mark created and initiated domestically, and then uses it internationally.

"Taboo" marks should be considered carefully. For example, a company would be certainly rather foolish to attempt to introduce products in South America under the brand-name, Yankee. This is a good example, however, of the sort of care that should be given, not only to the literal and formal translation, but also to the vernacular, which may be a quite different thing.

Changing Corporate Names

A final aspect of trademark considerations is that which flows from the changing of a corporate name.

As so well pointed out in *Industrial Marketing,* "the most expensive mania that modern business has fallen victim to is the compulsion to change the company name."

The excuse usually given by companies is that mergers or changes in product lines have made old names irrelevant and misleading. But the fact of the matter is that name-changing became fashionable, with the result that many fine old names—the handles by which markets identified trusted sources of suppliers— have given way to some absurd combinations of letters.

American Brake Shoe Company makes many other things besides brake shoes. Changing the name to anything else won't change the opinion the market already has of the company and its products. But changing the name surely will remove from the marketplace an identity that had been built up over the years at substantial cost of promotion and immense investment in good product and good service. And people have to start learning who ABEX is.

If you were naming an American automobile today, you surely wouldn't call it a Chevrolet—a name that's foreign and isn't pronounced the way it is spelled. But those reasons don't compel General Motors to change the name to something modern and American and more easily spelled.

If you made Hotpoint appliances and had built up a reputation for quality in heating appliances, you wouldn't panic and change the name just because a thing that is cold shouldn't have a name that is hot.

Westinghouse is a terrible name if you're going to worry about Western Electric. General Electric is a bad name because so many company names begin with "General." And either Goodrich or

Goodyear had better change its name because the names are so close.

Nonsense! The name is just a handle, and there is no reason why U.S. Steel should stay out of the chemicals business, or why Volkswagen should change its spelling because most people spell it wrong.

But the corporate image and industrial design geniuses have been having a field day doing research and dreaming up new names and designing new logos. As a result, the industrial market is now full of names nobody ever heard of before, and the degree of confusion in the marketplace is only matched by the fees the "imagers" have been dragging out of bug-eyed managements.

Advertising agencies and publications have been benefiting, too, from this craze. Managements that have been withholding funds from legitimate selling promotions eagerly pay for corporate-identification campaigns to tell people that they don't have the same name any more.

On the other hand, there may be valid reasons for changing a corporate name, especially when it is intelligently handled. Because of wide diversification, the severe limitations of the word Powder, and the very important fact that its name could be changed simply by shortening it without losing identity, Hercules Powder Company became Hercules Incorporated.

In announcing the change, the company said:

"For the first six years of existence, commercial explosives ... were its principal products. Diversification took the company, by 1931, into such new fields of chemistry as derivatives of pine trees and cotton, and materials for the paper and protective-coating industries. Today it is a producer of materials for such widely diversified industries as paper, plastics, coatings, agricultural chemicals, rubber, synthetic fibers, construction, mining, and quarrying.

"These broadening fields of interest in production, sales, and research have resulted in a need for changing its name from one descriptive of only a part of its business to one retaining the specific name and 53-year-old reputation and identity of Hercules. Therefore the name of Hercules Powder Company will be replaced by Hercules Incorporated ... The name Hercules Powder Company will be retained by a subsidiary and will be used and protected in the future."

Policing Your Trademark to Keep It

In an *Executive Newsletter* published by the United States Trademark Association, Ronald B. Coolen of Mason, Kolehmainen, Rathburn & Wyss, addressed this problem. Following is his advice on the subject, reported in the *Executive Newsletter* of the U.S. Trademark Association:

Your company may have just been granted a federal registration on a trademark. While this serves as notice of your ownership of it, you can not sit back, relax, and think it will remain your exclusive property if you fail to protect it. You must "police" the use of the trademark to prevent misuses of it and maintain rights to the mark. Policing involves creating a program that provides education to prevent innocent misuse of your trademark and allows aggressive legal action to stop intentional misuse. There are three levels to which the program can extend. The first, and most basic, is within your own company. The next reaches distributors, licensees, and franchisees and the third encompasses buyers of the goods and the general public.

The goals of a policing program are: to foster uniformity and consistency of use of the mark; lessen the chance of innocent misuse of it; bring instances of improper use to your attention; and prevent loss of the mark on the grounds of widespread use of it in a descriptive or generic sense. A trademark is a symbol you want the public to remember, recognize, and associate with your company. Consistent, correct depiction of it in print, art, and speech is encouraged by policing. Unchallenged misuse of the mark by its owner, the trade, or the general public can contribute to permanent loss of rights to a mark.

The In-house Program. The need for policing begins in-house. A proven starting point is the establishment of a committee staffed by your trademark attorney, and representatives from your advertising and marketing staffs. The committee should be charged with the task of advising on correct procedures for use of the mark within the company and outside of it.

You must make sure that your own employees use the trademark correctly in internal memos, correspondence, advertising, promotion, etc. Five basic rules should prevail:

1. Always follow the trademark with the generic designation of the product, e.g., "Band-Aid" adhesive bandage.

2. Use correct typographical treatment. Trademarks are proper adjectives and should always appear with an initial capital letter.

3. Use correct grammar. A trademark should not be used as a noun, verb, or in the plural.

4. Use the trademark in the same form in which it is registered.

5. Follow a registered trademark with a ®.

Unless typewriters are so equipped, it may not be possible to use the ® form of notice. In these circumstances, the other rules regarding capitalization and use of the generic term become even more important. Following these practices in internal communications forms a habit not likely to be broken in other correspondence. In the event of litigation at any point during the life of the trademark, the courts look to a company's efforts to foster proper use of the mark in-house as well as externally. Recognize that a trademark can be used in many different applications. It is often used on labelling, packaging, advertising, and displays. It may appear on the company stationery, invoices, order forms and even the company gate. In accordance with a sound in-house policing program, the review committee mentioned earlier should be consulted every time the trademark is used in a new or unique manner to clear the accuracy of the application.

Perhaps the best way to communicate your program to the proper people, and surely the time honored way, is the preparation and distribution of a trademark use manual. This manual, while primarily intended for education of and use by employees, can also be useful in educating the media and the general public. This manual may contain:

1. A short history of your company.

2. Definitions of trademarks and generic terms with examples of marks that have become generic.

3. Encouragement of employees to watch out for misuse and infringement of your trademark and to inform the policing committee of any misuse or infringement.

4. Rules and illustrations for proper use of your trademarks.

5. A list of your trademarks.

6. Measurements and directions for size, positions, and colors of logos.

7. Camera ready artwork for each trademark.

You should recognize that no matter how strong the language used in your manual, a manual alone will have the same resounding effect as clapping with one hand. The contents of the manual should be discussed in departmental orientation meetings. All departments within a company should at some point have the opportunity to attend a trademark orientation meeting but, since the advertising, marketing, and sales departments are usually most involved with a company's trademarks, they should be specifically targeted. Representatives of an outside advertising agency also have a significant impact on the use of a trademark and should also attend. Not only the "whats" but also the "whys" should be discussed at these orientation meetings. The technical and philosophical aspects of trademarks as they relate not only to law but also to marketing should be discussed. There should also be ample opportunity to raise and respond to questions. The overall test of any trademark orientation meeting is how well the practices discussed are understood by the people who must follow them. The clearer the presentation, the more effective it's likely to be.

The importance of in-house education is amplified by the realization that any company's employees are probably its best resource for monitoring any use of the trademark outside the company. Employees, especially sales forces, educated through in-house procedures, manuals, and meetings are exposed to and can examine media from all over and often discover both innocent and intentional misuse of trademarks.

Affirmative Action Outside the Company. Affirmative action to ensure that people outside the company do not misuse a trademark is also recommended. Failure to do so can diminish the chances of winning a trademark infringement lawsuit against a competitor who could commence using the same or a confusingly similar trademark. If a trademark owner fails to police its trademark, a competitor can point to this fact in defense of its action.

Policing efforts wisely extend to distributors, licenses, and franchises. Provisions on proper use of a trademark should be included in their contracts and require the following: that the distributor, licensee, or franchisee use your trademark only in accordance with your standards; and that you retain the right to control print applications of the trademark through prior inspection and approval of labelling, packaging, advertising, signs, or any other display of the mark. Further, this control must be exercised consistently and necessary action taken firmly and promptly to call attention to, and require correction of, any improper use of the mark.

Any decision to extend policing beyond this level is based on consideration of the following factors: the present value of a trademark; the future value of the mark; the financial position of your company; and the distinctiveness of your trademark. The greater the present and future value of your trademark, the better your financial position, and the more distinctive your trademark, the more you should extend your policing efforts to the third level—the media, customers, and the general public.

Having determined to extend a policing program, you must select the best policing procedures. In addition to the procedures mentioned, policing of the media can be accomplished using a clipping service. Such a service is an efficient way to check newspapers, magazines, books, radio, and television for misuse of your trademark. Clipping services review all media and send clippings of anything mentioning your trademark. The general public may be educated through advertisements placed in popular magazines that ask the public to remember that your mark is a trademark and should not be used descriptively. Some companies have gone beyond this and have prepared filmstrips for presentation to clubs and similar organizations and particularly to media associations and journalism schools. If a trademark is sufficiently famous the public may not always use it in a correct trademark sense. Instead, the public may use it to describe a quality or feature of the goods bearing the trademark, or generically as the common name for all of the same goods. This can contribute to loss of the trademark. Escalator, yo-yo, cellophane and aspirin were once attractive trademarks. They have all been found by courts to be generic and have been stripped of their trademark status. Each of these marks might still be a trademark if it had been properly policed by its owner.

It is particularly important to assure that your trademark is not improperly used in the print media or dictionaries. The large circulation of most newspapers, magazines, and similar publications will significantly harm your trademark if it is misused in these media. To minimize the likelihood of misuse in the print media, many companies publish advertisements in trade journals asking publishers, editors, journalists and other authors to follow the rules of proper usage.

Despite all your efforts to police a trademark and to educate the public, misuses of the trademark will occur. The question is how to approach the offender. Protests in letters from a trademark owner or an attorney can meet with varying reactions. The premise that honey wins more friends than vinegar applies. A letter written in a tone that assumes the misuse was committed in error should request voluntary cessation. The letter should cite the specific misuse and point out the proper usage of the trademark. The letter should further explain the effect of misuse of a trademark and conclude with a request that the misuse be immediately terminated. You may also include a copy of the pertinent pages of your trademark use manual illustrating the proper use of your trademark. Most offenders, when informed in a polite, informative manner of their error, will thank the informant, apologize, and cease improper use of the trademark. Another approach is to contact the offender personally through one of your salespeople or your advertising manager. A personal interview should be confirmed by letter to stress your concern in the matter.

Before sending a letter or contacting the misuser personally, be sure all the facts surrounding the misuse are known. The letter or personal contact could prompt the misuser to file a lawsuit claiming first use of the trademark. To avoid this, always determine when the misuser first used the disputed mark. Also determine whether your company has taken any inconsistent positions in the past. Then, take action. If the offender agrees to cease misusing your trademark, give him or her a reasonable amount of time to dispose of inventory and do not attempt to force an admission of wrong doing. Merely the promise to cease is generally sufficient. If after repeated requests the offender refuses to stop or ignores your requests, you should seriously consider the next step. Depending on the seriousness of the misuse, additional, more strongly worded requests to cease may be preferred. If, however, continued requests, letters, and personal interviews are unsuccessful and the misuse is causing substantial harm, filing a lawsuit must be considered. Filing a lawsuit can be expensive, but failure to do so can diminish your legal position in the future. If, at a later date, you decide to sue the same or another misuser, they most likely will point to your failure to prosecute in the past.

Conclusion. In order for a trademark to grow in value, it requires ongoing care in the form of policing. Policing is not difficult if you set up a program and properly implement it. A comprehensive policing program will ensure your trademark remains your property.

PART 5

Marketing Channels

Chapter 32

Distributors and Industrial Selling

Industrial distributors perform effective marketing services for manufacturers of production equipment, tools, technical supplies and related products. The distributor, operating efficiently and with a sound understanding of his role, fulfills an important function for both buyer and seller.

To the seller, the distributor offers a ready market, physical stocking close to the ultimate users, intimate knowledge of local customers and market requirements, active sales support, and credit.

To the buyer, the distributor often offers immediate delivery from warehouse stocks, a multiplicity of lines from a single source and catalog, product information and technical help, and demonstrable economy in stocking, purchasing, delivery, payment, and credit.

Locally-owned distributorships usually outperform company-owned distributorships for many reasons. The local distributor constantly works at improving his or her business, how to service customers better, take on more product lines to round out his or her expertise and service and thus, do a better job over the long haul. Company personnel in a company-owned distributorship tend to take a local, short-run view with in-company concerns taking priority. However, some companies start a distributorship in areas where good distributors don't exist. Once the distributorship is profitable, it is sold to a local entrepreneur.

Kinds of Distributors

There are basically four types of distributors that have replaced the mill supply houses of yesteryear. These types of distributorships are:

1. *The full-line distributor.* Despite changing times, the full-line distributor has remained the backbone of industrial marketing, particularly in the smaller markets. Sometimes stocking several hundred product lines, the "industrial department store" renders an invaluable service to both buyers and sellers. However, the very multiplicity and extent of his or her lines have limited the full-line distributor's ability to give intensive sales promotion to the products of *all* the manufacturers he or she represents. It has also limited the degree of technical service that can be offered.

2. *Specialized distributors.* Stepping into this "promotional gap" in the services of full-line houses has been a growing group of distributors who specialize in products that may require a high degree of product information, technical service, and application engineering. Common fields for specialization include cutting tools, abrasives, power transmission, materials handling, portable power tools, air and hydraulic equipment, power-plant equipment, welding equipment and supplies, electronics, etc.

3. *Limited-line distributors.* More recent has been the development of smaller distributors who specialize in a dozen or more profitable lines of unrelated products that require high salesmanship, technical service, rapid delivery, and depth of stock. Relying heavily on merchandising ability and competitive service, this class of distributor keeps an especially close watch on costs, margins, and profits for each line carried. Sometimes considered to be more a "stocking sales agent," the limited-line distributor is constantly seeking new "door openers"—readily salable, high-margin, fast-turnover products providing entrée for a specialty sales team.

4. *Combination distributors.* Aggressive, flexible *full-line* distributors are meeting the challenge of *specialized* and *limited-line* houses by setting up separate departments to sell and service their more profitable "key lines." Thus, in many large distributor organizations there are qualified de-

partmental sales managers and factory-trained salespeople concentrating on power transmission, materials handling, bearings, and other lines that need depth-of-product and application knowledge. This is the modern trend in full-line distribution.

The Industrial Distributor

Industrial-product distributors usually have greater stability as a group than those of consumer products because:

1. Their products are sold to buyers who are better capitalized and more durable than the retail buyers of consumer goods.

2. They seldom carry competing lines.

3. The cost of inventories makes new competition more difficult.

4. The demand for technical training and background keeps competition down and the quality of competition up.

5. They are more firmly established in their markets and are not easily substituted by other distributors or company branches.

6. Client relationships are generally stronger and on a higher level.

7. Most products are either on an exclusive or carefully selective contract basis.

8. They have better management know-how.

9. Good distributor associations have fostered high-competitive ethics and mutual respect, and contributed greatly to management education.

This stability has provided a sense of security that permits sound planning and greater effort toward advanced management and marketing. An increasing number of special distribution management courses are being scheduled at universities, consultants are being used more widely, and some of the most modern techniques are being tried and applied.

The industrial distributor's salespeople are the most qualified persons a buyer can consult outside his or her plant for counsel on how to achieve value-analysis objectives. Value analysis begins early in a product's planning and continues throughout marketing and servicing.

At every step in this process, there are vast opportunties for the industrial distributor's salespeople, as well as the buyer, to aid in reducing costs.

The Role of Research

Almost all failures in marketing industrial products can be traced to inadequate or faulty market research. The first thing to determine is the potential market. Too often manufacturers undertake an expensive sales and advertising campaign for a product on the assumption that every plant in the country "is a prospect." That is not true. The market for any product, industrial or otherwise, is limited by a number of factors. These include: 1) competition; 2) price; 3) design; 4) freight rates; to say nothing of such intangible factors as a customer's policy in practicing reciprocity in placing orders. It is not unusual for large corporations to go so far as to inquire as to who supplies its suppliers with parts or materials, so that every sales advantage may be considered.

Having determined factually the size of the potential market, the next step is to locate the market. What kind of plants are logical prospects, how many of them are there, and where are they located geographically? It may be more economical, in the beginning at least, to concentrate sales and advertising effort in a few areas rather than to undertake national distribution. It is customary in making such studies to use either a map and tack system or outline maps on which prospects can be "spotted" to visualize the sales management job involved. Colored tacks, or crayons, are used to indicate importance of potential accounts.

Establish a Relationship with Distributors

It is important when engaging a distributor that 1) reasonable agreements on goals and roles be reached, and 2) a good communications system be established that includes performance feedback data.

To achieve the best possible relationship, the process should include the following, as described by Donald Price in Dartnell's *Marketing Manager's Handbook:**

1. Establish well-defined distribution policies and objectives.

2. Develop and publish a distributor sales agreement.

3. Help the distributor determine what it costs to sell your product.

4. Provide training for distributor sales reps.

5. Establish performance evaluation procedures.

6. Educate your own sales force on the value of the distributor to your marketing effort.

7. Cooperate with your distributors in developing overall market potentials and sales quotas.

8. Provide the distributor with an adequate profit.

9. Develop efficient channels of communication with distributors.

Perhaps the most crucial and complicated part of the distribution channel relations management effort is that of deciding and obtaining agreement on various roles that the different channel members shall play; and the compensation (margin) they will receive for their role. Decisions on who does what must be made for all variables in the marketing mix; marketing intelligence, transportation and warehousing, advertising and selling, pricing and product adjustments.

---

*Stuart Henderson Britt, ed., *Marketing Manager's Handbook,* 1st ed. (Chicago: The Dartnell Corporation, 1978), pp. 726-727.

Donald Price lists the following subjects that could be considered as some of the role areas that need to be settled:

1. Definition of the geographic territory for which the distributor is to be primarily responsible

2. List of products to be sold by the distributor

3. List of sales exceptions (if the manufacturer reserves the right to sell direct, this should be specified in the sales agreement)

4. Specification of the conditions that apply when a distributor sells outside the assigned area of responsibility

5. Prices at which the distributor may purchase, and suggested retail prices

6. Payment terms

7. Delivery and shipping terms

8. Price protection policy

9. Inventory requirements and policies covering the return of unsalable stock

10. Sales promotion and advertising policies

11. Terms and conditions for termination of sales agreements

12. Product guarantees

13. Patent and infringement protection provisions

14. Financial information requirements

15. Procedures covering the handling of inquiries, orders, and the identification of customers

16. The support which the distributor can expect from the manufacturer's sales personnel

17. Programs and conditions covering training of the distributor's sales force

18. Conditions under which the manufacturer expects the distributor to hold sales meetings

The other major requirement of channel relations is the development of an effective channel communication system.

Reavis Cox and Thomas Schutte* make the following specific proposals.

1. Conduct a field study of how members of the channel perceive one another's needs, problems, programs, and results.

2. Recommend appropriate action by the company to overcome deficiencies in the flow of communication through its channels.

3. Communicate the findings and recommendations to all departments of the firm conducting the study.

4. Develop a company-wide program for appropriate changes in the firm's management of its channels.

5. Create a standing staff committee on channel management to be responsible for a continuing evaluation of communication flows and to make appropriate recommendations to the operating departments.

6. In support of the standing committee, develop a continuing program of perceptual studies to keep the company informed as to how its flow of communication is doing.

7. Introduce an in-house flow of communication among operating and planning departments that will bring into view problems for cooperation as a whole that arise in the channel.

One important and very essential type of channel communication is the control feedback form of information on the performance of channel members. The Conference Board conducted a major empirical study of what companies were actually doing in this area.

Marketing Manager's Handbook, p. 727.

Some companies limited their evaluation to current gross performance. Gross performance was usually measured through some feedback on sales performance. The measures actually used resemble in many ways those often used to measure salespeople's performance. For example, comparison of current sales with sales achieved in prior periods, comparison of sales between distributors, and comparison of distributor sales with assigned quotas were all used quite frequently.

Flexibility in Channels Used

It has been said that in industrial selling some 20 percent of a company's customers generally represent 80 percent of that company's business. Yet despite this, a conventional sales force typically makes only about 12 percent of its calls on customers who represent 70 percent of the organization's business. The answer could well be a strong emphasis on using national account executives who operate at upper management levels and look after the broader buying needs of a given customer. This way, a supplier can provide better service.

Many industrial companies start out with independent sales reps or distributors, then graduate to the use of their own sales forces. One of the largest manufacturers of electronic test instruments developed a system combining the best of both methods.

Under the system, this manufacturer set up 12 independent sales corporations based on geographical territories. Each of the 12 entities has 2 to 8 percent ownership, or a total of 40 percent in a separate sales subsidiary that is 60 percent owned by the manufacturer. The groups's 65 salespeople receive the normal commission for an independent rep, plus a stock interest in the subsidiary. With its system, the company retains the tight control of a conventional, internal sales structure, while preserving the entrepreneurial drive of an independent sales force. At the same time, the equity position encourages a new degree of loyalty and sense of participation.

Check Your Price Policy

The pricing of a product is far more important than generally realized. The following questions relating to price policy are listed in the United States Department of Commerce guidebook for manufacturers, *Developing and Selling New Products:*

1. Do you know, in general, what your price policy will be on this product?

2. Have you figured your profit margin as accurately as possible?

3. Have you clearly decided whether you want to follow a big-volume-small-margin price policy or a small-volume-big-margin price policy?

4. If in your price policy you are shooting at a relatively limited group of prospects, should you further reduce the total potential prospects?

5. Are you sure your price schedule on the new product will meet the requirements of all your logical prospects?

6. Have you considered insurance costs, as well as manufacturing and selling costs, in determining your price?

7. Have you considered all transportation costs, including basic rates, yard and switching charges, if any, and other handling costs?

8. Have you considered packaging and packing costs?

9. How will installation costs, if any, affect your price policies and those of your distributors?

10. Will you service or help service the product? If so, will the user pay you directly for the service?

11. Will you expect your distributor to help service the product?

12. How will performance guarantees, if any, affect your costs and prices and those of your distributors?

13. Will you sell spare parts at cost or at a profit?

14. Have you worked out a complete factory price schedule for spare parts?

15. If your distributors will also handle spare parts for your products, have you worked out spare-parts price schedules for sales to them and suggested prices for resale to users?

16. Have you decided what classes of customers will be entitled to trade discounts?

17. Have you determined the schedule of trade discounts to distributors? To users (for example, governmental agencies) to whom you may sell direct?

18. Will you offer a cash discount to your customers?

Line of Buying Authority

In industrial selling, it may be necessary for the salesperson to "sell" several people before he or she can walk out with an order. The salesperson may first have to "sell" the person who uses the product and get him or her sufficiently interested to suggest to his or her immediate supervisor that the product be specified the next time a requisition is placed. Since few workers are capable of effectively relaying a sales presentation, the salesperson must also "sell" the supervisor.

After the supervisor requisitions the product, the requisition may go to the works manager or the engineering department for approval. Again the salesperson has a selling job to do. He or she must make sure that these executives understand the engineering advantages of the product. Approved by the engineering or operating department, the requisition next may travel to the controller who approves the budgetary expenditure and passes it along to the purchasing department. The purchasing agent may or may not issue a purchase order, but will probably check the price against competition. Some similar product which the agent thinks is "just as good" may cost less money. So, unless the salesperson is on the job, the requisition may travel back to its point of issue to ascertain if the "just as good" product would not be acceptable in view of the "saving."

That is a normal procedure in industrial selling. In the case of equipment that involves a considerable outlay of money, it may be necessary to "sell" several executives *and* the board of directors. There are usually negative individuals in every organization who may not have much actual buying authority, but who can, if they are not sold, wreck a sale. A study made some time ago revealed that in less than 1 percent of the companies checked, one person had authority to place orders for industrial equipment. In 9 percent of the transations two or more people were involved; in 29 percent three persons were involved; in 26 percent four persons were involved; in 13 percent five persons were involved; in 23 percent six or more persons were involved. Even in the purchase of supplies such as oil, less than 16 percent of the purchases studied involved only one person.

Since the line of authority varies with the size and nature of the business, it is important in setting up an industrial sales operation to determine as accurately as possible 1) who actually influences the purchase of your products and 2) how best to reach *all* those in the line of authority with your sales message. Obviously it is impractical and much too costly to depend entirely upon the territorial salesperson to penetrate an entire organization.

The Industrial Catalog

The difficulty of maintaining close contact with industrial buyers makes it necessary to develop ways of helping the prospect order between the salesperson's calls. This can best be done by: 1) systematically working a carefully prepared and *well-maintained* list of prospects; 2) establishing your company in the prospective buyer's mind as headquarters for the products you sell; 3) furnishing the prospect with an easily used, well-illustrated catalog describing the products you sell, and issuing *periodic* price lists. In fact, the catalog, next to the salesperson, can be the most important factor in industrial sales management.

Millions of dollars are wasted on needlessly elaborate catalogs.

It is wiser to spend less for producing a catalog, and have more to effectively distribute it. Here are some of the trends observed in recently issued industrial catalogs:

1. *Format.* Neatly arranged pages, with inexpensive composition and clean illustrations, produced by the offset process.

2. *Paper.* Tough stock, suitable for offset reproduction, in place of highly coated enamel stock which tears easily and is hard to read. Exception is when illustrations show considerable necessary detail that must be faithfully reproduced by fine half-tones or color-process plates.

3. *Size.* The size of 8½ by 11 inches fits easily into a catalog file, a letter file, or a desk drawer. It permits issuing supplements that can be mailed in a standard No. 10 envelope. Being the same size as a business letterhead, supplements of that size can be used as enclosures. They can be filed in the customer's correspondence file.

4. *Binding.* Most are loose leaf—to permit adding price lists and supplements—or spiral-bound to lay flat when opened on a customer's desk. Since most catalogs are filed on edge, the preference is for post binding, which permits stamping the backbone. There is also less danger of contents being taken out and misplaced.

5. *Indexing Supplements.* A common weakness of loose-leaf catalogs is that there is no provision for easily inserting supplements in the proper place. It is therefore good practice to devise your own system in numbering the sections and pages of industrial catalogs, rather than to number the pages straight through the catalog. This permits giving each supplement a section, page, and reference number. It is a simple matter to insert each supplement in its proper place in the catalog.

The only sensible procedure to follow in distributing expensive catalogs is to make sure they go only to persons or companies known to have a use for them. If you can get such persons to ask for the catalog, fine, but to refrain from supplying potential customers with a catalog simply because they don't ask for it, seems unwise. It is, however, good practice when sending out catalogs to offer to send return postage if the recipient has no need for it. The same letter can explain how the catalog will be kept up-to-date and ask for the name of the person to whom supplements should be mailed.

"Run On" Cost of Catalogs

It is a common practice in arriving at the cost of a newly issued catalog to add together the editorial, typesetting, paper, printing and binding costs, divide by the number printed and come up with a "cost per copy." From an accounting standpoint that method of arriving at the cost is quite all right. But there is a danger that this cost will seem so high that top management will ask for restricted distribution.

For sales promotional pruposes the cost of getting the catalog ready for the press should be regarded as a necessary expense which would remain the same regardless of how many copies were printed. In other words, the pro rata cost of the catalog for the first 2,500 copies might be quite expensive. But the cost of running an additional 2,500 copies to distribute to less important customers might be considerably lower. This "run on" figure should be kept in mind when considering a wider distribution for the catalog, rather than the pro rata figure.

In the same way greater value may be obtained from the money invested in preparing a catalog by "fatting off" some of the pages and binding them as cooperative catalogs, of which there are several published. These cooperative catalogs are one of the most effective ways to secure orders for products which are usually specified by architects, engineers, or others not usually contacted by a salesperson.

Other Ways to Reach Buyers

While it may not be considered a catalog from many viewpoints, the telephone directory classified section (yellow pages) is the starting point for any basic classification of a company or its products. No purchasing department is complete without the yellow pages. Although the reference files of a purchasing department may be replete with directories and catalogs of all types, there are many occasions in all corporations when the yellow pages save the day for a harried purchasing agent.

Industrial users often hestitate to adopt a new material or process until consumer acceptance is assured. In such cases, direct advertising is almost essential.

Plenty of case histories prove the point. The garment industry, for instance, would have been much slower in accepting zippers if Talon hadn't done a big job of public education. But remember that building such demand is likely to be very expensive. The consuming public as well as the trade must be educated on a whole new product idea, not merely on a brand name.

Manufacturers selling a wide range of products under a name like General Electric, Goodyear, Du Pont, etc., have a definite advantage when it comes to promoting a material to consumers. Promotion cost per unit is small, and the company can trade on its established reputation. An appliance manufacturer who gets his motor from General Electric is anxious to publicize the fact. The prestige of the branded part is a major selling aid.

More and more industrial companies are moving closer to the ultimate consumers of their materials or products. They are implementing the marketing concept by becoming increasingly concerned with their customers' customers. They are becoming increasingly aware of the truth of the adage: "I'd rather own a market than a mill."

The U.S. Steel Corporation, for instance, used to run three promotions a year as part of a broad-range campaign to develop the market for its steel products among home-appliance manufacturers.

The company's marketing representatives organized promotions in 30 major markets and worked with local members of the industry in 15 secondary markets.

The campaign took the form of newspaper ads in 15 cities, provided dealers with free display material, sent out editorial material on appliances to 4,000 daily and weekly newspapers, and promoted local action committees.

The aluminum industry and nickel producers have conducted similar promotions on behalf of their metals.

Don't undertake promotion of a built-in item unless it has definite significance for the ultimate consumer. Failures on this point have been many and costly. A manufacturer of shoe eyelets started a consumer-advertising campaign some years ago; it didn't pan out because eyelets were a negligible selling point with consumers. The same was true of a company that undertook promotion of nuts and bolts; their unit value was too small to justify the expense, and they weren't sufficiently important for people to specify one kind over another.

It is a rough rule of thumb that standard materials or parts shouldn't be promoted directly because the superiority of a single brand is hard to establish. There are exceptions, however, where the item is an important component of a sufficiently important end product. The public can be educated to associate the brand with quality and reliability.

Timken, New Departure, Torrington, and other bearing companies, for example, have done considerable consumer advertising designed to make bearings an important selling point for the product in which they're incorporated.

The "Functional Consumer"

The National Automotive Parts Association (NAPA) is an organization of automotive-replacement-parts warehouses that supply the needs of automotive jobbers. The jobbers provide parts for many thousands of automotive service and repair shops.

In discussing how manufacturers try to reach this huge aftermarket, J. R. Degnan, former NAPA general manager, said:

> Who are the right people to talk to? Consider the "functional consumer"—the man who does the real consumer's work.
> The functional consumer is a person who makes product or brand selections and actually does the buying on behalf of a final user. In markets where they exist, functional consumers are the number one target for sales and communication efforts.

This was amply demonstrated by the "Buying Influences Study" done by Fry Consultants, Inc., for the Automotive Service Industry Association and the Automotive Advertisers' Council, which showed that trying to make car owners love your products, or even identify them, let alone insist that they be installed, is a losing battle.

Several manufacturers of replacement parts that lose their identity in an engine overhaul or tune-up, have attempted to establish brand recognition and consumer preference through national advertising.

Of all who have tried the consumer-advertising route, the spark-plug manufacturers, battery makers, and the filter manufacturers have come closest to establishing their brands in the car owner's mind—yet the number of car owners who go into a service station and demand Champion Spark Plugs over AC, or vice versa, is negligible.

A Marketing Plan for Industrial Distributors

Most industrial distributors recognize the need for an effective marketing program in order to compete and survive in today's business world. But many feel they don't have either the money or the manpower to develop such a program. As outlined in *Industrial Distributor News,* there is a simple five-step plan that almost any distributor can follow in developing a marketing program. It makes use of many sources of information already available to distributors and doesn't require any great expenditure.

In its barest form, it calls for 1) setting goals, 2) research, 3) planning, 4) action or implementation, and 5) review and evaluation.

Let's examine each phase in detail:

1. Setting Goals

    Distributor management must set realistic goals that are attainable. For example, to increase sales of air hydraulic equipment by 10 percent, or to add 48 new accounts during the coming year, sales to the 21 largest accounts should be increased 14 percent by selling items not now sold to these accounts.

2. Research

    The success or failure of a truly effective marketing program hinges on this phase of thorough research concerning market potentials, possibilities, competition, new territories, and methods of qualifying prospects. This means you determine the type of manufacturers that operate in your area, what types of products they make, and whether they are large or small. Knowing the type of products made will give you definite indication about the kind of supplies and tools required in their manufacturing processes.

3. Planning

Now you are ready to formulate a marketing plan. At the outset, you should analyze the three arms of marketing— advertising, sales promotion, and your sales force. Advertising and sales promotion are the functions necessary to reinforce your sales department. There are two methods of using persuasion. One is printed, the other personal; both have advantages and limitations. Advertising, for instance, can make a thousand calls in a day by direct mail and get the attention of people whose names are not available to the salesperson.

4. Action State

This presumes that the distributor is well organized to handle an order—it is properly selected from stock, packaged, and delivered on time. It also presumes that products will be kept in stock. The best promotion will not produce sales and profits if the distributor has poor inventory control and lacks service.

5. Review and Evaluation

A good marketing program is self-correcting; thus as certain goals are reached, other goals may then be set by management. As the effectiveness of the advertising and sales campaigns are measured, certain steps are eliminated or stepped up, depending upon their desirability and usefulness.

OEM or PRS?

An electric motor may appear as a part in many kinds of finished products—air conditioners, fans, furnaces, pumping systems, etc. In such cases the motors are called OEM (original equipment manufacturer). The same electric motor may also be used during the manufacturing process or repair of any or all of the products in which it appears as a part. For this kind of use, the motors are called PRS (processing, repair, and service). The only important difference may be the price that is paid and the distributor discounts allowed. Because of the quantities of the motors that may be sold as part of the product, motors qualifying as OEM would be sold (to the same buyer or distributor) at a lower price than the same motors used for PRS.

This two-price system for the same or an essentially similar unit has caused a great deal of difficulty among manufacturers, suppliers, and distributors.

The manufacturer of the motors, for instance, may sell direct to pump manufacturers on a lower basis at OEM, and allow distributors little discount on the motors when they are ordered for OEM use.

Some difficulty is experienced in defining the areas. Three views expressed by manufacturers at an industry convention illustrate this.

- "To qualify for an OEM discount, the purchaser must buy a component part of his or her machine as advertised on the open market. If it is not for sale on the open market, then he or she is not entitled to an OEM discount."

- "OEM pertains to a company that buys equipment on a repetitive basis for equipment used in the end product it turns out."

- "An OEM customer is a company that has an engineering department, sales department, and servicing group."

Some manufacturers feel that OEM sales are unprofitable, but by selling related items, the overall picture can be made to show a profit. Another manufacturer stated that since 75 percent of OEM sales are made at a loss by both manufacturers and distributors, industry should have a standard price system that gives consideration only for quantity. This, he said, would eliminate the OEM discount problem.

The Danger of Bypassing Distributors

The Norton Company, a major manufacturer of abrasive grinding wheels, announced a marketing plan some time ago that bypassed its established distributors on some important accounts. As described in *Industrial Marketing,* the company calculated, on computers, the usage trends and rates of big-volume customers and determined that they could order in large enough lots to provide manufacturing economies. To attract such orders, the company offered to share the savings by supplying customers direct from the factory at reduced prices. The customers had to order a minimum number of certain types and classes of wheels in a 12-month period to get the lower price.

Norton also agreed to set up a minimum inventory for customers who could meet the requirements, at no carrying cost to the customers. Distributors whose annual requirements meet the minimum qualifying quantity can order on the same terms as large customers.

In short order, Carborundum Company and Bay State Abrasives came out with similar plans. They differed to the extent that the qualifying customer could buy through his local distributor or direct from the factory, and distributors could have deferred payments on initial inventory. However, they had to pay the same price on replacement orders as the end users. If they elected not to use the deferred payment option, they could buy the items at a 3 percent discount from the end-user price.

Norton and Carborundum removed restrictions on direct accounts and encouraged distributors to solicit them. This, they said, would increase distributor sales.

The companies have claimed the plan is a success, but at least three large distributors dropped the Norton lines. The National Industrial Distributors' Association (NIDA) and the Southern Industrial Distributors' Association formally opposed the plan, and a former president of NIDA, Thomas Clynes, said that in several cases it had caused "a serious deterioration in what were formerly splendid distributor-manufacturer relationships."

Supplementary Lines

When operating warehouse branches a manufacturer frequently will stock and distribute supplementary lines to improve service to dealers. For example, a manufacturer of plumbing fixtures buys heating and electrical appliances, valves, fittings, pipe, kitchen cabinets, and other items for resale to plumbing dealers in order to supply all their needs and to promote the sale of his or her plumbing fixtures.

This manufacturer faces a policy decision: Shall the warehouse branch be run as a factory outlet for the plumbing fixtures or as a wholesale outlet? If the former, profit margins may be centered in the manufacturing effort and the warehouse merely expected to break even or possibly make a small profit. If the warehouse margin is small, it will be difficult for the warehouse manager to provide services that compete with those of other wholesalers. Furthermore, the factory may be inclined to produce those products most attractive to it, with scant regard to customer preferences.

If the warehouse is run in the manner of an independent wholesaler, then it is more attuned to customers' needs. It can be more demanding on its parent factory for quality product. If, in addition, the warehouse manager is permitted to buy from other than the parent factory and the factory manager is required to meet competitive prices and quality, a strong wholesaling program can be conducted.

Systems Selling

In discussing the significance of systems selling, a relatively new concept of marketing, Dr. Arnold Corbin, marketing consultant and instructor, said:

"A systems sale begins when the customer dumps a problem in a vendor's lap and closes when both sign a systems contract. The object is always to solve the problem, not to sell a product, and while the solution—the system—is often complicated, the output is usually extremely simple: power, steam, cement, pellets, thin metal strips, purified water.

"The systems vendor agrees to analyze and define the prospect's problem; to procure additional technology from other divisions within the company or from outside sources; to design, engineer, build, and test the system, and to train customer personnel in its operation and maintenance, agreeing to service the whole system for the length of the contract, which may be years. Every system is a multiproduct, multiservice operation and is wholly self-sustaining."

Why is systems selling a good idea? In the first place, it makes sense from the buyer's point of view, because is simplifies purchasing and engineering operations; it is much more convenient, and it increases the time and effort that can be spent on other aspects of business. From the seller's point of view, it also offers many advantages. The bigger "packages" (the larger units of sale) make a greater marketing effort worthwhile. Secondly, the seller gets control over all the elements in a sale, not just a specific product at a specific time. Furthermore, when you sell a whole system, in effect, what you are doing is building a continuous "aftermarket." As the customer develops needs for replacements of pieces of the system, coming back to you again as the source of supply makes sense, because the entire system was purchased from you.

Despite some problems, systems selling is here to stay, because it makes sense from the customer's point of view. And if that's the way the buyer wants to buy, then that must be the way the seller must sell, whether it is convenient or not. So even though systems selling involves a number of risks and complications, more and more firms are embracing this strategy.

But there's another side to the story. Many companies enamored of the idea of selling a product package rather than separate pieces of hardware, said Rockwell International's Richard E. Love, are bitterly disappointed.

"Producing systems may be something that a company is not equipped to do," said Love, whose company sells a multitude of products, involving hardware and systems. "If a company produces both systems and hardware, it may need two different people in every job."

The hardware salesperson, said Love, must be aggressive, have application and product knowledge, be able to solve problems on the spot, convey his or her message quickly and concisely, and be a lone wolf.

The systems salesperson, on the other hand, should be conservative. "When you think of a system," said Love, "you think of something that is going to entail not only a sale but also a responsibility after the sale. The systems person must be a team player, since the system is a team product."

The Systems Proposal

In selling complicated, expensive systems, marketing executives depend heavily on the engineering department for the development of a basic sales proposal. *Marketing Forum* described the Westinghouse policy as follows:

From the customer's viewpoint, the sales proposal is the most important medium of communication in the entire process of purchasing.

It is, first and foremost, a *sales* document—designed to persuade the customer. It's also a *technical* document—defining the entire project in sufficient engineering detail so the customer can fully understand what is being proposed. If the sale is made, it becomes also a *legal* document.

The proposal should incorporate the best in professional techniques to exploit the advantages of the system. Drawings, sketches, schematic diagrams, photo drawings, marked photographs, PERT charts, all should be used.

An abbreviated version is prepared for operating management. This tells what the system will do and how it will work, and stresses product quality, production efficiency, flexibility, customer service, and other benefits. For top management and sometimes corporate directors, a short summary is prepared.

Important as the proposal is, it's far from the only communication needed to sell systems. Advancing technology increases the need to simplify the visualization process. Westinghouse often used scale models at the final selling stage. A three dimensional model can transmit a concept and the details involved in a matter of minutes, saving hours or even days of poring over drawings.

Models can also serve to sell the general concept of systems, and may be used at any stage of selling.

Closely allied to models are exhibits, because they can reach audiences with a predictable interest in what the company offers. Motion pictures are another way to sell the systems concept.

Handling Inquiries and Sales Leads

In an address before the Eastern Industrial Advertisers, in Philadelphia, W. A. Phair, as director of information services, Chilton Company, quoted a statement by the Marketing Communications Research Center, as more fully discussed in Dartnell's *Sales Promotion Handbook**, which read:

"Inquiries can be thought of as a means by which the market is talking to suppliers. If the supplier will only listen carefully, he can learn much about the market's changing needs and problems with great profit to himself."

What makes a good inquiry-processing system? In his talk, Mr. Phair presented the following guidelines:

1. Do not send raw inquiries to a salesperson or distributor for follow-up. When you send out your literature, use a return postcard to locate prospects with current needs. Then send these on for mandatory follow-up.

2. The goal of your inquiry-fulfillment program is to segregate those with a current need from those with a long-term interest. Then the salespeople should be brought into the picture to work on the hot leads.

3. Set up a good accounting system so you will know the exact cost of your inquiries and the cost of the sales that result from them. Do the same with all your other sources of prospects, including trade shows and direct mail lists.

4. Don't sneer about "catalog collectors." If a man is serious enough to ask for your catalog, send him one.

---

*Ovid Riso, ed., *Sales Promotion Handbook,* 7th ed. rev. (Chicago: The Dartnell Corporation, 1979), pp. 141-142.

5. Set up your system to get as much marketing intelligence as possible out of it. This is a phase of inquiry handling that is generally overlooked.

Plugging "Profit Leaks"

Wasteful practices, too, creep into distribution and they must be constantly watched and corrected.

Summarizing all this, it will be useful to note the following list of "profit leaks" prepared for review by a West Coast manufacturer.

1. Unreasonably small shipments because of no planned buying procedure.

2. High transportation costs due to small shipments.

3. Allowing merchandise to be returned or exchanged means excessive and duplicated costs.

4. Burden of merchandise replacements made as matter of "policy" to avoid losing dealers' goodwill, and not because of defects in material or workmanship.

5. Cost of keeping up poor selling items showing unsatisfactory turnover.

6. Rush service because of dealers' starved stocks, which means peak load staff at all times.

7. Made-to-order size service for geographically undesirable or low-end buyers not regularly handling our lines.

8. Losses due to bad debts through not selecting best accounts for solicitation.

9. Long terms and high discounts increase cost of essential credit accommodation.

10. Chiseling deductions and improper claims allowed because "not worth fighting."

11. Annual dividends, rebates, etc., which are not reflected in retail prices.

12. Costly freight allowances that result in nearby customers carrying the overhead load of servicing far off customers.

13. Allowances for advertising, which are sometimes wasteful because some retailers don't spend the other fellow's money as carefully as their own.

14. Excessive solicitation, which must be paid for by someone.

15. Split shipments, which mean duplicated costs—usually unnecessarily.

16. Excessive number of errors due to excessive number of transactions per $1,000 of business.

17. Manufacturing costs higher and quality lower because of:

    • Too many varieties of merchandise.

    • Too many sizes made.

    • Excessive amount of made-to-order service.

    • Lack of continuity of sales.

    • Pressure of rush deliveries.

Many of the items in the list are obviously competitive and are probably continued at the demand of customers. It is not easy for one seller to refuse to do something which his competitors are doing. It is in this area of distribution that trade associations can be of great service to society. By means of agreements and voluntary action, distribution wastes can at least be restricted, if not entirely eliminated. Trade associations can and do prepare lists of inefficient marketing practices and constantly educate members to eliminate them as far as possible.

Chapter 33

Selling Through Wholesalers

Any purchase of goods for trade or business purposes is defined as a wholesale transaction. This is opposed to a sale made for personal use, leisure, or sustenance of an individual or household, which is defined as a retail sale.

The wholesaler enables a manufacturer to reach many buyers in one transaction. And, conversely, the wholesaler enables the retailer and industrial buyer to purchase from many manufacturers in a single transaction. Wholesalers are an important distribution channel because they are specialists in carrying out various marketing functions.

Classifications of Wholesalers

As Gary F. McKinnon states in Dartnell's *Marketing Manager's Handbook,** "There are many types of wholesaler, although two major classifications are traditional in marketing circles. The first, the merchant wholesalers, buy title to the merchandise and resell it to others. Agent wholesalers buy and sell merchandise for others but do not take title to the products sold." The following is a partial classification of wholesalers as defined by the Committee on Definitions of the American Marketing Association.

A wholesaler may be defined as a business unit that buys and resells merchandise to retailers and other merchants and/or to industrial, institutional, and commercial users, but that does not sell in significant amounts to ultimate consumers. Those who render all the services normally expected in the wholesale trade are known as service wholesalers; those who render only a few of the wholesale services are known as limited function wholesalers. The

---

*Steuart Henderson Britt and Norman F. Guess, eds., *Marketing Manager's Handbook,* 2nd ed. (Chicago: The Dartnell Corporation, 1983), pp. 768-769.

latter group is composed mainly of cash-and-carry wholesalers, who do not render the credit or delivery service; drop-shipment wholesalers, who sell for delivery by the producer direct to the buyer; truck wholesalers, who combine selling, delivery, and collection in one operation; and mail-order wholesalers, who perform the selling service entirely by mail.

The merchant wholesaler's customers vary according to the product mix and services. One class, lumber wholesaler, sells an expanding list of building materials to industrial users, large contractors, and retail lumber dealers. Another class is the paper wholesaler who sells to schools, institutions, manufacturers, other wholesalers, and retailers.

A third example is represented by automotive wholesalers (or jobbers). They have a mixed variety of customer arrangements, some selling only to other wholesalers, who in turn sell to the retailer. A fourth class specializes in sales to restaurants, hospitals, schools, processors, and institutions with lines of food, groceries, paper supplies, and other nondurable goods. Fifth is the wholesale distributor of machinery, equipment, store, hospital, restaurant, and institution supplies selling to the entire gamut of business enterprises according to market needs. Another class with the most diversified inventory is the wholesale grocer, with sales to manufacturers, other wholesalers, restaurants, and a variety of institutions, but whose major efforts are directed toward the retailer.

Finally, there is the specialty wholesaler. In contrast to the trend to diversification and expansion of lines as evident in the above classes, the specialty wholesaler enjoys exclusive or selected privileges from one or several manufacturers in specialty kinds of products. He or she pushes specific brands much more than is the case with the broad-line wholesaler. The expenses of these institutions are significantly higher, as they give specialized and varied service to their clients; and they are proliferating in type and growing in number. In studying wholesale operations and trends, the same basic factors, complexities, and pressures are occurring among all classes of merchant wholesalers. (Throughout this chapter the terms "jobber" or "distributor" are used as a synonym for "wholesaler." These terms are sometimes used in certain trades and localities to designate special types of wholesalers.)

Industrial wholesalers have grown in both volume and wholesaling product groups over the years, while consumer-product wholesalers have had a small decrease in their share of the national total. Consumer-product wholesalers are not as homogeneous as the industrials; even the basic classifications of convenience-shopping items and specialty goods are often inadequate because of the difference of products within each category, the variety of outlets, and the overlap of outlets used. At the same time, the three have enough in common to afford some important insights.

The principal headache for the wholesaler is the overhead and the slim profit margins, accentuated by price-cutting. Every manufacturer wants special attention given to his or her product, but the fewer items the distributor carries to make this possible, the better the unit profit has to be to pay the same amount of overhead. This conflict resolves itself to some extent in the degree of exclusiveness of the agency contract made; in fact, a pattern emerges that can be described as follows:

- The lower the price and more competitive the product, the more manufacturers lean toward extensive distributions.

- The higher the price and the more consumer deliberation in buying, the more is the leaning toward exclusive distribution.

- The greater the potential for industrial use, the greater the leaning toward exclusive arrangements.

Over the years many have been meeting the problems of cost by decreasing some services—no credit, no salespeople, sidewalk delivery, cash-and-carry—but at the same time increasing other services to meet the competition from chains, cooperatives, mail-order houses, and department stores. In effect, they have been eliminating those services retailers can do themselves and adding those they cannot.

Distributing Through Wholesalers

In spite of all the talk about eliminating the jobber, the fact is that selling through the wholesaler remains the most generally used channel. This is because manufacturers discovered that elimination of the wholesaler would not eliminate the cost of the service performed. Then, too, many jobbers or wholesalers have realized the importance of doing a more thorough merchandising job, and have not only set their own houses in order, but have also assisted their customers in organizing and modernizing their stores to help them compete with chains and co-ops. The wholesaler is still the backbone of American distribution as shown in the statistics on distribution channels for all manufacturing industries, and published by the U.S. Department of Commerce.

Wholesalers render a broad service to the trade. Because of the multiplicity of products and services they distribute, the cost of such service is distributed among more producers with potential for lower sales costs to each. This method is most desirable when the product is closely priced, and when sales volume is not a major consideration. The disadvantage of this method of distribution is that sales control, as a rule, rests in the hands of the distributor. When volume is a paramount consideration, it is sometimes difficult to get sufficient creative selling effort behind a product when marketed through this three-step channel.

However, it is noteworthy that companies like Procter & Gamble, which, some years back, elected to eliminate the jobber in order to more evenly spread sales and production, soon found selling costs excessively high in fringe territories. These were territories in which it was too costly to maintain salespeople selling P & G products exclusively. The plan of distribution was therefore changed so that the company now depends upon its own salespeople in large-volume areas, and jobbers' salespeople in fringe areas. However, changing conditions and a trend toward multiple sales organizations in distributing many products make the problems of the wholesaler very acute.

Function of the Wholesaler

Should a wholesaler consider himself primarily responsible to his *customers* or to his *manufacturing sources?*

If the former, the wholesaler acts as a buying agent and consultant to customers, stocks those products that are most suitable for customer needs, and may carry only partial lines of a number of manufacturers.

If the wholesaler is responsible primarily to the manufacturer, he or she is their representative, their local salesperson, promoting the use of their products and carrying their complete lines.

There is, therefore, considerable difference in the philosophy and manner in which a wholesaler conducts business under these two concepts. While granted that the concepts overlap, when the chips are down the manufacturer must follow one philosophy or the other. It is therefore better to make the choice in advance as a business principle and then pattern policies and conduct accordingly.

A distributor can be an active and aggressive part of your field sales organization. Unlike your own salespeople, however, the distributor can choose to sell your product or that of any one of several other companies. When distributors or wholesalers are involved in the marketing of your product, an improvement in their effort can greatly improve the efficiency of your own sales force.

What Should a Wholesaler Do?

One question for many years at all trade conventions has been "What is a wholesaler?" The reason for the discussion is because it became the vogue for retailers to claim wholesaler status in order to earn jobbing discounts. Sometimes they were entitled to it, sometimes not. Where should the dividing line be in deciding whether a company is a legitimate wholesale house or operates as a retailer with wholesale ambitions?

The National Association of Electrical Distributors adopted a "declaration" that applies with comparatively slight modifications to wholesalers in all lines of business. This "declaration" provides that a "legitimate" wholesaler must:

1. Maintain and warehouse an *adequate* stock of standard commodities sufficient to supply the trade.

2. Maintain a showroom to display commodities properly for the benefit of the trade.

3. Maintain delivery service and facilities for pickup service.

4. Maintain a selling organization trained to promote, specify, and quote on commodities, and to handle matters of service or misunderstanding with customers.

5. Be prepared to furnish promptly a variety of commodities in one order at a minimum of cost and with greatest convenience to the trade.

6. Advise the trade regarding the most suitable and reliable commodities to purchase and install.

7. Distribute catalogs showing and describing the most essential items in common use in the industry.

8. Extend justified credit to the buyer within the buyer's territory upon reasonable terms.

9. Maintain a repair and replacement service to supplement the facilities of the manufacturer and retailer in the handling of defective commodities.

Three Ways of Distribution

There are three ways of distribution through wholesalers:

1. Selling the product without restriction to any wholesaler who will handle it.

2. Selecting the two best wholesalers in a territory and giving them a special arrangement that will permit them to do a good promotional job for the product.

3. The exclusive wholesaler, dividing the country into territories and giving one wholesale distributor in each district the exclusive right to sell your product.

The theory behind the third plan is that the exclusive wholesaler will invest more time and money to build up sales volume for you, since the wholesaler is the certain and sole beneficiary from the effort. This supposition is more imaginary than real. Too often the wholesaler will add a line with the best intentions of energetically pushing it in return for the exclusive sale, but he or she has so many other lines and products to push that much less is done than intended. For that reason there has been a trend to use the "dual" system of wholesale representation, whereby in some districts two wholesalers, acceptable to each other, are given the line. The principle is that clean competition creates more business, and one will help the other in doing the needed promotional job. As a matter of fact, there are many instances where more than twice as much business has been taken out of a territory under the dual system, and that after the second wholesaler took over the line, the sales of the original distributor usually increased. Great care must be used, however, to make sure both distributors are the sort who will play fair and do a constructive selling job.

A wholesaler can cover his territory economically, because his truck makes many more stops than even a chain-store truck. In a small town, once the wholesaler's salesperson is there, he or she can make several calls at little more cost than if a few were made. In thinly populated country, the wholesaler provides the chief means of supply for essential merchandise. Few retailers could make the time to see salespeople from all the manufacturers whose goods they stock. Distant manufacturers could not give quick delivery. Most businesses need the wholesaler.

Some business is too small to be profitable, but not all small business is unprofitable. The extra volume it provides, beyond the break-even point, may mean the difference between profit and loss. Small customers may be the easiest for wholesalers to keep. Large customers are the easiest to lose to competing wholesalers or to direct-selling manufacturers.

The manufacturer needs wholesalers to obtain complete market coverage, and investigation may show that this means using wholesalers to a greater degree than at first anticipated.

The Strength of the Wholesaler

The strength of the wholesaler is service to customers. This is as true of the industrial distributor as of the wholesaler of consumer goods.

The wholesaler, among all those who sell the retailer, is likely to be the one who takes the most interest in the retailer's set of problems. The wholesaler is least likely to oversell the retailer—and it must always be remembered that overstocking is a principal cause of retail failures.

Wholesalers and retailers do more than "distribute" goods—they *move* them, sell them. They are part of the dynamic mechanism that raises standards of living and creates national wealth. No other nation in the world has developed to such an extent these two tremendous instruments for production of wealth—the instruments of mass production and organized distribution.

But the special opportunity of the wholesaler is and always has been to build close relations with customers. Over great parts of the nation, and through great parts of its history, the wholesaler has put retailers into business and kept them alive. The wholesaler has "made merchants out of storekeepers."

With 16 stores in Ohio, Indiana, and Kentucky, the Mr. Wiggs chain could have had a central warehouse and dealt directly with manufacturers but decided in favor of using key distributors as much as possible. As reported in *Mass Retailing Merchandiser,* when asked at a meeting of the Mass Merchandising Distributors Association to comment on, "Why would Mr. Wiggs use a distributor?" Stanley Coben, hard lines merchandising manager, gave the following reasons:

1. To reduce the dollar amount of my inventories and to increase the number of turnovers of my inventories.

2. I would readily select a distributor who could offer all of the following services to my organization:

   - A resource that could provide a proper selection of merchandise at competitive prices. I would select one who had a broad customer base and could place large commitments for merchandise. Therefore, he could secure volume discounts whenever they were available and pass the savings on to us.

   - A resource who could fill our orders on a minimum 90 percent in-stock basis.

   - An *experienced* sales staff to service my stores on an every two-week basis. A trained sales supervisor to supervise the salespeople who detail my stores.

- Delivery on their own trucks, or via a private or contract hauler. Delivery to all of my stores within ten calendar days from the date the orders are placed in my stores.

- A computerized preprint and a sales movement report, available on a quarterly basis.

"Were there to be a distributor available who could fulfill all of these requirements, the choice would be an easy one."

Wholesale Distributors

The wholesale distributor is a large distributor who sells to smaller wholesalers or jobbers, and whose operation takes the place of manufacturers' sales branches.

In reality, this is a fourth level of distribution, found particularly in the distribution of automotive accessories. Wholesale distributors receive scheduled shipments from their factory sources, carry large inventories, and sell to smaller wholesalers or jobbers, who carry limited stocks, frequently replaced, and who, in their turn, sell to garages, service stations, and similar outlets. These latter sell to the ultimate consumer or car owner, usually on an installed basis.

The function of the wholesale distributor was originally filled by manufacturers' sales-branch warehouses, which sold and delivered to both large and small wholesalers or jobbers. The large wholesalers began to buy in carload lots; then, when they sold to small wholesalers, they received a discount on these reshipments, which enlarged their profit on such transactions. Considerable abuse, which arose from the claiming of discounts on shipments not made to small wholesalers, led the manufacturers to seek other means of handling reshipments.

Manufacturers also save in factory handling costs and economical production runs by shipping on predetermined schedules attuned to cyclical and seasonal demand, without being required to maintain factory stocks.

The National Automotive Parts Association (NAPA) is a nationwide group of wholesale distributors, with more than 50 independent warehouses serving over 4,000 jobbers. The jobbers order weekly from the wholesale distributors, thus limiting their stocks, maintaining economical turnover, and permitting the wholesale distributor to place standing factory orders.

Other Classifications of Wholesalers

The census division gathers and classifies wholesale data on all those establishments that perform the wholesaling function, even though they are owned and managed by firms whose primary business is manufacturing or retailing. Thus, sales branches and petroleum bulk tank stations and chain store warehouses are classed by the U.S. Census of Business as wholesale establishments, even though they are owned and operated by firms whose principal business are manufacturing, processing, or retailing.

The census traditionally classifies the data on wholesale establishments under five headings:

1. *Merchant wholesalers.* The most significant in number and volume of those engaged in the wholesaling business, they both take title to the goods they buy and sell and with few exceptions take possession.

2. *Manufacturers' sales branches.* Selling stations and, in some cases, storage facilities or warehouses for manufacturers, these branches exist in instances where the manufacturer has sufficient volume and/or special needs which it is believed can best be served by an establishment under ownership control and management. Examples are sales branches of National Biscuit Company and General Electric Appliances Division.

3. *Petroleum bulk plants and terminals.* Physical distribution points for petroleum products, petroleum bulk plants and terminals provide storage and distribution near the retail market that serves the automotive service stations in specific population areas.

4. *Merchandise agents and brokers.* Firms that buy and sell for the account of merchants, merchandise agents and brokers do not take title to the goods in which they deal. They consist of auction companies, brokers, commission merchants, import and export agents, manufacturers' agents, selling agents, and purchasing agents. In some instances these firms carry stocks but they never take title to the goods; they serve as agents only.

5. *Assemblers.* In the same general category as agents, brokers, and wholesale merchants, assemblers operate exclusively in the area of farm products.

   For census purposes, wholesale trade is classified into one of the above five groups according to the characteristics of its operation, or to the nature of functions performed. Furthermore, the five groups are subdivided into 18 detailed subtypes according to SIC codes.

Factory Salesrooms

Manufacturers often maintain salesrooms for various purposes at or near their factories:

1. *Display rooms where goods are shown and selections made with delivery and billing of orders by independent dealer outlets.* This type is found in the building and furniture industries. List prices are frequently, but not always, shown on the goods, to assist the homeowners in making a choice. These display rooms are helpful to the manufacturer because they permit the goods to be displayed under attractive conditions; they are helpful to the dealers in that many cannot afford the cost involved for the volume of business they do. Manufacturers must be careful to show impartiality to their dealer customers, to find out which, if any, dealer sent the homeowner in, and be careful to notify only that dealer of selections made. Wholesalers also install display rooms operating them in the same manner. Manufacturers usually encourage, or help finance, wholesalers to install display rooms using their products; besides assuring good display

such investment ties the wholesaler more permanently to the manufacturer.

2. *Display rooms where seconds are sold.* This type is found in the furniture and the textile industries. Usually the goods have small flaws and are rejected by quality control; while they cannot be sold as top-quality goods, their usefulness is not entirely impaired and the goods are sold at a discount. Some bakeries and candy manufacturers sell broken goods which are still edible but are not up to salable quality.

3. *Display rooms where goods are sold to the consumer.* This type is found especially in the bakery and dairy industries, although any small manufacturer without dealer outlets may use them.

Advantages of Wholesale Distribution

Some sales managers fail to recognize the overall service that wholesalers render to business and to society. They are so concerned with their immediate problem of getting distribution that they don't stop to think what would happen to their retail outlets, and for that matter to the whole scheme of mass distribution as we know it today, if all retailers had to depend upon manufacturers' salespeople for the service they require.

The trend has been toward branch distribution, but only firms with a full line like General Electric can manage to make them self-supporting over the whole country. Shorter-line companies as large as Zenith, as well as companies in other industries, have balked at attempting it in more than the major metropolitan areas. They state their preference for independents (because of costs), but cannot afford to settle for what they consider second-rate distributors usually because lower-priced brands move better. In such cases, they settle for company-owned branches.

There are a dozen advantages to distribution through wholesalers, when such a procedure is logically within the type of operation and product concerned. These advantages may be listed as follows:

1. Availability of forward stocks

2. Handling broken stocks, and assembling order requirements

3. Provision of a ready-made sales force

4. Frequent customer contact at low cost

5. Intimate knowledge of local conditions and market demands

6. Intimate acquaintanceship in the local trade

7. More knowledgeable granting and handling of credits

8. Lowered transportation, storage, and delivery costs

9. Local representation for servicing and handling complaints

10. Assistance in obtaining local information for product development and market research

11. Effective means for distribution of product information and promotional literature

12. Elimination of capital investment in inventory and physical properties

Wholesale distribution is particularly advantageous for a manufacturer with a limited line, little concentration of customers, short margin of profit, low demand, or highly seasonal demand.

In the AMA *Marketing for Executives* series, John M. Brion, New York marketing consultant, commented:

"A manufacturer's major goal is to have distributors act as inventory and marketing agents in their territories, and, in this capacity, to:

- Carry the manufacturer's full line

- Carry a good stock of each item

- Not carry competing lines

- Not carry too many lines

- Carry sufficient spare parts or components

- Hire salespeople who will make the desired impression
- Train the salespeople on product knowledge and selling
- Develop a network of high-quality retailers
- Cover the product's market intensively and extensively
- Increase the product's marketing intensively and extensively
- Devote the needed time to sell each prospect
- Provide servicing quickly and efficiently
- Cooperate with the manufacturer on planning, sales campaigns, advertising, and promotion
- Provide local advertising and promotion
- Use effectively the advertising, promotion, and sales aids provided
- Give the line good window, counter, and floor advertising and display
- Keep facilities and equipment attractive and efficient in operation
- Give prompt delivery service
- Follow the manufacturer's pricing policies
- Provide needed market feedback
- Submit desired sales data on time for analysis
- Cooperate on strategy and tactics
- Make an adequate profit."

This adds up to meeting the demands that one could ordinarily expect only of one's own wholesaling operation; the nearest thing to it with distributors is "keyline status," so such status is frequently a basic goal.

The average distributor often has only a handful of salespeople. But his or her contacts, acceptance, and strategic position within his or her area make a well-planned network of franchised distributors unsurpassable in this respect. A manufacturer obtains maximum coverage, in number of accounts and calls in each geographic area, with resulting greater volume and lower price at a minimum of investment and expense.

Disadvantages of Wholesale Distribution

Disadvantages cited by sales executives generally include one or more of the following:

1. Reluctance by wholesaler to carry adequate stocks

2. Reduced profit spread to manufacturer

3. Competitive demand by other manufacturers for salespeople's time and interest

4. Lack of aggressive sales promotion due to multiple lines carried by the wholesaler

5. Loss of direct contact with the ultimate customer

6. Difficulty of providing necessary special and technical services

Maintenance of contact can be of considerable importance to a manufacturer, particularly should a wholesaler eventually decide to drop its line and replace it with a competitor's product.

Lack of merchandising ability is usually a major objection. Narrow profit margins and stiff competition place constant pressure on distributors to obtain high volume, and the more lines and brands carried, the less attention each gets. Well-advertised major brands as a result often move fairly well, while the products of small manufacturers without comparable ad budgets do not.

Closely related to this is the lack of intensive selling on minor product lines and those that are difficult to sell. Products that *must be sold* because of their nature, use, or competition have a rough time starting or growing through most distributors unless a strong incentive is given. This is because the salespeople are admittedly just order-takers for the majority of their products.

The manufacturer's lack of control over the marketing of the product is a third principal disadvantage. Many manufacturers complain that distributors do not always show enough interest in:

- Specialized selling
- Product success
- Ad and promotion care and effort
- Missionary work
- Service needs
- Handling of complaints
- Handling of inquiries and follow-up
- Analysis of markets and problems

In addition, manufacturers may also lose control of pricing and control of final condition of product and package. This totals up to inability of the manufacturer to execute marketing strategy because of remoteness from the actual marketplace, and the conflicting objectives and policies between the manufacturer and the market.

Manufacturers are prompted to seek new distributors by:

1. Efforts to gain greater geographic penetration, to sell a new product, or to find new prospects for old products

2. A need for better coverage in existing territories

3. Change in the distributive process, such as electing to use distributors instead of selling direct to end-users

A study conducted by the The Conference Board revealed that in some industries distributor selection is practically a continuous process, and in these a relatively new executive grade, manager of distributor sales (or development), has emerged. Usually, the job responsibility includes all aspects of distributor sales, but sometimes the principal function is to find, develop, and train new distributors or dealers.

Leads to possible new distributors are collected from several sources—trade associations, local civic and business interests, direct-mail solicitation, to name a few—but the brunt of collecting and evaluating information falls on the manufacturer's salespeople.

Sometimes the field sales staff will even make the final decision, but normally corporate headquarters exercises that right after a careful assessment of all relevant information.

What Does a Good Distributor Expect from the Manufacturer?

A study by The Conference Board presented some of the things a strong distributor considers before agreeing to take on a new supplier. They are:

- The manufacturer's record of financial capacity and stability

- Market potential for the supplier's product in the territory

- Major industries to be served by virtue of carrying the line

- National and local sales position and reputation of the product line

- National and local sales positions of the supplier's major competitors

- Information on other distributors and dealers handling the line

- Sales policies of the company (terms, discounts, minimal inventory requirements, and total initial investment required)

- Gross margin expectations

- Estimated annual sales volume and profits for the first and succeeding years should the line be added

- Warehousing requirements

- Packaging requirements for the products

- Advertising and sales promotion assistance

- Field sales assistance and training available from the supplier

In addition, "the principals of almost any well-established, reputable distributor firm will readily admit, or oftentimes complain, that too much of their time is spent seeing representatives of manufacturers who are trying to interest them in selling their product lines," the study discloses.

Distributing Direct to the Dealer

Sometimes there can be no specialized distributive channels that can make the contact between producer and seller. Other manufacturing operations lend themselves to direct dealings with the retailer because of the extent of the marketing, volume of business, and nature of product.

Among the major advantages of selling direct are: closer contact with the consumer than under systems that pass through more hands; centralized control over selling to dealers, permitting better promotional cooperation and closer contact with the buying public; and avoidance of the necessity of having to add distributors' margins to the price at which the product is sold to retailers.

The Food Machinery and Chemical Corporation found the advantages of direct dealerships to be as follows:

1. Closer relations with dealers who actually sell products to the public

2. Absolute control over distribution of available supply during periods of shortage

3. Elimination of distributor profit permits pricing of product at a competitive level

4. Greater profit for manufacturer

5. Ability to expand dealer organization rapidly by direct efforts rather than on a secondary basis through distributors

Keeping in close contact with the dealer is one of the headaches in this type of distributive pattern. If the manufacturer is able to get adequate coverage with his or her organization, the dealers can be one of the most efficient tools at the producer's disposal for measuring consumer product acceptance and for gauging market prospects.

This matter was emphasized by a producer of poultry and stock feeds:

"Dealers know—or should know—their potential customers, as well as their needs and the feeding problems they must solve, better than anyone farther removed from the consumer. Operation through dealers, we believe, enables the manufacturer to simplify administrative problems, and it eliminates the large staff of field personnel that any other method would necessitate. We do a minimum of direct selling because of the prohibitive costs of less-than-carload-lot shipments, and because this practice tends to break down the morale of some of the dealers."

What Wholesalers Must Do

To keep abreast of changing conditions, the wholesaler must study his or her relationship to the retailer who, after all, is the wholesaler's main source of income. The wholesaler should analyze customer accounts, their credit standing, service demands, dealer progressiveness as to location, efficiency of operations, delivery costs, and other factors. Market analysis is also of prime importance. The points to be considered here are:

1. Territorial analysis, such as population pattern, industrial trends, competition, transportation facilities, buying power, etc.

2. Sales quotas to guide executive control and set selling pace for salespeople.

Another important factor in the cost of distributing through wholesalers is the cost of handling orders in some houses. During the last few years various wholesalers have given this obstacle careful consideration, with the result that some of the larger houses have drastically reduced their handling costs, as well as speeded up the shipment of orders, by one-story plant "drag-line" and conveyor systems, short-cutting routines, and the latest mechanical equipment in all departments. Restricting sales to large units is another important development in wholesaling. This is aimed at the small-order headache.

It is the policy of many wholesalers today to organize their lines and facilities so that they will be in a position to supply their customers with merchandise of slightly better quality than what is offered by the chain stores and mail-order houses, and at a price that will enable them to compete successfully with these large-scale buying units. By means of special assortments, the excessive cost of handling small orders has been corrected to a large measure.

What are the principal problems distributors face in the conduct of their business?

1. *Profit margins.* Almost all face a continuous problem of survival; few can hope for better than a net profit of 3 to 5 percent of sales and many are consistently around ½ percent to 1½ percent.

2. *Accounts receivable.* A well-run firm may average about a 45-day turnover but still has to pay its sources in 15 days to get the small discount, and within 30 days to retain credit standing. Some manufacturers, in launching a new line, or, in an attempt to "load-up" dealers, sometimes extend much longer terms to both distributors and dealers, but these are special cases.

3. *Credit.* Distributors are excellent examples of business-persons who need credit for accounts receivable and high inventory costs, yet in periods of tight credit have a difficult time getting it.

4. *Inventories.* Even many large distributors do not adequately understand the cost of carrying inventories; sales forecasting; effective methods of analysis and purchasing; and the value of proper product mix and inventory balance.

5. *General management.* Large organizations usually have superior management, even go extensively into data processing, but small and newer firms generally take years to get down to sound management techniques: planning, budget-

ing, expense control, objectives and policy clarification, market analysis, and training.

6. *Promotion.* Distributors cannot always afford to carry out their sources' promotional campaigns. Merchandising displays are often costly; dealers will not pay even a small portion of this. Too, they will not pay for literature, which the distributor must buy from the manufacturer.

Sol Goldin, a guru in the retailing field, commented on a daylong seminar for dealers sponsored by a distributor in Harrisburg, Pennsylvania. He was impressed first by the number and caliber of retailers attending this seminar, and by their eagerness to learn the basics of merchandising and management. One dealer said, "Sooner or later we'll have to scratch for sales and then we'll need all the knowledge, skill, and help we can get." A major part of this help will be the merchandising experience of local distributors.

"Local" and "independent" were key words, said Goldin: "In *boom* times, it's all very well to have the factory and factory branches to manage distribution. But in the case of *bum* times, the wholesaler must be far more than an efficient warehouser, shipper, supplier. He or she also must be a sales manager, a financial adviser, a new product developer, a headquarters and clearinghouse for *all* services (not just product services), a first lieutenant on the merchandising front line."

The Wholesaler's Sales Organization

Another large area for improving the service that wholesale distributors can render without adding to their cost of operations is the selection, training, and supervision of their sales organizations. Relatively few salespeople calling on retailers do any creative selling. Most of them just take orders. The following checklist may be helpful to wholesalers who are not satisfied with the kind of sales job they are doing, or to manufacturer's salespeople who work with distributors in the field:

1. List sales functions and operations now being performed.

2. List other opportunities for promoting sales and expanding customers' sales that might be adopted.

3. Where a sales organization is already operating, draw up a chart of organization to make sure all jobs and personnel are covered, and that each has separate consideration.

4. Define the kind of selling job each type of salesperson has to perform, starting with a list of the separate operations each salesperson goes through. These are the job requirements. Salespeople can help in making this list.

5. Work out a standard operation for each type of salesperson. Include the experience of the most successful salesperson, and collect information from outside sources.

6. Set up a program for studying each job requirement continuously, having sales supervisors or the sales manager go along with the salesperson, so as to work out the best way of doing it.

7. Select for special emphasis the job requirements that prove most profitable.

8. In selecting new salespeople, list the best qualities of the present force and arrange in order of importance.

9. Collect information from outside sources on job analysis, sales force selection and training.

10. For new goods requiring specialty selling, consider a plan for sales training by manufacturers' salespeople, sharing the expense with the manufacturer.

11. Standardize the number of calls a salesperson should make per day, after analyzing the nature of his or her route.

12. Review salespeople's routes and territories.

13. Review present methods of compensation to see whether they suit the nature of the business and the job, are understood and accepted by the sales force, and provide incentive rewards for special ability and special sales events.

14. Analyze sales supervision to see whether it is actively conducted, with the manager regularly in the field with the salespeople.

15. Analyze costs and profitability of each operation performed in connection with sales, both inside and outside the house.

16. Where salespeople are responsible for collections, analyze methods to make sure they are constructive in building better habits of payment, and also are effective in reducing the average age of accounts and the total amount outstanding.

17. Evaluate the possibility of sales to each customer or potential customer, establish sales objectives, and allocate order solicitation time in accordance with the objectives.

18. Maintain records of sales achievement for review with the salespeople in the preparation and maintenance of sales strategy.

19. Program for the most profitable use of manufacturers' detail persons.

20. Examine lost effort and increased costs involved in the distribution of duplicate or competing lines, the carrying of unnecessary slow-moving stock, and poor housekeeping.

What Manufacturers Can Do to Help Distributors

A manufacturers-distributor inquiry on the subject of "What are the distributor sales aids?" produced these representative replies:

- "Hundreds of excellent aids are prepared by manufacturers for use by distributors and their salespeople. If as much care were taken in distributing these as there was in preparing them, everyone would benefit. The distributor must know what is available in order to use it."

- "Although we have the usual assortment of distributors' sales aids, there are times when specialized promotions are required to obtain maximum benefits."

- "The best aids for distributor use are self-contained direct-mail pieces. We favor them because they are relatively inexpensive to produce and more effective than circulars. Some distributors make effective use of these aids, but others do not. It depends on how forceful our distributor sales representative is and on the aggressiveness of the distributor's organization."

- "In my view, the best sales aids are personal calls. Users are impressed through personal selling and, through their own experience, with consistent service and competitive pricing. It is true that companies that can afford to hit the user with advertising in every form put their products in a favored position."

What Distributors Say They Need

A questionnaire was sent to all members of the National and Southern Distributors Association to determine distributors' problems with respect to manufacturers' merchandising and promotional programs.

In answer to the question: What does the average customer want to know about the products you handle, the distributors indicated price, use, and delivery as the most important.

In response to the question: How can distributors be further assisted by manufacturers, the answers were many and varied. But, in summary, they gave the manufacturers some excellent suggestions for improving their merchandising activities. For instance:

1. *Catalogs and bulletins*

   - Contain all the information needed.

   - Keep up to date.

   - Tell the story simply and show prices.

2. *Display material*

   - Limit size.

   - New items only.

- Occasional floor or counter units. (Some companies thought display was not important.)

3. *Direct mail*

    - Very useful.

    - Tie-up with distributor.

    - Should be colorful.

    - Distributors would rather handle.

4. *Advertising*

    - Very useful.

    - Direct to industrial distributors.

    - Use appropriate trade publications.

5. *Shipping practices*

    - Advise of any delays.

    - Use packaging lists.

    - Prompt mailing of invoices and documents.

    - Not too much weight in one package.

6. *Price lists*

    - Keep as simple as possible, but complete.

    - Make price lists understandable.

    - Standardize.

    - Separate from descriptive catalog pages.

In answer to the question, "What are some of the practices you would like to see remedied?" the answers were:

- Acknowledge orders promptly.

- Live up to promises of delivery.

- Have knowledgeable personnel.

Manufacturers' Distributor Policies

Most large companies have long recognized the need to render all the marketing assistance possible to their distributors and dealers in order to ensure their most competent and efficient performance.

It is not enough to send out sales representatives merely as order takers, or to mail out product announcements, advertising reprints or "pep" letters. These are too elementary except, of course, for companies with limited distribution and small budgets.

The established manufacturer with the necessary organizational facilities can and should provide distributors with marketing assistance in a number of ways. These include:

- Distributor and dealer counseling

- General management

- Financing and credit programs

- Merchandising

- Selection and training of salespeople

- Sales meetings

- Incentives for salespeople

- Legal aspects of pricing

- Cooperative advertising programs

- Dealer coverage

- Product presentations

- National advertising campaigns on TV and in trade and consumer publications.

How SKF Helped Its Distributors

To help distributors boost their sales, a Territory Management Plan was implemented by SKF Industries.

The plan was based on the concept that the only way to increase sales volume in a distributor territory is to "prepare and follow a well-defined, comprehensive plan." SKF gave distributors a working outline of the program, which covered creative selling, establishing new accounts, reinstating dormant accounts, follow-up in-plant seminars, territory sales forecasts by product, and planned expenses.

To assist the distributor, the plan included examples of how to establish sales quotas, increase coverage, and stimulate sales-call activities.

The effective use of maps—so that the individual distributor salesperson or management could see his or her territory at a glance—was also detailed.

"This plan reflected the best thinking of highly successful executives in the industrial sales field," said A.C. Johns, director of distributor program planning. "It grew from requests made by SKF's distributors during seminars held earlier throughout the United States."

Other Distributor Aids

There are many other examples of how manufacturers aid their distributors and dealers to increase sales:

Westinghouse merely asks its dealers to make the sale. Then Westinghouse takes over, making the delivery, installing the appliance, and servicing it. The retailer is relieved of these tasks. Procter & Gamble and General Foods developed new advanced techniques for improved materials handling and made these available to large food retailers. Campbell Soup Company runs management training seminars for retail food-store personnel.

An executive of an electrical equipment company described how his company helps its distributors and their sales forces:

"We use a variety of aids to help presell the prospect and also make the salesperson's time most productive during calls. This is done through several methods: extensive publication advertising, a continuous direct mail program, and displaying our products at most major industrial trade shows. All inquiries generated from these outlets are turned over to our distributors for follow-up.

"On the distributor level, in addition to personal calls from our district sales managers and factory personnel, we make continuous product mailings throughout the year covering individual models and accessories. This is sent to both inside and outside salespeople. Product mailings include samples or regular backup literature available for handing out. Special literature is also produced to point out and help salespeople better understand specific features.

"As an additional sales aid, we try to anticipate many of the questions that prospects will ask and furnish the salespeople with complete series of questions and answers to cover this area. Because we are asking the distributor salespeople to go "a little above and beyond" in becoming as familiar as possible with our equipment, we reward him or her in some way for this extra effort. For instance, we have run a product-knowledge contest that offers merchandise awards during the contest period, plus a choice from a number of worldwide trips as a grand prize.

"Our favorite type of distributor aid is direct-mail material. We have found that direct mail is the most effective means of getting past the front office and to the engineering and shop personnel, who specify equipment. You can't force a distributor to use promotional aids, but most of those who have, and who use up-to-date lists and mail with continuity, find that direct mail pays off in increased and traceable sales. Better still, salespeople have found many business opportunities that may not have popped up during their regular sales calls."

The Distributor Salesperson

Distributor salespeople have so many different products to sell that they can concentrate their efforts on only a small percentage of them. Second, they often lack complete knowledge of all of the products they handle and the applications of these products. Third, they must produce orders regularly, and hence, can spend very little time on long-range market-development projects.

For the most part, your success with distributors and their salespeople will depend on the quality and frequency of your communications with them. Therefore, part of your advertising program should concern itself with your distributors. It should inform them, motivate them, and help to make it easy for them to sell your product. Distributor salespeople can multiply your efforts in the field substantially, while freeing up your own salespeople to concentrate on the larger, more profitable accounts.

Not all wholesalers are equally dedicated or enlightened about the retailer's changing needs and wants. According to *Hardware Retailer,* many distributors cater to mediocre retailer's thinking and ignore those agressive retailers whose needs are different, whose desires are channeled more into merchandising and promotional assistance, not merely in procurement of goods.

It is because this type of retailer had been too much ignored—and still is being ignored in some areas—that types of wholesalers developed who singled these persons out to form the nucleus of their own wholesaling organizations that would concentrate efforts only on those services that the retailer felt he or she needed or wanted.

The idea of dealer-ownership of a wholesale concern is not new. It has boomed during recent years in the food field, where retailers have exhibited even more willingness to subject their individual independence and operational methods to group planning than have hardware retailers.

National Wholesale Distribution Associations Affiliated With NAW (National Association of Wholesalers)

This is a central group of alliance of wholesale associations. Its affiliates (as of the time of publication) include the following:

- Air-Conditioning & Refrigeration Wholesalers
- American Machine Tool Distributors' Association
- American Supply Association
- American Surgical Trade Association
- American Traffic Services Association
- Appliance Parts Distributors Association, Inc.
- Associated Equipment Distributors

- Association of Footwear Distributors
- Association of Institutional Distributors
- Association of Steel Distributors
- Automotive Service Industry Association
- Bearing Specialists Association
- Beauty & Barber Supply Institute, Inc.
- Bicycle Wholesale Distributors Association, Inc.
- Ceramics Distributors of America
- Copper & Brass Warehouse Association, Inc.
- Council for Periodical Distributors Association
- Electrical-Electronic Materials Distributors Association, Inc.
- Farm Equipment Wholesalers Association
- Federal Wholesale Druggists' Association
- Flat Glass Marketing Association
- Food Industries Supplier's Association
- Foodservice Equipment Distributors Association
- General Merchandise Distributors Council
- Hobby Industry Association of America, Inc.
- Laundry & Cleaners Allied Trades Association
- Lawn & Garden Distributors Association
- Mass Merchandising Distributors Association
- Material Handling Equipment Distributors Association
- National-American Wholesale Grocers' Association
- National Association of Aluminum Distributors
- National Association of Brick Distributors

- National Association of Chemical Distributors
- National Association of Container Distributors
- National Association of Decorative Fabric Distributors
- National Association of Electrical Distributors
- National Association of Fire Equipment Distributors
- National Association of Floor Covering Distributors
- National Association of Industrial Glove Distributors
- National Association of Marine Services Inc.
- National Association of Musical Merchandise Wholesalers
- National Association of Plastics Distributors
- National Association of Sporting Goods Wholesalers
- National Association of Textile & Apparel Wholesalers
- National Association of Writing Instrument Distributors
- National Builders' Hardware Association
- National Building Material Distributors Association
- National Candy Wholesalers Association
- National Electronic Distributors Association
- National Equipment Distributors Association
- National Fastener Distributors Association
- National Food Distributors Association
- National Frozen Food Association, Inc.
- National Independent Bank Equipment Suppliers Association
- National Industrial Distributors Association
- National Locksmiths' Suppliers Association
- National Marine Distributors Association

- National Paint Distributors, Inc.
- National Paper Trade Association, Inc.
- National Sash & Door Jobbers Association
- National School Supply & Equipment Association
- National Swimming Pool Institute
- National Welding Supply Association
- National Wholesale Druggists' Association
- National Wholesale Furniture Association
- National Wholesale Hardware Association
- National Wholesale Jewelers' Association
- North American Heating & Air Conditioning Wholesalers
- North American Wholesale Lumber Association, Inc.
- Optical Wholesalers Association
- Pet Industry Distributors Association
- Petroleum Equipment Institute
- Pharmaceutical Wholesalers Association
- Power Transmission Distributors Association
- Safety Equipment Distributors Association, Inc.
- Service Merchandisers of America
- Shoe Service Institute of America
- Steel Service Center Institute
- Toiletry Merchandisers Association, Inc.
- Toy Wholesalers' Association of America
- Truck Equipment & Body Distributors Association, Inc.
- Wallcovering Wholesalers Association

- Wholesale Florists & Florist Suppliers of America, Inc.

- Wholesale Stationers' Association

- Wine & Spirits Wholesalers of America, Inc.

- Woodworking Machinery Distributors Association

Manufacturers seeking ideas for establishing better relations with their wholesalers may receive valuable assistance from any or all of these groups.

There are, of course, many other associations for wholesalers; most of them make it a point to be helpful to manufacturers.

The National Association of Textile and Apparel Wholesalers is a group of wholesalers of ready-to-wear, piece goods, domestics, floor coverings, notions, underwear, hosiery, furnishings, infants' wear, and other lines. This group has developed timely marketing studies on subjects such as sales force compensation and ration analysis. It also has developed an excellent advertising program aimed at retailers expounding the advantages of purchasing from wholesalers. The association sponsors an annual convention, trade show, and educational seminar every year, open to wholesalers only, which makes it rather unique.

It seems probable that in the future much of the task of building better relations may be taken over by state associations of wholesalers and retailers, thus freeing the individual wholesaler for the actual work of warehousing and distributing merchandise. For example, a program of the Wisconsin Pharmaceutical Association, supported in large measure by the wholesale pharmaceutical houses of that state, comprised the following:

1. A pharmacy-school scholarship campaign

2. A store selling-and-buying service

3. Aid to pharmacists returning from the armed services

4. A store-remodeling service

5. Cooperation with universities

6. New professional-relations program

7. New public-relations program

At the top of the list of things producers can do to help their dealers is to share with them merchandising know-how based upon experience with so-called laboratory stores. This know-how could cover such phases of storekeeping as store arrangement, inventory control, credit policies, advertising and display, personnel problems, and customer services. Above all, dealers need help in increasing store traffic.

The Role of the Broker

In reaching appropriate markets, a grocery-product manufacturer or food processor has the choice of maintaining a sales force or using a food broker. To be successful, brokers must perform certain functions more efficiently than the manufacturers' own sales forces.

Brokers conduct continuing operations in the same area and thus are often able to develop and maintain more effective selling relationships than company sales representatives. They are flexible in their selling efforts, being able to employ extra sales manpower for special promotions or seasonal items. And because they represent several manufacturers, the cost of each sales call is proportionately lower.

HOW COMPANIES SELECT A BROKER

Before selecting a broker, a manufacturer should analyze his or her product and sales need in each market. Questions most frequently asked are:

1. Is the broker willing to represent the company aggressively?

2. Is he or she oriented toward selling the company's type of product to the buyers the manufacturer wants to reach?

3. Does the broker have contacts in his or her sales area that will facilitate effective selling to buyers in that area?

4. Does the broker have a reputation for integrity?

The manufacturer's evaluation of the broker's expressed interest, willingness, and reputation can best be done after personal interviews in the prospective broker's office.

A broker's value to a manufacturer depends on how well he or she helps the manufacturer achieve sales goals while holding costs at a reasonable level. To reach the target volume, broker and principal must work together to forecast sales accurately and to coordinate the broker's sales and merchandising activities with the manufacturer's promotion and marketing efforts.

MANUFACTURER CONTROLS MARKETING

General marketing management cannot be delegated to brokers. The manufacturer must be concerned with advertising, product development packaging, research, and pricing policies. The broker's primary objective is to maintain good selling relations between his or her principals and their customers, who are wholesalers, chain-store organizations, industrial users, and other buyers. However, the broker may assist in the physical handling of goods, credit investigation, invoicing, and other nonselling activities.

Food brokers were once free-lance sales representatives lacking any continuing relationship with the companies they represented. Now, they are integrated sales and service organizations operating under contract with the companies. Today's market-oriented brokers must be sufficiently flexible to adjust quickly to the changing requirements of both manufacturers and customers.

Future Trends in Wholesaling

In an article in *Marketing News,* Madhav Kacker, associate professor, Suffolk University, Boston, reported as follows:

- According to the Food Marketing Institute, more than 90% of wholesalers now offer a wide range of services, such as individual retail pricing, cooperative advertising, private labeling, gross margin reports by item, accounting and payroll services, equipment procurement, and providing product movement data.

- In the food industry, the Uniform Communication System is widely adopted to provide links between wholesaler's computers and those of suppliers. By 1990, it's estimated that 75 percent of all wholesalers will use on-line order entry systems.

- A 1983 study sponsored by the Distribution Research and Education Foundation (DREF) predicted, using the Delphi forecasting technique, that major changes would be experienced by the wholesale distribution industry in the 1980s and 1990s. The wholesalers/distributors, under pressure from end users and suppliers, will need to change their traditional business practices and make use of new technologies and systems to enhance productivity. They'll shoulder greater responsibility for inventory management by 1990.

Gary F. McKinnon made these observations in Dartnell's *Marketing Manager's Handbook:**

The development of the vertically integrated channel systems will continue in future years. Alert wholesalers will continue to offer assistance to customers in locating, leasing, designing, and managing their retail outlets. Wholesalers will continue to develop new types of integrated channels similar to their efforts in the past in forming voluntary chain store systems. They must continue to adapt their services to the needs of their target markets. They will likely continue to offer new types of services to the specialty outlets they serve. They will also continue to offer private or generic brands to their retail customers.

It is imperative that wholesalers seek new cost-reducing methods of doing business. Electronic scanning and merchandise control will continue to be growing forces in the channel systems. Wholesalers must react to the deregulation of transportation in order to further reduce costs. The FTC will now permit private carriers to solicit backhaul traffic. This new development may further reduce distribution costs for major wholesalers. Furthermore, material-handling costs will continue their decline for aggressive wholesalers willing to implement new procedures and electronic technology.

In summary, competitive forces will continue to drive out the inefficient wholesaler and many chains may more efficiently perform the marketing functions. However, the trends also suggest the aggressive and innovative wholesaler will continue to be an important part of an integrated channel system and the position of such firms will be strengthened in future years.

Marketing Manager's Handbook, p. 776.

Chapter 34

Retail Outlets

In the previous chapter a retail sale was defined as one made for personal use, leisure, or sustenance of an individual or household, as opposed to industrial users and intermediate buyers.

Retailing is perhaps the most diverse channel of distribution. It includes the independent dealer, department stores, discount houses, chain stores, mass distributors, supermarkets, and shopping centers/malls.

The Independent Dealer

The success or failure of a sales campaign comes to focus on the local retail dealer. That's where the action is. That's where the customer buys the product.

Despite the rapid growth of chain stores, discount houses, shopping centers, etc., the independent dealer is still an important factor in our system of mass distribution.

In fact, the independent merchant is today a better merchant, a better salesperson, and a more resourceful marketer *because* of the competition of the chains. By adapting new methods of display, self-service, checkout, and the rest, even the small merchant can often survive and make a profit in competition with the mass distributors. Although his prices may be higher, he depends on neighborhood trade and on the millions of consumers who prefer to do business with "the shop around the corner."

While it is customary to think of independents as small merchants, the classification also include the large-city specialty stores, department stores, some supermarkets, and exclusive dealers, as well as those tradespeople who operate in the shopping districts of big cities and small cities, suburban shopping centers, county centers, and rural communities, plus the thousands of filling stations and general stores still found at every crossroad.

SMALL-TOWN AND MEDIUM-SIZED CITY RETAILERS

One of the most intriguing units in the U.S. market is the small town and medium-sized city store. Competition for this business is especially keen, with many aggressive and well-managed chains in the field. But there are tremendous sales opportunities for manufacturers whose sales policy pivots around the independent merchant. Actually it is not always necessary to sell through one or the other outlet, for there are many nationally advertised products sold both through independents and through chains.

The key to successful distribution in the small-town market is selecting and selling the stores able and willing to get behind a product and really push it. While some cling to the idea of 100 percent coverage and seek to sell every store in town able to pay its bills, the more experienced sales executives operate selectively. They find it no longer desirable to leave dealer selection to their salespeople. The salesperson as a rule wants an order in a town. If he or she can't get a profitable order of sufficient size from the best store, the salesperson goes to the next best store, and so continues until some kind of an order from any store with any credit rating at all is obtained. Such a sales policy may yield volume, but it does not always yield a profit adequate to the effort expended.

CLUETT PEABODY STRATEGY

The makers of famed Arrow shirts sell to hundreds of key trading centers, including many small towns. This company does not sell to the mail-order chains or mail-order houses, but does sell to department-store chains, to some men's-furnishings chains, and to selected independent retailers. Cluett Peabody makes an intensive study of every community in which it sells, and makes its salespeople approach a dealer at least twice a year (in the big-city stores a Cluett Peabody salesperson calls daily) with a detailed plan for selling everything in the Arrow line, including a timetable of all advertising, special events, and promotions.

This organization maintains a continuous market research program, studying consumer preferences and buying habits. It also conducts in-store research to help retailers speed turnover and conduct their business on a profitable basis.

Constant checking on styles and consumer wants is maintained to produce merchandise attractive to consumers. The company, which has grown steadily over a period of more than 100 years, has been a consistent national advertiser. The image of the company is characterized by style and quality, foregoing entirely low-end merchandising.

Over the years, boys' wear and a Lady Arrow line of shirts and blouses have been added to the regular Arrow men's line of shirts, handkerchiefs, sport knits, jackets, and swim wear.

The manufacturer who is unwilling or unable to do a selling job at least partially similar to that of Cluett Peabody in the small cities may become discouraged. For unless the manufacturer's salesperson knows how to get goods pushed properly by the right merchants, and unless that merchandise enjoys consumer demand and is properly advertised, sales volume in the small-city stores may be disappointing.

HOW TO SELL TO THE SMALL-TOWN SECTOR

There are two major decisions to be made by the manufacturer who wants business from this small-town sector of the country:

1. To sell to the mass distributors; or

2. To set up selling machinery and methods that will enable independents to sell a fair share of the total, in spite of mass distributor competition.

Now suppose we look at the second alternative, assuming that the manufacturer wants small-town business, but is unwilling or unable to sell to the chains. To hold one's own in small towns, the manufacturer may have to use one or more of the following methods:

1. Organize and train salespeople to sell smaller merchants direct

2. Organize and train salespeople to sell independent merchants through wholesalers

3. Set up a distributing organization using distributors, branch houses, or warehouses

4. Organize or promote his own chain of stores

5. Organize or promote exclusive or "captive" stores to sell the line in question

Many of the electrical appliance manufacturers, working through distributors, depend almost wholly on specialty dealers who may handle several lines of appliances. These stores are usually rigidly supervised, and their franchises subject to quick cancellation, if volume fails.

For many years the Scholl Manufacturing Company of Chicago had "captive" dealers to sell its foot appliances and other products exclusively where local dealers produced in sufficient volume. It also had lines for general distribution.

Many other manufacturers have worked out franchise plans that require certain performances from all dealers who sell the lines. This seems to be one of the most successful methods, where the line is big enough to be important to a merchant. All these plans grew out of the fact that, when left to his or her own devices, the small retailer will seldom produce a profitable volume for any one manufacturer. Rather than develop sales through promotions, program selling, and close cooperation with the manufacturer, the small retailer is inclined to attempt to sell too many brands, to scatter his or her efforts, and to depend wholly upon voluntary "drop in" business.

HOW POLAROID HELPED BUILD DEALERS' SALES

When a new product is introduced, many companies organize sales and training meetings at which product features are demonstrated, their benefits are discussed, sales campaigns are announced, and dealer aids are presented. In preparing its dealers to sell its Model SX-70 several years ago, Polaroid Corporation conducted hundreds of meetings in more than 100 markets for several thousand dealers and their retail sales staffs.

Following the explanations of the product and the best techniques for demonstrating and selling it to prospective customers, the company unveiled a series of "dealer helps," which included a variety of store and window displays, an eight-foot demonstration center, a six-foot high rotating pedestal floor display, an illuminated counter display, color backdrops, and posters. In addition, of course, was a variety of consumer literature.

Companies in various industries allocate dealer costs of displays and other sales material in different ways. Manufacturers wish to sell their products and are not interested in making money out of their displays, so some items are offered free, and others at actual cost or less, while the cost of larger, more expensive units is shared among the manufacturer, the distributor, and the dealer. Other methods include package deals with expensive displays free with quantity orders, easy credit terms, and prizes for outstanding window or store displays.

WHAT THE DEALER WANTS TO KNOW

Manufacturer-owned retail shops are not a major factor in American retailing. Although a number of firms do own their own stores, the art of retailing is most difficult for manufacturers to understand, let alone master. It is hard for production people to comprehend what goes on in a merchant's mind. This is one of the main criticisms that can be made of manufacturers' salespeople who deal with retailers. Their sales approach is geared primarily to the product and its qualities or characteristics.

The retailer is not as interested in such information as in how the product will fit into the rest of his or her line, its markup and turnover, and ideas for promoting and merchandising it. The retailer is relatively unconcerned with its construction or composition. Unfortunately, too few manufacturers take the time and effort to learn about retailing, so that they can sell *from the point of view of their customers.* This represents a tremendous educational opportunity. The more marketing people learn about retail merchandising, the easier it will be for them to win a larger share of the retail market.

AN INDUSTRY PROMOTION FOR LOCAL DEALERS

Eleven manufacturers and a trade association banded together to increase summer sales in a classic example of cooperative marketing. The products all had peak sales during the outdoor season, so the group adopted the theme of "Leisure Living."

Styling themselves the Committee for the Great Outdoors were King-Seeley, Tupperware, American Gas Association, Cessna Aircraft Company, Johnson Motors, Champion Spark Plug Co., International Harvester, Jantzen, Inc., Johnson Reels, Inc., Mobil Oil Corp., Nimrod Division of Ward Manufacturing, Inc., and The Seven-Up Co.

The committee symbol was a stylized logo of a pine tree in a circle.

A Great Outdoors News Service was created, and a 20-page tabloid feature section full of general news stories on subjects ranging from camping in the desert to swimming and cooking in the backyard was made available to newspapers across the country, to be used and edited at will.

King-Seeley received over 800 newspaper requests for product information to include in expanded leisure-living stories.

The committee concentrated its program at the local level. Outdoor special sections were developed by individual newspapers, based on local recreational facilities.

Another industry-wide promotion was that conducted by the American Music Conference in which 166 musical instrument manufacturers participated and dealers were asked to purchase a modestly priced Discover Music kit to "increase sales, profits, and prestige."

COOPERATIVE ADVERTISING

Since the dealer is right on the firing line when it comes to contact with the customer, most manufacturers go to great lengths to provide advertising and promotional support. This usually takes two forms. The first consists of store merchandisers, window display, and consumer literature; the second assists the dealer to advertise in local newspapers and over the radio or TV stations in the dealer's area. For this purpose many major corporations selling through distributors and dealers have a cooperative advertising policy through which the cost of local advertising is shared among the producer, distributors, and dealer.

Basically, a cooperative reserve fund is set up by the manufacturer, based on a certain percentage of the value of each shipment to a distributor. A local dealer who advertises is credited by the distributor for 50 percent of the expenditure. The distributor in turn submits the statement to the manufacturer and receives a credit of 50 percent of his or her own share of the cost. Thus, in theory, at least, the net result is that the dealer pays 50 percent, the distributor 25 percent, and the manufacturer 25 percent, but these percentages may vary according to specific industries or companies. The point is that the policy must be uniformly applied to all accounts as required by the Robinson-Patman Act.

That is not to say, however, that in introducing a new line, a manufacturer may not increase the distributor's share of the cost. However, this must be done for *all* the manufacturer's distributors. The advantages or disadvantages of cooperative advertising from the standpoint of the manufacturer's interest are discussed in a later chapter.

Aside from newspaper advertising, the independent dealer does not always take full advantage of the manufacturer's promotional campaigns and advertising material. The reason for this is that the dealer is not too anxious to spend money and expects the manufacturer to do it instead. Unlike department stores, many dealers are not aware of the fact that their own store windows are one of their best advertising media. So when a manufacturer launches a very important campaign, in many cases he or she goes so far as to hire a window-display company to make sure that the dealer properly presents the product to the public.

Department Stores and Discount Houses

Department stores, discount houses, and independent dealers have separate retailing philosophies based on their specific responses to different categories of consumer needs and requirements.

With all its theoretical advantages, such as providing one-stop shopping in a prestigious atmosphere complete with charge accounts and delivery service, the department store is finding it increasingly difficult to compete with independent specialty stores and discount houses.

To meet this competition, many independently owned department stores have pooled their resources and formed cooperative groups. Federated Department Stores is a notable example of such cooperative action. Also, the modern department store avoids a lot of headaches by granting concessions to outsiders to run certain departments that are not greatly profitable or that require technical know-how. Concessionaires often run camera departments, tobacco shops, beauty salons, and millinery departments, among others.

The department store buyer, however, remains a key person in this industry. The title of buyer does not reflect his or her full importance—he or she makes a lot of advertising, merchandising, and promotion decisions and is responsible for buying the stock for a particular department.

The buyer will usually be found in a cubbyhole about the size of a broom closet, when not traveling to some large city or even abroad to look at new merchandise. Even when there is centralized purchasing, the buyer has the last word on what will be sold in his or her department.

Some independent department stores maintain buying offices in cities like New York, Chicago, St. Louis, New Orleans, Dallas, or San Francisco. Frequently a buying office may represent a group of stores.

A few of the largest department stores maintain buying offices in foreign cities; others send their buyers abroad every year to shop the foreign markets, while still others use agents as independent shoppers in the countries in which these agents live. Some of these agents may act as buyers for several U.S. department stores.

It is this wide diversity of practices that makes the problem of selling to department stores a complicated one that requires marketing executives to study the individual practices of the stores to which they wish to sell.

THE SHIFT TO THE SUBURBS

Retailers are one of the chief bulwarks of the economy of the United States, or of any other developed country. Many great corporations could not exist without the support of an extensive distributing organization and the effective retailing it provides. Many innovative and forward-looking marketing concepts come not from technical ideas but from the needs and demands of the market *as reflected by the retailers;* department stores account for most of the advances in the retail field.

Responding to the move from cities to suburban areas, department stores followed their customers, which aided the development of shopping malls and shopping centers, with the so-called dumbbell concept of a department store at each end of a row of independent shops.

ENTERING NEW FIELDS

Retail associations and economic research groups are aware of the increasing public need and demand for services in all fields. Merchants realize that, to build traffic, enhance store image, and increase sales, they must do more than offer merchandise at competitive prices to increase their sales volume. As a result, some of the national chains and the major department stores have entered the fast-growing and promising general services field.

The larger stores sell packaged travel tours; some sell tickets to cultural and sporting events or have greatly widened home decoration services.

THE MERCHANDISE MANAGER

The buyer's role is changing dramatically. He or she is becoming more of a specialist in the distribution of goods as he or she gives up responsibilities for supervising salespeople and for the collection and tabulation of inventory information.

This change is enhanced by the freedom to concentrate time and energy on the selection of merchandise, the preparation of assortments, and sales promotion plans.

The growth of branch operations has wrought the biggest

changes in buyer responsibilities. Branch operations have made it necessary in many cases for buyers to relinquish their sales supervisory roles to the branch department manager.

The computer and data processing are rapidly bringing about another change. Data processing is making it possible to relieve the buyer of responsibilities for inventory and stock-control operations. The buyer, no matter for what industry, can now be provided with a stream of fast and accurate information, allowing him or her to spend less time gathering information and more time interpreting it.

Classification-merchandising techniques will probably bring further changes in the scope and responsibility of the buyer's job. Under the classification-merchandising concepts, departments will gradually give way to classifications, with responsibility assigned by classification rather than by department.

This will give merchandise management more freedom to develop specialized buyers by types of related merchandise, particularly where the added complications of selling responsibilities are removed from the buyer's shoulders.

Divisional merchandise managers, like the buyers, are being relieved of many ancillary responsibilities, including the control of inventories.

The general merchandise manager will continue to be the person directly answerable to top management for merchandise sales and profits. He or she may be expected to assume the added responsibility of inventory management by classification.

Inventory management is creating a growing corps of new executives to service the merchandise division. The inventory manager (or merchandise controller) relieves the buying department of responsibility for control of merchandise after it is bought and also assumes responsibility for its replenishment.

The new function of inventory manager has been made necessary by the trend to multi-unit operations and the advanced development of data processing. His or her function is to centralize merchandise controls and to present the buying departments with the inventory information necessary to guide them in their buying operations. In some stores the inventory manager will have a rank comparable to that of a divisional merchandise manager; in others he or she will be attached to the general merchandise manager's office, while some will place him or her under general management, reflecting the high level of monetary responsibility the inventory manager will have.

SALES PROMOTION RESPONSIBILITY

The function of the sales promotion manager is also undergoing rapid evolution, particularly in larger stores. The sales promotion manager's role is no longer merely that of service to the merchandising departments, but is becoming more and more that of participant in every area that affects the store image and the store's relationship with the public.

For example, the rise of storewide events such as import fairs has brought the sales promotion manager into a closer working relationship with merchandisers, fashion coordinators, salespeople, and sales support personnel. The sales promotion executive must be concerned with every phase of such a promotion, from initial concept to final sale.

The proliferation of branch stores has presented retailing with a need for better coordination and a closer working relationship between advertising and merchandising. Telephone selling, once only a service or convenience to customers, is now a major promotional tool that the sales promotion division can help to expand.

THE BRANCH MANAGER

The branch manager has developed from a hybrid of both line and staff functions. He or she is expected to be an all-purpose executive, well versed in operations, personnel, merchandising, and sales promotion, as well as in the newer disciplines of data processing and credit management.

The branch manager, however, has a skilled corporate staff at headquarters on which to rely for guidance and assistance.

As branches become less reliant on the main store or corporate headquarters for the day-to-day decisions of store operations and merchandising, the branch manager will become more and more involved with top management concerns. He or she will participate in management decisions affecting future plans, rather than simply following instructions from headquarters.

MARKUPS AS A SALES TOOL

Not usually considered by suppliers to department stores is the importance of markup as a selling tool. Roger Dickinson, a former buyer for a major department store, wrote in the *Journal of Marketing:*

Markup is defined technically as the difference between cost and retail price, an amount usually expressed as a percentage of the retail price.

One notable contribution of markup is as a negotiation tool with actual and potential suppliers. The retailer can gain significant benefits by using markup effectively; and the supplier may benefit by understanding the retailer's use of markup to gain additional advantages.

The success of any commitment depends on the ability of the buyer to communicate it persuasively to the supplier. A buyer for a specific merchandise classification, therefore, might consider only vendor offers with a minimum markup of X percent. This minimum would be set at a realistic level after considering industry practices and those of competitors. If a vendor believes this markup constraint to be a commitment on the part of the retailer, he or she will meet these requirements in the hope of selling merchandise to the department.

Any supplier wishing to develop a substantial volume of business through department store outlets should consider markup requirements while establishing prices through the various channels of distribution. This should result in greater profits accruing to department store outlets as a group.

Markup is also an effective tool in negotiating with vendors for special merchandise. A buyer may ask a supplier for a mattress with features that, at a markup of 33 percent, will create an exciting value for the consumer. This gives the supplier some latitude, but puts pressure on for low cost because both buyer and supplier generally know the retail price that a promotional item with specific features must have to excite consumers.

In addition, when the buyer indicates the expected markup, he or she eliminates some price negotiation because the general range of the alternatives is specified in advance.

Actually, certain markup pressures may induce a buyer to violate the Robinson-Patman Act, by obtaining cost concessions on regular merchandise; but severe markup pressure may induce a buyer to create new products that may be entirely beyond the control of the Robinson-Patman Act.

THE USE OF DIRECT MAIL

Direct mail is widely used by department stores, as everyone with a charge account knows. In a study published by the National Retailer Merchants Association, two points were emphasized:

1. The bigger the store, the more direct mail.

2. Statement stuffers make up 75 percent of direct mail.

However, stores are not happy with statement stuffers, even though they continue to use them. They would like greater discrimination, better selection, and more personalization.

Since nearly all statement enclosures are supplied by vendors, a small drygoods store uses the same glossy mailer as a fashionable department store. As a result, more stores create their own direct mail pieces and insist that manufacturers pick up part or all of the cost.

Other facts revealed by the survey are that:

1. Most stores agree on the effectiveness of dated promotions.

2. Cosmetics and hosiery head the list of good direct mail items, with ready-to-wear at the bottom.

3. Most stores feel that selling the advertised product ranks third in importance. The first two are bringing customers to the store and increasing the use of charge accounts.

4. A breakdown of the direct mail dollar cost is 41 cents postage; 38 cents production; 21 cents processing.

5. The least-used forms of direct mail were postcards, letters, and broadsides.

6. In the stores' opinion, the merchandise itself outweighs the effects of art, copy, and price.

Of the stores surveyed, 95 percent said that direct mail would be increasingly important in the future.

TYPES OF RETAIL ADVERTISING AND PROMOTION

The great bulk of retail advertising is in newspapers, radio, and television.

Newspaper ads, in general, stress features and price. Some of the big department stores and other major retailers, often use a full page to allow the use of a full-size illustration as a means of creating customer attraction. In general, the practice is to stress illustration, description, and price.

Radio broadcasting has its own advantages. First, it follows the audience around the home, while traveling in the car or on a boat. Secondly, depending on the power, size of the station and the area covered, radio spots are relatively low in cost.

It should be remembered that the cost of commercials is, in most cases, negotiable as is evidenced by the rise of the brokerage and bartering techniques. It is essential that retailers monitor their schedules to ensure that their commercials are actually broadcast and at the proper time specified. There are not a few cases on record of double billing where, under cooperative advertising plans, one invoice is issued to the retailer while a different, higher one goes to the manufacturer for partial reimbursement.

The use of TV commercials by department stores and other large retailers has been increasing over the years and has proven to be quite effective.

When one picks up the Sunday newspaper these days, it's a hefty load caused by the tremendous amount of four-color multipage inserts by retailers.

STORE OPERATIONS

The profit squeeze of recent years has focused greater attention on better utilization of the money spent on store operations.

The challenge of efficient store operations in multiunit organizations has increased greatly, with a corresponding increase in the responsibilities of the operations executive. As this trend continues, the operations manager will have to become a stronger member of the top management team, being held more and more accountable for profits through more efficient organization and staffing of operating divisions.

It is possible that future department stores will have three pyramids of administration operating out of the central office. One would embrace merchandising and promotion; another would include the physical operations and control of parent and branch units, and the third would deal with coordination and control of all services.

There is a big communications gap from the point at which the manufacturer's salesperson sells the department store buyer and the point where the retail salesperson confronts the customer. The problem lies in the difficulty of transmitting to the selling floor the information the customer needs as the basis for making a decision to buy.

An executive of Carson Pirie Scott & Co., Chicago, said:

"The real problem is to get this information to the individuals who staff the floors of retail stores, having this communication coincide with the arrival of the merchandise, and giving our salespeople the benefit of all the product selling points as the manufacturer's salesperson gave them to the store buyer. The problem is to have the salesperson on the floor able to answer such questions as 'what has this one got that that one hasn't?' or 'what will this do for me?'"

TRAINING STORE PERSONNEL

The larger department stores carry on strenuous and continuous attempts to train sales personnel. One of the largest and best known, Marshall Field & Co., of Chicago, produced a film that was shown to all new salespersons; other large stores also have film programs, shopping clinics, and other types of training activities that try to overcome the inertia and disinterest of the average retail clerk.

Merging of stores in the larger cities, self-service, automated selling, and other devices have been tried as a partial answer to the difficulty of finding and keeping competent salespeople. Yet despite all efforts, nearly every large city—and many smaller ones—

can tell of once-prosperous stores that have fallen by the wayside due to the difficulty of securing adequate sales personnel.

A guide for retailers, published by the Committee for Economic Development (CED), emphasizes that people are more important than a building or merchandise. So a merchant who wants to see his or her business grow, or a manufacturer who wants to help his or her dealers to become better dealers, should study its personnel problem especially carefully. The following specific suggestions are offered by CED:

1. With the help of members of the organization, build up a manual even if it is only a good-sized notebook, covering the best way to handle each part of the selling job.

2. Include in the manual ideas that apply alike to all selling, and also special ideas related to different lines of goods.

3. Collect and file information about the merchandise from wholesalers, manufacturers, and other sources, which salespeople can learn to give them confidence in selling.

4. Train all salespeople carefully to make only true statements about the materials and qualities of goods. This will take on new importance as qualities of goods change for the better, as unfamiliar kinds of goods come into stores, and as prices change.

5. Experiment with methods of training that use "side-by-side" teaching, and active demonstration by salespeople.

6. Work out methods of incentive compensation for better performance, making them apply to both sales and nonsales personnel.

7. Try to work out a formula for incentive pay that gives better rewards to regular employees of proven ability than to rush-period help, even for equal sales, and that gives recognition to better results obtained in seasons when sales are normally dull.

In an effort to bring up-to-date fashion news to personnel in the branch stores, Lord & Taylor, New York, used a color video-cassette system to present new merchandise, fashion trends, and better selling ideas to both part-time and full-time employees in its branch stores.

"We wanted our salespeople to be authorities on all merchandise from the time it is introduced," a spokesperson said, emphasizing that salespeople must be capable not only of selling, but "of acting as fashion counselors to today's fashion-conscious shoppers."

"Our personnel must know everything about the merchandise they are selling," said Ted Bruce, senior vice-president, a strong believer in the "suggestive selling" technique that revolves around the ability to suggest new styles, accessories, color combinations and ideas.

The actors on the Lord & Taylor in-house TV circuit are store buyers, assistant buyers, manufacturers' representatives, and merchandise managers. All filming, production, directing and editing is done by Lord & Taylor employees. All merchandise presented on the video-cassette programs is also displayed on the scene by department branch managers, so that sales personnel can see the items and question the manager for detailed information in an effective two-way communication process.

THE RISE OF THE DISCOUNT HOUSE

In the 1950s a new kind of retailing establishment, the discount house, appeared in the United States. It was a tentative movement at first. Most of the early discount houses operated on a membership basis, issuing identification cards to government workers, members of labor unions, and similar kindred groups. Gradually, these closed-door discount houses opened to the general public.

The first public discount houses, operating from abandoned warehouses and similar structures, carried little in the way of nationally advertised brands of household goods and appliances. Their development was quite similar to that of the supermarket in food retailing, in that long-established manufacturers were hesitant to sell their merchandise for fear of offending independent retailers.

Like the supermarkets, however, the discount houses prevailed upon brand-name manufacturers to sell them goods. Many discount houses were a double threat to established retailers, in that they carried food, as well as soft goods, hardware, and appliances.

The early appeal of the discount houses was on price alone. First-quality merchandise was rare, and surroundings were plain and unattractive. Everything was, of course, sold on a self-service basis and no delivery service was offered.

As discount merchandisers multiplied and competition grew brisk, some upgraded their quality, decorated their stores, and offered some limited but helpful service. In the early 1960s, competition was so brisk that many discount houses failed. But the strongly-financed and wisely-managed houses survived, and were joined by many old-line retailers.

Today many discount houses rival department stores with their fine buildings and interior appointments. Most continue to be largely self-service, and no delivery service is available. But the advent of the bank credit card has made charge account purchases as easily available in the discount house as in the department store.

The discount house today can justify its claim as a major distribution outlet, according to a study by Perry Meyers, Inc., management consultant firm. Although the survey was restricted to 200 housewives in a New England community, it is of interest in helping to assess the place of the modern discount store in the nation's system of distribution.

Strangely enough, price, the theme of discount-house advertising for years, rated fifth in the reasons given for shopping at these stores. The most common reason given was convenience of location, mentioned by 28 percent of the group. Next most popular reasons were "good parking facilities" and the fact that the women "liked self-service" (each factor rating a 27 percent response). Ten percent of the group interviewed cited evening openings as an advantage.

Voiced as the principal disadvantage by the group, however, was the need to wait in line to check out purchases, with "too few clerks" given as a second disadvantage. Another peeve (cited by 10 percent) was the "generally poor merchandise" available at discount stores, although only 18 percent thought the wares below average.

The survey further showed that the discount shopper averaged 5.2 visits a month, and the lower the income the more frequent the visits. Children's wear, household goods, and curtains are the top merchandise "buys" at the discount stores, according to the majority of the group, with furniture and major appliances at the bottom of their list.

HOW A DISCOUNT CHAIN OPERATES

In an interview reported in *The Discount Merchandiser,* Mark Goldman, chairman of the board of Goldmans Bargain Barns, described some of the policies of his chain of discount stores. He noted:

> We have upgraded our stores with the newest and most modern fixtures available. We have engaged companies who specialize in store decor. In our new stores, on main traffic aisles, we have changed from tile to terrazzo because the maintenance and housekeeping problem is simpler that way.
>
> We have reappraised our buying staffs and have hired people who are specialists in all areas. We are now buying higher-priced lines than ever before, and are giving our customers more fashion instead of just the lower-end merchandise. In other words, we are taking advantage of the increased gross national product. We know that people want better things.
>
> We don't buy special promotional merchandise. *We do not want to buy someone else's mistakes.* Of course, if we've been buying an item at $10 and the manufacturer came out with a special on it at $7.50, we'll go out and heavily promote the item. Our markdowns on that particular sale would be very heavy. However, the total markdown at the end of the season would not be heavy, and it wouldn't affect our gross margin because the thing that kills most stores is the promotional remainders. We eliminate them by promoting from within our stock. After the sale the merchandise goes back to the original price.
>
> We have developed a work schedule whereby we show a break down of hours of the day in quarters: 9 to 12, 12 to 2, 2 to 5, and 5 to 9. We know where our peak selling periods are, and therefore, we can schedule our help accordingly.
>
> We give the store managers a budget each quarter, broken down by weeks. Then they have a schedule sheet and break down their sched-

ule by periods during the day. We have a 40-hour week, five days. We'll have part-timers cover the peak periods, and we merchandise our help like we merchandise our merchandise.

In our method of operation we take 95 percent of our promotions out of our everyday merchandise; we don't re-mark items. We count the items and take a markdown on the entire quantity. Then, at the end of the promotion, we recount the items and take a markdown cancellation showing a net markdown on the group.

Chain Stores and Mass Distributors

Compared with the independent retailers, the chain stores must be doing *something* right; perhaps more than one "something." The fact is that, in many communities, they have become the main retail centers around which other retailers have clustered, as in the shopping malls. Actually, no shopping mall is complete without a chain department store at each end, giving rise to the term "dumbbell design."

Buying power is not the only important factor in the amazing success story of the chain store. Of equal—and sometimes even greater—importance is the attractiveness of interior display.

Go into any independent store today, and with rarest exception there is not enough merchandise visible. Stocks may be good, but too much of the merchandise is high on shelves, in blind packages, under the counters, and generally out of reach and out of sight of the customer who has money to spend.

Go into a chain store and the merchandise is piled neatly on open counters. Oceans of merchandise seem to rise up and tempt the dollars right out of your pocket. Interior display of the merchandise itself is all-important, yet the average independent does not seem to grasp this. In a typical independent drugstore you will see a great collection of lithographed "cut-outs" advertising cosmetics, laxatives, and hair oil. In a nearby Walgreen store few if any of these lithographic nightmares are on display; instead there are great stacks of merchandise to create impulse sales. Factors in the success of chains include better prices, featuring one low-priced item as bait, but selling higher-priced lines; better selection; better packages; lighter, brighter stores; better advertising, plus a constant succession of events that create customer traffic. Most important is the fact that you can stand at almost any spot in a chain store and find, within arm's reach, 50 to 100 tempting items of merchandise. In addition, the chain is more mobile than the independent. If a store in one community proves unprofitable, it is promptly closed and the fixtures and merchandise moved to a new location.

According to *Chain Store Age,* drug chains have been opening new stores at an unprecedented rate, most of them in shopping centers. Remodelings of old stores have also been numerous, with an increase anticipated in the years ahead.

Today the drugstore chains are becoming more and more important to all manufacturers in the health and beauty-aids field, as well as in photo, candy, tobacco, stationery, and mass-selling sundries. Pharmaceutical manufacturers are finding that chains, with their professional know-how, the confidence they've earned from both patients and doctors, and their ability to fill the prescription needs of the communities they serve at reasonable prices, account for an increasing share of the nation's prescription business.

In the area of cosmetics, chain volume in the past few years has been phenomenal as chains expand their lines and intensify their training efforts. Toiletry and proprietary-goods manufacturers are returning to their old friends in the chain-drugstore field for promotional exploitation because they know it is the chains that give momentum to new products and promotions.

HOW CHAIN STORES SELL

The principal reason, aside from its buying advantages, that the large chain is able to outsell the independent in most communities is better merchandising—particularly in store display. The chain store theory is that goods well displayed sell themselves if the price is right. Manufacturers interested in chain store distribution therefore have the problem of adapting their product to display selling, or concentrated selling as it is called by merchandisers. Some of the factors that enter into self-service merchandising, as set forth by *Chain Store Age,* are as follows.

1. The package is paramount. Included in the package is descriptive, informative labeling or a clear view of its con-

tents, or both. The package must stack or be otherwise easy to handle and display. And a recognized brand name helps considerably.

2. The supply lines must be kept open and the merchandise in constant movement. Ordering, warehousing, and transportation systems will undoubtedly receive considerable overhauling as the full weight of concentrated self-service selling makes itself felt.

3. Store layout will be viewed afresh. Customer traffic patterns will take on new meaning. The entire store will be designed as a selling mechanism, with related selling, trading up, and all the other sacred cows of service selling taken care of through carefully conceived display, merchandise placement signs, and labels.

4. Mass displays will be punched up by light coming from fixtures designed for flexibility, as part of the overall scheme to make the display sell.

5. Mechanized handling of merchandise will assume greater importance at the store level.

THE INCREASE IN SELF-SERVICE

The phenomenal increase in self-service in grocery and drugstores has been repeated in hardware, stationery, and discount stores throughout the country. In the grocery field, the increase of self-service has grown considerably in the past decade.

Paralleling the growth of self-service has been the number of items carried in stock. In food distribution, the average supermarket of today carries approximately six times as many items as the food stores of 20 years ago. Statistics on the drug industry indicate that the average number of items carried increased more than fivefold in 25 years.

What does self-service accomplish? First and foremost, the installation of self-service techniques increases sales volume. Customers tend to buy more on each visit to the store and, in addition, store traffic itself tends to rise. Other benefits that flow logically from increased sales volume are decreased costs of doing business (as a percentage of sales) and the opportunity to show an improved net profit position.

How can increased traffic and sales be handled, assuming no increase in total floor space? One variety store operator reports that conversion to self-service added 49 percent more effective space. Self-service fixtures (with no dead space for clerks), and gondola and tiered displays increased the size of selling areas. Step-up selling displayers against a rear wall contributed their share to the total added space.

The principal area of chain-store expansion used to be in the big cities. Then the chain store invaded the small city and town market.

It was probably J. C. Penney Co., Inc., that really discovered the possibilities of the smaller-sized city for chain operations. Although Penney is concentrating its efforts more and more on larger-sized markets, 25 percent of its sales still come from towns and cities of less than 100,000 population. With the abandonment of the cash-and-carry policy of the founder and the provision of credit facilities, the company has followed a trend that started long ago in the nation's department stores. The "famous five principles" upon which the Penney stores were originally operated and under which they still function, according to the management are:

1. To serve the public, as nearly as we can, to its complete satisfaction.

2. To offer the best possible dollar's worth of quality and value.

3. To strive constantly for a high level of intelligent and helpful service.

4. To charge a fair price for what we offer—and not all the traffic will bear.

5. To apply this test to everything we do: "Does it square with what is right and just?"

CHAIN STORE SALES POLICIES

Study of the established principles used so profitably by the chains is useful not only to independent retailers but also to the people who sell to them. You do not find the chain stores going in for any such foolishness as 28 different sizes of shears; nor do you find dead merchandise in their stocks. The reason for this is that the buyers for chains determine accurately what people will buy and stock that and nothing else. In setting up sales policies that will click with the dealers in towns of less than 50,000 population, it is a good idea to study chain buying and selling methods and to develop a sales pattern patterned after their methods.

The chains have learned to adjust stocks for regional preferences, climatic conditions, and many other factors. The mail-order houses, at least the larger ones, issue different catalogs for different sections of the country.

THE CHAIN STORE TEST METHOD

For new merchandise, the average chain store buyer will probably place a small order for tests in typical stores. If the tests prove satisfactory, the buyer may begin negotiations for merchandise to stock the entire chain, or parts of it. Manufacturers who are developing plans to sell merchandise to small-city merchants will be smart to follow this same principle. Tests should be made in typical towns, in several areas, then sales plans built around these tests. In making these tests remember that there are many differences, even in the same states. East Texas and West Texas are very different. There is a considerable range of climate between Florence in northern Alabama and Dothan in southern Alabama. Conditions in the West may depend on which side of a range of mountains a town is situated; in developing any sales plan check every condition that may be a factor in sales: climate, snowfall, rainfall, crops, industry, temperatures, whether the water is hard or soft.

AFFILIATED INDEPENDENTS

In order to meet the competition of the large chains, many of the smaller independent retailers in some cities have banded together in buying groups. Their central buying activities led to the organization of central supply houses, the stock of which was owned by the retailers.

In other cities, wholesalers took the initiative themselves. They organized the best retailers in each community, induced them to modernize their stores, and encouraged them to feature private brands.

There are at present the following types of affiliated independents (sometimes referred to as "voluntary chains"):

1. *The individual voluntary chain.* Operated by a wholesaler, this type has no affiliations except local cooperatives.

2. *Syndicate voluntary chain.* This type is operated by a wholesaler on a franchise plan. National name and trademark used by the wholesaler in an exclusive territory. All buying is done by each individual wholesaler.

3. *Retailers' voluntary chains.* Primarily operated as a buying pool, but cooperative efforts also are extended into advertising, selling, and merchandising channels. Buys through any source of supply.

4. *Retailers' voluntary chains (owning wholesale house).* A cooperative buying and advertising group that functions also as a wholesaler. Purpose is to reduce the cost of merchandise to retailer.

5. *Retailers' voluntary chains (cooperating with wholesalers).* A cooperative buying and advertising group, purchases being made through cooperating wholesalers, with no responsibility on the part of the wholesalers for the voluntary chain.

6. *Participating ownership voluntary chains.* Under complete control of the wholesaler, with the original owner participating in ownership and profits. Store operating, buying,

and management, however, are dominated by headquarters.

7. *Syndicate voluntary chain (complete service).* This type is operated by the wholesaler on a franchise plan and includes national name, private brands, and trademark. Most of the buying is done by headquarters, all wholesale members pooling their purchases. Includes complete merchandising service.

The chance to buy at a lower price has attracted many retailers to join voluntary groups. Some who previously bought from wholesalers with a 15 to 20 percent markup found they could get the same goods through a co-op or voluntary group at a much smaller markup. "Our members save 3 to 4 percent over what it would cost them to buy from a regular wholesaler," says the chairman of one cooperative in the Chicago area, the Certified Grocers of Illinois, Inc.

MAIL-ORDER HOUSES

Another type of mass distributor, closely allied with the national chain store group, is the publicly financed company that sells by mail from merchandise catalogs. These distributors principally serve the rural market. To meet the growing competition from the national chain store organizations, and because the automobile has made buying from a catalog less necessary to a farmer or small-town resident, these mail-order houses have supplemented their volume by opening up catalog stores throughout the country. Since the buying policies and methods of these big mail order houses follow closely those of the chain store, they require the same sales methods and techniques as prove successful in selling to large chains. The importance of mail order houses that do not operate chain stores is decreasing.

While some of the larger mail order houses promote and sell their own brands, others feature national brands. The total volume in the mail order field is quite impressive, and the companies make their profit on rapid turnover, using highly mechanized order-picking and handling methods.

CONSUMER CO-OPS

High distribution costs have opened the door for consumer cooperative enterprises in the United States. A group of consumers, usually those living in an agricultural or rural community, pool their resources to obtain greater buying power. They establish a community store. They pay regular retail prices for what they buy from the warehouse or store, and at the end of the year, after all expenses are met, a dividend is paid to the shareholders. Generally speaking, the importance of these co-ops, both in wholesaling and retailing, has been greatly overemphasized.

Supermarkets and Shopping Centers

The supermarket of today is defined by Super Market Institute as a retail food store with a self-service grocery department, with meat, dairy, and produce departments. Two factors that have favored the growth of the supermarket are the opening up of outlying districts for both low-cost and luxurious housing developments and the constantly increasing number of automobiles on the road. Another factor is the continued popularity of self-service.

As the idea of shopping at supermarkets spread, there was a tendency to build more suitable homes for them, and some of the supermarkets on the Pacific Coast, such as the Portland Public Market and the Farmer's Market of Los Angeles, became quite famous. Their success touched off a wave of building and investing. It was not uncommon for as much as $1,500,000 to be invested in a single market. R. H. Macy & Company, Inc., invested $6,000,000 in the Hillside Shopping Center in San Mateo, California.

There are three principal types of supermarkets, as follows:

1. Complete combination food market, highly departmentalized, carrying full lines of groceries, meats, delicatessen, dairy products, bakery goods, fruits, and vegetables. Each line is operated as a fully equipped department, generally in charge of a department head who is responsible for a certain percentage of the total profit. These markets are usually lo-

cated in the so-callled shopping centers, in fine buildings. Some operate in the main street areas. They are large advertisers, sell for cash, and frequently offer a delivery service. Their prices usually meet the competition and their net profit, which is small, is based on their huge sales volume.

2. A complete food department, but in addition a confectionery, soda and lunch department, gas station, cut-rate drug and toilet-goods department, and a cigar and tobacco department. Occasionally, it features novelties and household articles as special promotions. This type of market also renders limited service, selling mostly on a cash-and-carry basis. Its huge volume is obtained through circus-like promotions and substantial advertising in all types of media.

3. The third type of supermarket features the complete food departments, but, in addition, has added concessions of specialty lines such as hardware, paints, radios, auto accessories, women's apparel, shoes, and shoe repairing, barbershop, beauty parlors, etc. The number of the departments will vary from a dozen to more than 30. The sponsor—usually a wholesale grocer—uses the grocery department as the leader and counts on concessions to provide net profits.

As a rule, the complete food supers are owner-controlled. There are some supers, however, that rent out the meat concession, retaining the rest of the operation for themselves. If the supermarket is opened by a wholesale grocer, as a rule the wholesaler retains only the dry-grocery department and rents out the remaining concessions on a straight rental or a percentage basis. The latter method prevails in the majority of cases. Most of the independent operators follow the procedure of the wholesalers. Worth mentioning is the cooperative supermarket, where the concessionaires pool together and rent a building. Each pays its pro-rata share of the operating costs, based on the volume of each department.

NONFOOD MERCHANDISING

More and more the supermarkets are coming to rely on higher profits from health and beauty accessories and from general merchandise. As publisher and editorial director of *Supermarketing,* Howard S. Rauch estimated that by 1989, total grocery store sales will rise to more than $250 billion. Of this amount 4½ percent will be health and beauty accessories plus Rx and 7⅓ percent will be other general merchandise. Incidentally under HBA and Rx come the following: dieting aids, cosmetics, hand and hair products, health aids, infant formulas, oral hygiene products, shaving products, deodorants, and packaged medications.

Supermarkets have for some time emphasized the role of proprietary drugs and some have leased space for prescription services. A number of leading chain store companies have invaded the business even further; Jewel Tea Company bought a 30-store drug chain (now more than 80) which it is operating under the name of Osco Drugs under one roof; Dominick's Finer Foods added drug outlets.

THE UNIVERSAL PRODUCT CODE

After many years of study and negotiation, the $100 billion plus food industry developed a universal product code (UPC) by labeling food according to a single industry standard. Retailers, wholesalers, and manufacturers can cut costs and raise profits by speeding the industry's conversion to electronic cash register systems.

The code identifies thousands of food items sold by the average supermarket and provides a standard labeling language that can be read by electronic scanners plugged into a central computer. By changing the bar widths in the code and the spaces between bars, a system user can accommodate all the variations needed to identify each grocery product and size. (See Figure 1, page 710.)

In an address before the American Association of Millers, Milton Field, product manager, J. H. Mathews & Co., described the Universal Product Code Symbol as follows:

"The image contains the code numbering system, adopted for the grocery industry, of 10 numeric digits. The standard symbol is in the form of a series of parallel white and black bars of different widths and is called a bar code symbol. This 10-digit system also includes growth capacity for longer codes (12, 14, or more) to facil-

Figure 1. XYZ Food Company 8 Oz. Juice

The Universal Product Code Symbol consists of 59 black or white bars which combine, in "digits" and "modules" to provide data for the electronic cash register and the mini-computer system in the store. The first five digits represent the manufacturer's number; the second five digits represent product code numbers. The symbols are "read" by an electronic scanner.

(Courtesy: J. H. Mathews & Co.)

itate compatibility with other distribution industries, which will be coming in the future.

"The basic symbol has the following characteristics:

1. A series of white and black parallel bars (30 black and 29 white for any 10-digit code), with a white margin on each side.

2. It is a rectangular shape.

3. Each character, or digit, is made up of two black bars and two white spaces.

4. Each character (digit) is made up of seven data elements; these data elements are called modules.

5. A module may be either white or black.

6. A single bar may be made up of one, two, three, or four modules.

7. Each character is independent.

8. The symbol also includes two digits beyond the 10 needed to encode the Universal Product Code:

   • One character, a modular check character, is at the right-most position of the symbol to ensure proper encoding of the symbol digits.

   • Another character, located in the left-most position of the symbol to show which number system a particular symbol encodes. In this case, "O" represents grocery products. Redundant number sets are used to accommodate such things as meat and produce without the need to set aside code numbers in the UPC.

9. To complete the symbol, there are left and right guard bars, and center bars that separate the 10 numeric digits into two groups of five. The first five digits represent the manufacturer's number, and once it is assigned to a company it remains constant for that manufacturer on all packages. The second group of five digits on the right-hand side of the center bars represents the product code number, and the grocery manufacturer assigns these codes to his or her products. Thus, if you produce 10 or 10,000 products, you will always have the first five digits reading the same on all of them, and a different five-digit product code on each product package. The 10-digit code is thus translated into a standard symbol that can be preprinted on each consumer package by the food manufacturer, and read or scanned by a unit at the checkout end of the supermarket. It is estimated that the code has an error detection capability of one in ten million. It is omni-directional, which means that an opera-

tor at the checkout counter can pull the package across the scanner diagonally from top to bottom or bottom to top, or directly through the center.

Just a few of the things UPC can do:

1. Reduce labor costs

2. Speed customer traffic at the checkstand

3. Eliminate the cost of price marking every item and cost of price changes

4. Reduce store losses due to error (misrings, etc.)

5. Pinpoint stock shortages by item—a new method to reduce pilferage

6. Allow your customers to keep accurate inventory records

7. Enable faster, more accurate communication from store to warehouse to you as a manufacturer

8. Provide faster, more accurate measures of the effectiveness of the marketing ... which includes the advertising and promotion by the retailer and the food manufacturer."

THE SHOPPING CENTER

According to the International Council of Shopping Centers, retail sales in shopping centers account for nearly 30 percent of the total retail sales in the United States. Adjusting for such non-shopping center retail activities as sales of automobiles, gasoline, lumber and building materials, and fuel, it is estimated that shopping centers account for as much as 42 to 46 percent of the remaining gross retail sales.

In 1985, there were 24,700 shopping centers in the United States, 1,150 in Canada. (See Table 1, page 713.)

Retail sales in shopping centers exceed $475 billion. The growth of shopping centers in the noncentral communities of the metropolitan cities and larger towns and especially in the metropolitan suburbs, has greatly stimulated the increase in the number of supermarkets.

Table 1. Total Shopping Centers in the United States by Type, 1985

Type	Number
Neighborhood	12,350
Community	9,880
Regional	2,470

A drawback to the supermarket, at first, was the noncompetitive feature. Inasmuch as they were usually located in areas where there were few other comparable stores, there was little or no opportunity for the shopper to "shop." On the theory that clean competition makes for more business, the current practice is to locate supermarkets close to competitors so that when a person drives out to the shopping center he or she will have an opportunity to compare values and prices without having to move the car.

It is not unusual for a modern shopping center to include one or more supermarkets. A typical example is the Colonial Shopping Center in Orlando, Florida. Its key attraction is Belk's, a full-scale department store equal in size and choice of merchandise to any in the downtown area. It makes excellent use of publicity to build store traffic for its tenants. A typical promotion was a Mardi Gras Day, when prizes scaling from $2,500 down were awarded by the landlord for the most original costumes worn by salespersons working in the center. Full-page newspaper ads invited the public to come and see the fun. And how they came! You could hardly get around the streets.

There are a number of factors that affect the volume of trade that a primary trading center attracts to its stores. The most important of these are: 1) its relative size as compared with rival trading centers (generally the larger cities have the more attractive stores); and 2) its relative distance from consumers as compared with the rival centers. Obstacles to the movement of traffic, such as mountains, toll bridges, congested roads, etc., could have important effects too. Other factors that may affect the volume of trade drawn to a city are its qualities as a shopping center—the number, size, and character of its stores, parking conditions, variety and types of merchandise carried, prices, and all the other elements that community residents will consider in determining whether it is a "good place to shop."

The principle that the volume of trade attracted varies with the sizes and distances of riyal trading centers has been expressed in a formula known as the law of retail gravitation. It is that the relative volume of trade that two such centers will draw from an intermediate point is in direct relation to the relative populations of the two centers and in inverse relation to the squares of their distances from the intermediate point.

Annual traffic-building events, such as outdoor art exhibits during fine weather and annual rummage sales (perhaps featuring handcarts and street stalls) are conducted with great success by many shopping centers. Some centers now include "kiddielands" where shopping parents may park their children while shopping.

Whether this trend toward community drive-in shopping centers will become increasingly pronounced in the years ahead depends, experts believe, upon how soon the saturation point in automobile operation is reached. The whole problem of traffic and parking is so bad in a great many trading areas, especially suburban areas, that self-protection requires merchants to do something about it. The drive-in store makes it possible for the customer to make many types of purchases without getting out of the car.

While shopping centers are still being developed in the suburbs, retailers are reevaluating the possibilities in downtown areas of large cities, especially those with rebuilding programs.

WHAT CUSTOMERS LIKE

A survey reported in *Display World,* sponsored by the Glendale, California, Chamber of Commerce was conducted by Latta and Company among local merchants and shoppers to obtain answers to the following question: What do you believe is the most important influence on selling practices and buying habits in the central shopping district? The answers, ranked in order of importance, were:

- Fair or competitive prices
- Service
- Personnel (trained, or courteous)
- Ample selection of merchandise
- Good or quality merchandise
- Attractive stores and displays
- Parking
- Variety of shops close to each other
- Advertising and promotion
- Good merchandising
- Style (related to fashion goods)

Another phase of the survey showed that 62 percent of the shoppers were influenced by attractive window displays, 58 percent by newspaper advertising, 4 percent by radio, and 18 percent by TV.

POINT-OF-PURCHASE ADVERTISING

As unbelievable as it may sound, in some retail outlets on-the-spot decisions—made *inside* the store—account for almost two-thirds of all sales. As retail stores have become a crucial battleground in the war of consumer goods manufacturers to win customers, point-of-purchase—or point-of-sale—advertising has become an important sales weapon. Well-designed displays, distinctive packaging, and in-store advertising can provide the competitive edge.

The E. I. DuPont Company has been monitoring consumer buying habits at supermarkets since 1935. Its most recent study was in collaboration with the Point-of-Purchase Advertising Institute, Inc. (POPAI). This survey recorded 53,000 purchases made by 4,000 shoppers at 200 supermarkets nationwide, then compared these items with what consumers said they would buy as they entered the store.

Researchers found that an overwhelming 64.8 percent of all purchase decisions were made inside the store. This included impulse purchases, along with substitutions and generally planned buys (the shopper had an item in mind, but no brand). Another study of first-time purchases conducted by Ralph Head and Affiliates showed that more than half were unplanned. The primary motivating reason most frequently cited by these shoppers was; "I bought it because I saw it displayed."

These in-store decisions, then, are largely a product of *environmental* influences, such as pricing, availability of new or different products, and the existence of POP displays and signs. In other words, customers are highly motivated by their visual experiences at the store.

"Environmental marketing" is the term given to modifying the conditions at the retail level to create a more persuasive sales atmosphere. Layout, fixtures, lighting, product placement can all be manipulated to achieve different effects. And among the most important environmental marketing tools for both goods and services are POP signs and displays.

Highlights of the POPAI/DuPont Consumer Buying Habits Study are shown in Figure 2, page 717.

PROOF POSITIVE

Kenwood Electronics considered the need to communicate directly with prospective consumers when launching its new line of car stereo products. Their sophisticated counter-top demonstration unit was designed to educate consumers and the dealer's salesperson as well. The professional display showed all four components of Kenwood's new system, while the copy highlighted important features. When an interested customer turned the ignition key, the antenna emerged and the equipment was functional. This action display not only promoted Kenwood's image as a technical leader, but also directly and successfully sold the consumer through a combination of product information and "hands on" testing. Kenwood reported that stores using these POP displays outsold stores without the units by 80 percent.

POP materials often tie in with a seasonal sales promotion. But

Figure 2. In-Store Buying Decisions

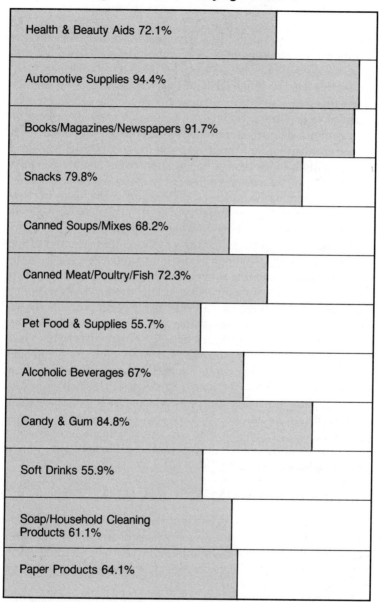

Health & Beauty Aids 72.1%

Automotive Supplies 94.4%

Books/Magazines/Newspapers 91.7%

Snacks 79.8%

Canned Soups/Mixes 68.2%

Canned Meat/Poultry/Fish 72.3%

Pet Food & Supplies 55.7%

Alcoholic Beverages 67%

Candy & Gum 84.8%

Soft Drinks 55.9%

Soap/Household Cleaning Products 61.1%

Paper Products 64.1%

Highlights from DuPont POPAI Consumer Buying Habits Study. Percentages of total supermarket sales for each product category resulting from a consumer decision made in the store are shown.

when POP is developed into a coordinated, storewide event, the results can be remarkable. STP Corporation created such a program for a refund promotion for STP oil and gas treatments, endorsed by racers Kyle and Richard Petty. A model race car was one of the two free-standing displays designed for the program which included case posters, shelf cards, banners, and trade promotion folders. This colorful, comprehensive campaign stimulated consumer enthusiasm and interest in the product. During the peak selling period, more than a half-million cases of STP products were on display in mass-merchandising stores, chain auto stores, drugstores and hardware stores. STP reported that sales in these stores incorporating the integrated POP materials were an astounding 900 percent above normal.

POP has been an effective sales generator in supermarkets from the very beginning. And one of the most productive places is the check-out line where idle customers are "trapped," awaiting their turn. The William Wrigley Jr. Company, producer of top-selling gum and candies, worked with a wire display firm to develop a permanent POP floor merchandising unit. The result was the creation of an 11-shelf display that exposed all products to full view, held adequate inventory, and was easy to assemble, load, and handle. More than 7,000 of these Top Sellers were distributed. The unit functions as a "confectionery department" by displaying and merchandising the top-selling product categories of all the leading manufacturers, in addition to Wrigley's own line on the higher, prime shelves. The results were outstanding. One food chain that installed 350 of these POP units reported a 130.3 percent jump in sales in a single quarter.

TRENDS IN RETAILING

John Naisbitt, business consultant and author, states, "The retailer who is able to identify a market niche and meet consumer expectations will fare well. Retailers who try to be all things to all people, or who miss a key component, will be washed away in a tidal wave of competition."

As of this writing, "warehouse clubs" have become the new darling of the retail trade. San Diego-based Price Clubs report an average of $60 million in annual sales for its 20 outlets with net profits of 3.4 percent.

Manufacturers' rebate coupons are the current hot retail promotional tool. The bet here is that, while it makes the final product price attractive, relatively few purchasers will bother to claim the rebate.

Chapter 35

Global Marketing

Global markets represent a great source of sales and profits, as indicated by the percentage of sales attributed to international operations by many companies in all fields. That more companies do not develop their overseas sales is due simply to a lack of knowledge of the technical requirements of export procedures, which are actually simple enough to easily become a routine process.

"Foreign trade is easy to get into," according to Thomas H. Coulter, director of the Chicago-Tokyo Bank and who has served as president of the Japan America Society of Chicago. He cites these factors as conducive to American exports:

- Pricing structures overseas provide greater margins, more profits.

- Less competition than in American markets.

- Every state has an Export Council.

- The U.S. International Trade Commission provides a wealth of help and information.

- In the case of Japan, the Japanese Trading Company is constantly and eagerly looking for imports.

- World trade has expanded at a rate of 15 percent compounded each year.

- International Trade Clubs are on the rise in the United States.

- Exports of services are a growing factor.

The big challenge to American marketing ingenuity and initiative lies in international trade. There is a world of markets, singly and in groups, private and governmental, industrial and consumer, waiting for U.S. goods and services. That it is a fertile field for sales and profits is evidenced in the annual reports of numerous corporations.

Four Kinds of Markets

International marketing usually falls into four classifications. Most companies sell to independent overseas distributors, who are responsible for local (in the foreign country) distribution. As a rule, payment is made through letters of credit and bank drafts. Freight forwarders handle all the details of making shipment abroad. Another channel for international distribution is through export-sales agencies, which usually pay for the merchandise in the U.S., have their own local outlets, and take care of all the shipping details.

Many markets, however, have import restrictions imposed by local governments, either to control the flow of their limited supply of United States dollars, to protect local industry, or to encourage the development of new industries.

In this case major American corporations establish manufacturing subsidiaries that import raw materials or the technical components to assemble or manufacture the product locally. These subsidiary companies often enjoy a large measure of autonomy from the parent company, since they are in the market and must act quickly to meet changing conditions. In addition, since they must meet local consumer demand by introducing products, models, or parts not made by the parent company, large corporations permit their subsidiaries to buy their requirements from company plants as well as outside plants in any country. This multinational policy is justified on the ground that sales would otherwise be lost. Also, it produces dividends that eventually find their way to the home office.

The fourth international marketing channel is through licensees. Licensing arrangements are justified where imports are restricted or the market is too small to warrant the cost of establishing a subsidiary company plant. Manufacturers license foreign companies to produce their products and to use their trademark, for a contractual fee. Though the fee is usually based on a percentage of sales, the parties may agree on a lump sum or annual fee.

For this, the U.S. manufacturer provides management, technical, and marketing assistance to the local licensee. The advantages of licensing are twofold: It eliminates the cost and headaches of building a plant and the U.S. manufacturer acquires a ready-built distributing organization. The major disadvantage is reduction of quality control.

For most companies, however, selling to independent distributors is the preferred method. As in the domestic field, the selection of the proper distributor will make or break the position of the manufacturer in any market. Major companies have regional managers or field representatives who will go to a country to investigate the possibilities and to compare the capabilities and resources of local organizations. Other companies depend on information supplied by the U.S. Department of Commerce, banks with international departments, or international transportation firms. The Department of Commerce supplies specific leads and will obtain special reports from U.S. consulates and commercial officers abroad at very nominal cost.

U.S. Export Restrictions

Although no formal or special license to engage in an export business is required, permission or a license to export most goods from the United States is required. Most items that require special permission or license for exportation are under the control of the Department of Commerce. Other departmental responsibilities include: 1) arms and implements of war, Department of State; 2) atomic and fissionable energy material, Atomic Energy Commission; 3) gold and U.S. silver coins, U.S. Department of Treasury; 4) narcotic drugs, Department of Justice; 5) natural gas and electric energy, U.S. Federal Power Commission; and 6) endangered wildlife, Interior Department.

Unless an exporter's products fall into one of the six exceptions listed, the exporter must consult the Department of Commerce to determine whether a specific license to export a product is required. The export licensing controls administered by the Department of Commerce apply to: 1) exports of commodities and technical data from the United States; 2) re-exports of U.S.-origin commodities and technical data from a foreign destination to another foreign destination; 3) U.S.-origin parts and components used in foreign countries to manufacture foreign products for exports; and 4) in some instances, the foreign-produced direct product of U.S.-origin technical data.

All regulations imposed by the Department of Commerce are published in the *Export Administration Regulations,* which is periodically revised and supplemented by the *Current Export Bulletin.* The respective department or bureau should be contacted for the current control regulations.

Types of Licenses. There are two types of licenses for exporting from the United States: a general license and a validated license.

- A general license is a privilege permitting exportation within limits without requiring that an application be filed or that a license document be issued.

- A validated license is a document authorizing exportation within the specific limitations it sets forth; it is issued only upon formal application.

Application must be made in accordance with procedures set forth in the *Export Administration Regulations.* Most commodities can be exported from the United States to free-world countries under a general license, but a validated license is required when exporting strategic goods and when exporting to unfriendly countries. Two criteria—the country of destination and the type of commodity to be exported—determine which type of license is needed for exportation requiring authorization by the Department of Commerce.

Joint Ventures

When doing business with foreign countries, exporting is always the primary objective. However, this may not always be possible. A second choice is to assemble, package, and partially manufacture the product in the host country. If neither is possible, a third choice is to wholly manufacture the product there. In the latter two cases, a joint venture arrangement may be desirable. The relative percentages of ownership are based on whether there is a requirement that majority interest be held by the national or the host country and whether the U.S. firm desires to minimize or limit its initial investment.

The equity contributed by the U.S. firm can vary according to the circumstances. An indication of serious interest will greatly enhance the relationship's desirability to the potential business partner. In this way your associates' nationalistic pride is preserved.

A careful review of relative costs and tax implications should be made in order to weigh the advantages of all available options.

The Multinational Company

In the face of the shifting economic patterns of world markets, the multinational corporation has emerged as the force to bridge the gaps of marketing systems. Leaping over tariff barriers and smoothing the path through local taxes and monetary differences, profitable operations become possible.

The multinational corporation is not unique to the United States. Every major country in the world is represented with trading companies in the ranks of industry. As money values fluctuate, the importance of diversified investment becomes essential to maintain a balanced financial structure and profitable sales. As costs ebb and flow, diversion of material and labor is manipulated back and forth among favorable manufacturing bases to take advantage of local factors.

In recent years, the major companies of the world have truly become international. Technologies have been licensed and cross licensed. Joint ventures have been based on the most compatible arrangements possible. Giants of industry have come to realize that to survive in the major markets of the world, they must be located within them.

Common Markets—International Trade Blocs

Over the past decade, regional economic organizations have had a significant impact on world trade in agricultural and industrial products. A free trade area becomes a customs union when its members agree to maintain a common external tariff on imports from nonmembers. A customs union that removes all internal barriers to permit the free flow of labor, capital, goods, and services becomes a common market.

Among these regional organizations are the European Economic Community, the European Free Trade Association, the Andean Common Market, the Latin American Free Trade Association, the Central American Common Market, the Caribbean Free Trade Association, and the Association of Southeast Asian Nations. Foreign trade of the People's Republic of China, the USSR, and the countries of Eastern Europe is handled by government monopolies.

The First Steps in Exporting

To get started, the novice exporter must assess the overseas appeal of the product to be offered. If it has appeal, the exporter must develop a sales plan and then must decide whether to sell directly or indirectly to foreign customers. Although even these preliminary steps may sometimes seem bewildering, plenty of help is available, starting with the U.S. Department of Commerce. The many sources of export assistance are discussed in the opening chapters of the Department's new *A Basic Guide to Exporting*, summarized in the following passages. The publication (stock number: 003-009-00487-0) may be obtained for $8.50 from the Superintendent of Documents, U.S. Government Printing Office, Washington, D.C. 20402; telephone (202) 783-3238.

There are several ways to measure a product's potential in overseas markets. One of the most important is its success in domestic markets. If a company is successful in selling a product in the U.S. market, there is a good chance that it will be successful in selling in markets abroad, wherever similar needs and conditions exist. In markets that differ significantly from the U.S. market, some products may have limited potential. Significant differences may relate to climate and environment factors, local availability of raw materials or product alternatives, lower wage costs, and lower purchasing power. If a product is successful in the United States, its success in export markets may necessitate a careful analysis of why it sells here and then the selection of similar markets abroad. In this way, little or no product modification is required.

If a product is not new or unique, preliminary and low-cost market research is probably already available that can facilitate the assessment of its overseas market potential. Trade statistics, available in many local libraries, can give a preliminary indication of markets for a particular product in most countries. If a product is unique and has important advantages that are hard to duplicate abroad, market data may not be available, yet chances are very good for finding an export market.

Finally, even if the sales of a product are now declining in the United States, sizable export markets may exist, especially if the product once did well in the United States but is now losing market share to more technically advanced products. Countries that are less developed may not need state-of-the-art technology and may instead have a surprisingly healthy demand for U.S. products that are older, less expensive, and less sophisticated.

Making the Export Decision

Once a company determines that it has exportable products, it must still consider other factors, such as:

- What does the company want to gain from exporting? Is exporting consistent with other company goals?

- What demands will exporting place on the company's key resources—management, personnel, production capacity, and finance—and how will these demands be met?

- Are the expected benefits worth the costs or would company resources be better used for developing new domestic business?

The Value of Planning

Many companies begin export activities without a careful screening of markets or options for market entry. While these companies may encounter a measure of success, they may overlook better export opportunities. In the event that early export efforts are not successful, the company may unwisely abandon exporting altogether. Formulating an export strategy, based on good information and assessment, makes it more likely that the best among several options will be chosen, that resources will be used effectively, and that efforts will be carried through to completion.

The purpose of the export plan is to assemble facts, constraints, and goals, and to create an action statement. The statement includes specific objectives; it sets forth time schedules for implementation; and it marks milestones in order to measure the degree of success and help motivate personnel.

The basic elements of a plan need not be elaborate or detailed—nor should they be the first time around. However, at a minimum, the following questions should be answered:

1. What countries are targeted for sales development?

2. What strategy is to be exploited in these markets?

3. What specific operational steps must be taken and when?

4. How many dollars and how much management time can be committed to each element of an export plan?

5. What will be the framework for implementing different elements of the plan?

6. How will results be evaluated and used to modify efforts?

One key to developing a successful plan is the participation of all personnel who will be affected and involved in the exporting process. All aspects of an export plan should be agreed upon by those who will ultimately execute them.

A clearly written marketing strategy offers five immediate benefits:

1. Written plans help ensure a commitment to exporting for an evaluation of results.

2. Written plans display their strengths and weaknesses more readily. This will be of great help in formulating and polishing an export strategy.

3. Written plans are not as easily forgotten, overlooked, or ignored by those charged with executing them. If deviation from the original plan occurs, it is likely to be due to a deliberate choice to do so.

4. Written plans are easier to communicate to others and are less likely to be misunderstood.

5. Written plans allocate responsibilities and provide for an evaluation of results.

All of these advantages of written plans are important, but the first is especially noteworthy. Unless top management is willing to commit itself to the steps of a clearly written plan, it is all too easy to let initial effort die for lack of follow-through.

The Planning Process and the Result

A crucial first step in planning is to develop broad consensus among key management officials on the company's goals, objectives, capabilities, and constraints.

The first time an export plan is made, the efforts should be kept simple. The initial planning efforts can generate much information and insight that can later be incorporated into more sophisticated planning.

Once the groundwork has been laid, the export plan should be written. It need only be a few pages long, especially for a first draft, since important information may not yet be available. The plan should be a working document that can be used actively as a management tool. The objectives in the plan should be used to measure the success of different strategies when compared to actual results. As more information and experience are gained, the company can modify the plan and make it more specific.

A detailed plan is recommended for companies that intend to export directly. Companies choosing indirect export methods may need much simpler plans.

Approaches to Exporting

The way a company chooses to export its product can have a significant effect on its export plan and specific marketing strategies. The basic distinction among approaches to exporting concerns the level of involvement of the firm in the export process. There are at least four approaches, which may be used alone or in combination:

1. *Filling orders from domestic buyers who then export the product.* These sales are indistinguishable from other domestic sales as far as the original seller is concerned. Someone else has decided the product in question meets foreign demand. That party takes all the risk and handles all of the exporting details, in some cases without even the awareness of the original seller. Many companies take a stronger interest in exporting when they discover that their product is already being sold overseas.

2. *Seeking out domestic buyers who represent foreign end-users or customers.* There are a large number of U.S. and foreign corporations, general contractors, foreign trading companies, foreign government agencies, foreign distributors and retailers, and others in the United States who purchase for export. These buyers are a large market for a wide variety of goods and services. In this case, a company may know its product is being exported, but the risk is on the buyer as to whether or not the product meets foreign demand. The buyer also handles all the details.

3. *Exporting indirectly through intermediaries.* With this approach, a company engages the services of an intermediary firm capable of finding foreign markets and buyers for its products. Export management companies (EMCs), Export Trading Companies (ETCs), international trade consultants, and other intermediaries can give the exporter access to well established expertise and trade contacts. Yet, the exporter can still retain considerable control over the process and can realize some of the other benefits of exporting, such as learning more about foreign competitors, new technolo-

gies, and other market opportunities. While risks increase with this option, so do the potential profits.

4. *Exporting directly.* This approach means nearly total involvement in the process. That is, almost complete control is exercised from market research and planning through foreign distribution. It also involves significant commitment of management time to achieve success. This approach is not appropriate for everyone nor for every foreign market, but for some it represents the best way to achieve maximum profits and plan for long-term growth.

Obtaining Export Advice

For companies making initial plans to export or to export in new areas, considerable advice and assistance is available at little or no cost. It is easy, through lack of experience, to overestimate the problems involved in exporting or to get embroiled in difficulties that can be avoided. For these and other good reasons, it is important to get expert counseling and assistance from the beginning.

A brief overview follows of sources of assistance available through federal, state, and local government agencies and in the private sector.

Department of Commerce. The scope of services provided by the U.S. Department of Commerce to exporters is vast but often overlooked by many businesses. The primary organization within the Department dealing with U.S. exports is the International Trade Administration (ITA).

Although ITA itself has many important divisions, each with a variety of services and products, the process of using these services has been streamlined. In each local area, it is only necessary to contact a single agency: the District Office of the U.S. and Foreign Commercial Service (US&FCS). Through the local district office, the exporter has access to all assistance available through ITA and to trade information gathered overseas by US&FCS commercial officers in U.S. embassies and consulates.

The US&FCS has 48 district offices and 24 branch offices located in industrial and commercial centers throughout the United

States and Puerto Rico. These offices provide information and counseling to the business community. Each District Office can give information about:

- Trade and investment opportunities abroad
- Foreign markets for U.S. products and services
- Services to locate and evaluate overseas buyers and representatives
- Financing aid to exporters
- U.S. Export-Import Bank
- Tax advantages of exporting
- International trade exhibitions
- Export documentation requirements
- Economic statistics of foreign countries
- U.S. export licensing and foreign nation import requirements

A key element in the aid offered by the district office is the professional counseling provided by trade specialists to interested firms. Each office is headed by a director and is supported by a contingent of trade specialists and other staff. These professionals can first help a company's decision makers gain a basic understanding of profitable opportunities in exporting and assist them in evaluating the company's market potential overseas.

The next step may be to guide the company through the entire process from evaluating and choosing a market to making its first shipment. Once a firm has made its first overseas sale, chances are good the company will want to make more. The US&FCS District Offices and overseas commercial posts can actively identify additional sales leads for the firm and search for new market opportunities.

To encourage and assist U.S. businesses to enter international trade, US&FCS trade specialists draw upon the resources of the entire Department of Commerce for many export marketing aids and services. These services include the following:

- Market research

- Assistance in promoting U.S. products in overseas markets

- Computerized trade opportunities

- Help in locating overseas agents or distributors

- Trade missions and introductions between foreign buyers and U.S. firms

- Export seminars and conferences

- Participation in major international trade fairs

- Customer evaluations

Small Business Administration. Through its field offices in cities throughout the United States, the U.S. Small Business Administration (SBA) provides counseling to potential and current small business exporters. These services, available at no cost to eligible recipients, include the following:

1. *Export counseling.* Export counseling services are furnished to potential and current small business exporters by executives, advanced business students, and professional consultants. Members of the Service Corps of Retired Executives (SCORE) and the Active Corps of Executives (ACE), with years of practical experience in international trade, assist small firms in evaluating their export potential and strengthening their domestic operations by identifying financial, managerial, or technical problems. These advisors also can help small firms develop and implement basic export marketing plans, which show where and how to sell goods abroad.

2. *Small Business Institute/Small Business Development Centers.* Through the Small Business Institute, advanced business students from more than 450 colleges and universities provide in-depth, long-term counseling under faculty supervision to small businesses. Additional export counseling and assistance are offered through Small Business De-

velopment Centers, which are located within some colleges and universities. Students in these two programs provide technical help by developing an export marketing feasibility study and analysis for their client firms.

3. *Call Contact Program.* A third facet of the SBA counseling service is the Call Contact Program, which uses professional management and technical consultants. This program is employed where firms require highly sophisticated marketing information and production technology to identify and service overseas markets.

4. *Export training.* SBA Field Offices co-sponsor export training programs with the Department of Commerce, other federal agencies, and various private sector international trade organizations. These programs are conducted by experienced international traders.

5. *Financial assistance.* The SBA operates loan guarantee and direct loan programs to assist small business exporters.

6. *Legal advice.* Through an arrangement with the Federal Bar Association (FBA), exporters may receive initial exporting legal assistance. Under this program, qualified attorneys from the International Law Council of the FBA, working through SBA Field Offices, provide free initial consultations to small companies on the legal aspects of exporting.

For information on any of the programs funded by SBA, contact the nearest SBA field office.

Department of Agriculture. The U.S. Department of Agriculture's (USDA) export promotion efforts are centered in the Foreign Agricultural Service (FAS), but other USDA agencies offer services to the U.S. exporter of agricultural products. These include the Economic Research Service, the Office of Transportation, the Animal & Plant Health Inspection Service, the Food Safety and Inspection Service, and the Federal Grain Inspection Service. A wide variety of other valuable programs is offered, such as promotion of U.S. farm products in foreign markets, services of commodity and marketing specialists in Washington, D.C., trade fair exhibits, publications and information services, and financing programs. For more information on programs contact the Director of Export Programs Division, FAS, U.S. Department of Agriculture, Washington, D.C.; telephone: (202) 447-6343.

State governments. State development agencies, Departments of Commerce, and other departments within state governments often provide valuable assistance to exporters within the state. State export development programs are growing rapidly. In many areas, county and city economic development agencies also have export assistance programs. The aid offered by these groups typically includes:

- *Export education.* Helping the exporter analyze export potential and orienting the firm to export techniques and strategies. This help may take the form of group seminars or individual counseling sessions.

- *Marketing assistance.* Markets for U.S. products or services, including trade leads, are identified.

- *Market development.* Assistance is provided in selecting export strategies and obtaining financing and counseling on packaging, shipping, etc.

- *Trade missions.* The organization of trips abroad enabling exporters to call on potential foreign customers.

- *Trade shows.* The organizing and sponsoring of exhibitions of state-produced goods and services in overseas markets.

Readers interested in the role played by state development agencies in promoting and supporting exports may also wish to contact the National Association of State Development Agencies (NASDA), 444 North Capitol Street, Washington, D.C. 20001; telephone: (202) 624-5411.

To determine if a particular county or city has local export assistance programs, contact the appropriate economic development agency.

Commercial Banks. More than 300 U.S. banks have international banking departments with specialists familiar with specific foreign countries and various types of commodities and transactions. These large banks, located in major U.S. cities, maintain correspondent relationships with smaller banks throughout the country. Larger banks also maintain correspondent relationships with banks in most foreign countries or operate their own overseas branches, providing a direct channel to foreign customers.

International banking specialists are generally well informed about export matters, even in areas that fall outside the usual limits of international banking. If they are unable to provide direct guidance or assistance, they may be able to refer inquiries to other specialists who can. Banks frequently provide consultation and guidance free of charge to their clients, since they derive income primarily from loans to the exporter and from fees for special services. Many banks also have publications available to help exporters. These materials often cover particular countries and their business practices and can be a valuable tool for initial familiarization with foreign industry.

The many services a commercial bank may perform for its clients include:

- Advice on export regulations

- Exchange of currencies

- Assistance in financing exports

- Collection of foreign invoices, drafts, letters of credit, and other foreign receivables

- Transfer of funds to other countries

- Letters of introduction and letters of credit for travelers

- Credit information on potential buyers overseas

- Credit assistance to the exporter's foreign buyers

Trading Companies. Trading companies are of many different types, ranging from giant international companies, many foreign owned, to highly specialized, small operations. Export Management Companies and Export Trading Companies are similar types of trading companies that provide a multitude of services, such as performing market research, appointing overseas distributors or commission representatives, exhibiting a client's products at international trade shows, advertising, shipping, and arranging documentation. In short, the trading company can take full responsibility for the export end of the business, relieving the manufacturer of all the details except filling orders. Trading companies may work simultaneously for a number of exporters, and they may buy and sell or work on the basis of a commission, salary, or retainer plus commission. Often, products of a trading company's clients are related, although the items usually are noncompetitive. The advantage of a trading company is that it can immediately make available marketing resources that would take years for a smaller firm to develop on its own. Many trading companies also finance sales and extend credit, facilitating prompt payment to the exporter.

World Trade Clubs. Local or regional world trade clubs are composed of area business people who represent firms engaged in international trade and shipping, banks, forwarders, customs brokers, government agencies, and other service organizations involved in world trade. These clubs conduct educational programs on international trade and organize promotional events to stimulate interest in world trade.

By participating in a local association, a company can receive valuable and timely advice on world markets and opportunities from business people who are already knowledgeable on virtually any facet of international business. Another important advantage of membership in a local world trade club is the availability of benefits—such as services, discounts, and contacts—in affiliated clubs from foreign countries.

Chambers of Commerce and Trade Associations. Many local chambers of commerce and major trade associations in the United States provide sophisticated and extensive services for members interested in exporting. Such services include:

- Export seminars, workshops and roundtables geared to specific industry interests

- Documenting (providing certificates of origin)

- Trade promotion, including overseas trade missions, mailings, and event planning

- Organization of U.S. pavilions in foreign trade shows

- Contacts with foreign companies and distributors

- Transportation routings and consolidating shipments

- Hosting of visiting trade missions

- International activities at their own domestic trade shows

In addition, some industry associations can supply detailed information on market demand for products in selected countries and refer members to export management companies.

Industry trade associations typically collect and maintain files on international trade news and trends affecting manufacturers. Often they publish articles and newsletters that include government research as soon as it is made available.

American Chambers of Commerce Abroad. A valuable and reliable source of market information in any foreign country is the local American chamber of commerce. Secretaries of these organizations are knowledgeable about local trade opportunities, actual and potential competition, periods of maximum trade activity, and similar considerations. American chambers of commerce abroad usually handle inquiries from any U.S. business. Detailed service, however, is ordinarily undertaken free of charge for services rendered to non-members.

International Trade Consultants and Other Advisors. International trade consultants can advise and assist a manufacturer on all aspects of foreign marketing.

These consultants can locate and qualify foreign joint-venture partners and conduct feasibility studies for the sale of manufacturing rights, the location and construction of manufacturing rights, the location and construction of manufacturing facilities, and the establishment of foreign branches. After sales agreements are completed, trade consultants can ensure that follow-through is smooth.

Trade consultants usually specialize by subject matter and by global area or country. For example, firms may specialize in high technology exports to the Far East. Their consultants can advise on which agents or distributors are likely to be successful, what kinds of promotion are needed, who the competitors are, and how to deal with them. They are also knowledgeable about foreign government regulations, contract laws, and taxation.

Many large accounting firms, law firms, and specialized marketing firms provide international trade consulting services.

Consultants are of greatest value to a firm that knows exactly what it wants. For this reason, and because private consultants are expensive, it pays to take full advantage of publicly-funded sources of advice before hiring a consultant.

Global Market Research

At the outset, a firm wishing to expand into exporting must conduct market research to determine which foreign markets have the best potential for its products. Results of this research inform the firm of:

- The largest markets for its product

- The fastest growing markets

- Market trends and outlook

- Market conditions and practices

- Competitive firms and products

A firm may begin to export without conducting any market research if it receives unsolicited orders from abroad. While this type of selling is valuable, the firm may discover even more promising markets by conducting a systematic search. A firm opting to export indirectly by using an export management company may wish to select markets to enter before selecting the EMC, since many EMCs have strengths in specific markets but not in others.

A firm may research a market by using either primary or secondary data resources. In conducting primary market research, a company collects data directly from the foreign marketplace through interviews, surveys, and other direct contact with representatives and potential buyers. Primary market research has the advantage of being tailored to the company's needs and provides answers to specific questions, but the collection of such data is time-consuming and expensive.

In conducting secondary market research, a company collects data from compiled sources, such as trade statistics for a country or a product. Working with secondary sources is less expensive and helps the company to focus its marketing efforts. Although secondary data sources are critical to market research, they do have limitations. The most recent statistics for some countries may be over two years old. Product breakdowns may be too broad to be of much value to a company. Statistics on services are often unavailable. Finally, statistics may be distorted by incomplete data gathering techniques. Yet, even with these limitations, secondary research is a valuable and relatively easy first step for a company to take. It may be the only step needed if the company decides to export indirectly through an intermediary, since the other firm may have advanced research capabilities.

Because of the expense of primary market research, most firms rely on secondary data sources. Secondary market research is conducted in three basic ways:

1. The first is by keeping abreast of world events that influence the international marketplace, watching for announcement of specific projects, or simply visiting likely markets. For example, a thawing of political hostilities often leads to the opening of economic channels between countries.

2. The second method is through analysis of trade and economic statistics. Trade statistics are generally compiled by product category (often by SIC code) and by country. These statistics provide the U.S. firm with information concerning shipments of its products over specified periods of time. Demographic and general economic statistics, such as population size and makeup, per capita income, and production levels by industry can be important indicators of the market potential for a company's products.

3. The third method is to obtain the advice of experts. A company may accomplish this by:

- Contacting trade specialists at the Department of Commerce and other government agencies

- Attending seminars, workshops, and international trade shows

- Hiring an international trade and marketing consultant

- Talking to successful exporters of similar products

- Contacting trade and industry association staff

Gathering and evaluating secondary market research can be complex and tedious. However, there are several publications available that can help simplify the process. The following approach to market research refers to these publications and other resources.

A STEP-BY-STEP APPROACH TO MARKET RESEARCH

The U.S. company may find the following approach useful:

- **Screen potential markets**

   1. Obtain export statistics that indicate product exports to various countries. *Export Statistics Profiles (ESP)* from the Department of Commerce can assist. If ESPs are not available for a certain product, the firm should consult the *Custom Statistical Service* (Commerce), *Foreign Trade Report, FT 410* (Census), *Export Information System Data Reports* (Small Business Administration) or *Annual Worldwide Industry Reviews* (Commerce).

   2. Identify five to ten large and fast growing markets for the firm's product. Look at these over time (the past three to five years). Has market growth been consistent year to year? Did import growth occur even during periods of economic recession? If not, did growth resume with economic recovery?

3. Identify some smaller but fast-emerging markets that may provide ground floor opportunities. If the market is just beginning to open up, there may be fewer competitors than in established markets. Growth rates should be substantially higher in these countries to qualify as up-and-coming markets, given the lower starting point.

4. Target three to five of the most statistically promising markets for further assessment. Consult with Commerce Department district offices, business associates, freight forwarders and others to help refine targeted markets.

- **Assess targeted markets**

1. Examine trends for company products, as well as trends regarding related products that could influence demand. Calculate overall consumption of the product and the amount accounted for by imports. *International Market Research (IMR), Country Market Surveys (CMSs), Country Trade Statistics, Export Statistics Profiles, Annual Worldwide Industry Reviews,* (all Commerce), give economic backgrounds and market trends for each country. Demographic information (population, age, etc.) can be obtained from *World Population* (Census) and *Statistical Yearbook* (United Nations).

2. Ascertain the sources of competition, including the extent of domestic industry production and the major foreign countries the firm is competing against in each targeted market. *IMR Studies* and *CMSs* (both from Commerce) can be helpful. Look at U.S. market share.

3. Analyze factors affecting marketing and use of the product in each market, such as end-user sectors, channels of distribution, cultural idiosyncrasies, and business practices. Again, *IMR Studies* and *CMSs* are useful.

4. Identify any foreign barriers (tariff or non-tariff) for the product being imported into the country. Identify any U.S. barriers (such as export controls) affecting exports to the country. *IMR Studies* and *CMSs* are useful.

5. Identify any U.S. or foreign government incentives to promote exporting the product or service. Once again, *IMR Studies* and *CMSs* are helpful.

DRAW CONCLUSIONS

After analyzing the data, the company may conclude that its marketing resources would be better used if applied to a few countries. In general, company efforts should be directed to fewer than 10 markets if the firm is new to exporting; one or two countries may be enough to start with. The company's internal resources should help determine its level of effort.

Indirect and Direct Exporting

The question for beginning exporters is whether to sell overseas directly or to find a go-between to do it for you.

Several factors should be considered when deciding whether to market indirectly or directly, including:

- The size of the firm

- The nature of its products

- Previous export experience and expertise

- Business conditions in the selected overseas markets

The paramount consideration is the level of resources a company is willing to devote to the international marketing effort.

INDIRECT EXPORTING

The principal advantage of indirect marketing for a smaller U.S. company is that it provides a way to penetrate foreign markets without getting involved in the complexities and risks of exporting. There are several kinds of intermediary firms that provide a range of export services; each type offers distinct advantages.

Commission agents. Commission or buying agents are "finders" for foreign firms that want to purchase U.S. products.

They seek to obtain the desired items at the lowest possible price and are paid a commission by their foreign clients. In some cases, they may be foreign government agencies or quasi-government firms empowered to locate and purchase desired goods. Foreign government purchasing missions are one example.

Export management companies. An export management company acts as the export department for one or several manufacturers of noncompetitive products. It solicits and transacts business in the names of the manufacturers it represents or in its own name for a commission, salary, or retainer plus commission. Some EMCs provide immediate payment for the manufacturer's products by either arranging financing or directly purchasing products for resale. Typically, only larger EMCs can afford to purchase or finance exports.

There are more than 2,000 EMCs in the United States, the majority of which are small. Due to their size limitations, EMCs usually specialize either by product, by foreign market, or both. Because of their specialization, the best EMCs know their products and the markets they serve very well and usually have well-established networks of foreign distributors already in place. This immediate access to foreign markets is one of the principal reasons for using an EMC, since establishing a productive relationship with a foreign representative may be a costly and lengthy process.

One disadvantage in using an EMC is that a manufacturer may lose control over foreign sales. Most manufacturers are rightly concerned that their product and company image be well maintained in foreign markets. An important way for a company to retain sufficient control in such an arrangement is to carefully select an EMC that can meet the company's needs and maintain close communications with it. For example, a company may ask for regular reports on efforts to market its products and may require approval of certain types of efforts, such as advertising programs or service arrangements. If a company wants to maintain this type of relationship with an EMC, it should negotiate points of concern before entering an agreement, since not all EMCs are willing to comply with the company's concerns.

A description of services rendered to exporters by EMCs (and suggestions for choosing an appropriate firm) is available through the U.S. Department of Commerce pamphlet, *The EMC—Your Export Department* (Publications Distribution, Room 1617D, U.S. Department of Commerce, Washington, D.C. 20230). Also, the Association of Export Management Companies in New York has a list of EMCs in different regions: *The Directory of Leading U.S. Export Management Companies* is available for $45 from Bergano Book Company, P.O. Box 190, Fairfield, Conn. 06430.

Export trading companies. An export trading company is an organization designed to facilitate the export of U.S. goods and services. It can be either a trade intermediary, providing export-related services to producers, or an organization set up by producers themselves. An ETC is similar to an export management company. Traditionally, however, EMCs do not take title to goods being exported and typically provide only export facilitation services. An ETC is generally understood to be an organization that provides a broader range of services than an EMC, though there may be little practical distinction.

The goals of the Export Trading Company Act, passed in 1982, are to stimulate U.S. exports by: 1) promoting and encouraging the formation of export trading companies, 2) expanding the options available for export financing by permitting bank holding companies to invest in export trading companies and reducing restrictions on trade finance provided by financial institutions, and 3) reducing uncertainty regarding the application of U.S. antitrust law to export operations.

Firms can obtain further information from the Office of Export Trading Company Affairs, Room 5618, U.S. Department of Commerce, Washington, D.C. 20230; tel. (202) 377-5131. The *Export Trading Company Guidebook* and *Partners in Export Trade,* a contact facilitation services directory, can be obtained from that office.

Export agents, merchants, or remarketers. Export agents, merchants, or remarketers purchase products directly from the manufacturer, packing and marking the products according to their own specifications. They then sell overseas through their contacts in their own names, and assume all risks for accounts.

In transactions with export agents, merchants, or remarketers, a U.S. firm relinquishes control over the marketing promotion of its product, which could have an adverse effect on future sales efforts abroad. For example, the product could be underpriced or incorrectly positioned in the market, or after-sales service could be neglected.

Piggyback marketing. Piggyback marketing is an arrangement in which one manufacturer or service firm distributes another's product or service. The most common piggybacking situation is when a U.S. company has a contract with an overseas buyer to provide a wide range of products or services. Often, this company does not produce all of the products it is under contract to provide, and it turns to other U.S. companies to provide the remaining products. The original U.S. producer piggybacks its products to the international marketplace, generally without incurring the marketing and distribution costs associated with exporting. Successful arrangements usually require that the product lines be complementary and also that they be appealing to the same customers.

State-controlled trading companies. Some socialist countries have state trading monopolies that control all foreign trade. Worldwide changes in foreign policy, however, can have a profound impact on international trade with these countries. Because of this, they may become important markets in the future. For the time being, however, export opportunities to most socialist countries are found primarily for such items as raw materials, agricultural machinery, and manufacturing equipment, rather than high-technology products, consumer, or household goods. This is due to the shortage of foreign exchange and the emphasis on self-sufficiency, as well as national security concerns.

DIRECT EXPORTING

The advantages of direct exporting for a U.S. company include more control over the export process, potentially higher profits, and closer relationship to the overseas buyer and marketplace.

These advantages do not come easily, however, since the U.S. company needs to devote more time, personnel, and other corporate resources than are needed with indirect exporting.

When a company chooses to export directly to foreign markets, bypassing the use of EMCs or other intermediaries in the United States, it usually makes internal organizational changes to support more complex functions. A direct exporter normally selects the markets it wishes to penetrate, chooses the best channels of distribution for each market, and then makes specific foreign business connections in order to sell its product.

Organizing for exporting. A company new to exporting generally treats its export sales no differently from domestic sales, using existing personnel and organizational structures. As international sales and inquiries increase, however, the company may separate the management of its exports from that of its domestic sales.

The advantages of separating international from domestic business include the centralization of specialized skills needed to deal with the international marketplace. Another advantage is a focused marketing effort, one that is more likely to lead to increased international sales. A possible disadvantage of such a separation is the less efficient use of corporate resources due to segmentation.

When a company separates international from domestic business, it may do so at different levels within the organization. For example, when a company first begins to export, it may create an export department with a full- or part-time manager who reports to the head of domestic sales and marketing. At later stages a company may choose to increase the autonomy of the export department to the point of creating an international division that reports directly to the president.

Larger companies at advanced stages of exporting may choose to retain the international division or to organize along product or geographic lines. If a company has distinct product lines, it may choose to create an international department within each product division. A company with products that have common end-users may choose to organize geographically; for example, it may form a division for Europe, another for the Far East, etc.

These examples of organizing a separate international structure within a company generally apply once international sales become significant or within a large company with substantial financial resources. A small company's initial needs may be satisfied by a single export manager who has responsibility for many international activities.

Regardless of how a company organizes for exporting, it should ensure that the organization facilitates the marketer's job. Successful marketing skills can help the firm overcome the handicap of operating in an unfamiliar market. Experience has shown that a company's success in foreign markets depends less on the unique attributes of its products than on its marketing methods.

Once a company has been organized to handle exporting, the proper channel of distribution needs to be selected in each market. These channels include agents, distributors, retailers, and end-users.

Sales representatives or agents. Overseas, a sales representative is the equivalent of a manufacturers' representative here in the United States. The representative uses the company's product literature and samples to present the product to potential buyers. The sales representative usually works on a commission basis, assumes no risk or responsibility, and is under contract for a definite period of time (renewable by mutual agreement). The contract defines territory, terms of sale, method of compensation, and other details. The sales representative may operate on either an exclusive or nonexclusive basis.

Distributors. The foreign distributor is a merchant who purchases merchandise from a U.S. exporter (often at substantial discount) and resells it at a profit. The foreign distributor generally provides support and service for the product, relieving the U.S. company of these responsibilities. The distributor usually carries an inventory of products, a sufficient supply of spare parts, and maintains adequate facilities and personnel for normal servicing operations. The distributor normally carries noncompetitive but complementary products.

The payment terms and length of association between the U.S. company and the foreign distributor is established by contract.

Some U.S. companies prefer to begin with a relatively short trial period and then extend the contract if the relationship proves satisfactory to both parties.

Foreign retailers. A company may also sell directly to a foreign retailer, although in such transactions, products are generally limited to consumer lines. This method relies mainly on traveling sales representatives who directly contact foreign retailers, though results may be accomplished by mailing catalogs, brochures, or other literature. While the direct mail approach can eliminate commissions and traveling expenses, a firm that uses it may find that its products are not receiving proper consideration.

Direct sales to end-users. A U.S. business may sell its products or services directly to end-users in foreign countries. These buyers can be foreign governments, institutions—such as hospitals, banks, and schools—or businesses. Buyers can be identified at trade shows, through international publications, or through U.S. government contact programs, such as the Department of Commerce's Export Mailing List Service.

The U.S. company should be aware that if a product is sold in such a direct fashion, the exporter is responsible for shipping, payment collection, and product servicing, unless other arrangements are made. If the cost of providing these services is not built into the export price, a company could end up making far less than originally intended.

Locating foreign representatives and buyers. A company that chooses to use foreign representatives may meet them during overseas business trips or at domestic and international trade shows. There are other methods that are effective and can be employed without leaving the United States. The availability of good secondary sources of information does not imply that travel is not necessary; however, a company can save time by first doing homework in the United States. These methods include use of the contract program of the U.S. Department of Commerce's U.S. and Foreign Commercial Service, banks and service organizations, and publications.

Contacting and evaluating foreign representatives. Once the U.S. company has identified a number of potential agents or distributors in the selected market, it should write directly to each. Just as the U.S. firm is seeking information on the foreign representative, the representative is interested in corporate and product information on the U.S. firm. Therefore, the firm should provide full information on its history, resources, personnel, the product line, previous export activity, and all other pertinent matters. The prospective representative may want more information than the company normally provides to a casual buyer. The firm may wish to include a photograph or two of plant facilities and products.

A U.S. firm should investigate potential representatives carefully before entering into an agreement. To evaluate the qualifications of potential overseas agents and distributors, the U.S. firm needs to know the following information:

- Current status and history of the firm, including the background on the group's principal officers;

- Personnel and other resources (salespeople, warehouse and service facilities, etc.);

- Sales territory that the representative covers;

- Methods of introducing new products into each respective sales territory;

- Names and addresses of U.S. firms that the agent or distributorship currently represents; and

- Data on whether the representative can meet special requirements of the U.S. company.

A U.S. company may obtain much of this information from business associates who currently work with foreign representatives. In addition, the company may wish to obtain at least two supporting business and credit reports to ensure that the distributor or agent is reputable. By using a second credit report from another source, the U.S. firm may gain new or more complete information. Reports are available from commercial firms and from the U.S. Department of Commerce's World Traders Data Reports (WTDR) program.

A WTDR is a background report prepared on a specific foreign firm by the US&FCS commercial officers overseas. WTDRs give such information as the type of organization, year established, relative size, number of employees, general reputation, territory covered, language preferred, product lines handled, principal owners, financial references, and trade references. Each also contains a general narrative report by the U.S. commercial officer conducting the investigation concerning the reliability of the foreign firm. Reports are not available for all countries. A fee is charged per report. Request forms and further information on this service are available from any US&FCS district office.

Commercial firms and banks are also sources of credit information on overseas representatives. They can provide information directly or from their correspondent banks or branches overseas. Directories of international business may also provide credit information on foreign firms.

If the U.S. company has the information necessary, it may wish to contact a few of the foreign firm's U.S. clients to obtain an evaluation of the representative's character, reliability, efficiency, and past performance. It is important for the U.S. firm to learn about other product lines that the foreign firm represents to protect itself against possible conflicts of interest.

Once the company has established correspondence with foreign representatives, it may wish to travel to the foreign country to observe the size, condition, and location of offices and warehouses. In addition, the U.S. company should meet the sales force and try to assess its strength in the marketplace.

Negotiating an agreement with a foreign representative. When the U.S. company has found a prospective representative that meets its requirements, the next step is to negotiate a foreign sales agreement. US&FCS district offices can provide counseling to firms planning to negotiate foreign sales agreements with representatives and distributors.

The potential representative is interested in the company's pricing structure and profit potential. Representatives are also concerned with the terms of payment, product regulation, competitors and their market shares, the amount of support provided by the U.S. firm (sales aids, promotional material, advertising, etc.), training for sales and service staff, and the company's ability to deliver on schedule.

The agreement may contain provisions that the foreign representative:

1. Not have business dealings with competitive firms (this provision may cause problems in some European countries, and may also cause problems under U.S. antitrust laws);

2. Not reveal any confidential information in a way that would prove injurious, detrimental, or competitive to the U.S. firm;

3. Not enter into agreements binding to the U.S. firm; and

4. Refer all inquiries received from outside the designated sales territory to the U.S. firm for appropriate action.

To ensure a conscientious sales effort from the foreign representative, the agreement should include a requirement that the foreign representative apply the utmost skill and ability to the sale of the product for the compensation named in the contract. It may be appropriate to include performance requirements regarding a minimum sales volume and an expected rate of increase.

The U.S. company should seek to avoid provisions that could be contrary to U.S. antitrust laws. The new Export Trading Company Act provides a means to obtain antitrust protection when two or more companies combine for exporting. In addition, the U.S. firm should obtain legal advice when preparing and entering into any foreign agreement. The exporter should be aware of U.S. and foreign laws that govern such contracts. In some countries national laws give extraordinary protection to the representative at the expense of the exporter and may make termination of the contract difficult or costly.

World Commercial Holidays

Liberia is unlikely to attract American business visitors, particularly on March 11—on that day Liberian business establishments will be closed in observance of Decoration Day. Little business will be conducted in Australia on January 26—Australia Day, or in Canada on its national day—July 1. Regional holidays will close businesses in parts of many countries on certain days. Business in Arab nations will be suspended for several days at a time in observance of the variable Moslem feasts, the exact dates of which depend on sighting of the moon and are not known until shortly before they occur.

There are hundreds of commercial holidays around the world each year, as well as longer periods when the conduct of business is discouraged in particular countries. In fact, there were only a few days in 1987 when there were no commercial holidays somewhere in the world that closed both business and government offices in the celebrating countries.

Many commercial holidays occur on different calendar dates from year to year. Holidays and even weekends often vary from country to country and from region to region.

In cases where holidays fall on Saturday or Sunday, commercial establishments may be closed the preceding Friday or following Monday.

For many countries, such as those in the Moslem world, holiday dates can only be estimated because they are based on the lunar calendar. Businesses in many Moslem countries are closed on Fridays.

Department of Commerce District Offices

District offices of the Department of Commerce are listed here by region.

Northeastern Region I
CONNECTICUT
Hartford, 06103, Room 610-B, Federal Bldg., 450 Main St., (203) 722-3530
MAINE
Augusta, 04330, 1 Memorial Circle, Casco Bank Bldg., (207) 622-8249

MASSACHUSETTS
Boston, 02210, World Trade Center Boston, Commonwealth Pier, (617) 223-2312
NEW HAMPSHIRE
Serviced by Boston District Office
NEW YORK
Buffalo, 14202, 1312 Federal Bldg., 111 W. Huron St., (716) 846-4191
New York, 10278, Rm. 3718, Federal Office Bldg., 26 Federal Plaza, Foley Square, (212) 264-0634
Rochester, 14604, 121 East Ave., (716) 263-6480
RHODE ISLAND
Province, 02903, 7 Jackson Walkway, (401) 528-5104
VERMONT
Serviced by Boston District Office

Mid-Atlantic Region II
DELAWARE
Serviced by Philadelphia District Office
DISTRICT OF COLUMBIA
Serviced by Baltimore District Office
MARYLAND
Baltimore, 21202, 413 U.S. Customhouse, Gay and Lombard Sts., (301) 962-3560
Rockville, U.S. Department of Commerce, Herbert C. Hoover Bldg., Rm. 1066, 14th and E Sts. N.W., Washington, D.C. 20230, (202) 377-3181
NEW JERSEY
Trenton, 08608, 240 West State St., 8th Fl., (609) 989-2100
PENNSYLVANIA
Philadelphia, 19106, 9448 Federal Bldg., 600 Arch St., (215) 597-2866
Pittsburgh, 15222, 2002 Federal Bldg., 1000 Liberty Ave., (412) 644-2850

Appalachian Region III

KENTUCKY
Louisville, 40202, Rm. 636B, U.S. Post Office and Courthouse
Bldg., (502) 582-5066
NORTH CAROLINA
Greensboro, 27402, 203 Federal Bldg., 324 W. Market St., P.O.
Box 1950, (919) 333-5345
SOUTH CAROLINA
Columbia, 29201, Strom Thurmond Federal Bldg., Suite 172,
1835 Assembly St., (803) 765-5345
Charleston, 29401, 17 Lockwood Drive, (803) 724-4361
TENNESSEE
Nashville, 37219-1505, 1114 Parkway Towers, 404 James
Robertson Parkway, (615) 736-5161
Memphis, 38103, 555 Beale St., (901) 521-4137
VIRGINIA
Richmond, 23240, 8010 Federal Bldg., 400 N. 8th St.,
(804) 771-2246
WEST VIRGINIA
Charleston, 25301, 3000 New Federal Office Bldg., 500 Quarrier
St., (304) 347-5123

Southeastern Region IV

ALABAMA
Birmingham, 35203, 3rd Floor, Berry Bldg., 2015 2nd Ave.,
(205) 731-1331
FLORIDA
Clearwater, 33515, 128 N. Osceola Ave., (813) 461-0011
Jacksonville, 32202, 3 Independent Dr., (904) 791-2796
Miami, 33130, Suite 224, Federal Bldg., 51 S.W. First Ave.,
(305) 536-5267
Orlando, 32802, 75 E. Ivanhoe Blvd., (305) 648-6235
Tallahassee, 32304, Collins Bldg., Rm. 401, 107 W. Gaines St.,
(904) 488-6469

GEORGIA
Atlanta, 30309, Suite 600, 1365 Peachtree St., N.E.,
(404) 881-7000
Savannah, 31401, 120 Barnard St., Federal Bldg., (912) 944-4204
MISSISSIPPI
Jackson, 39213, Suite 328, 300 Woodrow Wilson Blvd.,
(601) 965-4388
PUERTO RICO
San Juan, (Hato Rey), 00918, Room 659, Federal Bldg.,
(809) 753-4555

Great Lakes Region V
ILLINOIS
Chicago, 60603, Room 1406, Mid-Continental Plaza Bldg., 55 E.
Monroe St., (312) 353-4450
Palatine, 60067, W. R. Harper College, Algonquin & Roselle Rd.,
(312) 397-3000, Ext. 532
Rockford, 61110-0247, 515 North Court St., P.O. Box 1747, (815)
987-8128
INDIANA
Indianapolis, 46204, 357 U.S. Courthouse & Federal Office Bldg.,
46 E. Ohio St., (317) 269-6214
MICHIGAN
Detroit, 48226, 1140 McNamara Bldg., 477 Mich. Ave.,
(313) 226-3650
Grand Rapids, 49503, 300 Monroe, N.W., Rm. 409,
(616) 456-2411
MINNESOTA
Minneapolis, 55401, 108 Federal Bldg., 110 S. 4th St.,
(612) 349-3338
OHIO
Cincinnati, 45202, 9504 Federal Office Bldg., 550 Main St., (513)
684-2944
Cleveland, 44114, Room 600, 666 Euclid Ave., (216) 522-4750

WISCONSIN
Milwaukee, 53202, 605 Federal Bldg., 517 E. Wisconsin Ave., (414) 291-3473

Plains Region VI
IOWA
Des Moines, 50309, 817 Federal Bldg., 210 Walnut St., (515) 284-4222
KANSAS
Wichita, 67202, River Park Place, Suite 565, 727 North Waco, (316) 269-6160
MISSOURI
Kansas City, 64106, Rm. 635, 601 E. 12th St., (816) 374-3142
St. Louis, 63105, 120 S. Central Ave., (314) 425-3302
NEBRASKA
Omaha, 68102, Empire State Bldg., 1st Floor, 300 S. 19th St., (402) 221-3664
NORTH DAKOTA
Serviced by Omaha District Office
SOUTH DAKOTA
Serviced by Omaha District Office

Central Region VII
ARKANSAS
Little Rock, 72201, St. 320, Savers Federal Bldg., 320 W. Capitol Ave., (501) 378-5794
LOUISIANA
New Orleans, 70130, 432 World Trade Center, 2 Canal St., (504) 589-6546
NEW MEXICO
Albuquerque, 87102, 517 Gold S.W., Suite 4303, (505) 766-2386
OKLAHOMA
Oklahoma City, 73116, 5 Broadway Executive Park, Ste. 200, 6601 Broadway Extension, (405) 231-5302
Tulsa, 74127, 440 S. Houston St., (918) 581-7650

TEXAS
Dallas, 75242, Room 7A5, 1100 Commerce St., (214) 767-0542
Austin, 78711, P.O. Box 12728, Capitol Station, (512) 472-5059
Houston, 77002, 2625 Federal Bldg., Courthouse, 515 Rusk St., (713) 229-2578

Rocky Mt. Region VIII
ARIZONA
Phoenix, 85025, Federal Bldg. & U.S. Courthouse, 230 N. First Ave., (602) 261-3285
COLORADO
Denver, 80202, Room 119, U.S. Customhouse, 721 19th St., (303) 844-3246
IDAHO
Boise, 83720, Statehouse, Rm. 113, (208) 334-9254
MONTANA
Serviced by Denver District Office
NEVADA
Reno, 89502, 1755 East Plumb Lane, Rm. 152, (702) 784-5203
UTAH
Salt Lake City, 84101, Rm. 340, U.S. Post Office Bldg., 350 S. Main St., (801) 524-5116
WYOMING
Serviced by Denver District Office

Pacific Region IX
ALASKA
Anchorage, 99513, P.O. Box 32, 701 C St., (907) 271-5041
CALIFORNIA
Los Angeles, 90049, Rm. 800, 11777 San Vicente Blvd., (213) 209-6707
San Diego, 92138, P.O. Box 81404, (619) 293-5395
Santa Ana, 92701, 116-A W. 4th St., Ste. 1, (714) 836-2461
San Francisco, 94102, Federal Bldg., Box 36013, 450 Golden Gate Ave., (415) 556-5860

HAWAII
Honolulu, 96850, 4106 Federal Bldg., 300 Ala Moana Blvd., P.O. Box 50026, (808) 546-8694
OREGON
Portland, 97204, Room 618, 1220 S.W. 3rd Ave., (503) 221-3001
WASHINGTON
Seattle, 98109, Rm. 706, Lake Union Bldg., 1700 Westlake Ave. North, (206) 442-5616
Spokane, 99210, P.O. Box 2170, (509) 456-4557

Department of Commerce — International Trade Administration Regional Information Sources

Area Served	Telephone	Address
AK	(907) 271-5041	701 C. St. (mailing address: P.O. Box 32), Anchorage, AK 99513.
AL	(205) 254-1331	2015 2nd Ave. N., Birmingham, AL 35203.
AR	(501) 378-5794	320 W. Capitol Ave. (Savers Federal Bldg.), Little Rock, AR 72201.
AZ	(602) 261-3285	201 N. Central Ave., Phoenix, AZ 85073.
CA	(213) 209-6707	11777 San Vicente Blvd., Los Angeles, CA 90049.
	(415) 556-5860	450 Golden Gate Ave. (mailing address: P.O. Box 36013), San Francisco, CA 94102.
CO, MT, WY	(303) 844-3246	721 19th St., Denver, CO 80202.
CT	(203) 722-3530	450 Main St., Hartford, CT 06103.
DC, MD	(301) 962-3560	Gay and Lombard Sts., Baltimore, MD 21202.
DE, PA	(215) 597-2866	600 Arch St., Philadelphia, PA 19106.
	(412) 644-2850	1000 Liberty Ave., Pittsburgh, PA 15222.
FL	(305) 350-5267	51 S.W. 1st Ave., Miami, FL 33130.
GA	(404) 881-7000	1365 Peachtree St. N.E., Atlanta, GA 30309.
	(912) 944-4204	27 E. Bay St., Savannah, GA 31401.

Area Served	Telephone	Address
HI	(808) 546-8694	300 Ala Moana Blvd. (mailing address: P.O. Box 50026), Honolulu, HI 96850.
IA	(515) 284-4222	210 Walnut St., Des Moines, IA 50309.
ID, UT	(801) 524-5116	350 S. Main St., Salt Lake City, UT 84101.
IL	(312) 353-4450	55 E. Monroe St., Chicago, IL 60603.
IN	(317) 269-6214	46 E. Ohio St., Indianapolis, IN 46204.
KS, MO	(314) 425-3302	120 S. Central Ave., St. Louis, MO 63105.
	(816) 374-3142	601 E. 12th St., Kansas City, MO 64106.
KY	(502) 582-5066	U.S. Post Office and Courthouse Bldg., Louisville, KY 40202.
LA	(504) 589-6546	2 Canal St., New Orleans, LA 70130.
MA, ME, NH, RI, VT	(617) 223-2312	441 Stuart St., Boston, MA 02116.
MI	(313) 226-3650	231 W. Lafayett St., Detroit, MI 48226.
MN	(612) 349-3338	110 S. 4th St., Minneapolis, MN 55401.
MS	(601) 960-4388	300 Woodrow Wilson Blvd., Jackson, MS 39213.
NC	(919) 378-5345	324 W. Market St. (mailing address: P.O. Box 1950), Greensboro, NC 27402.
ND, NE, SD	(402) 221-3664	300 S. 19th St., Omaha, NE 68102.
NJ	(609) 989-2100	240 W. State St., Trenton, NJ 08608.
NM	(505) 766-2386	517 Gold Ave. S.W., Albuquerque, NM 87102.
NV	(702) 784-5203	1755 E. Plumb Lane, Reno, NV 89502.
NY	(716) 846-4191	111 W. Huron St., Buffalo, NY 14202.
	(212) 264-0634	26 Federal Plaza, New York, NY 10278.
OH	(513) 684-2944	550 Main St., Cincinnati, OH 45202.
	(216) 522-4750	666 Euclid Ave., Cleveland, OH 44114.
OK	(405) 231-5302	4024 Lincoln Blvd., Oklahoma City, OK 73105.
OR	(503) 221-3001	1220 S.W. 3rd Ave., Portland, OR 97204.

Area Served	Telephone	Address
PR	(809) 753-4555	Federal Bldg., Hato Rey, PR 00918.
SC	(803) 765-5345	1835 Assembly St., Columbia, SC 29201.
TN	(615) 251-5161	1 Commerce Place, Nashville, TN 37239.
TX	(214) 767-0542	1100 Commerce St., Dallas, TX 75242.
	(713) 229-2578	515 Rusk St., Houston, TX 77002.
VA	(804) 771-2246	400 N. 8th St., Richmond, VA 23240.
WA	(206) 442-5616	1700 Westlake Ave. N., Seattle, WA 98109.
WI	(414) 291-3473	517 E. Wisconsin Ave., Milwaukee, WI 53202.
WV	(304) 347-5123	500 Quarrier St., Charleston, WV 25301.

Chapter 36

Franchising

The following text was excerpted from *Franchising in the Economy 1985-1987,* a recently published Commerce Department report providing franchising statistical data on sales, units, and employment in 22 major franchised business categories. The report also includes statistical data on total investment and start-up cash required; average sales per establishment; changes in ownership; international franchising, minority franchisees, franchise agreements; and renewals, terminations, and transfers. Copies of the publication are available from the Superintendent of Documents, U.S. Government Printing Office, Washington, D.C. 20402 (Stock No. 003-008-00202-1).

Franchising Today

Franchising is increasingly important to the U.S. economy and continues to prove its validity as a marketing method adaptable to an ever-widening array of industries and professions. Because of its acceptance by the public, prospective entrepreneurs doing business under a franchise receive immediate identity and recognition. Established companies also are turning to franchising as a means of expanding their distribution by either converting their wholly owned outlets or by launching new programs.

Franchising sales of goods and services in more than 498,000 outlets reached more than $591 billion in 1987, about 6 percent higher than a year earlier and about 77 percent over the level of sales at the start of the 1980s. Employment in franchising, including part-time workers and working proprietors, was 6.3 million in 1985 and reached more than 7 million by the end of 1987. Movement by U.S. franchisors to foreign markets continues to grow at a rapid rate, and in 1985 there were 342 U.S. franchisors with over 30,000 outlets located in most countries of the world. Additionally, accelerated growth is being experienced in the establishment of new franchising companies, advisory councils, franchise consultants, and franchise attorneys.

Product and trade-name franchising began in the United States as an independent sales relationship between supplier and dealer in which the dealer acquired some of the identity of the supplier. Franchised dealers concentrate on one company's product line and to some extent identify their business with that company. Typical of this segment are automobile and truck dealers, gasoline service stations, and soft drink bottlers. Together they dominate the franchise field, accounting for an estimated 71 percent of all franchise sales for 1987 compared with 74 percent for 1985.

Total sales by product and trade-name franchisors reached an estimated $421 billion in 1987 compared with $403 billion in 1986 and $402 billion in 1985. Since 1972, the establishments of product and trade-name franchisors declined at a rapid rate; for example, there was a net loss of over 106,000 gasoline service stations between 1972 and 1986 alone. The attrition rate is expected to slow in the next few years, and in 1987 the number of these establishments was expected to decline to 146,000—from 149,050 in 1986 and 153,531 in 1985.

Business format franchising is characterized by an ongoing business relationship between franchisor and franchisee that includes not only the product, service, and trademark, but the entire business format itself—a marketing strategy and plan, operating manuals and standards, quality control, and continuing two way communications. Restaurants, non-food retailing, personal and business services, rental services, real estate services, and a long list of other service businesses fall into the category of business format franchising. Business format franchising has been responsible for much of the growth of franchising in the United States since 1950 and will continue to offer opportunities for those individuals seeking their own businesses.

The volume of sales and the number of units owned or franchised by business format franchisors have been steadily on the rise since 1972. Sales of business format franchisors were almost $171 billion in 1987, compared with $153 billion in 1986 and $141 billion in 1985. In contrast to product and trade-name franchises, the number of establishments of business format franchisors increased to almost 353,000 in 1987, compared to 317,751 in 1986 and 301,689 in 1985.

Many franchisors are currently involved in testing a new form of franchising comprising different products under the same roof—in other words, a franchisor who would sell products and/or services within the unit of another franchisor. Most of those involved in this new trend, known as a combination franchise or a franchise within a franchise, are currently in food-related services.

An increasing trend is the movement of new and small companies into the franchise system of distribution. In 1985, the net gain of companies converting to franchising jumped dramatically to almost 8 percent, the highest percentage increase for the last five years. A total of 273 firms turned to franchising in 1985, and this growing trend is expected to continue for the next few years.

All services related to various types of business aids are growing strongly and should continue. This can be attributed to the large numbers of both small and large companies going outside of their own organizations to fulfill many service functions previously performed internally. This is demonstrated, for example, by the rapid rise of franchising services in accounting, collection services, mail processing, advertising services, message taking, package wrapping and shipping, business consulting, security, business record keeping, tax preparation, personnel services, and others.

Other areas in franchising that are expected to advance rapidly for the remainder of the 1980s are weight control centers, hair salons, temporary help services, printing and copying services, medical centers, and clothing stores.

The Department of Commerce survey reveals that 342 U.S. franchising companies operated 30,188 outlets in foreign countries in 1985, compared with 328 franchisors with 27,021 outlets in 1984. Further, an additional 192 companies have indicated that they are considering extending their U.S. operations to foreign countries by the end of 1988. This interest has been expressed mostly by small- and medium-sized franchisors, marketing a variety of services and products. Of the companies seeking foreign markets, 44 are franchisors of business aids and services and 39 are restaurant franchisors.

Canada continues to be the dominant market for U.S. franchisors despite its delining share of U.S. foreign outlets. In 1985, 30 percent of all U.S. foreign franchised outlets were located in Canada, down from a high of 46 percent in 1971. A total of 239 U.S. franchising firms with 9,054 units operated in Canada in 1985, predominantly in restaurants (1,542), non-food retailing (1,599), and business aids and services (1,279). Japan continues to be the second largest market for U.S. franchisors with a total of 7,124 units, of which 67 percent represent various food categories such as restaurants, donut shops, ice cream stores, and convenience food stores. The United Kingdom ranks third with 2,291 outlets, while 4,398 outlets are located in all of continental Europe. Table 1 on page 764 lists countries of foreign regions where U.S. franchisors operated in 1985.

For the businessperson with the right talents, a franchise with a successful and reputable firm offers high profits and independence, along with a reassuringly low degree of risk. Many a fortune, in fact, has been built up by those who staked their capital on a franchise, and through flair or good luck, or both, turned it into a gold mine. The sales manager will want to consider the industry as a whole as a potential market.

Table 1. County or Foreign Region	Number of Franchisors
Canada	239
Caribbean	88
Australia	75
Asia (other than Japan and Middle East)	74
Continental Europe	73
United Kingdom	68
Japan	66
Middle East	41
Mexico	36
South America	35
Africa	28
Central America	27
New Zealand	22

How Franchises Work

The reasons for the high rewards of franchising are not hard to find. The word *franchise* means many things to many people, but the basic principles of franchising are as follows:

The parent company, or franchisor, sets up a chain by licensing independent businesspeople to run its establishments, using its trade or brand name and dispensing its services along lines approved by the company. The businessperson usually pays a licensing fee and thereafter gives some kind of consideration to the company each year for the privilege of belonging to the chain. He or she must also have the required sum of capital to put into the business at the outset.

Once the franchise is obtained, a businessperson will have to make additional payments, such as a mortgage or a bank loan. The franchisee will have to reinvest part of his or her earnings in the business as it grows. And most franchising arrangements involve a yearly payment to the franchising company as well as any initial fee. This may be in the form of rent for the premises, or it may be a percentage of the gross sales—usually considerably less than 10 percent.

In return for any payments made to the parent company, however, the franchisee receives benefits that are worth far more, including the leverage offered by the resources of a far larger organization. For one thing, the franchisee is selling goods or services that have the incalculable support of a well known brand name. In addition, whenever the franchising firm conducts a national advertising campaign, the franchisee gets a free ride. The franchisee will probably be able to buy supplies at a favorable price through the bulk buying of the "parent" company, and will share in the benefits from any improvement and upgrading of the product by the parent company.

But perhaps most important of all, the parent company puts management guidance, backed by far larger resources and wider experience than the licensee can hope to demand, constantly at his or her disposal. As well as providing continuous advice to their franchisees once they are in business, the parent companies usually give them an intensive training course beforehand.

A recruiting brochure issued by 7-Eleven Stores, while it does not specify costs, very briefly outlines some of the major provisions for a company franchise as follows:

- Franchisee benefits and responsibilities

    1. Operate your own store

    2. Control your own inventory

    3. Benefit from mass producing power

    4. Keep records of your purchases, sales, and deposits

    5. Hire and supervise your own employees

    6. Be eligible for medical and life insurance

- 7-Eleven franchisor responsibilities

    1. License you to use the 7-Eleven trademark, copyrights, and business systems

    2. Lease you the building and equipment

    3. Keep your books

4. Permit you to use the 7-Eleven Merchandising System

5. Provide continuing management services

6. Provide advertising services

7. Finance a portion of your investment

The Franchise Agreement

The contractural basis for the franchisor-franchisee relationship is the franchise agreement. The origin of much of the unfairness that exists in franchising is to be found in the agreement, states Dr. G. C. Udell in *The Franchise Agreement Handbook,** published by Purdue University.

Examining 172 franchise agreements, Dr. Udell found that, in general, most contracts favor the franchisor. For instance, not one agreement studied contained any provision dealing with franchisor's nonperformance. A second element of imbalance is in the wide range of requirements on the franchisee and the paucity of the franchisor requirements, as pointed out by U. B. Ozanne and S. D. Hunt, authors of *The Economic Impact of Franchising.*†

"There are many honest and fair franchisors," states Udell, "who work diligently to meet the needs of their franchisees and who honor their commitments. They do not need vaguely worded or limited provisions. They have nothing to fear from equal rights of termination and enforcement."

Since 1979, every franchise offered for sale in the United States has been subject to the Federal Trade Commission's Franchising Trade Regulation Rule (FTC Rule). The FTC Rule requires franchisors to provide information about all material aspects of the franchise offered to a prospective franchisee before a franchisee agreement can be signed. The materials are known as disclosure documents, offering circulars, or prospectuses.

---

*G. C. Udell, *The Franchise Agreement Book* (Lafayette, Indiana: Purdue University, 1973).
†U. B. Ozanne and S. D. Hunt, *The Economic Impact of Franchising* (Madison, Wisconsin: Graduate School of Business, University of Wisconsin—Distributed by Superintendent of Documents, U.S. Printing Office, Washington, DC, 1971).

In addition, at least 13 states require franchisors to submit similar materials. Unlike state regulatory agencies, the Federal Trade Commission does not review any of the disclosures it requires franchisors to make. The FTC, however, is empowered to respond to complaints and bring lawsuits in its own behalf and on behalf of defrauded franchise buyers.

The tool that most experts agree is key in evaluating and comparing franchise offerings is the FTC Franchise Disclosure Statement, according to Carl E. Zwisler in *1987 Franchise Yearbook*. This document is also known as the Uniform Franchise Offering Circular (UFOC), which every franchise buyer must receive at least 10 business days prior to signing a franchise or related contract or to paying money (or other remuneration) to a franchisor or his or her representative to discuss the proposed sale or purchase of a franchise: if the conversation results in a serious sales presentation, the franchisor must provide the potential franchisee with a disclosure document at that time.

Franchisors must disclose to the franchisee the initial franchisee fee, the initial investment required to establish the franchise business, and the cost of buildings, equipment, and related services. Because of fluctuating prices for real estate, utilities, labor, transportation, etc., franchisors often state a range of estimates within which they think any given franchise business will fall.

What the Franchisee Should Know

The U.S. Small Business Administration and the Commerce Department's International Trade Administration provide some information about franchising as suggested in an article in *Nation's Business*.

Franchisors' advertising in business publications is a source of information about specific opportunities. Another is the International Franchise Association, sole trade organization for franchisors. Its membership directory gives information on costs, types of business, locations, and contacts. All members must comply with a code of ethics.

Experts say the first thing a person who wants to invest in a franchise should do is examine personal characteristics. Can your family (if there is one) handle the time commitment necessary for success in business? Are you really the go-my-own-way type, or do you need a boss? Is the business suited to your personal tastes and training?

The International Franchise Association recommends that a person also consider such questions as:

- Is the product or service obsolete?

- Is the franchisor experienced, successful, financially strong, and reputable?

- What is the experience and financial history of the company's officers and directors?

- What is the litigation history, if any?

- What are the profit projections?

- What is the cost—initial fees, cash requirements, royalties, other fees?

- What are the company's operating practices, assistance, and controls like?

- What is your right to sell?

- How long is your contract for, can you terminate it ahead of time, and can you renew it?

Experts say the contract should be carefully examined and thoroughly understood by the prospective franchisee. If you do not understand it, hire an attorney who does. Things to look for, and question, include the scope of the contract. Does it cover all aspects of the franchises, including training and management advice? Will you be required to buy a certain amount of materials? From whom? How are any disputes between the franchisor and the franchisee settled? And, finally, will you have exclusive rights to a territory and for how long?

The International Franchisee Association publishes an annual membership directory that can be obtained from that association at 1025 Connecticut Avenue, N.W., Suite 707, Washington, D.C. 20036.

Failure Rate Is Low

The rewards of running a franchise business, however, are not measured only in terms of yearly profits. A franchise also offers the businessperson a greater degree of security than one could hope for in setting up one's own business. The reason is simple: Most companies will go to great lengths to avoid having failed franchisees on their hands. "The franchisor cannot afford failure," said the president of a restaurant chain. "It's not only bad for profits, it's bad for his image."

The image of its chain is important to the franchisor because its prosperity depends heavily on the abilities of its franchisees as businesspeople and managers. The spectacle of numerous failures would obviously deter the shrewder, more capable, and better-financed prospects.

Because the franchisors cannot afford to let franchisees sink, they frequently will go to great lengths to keep them afloat. The result is a phenomenally low failure rate for the industry as a whole. "The experience of the industry," said the executive secretary of the International Franchise Association, "is that fewer than 10 percent of all franchisees fail in business." In dramatic contrast with this is the fact that perhaps one out of every two businesspersons who start on their own fails within two years.

To qualify for prompt and effective help in business, a franchisee does not even have to be foundering, but merely has to be making less out of his or her business than the chain thinks is reasonable. Mister Donut of America, for example, claims that the failure rate among its established franchisees is less than 1 percent. "This," said Chairman Harry Winokur, "is because we make it almost impossible for a franchisee to fail."

It is impossible to generalize about the amount of capital necessary to obtain a franchise. However, Table 2, page 770, gives a few examples of the equity capital needed and whether or not financial assistance is given in a sampling of franchises listed in the *1987 Franchise Yearbook* published by *Entrepreneur*. Some 1500 franchises are listed in the publication.

Table 2.

Franchise	Equity Capital Needed	Financial Assistance
Mister Donut	$75K-100K	Yes
Kentucky Fried Chicken	$360K +	No
McDonald's	$400K +	No
Pizza Hut	$100K	No
Computerland	$250K	Yes
Superlawns, Inc.	$40K	Yes
Culligan (water softener)	$42K +	Yes
Postal Instant Press	$15K	Yes
Century 21	$15K-25K	Varies

Chapter 37

Trends in Distribution Channels

The Conference Board conducted a research study, "Rethinking the Company's Selling and Distribution Channels,"* authored by Howard Sutton.

In describing why this report is important to today's marketers, James T. Mills, president of The Conference Board said: "Driven by pressures of cost and competition, manufacturers are looking for more efficient ways to reach present and potential customers.

"Some companies, for example, are reorganizing their direct sales forces to provide greater specialization by types of users or products. Others are shifting their emphasis from direct sales channels to indirect reseller channels, or vice versa. Still others are increasing their use of supplementary forms of customer contact, such as telemarketing and computer-to-computer ordering.

"Choosing the right mix of distribution channels and contact methods is a complex, crucial decision today. Management needs a broad understanding of the issues to evaluate its choices. This report presents the findings of a Conference Board study that shows how companies have been analyzing their various selling options, how they have gone about making appropriate changes, and how such changes have affected marketing efficiency."

The first section of this comprehensive report is presented as follows.

Reviewing the Manufacturer's Options

Within the last few years, manufacturers in the United States have been faced with three serious problems: The economy has been growing slowly, competition from overseas producers has in-

---

*The complete report is copyrighted and is available from The Conference Board, 845 Third Avenue, New York, NY 10022.

creased dramatically, and marketing costs have continued to rise rapidly. One consequence of this confluence of events is that many companies have been compelled to reexamine their selling and distribution channels and to look for more efficient alternatives. The Conference Board study of the practices and experiences of more than 200 U.S. companies reported here confirms that managers are asking such questions as these:

- Are we using the most efficient channels of distribution?

- Do our distributors have enough technical know-how to sell newer, more complex products?

- Are our customers beginning to think of our product as a commodity? If so, does that mean we should put more emphasis on selling through distributors and less on direct selling?

- Should we reorganize the sales force to make better use of salespeople's time?

- How can we use computers to back up our salespeople and distributors?

- Does telemarketing make sense for this company?

- How about computer-to-computer ordering?

True, manufacturers have always paid a lot of attention to logistic problems: How many warehouses should we have? Where should the warehouses be? What are optimum and minimum order quantities? But many companies have yet to concentrate on the strategic problems: How much weight should be given to each of the sales channels now in use? And are there some more efficient alternatives?

However, a number of manufacturers have concentrated on such problems, and some have made significant changes in their selling and distribution methods. The purpose of this report is to consider some of the ways that company managements have analyzed their options, how they have implemented change, what problems they have run into, and how the changes have worked out. The report focuses mainly on the industrial sector, because that is where many of the most significant changes are taking place.

DEFINING THE OPTIONS

Manufacturers generally have three options for reaching prospects and customers: selling directly through their own company channels, selling through indirect channels, and employing supplementary methods of contact. These possibilities are not mutually exclusive; most companies are making increased use of a variety of channels.

Direct channels. The main method of direct contact is through the company's field sales force, which may include both generalists and specialists. Generalists sell the company's product line to all kinds of customers. Specialists, as the word implies, cover only part of the market. Among other possibilities, they may deal only with large-volume customers, only with certain products in the company's line, only with a particular industry, or only with a particular type of distributor. For the purposes of this report, various kinds of sales agents, such as manufacturers' representatives, are included among direct-selling channels.

Indirect channels. Companies reach their prospects and customers indirectly through resellers. These are middlemen—typically industrial distributors, wholesalers or independent retailers—who buy products from the manufacturer and sell them to end users. (A few firms maintain company-owned wholesale or retail outlets.) Indirect channels are often referred to collectively as distributors or, sometimes, just "distribution."

Other contact methods. Beyond these, the most important contact methods referred to here are telemarketing, computer-to-computer ordering, and catalogs.

Table 1, page 774, shows the main channels that were reported, usually for the largest or most typical unit of the company.

SURVEY METHOD

This study was conducted in two steps. First, a short questionnaire went to senior marketing and sales executives in large manu-

Table 1. Channels Now Used by Manufacturers

Selling channels and contact methods used	Percentage of reporting companies*			
	Total companies	Industrial product producers	Consumer product producers	Both
Direct channels				
Company's sales force				
Specialists	68%	75%	55%	75%
By type of product	54	63	38	63
By type of industry	30	37	13	46
By trade channel	23	16	28	42
By size of account..........	21	19	25	17
By type of user	18	23	8	25
Generalists...................	64	66	58	71
Company agents				
Manufacturers' representatives ...	32	37	19	42
Independent agents	16	21	13	4
Brokers	14	9	23	17
Commission merchants.........	4	3	5	8
Independent telemarketers	1	1	3	—
Company-owned retail outlets......	12	7	17	1
Company-owned wholesale outlets..	9	9	5	25
Indirect channels				
Wholesalers...................	49	34	69	80
Industrial distributors	42	54	11	58
Independent retailers.............	39	15	70	80
Franchise outlets	16	12	23	13
Drop shippers	9	6	13	8
Other contact methods				
Telephone sales.................	25	25	20	38
Computer-to-computer ordering	12	10	19	9
Catalog sales	8	6	11	8
Number of companies	214	126	64	24

*Multiple responses

facturing corporations. The 214 replies form the basis for the tables in the report. According to Table 1, 59 percent of the companies sold industrial products, 30 percent sold consumer products, and 11 percent sold both. (Most survey participants from companies with multiple operating units and selling operations restricted their reporting to just one of those units, the largest or most typical.)

The second step was to conduct a series of telephone and personal interviews with selected marketing and sales executives, many of whom had responded to the questionnaire. Each executive had been involved in a decision to make, or to not make, a significant change in a company's selling channels or sales-contact methods. Some independent consultants, known for their work on sales management and channels of distribution, were also interviewed.

TRENDS

Costs are the driving force behind the major changes in sales channels. As companies respond to that force, a number of trends are apparent.

Manufacturers are becoming increasingly aware of the economic costs of soliciting sales and getting their products from the plant to the customer. Since economic costs are not only current out-of-pocket costs, they may not always be fully recognized.

For example, inventory includes the cost of the capital that is tied up in the products—money that might be used more profitably elsewhere—and the cost of storing and insuring the materials and finished products. According to some estimates, holding inventory for a month costs about 2½ percent of the product's factory price.

Most companies do not charge their divisions for the use of that capital, but some are beginning to. This contributes to acceptance of the just-in-time idea—a concept that may have a seismic effect on many industries. Many end users are demanding that the supplies or components they purchase be delivered on a specific day, at a specific time. That obviously reduces their costs of storing and handling items on the way into the manufacturing process.

Many end users are also relying on fewer and fewer suppliers. The end users are giving their business to stable, reliable sources of supply and help in solving manufacturing problems.

Since few manufacturers are set up to make just-in-time deliveries all over the country, many companies—at least those supplying components and finishing materials for other manufacturers —will probably become more dependent on those distributors that have become especially proficient in managing warehouses and transportation operations. Those manufacturers that lead the way into these closer alliances may be in a better position to compete.

According to one marketing executive, "If manufacturers develop loyal partnerships with distributors in this country, they probably can hold off or neutralize foreign competition. I'm not sure a lot of manufacturers appreciate that, but it's a very viable defense."

Table 2, page 777, shows a trend, for the sample as a whole, toward increased use of other-than-direct selling. Roughly a fifth of the companies expect to become more dependent on industrial distributors. Independent retailers and wholesalers were mentioned with nearly equal frequency. An industrial marketing consultant uses a similar trend: "Distribution seems to be growing as a percent of sales in almost all the markets we're involved with."

Along with this shift, there are apparently changes ahead in the role of the manufacturer's sales force. These people are increasingly likely to be specialists of some sort. And they are likely to be spending less time in selling and more in providing technical advice and solving problems.

Most companies employ both generalists and those who are, in some way, specialists. In a majority of cases, the generalists now outnumber the specialists, as Table 3 on page 778 shows. Half of the companies report, however, that they expect to become more dependent on specialists over the next five years.

Product Life Cycles

A shift from one type of sales channel to another may come as a company's product matures. This is particularly true where a product has fairly technical applications. When such a product is introduced, the manufacturer is likely to have high selling costs, partly because most of the selling is done by a technically trained, direct sales force. As the product becomes more standardized and

Table 2. Manufacturers' Expectations of Channel Use

In five years, expect to be more dependent on	Percentage of reporting companies*			
	Total companies	Industrial product producers	Consumer product producers	Both
Direct channels				
Company's sales force				
Specialists	49%	50%	48%	54%
Generalists	15	14	23	4
Company agents				
Manufacturers' representatives	10	8	14	4
Independent telemarketers	4	2	5	4
Brokers	4	2	6	8
Independent agents	3	4	2	—
Commission merchants	—	—	—	—
Company-owned retail outlets	6	2	13	4
Company-owned wholesale outlets	2	1	—	13
Indirect channels				
Industrial distributors	22	30	2	25
Independent retailers	21	10	34	33
Wholesalers	19	14	25	29
Franchise outlets	6	6	14	4
Drop shippers	1	—	5	—
Other contact methods				
Telephone sales	22	20	17	38
Computer-to-computer ordering	20	18	23	21
Catalog sales	8	6	13	4
Number of companies	214	126	64	24

*Multiple responses

users become accustomed to it, much of the selling job can be shifted to resellers. Then the direct-salesperson's role may be increasingly confined to providing technical advice to large-volume purchasers or those with more complex application problems.

A manufacturer may also try to fine-tune its distribution channels by using one type of distributor in the earlier stages of a product's life cycle and a different type in later stages. The manu-

Table 3. Composition of Company's Direct Sales Forces

Composition of sales force	Percentage of reporting companies			
	Total companies	Industrial product producers	Consumer product producers	Both
Mostly generalists	58%	53%	68%	70%
Mostly specialists	39	47	32	30
Not reported	3	—	—	—
Number of companies	214	126	64	24

facturer might start out with distributors that are equipped to do market development work. These distributors locate prospects that might be able to use the product, show them how to do so, and provide users with most of the necessary support services.

Later on, the manufacturer will perhaps have a network of distributors that simply service accounts. These distributors do not spend any time looking for new customers; they just stock the product and sell to present customers.

If the manufacturer has made these shifts efficiently, marketing costs may decline significantly in the course of the product's life. According to some estimates for industrial goods, total marketing costs are generally about 50 percent of the product's price at the beginning of the life cycle and about 40 percent at the end.

The problem, of course, is that it is all too easy to miss opportunities. Some companies wait until their products are well into middle age before they shift into less costly distribution channels. But more and more managements are thinking in terms of product life cycles and the possible need to reorganize their mix of channels. Conspicuous examples are to be found in the computer industry: As profit margins have decreased, computer manufacturers have been forced to search for new markets and resort to new distribution channels. Many have realized that small businesses, which represent a large part of the potential market for their products, can not be reached efficiently by the direct sales force but can be reached by independent resellers, computer dealers, or in particular, by value-added resellers or remarketers. (Value-added resellers, or VARs, specialize in designing computer programs for particular types of businesses, to work with particular pieces of equipment. A VAR buys the equipment from the manufacturer at a discount and resells it along with a tailor-made program at something approximating the manufacturer's list price.)

Telecommunications

Another important development is that marketers are coming to see the telephone as an alternative mode of customer contact. According to Table 1, page 774, a quarter of the companies surveyed are now selling by telephone. Table 2 on page 777 indicates that a quarter of the responding companies are likely to become more dependent on telephone selling in the five years ahead.

Among other things, telemarketing, in its many forms, can be an efficient way to solve two chronic problems: how to reach new prospects and how to reach the small-volume buyer. But the telephone has been around for a long time. Why is telemarketing a new trend? One answer is cultural inertia. Many companies have assumed that the face-to-face meeting of salesperson and customer was the only way to do business. Another answer is that some of the computer-oriented support systems for telemarketing have appeared only recently. A telemarketing specialist can now work in front of a monitor, reading a carefully prepared script, and sending orders and follow-up information to a central computer by keyboard. Possibly the best answer, as some executives have observed, is that many manufacturers did not really have much incentive to look for such customer-contact alternatives as telemarketing until fairly recently.

Tables 1 and 2 also confirm a trend toward computer-to-computer ordering—with a purchase order originating in a computer terminal in the customer's office, transmitted by telephone cable to the supplier, and processed at the supplier's office. At the present, this is not always easy to do because of requirements or hardware and software at both ends of the line. But the potential for saving time and money is enormous, and about a fifth of the companies expect to depend more on computer-to-computer ordering in the next five years.

Ultimately, the customer will decide how far a manufacturer can go in this direction. Many customers—especially those that buy relatively standard products—may find the idea of computer-to-computer communication extremely attractive. A marketing professor makes this point in an interview: "If you follow the high-tech versus the high-touch theory of decision-making processes, lots and lots of people would like to avoid having to deal with salespeople. They think they know enough about the product or the service. They don't want to be terribly involved with it, so they can be very well served by more mechanical means—on-line computers, electronic data systems, and such. They simply want to replace effort with technology."*

Focusing on the Customer

Several reporting executives say their companies have made, or are trying to make, an important strategic change toward less concentration on their products and more on their customers. In effect, they are trying to define their businesses more in terms of customers' needs which, in turn, affects the company's decisions about sales channels.

This is not a new idea, of course. It surfaced in the 1950s, but some companies have apparently taken it seriously only recently. Why?

One marketing vice-president offers this view: "There's a very definite change in the marketing focus. Companies are trying to get away from an internal product focus to a customer focus. They did not change earlier because they didn't have to. But now we are on a real upswing in terms of urgency—foreign competition, a lot of overcapacity, a lot of companies searching for new things to do."

---

*See also Louis A. Wallis, *Computers and the Sales Effort*. The Conference Board, Report No. 884, 1986.

The Reviewing Process

How do managements go about deciding to make a change in selling channels? Some have their marketing-research units perform formal investigations, some enlist their salespeople to conduct surveys, some hire consultants to do the research and make recommendations, and a few do a formal profit-and-loss analysis, channel by channel. But the reviewing process for many companies may amount to little more than deciding to do what other companies seem to have done successfully.

At least one major company, 3M, has set up an internal consulting group to help its divisions review, among other things, selling and distribution channels.

Reviewing Channel Options at 3M

3M's Market Development Services group was established early in 1985. Its head reports to the director of planning who, in turn, reports to the vice-president of staff marketing services.

The main missions of the group are to evaluate marketing productivity and to recommend alternatives for achieving it. If a particular division wants help, the group will analyze its market coverage and selling and distribution methods, and then suggest ways of improving them. Some of its analyses and recommendations relate to sales channel and customer-contact options.

According to Richard Getchell, the head of the group: "When we started, we couldn't find any meaningful studies on how to measure marketing productivity. And so we've pretty much developed our own methods. Our job is to help managers in the divisions reach a decision.

"Often, they know they have a problem, and they may know what the solution is, but they really don't want to accept it. The solution may mean eliminating people, or moving people, or going against tradition.

FOCUSING ON THE PROBLEM

"We go in and try to put things in focus for them. We present the information in a way that's logical and systematic. It begins to form a picture. For example, we may discover that they're spending 40 percent of their effort on certain products, but getting only 20 percent of their total sales from those products. They may not realize that until we get it up on the board in front of them. Before we're through, they usually see for themselves what they can do. And it's hard to avoid making some of these decisions when they see it in black and white in front of them.

"If we bring in a group of fairly high-level managers for an all-day meeting, we can get the information on sales and distribution that we need in a few hours. We really don't have to have hard numbers. What we need is information on trends and on the managers' perceptions.

ADDING TELEMARKETING

"One of the first things divisions want to do is move into telephone sales and telephone marketing, because they can do that without upsetting everything. It's relatively easy at this point. For example, if one of their salespeople leaves, rather than fill that territory, they may bring in a person to start telephone sales and realign the territories. It's a great opportunity for reducing costs. However, one of our responsibilities is to reassess and say: 'Wait a minute. Let's sit down and work this out. Let's see what you really need.'

"We offer expertise in telemarketing. As a corporation, we really needed some direction, because divisions were getting into telemarketing without any comprehension of what it takes. They were going to outside vendors, or hiring people to sell over the telephone. Now they are coming to us and asking for ideas and help.

ANALYZING DISTRIBUTION SYSTEMS

"Divisions are also taking a close look at their distributors. Large distributors are becoming larger, and smaller ones are merging. With computer ordering and so on, it takes a pretty sophisticated distributor to do a lot of these things.

"How to pay these distributors today? Do we pay them the same way we paid them for the last 40 years—or do we pay them for what they really do? This is one of the biggest questions that has come up recently.

"We're studying all the distributors' costs—inventory, sales, and so on—and then we're looking at our costs. Maybe we will want to pay the distributor to assume more of the functions we now do. Or maybe we can absorb some activities back here and reduce the distributors' margin. But somebody has to pay for it. We're trying to come up with a classification system so divisions can have different levels of distributor margins, depending on what services the distributor provides.

"We weigh ideas carefully, test them, and feel our way along. We may try them out in a district or a region first. We are very careful about making changes."

THE DIFFICULTIES OF CHANGE

Once management decides to make a significant channel change, it may encounter unexpected consequences. As noted, many manufacturers are relying more and more on distributors. A company's field sales force may resist the idea, especially in an older company with a large, well-established sales force. By contrast, the sales force in a newer, rapidly growing company may be less resistant to turning a larger part of the selling over to distribution.

In some older companies, once heavily dependent on direct selling, there may be lingering doubt about the distributors' ability to perform a useful service. For example, over a period of 15 or 20 years, one abrasives manufacturer has given up most of its warehouses and has gradually shifted those accounts that do not have technical-application needs to distributors. The marketing vice-president describes the situation: "I believe the distributor can handle inventory, order filling, and shipping much better than we can, and do so at a fair price. The only problem I have is convincing the rest of the company, because most of them weren't around in the days when we used to do it ourselves."

Another problem is that a company may find it hard to treat the distributor as a partner. In some industries, manufacturers have paid distributors little more than enough to allow them to survive. That seems to be changing, however, as many manufacturers have come to see that a strong distributor network is essential. And as promising distributors have become more experienced in dealing with technology, finance, and marketing, some manufacturers have provided them with capital to expand their operations.

When relying increasingly on resellers, a related issue has to do with serving small-volume customers. Some manufacturing executives have observed that fast-growing distributors may tend to shift their attention to large customers and ignore the small ones. In those cases, a manufacturer may lose touch with large groups of potential customers.

CHANGING THE DISTRIBUTOR MIX

The problem of reaching the small-volume buyer is a common one. As a solution, some firms have considered adding more distributors. But, as one manager says, "If we run around and appoint everybody and his brother a distributor, then we're in trouble with our major distributors."

In some industries, signing up increasing numbers of distributors has been a competitive tactic. But the tactic reportedly can be dangerous. Eventually, as the quantity of distributors increases, the quality of the network may disintegrate. In that case, the solution may be to abandon the old distributors and replace them with a few high-quality distributors.

As a product line matures, the manufacturer may feel compelled to make a shift from one type of distributor to another. This can be a touchy situation, partly because the company's field representatives may have developed very strong personal relationships with the present distributors and be reluctant to make any changes at all. If the new distributor can underprice the old one, which is usually the reason for the move, the old distributor's business may be in jeopardy.

In fact, however, the move from one type of distributor to another may be dictated by the end user. At some point, the latter may refuse to pay for unnecessary services provided by the old type of distributor.

Emphasizing Direct Selling

Those manufacturers that have elected to put greater emphasis on direct selling in the future face an entirely different set of problems. One is that markets are maturing faster than they used to, and manufacturers that are new to the market may not have time to build effective sales organizations. As one consultant says: "A company has to acknowledge that it takes a long time to build a sales force—years. If it is going to put 60 people out in the field, it is going to take two or three years. In an area of rapidly moving technology, it may have to go through reps."

Manufacturers' representatives are often viewed as an interim solution. As some managers have observed, they can be valuable to companies if they are appropriately supervised. However, many sales managers cannot handle independent agents as well as they handle their own salespeople.

Manufacturers accept the fact that certain of their customers would prefer to buy from distributors. Also, when a company shifts its selling emphasis from distributors to its field sales force, former distributors may end up as competitors. For example, in some heavy-equipment industries, much of a manufacturer's revenue may come from selling replacement parts. If the manufacturer severs its ties with distributors, they may be strongly tempted—and in a position—to sell parts acquired from other sources.

Reorienting the Sales Force

Whatever adjustments in channels and selling focus management hopes to achieve, the internal inertial effects are often strong. "It's like turning an aircraft carrier around," says one consultant. "To make a major change in a marketing program, it is going to take years to change the field sales force's way of thinking."

One company, a manufacturer of centrifuges and other processing equipment, found it very difficult to shift to a market orientation. The problem was that the company's salespeople, mainly chemical engineers, were used to thinking about products instead of the needs of a particular industry—paper, food or mineral processing—the company might serve. However, the marketing vice-president acknowledges that some of the best ideas for serving those industries have since come from the sales force.

A manufacturer of medical equipment is revising its strategy to cope with the drastic changes in its market. When Congress put tighter limits on Medicare reimbursements in 1984, the entire health-care industry went into what one manager calls "a catatonic state." Hospitals began sharply reducing their purchases of expensive diagnostic equipment, no longer being able to pass on most of these expenses to the government. To meet the continuing demand for high-tech diagnostic services, entrepreneurs began to build diagnostic-imaging centers. For this equipment manufacturer, the appropriate strategy has been to move away from selling equipment piece by piece to hospital administrators and to move instead toward selling equipment systems to imaging centers in this rapidly growing part of the market. So far, however, the company's salespeople, who are specialized by type of product, are extremely uncomfortable about the prospect. Management finds they are not at all prepared to become part of a disciplined team effort to undertake a systems-selling approach.*

Adding a Channel

The idea of adding a new channel or a new method of contact can be very difficult to sell within a company. A marketing executive in an old-line manufacturing firm says: "What happens in a big company, I think, is that the main core business drives the company. Everybody's so busy with that business that they just can't cope with a new idea."

In some cases, marketing managers may be apprehensive about

*James K. Brown, *Refocusing the Company's Business.* The Conference Board, Report No. 873, 1985.

establishing a telephone sales operation because they have had unfortunate experiences with telephone solicitations at home. However, as telemarketing specialists note, business-to-business telephone selling is generally much more professional, and customers are beginning to recognize that both buyers and sellers can benefit from this increasingly efficient form of contact.

Another reported problem with setting up a telephone sales operation is that field salespeople may regard it as a threat. In most companies, it is said to be important to present telephone selling as a supplement to the field sales force's efforts. The idea is that it frees the regular salespeople to do what they do best—concentrate on larger accounts that may require face-to-face selling. The threat is also diminished if members of the field sales force receive some credit for telephone sales in their territories.

Adding value-added resellers is yet another potential cause for conflict. For example, a VAR might design a computer program for a particular market (hospitals or tool makers) with the program fitting a particular brand of computer. For the manufacturer, the VAR offers a way of selling its products to many customers that would be beyond the reach of the direct sales force. A problem arises, however, when VARs try to sell to customers that are large enough to be called on by the manufacturer's own salespeople. The question, then, is whether this should be considered healthy competition or unhealthy conflict.

PART 6

Managing the Sales Force

Chapter 38

Recruiting

The high cost of selling underscores the importance of proper recruiting, selection, hiring, and training methods.

Dartnell's 24th Biennial Survey of Sales Force Compensation revealed some relevant facts derived from Dartnell's Profile of the American Sales Professional, shown in Figure 1, page 791.

If you take the average pay of $23,000 of the sales trainee (on all compensation plans), add the field expenses of $14,666, plus the average value of benefits received of $8,218, you have a basic investment of over $45,000—and that's probably a pretty conservative figure.

Then $14,435 for training, and the first-year investment totals over $60,000. After you drop the trainee costs, compensation increases bring the cost of an experienced salesperson to approximately the same figure—over $62,000.

If the salesperson leaves after 4.7 years, as the survey revealed, you've invested over $282,000—more than a quarter of a million dollars—to be repeated again. It thus behooves the sales manager to protect that investment with proper recruiting, selection, hiring and training techniques, and sound compensation planning and design for increased profitable sales growth and a healthy degree of retention of professional sales producers.

The American Sales Professional

Who is this person we're talking about—the person being paid to get sales? The Dartnell survey provides some interesting insights for the sales manager.

Figure 1. Dartnell Profile: The American Sales Professional—National Averages

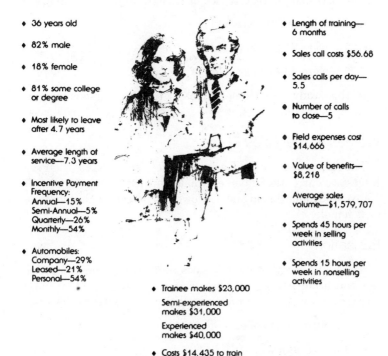

- 36 years old

- 82% male

- 18% female

- 81% some college or degree

- Most likely to leave after 4.7 years

- Average length of service—7.3 years

- Incentive Payment Frequency:
  Annual—15%
  Semi-Annual—5%
  Quarterly—26%
  Monthly—54%

- Automobiles:
  Company—29%
  Leased—21%
  Personal—54%

- Length of training—6 months

- Sales call costs $56.68

- Sales calls per day—5.5

- Number of calls to close—5

- Field expenses cost $14,666

- Value of benefits—$8,218

- Average sales volume—$1,579,707

- Spends 45 hours per week in selling activities

- Spends 15 hours per week in nonselling activities

- Trainee makes $23,000

Semi-experienced makes $31,000

Experienced makes $40,000

- Costs $14,435 to train

Copyright 1988. Compiled from *Sales Force Compensation—Dartnell's 24th Biennial Survey:* The Dartnell Corporation 1988.

Selling Is a Young Person's Game

The average age of a salesperson is 36. This age characteristic has remained virtually unchanged over the past eight years. This places our sales professional in the leading edge of the baby boom, members of which are now in their late thirties. It's interesting to compare these facts with a research study conducted by Xerox Learning Systems a few years ago. They observed the sales behaviors of 176 salespersons in 24 different organizations representing a variety of industries.

The personal characteristics of this group were as follows:

- 40% were 30-39 years old

- 37% were 21-29 years old

- 23% were 40-61 years old

In this study over three-fourths of the salespersons were less than 39 years old.

Women in the Sales Force

The respondents to the Dartnell survey reported that their sales forces are currently 82 percent male and 18 percent female. The Xerox study mentioned above showed 79 percent male and 21 percent female.

Education

Some 80 percent of today's sales professionals have some college education or a degree. The survey response to what formal education and/or special training is required showed these results:

- 42% with some college

- 39% with a degree

- 26% with a high school education

- 9% with technical school training

The total exceeds 100 percent, because some companies required technical training in addition to the usual formal schooling.

Selling Experience

The average sales professional is most likely to leave after being with a company about five years, and the average length of service is 7.3 years.

Over half of the sales forces have less than six years' experience.

And interestingly enough, that figure remains virtually unchanged over the past eight years.

What does all this tell us?

To repeat an earlier comment, selling is a young person's game. Today's sales professionals are brighter, better educated than their predecessors, and they need to be challenged.

They aren't afraid to move on if they are not satisfied. It would not appear that their values of loyalty are very strong. On the other hand, there is growing evidence that companies are separating poor performers more quickly than in the past.

The figures don't say much for longevity of service as compared to many inside company jobs. This may be due primarily to the function and characteristics of the selling job. How much of this is due to restlessness, job dissatisfaction, arbitrary cuts in the sales force, economic downturns in individual sales territories, and other factors is largely anyone's guess.

At a Conference Board Marketing Conference, Richard J. Haines, general sales manager of The Maytag Company, made these observations:

"Today's younger employees tend to find securities in their own abilities and self-confidence, and loyalty is more to one's peer group than to one's employer. Career growth often demands change. Mobility is highly desirable. Relocation, on the other hand, is sometimes rejected.

"The situation is further complicated because we are dealing with college graduates with schooled attitudes of a professional marketer. These individuals educated in the marketing sciences feel they can work for anybody. They arrive committed to specific career plans and are prepared to move on if promotion and recognition do not come quickly."

This underscores the need for two things:

1. To hire and train carefully. Because of their college backgrounds, sales trainees can absorb training quickly and put it to immediate use. This means training techniques must be up-to-date and a bit more sophisticated than in the past. While the basics of salesmanship have not changed that

much in the past 20 years, they must be taught in a manner compatible with the age of the computer.

2. To provide the kind of incentive in the compensation plan to keep top-performing salespeople with the company longer.

Tied into this segment of survey data is the turnover rate. The average turnover for all industries was 20 percent, up from 18 percent reported in the previous survey.

Keep in mind that *some* turnover is healthy and desirable. The important point is to determine the reasons *why* people leave or are discharged. If the reasons are sound, there is no reason for concern. A standard practice of exit interviews can be helpful.

Is Your Job Offer Attractive?

George J. Lumsden, author of Dartnell's *Building a Winning Sales Force,** states: "Although making a job offer to candidates comes very late in the staffing process, consideration of what the offer will be belongs in the planning. Why go through all the rigors of advertising, promoting, screening, and interviewing candidates when the job you will offer is likely to be turned down? Or why be put in the untenable position of having to rewrite your compensation plan on the spot in order to snag what you believe to be a promising candidate? Lemuel Boulware, former vice-president for employee relations at General Electric Company used to say of job packages, 'Think of the job as a product you have to sell. Make that job as attractive as you can, then sell it for all you're worth.' Not bad advice for anyone who is trying to fill openings with the best individuals he or she can find."

The Job Package

Lumsden recommends the job package should include the following elements:

- *Compensation.* Know what similar sales jobs currently are

---

*George J. Lumsden, *Building a Winning Sales Force* (Chicago: The Dartnell Corporation, 1986).

being compensated in your industry, your community, or your trading area. Develop a complete plan that includes not only earnings, but benefits and any other perquisites unique with your company. And be sure the plan rewards productivity.

- *Benefits.* They are not only expected, but are closely analyzed by people to whom jobs are offered. Who pays for the employee insurance plan? The hospital/medical plan? What are the coverages? What are the details of the company retirement plan and can an employee buy stock in the company? What is the company policy regarding company cars and car expenses?

Your job has other items of incalculable value—training, working conditions, market growth, advertising, sales promotion, career growth, and potential for promotion. Each deserve preplanning and identification in the job package. The more perceptive and circumspect of your candidates will certainly want to know about these things.

The above are merely examples of some benefits that may be offered. Also, applicants may ask questions about these benefits. It is better to have these items lined up in advance of any recruiting effort, and certainly before any applicant is interviewed. A Job Package Feature Planner is shown in Figure 2, page 796. This is for use as a reminder and not to be issued to candidates.

Job Specifications

George Lumsden suggests working from job descriptions already on file to underline the key duties and transferring them to a Sales Personnel Specification Guide. A sample is shown in Figure 3, page 797. Only after you have completed this hard look at the job itself are you ready to think about the kind of individual you want to fill it.

What to Look For

Practically all sales managers have differing opinions as to the characteristics of a good salesperson. One sales executive listed them as follows: 1) good appearance, 2) a pleasing, well-wearing

Figure 2. Job Package Feature Planner

The following features apply to the successful candidate for this employment opportunity:

Job Title_____

First assignment_____

Title of supervisor_____

Beginning compensation

_____Salary _____Commission _____Combination

Anticipated increases based on performance_____

How compensation plan works_____

_____

How payment is made ____Weekly ____Monthly ____Draw vs. Pay

Benefit Plans:

  Insurance_____

  Hospital/Medical_____

  Pension_____

  Other_____

Car Expense_____

_____

Working hours_____

Vacations/Holidays/Personal Time_____

_____

_____

Sales Support_____

Career Potential_____

Company Reputation_____

personality, 3) stability, tenacity, and perseverance; 4) basic character and integrity, and 5) industriousness—willingness to work.

Other sales managers may look for the same qualities in a person but rank them in a different order of importance. It is very interesting to note that many lists place experience at the bottom of the list or omit it entirely.

Charles E. Hummel, sales manager for Standard Shannon Supply Company, Philadelphia, for many years, drawing on his lengthy experience and talks with other sales managers, listed the following rules for hiring salespeople for readers of *Industrial Distributor News:*

  1. Overcome your prejudices.

Figure 3. Sales Personnel Specification Guide

Key Work Assignments and Responsibilities
Travel_____
Inside Sales_____
Proposal writing_____
Negotiation_____
Paperwork_____
Other_____
_____
_____

Qualities Demanded or Desired in Candidates
EXPERIENCE:
Work within the industry_____
Type?_____
Selling outside the industry_____
Type?_____
Selling within the industry_____
Where?_____
No prior experience needed_____
Why?_____
EDUCATION:
High School_____
Some College_____
College Grad_____
Degree_____
Advanced Degree_____
APPEARANCE:
_____
PERSONALITY:
_____

EVALUATE THE JOB. FIND THE PERSON TO FILL IT.

2. Don't insist on experience.

3. Advertise your name. Why hide behind a blind box number in your ad? Let the prospect know who you are.

4. Don't hide your story. Has your company experienced terrific growth? Say so in your ad.

5. Keep a reverse file. Even if you don't hire a candidate on the first call, don't throw away all of your applicants' resumes. Keep a file of those candidates who came close.

6. Let someone else interview, too. This is no reflection on your ability to judge applicants. But two heads are better than one in most cases.

7. Check references carefully. Many a poor salesperson has listed references that won't check out, figuring you won't check them because you'll assume he or she wouldn't list a bad reference.

8. Be wary of competitors' people. This is a tough rule and not everyone will agree with it. But the disadvantages may offset any advantages; their asking price may be high; they may be castoffs who couldn't produce, or prima donnas who won't work your way, or they may simply be jobhoppers who'll leave you the minute a better opportunity shows up.

9. Hire persons from related fields. This gives you a person with some experience, yet you avoid the disadvantages of hiring competitors' people.

10. Be flexible. When you hire a person, give him or her a fair trial. If the person is not working out after a reasonable time, be prepared to change your own training techniques.

Where to Look

One of the basic decisions to be made is whether to concentrate upon hiring experienced salespeople or to emphasize the hiring of sales trainees. The decision to concentrate upon hiring experienced people may provide for rapid expansion, and it may also lessen the need for, and cost of, a more elaborate training program. Despite some of the obvious advantages in hiring experienced salespeople, many companies—especially the larger firms— depend heavily upon the recruitment of trainees and their development through training programs.

Sales trainees are recruited from colleges and universities, junior colleges and other educational institutions, from among employees in other departments of the firm, and from the labor market in general.

Most of the trouble in employing salespeople who will make good can be traced to the method of selection. There are two approaches to this problem: 1) Picking the best people who apply to you for selling positions, and 2) "spotting" likely people and going after them. The trouble with the first method is that, as a rule, the people who will make the best salespeople are usually not out of jobs nor even thinking about changing jobs. They usually have jobs and are making good at them. In the opinion of one sales executive: "The best way of securing salespeople is to go right out after them personally by spotting alert, ambitious people who are already employed in chain stores, on farms, in department stores, as preachers, as teachers, as painters, as carpenters, as machinists, etc., and inducing them to take up salesmanship.

"Practically every field of endeavor is a source from which to draw salespeople. Specialty salespeople who are lured from one line to another on the whole are not particularly satisfactory unless you have a proposition of exceptional earning possibilities, which tends to advertise itself to other salespeople in other lines."

Some organizations of specialty salespeople are recruited through home-office training schools. Technically equipped salespeople also are hired from retailers or jobbers. As a rule, people whose services are sought, rather than the individual who seeks the job, are more desirable from the standpoint of results. However, such a method of waiting for unsolicited applications would hardly be feasible for companies that employ large staffs of specialty salespeople.

The NCR Corporation, IBM, Pitney Bowes, and many others in the office-equipment field recruit their best salespeople from the ranks of their servicepeople. In fact, it is a rule with many of these companies that in engaging a serviceperson, he or she must have the qualifications that make a good salesperson. In other industries, the most dependable salespeople are those who come up through the stockroom and know the business thoroughly.

Classified Advertisements

The preponderance of experience is decidedly against depending on classified advertisements as the sole means of finding good salespeople. But it is only fair to say that some sales managers still get most of their salespeople that way, and would not think of changing their methods. One sales executive is against classified advertisements on the ground that, "It is a good, reliable, lazy way to get salespeople, but after the prospective salespeople are secured through classified advertising, there is a tremendous amount of work that has to be done in sifting out the applicants and in training the very small percentage that finally stick and develop."

Most classified advertisements bring a flood of applications either in person or by mail. The professional ad-answerers are legion. They are the type of persons who seem constitutionally unable to hold any position very long. They are the floaters, and advance seekers. Weeding out these people requires a lot of interviewing, examining many application blanks, and endless investigating of references. Unless an organization is set up to handle applications on a wholesale scale, classified advertising may often prove the most difficult and costly method of recruiting salespeople. This may prove particularly true when only a few persons are needed.

While it is true that it requires time and work to weed out the undesirables who answer classified advertisements, many sales executives feel that this work and time are justifiable. In view of the cost of training new salespeople, and in view of the difficulties of finding good salespeople, even one promising letter out of a hundred applications is worth investigating. Many hundreds of letters of application can be scanned in a day, and the good ones can be set aside for further investigation; to find even one good person is worth the effort.

Here are a few things to remember when newspapers and other media are used:

- Sunday editions of metro papers get a good reading by people who are considering making a job change. Most metro dailies get statewide circulation, so you get more than a city audience for your ad. Even if your search is away from the city in which the paper is published, you may be sure that the people you're trying to reach will see it.

- An ad in a Sunday paper is worth more than two ads in a daily edition. However, you may find good candidates if you run the same ad the following Monday in a business section. The Sunday reader may become interested, but he or she is reinforced in enthusiasm and resolve when the same ad runs on two consecutive days.

- Consider suburban papers, particularly if those papers are published in communities populated by upwardly mobile people. Where are the singles apartments and the new small family homes? Where are the new shopping malls going up? Many suburban weeklies are well read by local residents.

- Don't neglect papers that have an appeal for special interest groups. If your objective is to balance your sales force by way of affirmative action, these papers may produce minority candidates for you.

- Trade journals or industrial papers are a good bet if you're looking for people in a specific industry. The closing dates or deadlines for accepting an ad in these publications require much more lead time than the normal newspaper, so they don't help in last-minute searches.

- Consider your corporate image when selecting media. If you wouldn't want to be represented by a certain type of person, don't run ads in the type of paper he or she is most likely to read.

Below and on the following pages are some sample employment ads with short critiques.

The series of ads, shown below, are very characteristic of the help wanted ads seen in most papers. They are too short and contain little real information to convince an applicant of the merits of the job.

The single ad on the right is an improvement over the others, but it still has too little sell copy. Keep in mind that your ad is designed to build traffic of the best quality and in the largest numbers. Consider the economics, too. Run a small ad many times, or run a large ad once or twice. You'll spend about the same either way.

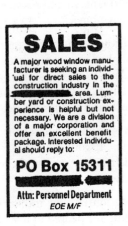

This ad tells the name of the employer, but solicits no resumes or applications. By putting just a telephone number, the employer will have to spend a lot of time just talking to a number of candidates, many of whom will not be qualified.

This ad is much better. It retains the confidentiality of the company by listing just a box number, but it will get responses.

SALES ENGINEER

A growing international automotive components corporation is seeking to fill this newly created position. The position will report to the Product Manager of the Small Motors Division. Primary responsibilities include contacting the Engineering Quality and Purchasing Departments of major automotive manufacturers as well as contacting major systems suppliers in the development of motor production from design conception to production introduction including economics negotiations on a yearly basis. Knowledge of front wiper motors, rear reciprocating wiper motors, wiper systems, seat track motors, window regulator motors and fan cooling motors is desirable.

Minimum requirements for this position include but are not limited to:

- 4 year Electrical Engineering degree or 4 year Electrical Technology degree or equivalent experience.
- 2 years experience dealing with major automotive engineering product groups or purchasing.
- French language skills desired but not mandatory

Some domestic and international travel may be required.

Salary and benefits commensurate with experience and qualifications. Please send resume to

Attn:

EOE

This ad presents itself well, with graphic border and type to fit the format. It contains a lot of information about the job itself. It is specific about all educational and experience requirements. Although it does not use an excessive sell on the salary and benefits, the reader will know they are there. This ad will draw the type of applicants you really want.

"Situations Wanted"

A salesperson is always a salesperson, and usually displays his or her resourcefulness in the manner in which he or she sells himself or herself. For this reason, a number of concerns make a practice of scanning the Situations Wanted columns, claiming that they get a better class of applicants as a rule than through their own advertising. A salesperson who takes the trouble to prepare an advertisement and makes the investment in the space is not apt to be a floater. The Equitable Life Assurance Society is a strong believer in this method of securing leads for good life insurance agents.

Developing Salespeople Within the Company

There is no question that this method is more effective than any other for the smaller organization, although many large organizations that maintain sales schools also claim that it pays in the long run. Those companies that have been most successful in developing raw material through their factory and office make this distinction, which is well to bear in mind: Salespeople are not recruited by accident from the shop or the warehouse, but rather careful attention is given to the employment of these persons when they first join the company. Even though a person may be given a job as a delivery person when he or she is hired, he or she is sized up at the time as a potential road salesperson. In one large tire company, the employment department schedules a certain number of jobs in each department of the factory for future salespeople—these jobs being occupied at all times by persons who will later be moved up to positions in the office and then to the sales force. In the automobile-accessory line, it is common practice to promote from stock room to city counter, to city sales, and to the road. The same is true of electrical jobbers. Lumber yards promote from the yards to the mill, to the office, the city counter, and then to road positions.

Recruiting College Graduates

Many companies seem to stress the recruiting of college graduates. The college graduate has been through something of a screening program and he or she is perhaps a person of appreciable potential. Some firms overemphasize the recruitment of the graduate. Some sales positions are such as to offer the graduate a satisfying career over a prolonged period. In perhaps too many cases, however, the graduate is hired with the impression that the sales job is a short-termed step along the way to an executive management position. Unless the firm is undergoing great expansion, it may be impossible to move large numbers of people recruited as salespeople into executive management. Unrealized expectations lead to a high rate of turnover among the sales force.

The manager of employment and college relations of Armstrong Cork Company (now Armstrong World Industries, Inc.), after checking with divisional general sales managers in early September to determine salespower needs for the next year, has scheduled visits to selected colleges by the company's recruiting team to meet with members of the administration and faculty, and to interview candidates for Armstrong sales positions.

"In our visits," an Armstrong recruiter explained, "we outline in detail the job opportunities and training offered. We give complete information on our company facilities, products, and scope of activity. When visiting a college, we take a list of its graduates who work for us. This indicates the type of person in whom we are interested and is a good advertisement for the company, since college students look up to graduates and the companies for which they have chosen to work.

"We regularly visit some 100 campuses and interview some 2,500 young persons, of whom about 400 are invited to visit our general offices for a day at the expense of the company. Approximately one-half of this number are for the sales divisions. While it is the employee relations department's responsibility to make the primary selection of candidates, it is the prerogative of the sales divisions to make the final selection. Therefore, at the home office interviews are conducted by as many marketing managers and other executives as possible, as well as by several staff executives who have had long experience in judging and selecting candidates. Unless there is full agreement on an individual by the sales division personnel, staff executives, and employee relations department personnel, he or she is not offered a job."

If the employing organization's size does not permit such an extensive canvass, recruiting in local colleges can be used to great advantage. It is imperative that such an organization sell the college on the opportunities offered, for it is only natural that the larger national organizations that have been conducting major recruiting programs hold the appeal for the majority of the students. Local companies will have to draw active attention to their opportunities to be successful in such a program.

Each year, eager, ambitious young people arrive at corporate offices seeking careers in selling and marketing.

"If the potential of today's youth is to be fully exploited and developed it is necessary not only to provide immediate compensation but to demonstrate prospects for future reward," states a report from The Conference Board based on a survey of 110 senior marketing executives.

Following are some of the elements they suggested as the basis for the development of a successful recruiting and sales personnel development policy:

- Rigorous hiring criteria

- Training and development

- Challenging assignments

- Rotation and "exposure"

- Team projects, task forces

- Frequent evaluation

- Promotion and other recognition

- Money

- Pride in selling

- The need to recognize marketing's value

What to Look for in College Graduates

While the qualities which contribute to the success of a college graduate in sales work are the same as those needed to make any salesperson successful, there are special considerations to be weighed in recruiting college graduates. These have been summed up by one sales executive as follows:

1. *Education.* Except for jobs requiring specific technical training, the course studied is unimportant. We are interested primarily in whether or not the candidate has been taught to think problems through logically and clearly and whether or not he or she has ability to reach a satisfactory conclusion. We must make certain, nevertheless, that he or she has a good command of the English language and is able to spell. The breadth of a candidate's vocational interests can be spotted sometimes in educational likes and dislikes.

2. *Earnings for school expenses.* We are quite interested in persons who have worked all or a part of their way through school. We have found that this type of candidate gains valuable practical experience, certainly demonstrates ambition, initiative, self-reliance, and knows the value of a dollar. He or she usually has confidence, cannot be discouraged easily, and has a more mature attitude toward job procurement and business in general. He or she views life somewhat more seriously than the student who has been given everything during his or her college career.

3. *Leadership.* Is the candidate a leader? Participation in extracurricular activities is very important to us. Is the candidate sufficiently interested and well-rounded to go beyond the scope of the books in order to obtain a well-rounded education? The ability to get along with others and to gain their respect is essential. Whether a person's interests are in athletics, fraternities, church or welfare work, campus politics, dramatics, or publications is not important to us. Our chief interest is in whether he or she has the ability to be a leader. Along with this, we are interested in his or her hobbies, since at times these are indicative of interests, versatility, ambition, and ability to lead.

4. *Character.* Good character is naturally a most essential quality. The school record, with faculty impressions and recommendations, should show readiness to accept responsibility and give an indication of the candidate's reputation on the campus. Self-reliance without conceit, and real initiative coupled with tact, are very desirable.

5. *Family and school background.* In considering family and social background, our purposes might easily be misconstrued; however, we have obtained some clues from this as to the individual's possibility of success. A young person's background and family life are very important. An applicant who has been given good work habits in childhood will usually make a better salesperson than one who has not had such training.

6. *College grades.* Once, concerns tended to emphasize scholastic attainments. But in our case, although there is a general feeling that an outstanding person should be in the first quarter of the class, we are not looking for this type if scholastic standing has been attained at the expense of a balance between outside work, social life, and leadership and development activities. I might mention here that in the larger group of average or above-average students, some have considerably more to offer than some of those who are in the upper one-tenth or so of the class.

Other Recruiting Sources

The following additional sources for recruiting salespeople are digested from the plans of more than 1,000 concerns that have gone out of the beaten path in their methods. These plans point out fruitful sources for a number of lines of business that have not heretofore taken advantage of them.

Employment Agencies. Comparatively few sales managers use employment agencies as a means of getting applicants for sales positions. As one states, "They are excellent media for securing labor, factory help, typists, stenographers, and often executives, but they seem to lack the prerequisites for choosing the type of person that makes a good salesperson." However, other executives report good success in recruiting through employment agencies when care is taken to give the selection executive detailed specifications as to exactly the type of person required.

Trade Associations. An activity undertaken by some trade associations on behalf of their members is to plan, either on their own or in cooperation with a university, a practical training course for salespeople. The industry as a whole is in a position to attract young persons for sales work, finance the general training required, and then make the salespeople available to members of the association. This idea has been used in recruiting and training printing salespeople, and can be widely applied.

Advantage of this plan is that it would provide the machinery to indoctrinate properly young men and women sincerely interested in selling with a constructive and forward-looking attitude toward their work. If reasonable care in selection is used, the percentage of persons who succeed should be relatively high. One good salesperson would yield enough profit over a period of time to repay the whole cost.

Competitors' Salespeople. Experience shows it does not pay to hire salespeople from competitors except under unusual circumstances, as when a weak competitor holds a high-class salesperson who is bigger than his or her job. The ethics of modern business demand that the competitor's salesperson must make the first advance, and even though he or she may be hired, there are several reasons why he or she does not as a rule make as reliable a salesperson as a person recruited by another method, or who has been developed within the organization. First, if he or she is a good person for you, he or she is worth just as much to his or her present employer, who would not be apt to let him or her go. Second, he or she will leave you as quickly as he or she left the competitor, carrying away in the bargain your confidential house policies. Furthermore, he or she has a lot of "old tricks," learned in another organization, which make it difficult for you to educate this individual in the policies of your house—so that in the long run the same amount of effort expended on another person will produce equal or better results. Of course, the lure is that he or she is already trained and has demonstrated what he or she can do at someone else's expense.

Drawing from Retail Clerks. This is an excellent source for companies selling a seasonal line that may alternate with the busy season in certain retail lines. The salespeople employed can develop their retail connections during one season, and go out on the road for the manufacturer or wholesaler during another season. One company gets most of its applications from people connected with shoe stores—proprietors, buyers, clerks, etc.—who have handled its line at retail. The selling season starts shortly after the first of the year and lasts from three and one-half to five months, and as these months are usually dull ones in the retail shoe store, many of its salespeople are able to handle both jobs satisfactorily. Retailers are also drawn upon by a large number of organizations to recommend salespeople who visit their territory and who they know might be interested in another connection that can be combined with their regular line.

Through Jobbers. Most jobbers' salespeople look upon the position of manufacturer's representative as a step upward and it very often happens that a jobber's salesperson will take a particular interest in a certain manufacturer's line, and the jobber is glad to recommend him or her, as it is a certain advantage to deal with the manufacturer through a person formerly on his or her staff.

Chapter 39

Selection and Hiring

The next steps after the recruiting efforts have been completed are:

- Pre-interview screening and preparation
- The interview process
- Reference checking
- Hiring

Pre-Interview Screening

George Lumsden* suggests that all of the resumes and application letters be given a first screening to knock out the candidates who obviously do not qualify on the basis of the information they sent to you. For instance, there may be candidates whose educational standards or experience are far below what you are looking for. On the second go around, separate those remaining into two piles—one for *must-see* applicants and one for *maybes*. Review the *maybes* one more time to see whether someone deserves more attention.

On each of the resumes you use for pre-interview screening are items of information—or lack of information—sufficient to make you ask questions. One thing that may be helpful to you is the Dartnell Sales Applicant Interview Guide shown in Figure 1, pages 813-819. This is something you can use during the interview, but it will also help you prepare beforehand. You may not fill it in completely prior to the first interview, but you'll have a lot of marks on it before you conduct a second interview with the same applicant.

---

*George J. Lumsden, *Building a Winning Sales Force* (Chicago: The Dartnell Corporation, 1986).

Figure 1. Sales Applicant Interview Guide

To the interviewer: This Applicant Interview Guide is designed and intended to assist you in selecting and placing sales personnel. When it is used for all applicants for an available position, it will help you judge among them and provide more objective information than you will obtain from unstructured inerviews.

Because this is a general guide, not all of the questions may apply for each position. Skip those that do not apply and add any additional questions you believe to be necessary. Be sure to use the same questions for each applicant for the opening.

Federal law prohibits discrimination in employment on the basis of sex, race, color, national origin and, in most cases, age. The laws of most states also ban some or all of the above types of discrimination in employment, as well as discrimination based upon marital status, physical or mental handicap or disability, or ancestry. Interviewers should take care to avoid asking any questions that suggest that an employment decision based upon such factors may be made.

Job Interests

Name: _____
Position applied for: _____
What do you think the job involves? _____
Why do you think you are qualified for it? _____

What would your salary or earning requirement be? _____
What do you know about our company? _____

Why are you interested in working for us? _____

Current Employment Status

Are you currently employed? _____ Yes _____ No. If not, how long have you been out of work? _____ What have you been doing? _____ If employed, why are you applying for this position? _____

When would you be available to begin work? _____
(continued)

Figure 1. Sales Applicant Interview Guide

(continued)

Employment Experience

(Begin with the current or most recent position and work back in time. Account for all periods of time, for at least 12 years. Military service should be considered as employment.)

Current or last job:

Company name _____ Address/location _____

Starting date _____ Date left _____ Current or last job title _____

What are (were) the major duties of the job? (Be specific and complete)

_____

_____

Have you held the same job the entire time you have been with this Company? _____ Yes _____ No. If not, describe the various jobs you held, the dates of each and the duties of each of the jobs: _____

_____

_____

What was your starting salary? _ What are you currently earning? _ How much of that is salary? _____

Bonus _____ Commission _____ Other _____ Comments: _____

Name of your current or last supervisor: _____

May we contact him/her? _____ Yes _____ No.

What did you like most about this job? _____

What did you dislike most about it? _____

How well do you think you did on that job? How do you think your work compared with that of others in the same or similar work with that company? _____

_____

(If the applicant indicates that he or she did not do very well:) Why do you think you were not more successful? What accounted for that? _____

_____

(If still employed) Why do you want to leave your current job? (If not still

(continued)

Figure 1. Sales Applicant Interview Guide

(continued)

employed) Why did you leave that job? _____
_____
_____

Job before the current or last one:
Company name: _____ Address/location _____
Started _____ Left _____ Last job title _____
Duties of your job at the time you left: (Be specific and complete) _____
_____

What were you earning when you left? _____ Please break that down
between salary _____, bonus _____, commission _____,
and any other forms of compensation _____ Comments: _____

Who was your last supervisor? _____
May we contact him/her? _____ Yes _____ No.
What did you like most about that job? _____
What did you like least about it? _____
Did you have other jobs with that employer before the last one?
_____ Yes _____ No. If so, describe them, their titles, dates, and your
duties. _____
_____

How well do you think you did with that company? Relative to others doing
the same or similar jobs, how did you do? _____
_____

(If the applicant indicates that he/she did not do well, ask for a further explanation.) _____

Why did you leave that company? _____

Any other comments about the company or your job with them? _____
_____

Job before that one:
Company name: _____ Address/location _____
Started _____ Left _____ Last job title _____
Duties of your job at the time you left: (Be specific and complete) _____

What were you earning when you left? _____ Please break that down
between salary _____, bonus _____, commission _____, and any
other forms of compensation _____ Comments: _____

(continued)

Figure 1. Sales Applicant Interview Guide

(continued)

Who was your last supervisor? _____

May we contact him/her? _____ Yes _____ No.

What did you like most about that job? _____

What did you like least about it? _____

Did you have other jobs with that employer before the last one? _____ Yes _____ No. If so, describe them, their titles, dates, and your duties. _____

_____

How well do you think you did with that company? Relative to others doing the same or similar jobs, how did you do? _____

_____

(If the applicant indicates that he/she did not do well, ask for a further explanation.) _____

Why did you leave that company? _____

Any other comments about the company or your job with them? _____

_____

Interviewer: If the total length of employment in the last three jobs is insufficient, use additional sheets to go back further.

If there were any gaps in the applicant's employment history:

There is a gap between your employment at _____

and your employment at _____

of _____ months. Can you explain this? _____

What were you doing during this period to support yourself?_____

_____

Sales Experience

What kinds of sales work have you done? When, where, and for how long?

_____ Retail _____

_____ Door to door _____

_____ Delivery or route _____

_____ Missionary _____

_____ Technical _____

_____ Specialty: Tangibles _____

_____ Specialty: Intangibles _____

_____ Big ticket _____

_____ Other _____

(continued)

Figure 1. Sales Applicant Interview Guide

(continued)

How do you feel about selling to:
Consumers _____
Jobbers/wholesalers _____
Retailers _____
Industrial users _____
Government _____

Do you have experience in:
(If the answer is yes, ask for details)

	Yes	No	Comments
Starting new accounts			
Display work			
Product demonstrations			
Negotiating prices			
Telephone sales			

What types of sales work do you enjoy most? _____
_____

What types of sales work do you like least? _____

Have you traveled in previous jobs? _____ Yes _____ No. If yes, how much? _____

Did you like travelling? _____ Yes _____ No. Did travelling create any family problems? _____ Yes _____ No. Comments: _____

If the job you are interviewing the applicant for has travel, ask the applicant how he/she would feel about it. _____

If applicant has indicated that some prior travel caused family problems, ask how these will be handled if he/she gets this job. _____

Education

What is your highest level of education? _____
If it is a college or graduate degree, in what area? _____
Name of college or university _____
What scholastic awards or prizes did you receive? _____
What activities did you participate in? (Caution applicant to omit those which indicate religion, race, color, sex or national origin.) _____

(continued)

Figure 1. Sales Applicant Interview Guide
(continued)

Further educational or training activities which might be pertinent to this
job: _____
_____

Health

The purpose of this section is to help determine if you have any health-
related problems which might interfere with your ability to perform this
job.
How is your general health? _____ In recent years, have you had
any health-related problems? _____ Yes _____ No.
If you have such problems, please describe them _____
How much time have you lost from work due to health in the last five
years? _____
Do you have any physical or mental conditions which might affect your
ability to perform the job for which you have applied? _____ Yes
_____ No. If so, describe the problem _____
Have you had a physical examination recently? _____ Yes _____ No.
When was your last physical? _____
If employed, would you be willing to take a physical at our expense?
_____ Yes _____ No.

Citizenship

Are you a U.S. citizen? _____ Yes _____ No. If not, what kind of visa do
you have? _____ Are you legally permitted to work?
_____ Yes _____ No.

Miscellaneous

What off-the-job activities do you enjoy?
_____ Part-time job   _____ Clubs   _____ (other) _____
_____ Athletics   _____ Reading   _____
_____ Spectator sports   _____ Youth work   _____

Personal

What do you think are your strong points? _____
_____

What do you think are your weak points? _____
_____

(continued)

Figure 1. Sales Applicant Interview Guide*

(continued)

Interviewer: If there are any discrepancies between the employment application or resume and the interview, try to clear them up at this point. Ask the applicant about them. _____

_____

Before the applicant leaves the interview, the interviewer should explain the job in more detail and generally discuss the company, the work location, and other factors that might affect the applicant's interest in pursuing the position further.

_____ Job details discussed   Interviewer's initials _____

Interviewer's impressions:

Personal characteristics—rate 1 to 4, with 1 being the highest:

	1 2 3 4	Comments
Neatness, cleanliness		
Dress		
Poise, manner		
Speech		
Cooperation with interviewer		
Job-related characteristics:		
Experience		
Knowledge of job		
Interpersonal relationships		

Overall rating for the job:

_____ Superior   _____ Above Average   _____ Average
                        (Well qualified)   (Appears qualified)

        _____ Marginal   _____ Unsatisfactory
        (Barely qualified)

Comments or remarks _____

_____

        Interviewer _____ date _____

---

*"Sales Applicant Interview Guide," Form S-2, an 8½″ x 11″, 6-page form, can be ordered in quantity from Dartnell, 4660 Ravenswood Avenue, Chicago, IL 60640.

Screen first. Don't make decisions other than, "These are the people I want to see most." Cut the pile down, but don't cut it down too far. If you're interviewing 20 people, you're seeing too many. If you're seeing only one or two, you're seeing too few.

There Are Laws to Obey

Whatever we may feel about current labor laws, we are obliged to obey them. To some employers, they pose restrictions. To others, they are meddlesome. To most sophisticated and well-run businesses, they are constructive efforts to do away with some of the discriminatory hiring practices of the past. Prior to the interview, condition yourself mentally to adhere to them completely.

The laws involved are these:

- Civil Rights Act of 1964, including Title VII
- Age Discrimination in Employment Act
- Fair Labor Standards Act
- Equal Employment Opportunity Act of 1972
- Equal Pay Act of 1963
- Executive Orders

If we were to summarize these laws in a single statement, that statement would be:

Federal Law prohibits discrimination in employment on the basis of sex, race, color, creed, national origin, and age. Most states also ban discrimination based on marital status, physical or mental disability, or ancestry.

In short, care must be taken to adhere to these restrictions so that nobody can make the case that a hiring decision has been made with any of these conditions in mind. Go to the extreme in order to avoid difficulty with the laws.

Begin with a Legal Application Form

If your company's application form has not been checked by legal counsel in recent years, have it checked. The form should not ask for more information than the law allows. If the applicant provides you with information beyond what is asked for, that is his or her own choice.

If a resume is attached, that is also the applicant's choice. Do not require pictures to accompany resumes or applications. If a picture is sent, return it to the applicant.

What You May Ask and What You May Not

"It's getting so that you can't ask anyone anything anymore, except name and address, and I'm not really sure you can do that," said one sales manager. It may seem that way, but you can find out a lot in a perfectly legal manner if you ask the right questions.

AGE

You may inquire whether or not an applicant is at least 18 years of age. That's all. You can't ask date of birth, nor should you ask applicants to indicate what year they completed high school or college; those are clear indicators of age.

SEX

You may ask a female applicant whether the travel required in a job poses any problem to her, but you may not ask how her husband feels about it, or how her children will be cared for if she does travel. Such questions imply that a woman's role is as wife or mother. Do not ask a female about her typing or clerical skills; this may suggest that you are trying to fit her into a traditional female work role. Do not suggest that her qualifications for your sales job are under your requirements, but that you have an in-house clerical job she might consider. Keep your entire conversation riveted to the job at hand.

If a female applicant indicates she is married, do not ask her maiden name, nor ask any questions regarding her feelings on any of the women's rights issues.

MARITAL STATUS

If an applicant volunteers information regarding his or her marital status, simply acknowledge the fact. Do not solicit such information or ask if he or she has children, whether the spouse is employed or what the spouse's name is.

CREED OR RELIGION

Do not inquire as to an applicant's religious denomination or affiliation, religious holidays observed, or mention priest, rabbi, or minister.

NATIONAL ORIGIN

You may not ask an applicant who has an unusual name to identify what nationality it is, where he or she was born, or the birthplace of his or her parents. You cannot require a birth certificate or baptismal record.

CITIZENSHIP

You may ask an applicant whether he or she is a citizen.* If the answer is *no,* you may ask whether the individual intends to become a citizen, and you may also ask if he or she has the legal right to remain permanently in the United States. You may not ask of an applicant what country he or she has citizenship in.

If the answer is *yes,* you are not allowed to ask whether that citizenship is native-born or naturalized, require presentation of naturalization papers, or ask about the citizenship of parents or spouse.

RACE OR COLOR

You may not make any comment or ask any questions regarding the applicant's complexion or color of skin. You may not suggest that a photograph is vital to the employment process.

---

*Since the passage of the Illegal Alien Amnesty law in 1986, it became the employer's responsibility to ask job applicants if they are U.S. citizens. If they are not, the employer needs proof that they are not illegal aliens.

HEALTH

You may ask applicants about any impairments they may have that would interfere with the job for which they have applied, but you may not ask about disabilities and handicaps in general, or whether they have been treated for specific diseases, or whether they use any adaptive device or aid. You cannot require females to have pelvic examinations. You may ask about any contagious or communicable diseases that may endanger others.

You should not make inquiry into an applicant's height or weight. You may ask the applicant if he or she will take a physical examination, if hired, at company expense.

CONVICTIONS

You may ask an applicant about convictions, but not about arrests. Our legal system presumes innocence unless proven guilty. If a conviction is indicated, you are allowed to ask the nature of the offense and when it occurred.

AFFILIATIONS

You may inquire about an applicant's role in an organization so long as that organization does not have a name or character that indicates race, color, religion, national origin or age. Your application form should, if it asks such information, have the disclaimer displayed—"Omit any organizations that reflect . . ."

EDUCATION

You are free to inquire fully into an applicant's academic, technical, or professional education, including public and private schools attended and levels of achievement.

EXPERIENCE

You may inquire fully into work experience, positions held, nature of work done, supervisor, reasons for leaving. The applicant should be told that you will check work references, and you should ask if there are any employment references he or she would prefer you not check. This is especially important in the case of a present employer.

PERSONAL DATA

You may ask name, address, telephone number, social security number, name of any person to be notified in case of emergency (but not the relationship), and personal aspirations and expectations in making application for this job.

GENERAL

The safest line of inquiry is to stick close to education and work experience. What you want to know is whether or not the individual will be able to perform in the sales job you have to offer. Whatever the applicant volunteers in an interview or in a resume is entirely legal, but you should exercise care not to pursue areas of volunteered information that have legal implications.

The laws tell us, principally, to stay out of personal lives. They were written to eliminate hiring decisions based on prejudice. You will, in any carefully designed and controlled interview, uncover enough about an individual's disposition and character, his or her attitudes and interests, to make a sound hiring decision.

You know what kind of person you are looking for. As you interview, you may discover that early opinions vanish in the face of what you learn in an interview. If you have prejudices, subdue them. If you haven't, take care not to appear to have them.

Since the laws were written, many employers have discovered that the kind of people they once thought wouldn't work out have done very nicely. Once you discipline yourself to stay within the law, you'll discover that you can deal with job-related issues and hire competent individuals of all ages, sexes, national origins, religions, races, married or single.

Preparing for the Interview

The next step is to have the applicant fill in your standard application form after he or she has arrived for the interview but prior to the interview. The contents of the Dartnell Application for Employment-Sales are shown in Figure 2, pages 825-829.

Prior to having the applicant come into your office, review his or her completed application against the resume and the Interview Guide.

Figure 2. Application for Employment—Sales*

To the applicant: Thank you for your interest in our organization. Your application will receive consideration without regard to race, creed, color, sex, age, national origin or handicap. To enable us to properly and fairly evaluate your application, please answer all of the questions as carefully and completely as possible.

Personal Data

Name _____

Address _____

Do not write here

Telephone No. _____ Soc. Sec. No. _____

Position applied for: _____

Salary expected _____ When could you start? _____

General Information

Previously employed here? ___ Yes ___ No. If so, what were the dates of your employment? From _____ to _____. Supervisor's name _____

Your position _____

Can you furnish proof of age, if necessary, to comply with legal restrictions? ___ Yes ___ No.

What prompted you to apply to our company? _____

Employment Record

Please provide information covering your employment history. Cover at least your last four jobs and at least the last 12 years. Include periods of military service, if any. Note any gaps in your employment. Begin with your most recent job and work back.

Name and address of Company	From Mo.	Yr.	To Mo.	Yr.	Starting Salary	Last Salary	Reason for Leaving	Name of Super.

_____ In detail, describe your duties _____

_____

_____

_____

Tel. No. _____

Type of business _____

(continued)

*"Application for Employment—Sales," Form S-1, an 8½"x11", 4-page form, can be ordered in quantity from Dartnell, 4660 Ravenswood Avenue, Chicago, IL 60640.

Figure 2. Application for Employment—Sales

(continued)

Name and address of Company	From		To		Starting Salary	Last Salary	Reason for Leaving	Name of Super.
	Mo.	Yr.	Mo.	Yr.				

_____ In detail, describe your duties _____

_____

_____

_____

Tel. No. _____

Type of business _____

Name and address of Company	From		To		Starting Salary	Last Salary	Reason for Leaving	Name of Super.
	Mo.	Yr.	Mo.	Yr.				

_____ In detail, describe your duties _____

_____

_____

_____

Tel. No. _____

Type of business _____

Name and address of Company	From		To		Starting Salary	Last Salary	Reason for Leaving	Name of Super.
	Mo.	Yr.	Mo.	Yr.				

_____ In detail, describe your duties _____

_____

_____

_____

Tel. No. _____

Type of business _____

(continued)

826

Figure 2. Application for Employment—Sales
(continued)

Current or most recent employer:
May we contact these employers? ___ Yes ___ No
List by name any previous employer you do not wish us to contact. ___

___

Is there anything further we should know about your employment history?
Other jobs, skills, periods of unemployment, etc. ___

___

___

What specific kinds of selling experience have you had?
- ___ Calling on the trade   ___ Delivery or route
- ___ Retail (over the counter)   ___ Missionary
- ___ Specialty (tangibles)   ___ Technical
- ___ Specialty (intangibles)   ___ "Big Ticket"

For each of the above where you had experience, list the firm, lines sold
and amount of experience. ___

___

___

___

Education

Level	Name/city	Major field	Graduate?	Degree/certificate
Elementary				
High School				
College				
Bus/Trade/Technical				
Other				

Other activities: list past or present activities. Omit any organizations which
reflect race, color, creed, sex, religion or national origin.

Type	Name/description	Active from	to	Offices/ dates	Still active?

(continued)

Figure 2. Application for Employment—Sales
(continued)

Health

In the last five years, how much time have you lost from work due to health? _____ When was your last physical examination? _____
What was your physical condition? _____
What is your present physical condition? _____
Do you have any physical or mental conditions which might interfere with your ability to perform the job for which you have applied? ___ Yes ___ No.
If so, please describe the condition _____
If hired, would you be willing to take a physical examination at our expense? ___ Yes ___ No.

Personal References—do not list relatives or former employers

	Name	Address	Phone No.	Relationship
1				
2				
3				

Self-Assessment

What do you think are your greatest strengths as a salesperson?
_____
_____
_____

What do you think are your greatest weaknesses as a salesperson?
_____
_____
_____

What else could you tell us which might enable us to make a more accurate assessment of your qualifications to work for our Company? _____
_____
_____
_____

Please read the completed application over carefully before signing it below.
The answers to the above questions are true and complete. I understand that any inaccurate or misleading information will cause rejection of this application or dismissal. I grant permission for the Company to investigate my references and I authorize my references to provide any information to the Company that they deem appropriate. I authorize the Company to make an investigative consumer report which may contain information obtained through personal interviews with my friends, neighbors and acquaintances. If made, this inquiry may include information as to my character, general reputation, personal characteristics and mode of living. I understand that I

(continued)

828

Figure 2. Application for Employment—Sales

(continued)

will have the right to make a written request within a reasonable period of time to receive additional information concerning the nature and scope of any investigative inquiry.

In consideration for my employment, I agree that my employment and compensation can be terminated with or without cause, and with or without notice, at any time at the option of either the Company or myself. Further, I understand that this agreement can only be modified by the Company President or Vice President, and only in writing.

Signature _____ Date _____

Interview scheduled for _____ at _____

Interview by _____

Second interview ___ Yes ___ No

Scheduled for _____ at _____

Interview by _____

Third interview ___ Yes ___ No

Scheduled for _____ at _____

Remarks _____

Conducting the Interview

The interview is by far the most important step in the selection procedure. Successful interviewing is more than a knack. It involves techniques shown by experience to be the best ways to draw from an applicant the information the applicant prefers to withhold.

Ask Proper Questions Properly. Your objective is to pull out of the applicant as much information as you need to make a sound hiring decision. You want the applicant to provide you with that information as completely and freely as possible. That means that your tone of voice will be inviting, not demanding. You will seek, not intimidate. Here are some suggestions on the kinds of questions you'll ask and how you'll ask them:

1. *Ask open questions.* An open question is one that cannot be answered by a simple *yes* or *no*. It is characterized by the use of what are often called journalistic words — how, why, when, where, what. Use any of those words as the lead-in to a question, and it has to produce information. For instance:

   • How long have you been thinking about selling as a career?

   • Why do you feel that working for XYZ Company will be a good career move for you?

   • When did you first enter the field you are now in?

   • Where do you feel you should be, say five years from now?

   • What sort of things challenge you most—in work or at play?

   Questions such as these will produce conversation between you and your applicant. And the information you get will be fuller and more revealing than if you had asked what are called *closed* questions.

2. *Use closed questions.* Closed questions, although they will not produce the type of information open questions can, are

valuable in checking and confirming what has already been said. They can also be useful in introducing new subjects, and then open questions can be employed. For instance:

- Are you currently employed? (Yes) Where?

- Did you graduate from college? (Yes) Which one?

Their biggest asset is in the area of checking and confirming:

- Let's see. It says here that your degree was in marketing. It that correct?

- I notice that you were employed for only six months with Uptown Industries. Is that right?

- And you are definitely interested in selling?

3. *Extend the applicant's response.* There will be times when the applicant volunteers information, or presents only a part of what you want to hear. It is the interviewer's job to pull out more of the story invitingly. For example:

- I think that's interesting. Tell me more about that.

- Well, you really were on the spot when that happened. Go on with your story.

Get to the Heart of the Matter. If all there was to interviewing was a review of what is on the resume and application, it would be a simple task. You want to go beyond the documentary information and get the background. Significantly high on your priority list should be:

- Unexplained time gaps in employment

- Voids in educational information

- Reasons given for leaving jobs

- Numbers of jobs and duration of employment

Some questions you will want to ask are:

- Regarding your present job, what do you like most and least about it?

- In what way does your present job and other experience seem to fit the job you're applying for?

- In your school career, what kind of activities were you involved in beyond the classroom, and which were most satisfying to you?

- What sort of growth have you seen in your past employment?

- What sort of growth do you anticipate if you were to take employment with this company?

- What are your real reasons for wanting to leave your present job and seek employment elsewhere?

Watch Your Time. Some applicants are more interesting and more vocal than others. Some prompt you to ask more questions than others. Time can get away from you if you don't watch it carefully.

- Don't rush the interview, but be selective of areas of inquiry.

- Listen carefully and make notes you can refer to later if it becomes necessary.

- When interviews seem less than productive, as with candidates who aren't particularly interested or well suited, find ways to cut the interview off early. Don't do this until you are very sure you have heard what you wanted to, and that the applicant will feel that he or she has had a fair hearing.

- Schedule interviews far enough apart so that if you do need more time, you can take it.

Interview, Don't Sell. A common mistake some interviewers make is to get lost in describing the job to the applicant; they sell instead of interview. Keep detailed information about the job in reserve until you are very sure the candidate is one of several you will consider seriously. For example:

- Make your preliminary remarks about the job brief and keep any hint of a sales pitch out of them.

- If you must go into detail, say, "The individual who will be selected for this position will.." Never phrase a comment, "You'll be expected to . . ." That sounds too much as though the selection has been made.

- Keep the focus on the applicant, listen, ask, don't talk too much.

Avoid Any Hint of Illegality or Entrapment. We have covered the legal aspects of interviewing, so you are well aware of specific areas you can't explore. However, you may—if you're not careful—fall into other illegal areas. Here are a few examples:

- You said that you were married and that you have no children (volunteered information). Is that because you choose not to, or can't? (Very personal—very illegal.)

- You say you speak German fluently. Did you learn that at school or at home? (National origins are taboo.)

Entrapment is almost as bad. It puts people on the defensive. As much as you might like to know about something, don't entrap or lead answers:

- Your transcript says that you majored in education. Couldn't you get a job as a teacher?

- You say you didn't like the management policies at your last place of employment. What makes you think you know what good management policies are or are not?

- You don't like your present manager, do you? What does he or she do wrong?

Multiple Interviews

If your company policy is to have more than one person interview an applicant, advise the applicant accordingly. Normally, you will not have another person interview your applicant if the applicant doesn't please you. Or, it could be the opposite way around; you may have an assistant interview first, then refer only the better candidates to you. It's a matter of company policy and/or personal preference.

If it is convenient, arrange any multiple interviews to take place on the same day and in the same place. Applicants are often taking time away from their present jobs, and we should always consider their situation.

Second Interviews

If candidates appear to be promising, and you can't make a decision in a single interview, suggest that you will want to see them again after your first round of interviews. Again, don't give false signals. If you have three good candidates and can choose only one, put it that way to the applicant.

Second interviews are likely to be shorter, and you may be asked to make a decision quickly. Don't let an applicant push you for an answer. But be sure you crowd second interviews into a short span of time, and give responses fairly quickly afterward.

Approvals for Reference Checks

You will run reference checks only on your best applicants; to do all of them would not only be time-consuming, but it could also be a breach of confidence for some applicants.

Any applicant on whom you wish to check references should be asked prior to any checking. The question can be as simple as this:

- May we have your permission to check with the people you have listed as references in the event we want more information on your background?

You will certainly not check with a present employer, and you should tell the applicant that you will not do so.

Candidate Ratings

A candidate evaluation form is shown in Figure 3, page 835. This form should be used by multiple interviewers, if that is the policy, and it should also be used by you, the prime interviewer. It

Figure 3. Candidate Evaluation Form

Person interviewed	Date	Comments	G*	F*	P*	Recall?

*Good
Fair
Poor

is, for the most part, a simple check-off sheet that lets you condense your findings and feelings about an applicant. In the event you interview many individuals, it will help you keep them in proper perspective.

Again, as with your initial grading of candidates from the resumes, you will probably end up eliminating some and keeping top candidates for further examination.

For Those Who Don't Make It. You owe applicants who have taken time to interview a letter of thanks and, perhaps, a word of encouragement. You are not obliged to be specific regarding your turndown, just polite.

Making the Right Hiring Decision

It is frequently easier to make an ongoing business decision than to make a hiring decision. In the normal course of business you are dealing with known factors, but in hiring situations you are dealing with a few unknowns. Your best bet is to rid yourself of as many unknowns as possible. That means probing around, asking others and checking references.

Reference Checks

A properly designed applicant form will have on it a disclaimer such as:

The answers to the above questions are true and complete. I understand that any inaccurate or misleading information will cause rejection of this application or dismissal. I grant permission to the company to investigate my references and I authorize my references to provide any information to the company that they deem appropriate. I authorize the company to make an investigative consumer report that may contain information obtained through personal interviews with my friends, neighbors, and acquaintances. If made, this inquiry may include information as to my character, general reputation, personal characteristics, and mode of living. I understand that I will have the right to make a written request within a reasonable period of time to receive additional information concerning the nature and scope of any investigative inquiry.

So your applicant, in signing the application, is well aware of reference checking. You will have further alerted him or her to it by asking at the close of the interview for permission.

The investigative consumer report is a credit check done by organizations like Dun & Bradstreet and Merchant Credit. If you have a candidate pretty well selected, you'll run such a check while you make other reference checks yourself.

Telephone Checking

Your simplest way to get a lot of references checked in a hurry is to use the phone. The important factor, however, is knowing the kind of questions to ask. A copy of the Dartnell form Pre-employment Telephone Reference Check—Sales Applicant is shown in Figure 4, pages 838-840.

As you review the form, note how the questions are asked. In the beginning, the checking is done on the basis of initial information supplied by the applicant. After you have won the confidence of the reference—and assured yourself of his or her honesty—you will ask more personal questions. Probably the most important question is: "Would you rehire this individual?"

Assemble the Evidence. Your best candidates are those who gave you impressive information on the application, interviewed well, and came out clean on reference checks. You will now be able to invite the individual back for a final interview.

You have an application, rating sheet, reference check, and resume before you. Now your concern is whether a second impression is as good as the first. If it is, you're on the verge of the hiring process.

Decision time. It's easy to cull out the poorest and the best. The real problem lies in deciding between the best. Here are a few suggestions:

- Go back to your spec sheet. Which one has all or most of the qualifications you are looking for in the first place? That's an important step, because when we interview, we are attracted

Figure 4. Pre-Employment Telephone Reference Check
Sales Applicant*

Name of Applicant _____ Social Security No. _____
Current Address _____
Under consideration for the position of _____
                    Reference checked by _____
Prior employer: Name of employer _____
        Address _____ Tel. _____
        Person contacted _____ Position _____
I'd like to verify some of the information given to us by Mr./Mrs./Ms
_____ who has applied to our
organization for a position in _____ .
Do you remember the person? (If not, try to obtain the name of someone
who would recall the applicant.) I would greatly appreciate your assistance
in verifying some of this information and in obtaining your assessment of
the individual. We will hold any information you provide in confidence.

Note: Try to take as many notes as possible of any exceptions to the information furnished by the applicant, as well as of the respondent's assessment of the candidate. Do not trust to memory.

Some questions may be inappropriate for the particular position you are filling. If so, skip over those items.

1. The applicant says that he/she was employed with your company from _____ until _____ . Is that correct? If not, what were the correct dates?

2. What was the applicant's first job with you? What was he/she doing at the time of termination? What other jobs did the applicant hold with you?

(continued)

*"Pre-employment Telephone Reference Check Sales Applicant, Form S-3, an 8½"x11", 2-page form, can be ordered in quantity from Dartnell, 4660 Ravenswood, Chicago, IL 60640.

Figure 4. Pre-Employment Telephone Reference Check
Sales Applicant

(continued)

3. At the time of termination, the applicant says he/she was earning _____ per _____ . Is this correct? If not, can you give me the actual earnings?

_____
_____
_____

4. How much of this was salary?
        commission?
        bonus?
        other (explain)
What was the basis of pay?

_____
_____
_____
_____
_____
_____
_____

5. What type of selling did the applicant do?

_____
_____

6. How did the individual's results compare with those of others who were doing the same kind of work? (If not good) What do you think was the reason that results were not better?

_____
_____
_____
_____
_____

7. How did the person get along with others?

Customers _____
Supervisors _____
Fellow employees _____
_____

8. Were there any problems with customers?

_____
_____

9. Compared to others, was the applicant a hard worker?

_____
_____

(continued)

Figure 4. Pre-Employment Telephone Reference Check
Sales Applicant

(continued)

10. How was attendance?
    Were there any problems
    which affected attend-
    ance?

    _____

    _____

11. Did you know of any do-
    mestic or financial prob-
    lems which interfered with
    work?

    _____

    _____

12. Any problems with gam-
    bling or drinking?

    _____

    _____ _____

13. Why did the applicant
    leave your employ?

    _____

    _____

14. Would you rehire? If not,
    why not?

    _____

15. What were the applicant's
    strong points?

    _____

16. What were the weak
    points?

    _____

17. What type of sales work
    do you think the applicant
    could do best?

    _____

    _____

18. In your employ, did the ap-
    plicant travel?
       If so, how much?
       How long away from
       home?

    _____

    _____

    _____

Interviewer:

19. List here any other ques-
    tions you wish covered.

20. Other comments

to certain individuals, and sometimes make an emotional choice.

- What are the greatest lacks in your two or three best applicants? Remember, you can't rebuild character or personality quickly or easily, but you can train people in how to do the job. Favor the individual whose deficiencies are most easily corrected.

- Consider which of your applicants will interact best with your type of clientele. Which one will have the greatest credibility? Which one has the social aptitudes which will connect best?

- Which one would represent you most satisfactorily? Members of a business organization are extensions of their managers.

- We have all seen salespeople work effectively by themselves, but who never seem to fit into the organization. If you're content with a mismatch of this sort, fine, but bear in mind that somewhere down the road you'll be looking for promotables, assistants, people to bring into the home office. That's what you have to consider, as well.

In a sense, you are doing a computer function on the various people you have interviewed. Maybe you'll end up hiring nobody, because no one in your battery of applicants meets your specifications. That's not all bad, either. Just start again. Maybe, as sometimes happens in large and growing organizations, you'll hire two instead of one. One, two, or none ... know the reasons why.

The Value of Consultation

If you set up multiple interviews, here's your opportunity to take advantage of the opinions of others. Seek out points of view, then express your own. The more opinions you get, the better off you are, even though you will make the final decision yourself. Multiple interviews, incidentally, make a great training ground for assistants; they learn from the interviewing and from observing your decision-making skills.

Call Them in Again. If it takes a second or third interview to make a decision, don't hesitate to ask for them. Something might happen the second or third time that will change your opinion of a candidate completely. Win or lose, the applicant who is finally chosen knows the care with which he or she has been selected, and will realize what the performance expectations will be.

The Loser. Winners get the job. You'll see more of them in your hiring procedure. Losers are gone. That's a point to bear in mind—the loser you let go today may be the candidate you want to talk to next week, next month, six months from now. For instance, the winner is hired contingent on the satisfactory completion of a physical examination, and what happens if he or she fails it? Or, you may discover that after you hire and think all your slots are filled, you have a salesperson quit on you. The person you struggled over and finally passed over may be the best deal in town.

Be sure to write or talk to the losing candidate. Don't make any promises, but don't leave any scars. One sales manager said, "I treat every applicant as a potential customer." That's not a bad way to leave the subject.

Psychological Testing

The subject of psychological testing has produced two schools of thought—sales managers who swear by it, and sales managers who swear at it.

Aptitude testing for selecting salespeople is frowned upon in those situations where do-it-yourself aptitude tests were sold to industry and applied by the inexperienced. A specialist in the field of psychological testing has said, "Do-it-yourself psychological testing has as much validity as do-it-yourself cancer cures." Seeming to substantiate this statement are a number of sales executives who tried this type of testing and were disappointed.

There are, of course, large corporations with psychologists on their staffs or under contract who test all salespeople routinely before employment. Obviously, these companies are convinced of the value of such tests when administered and interpreted by professionals.

Two Types of Tests

The fundamentals of testing salespeople are generally considered in two categories:

1. Personality

2. Sales aptitude

Tests in the first category are intended to answer the question, *"Does this person have a good sales personality?"* In the second category are tests intended to answer the question, *"Does he or she have the proper aptitudes for selling?"*

Sometimes these tests are combined, sometimes separate, sometimes administered by the sales executive (who "grades" them with a set of prepared answers and a scoring chart), sometimes by a psychologist on the staff, and sometimes by outside consulting firms, with or without psychologists. Considering the wide variability of practices, it is not surprising that evaluation of such testing is statistically hard to come by.

PERSONALITY TESTS

Tests for "sales personality" run a gamut of desirable and undesirable factors from A to Z. For example, one company specializing in this type of testing lists such factors as:

1. Aggressiveness

2. Business sense

3. Confidence

4. Dominance

5. Enthusiasm

6. Foresightedness

7. Group sociability

8. Happiness

9. Incisiveness

Those who feel that question-and-answer psychological tests are of limited value list a number of defects. These include:

1. Oversimplification

2. Neglect of potential for personality development

3. Varying degrees of articulateness of respondent

4. Lack of standards for comparison

5. Lack of statistical validity

6. Lack of self-knowledge

7. Tendency to "fake" replies

SALES APTITUDE TESTING

Included in, or separate from, the personality tests, a series of "sales aptitudes" is often evaluated.

Practically everything that has been said pro and con with regard to the sales personality tests is repeated with reference to testing for sales aptitudes.

The usual sales aptitude evaluation covers such factors as the following:

1. Verbal intelligence

2. Ability to communicate ideas

3. Controlled aggressiveness

4. Sales sense

5. Insight into higher motivation

6. Diplomacy and tact

7. Ability to accept criticism

8. Resistance to discouragement

9. Sales motivation

10. Self-discipline

The overlapping between sales aptitudes and personality qualifications is quite frequent.

Additionally, potential sales executives may also be evaluated for such factors as:

1. Administrative ability

2. Emotional stability

3. Ability to inspire others

4. Business judgment

5. Supervisory capacity

6. Initiative

7. Resourcefulness

8. Maturity

9. Organizing ability

10. Training skills

There can be no difference of opinion on the value of determining how a prospective salesperson measures up in such factors as those listed above. The difference of opinion arises in the concept of whether valid tests can be made of such factors.

In commenting on aptitude testing, an officer of a highly succesful sales organization in the textiles field reports that his company uses aptitude and psychological tests primarily:

- When hiring a person, to be assured that he or she will properly fit in with the company and in the job requirements;

- When wishing to upgrade a person to see if he or she has the capacity to handle a more complex job.

We never conduct mass testing, believing that:

- The disturbance caused outweighs the added knowledge gained.

- Little will be added to our present knowledge of the individuals. Management already knows if they are doing a good or bad job. If management has been periodically reviewing their work progress and has been counseling with them as it should do, a program for their development is already in progress.

But for even these limited applications there is a considerable difference of opinion among sales managers as to how much dependence can be placed on psychological tests.

On the other hand, you find considerable enthusiasm for psychological testing in the insurance field. Some years ago, the Life Insurance Sales Research Institute, worked out what it calls the "Aptitude Index" for use among member companies, and it proved helpful. Obviously, developing a battery of tests to be applied to applicants selling a special and similar service offers less opportunities for error than when the test is general. It should be noted, however, that these tests are not represented to institute members as a means of doing the entire selection job, but rather as a tool for checking judgments of supervisors after applicants have 1) been screened 2) been interviewed, and 3) had their references checked.

An executive of one of the major automobile sales organizations had this to say: "We have experimented off and on for about six years with psychological tests and aptitude testing for salespeople. I am personally sold on the value of such tests in general, but I am convinced that there is a lot of testing being done that is far from hitting the mark, not because the idea is unsound, but because the tests themselves are improperly designed, executed, or both. I believe there is a place for scientific testing but there is still a lot of work to be done before a sales manager can feel safe in depending on such tests."

Even though tests are carefully validated—that is to say, tested on the best and worst people in your sales force—they must still be checked for reliability to fully determine their value in the selection procedure. This requires about two years' time.

Personality tests have been the most vulnerable to attack. According to one report, the greatest success to date in selection techniques has been with what psychologists call the *Biographical Information Blank* or *Background Survey*. These are based on the premise that the best predictor of the future is the past. In this technique questions are asked about early family background, childhood hobbies and activities, past school performance and extracurricular activities, attitudes toward past experiences, etc. But instead of the applicant answering in his or her own words (as he or she would in an interview), he or she checks one of the several alternative answers that are provided in the questionnaire.

Experience indicates that some types of tests are more likely to predict job success accurately than others, and this is as specific as one can be until the tests have been tried in actual situations.

Efficient Appraisal Procedure

Any appraisal system should include a minimum of four tests and inventories to aid in the appraisal of mental equipment, aptitude for selling, stability, and vocational interest in selling activities. To add more tests frequently measures the same general factor a second time and decreases the emphasis upon and the time for interviews and investigations in the appraisal of personal history.

The appraisal system should include a good personal history blank to aid in the appraisal of physical qualifications; education; occupational experience; financial status and achievement; activities; contacts; financial capacity to survive, and all other factors known to be important. The factors mentioned are best appraised by interviews and investigations, although supplementary steps are recommended to ensure sound conclusions.

The system should include a convenient manual of instruction and a good rating form to facilitate appraisal procedure.

Appraising Health and Vitality. The majority of people think of health as the absence of illness. Few understand the substantial differences in the degree of vitality that exists even among persons who appear to be in good health. Far too many salespeople are handicapped by the lack of full vitality, so important to the generation of enthusiasm while engaged in selling activities. This means that the employer and the medical examiner should look for vitality, as well as for the negative factors of illness and impairments, that will hinder a salesperson.

Appraising Mental Equipment. The mental equipment of an individual cannot be appraised as a single unit factor, but must, instead, be appraised in several dimensions. It cannot be appraised by the use of intelligence tests alone, since some highly intelligent people have not yet acquired much knowledge and experience. Neither is mental equipment determined by the number of years of education, nor by the degrees and diplomas received. It has been clearly demonstrated that some high school graduates are the equal of others who have been graduated from college. It is necessary, therefore, to appraise mental ability, education, and experience. (See Table 1, page 849.)

An accepted method is through the use of a standard mental-ability test with proper adjustments for differences in age. It has been found that as people grow older the speed with which they can complete test items decreases even while their knowledge and experience increase.

The appraiser also must bear in mind that the graduates of each high school and college vary a great deal in the type of courses completed and the quality of work done. Without question, the graduates who earned high grades in recommended courses possess more useful knowledge, on the average, than graduates who earned average or low-average grades, or high grades in courses of doubtful value in business.

The amount and soundness of knowledge possessed by a salesperson as related to a given field of work are best determined by a special objective examination developed for the purpose. Such tests are helpful in appraising experienced salespeople or applicants for promotions but are much less so in the appraisal of applicants for employment on an apprentice basis. Without such tests, appraisals must be made with interview.

Table 1. Ability Factors (Ability to)

ITEM	Class 1	Class 2	Class 3	Class 4
1. Analyze	Develops essential facts in any situation	Usually gets to bottom of problems	Unable to form conclusions	Often misinterprets facts
2. Create or Invent	Develops and expands his work	Occasionally creates and executes ideas	Fairly aggressive	Waits to be told
3. Visualize or Imagine	Possesses unusual foresight	Quick to grasp possibilities of new plans	Slow to show enthusiasm over changes	Can only comprehend facts proven by experience
4. Make Decisions	Prompt and accurate in conclusions	Makes few errors in judgment	Usually hesitates between two courses of action	Does many ill-considered things
5. Select and Develop Others	Picks winners and develops them	Chooses good salespeople and trains them well	Occasionally develops a good salesperson	Sometimes spoils potential executives
6. Organize	Creates harmonious efforts among individuals to a constructive end	Secures concrete results by directing efforts of others	Secures loyalty of workers but cannot get results	Cannot secure team work
7. Cooperate	Will help others at personal sacrifice	Good team worker	Strictly an individualist	Selfish and obstructive
8. Be Tactful	Contacts always pleasant	Approach usually good	Occasionally in wrong	Gets in wrong continuously
9. Be Efficient	Puts effort where it counts the most	Discriminates between important and unimportant matters	Does not always apply himself or herself to best advantage	Takes everything as it comes
10. Express Ideas Clearly and Convincingly	Uses forceful words in effective manner	Logical but not impressive	Cannot put ideas in understandable form	Cannot interest people in his subjects
11. Work Accurately	Others always agree with results	Usually accurate	Makes a few errors	Work always has to be checked
12. Work Rapidly	Exceptionally quick	Can speed up under pressure	Usually behind others	Very slow
13. Remember	Never forgets a thing	Can usually recall salient facts	Has to be occasionally reminded	Cannot retain facts or details

Miscellaneous Factors

1. General Knowledge	Talks intelligently on all subjects	Knows something about most subjects	Well read on a few subjects	Limited to superficial facts
2. Specialized Knowledge	Is an authority on his or her subject	Thoroughly conversant in his or her field	Not always certain of facts	Makes incorrect statements
3. Health Habits	Takes best possible care of self	Follows consistently good habits	Slightly impaired by occasional dissipation	No care of self—habitual dissipation
4. Physical Constitution	Rugged—never sick—stand anything	Occasional sickness	Must take care—cannot overwork	Work impaired by poor health
5. Neatness	Immaculate	Always presentable	Sometimes lax	Careless in appearance of person or work

Executives should be asked to fill out the form to the extent of their personal observation and knowledge of the person in question. During the salesperson's employment with a company, such a record, made by a person qualified to do so, is of great value in rating him or her on present work or for promotion.

Chapter 40

Training the Sales Force

Sales training has been recognized as a vital factor in the success of a salesperson. Training programs range from the elaborate, complex procedures of giant corporations to the simplified plans employed by smaller companies.

Forty Years of Sales Training

To gain a proper perspective of the development of sales training over the past 40 years, Robert Whyte of the Porter Henry Company, New York City-based training experts, summed it up in a presentation to the National Society of Sales Training Executives. Here's what he said:

The 1940s

The 1940s saw the development of the famous Job Instruction Training formula that was developed during World War II to teach skill training to factory workers. It was a four-step process:

- 1. Tell 'em.
- 2. Show 'em.
- 3. Let 'em do it.
- 4. Review it.

The JIT formula was used for a good many years after World War II and for jobs other than factory training. It's still a pretty sound approach to almost any kind of training, as the success of this method brought the realization that people learn best by *doing* combined with feedback on their performance.

Also, with the realization that *salespersons are made and not born,* sales training became recognized as an essential marketing function.

Now, think about that for a moment. Research has undeniably shown that most persons in the profession of selling come to it after having one or two other jobs. And therein lies the need for proper sales training and its importance in your sales operation.

During the postwar period, tools and techniques such as job profiles, employment criteria, interviewing techniques, and aptitude testing emerged. Trainers were teaching *product, product, product* and *features, features, features*. The sales presentations that existed were 100 percent canned.

The AIDA formula was conceived—get their *attention,* then their *interest,* arouse *desire,* and then comes *action.* Training techniques were short and sweet, consisting of lecture, lecture, and more lecture.

The '50s

This decade saw the emergence of *field* sales training as opposed to classroom training.

On-the-job coaching and the "curbstone conference" became regular operating procedures.

Sales training films, produced by Dartnell and featuring sales training actors Borden and Busse, dramatized on screen how to make sales talks more effective. Their classic films, "Opening the Sale," "Closing the Sale," "Overcoming Objections," "Presenting Your Case Convincingly," and "Developing Your Sales Personality,"—all produced in the '50s and early '60s—all left their mark on trainer and salesperson alike.

In the '50s, training started to pick up steam. John McCarthy was the first person to talk about *the psychology of selling.* He taught us what the word *empathy* meant, and we turned our attention to the needs and concerns of the buyer, the prospect, and the customer. This led to *benefit selling* and the *features-benefits* approach.

Dale Carnegie wrote *How to Win Friends and Influence People* and *The Five Great Rules of Selling.* Elmer Wheeler turned a wisecrack, "Don't sell the steak, sell the sizzle," into an imposing business philosophy; Red Motley taught us that "nothing happens until something is sold.''

In the late 1950s and into the '60s, we learned about *the laws of learning.* We involved trainees in the learning process and spawned a wide range of training methods such as the buzz session, brainstorming, case studies, games, debates, team exercises, and so on.

The hardware revolution began in the '50s. Trainers rushed out to buy the opaque projector, and later, the overhead transparency projector; 35mm slide and film strip projectors; record players; magnetic audio tape recorders, reel-to-reel 16mm motion picture projectors, screens, and films; and flannel boards and special lighting effects.

Recruiting, selecting, and hiring of salespeople received increased attention, led by Dr. Robert McMurry with his important Dartnell manual and forms designed for this critical selection process.

The '60s

Probably the most significant of the four decades for sales trainers, the '60s were filled with enormous ferment, searching, and innovation. The behavioral scientists dumped an endless stream of concepts and theories on us. Everyone was urged to help everyone else to achieve self-actualization!

We had Abraham Maslow and his *hierarchy of needs;* Douglas McGregor's *theory X and theory Y;* Frederick Herzberg and his lists of *satisfiers* and *dissatisfiers* and *hygiene factors;* Dr. Livingston and his *pygmalion effect;* plus Odiorne, Lippitt, Lickert, and scores of others.

The trouble was that behavioral jargon was substituted for clear, simple English and we had a heck of a time figuring out what they were saying to us.

We experienced an electronic revolution in the '60s—videotape recording systems, color cameras, videotape cassettes, audiocassettes, and tape recorders.

With videotape recorded playback, skill-building and role play practice became a more effective learning experience.

One highly touted training technique held sway for a short time and then bit the dust—*sensitivity training.* Most trainers were glad to see it disappear.

Off-the-shelf audio-visual training programs began to appear and found application in many sales training curricula.

The '70s

The '70s were marked by a curious phenomenon. After the dizzying deluge in the '60s, the behaviorists faded into silence. We haven't been offered a "universal solution" in years!

While their influence will undoubtedly continue to be felt, the social scientists will be forced to do two things in the years ahead: 1) support the relevance and application of their concepts to salespeople; and 2) speak to us in English.

One fad in the '70s—Harris and Berne's *Transactional Analysis*—was an overnight sensation. It was an intriguing new method of using the logic box, but like most fads, not much is heard about it today.

A new word came into being—*Salesperson*— recognizing the many females joining the ranks. We learned how to train Blacks and Hispanics.

Management by objectives, conceived by Dr. George Odiorne, became a corporate way of life in the 1970s and sales trainers were challenged to adapt it and teach it to field salespeople. The only problem was that field salespeople already had a very tangible set of goals imposed on them—the sales numbers. This led the way in wedding the numbers to a development of a set of supportive goals.

Field sales management was under enormous pressure to do a better job *right now,* so training became more practical and reality-oriented and less theoretical in nature.

Training began to focus on the basics like:

- Recruiting, selection, and interviewing
- Field coaching
- Performance evaluation
- Counseling
- Planning and conducting sales meetings
- Management by objectives

We taught sales reps how to find out the needs of their buyers and then how to satisfy them. In order to do that, we had to teach them how to engage in a meaningful dialogue.

What a far cry from the canned presentations—the one-way communications—of the '40s and '50s.

Sales reps had to learn how to become a genuine resource to their customers and prospects. The implications to training departments and training techniques were enormous and continue to be so.

Sales call planning and time and territory management both came in for far more training attention then they had ever received before. This healthy trend continues.

We're still hung up on motivation theory. Any presentation of theory on motivation will always draw a crowd. I guess we'll always be looking for the "quick fix."

Maybe we never *will* identify all those things that genuinely get people moving and maybe that's as it should be.

The '70s brought another big change and a happy one—the kind of people you're training. They are bright, they are challenging, and I think they are more fun to train. They are also quick to question; they don't simply accept things. They want to be heard and they feel they have the right to question. We have shaped our forums accordingly. Because of this, you are better trainers and they, in turn, are better trained.

During the 70s, the *Career Path* concept was developed, along with its logical companion—*assessment centers.*

In terms of classroom training techniques and philosophy, the '70s seem to have been a period of maturing and refinement rather than one of explosive innovation.

The technical/electronic explosion has continued. Closed-circuit television got better and is easier to operate.

One of the most important developments in the '70s was the introduction of methods and systems to properly identify training objectives and to analyze performance problems.

And an exciting change has occurred in the attitude of management toward the training function. Companies, by and large, have come to accept and support the importance of training to a company's success.

It is also reassuring to see how many more bright and dedicated people are entering the training field, not merely as a stepping-stone, but as a career. There is room for both.

In the early days, training was primarily concerned with business problems and not very much with people problems.

In the '60s, the social scientist told us that if we just took care of the people problems, the business problems would take care of themselves.

Today, I believe it is fair to state that trainers are concerned about both business *and* people problems.

And it is you who are achieving an appropriate and a real-world balance.

The '80s (and the '90s)

Well, with all of the accumulated knowledge, experience, experimentation, and innovation of the past, we should carefully distill and refine all that's available and apply it in a maturing sense to each of our specific training functions. Not all will work in every situation and some of it can be rather suspect. Do not neglect the basics and fundamentals and get caught up too much in the new catch words, phrases, and theories.

Training and trainers are maturing. We are heading into a more business-minded era. There will be more emphasis on getting trainees ready to produce faster and weeding them out quicker.

One key element in a successful training program is to make sure that you, line sales management, *and* the trainee are in full accord, and in step with, what your training and results should be.

As a major step in that direction, I refer to a research study by Dr. Alan Dubinsky* of how sales managers, sales trainers, and sales personnel independently rate eight steps in the selling process as important or unimportant.

The significance of this study is that if the salespeople aren't being trained in those areas that at least both their boss—the sales manager—and the sales trainer agree are important, you can have some pretty mixed-up people out there making sales calls.

Trainees must be taught the skills upon which their bosses will be measuring and rewarding them.

---

*Alan J. Dubinsky, *Sales Training: An Analysis of Field Sales Techniques.*

The Three Phases of Training

The training of new salespeople, as distinct from "refresher courses" for experienced people and continuous training activities such as sales meetings, educational contests, etc., has three phases: 1) Group-training the new person at the outset of his or her employment, similar to the "vestibule" training of production employees; 2) field-coaching new people; and 3) formal classroom training.

In these three broad divisions of sales training there are four steps essential to effective training: 1) Tell them; 2) show them; 3) let them do it; 4) check to be sure they are doing it.

What are the gains to be expected from a sales-training program? Does formalized sales training really pay off?

We know that the experience of hundreds of successful companies proves that sales-training programs can pay off in many ways. New business and more sales can be obtained from new customers; larger territories can be covered with less waste of time and effort; company policies and procedures will be better known and understood; the time and cost of supervisory and administrative efforts can be reduced; costs of turnover can be lowered; goodwill can be increased and returns reduced through reduction, if not total elimination, of ill-advised sales and wrong recommendations.

But these desired accomplishments require careful advance planning and experienced guidance.

The amount of training to be given depends on too many variable factors for generalization: on the product or service to be sold, on its degree of simplicity or complexity, on the market and type of buyers, on the education and previous experience of the sales trainees, and on the extent of information needed to be passed along to salespeople on company policies and procedures. All these factors must be qualified in advance of launching the program.

Sales executives in charge of planning sales training might be guided by considering the following points, in terms of company operations, needs, and special conditions:

1. To what extent do new salespeople need to be indoctrinated and trained before being sent out to sell?

2. How much training is needed and justified for established salespeople whose selling efforts are not up to a reasonable par?

3. How much, and what kind of training, is needed for established salespersons at such times as the following:

- When new program or products are being introduced;

- When market conditions are changing;

- When marketing methods or policies are being changed;

- When changes are being made in distribution or pricing policies;

- When the status or the organizational position of established salespersons is to be changed.

Whether you are dealing with a single trainee or a group, the sales manager or his delegated substitute must have a planned schedule so that things will start to happen as soon as the trainee walks in and will continue in an orderly fashion. Unfortunately, some managers look upon the indoctrination of a recruit as a necessary but irritating interruption of their usual (and more or less comfortable) routine. They forget that whenever a person reports for duty he or she already represents a substantial investment in recruiting, screening, investigating—and finally—employment, whether this is done by a central staff office or by the manager. An orderly, planned, and organized program to get the new person into productivity with a minimum investment of time and further dollars is one of the job responsibilities of any sales manager.

These same questions should be asked with regard to training order clerks, sales supervisors, and department heads in the sales department, who are too often overlooked in the sales-training program. It is sometimes as important, for example, that the order clerk be aware of sales policies as that the salesperson keep abreast of them, since in many cases the people in the home office can contribute to the overall efficiency of the selling operation to a much greater extent than they do when merely blindly following routine.

Why Special Training Is a Necessity

True, a salesperson's merely being on the job and going through the process of calling on people, presenting his or her products or service for purchase and the acceptance of orders, will result in some training. But how good the training will be, what the salesperson learns or does not learn, what work habits and attitudes he or she does or does not acquire—these are something else. If the salesperson is wide awake and above average in observance, he or she may acquire many favorable fine skills from watching the reactions of customers. On the other hand, he or she may learn to be biased in favor of his or her customers.

Through conversations with other salespeople, he or she may learn what the outstanding salespeople do, or he or she may learn the wrong things. Such "training" is a gamble with the odds against the company. Special training is the only answer.

To be sure, training costs money. For the company to train its salespeople is expensive; so, too, is it expensive for its salespeople to be *mistrained* by customers or other salespeople. If the company does the training, it can at least appraise and budget all costs. If others do the training, it is anyone's guess how much the cost will be in lost orders, in the poor handling of complaints and requests for undue credits, in the expense of poor routing or indifferent effort, in the headaches of abnormal managerial supervision, and in the hiring and eventual rehiring of replacements when the unsuccessful salespeople leave. (See Table 1, page 858, for typical sales training costs.)

If the cost is to be incurred anyway, what will it probably be and how much can a company afford to spend on training? It is difficult to generalize.

For a small company, the training would probably have to be done by the sales manager and the training course would be quite informal.

With a medium-sized company, the sales-training course might be prepared by staff personnel and some class work given, supplemented by on-the-job direction.

With a large company, there might be a fully staffed training department, well equipped for research and with training tools.

Table 1. Sales Training Analysis by Industry*

Industry	Number of Companies	Training Cost Per Sales Trainee	Most Used Method of Compensation During Training	Length of Training Period (in Months)
Aerospace	3	$21,666.67	Salary	12
Appliances (household)	2	11,500.00	Salary	6
Automotive parts/Accessories	4	15,875.00	Salary	4
Auto and truck	3	6,750.00	Salary	3
Banks/Bank holding/ Finance co.	3	12,000.00	Salary	4
Beverages	7	12,571.43	Salary	4
Building materials	6	7,583.33	Salary	4
Chemicals	12	10,891.67	Salary	4
Computer products/Services	20	18,074.95	Salary	6
Drugs/Medicines	5	24,440.00	Salary	8
Electrical equipment/Supplies	5	12,000.00	Salary	6
Electronics	9	14,222.22	Salary	7
Fabricated metal products	14	13,907.14	Salary	6
Food products	10	10,104.20	Salary	6
Glass/Allied products	2	14,771.00	Combination	6
Healthcare products/Services	18	8,011.11	Combination	4
Housewares	1	3,500.00	Commission	2
Instruments/Allied products	7	15,357.14	Salary	6
General machinery	6	23,333.33	Salary	5
Iron and steel	3	30,000.00	Salary	9
Life insurance	5	29,400.00	Salary	11
Casualty insurance	5	24,091.20	Combination	19
Non-ferrous metals	3	46,666.67	Salary	11
Office machinery/equipment	10	15,100.00	Salary	6
Paper/Allied products	1	70,000.00	Salary	24
Petroleum/Petroleum products	5	7,900.00	Salary	3
Printing	6	30,333.33	Salary	12
Publishing	8	5,362.50	Combination	5
Radio and television	2	4,250.00	Salary	4
Rubber, plastics, leather	5	16,500.00	Salary	11
Service industries	23	11,750.00	Salary	4
Textile and apparel	2	26,000.00	Salary	7
Tobacco	1	6,000.00	Salary	3
Tools and hardware	2	10,000.00	Salary	4
Transportation	6	6,020.83	Salary	4
Transportation equipment	2	9,600.00	Salary	4
Utilities	3	6,666.67	Salary	5
Other	45	13,192.96	Salary	6
All Industries	**274**	**$14,435.00**	**Salary**	**6**

*Dartnell's 24th Biennial Survey of Sales Force Compensation

However, the cost per trainee might be about the same in all three types of companys, when all expenses, direct and otherwise, are considered.

Who should be trained? Obviously, new salespeople should be trained, and established salespeople should be retrained when the luster goes out of their performance. Sales personnel should be trained in *their* work, to assure effective operations and to give them an awareness of how they mesh in with other departments and activities.

Then the trainers themselves should be trained, to be sure they train the way the company wishes them to train.

What Should Training Cover?

The training process is aimed at creating more sales volume through better sales presentations and the better closing of orders. It is also aimed at improving the atmosphere in which the salesperson works. It is aimed at improving his or her knowledge about the history and objectives of the company, its products, its services, its policies, its procedures, and formalities.

It is aimed at contributing to his or her personal development and advancement in the company, and to creating interest in staying with the company.

Determining Training Needs

In Dartnell's *Building a Winning Sales Force,** George Lumsden offers suggestions and guidance.

The formula for determining training needs is simple: What the job requires in terms of skill and knowledge minus what the individual already knows and can do equals what needs to be taught and practiced.

This is one reason why sales managers like to hire experienced people; they have less training to do. A person who already knows the product, for instance, may need skill development in how to

*George J. Lumsden, *Building a Winning Sales Force* (Chicago: The Dartnell Corporation, 1986).

sell it. A person who has proven selling skills may need only knowledge of the product to function well.

KNOWLEDGE

There is more to selling than knowing the product or service. A good rep will know what his or her customer's business is, what the market involves, and how customers think, feel, and function. That is knowledge. What one does with knowledge is skill. To be effective, sales reps should be thoroughly familiar with the following kinds of information.

1. Product

   - How it is used

   - What its features are

   - What benefits those features provide

   - What advantages our product has over competition

   - What limitations our product has

   - How the product is made

   - What the product is made of

   - What makes the product work

   - How the product functions

2. Customer's business

   - The nature of the customer's business

   - What the customer will do with the product—retail it, use it to produce his or her own product, use it as a necessary support to a business, use it personally

   - How the product is especially important to the customer

   - Why our product fits the customer's needs better than a competitive product—use, versatility, delivery, price, service, etc.

- If the customer is a retailer, how consumers need and use the product and how to merchandise it, display it, advertise it, and sell it

3. Market

  - Where the greatest use for our product is
  - Where the greatest volume potential lies
  - What other industries can find use for the product
  - What other uses can be made of the same product in a given industry
  - What competition is doing in the same market
  - How to find ways to overcome competition

4. Customers

  - How customers tend to think, feel, and function
  - How we gain attention, confidence, and approval

It is possible to know all of the above—product, customer's business, market, and customer—and still not be able to do anything with all that knowledge. That's where skill comes in.

SKILL

Skill is what you do with what you know. It the case of the product, for instance, the skill is being able to translate the product into benefits that fit the customer's needs, attach features and functions to support the benefits, and communicate effectively.

Here are some of the interpersonal skills a good sales rep must possess if he or she is to succeed.

- How to connect with people on a friendly basis
- How to establish rapport that opens and cements relationships
- How to listen and respond

- How to display confidence and develop it with customers
- How to behave in social settings
- How to be friendly and businesslike at the same time

Basic Selling Skills

The following skills are essential components of good salesmanship.

- *Planning—the call, the time, and the territory.* The salesperson who can't plan will see fewer prospects, make fewer presentations, convert fewer customers and make fewer sales than the salesperson who can.

- *Prospecting—finding new people to sell to and broadening the market.* What every business needs is a larger share of the market, and not all of it can be done with existing customers.

- *Qualifying—determining buyer needs and diagnosing buyer habits.* Too many salespeople begin a presentation without understanding their audience. They're like the cowboy in the old cartoon—standing in front of the western saloon, right foot heavily bandaged. The caption reads, "Quick on the trigger, but slow on the draw." Knowing where the target is, is worth a lot in any shoot-out.

- *Presenting—explaining the product in such a way that the buyer understands, is interested, and feels compelled to buy.* No product sells itself; the interpretation the salesperson provides enhances the product's value in the buyer's mind. Communication skills—speaking, listening, handling objections— are vital at this step.

- *Demonstrating—showing the product to its best advantage.* A demonstration is proof of the presentation. "A picture is worth a thousand words."

- *Trial closes—using checking and confirming questions to test the customer's understanding and interest.* Such questions should be used throughout the sales encounter.

- *Negotiating—coming to grips with prices, terms, and conditions.* Some products are not subject to negotiation, some are. Whatever the situation, salespeople must have the skill to cope with prospects who are going to make buying decisions based on one or several variables.

- *Closing—finalizing the sale or getting a commitment.* This is often perceived as the most difficult step in the sale, and indeed it is—if the other steps haven't been handled properly.

- *Following up—making sure the customer is wholly satisfied or making adjustments if the customer is not.* This is probably the most neglected part of the selling process. Here is where objection-handling skills are often as useful as they are in the presenting, negotiating, or closing steps.

Experienced sales pros develop these skills, but where they haven't been developed—especially to your satisfaction—there's a training need indicated. Without experience, the whole battery of basic skills constitutes a curriculum in itself.

In addition to the development and practice of good skills, knowledge and attitude are vital factors in sales performance. They differ in these ways:

- Knowledge is *learned* from many sources—instructors, association with product, customer, and market. The more a salesperson knows, the better he or she will function in the sales responsibility. Read a book and you acquire knowledge.

- Attitudes are *developed.* They are encouraged, complimented, criticized, copied, counseled, acquired. This is not a matter of training, but of motivation. However, a well-trained individual who possesses knowledge and performs skillfully is generally the individual with the best attitude.

A FORMULA

Skill + Knowledge = Competence

Competence × Attitude = Performance

Put numbers to that formula, if you will. Using 10 as tops, you can quantify it easily.

Skill (9) + Knowledge (9) = Competence (18)

Competence (18) × Attitude (5) = Performance (90)

Raise the attitude level to 6, 7, 8, 9, or even 10, and see what happens to performance.

Competence (18) × Attitude (7) = Performance (126)

Or see it in another perspective:

Skill (7) + Knowledge (8) = Competence (15)

Competence (15) × Attitude (10) = Performance (150)

This is not an argument against training. This is mere recognition of the fact that some individuals, with less than superior knowledge and skill, can outperform those with greater knowledge and skill if they have an edge on attitude. Again, the trained person—the individual who appreciates the fact that you have spent time, money, and patience on his or her training—will generally respond with a better attitude.

Training Programs—Make or Buy?

A serious question—even in larger companies where training departments exist—is whether to create your own programs or buy them on the outside. There are good reasons on both sides of this issue, and most of them rely on the nature of your business and the size of your organization.

ONE OR MANY?

Larger sales organizations are generally supported by an in-house training department. Some training departments are complete organizations—program developers and instructors capable of building and presenting a complete program. Some training departments are no more than a single manager whose responsibility it is to define training needs and acquire the necessary resources to satisfy those needs. Such departments are capable of organizing instruction, but they must buy outside professional services to create programs and deliver them. If you manage within a larger structure, contact your training manager and discuss your needs with him or her.

Smaller organizations may not have the benefit of training organizations. The training problem is squarely up to the sales manager. You may not have enough people at any one time to offer classroom training. Instead, everything comes one-on-one and on-the-job. You can still organize a curriculum, buy the materials needed to support that curriculum, present some of it yourself, and let your salespeople develop with home study courses. One thing some sales managers do is call their organizations together quarterly, semi-annually or annually, and make a day or two of the meeting into a training session.

In such cases, it is common to find a person who specializes in certain fields—time and territory management, communication skills, basic or advanced selling techniques, sales psychology, or customer relations—and let that person provide instruction to the group. Exercise care in the choosing of such consultant help; they should provide you with a course outline or proposal that defines the content and describes the style of instruction.

The conclusion we ultimately reach in deciding which technique is best is that all techniques should be used at various times and for various reasons. For instance, product knowledge is a good subject for self-study if it is reviewed and clarified in a class setting, then tested on the job. We might teach *about* a skill in a classroom and reinforce the concepts with good self-study materials, but skills can be best learned in practical use—on the job.

Different Industries—Different Demands

The judgment about what training is needed, how it is applied, and whether it should be created inside or purchased outside depends greatly on specific industries. For instance:

Pharmaceuticals. Companies that make and sell prescription medications are seriously concerned about product information in the training of their sales personnel. Salespeople must know their own product and how it compares with similar products of other companies. But they must know more than that; they have to know what the drug does, what illnesses or conditions call for its use, what its limitations and hazards are, and so on. Such training must be precise, and it is unlikely to find an outside training program that can do what needs to be done.

Some pharmaceutical companies use outside materials and

trainers for selling skills training if such programs lend themselves to the type of selling pharmaceutical salespeople do. Case in point: Detail salespeople are not "closers" in the same way most salespeople are—they recommend and get commitments from doctors who do not buy the product. With drug stores, they do a modest type of close based on the fact that the product should be on hand when the doctor prescribes it.

Technical Sales. Technical sales personnel are more likely to function as consultants and advisors than as product sellers. The product is collateral to the advice. To be sure, the product knowledge is important, but more important are sales techniques that generate long-term relationships. The technical salesperson has to know a lot about the nature of the business to which he or she is selling and how the product applies in a given application. This calls for a different kind of sales training.

Sales to Retail. The wholesale salesperson will probably deal with two very different types of buyers—the central office professional buyer who purchases merchandise for a chain of stores, and the individual store proprietor who is interested only in one retail outlet. And then there are the products that are for the mass merchandise outlet, versus the products that are more suitable for boutique retailing.

Some wholesale salespeople are more business counselor than seller. Automotive representatives help dealers with business problems—merchandising, advertising, display, selling systems, business management, and operations. The success of the outlet dictates the volume of wholesale sales. It is possible, in this case, to know very little about the product and still be successful in the sale of it.

Packaged goods salespeople vie for shelf space more than sell the product. Soft drinks, cereals, soaps, and staple items fall into this classification. This type of salesperson can be marginally trained in the product and heavily trained in human relationships.

Retail Sales. Here, too, is a different type of training. Some retail selling requires little more than interpersonal skills; the customer decides on the product, and the salesperson facilitates the sale. Some retailing is more product-oriented; hardware salespeople have to be Mr. Fixits, helping buyers know what to choose for the job to be done. Some retailing is more financial counseling than selling; a car salesperson may spend time selling the vehicle, but even more time selling the deal. An insurance salesperson has to be effective in selling the idea of insurance even more than the product itself.

Shelf Programs

The training business has some very fine people in it. Some are very pedantic, others very practical. Some are sincere in the programs they present, others are snake oil merchants of the highest rank. The best advice is to look at a few of the many shelf programs available, and select the one most closely suited to your needs. Nobody can tell you anything better than that. It doesn't mean a thing that a hundred thousand people have gone through a given course of instruction if that course of instruction can't teach your salespeople how to sell your product or service to your particular market.

Most shelf programs are generic. Your problem will be to make the generic program company and product specific. That, in most cases, is a real task.

What you might do with a generic program is take the central ideas and present them, creating your own examples and roleplays. Or, if a self-study, programmed instruction package is available, you might buy such a package and have salespeople go through it. Don't expect a generic program to do the whole job; it can provide structure and basic concepts, but you'll have to make it fit your own purposes. Use outside materials for support and teach your own way. Before you rush out and buy an off-the-shelf program, you might want to study the training program outline supplied in Figure 2 at the end of this chapter, pages 891-893. It is basic, generic, and simple, allowing you to add your own materials and your own instruction. With it, you may also measure the appropriateness of some standard program you'd like to buy. It is designed to give you an idea of what the typical sales training program should have. A booklet series is available and specifically designed to complement this outline. Extra copies of the booklets may be ordered for each of your sales reps. For information, call the customer service department at Dartnell. The telephone number is (312) 561-4000.

The Outside Training Consultant

There are many competent trainers whose services are purchased by companies to handle training when inside specialists are not available. A really good trainer will acquaint himself or herself with your specific product, service, system, or market in advance of any training done. That same trainer will also supply you with information like:

- Other companies for which training has been done

- The names of people within those companies who can tell you how the individual performs and what may be expected

- A content outline of the materials to be covered

- A style definition—lecture, workshop, roleplaying, a/v use, study or work materials supplied, etc.

You may want to use a professional training consultant as part of your training effort, or you may want to delegate such a consultant to do almost all of it. Bear in mind that consultants are generally skill trainers, not product-knowledge trainers, so there is still a fair share of training you'll have to do for yourself.

Unless you want to use a trainer as an entertainer, steer clear of showboaters. There are many speakers who are not trainers. They can excite audiences, inspire people, tell entertaining stories and put on memorable performances, but they don't teach anyone much about the business of selling. In fact, some showboaters are so proficient in what they do that they literally discourage their listeners from trying to do it. We have all heard salespeople come away from such performances saying, "I wish I could do that, but I know I can't."

If you want an after-dinner speaker or a keynoter or a wind-up motivator, hire one. If you want a trainer, find someone who is less likely to use the platform as his or her own playground, but who has a reputation for getting results from students.

Need help in finding the right person to help with your training? Here are a few sources and the kinds of people they are likely to recommend to you:

- *American Society of Training Directors.* You'll find a local chapter near you. This organization has recently added sales trainers to its list. Some are already in place with their own companies. Others are self-employed and available to you.

- *National Society of Sales Training Executives.* This organization is wholly dedicated to sales and sales management training. Most members are actively engaged in a given company, but there are associate members who have their own training organizations or are free-lancers. Call their Sanford, Florida headquarters for a list of associates. Their telephone number is (407) 322-3364.

- *National Speakers Association.* This organization of speakers is headquartered in Phoenix, Arizona. While many of their members are keynoters and after-dinner speakers, many are also sales trainers and/or specialists in some aspects of training. Ask them to send you a copy of their current *Who's Who.* Telephone: (602) 265-1001.

Audio-Visual Aids

Why struggle with explaining something when a professionally made motion picture or videotape can do it more dramatically and more memorably? What we know is that most producers make films or videos for the widest possible market, so such products are generic. They will not—nor should they be expected to—handle your product instruction or your specific sales procedure, but they can be both interesting and helpful if you can effect what is known in the educational business as "transfer." That, in a nutshell, means you can use the ideas shown in the film and build on them for your own purposes. If your salespeople sell cloth and the illustration in the film talks about china, you make the transition, or transfer.

As an example, the Dartnell classic film feature, *Second Effort,* has Vince Lombardi, the legendary coach of the Green Bay Packers, as the central figure. Lombardi wasn't a salesman. But he had ideas about success that salespeople should know. The film is full of hard-hitting blocks and tackles, dramatic open-field running and sensational pass catching, but those elements were designed to hold attention. In more quiet and deliberate passages, the great coach passes on good advice that anyone could use. That's where the instruction really comes in.

If you are to use such a film, your procedure should be there to preview it, get the hard points down, and introduce it properly. This means telling your audience what to look for and how they might apply some of the ideas to their own work. That also means conducting a post-showing discussion about the central ideas—transferring, of course, to the application you want your salespeople to make of those ideas.

Visual aids are just that—visual aids. Audiotapes are helpful if you use them to help. They do not constitute a training program of their own, but they make *your* training program more effective.

Role Playing

One of the most effective techniques in sales training is role playing.

This is as close to a real selling situation as you can get without actually being face-to-face with a prospect. It can be employed whenever the learner has an understanding of what he or she is supposed to do—meeting the prospect for the first time, qualifying or probing for buyer needs and motives, making the presentation and/or the demonstration, checking interests, moving to the close—any of the interpersonal activities in selling. It is to the salesperson what batting practice is to the baseball player.

Role playing is done best when the trainer sets up the situation, details the conditions of the sales encounter, and prepares the role player in advance. It works poorly when it is extemporized and uncontrolled. Each player should have a sheet describing his or her role and the objective of the role play. Each should be advised that this is merely practice, not a test. The role play should be monitored by the instructor and constructive criticism should be given following the exercise. An audiotape recorder is helpful in the monitoring and review.

The use of videotape is sometimes used, but many trainers feel that the learner is so concerned about appearance that much of the real learning suffers in favor of playing to the camera. Also, much valuable time can be lost in handling the equipment.

Testing

There are two basic reasons for testing—to check learning progress and to teach. We opt for the emphasis on the teaching, because the real benefit of a test is the review that follows it. Here are some suggestions on the use of testing as a teaching tool:

- Build the test so that it covers only the subject matter currently being taught.

- Make questions clear with specific answers in mind.

- Use no trick questions.

- Vary question type—true/false, fill in the blanks, essay.

- Put a time limit on completion.

- Announce that the test is for the purpose of discussion, not to be turned in for grading.

- Use the test as the basis for discussion immediately following its completion.

- Involve everyone in responses.

When testing is done in this manner, correct answers reinforce and incorrect answers reteach the material. The more thorough the post-test discussion, the better the instruction.

Field Trips

Whenever possible, new salespeople should be taken on a tour of the plant or laboratory or engineering department that is responsible for producing the product. The earlier this is done, the better. What this does for the salesperson is give him or her a sense of belonging and the ability to connect, personally, with the product being sold. It also makes it possible for the salesperson to say to a customer, "In our plant, we ..." This is good sales support for anyone.

Helpful Hints

The old song that has the line, "The more we get together, the happier we'll be ..." has good sense in it. There is something about sitting in a classroom with peers that gives the learner support. He or she knows that others are struggling over the same rocky places. This is true of new hires and old hands in much the same way. And classroom instruction provides management with some interesting feedback that might not come in one-on-one instruction.

If your sales organization is big, and you can run classes for newly hired salespeople, that's a good way to get people started properly. If your organization is small, it is to your advantage—and theirs—to assemble the force periodically for sales meetings. A part of each meeting should be given over to training. Whether you do it yourself, have some expert come in and help, or have an internal training operation handle it, good classroom training will help you put your organization up front with the best available knowledge and skills.

The following suggestions will help you successfully train a new person:

1. *Have a detailed plan and follow it.* Insist that assistants do likewise.

2. *Work at full capacity.* Start early and finish late. Remember, nothing that the trainee hears or reads later will affect him or her as much as what he or she sees right now. So demonstrate the hard work necessary for success.

3. *Make company policies clear.* No matter what items concerning policy come up, be sure they are fully understood. Explain each one by specific example whenever possible. Where this is not possible, point out how the policy makes sense and assure him or her that if it were not important to the success of the business it would not exist as a policy.

4. *Put your best foot forward.* Remember that the trainee is going to want to know what kind of people he or she is working for. It will not take him or her long to get to know you. As a new person, he or she is likely to respect your opinions.

5. *Emphasize the need for teamwork and cooperation.* Do this by stressing the importance of each person in your organization. Emphasize the importance of clear, intelligent, factual, and on-time reporting.

6. *Stimulate the trainee's enthusiasm.* Discuss success stories in connection with every phase of the work. Give him or her some of the romance and history of the organization—its stature in the industry, its growth, and its apparent future.

7. *Earn the trainee's respect.* Conduct yourself at all times as a businessperson. Show a good front in all things—in your appearance as well as the appearance and condition of your office, warehouse, and equipment. Bear in mind that, even if he or she does not indicate it, any trainee is studying you very carefully.

8. *Give the trainee field experience as early as possible, in your presence.* Let the trainee carry the ball. Encourage him or her to think independently. Correct any errors later, away from the customer.

9. *Make the trainee understand that future development is up to him or her.* Future training and development cannot be handed to any person on a silver platter. He or she must do something about them himself or herself.

Selection of Trainers

The success of your orientation program depends on the care used in the selection of the people who will assist you in getting your new people off to a sound start. The trainee is quite likely to pattern his or her own future work habits after those of the people who trained him or her. If they are prompt in keeping appointments, the trainee will probably be prompt. If they go about their work in a well-planned, organized, and businesslike manner, the trainee will accept these things as standards by which to govern his or her own future activities. Sound selection of instructors, of course, depends on the objectives desired.

Obviously, in view of the wide diversity of products, company policies, industry conditions, and so forth, it would be folly to try to detail a list of objectives that would apply to all cases. In setting up this program and selecting the people who are to help implement it, the sales manager will want to keep in mind that the function at this point is threefold:

- To impart knowledge of product, company, methods, procedures, etc.

- To impart and develop skills in performance

- To inspire enthusiasm for and confidence in the company, product, and industry, as well as self-confidence in the trainee

Before discussing what should go into such a program, however, let's discuss the kind of person who should handle this kind of assignment.

The Trainer's Qualifications

Whether he or she be a full-time trainer or a person who works with new personnel along with his or her other duties, there are certain qualifications that must be fully considered if such an appointment is to be successful.

The "natural born" salesperson, of whom there are probably a few, rarely makes a good trainer. He or she intuitively does the right thing at the right time to the right people to get the order, but he or she seldom knows why he or she does these things and, since he or she does not know "why," he or she is seldom capable of passing on either the "why" or the "how" to someone else. Just as the strong "personal producer" so often fails as a sales manager, he or she will usually fail to measure up as a successful trainer of new salespeople.

Before a person is appointed to training responsibilities, there are at least three factors which need to be thoroughly investigated.

With respect to his or her experience and background with the company, such questions as these need to be resolved:

Is he or she loyal to his associates, company, and customers?

Does his or her experience have breadth and depth in respect to the geography of the territory and acquaintance with all types of customers and industries served, as well as with your full line and the application of each line to the customer's needs?

Assuming that he or she has know-how, to what degree can he or she pass it along to others so that they, too, can put it to work?

Does he or she discuss all facets of the work well and effectively, or does he or she concentrate on those phases which he or she personally enjoys—like a salesperson high-spotting his or her territory, spending most of his or her time and effort on the accounts he or she personally likes, without regard to their buying potential?

The Trainer's Personality

Some feel that all successful salespeople like people and want to be helpful—but experience has proved that too many salespeople are interested only in themselves.

The successful trainer must have a sincere desire to help others and must gain great personal satisfaction from helping others to learn and develop. Many of us can remember certain personalities among the professional teachers under whom we studied who obviously did not possess this attribute. These people, though making their living as teachers, were not truly successful and would not last long as trainers of adults.

Some attributes to look for in trainers are:

- *High personal integrity.* You are entrusting this person with your trainee's career. You can't afford to settle for less.

- *Thorough knowledge of company policies and philosophies.* Ability to explain them lucidly and "sell" them.

- *Good grooming.* Never flashy, but dressed to fit the situation, and always in good taste.

- *Clear and objective thinker.* Who gets to the point and is not lured into meaningless bypaths of time-consuming and unrelated discussions.

- *Good vocabulary and diction.* He or she must do 80 percent of his or her work through the use of words, so he or she must have an adequate vocabulary to make his or her point, and clear diction so the trainee will not have to strain to understand what is being said.

- *Mental and physical alertness.* The trainer is always under scrutiny—and always sets the pace—which means he or she must be the source of both physical and mental energy all the time he or she is training.

- *Teaching ability.* A person may have all other attributes, but without teaching ability he or she is "dead in the water." Unless he or she has the ability to impart knowledge, develop skills, and inspire enthusiasm for his or her subject, he or she is utterly useless as a trainer.

Where do we find such paragons? We don't! Perfect people don't exist. No one possesses all the desirable attributes to the fullest degree, but the real trainer prospect will have most of them in some degree, and be objective enough to try to improve in areas where improvement is needed when called to his or her attention.

A wise procedure for the first-line sales manager who is selecting people to help break in new salespeople—and is perhaps checking on his or her own attributes—is to develop a checklist, or set of standards, against which to score each prospective trainer, as shown in Table 2, page 877.

After applying this yardstick, the sales manager at least knows where he or she stands with respect to trainer talent, how much he or she can delegate, and how much must be done personally. A side benefit is that the manager will discover weak spots in the regular force that need his or her action since, ideally, all salespeople should be available to do a good job of breaking in a new salesperson on the staff.

Table 2.

	Below Average	Average	Above Average
Personal Integrity	___	___	___
Knowledge of Company Policy	___	___	___
Knowledge of Product	___	___	___
Personality	___	___	___
Thinking Ability	___	___	___
Teaching Ability	___	___	

Evaluation of Training

The results of the training effort should be evaluated in order that mistakes can be corrected in future courses and so that salespeople who failed to learn can be replaced or properly trained. As distasteful as formal examinations are, it is hard to beat them. There can be a series of informal quizzes; salespeople can be asked to demonstrate sales situations that will show what they have learned, their work can be critically appraised in the field, and they can answer "situation" questionnaires.

It is an inevitable responsibility of sales executives to test and find out what their salespeople know and believe, and take remedial action when necessary. To do it subtly is better than to do it crudely; not to do it at all is worse than doing it poorly.

An insight into how one major company evaluates sales training is provided by the manager, marketing administration, of Westinghouse Electric Corporation. He states:

"We feel we must increase the efficiency of the salesperson (i.e., his or her ability to handle more profitable volume), at the same time realizing that his or her cost to us is going to increase. The demand for our products and services will continue to increase and this will be matched by growth in our physical capacity. However, we do not anticipate that this demand will be matched with a proportionate increase in salespeople. In fact, we anticipate that we would have a great deal of difficulty obtaining and training them if we attempted to do so. Our program to make salespeople more productive consists of these things:

- Position their managers as managers and not as super sales-people. This we are doing through a continuing series of nine-day courses to increase managers' understanding of their re-sponsibilities and functions in the areas of planning, pricing, and directing the sales forces, as well as inspiring them to im-prove their own self-development.

- A six-day marketing course for salespeople who have demon-strated high performance and have exhibited potential for growth.

"The two courses focus on sales management as the keystone of our approach to more effective use of salespeople. However, to get at the salesperson, we have two additional steps:

- Free the salesperson from routine paper work, order handling, and follow-up. Here we are doing such things as "wired order-entry procedures," computer-order follow-up programs and tape-player communications programs for internal correspon-dence and product training.

- Improve the salesperson's selling techniques. Much of our business is obtained in large "hunks" or annual commitments. The loss of a single order can be the loss of a single customer's business for the year."

James (Jim) Evered, president of HRD Services, Denton, Texas, and past president of National Society of Sales Training Executives, devised the following regional sales manager's evalua-tion form, which can be used to evaluate training needs for sales-people. It is reprinted with his permission.

Regional Sales Manager Evaluation*

One of the primary responsibilities of a sales manager is to con-duct an objective and accurate evaluation of his or her personnel. Only through such an analysis will you be able to pin-point areas where additional help is needed. You are then able to plan your training around these specific areas.

*Copyright 1986, HRD Services, Inc.

However, in planning training for your salespeople, it is important that you consider the salesperson's perception of his or her needs. If a salesperson does not perceive a need for training and development in certain areas, he or she is not likely to absorb it and may even resent it.

The Regional Sales Manager Evaluation Form in Figure 1, page 880, will help both of you gain an objective perspective on training needs, and will help your salespeople gain some valuable insight into their own needs.

In order to gain maximum effectiveness from this analysis, the following procedure will get the job done:

1. Give the salesperson a copy of the Regional Sales Manager Evaluation sheet, asking him or her to be as objective and honest as possible in evaluating himself or herself on the items indicated. Allow one week to complete the evaluation. Advise the salesperson that you are also going to complete an evaluation on him or her and that one week later the two of you will sit down and compare evaluations, item by item, and reconcile any differences. Establish the date for the meeting.

2. You complete the form for each of your sales reps, being as objective and honest as possible. Both you and the salesperson are free to check the "Needs Help" box for any item listed. This helps both of you pin-point any areas as training targets. Be sure to check the box that indicates your evaluation and have the salesperson check the box indicating his or her own evaluation.

3. On the day indicated (one week later), sit down with the salesperson and thoroughly discuss any item where your evaluations differ more than two points. Determine why the difference exists. Listen to your salesperson's reasons for his or her own rating, and be honest as you defend your own answers. DON'T CHANGE ANY ANSWERS: leave them as originally rated.

Figure 1. Regional Sales Manager Evaluation Form

Reg. Mgr:_____   Evaluation Conducted by
                                          ☐ Self   ☐ Gen. Sls. Mgr.

	Excellent								Poor		Needs Help
Handling of reports	10	9	8	7	6	5	4	3	2	1	☐
Accuracy of reports	10	9	8	7	6	5	4	3	2	1	☐
Budgets time wisely	10	9	8	7	6	5	4	3	2	1	☐
Maintains account records	10	9	8	7	6	5	4	3	2	1	☐
Records well organized	10	9	8	7	6	5	4	3	2	1	☐
Pre-call analysis	10	9	8	7	6	5	4	3	2	1	☐
Post-call analysis	10	9	8	7	6	5	4	3	2	1	☐
Competitive knowledge	10	9	8	7	6	5	4	3	2	1	☐
Product knowledge	10	9	8	7	6	5	4	3	2	1	☐
Telephone sales presentations	10	9	8	7	6	5	4	3	2	1	☐
Face-to-face presentations	10	9	8	7	6	5	4	3	2	1	☐
Strong opening statements	10	9	8	7	6	5	4	3	2	1	☐
Presents customer benefits	10	9	8	7	6	5	4	3	2	1	☐
Answers objections well	10	9	8	7	6	5	4	3	2	1	☐
Uses strong closes	10	9	8	7	6	5	4	3	2	1	☐
Use of probing questions	10	9	8	7	6	5	4	3	2	1	☐
Listens with comprehension	10	9	8	7	6	5	4	3	2	1	☐
Persistence	10	9	8	7	6	5	4	3	2	1	☐
Use of sales aids	10	9	8	7	6	5	4	3	2	1	☐
Trains retail salespeople	10	9	8	7	6	5	4	3	2	1	☐
Reliability	10	9	8	7	6	5	4	3	2	1	☐
Establishes priorities	10	9	8	7	6	5	4	3	2	1	☐
Sets personal objectives	10	9	8	7	6	5	4	3	2	1	☐
Self-development objectives	10	9	8	7	6	5	4	3	2	1	☐
Uses good judgement	10	9	8	7	6	5	4	3	2	1	☐
_____	10	9	8	7	6	5	4	3	2	1	☐
_____	10	9	8	7	6	5	4	3	2	1	☐
_____	10	9	8	7	6	5	4	3	2	1	☐
_____	10	9	8	7	6	5	4	3	2	1	☐
_____	10	9	8	7	6	5	4	3	2	1	☐
_____	10	9	8	7	6	5	4	3	2	1	☐

4. Set your target dates for working with the salesperson on any items where you feel improvement is needed. Be specific. Let him or her know exactly what improvement you expect, by what date you expect it to be improved, how you are going to evaluate the improvement, and what help you are going to give him or her to improve.

5. A plan for improvement should be developed for all items *you* rate as "6" or less.

6. A WORD OF CAUTION: Don't "whitewash" the evaluations in order to make your sales group look better. That is a sure way to defeat the purpose of the evaluation. Be absolutely honest and objective in each rating. The purpose of the entire analysis is "improvement." We won't get improvement by sweeping problems under the rug.

Let's improve our sales department by pin-pointing those areas where specific improvement is needed, and then working with our salespeople to get that improvement.

Retraining Salespeople

Retraining has been found most valuable to "refresh" salespeople who need to be brought up-to-date on new techniques and also as a device to correct ineffective working habits and improve the selling strategy of older salespeople.

In some cases, the salespeople to be retrained are brought together at some central point for a two-week conference. These are usually people with five or more years of experience. Such a conference is usually presented as a leaders' clinic, executive seminar, or sales management conference rather than as a training program, to get away from the going-to-school idea. One firm, for example, calls the retraining program a business management conference. But it is a continuing program, and as fast as one group of dealers is retrained, another group comes in. The company took over a private home that has been especially equipped to house this activity.

Retraining is a continuous process. New demands for volume sales have brought sales managers face to face with the fact that the only way the required business can be produced at a profit is by more and better training of the salespeople. This is valid for the 30 percent who produce 70 percent of the company's business, as well as the newcomers to the organization and the 70 percent who are not doing the business they should. For the topflight people, unless they are exceptions to the rule, run down and get into a groove. They call on many different buyers, most of whom have gripes about the company, the product, or the price. Constant exposure to that sort of thing will wear down any salesperson in time.

Then, too, salespeople on their own too long develop short cuts that are not always good—such as leaving a sales kit in the back seat of the car instead of using it to get larger orders. It is to guard against salespeople getting off the beam, and to periodically rekindle their enthusiasm by feeding them new ideas, that a number of companies require every salesperson who completes his or her initial training to come back for retraining at least every five years. These companies are too astute, and too experienced in the ways of salespeople, to think the training job is done when the new person graduates from training school. And they have learned the hard way that getting the salespeople together once a year for an annual convention helps, but it still does not do the job of correcting unprofitable work habits.

Refresher training differs from other types of training because it depends upon salesperson participation. The salespeople are taught as much as possible by the discussion technique—by far the best way to teach. But it is not always feasible in the case of new salespeople, who might be confused by the arguments. They would lack the field experience necessary to enable them to properly evaluate selling ideas. Then, too, retraining requires, as a first step, ridding the minds of those in the group of any negative ideas that might be impeding their progress. That, of course, is not so important in the case of trainees with little or no sales experience. In fact, it would do more harm than good.

Field Application of Training

To make sure that the utmost return is obtained from the time and effort expended for sales training, Johns-Manville gives particular attention to the use of the training, as well as the training itself. On this particular point, an executive says:

We based the entire Johns-Manville plan of selling on methods developed by successful salespeople in the field. We began surveying and collecting this material six years ago, and we have been at it ever since. Nothing has been passed on to the sales force until it proved itself and until it was proved that average salespeople could use it effectively.

Of course, it costs money, good money, to survey the entire field and find the best selling methods. It's much easier to say, "I guess we ought to know what to tell our salespeople to do." It seems cheaper, too. But it's terrifically expensive to pass on fancy opinions and pet ideas that won't meet the actual needs in the field.

When we provided sound training material we provided also for its use and application in the field. We provided for field supervision and checkups to see that every salesperson actually used the recommended methods. We kept checking each one until we knew he or she was using them properly and effectively. We didn't consider that our job was done when we showed training films at a sales meeting.

There are sales executives who think they have done their duty when they have passed the information along. The we-did-our-part attitude has cost thousands and thousands of dollars and wrecked many an otherwise worthy training effort. Unless you can follow through to actual, universal use at the point of sale, dissipation of effectiveness is going to increase by the square of the distance from the home office.

The value of refresher training depends upon the use the salesperson makes of the information he or she has been given. Sales executives know this, yet we find many companies do little or nothing to keep the training alive after it has been given to the salespeople. As a result, the salespeople go back to their territories, apply the new methods they have discussed for a while, and soon settle down to using their old methods.

Even the best salespeople forget what they have learned. To make sure salespeople do not forget, and that the company gets continuing dividends on its investment, it is the growing practice to follow up refresher courses, as well as training courses for new salespeople, with better-methods bulletins.

What are some of the symptoms and signals that suggest it is time for a retraining program?

The following should be considered warning signs that it is time to consider refresher courses of some kind:

1. When the normal keenness of established salespeople appears to dull

2. When turnover of salespeople increases

3. When submittal of expense and call reports begins to drag abnormally

4. When the feed-back about field conditions becomes sluggish or drops off

5. When sales decline more drastically for the company than for the industry as a whole

6. When new salespeople outsell established salespeople

For companies that conduct seasonal programs or campaigns, the occasion of planning and introducing the new program offers an ideal opportunity to retrain the sales force. What baseball or football team would start the new season without an intense rehearsal of the fundamentals and advanced strategy and with no players excused?

When thus closely related to current programming, the cost in time and money of such refresher training will not be considered as extra, but rather as an integral and necessary activity to ensure accomplishing the desired selling results.

Besides bringing distributors' salespeople to the home office or other locations for formal training, there can be considerable advantage in holding training meetings at the distributors' places of business. There, meetings are usually handled by manufacturers' salespeople, with various degrees of success. Some companies use specially trained field trainers for such work.

If the company's salespeople do the job, they should be given training in how to conduct these meetings, and they should be supplied with interesting props and other materials. It goes without saying that a manufacturer's salesperson who can train his or her distributor's salespeople to sell the company's products properly will help multiply sales manyfold.

Training Retail Salespeople

Because of the increasing complexity of merchandise and the growing number of new and different items being added daily to the shelves in the stores, retail training is more important today than ever before. Stores must maximize the efforts of every person regardless of his or her assignment to do a clean-cut job of public relations and selling.

Large retail stores have training directors and staffs; their own training manuals, printed materials, and visual aids; and department heads and buyers to conduct a continuing in-store training program. Others, however, need the help of manufacturers, and sales managers should be alert to the opportunities afforded by their need.

Motivation and morale are the basic purposes of training. Training increases employees' productivity, standardizes store procedure, reduces personnel turnover, and produces a source of trained and experienced personnel to fill supervisory and managerial positions. The employee benefits from greater self-confidence and increased earnings. Training affords the employee additional job security and enhances his opportunity for advancement.

Every store should have a plan for training the new employee and for carrying a continuing training program for all store employees. The plan should include all levels of employees: management, supervisory, sales, and service personnel. New employees should be given information about the operation of the business, store policies, store clientele, employee pay plan and benefits, mechanics of making sales, layaway and credit procedures, stockkeeping procedures, identification of lines of authority, and specific work assignment, stock location, and inventory system.

All employees should be given continuing training in product information and sales techniques.

Supervisory personnel should be given instruction in human relations, psychology, and basic principles of getting work done through other people.

State and local boards of education offer assistance to small stores through distributive education.

Distributive education is a part of the curriculum of many high schools and junior colleges. Students enrolled in distributive education attend school part time and work in local stores part time. Both the student and the store benefit.

Adult classes are also available through distributive education. Classes are conducted for management, supervisory, sales, and service personnel in all types of retail and wholesale establishments.

Numerous colleges and universities now offer noncredit short courses for the retail field. In addition, many undergraduate and graduate courses are available. The student may elect to take the course as a student for degree work or as an auditor for no credit.

Information about instructors and courses may be obtained from the colleges themselves, the state supervisor of distributive education, or the nearest Small Business Administration regional office.

Most trade associations now include educational programs among the services offered to their members. Correspondence courses, films, materials for conducting training programs, management and sales institutes, and traveling instructors are some of the aids provided by trade associations. Many of these services are provided through arrangements with universities and distributive education.

A Program for Retail Salespeople

The National Shoe Retailers Association, in its Operating Guide No. 5, outlines its recommendations for designing and developing a training program for store salespeople. It stresses the following points:

1. Determine the basic and specific objectives you want the training program to accomplish. Complete a full realization of the conditions that prevail, the possibilities of improving

them, and the basic objectives that may be attained by action.

2. Assign responsibility for developing more effective sales effort. First, top management personnel must take part initially to develop the correct attitude and to assure those in the organization that the training program is extremely important and worthwhile.

3. Complete a preliminary analysis. The key is to pinpoint strong and weak performances of individuals on the sales staff. Knowledge along these lines will suggest the content of the training program.

4. Develop the content of the training program and set up topics to be covered on a timetable basis. Moreover, for each item indicated below ask yourself:

   • What the salesperson has to do

   • What the salesperson has to know

   • What the salesperson must learn

   • How it should be taught—by whom?

Sales Training Aids

The sales training manager has a wealth of material, in films, slide films, video cassettes and printed form, to aid him or her in training and motivating salespeople. Dartnell Corporation films include:

1. "Make It Happen," starring golf great Julius Boros. "A beautifully-produced sales film." Color.

2. "The Professional," with Van Johnson and Forrest Tucker. "Every salesperson should see this great film at least once."

3. "Second Effort," starring the immortal Vince Lombardi. The largest selling sales training film in history. A true classic. Color.

4. "Ask for the Order and Get It," the first in a series called Tough-Minded Salesmanship. This has been acclaimed as one of the most effective and important sales training films ever made. It gives key principles of how to get an order and Joe Batten is very effective as a narrator. Color.

5. "Your Price Is Right ... Sell It," is the second in the series and basically tells how to sell quality. Once a salesperson sees this film, he or she will no longer fear high prices. Color.

6. "Manage Your Time to Build Your Territory," the third in the Joe Batten series, is valuable for managing the salesperson's most precious commodity, "time." The vignettes dramatize how every salesperson can increase sales volume. Color.

7. "When You're Turned Down ... Turn On," the fourth in the Joe Batten series, deals with handling objections. Batten shows how a true rejection can be turned into a solid order. Color.

8. "Charge." Since so many salespeople are interested in golf and everyone knows Arnold Palmer, this ideal film shows how the same principles that apply to successful golf apply as well to salesmanship. Color.

9. "Salesman," film won the Silver Medal at the International Film Festival. Wayne Tippet is perfect as the dedicated "salesman." Every salesperson will identify with this day in the life of a successful, proud salesman. Color.

10. "Sell Proud." Earl Nightingale, the dean of successful motivation, does a superb job of instilling confidence in even the average salesperson. This is guaranteed to get results at any sales convention. Color.

11. "Think Win," featuring George Blanda, shows how Blanda used his secrets of success on the football field in his life as a salesman. Color.

12. "Dealing With Price Resistance." A film to help salespeople overcome the biggest roadblock in selling—objection to price.

13. "The Challenge of Objections." A touch of humor and irony highlights this serious look into the problems, frustrations, and challenges of selling.

14. "Wickersham" shows a salesperson how to be better than the competition.

15. "Selling Benefits" is a fresh new twist on a very basic technique of salesmanship.

16. "Keep Climbing" gives a new outlook to the age-old selling problem of complacency.

17. "Two Guys Named Mike" was produced especially for field service representatives.

18. "Salesmanship on the Line" shows salespeople how to sell by solving problems.

19. "Time Well Spent" shows why planning and organization are as vital as calling on the customer.

Sales Training Kit

Dartnell's 15-Session Sales Training Kit, organized and packaged in a permanent and sturdy vinyl container, offers 15 stimulating, ready-to-go sales training sessions covering all the critical areas of improving basic sales skills. Each session includes meeting leader's script, two thematic banners, and "Technique Builder" handout sheet, plus a complete meeting leader's guide.

A Typical Sales Training Program

On the following pages (Figure 2) you'll find a condensed outline from *Building a Winning Sales Force* that is typical of most sales training efforts. It may not fit your needs; some portions of it you may want to expand and others treat differently. (Figures 3 and 4 on pages 894 and 895 provide you with a Feature/Function/

Benefit Worksheet and a Post-Call Evaluation form respectively.)

The outline is, essentially, a classroom-type program of instruction. For that reason, notes are included to indicate the teaching technique recommended at various stages of the program. You may, however, do this program on an individual basis, because the same content applies in either case.

The program is built on two assumptions:

- Suitable orientation of the new hire has been accomplished.

- The trainee is destined for a territory—outside selling. With modest changes, you can adapt this to other types of selling.

Sessions can be presented in a different order. However, there is a basic logic in most of the outline. It requires qualifying to make proper presentations and demonstrations, and one doesn't attempt to close a sale until those steps have been taken. Time and territory management, for instance, can come early or late in the instruction. Pre-call planning and post-call evaluation are sometimes taught at the same time, because they interrelate in content, if not in time.

The duration of instruction is open to judgment. Keep in mind the individual training needs and job requirements.

Building a Winning Sales Force is a comprehensive sales management package providing guidance on how to recruit, select, train, and coach a sales force to success. Included is an audiotape to facilitate candidate interviewing, and a series of 12 selling skills training booklets that serve as the core of a sales training program. It is available from the Dartnell Corporation.

Figure 2. Training Program Outline

Session 1

Pre-Call Planning

- The Importance of Pre-Call Planning (Lecture-Discussion)
- Steps in Pre-Call Planning (Lecture-A/V support)
- Case Studies in Pre-Call Planning (Workshop-Discussion)
- Creating a Real Plan for Future Use (Workshop)

Session 2

Opening the Call

- You Never Get a Second Chance to Make a Good First Impression (Lecture)
- Calling on a New Prospect (Lecture-Demonstration-Discussion)
- Calling on Familiar Customers (Workshop-Role Play)
- Leaving the Door Open for the Future (Discussion-Role Play)

Session 3

Uncovering Buying Motives and Qualifying Prospects

- Customers Buy for *Their* Reasons—Not Ours (Lecture-A/V-Discussion)
- How to Ask Questions That Define Buying Motives (Lecture-Role Play)
- Processing Information to Set up a Presentation (Discussion-A/V-Role Play)

Session 4

Selling Benefits

- Turning Nuts and Bolts into Reasons to Buy (Lecture-A/V-Workshop)
- Tell Me Less of How It Came to Be and More of What It Means to Me (Role Play)
- Practice Makes Perfect (Case study-Role Play)

(continued)

Figure 2. Training Program Outline

(continued)

Session 5

Building Agreement and Handling Objections

- Big Sales Are Made of Small Agreements (Lecture-Discussion)
- Asking Questions That Generate Agreement (Lecture-Discussion-Role Play)
- Handling Objections That Might Arise (Discussion-A/V-Role Play)

Session 6

Demonstrations: Proving What You Say

- If a Picture Is Worth a Thousand Words, the Real Thing Is Worth Millions (Discussion)
- Making an Effective Demonstration (Lecture-Demonstration)
- Getting the Prospect Involved (Discussion-Workshop)
- Moving from the Demonstration to the Close (Lecture-A/V)
- How to Use Visual Aids in Cases Where the Real Thing Isn't Available (Demonstration)
- Putting the Show on the Road (Workshop-Role Play)

Session 7

Closing

- Two Closes in Every Sale (Lecture-Discussion)
- Closing on the Product/Service (Lecture-A/V-Discussion)
- Closing on Price (Discussion-Workshop-Role Play)
- Closing on Objections (Discussion-Role Play)
- How to Ask for the Order (Role Play)

Session 8

Post-Call Evaluation and Follow-Up

- The Importance of Post-Call Evaluation (Discussion)
- Doing a Post-Call Evaluation (A/V-Workshop)
- Follow-Up Is More Than a Courtesy (Lecture-Discussion)
- Making a Post-Sale Follow-Up Call (A/V-Role Play)

(continued)

Figure 2. Training Program Outline
(continued)

Session 9

Developing Sales Volume

- Setting Workable Goals (Lecture)
- Increasing Volume with Present Customers (Discussion-Workshop)
- Prospecting for New Buyers (Demonstration-Role Play)

Session 10

Time and Territory Management

- Sales Performance Depends on Skill, Knowledge, Attitude, and Time (Lecture-Discussion)
- Planning a Territory Uses Time Effectively (Discussion-Workshop)
- Setting Priorities Consistent with Plans (Actual Workshop)
- Coping with Time-Wasters (Discussion)

Session 11

Motivation: The Key to Success

- All Motivation Is Self-Motivation (Lecture-Discussion)
- Goal Setting—Something to Shoot for (Workshop)
- Attitudes—How Work Becomes Enjoyment (Discussion)

Figure 3. Feature/Function/Benefit Worksheet

Product_____

Product Features	Product Functions	Buyer Benefits

Figure 4. Post-Call Evaluation

Name of Company_____

Name of individual called on_____

Title_____

Present customer?_____ New prospect?_____

Did the call result in an order?_____ Why?_____

Did the call fail to produce an order?_____ Why?_____

Which of these major areas can be credited with the failure of the call:

_____Wrong product/service

Which product/service might have sold better?_____

_____Wrong-decision maker

Who should be seen on a second call?_____

_____Incomplete presentation/demonstration

What went wrong?_____

_____Competition

What is competition doing we are not?_____

Are there other problems we should look into?_____

What are they?_____

Is another call scheduled or planned?_____ When?_____

What should we plan for that call?_____

Chapter 41

Coaching and Evaluating Sales Performance

Sales managers have to work with their salespeople, or salespoeple aren't going to work effectively. While this may not always be true, it's true often enough to make the concept valid and hard to ignore.

Two management activities—coaching and counseling—have much in common and that is one-on-one attention to bring a salesperson's performance up to optimum levels. Where they differ is in their concepts. Coaching is concerned with skill development, and counseling is concerned with attitude development. Some people don't know how—they need coaching. Some people know how, but don't—they need counseling.

What Is Coaching?

In a special series of articles for Dartnell's *Sales & Marketing Executive Report,* Harry L. Bullock, a training executive of note, covered the subject in depth, as follows:

Basically, coaching is a technique by which a manager helps each of his or her sales reps:

- Achieve a more exacting degree of job knowledge

- Acquire greater skill in effectively carrying out job responsibilities

- Attain a higher level of job satisfaction through improved performance

- Assure continuing progress by expanding viewpoints, improving attitudes and behavior, bringing out latent or dormant capabilities

Coaching emphasizes the job, not the sales rep. It concentrates on the *acquisition of knowledge* and the *development of skills.*

Though coaching does require that a manager be aware of the personality characteristics of his or her people individually, this awareness serves as a background for the activity.

The Importance of Coaching

Many management experts agree coaching is one of the most important training techniques available to sales managers. Properly handled, they said, it permits them to:

- *Measure results.* The manager can observe results—or lack of results—immediately. Equally important, he or she is in a position to share his or her thoughts with sales reps concerning problem areas inhibiting progress—and recommend methods most likely to overcome them.

- *Study techniques.* Because the sales rep is actually accompanied on calls, the manager can note the depth of the person's planning, the approaches to various selling situations, the validity of objectives, and the methods used to achieve them.

- *Evaluate training.* A conscientiously conducted coaching session helps the manager determine how effective a salesperson's training has been to date, and what the needs are for further training in terms of what is now being accomplished.

- *Influence improvements.* During coaching, the manager has a unique opportunity to simultaneously observe, demonstrate as necessary, teach all elements of the job, pinpoint flaws in the salesperson's techniques and help to correct them.

- *Recognize progress.* With regular and well conducted coaching sessions the manager can reinforce good selling habits and aid his or her people in eliminating those that are causing sales and service failures. Moreover, the manager can spot people with real potential for growth, as well as those he or she must work with more frequently.

To coach effectively, the manager must have an attitude consistent with coaching principles. Its success or failure—partial or complete—depends upon the knowledge, skill, and understanding of the manager. In a very real sense, coaching's success depends on the spirit in which it is used. If employed as a gimmick, it will fail. But if used in the spirit of developing greater understanding of what the sales and service job is all about, its success will be assured. What follows is an overview of the coaching process.

COACHING

- **During Call**

  1. Set the mood

     · Put sales rep at ease

     · Let sales rep talk

     · Explain what you want to do

  2. Prepare for calls

     · Observe and listen during first few calls

     · Watch manner in which sales rep is received in accounts

     · Avoid involvement

  3. Critique

     · Demonstrate

     · Concentrate on only one or two major aspects of sales rep's actions

     · Avoid harsh criticism

     · Stress basic skills of selling

     · Encourage!

- **After Call**

  1. Compliment strengths noted

     · Stress good performance

     · Suggest changes, possible new approaches

2. Define problems observed

   · Explain effect on selling activities

   · Pinpoint difficulties

   · Offer your help

3. Encourage self-improvement

   · Outline corrective actions sales rep is to take

   · PUT IT IN WRITING!

   · Give salesperson a signed copy

   · Keep a copy for your files

- **Remember to:**

  1. Observe!

  2. Listen!

  3. Question!

  4. Analyze!

- **Before Call**

  1. Analyze to:

     · Determine sales rep's capabilities

     · Consider courses of action

     · Decide on follow-through

  2. Prepare by evaluating:

     · Training provided

     · Sales effort

     · Sales rep's records and reports

     · Condition of sales rep's accounts

3. Make notes of:

  · Key areas to cover during coaching session

  · Results of last coaching session

  · Schedule of calls sales rep is to provide for current coaching session

Coaching Principles

Coaching sessions are the actions taken by the manager to improve performance of those representatives who report to him or her. To do this effectively requires:

- Focusing attention on those aspects of the representative's job requiring immediate and long-term improvements;

- Respect for the worth and dignity of the representative as a human being;

- Evaluating the representative's intelligence, aptitudes, knowledge, and skills—as well as the environment in which he or she must operate;

- Acquiring not only more knowledge about the person as an individual, but a deeper understanding of his or her job;

- Active listening on the part of the manager, plus a high degree of questioning skill;

- Holding each representative accountable for responsibilities either delegated to him or her, those he or she has accepted, or which are an inherent part of the job.

Coaching Techniques

To achieve maximum results from coaching requires mastery by the manager of specific skills. In essence, the manager must be able to:

- Observe objectively

- Listen actively

- Question intelligently

- Analyze effectively

OBSERVE OBJECTIVELY

To increase your powers of observation, keep the following points in mind:

1. Organize to observe

   - Understand the ramifications of the sales rep's job, including primary responsibilities, limits of authority, skills required, aptitudes, and training.

   - Familiarize yourself with the standards by which performance, productivity, and progress are measured.

   - Know the person you'll be coaching: his or her aptitudes, aspirations, strengths, and weaknesses.

2. Observe to learn

   - Remain physically and mentally alert through the coaching session.

   - Concentrate on what you see by overcoming preoccupation and shutting out distractions that divert attention.

   - Compare your version of what you have observed with others. Where yours differs, try to determine how and why. This will also help you remain alert and interested.

3. Remember what you observe

   - Reflect on what you have observed, otherwise what you have seen will remain in a set, brittle state.

   - Put what you have observed in proper sequence so that you can group facts meaningfully. This will help you grasp and remember them.

   - Maintain a questioning attitude. Avoid seeing only what past experience tells you will be there. Look for differences in people, places, and things. This will help you gain a clearer insight into situations and conditions.

- Note down key points observed so that later, recall can be done more easily.

LISTEN ACTIVELY

Not only must the manager listen attentively, he or she must also create opportunities for listening. In almost all manager-to-sales rep situations, the manager must use listening as a tool to allay suspicions, uncover the real reasons behind problems, denote respect and consideration, and forge a connecting link in the chain of understanding.

To stimulate listening efficiency, put the steps below to work:

1. Prepare to listen

    - Give the sales rep time in which to say what's on his or her mind.

    - Become physically alert. As the sales rep talks, look him or her in the eye. Reflect your interest and attention by your facial expressions and body posture (tense slightly and lean toward the person).

    - Avoid nervous mannerisms that can distract you and the sales rep.

    - Clear your mind of any extraneous thoughts so that your full attention is focused on the sales rep.

    - Watch the sales rep's facial expressions, posture, and gestures for clues as to his or her attitudes, feelings, and desires.

    - Note voice tone and inflection to help you determine the real meaning or importance behind his or her words.

2. Listen to learn

    - Don't allow the sales rep's appearance, mannerisms, or

speaking ability to prejudice you so that you fail to listen attentively.

- Keep pace with the sales rep as he or she talks by avoiding mental irrelevancies.

- Pick up the central theme or idea the sales rep is trying to convey by getting supporting facts, ideas, and statements clearly in mind.

- Listen with your mind, not your emotions. If the sales rep makes a point contrary to your beliefs, don't stop listening—you'll only be defeating yourself. Rehearsing devastating rebuttals to hurl will prevent you from hearing additional, perhaps qualifying, comments.

- When appropriate, ask questions to ensure that you have all the facts straight. Request additional information to ensure that you understand.

- Feed back your interpretation of the sales rep's replies. This will help determine if he or she has been clear, or if additional information or amplification is required.

3. Make notes

- As you listen, jot down key words or phrases. This will aid in reviewing important points and improve recall. Be sure to note questions you will want to ask, as well as specific points of disagreement if any.

QUESTION INTELLIGENTLY

Skillfully asked questions can be a powerful coaching technique because they compel answers. Their power, however, also makes them dangerous. Asking the wrong question at the wrong time or in the wrong way can result in pat answers that may confirm preconceptions that later prove false. Questions should be asked to get facts and opinions, ideas and explanations. Questions should also be used to give information and encourage decisions.

To increase your skill in asking questions, keep these tips in mind:

1. Create a receptive mood

   - Reveal your personal interest in the sales rep so that he or she will be willing to cooperate and answer accurately.

   - Dissolve tensions by making the sales rep aware that you are considering his or her needs and feelings.

   - Let the sales rep know what it is you want to learn—and why.

   - Familiarize yourself with the sales rep's frame of reference. This will enable you to anticipate the way in which questions will best be understood.

2. Formulate questions carefully

   - Phrase questions so they will not antagonize, or sound threatening or challenging.

   - Indicate your concern for facts rather than the placement of blame, or the need for lengthy excuses.

   - Suit each question to the purpose for which it is asked. Specifically, will it communicate what you know about the situation or condition that prompted the question in the first place? Will it communicate any information that will help the sales rep arrive at an answer?

   - Ask questions that cannot be answered with a simple "yes" or "no". Rather, ask questions requiring descriptions, explanations, amplifications.

3. Evaluate answers

   - Try to get some idea of the direction of sales rep's thinking, and to learn additional information you may not have thought to ask specifically.

   - Listen for comments or remarks that seem out of order, and draw out the sales rep to learn why he or she answered in that way.

   - Summarize your understanding of the sales rep's answers.

Table 1, page 906, provided examples of several types of questions you will want to put to work when contacting your people.

ANALYZE EFFECTIVELY

Through his or her powers of listening and questioning skills, a manager is usually in a position to analyze weaknesses and strengths that affect the sales rep's performance. The purpose of analysis is to determine what steps should be taken so that the manager and the sales rep, working together during the coaching session, can overcome obstacles and stimulate sales results.

Careful analysis and diagnosis before a coaching session can prevent it from deteriorating into a social visit, inquisition, cross-examination, or outright argument. It can result in a fair exchange of ideas, greater understanding, and reaching mutually agreed-upon decisions.

The following steps suggest a method for analyzing more efficiently:

1. Determine sales rep's capabilities

   - Develop sufficient background information about the person so that you are aware of personal goals and ambitions; acquainted with the values by which he or she can be motivated; apprised of personal needs, wants, interests, and desires.

   - Review facts and information pertaining to sales activities, customers, competition, territorial potential, and other vital factors.

   - Evaluate the sales rep's strengths and weaknesses in terms of what he or she is not achieving, or could achieve.

   - Compare what he or she is accomplishing in relation to his or her experience, knowledge, and skill with those of other sales reps reporting to you.

   - Consider the extent of training received and its effect on the rep's performance. Has training provided him or her with essential information and skills?

Table 1.

TYPE OF QUESTION	IN-USE SITUATION	COACHING EXAMPLE
SPECIFIC	As the term implies, this type of question attempts to elicit detailed, factual information from the respondent.	If you had the chance to make that call all over again, what might you do differently—and why?
DIRECT	Employed when it is certain the person to whom a question is addressed has, or can get, information requested in the question.	Last year, what were our sales to that account?
LEAD-OFF	Helpful for stimulating a discussion.	With what you now know about the customer, why do you think he refused to buy?
OPEN-END	Does not specify what is required in the way of an answer. Respondent is free to answer any way he or she wishes.	How are things?
ALTERNATIVE	Used to bring a discussion to a head and force a decision.	Isn't the real question whether or not we're seeing the person who can make the decision to buy?
SHIFTING GEARS	Such questions are useful for opening a discussion, or introducing a new phase of a subject to ensure that the person you're with has the chance to comment.	Why didn't you stress the 30 percent discount he'd make by placing his order now?
FOLLOW-THROUGH	Designed to pursue a discussion further.	Last time we were together you mentioned closings were tough for you to handle. Any progress since then?

2. Consider courses of action

- Determine what must be done and then outline steps in logical sequence.
- List values and benefits to the sales rep.

3. Decide on follow-through required

- Reflect on the courses of action your analysis has revealed so that you have time to marshal facts and ideas, think up revealing questions to ask, and be prepared to help overcome problems and exploit opportunities.
- Set deadlines for the achievement of any assignments, goals, or objectives established.
- Provide sufficient time in which to conduct the coaching. Certainly it must never be less than a full working day. Anything less is likely to be a waste.

Conducting the Coaching Session

BEFORE COACHING

Adequate preparation for coaching is necessary for the same reason a good sales rep prepares for every important call. The sales rep knows that an intelligent proposal is always based on a thorough knowledge of the account. He or she also knows that the account is favorably impressed with a sales rep who has taken the trouble to learn about their needs. Similarly, a manager cannot do an intelligent job of coaching until he or she knows as much as possible about the person with whom he or she will work.

During coaching it is imperative that the manager establish his or her authority. He or she does this not by dominating the sales rep, but by having a storeroom of facts and experiences far beyond those of the sales rep. This information lets the manager speak with authority. The manager's thorough knowledge of the person's job impresses him or her and stimulates that individual to work hard on suggestions or recommendations offered.

To make the coaching session pay off:

1. Get ready

   a. Determine the extent and quality of training the sales rep has received.

      • Review any training materials and assignments provided.

      • Evaluate results in terms of the person's involvement during training sessions; contributions made, degree of understanding evidenced; results achieved.

      • Note strengths and weaknesses.

   b. Analyze the person's sales efforts.

      • Is the representative doing well with certain types of customers or accounts, but not so well with others?

      • Is he or she selling the full line?

      • Is he or she getting the proper mix of sales and service calls?

      • How does his or her performance compare with your other people?

   c. Check the various records and reports maintained on the sales rep, or submitted by him or her to you.

      • What do they reveal?

      • What do they fail to tell?

   d. Familiarize yourself with the sales representative's major customers.

      • What trends or patterns seem to be developing?

      • What changes are taking place within them?

      • What inroads is competition making, and to what extent?

2. Get set

   a. Jot down key areas you will want to cover in detail during the coaching session, including:

      • A brief description of the situation or reason for the coaching session.

      • Specification of goals or objectives to be achieved.

      • Tools and materials required during the coaching session, and the order in which they will be used.

   b. Review results of any previous coaching sessions, evaluations, appraisals.

   c. Provide advance notice of the coaching session.

      • Select day or days for coaching each representative.

      • Give sufficient advance notice so sales rep can complete whatever preparatory work he or she feels may be necessary.

      • Explain briefly the purpose of the coaching session.

   d. As far as practical let the sales rep arrange the schedule of calls to be made during coaching, and then inform you.

      • Evaluate what the schedule of calls submitted by the sales rep tells you about his or her selling strengths and weaknesses. Is he or she going to show you only "set-ups," or a typical mixture of accounts?

      • Adjust schedule of calls as necessary to ensure cross section of calls, while you are with the sales rep (service, sales, prospecting, etc.).

      • Decide what calls you will want to handle for demonstration purposes.

   e. Determine length of coaching session.

- Provide time for a discussion with the sales rep prior to making any calls during the coaching session.

- Decide when calls will be made. (Remember! The calendar day isn't necessarily the best coaching unit. Sometimes more can be learned by working with the sales rep from noon to noon, than from morning to night.)

- Include sufficient time for a summary and discussion at end of the coaching session.

DURING COACHING

It is during the coaching session that the manager's advanced planning preparation pays off! To get the session off on the right foot it is vital that you:

1. Set the mood

   a. Put the sales rep at ease by indicating your awareness of the pressure he or she is under.

   b. Give him or her a chance to say anything that may be relative to the coaching session.

   c. Impress him or her with the fact that the coaching session does not imply any personal criticism. Its sole purpose is to help make him or her a better sales rep.

2. Prepare for calls

   a. For the first few calls let the sales rep set the pace. Before probing with questions *observe* and *listen* for:

      - Evidence of effective planning.

      - Objectives for each call.

      - Degree to which he or she analyzes needs, wants, and opportunities in each account.

      - Way in which he or she fields questions and handles objections.

- Skill with which he or she highlights benefits.

- Strength and persistence of closes.

b. Pay particular attention to reception given in accounts (the cold shoulder treatment can indicate past difficulties); courtesy and decorum exhibited by sales rep; use of waiting time.

c. Avoid involvement

  - During calls stay on the sidelines unless you have told the sales rep exactly under what circumstances you will take over.

  - Tactfully redirect the discussion when the account attempts to involve you in the sales interview.

d. Demonstrate

  - From time-to-time you may want to handle a complete call, giving the sales rep a chance to watch you in action. This is an excellent coaching technique, particularly on cold calls when no relationship has been established.

e. Critique after the first several calls.

  - Find something about the rep's performance during the call you can *honestly* compliment.

  - Concentrate on only one or two major aspects of the sales rep's actions during the call.

  - Focus attention on specific weaknesses observed during the call as well as strengths that deserve reinforcement.

  - Avoid harsh criticism that can undermine the sales rep's confidence so that his or her performance for the rest of the coaching is anything but typical.

  - Give the sales rep an adequate opportunity to tell his or her side of the story.

- Probe with questions that will stimulate thinking.

- Stress basic sales skills, particularly those covered in training.

- Ensure understanding by the sales rep of what you want done.

- End the critique on a note of encouragement. If you had to discuss a weakness, point out how valuable it is to get it out into the open and talk about it. The biggest hurdle in overcoming any weakness is simply recognizing that it exists.

AFTER COACHING

At the end of the coaching session—when all joint calls and critiques immediately following each call have been completed—the manager should sit down with the sales rep and review thoroughly what has been accomplished. In this review it is important to:

1. Compliment strengths noted

   a. Point out their importance to the person's performance and how they helped achieve results.

   b. Encourage their continued use.

   c. Suggest how they can be tailored or adapted for use in other sales situations.

2. Define problems observed

   a. Explain exactly what the problems are, and their effect on the sales rep's selling activities.

   b. Sell these ideas:

   - That his or her sales performance is not all that it should be.

   - That your aim is to help pinpoint difficulty.

   - That you can help if he or she will let you.

3. Emphasize self-improvement

   a. Outline the corrective actions you want him or her to take.

   b. Put them in writing. Give him or her a copy and keep one for your file.

- Emphasize the means by which he or she can increase his or her effectiveness and potential.

- Specify specific portions of training the sales rep may have undergone for review and study. Tell him or her how, when, and where he or she can apply the training received to the various sales situations he or she encounters.

   c. Set up a schedule for him or her to follow in taking the corrective actions you recommend.

   d. State the results you are confident he or she is capable of achieving.

- Tell him or her when you will get together for a review of assignments.

- Let the sales rep know you are available at any time to lend assistance.

Out of the total coaching effort with all sales reps, it is possible for a manager to learn *what* each one is doing, *how* well he or she is doing it, and *where* progress is being made. This information will provide an accurate measure by which the manager can determine the effectiveness of training, use of skills in selling, and what areas require further improvement for all of his or her people.

Performance Management System

After salespeople are hired, trained, coached, and are in the territories producing sales, a periodic evaluation of their individual sales performances is essential to keep the sales force operating at a peak level. Performance appraisals should be looked upon as a management system.

When viewed as a management system, it:

- Becomes a tool for you, the manager, to use in the overall maintenance and improvement of your sales force.

- Becomes systematic. Rather than a single event at each appraisal period, the system yields a culmination of many events and observations which find expression in a formal document and a professional interview.

The performance appraisal in the hands of some managers is a perennial club to be held over the heads of salespeople, but most others see it as an opportunity to:

- Keep communications open between employees and manager

- Provide opportunity to measure performance on a formal basis

- Advise the employee with respect to goals and expectations

- Remind the employee of the various responsibilities, functions, tasks, and objectives of the job

- Reestablish standards of performance in the employee's mind

- Encourage continued effective performance and correct poor practices wherever they may exist

- Motivate further development by indicating areas where the employee could improve performance

- Counsel wherever attitudes and behavior indicate the need for it

- Discover the employee's feelings about himself or herself, the job, the company, and even the manager.

If you already have a corporate appraisal form use it. A Dartnell Performance Evaluation Form is included in Figure 1, pages 915-920, for use if you do not currently have an official document within your organization, or if you are contemplating replacing your present form. What you may not have are two items that can be very helpful in building your performance management system. These two items are:

- Performance Objectives and Planning Sheet (Figure 2, page 922.)
- Contacts and Observations Form (Figure 3, page 923.)

Performance Objectives and Planning

Salespeople need more than quotas; they need direction. The use of the Performance Objectives and Planning Sheet is the manager's best single opportunity to apply consultative or participative management techniques. That's because:

- The salesperson fills it in first.
- You review it.
- You and the salesperon discuss it and amend it.
- The salesperson commits to it.
- Both of you retain a copy of it—the salesperson for his or her constant reminder of the commitment, and you for interim checking and for final evaluation leading to performance appraisal.

Figure 1. Performance Evaluation Form

Name _____ Social Security No. _____

Position _____ Department _____

Date of evaluation _____ Date of last evaluation _____

Appraised by:

Name and title _____ _____

Signature _____
(continued)

Figure 1. Performance Evaluation Form

(continued)

Reviewed by:

Name and title_____ Date _____

Signature _____

Purpose: The employee should know his/her supervisor's goals for him/her and how well the supervisor believes the employee is achieving these goals, together with a plan for improvement in those areas where it may be desirable. Communication on performance, goals, and achievements is a two-way street, so the supervisor should also know and understand the employee's point of view.

Instructions: On a regular basis, either annually or more frequently if desirable, a formal employment evaluation should be conducted. The employee should be told in advance of the evaluation and a period of time should be set aside for it. Both the employee and the supervisor should complete the form. Each should have the opportunity to read the other's comments. They should then meet to discuss the comments, to examine the employee's achievements and performance over the period and to map out a program for future development. The form should be placed in the employee's records jacket; both the supervisor and the employee should retain a copy of the form. In preparing for the evaluation, the supervisor should review the previous evaluation form.

Dos and don'ts:

1. Don't make the common error of rating everything as "average."
2. Don't be afraid of hurting people's feelings or angering them. No one is perfect. Few people are superior in every aspect of the job.
3. Don't dwell only on negatives. Do show recognition of progress and accomplishments, and of qualities the employee possesses.
4. Do take the time and effort to do a complete, comprehensive, and adequate evaluation. The evalution and development of your subordinates is one of your most important functions.
5. Don't let the evaluation be rushed, or interrupted by telephone calls or messages. It should take place in privacy, without interruption, and with enough time to enable both of you to fully participate.
6. Don't make the evaluation a lecture. Ask questions and listen to the answers. This is a good time to learn how the employee really feels about his/her job and how he/she perceives his/her relationship to the organization.

(continued)

Figure 1. Performance Evaluation Form

(continued)

I. General Criteria:

Evaluate employee's performance on each of the criteria below. Indicate specific achievements and accomplishments since the last review. Also list areas where goals have not been met, and problems or job-related weaknesses that may have developed. Indicate whether the employee showed improvement in areas previously discussed.

	Supervisor's Comments	Employee's Comments
Job Knowledge Understanding and application of fundamental knowledge, skills, procedures, and methods required in the job.		
Fiscal Responsibility Maximum use of available resources, efficiency of production with cost containment.		
Planning for Results Determination of realistic goals and methods of achievement.		
Judgment Ability to examine all facets of problems, resourcefully solving problems and reaching sound decisions.		
Leadership Organizing, directing, motivating and evaluating staff to achieve common goals set by company.		
Interpersonal Relationships Ability to deal effectively in all types of situations with subordinates, superiors, peers, customers, vendors, and others.		
Performance Achievement of company goals within the organization's overall policies, including budget, affirmative action, safety policies, etc.		

(continued)

Figure 1. Performance Evaluation Form
(continued)

II. Overall Evaluation

Note that this part of the evaluation is concerned with employee's future performance in his or her current position. This part of the discussion with the employee should emphasize the future. What are the department's objectives and how can the employee best help to achieve them? How can he/she improve or moderate behavior to better assist in reaching these goals?

1. What are the employee's major strengths?

_____

_____

_____

2. What should the employee do to build on these strengths?

_____

_____

_____

3. What are the major areas in which the employee needs improvement?

_____

_____

_____

4. What should the employee do to improve in these areas?

_____

_____

_____

5. What overall developmental actions are suggested for the employee?

_____

_____

_____

(continued)

Figure 1. Performance Evaluation Form
(continued)

6. How well has the employee done in meeting the objectives and developmental actions agreed on previously?

_____

_____

_____

Past Objectives   Results and comments

_____   _____

_____   _____

_____   _____

_____   _____

III. Future Objectives and Timetable
The supervisor and the employee should mutually discuss and agree on these objectives:

Objective   Date to be accomplished by:

_____   _____

_____   _____

_____   _____

_____   _____

IV. Employee Potential
☐ This employee appears to be suited for his/her current job.

☐ This employee is not satisfactory in his/her present job. Termination or a job transfer should be considered.

☐ This employee's performance is not completely satisfactory. Goals and timetables for improvement have been set and another evaluation should be held on _____.

☐ This employee is ready for promotion now, to the job(s) indicated below.

(continued)

Figure 1. Performance Evaluation Form

(continued)

☐ This employee, with additional experience and/or training, should be promotable to the job(s) indicated below.

Job Title _____

Comments:

_____

_____

_____

_____

Signature _____ Date _____

Employee's Comments

After you have reviewed the form and discussed it with your supervisor, briefly list your comments about the overall evaluation or any part of it. (If you have no comments, indicate "none.")

_____

_____

_____

_____

_____

_____

_____

_____

Employee Signature _____ Date _____

The management objective then becomes the salesperson's objective, and he or she has had a hand in the setting of it. The plan becomes your mutual judgment regarding how the objective is to be met. What we know about employee involvement in goal setting is:

- Goals set by employees tend to be higher than their managers would dare set them.

- Employees work harder on goals they have set, or have participated in setting, than they would on employer-set goals.

- Employees tend to demonstrate a better attitude toward their goals because they understand them, feel challenged by them, and take pride in their achievement of them.

The Performance Objectives and Planning Sheet is literally what integrates the system. It is used at the outset of an appraisal system, is monitored throughout the system by both the salesperson and manager, and is used in the building of the final appraisal. It, rather than the performance appraisal, becomes the focal point of manager-employee effort; the appraisal is merely the final and formal result.

How to Write Clear Objectives

Using the Performance Objectives and Planning Sheet (Figure 2, page 922) as an example, we note a distinction between objectives, plans, and target dates.

- Objectives indicate what we hope to accomplish.

- Plans indicate our method of doing so.

- Target dates put a priority on the activity and an acceptable completion date.

Examples of clear objectives might be:

- To increase unit volume in the next six months by _____ units.

Figure 2. Performance Objectives and Planning Sheet

Sales Representative _____

Assignment _____

Length of time on assignment _____

Date of last establishment of objectives/plans _____

Estimate of success on those objectives/plans _____

NEW BUSINESS OBJECTIVES/
PLANS FOR PERIOD _____ to _____

OBJECTIVE	PLAN	TARGET DATE
1.		
2.		
3.		
4.		
5.		

NEW PERSONAL OBJECTIVES/PLANS FOR SAME PERIOD

OBJECTIVE	PLAN	TARGET DATE
1.		
2.		
3.		

Concurrence   Approval
(Sales Representative)   (Sales Manager)

_____   _____

Figure 3. Contacts and Observations Form

Representative _____

Date	Situation	Observation	Action

- To increase dollar volume in the next year by _____.
- To achieve unit sales of Product A by _____ %.
- To add _____ new accounts within the territory.
- To achieve an account service call rate of _____ %.
- To reduce customer complaints by _____ %.
- To reduce sales expense by $_____ in the next 3 months.

Or, on a personal level:

- To complete four additional credit hours toward a B.S. degree.
- To improve appearance and timeliness of all reports.
- To minimize sick days within corporate limits.

You will note that each of those objectives is specific, brief, and unqualified. It is best to write objectives in that way so that there will be little misunderstanding about them. Since your salesperson will take the first pass at writing his or her own objectives, you will want to offer counsel on what should be done.

Contacts and Observations

The other recommended form is the Contacts and Observations Form shown in Figure 3, page 923. This is a means for you to make note of any particularly good or bad business, or personal achievement or attribute you may notice in your ongoing relationship with the salesperson. It should be kept in the individual's personnel file, and it will make your appraisals more specific. After any day in the field, meeting in which the salesperson participated, telephone contact, or report submitted from the field, you will have occasion to record your observations. They may be like these:

- 3/12. Calls in field. Exceptional presentation to buyer at Magnum, Inc. Sample order taken. New account that shows potential.
- 4/17. Staff meeting. Assigned role to make new product presentation. Did a good job, but demonstrated a superior and ar-

rogant attitude towards peers who lacked his or her understanding of the product.

- 6/13. Good field report. Provided helpful information to marketing people who are studying new product potentials.

Here you have an individual whose business acumen and performance is outstanding, but who demonstrates an attitude that may become very damaging.

With information such as this, you will be able to write an appraisal that rewards performance, but alerts the individual to his or her interpersonal relationships problem.

The Contacts and Observations Form is your own private information. It need not be shown to the employee. What it will provide you is specific information on which to write an appraisal over the period covered.

Conversely, the Performance Objectives and Planning Sheet is one on which you and the salesperson work jointly. This is shared information that delineates goals and action needed to reach those goals. It, too, gives you information on which to base the written appraisal. Using both devices together will result in an appraisal that is beneficial to both you and the employee.

Conducting the Appraisal Interview

Here's where it all comes together. Or where it falls apart. Appraisal interviews traditionally don't rank high on wish lists of either employees or managers. The appraisal interview should have no surprises. The manager who works with his or her salespeople on a regular basis—coaching and counseling on day-to-day needs—will have communicated appraisal elements as they have occurred. If, indeed, there are surprises to the employee, they will come in the form of compliments for having overcome an earlier difficulty.

The sales manager who is well prepared, and who has written a sound appraisal, will enter the appraisal interview with assurance. There is not an employee question that can't be answered or an objection that can't be overcome. The substance is all there. Now is the time to discuss how to handle the interview effectively. Here are the essential guidelines for conducting the interview or conference:

- Assure privacy.
- Put the salesperson at ease.
- Encourage participation.
- Take the appraisal item by item.
- Sell the point.
- Handle objections.
- Develop agreement.
- End on a note of commitment.

Chapter 42

Sales Time and Expense Control

At least two factors lend importance to efficient time utilization by salespeople; the nature of time itself and the rising cost of salespeople's time. As the Sales Executives Club of New York puts it: "Time itself is nothing but a measured duration, and as such is simply a limited resource. However, it differs from every other resource in that it cannot be accumulated but can only be used as it becomes available. Further, it becomes available constantly, and evenly, increment by increment. Managers plan for the use of most resources and hold back additional amounts of those resources until they can be put to a planned use. Not so with time—it keeps coming at the executive in even doses, and if there is no plan for its use, it is wasted. In addition, the cost of a sales call has risen incredibly."

The main elements of territorial management are planning, implementation, and control.

Planning is a predetermined course of action that establishes goals and objectives, estimates the resources necessary to accomplish them, designs strategies for the best allocation and use of these resources, and controls activities to assure the realization of objectives. Too often salespeople indicate that they cannot plan because of the many emergencies that interrupt their schedule. Planning is not scheduling. All of the excuses salespeople use for not planning are actually all the reasons why they must plan. The emergencies will occur with or without a plan.

A plan enables the salesperson to evaluate the emergency and decide if he or she should drop everything for it and how much time he or she can afford to devote to it. It also provides a track to get back to after each emergency. It begins by analyzing the accounts in a given territory to determine their potential and to gather as much information as possible about the account in order to realize its potential. This analysis enables management to set goals and objectives for territorial coverage.

The concept of "expected value" of accounts is developed at this point. An estimate of the work load required to cover the territorial potential is made in order to measure the salesperson's available time and the time required to cover the territory. Adjustments in this estimate must frequently be made. The next step is resource allocation, whereby a value is placed on the salesperson's time in terms of how much each unit of time must contribute to accomplishing objectives. Activities are evaluated on the basis of their potential contribution to the objectives and time is allocated according to this potential.

At this point, a system of priorities evolves for a salesperson's activities. Selling strategies are then designed to use the resources in a way that will result in accomplishing objectives. After this careful planning, the salespeople are now ready to begin their field activities.

Implementation involves those activities required to call on accounts and cover the territory efficiently. As such it includes identifying decision-makers to be called on in accounts, developing call schedules, planning and making the actual sales call, and designing routing plans and prospecting.

Control of these activities is essential to assure that they are contributing to the planned objectives. Informal inputs, including reports and records, provide the salespeople with the critical data needed to evaluate actual performance against predetermined standards. Control over essential but unproductive nonselling activities is important in this phase. Finally, the self-discipline of time control is included in this area.

Basic Requirements for Time Control

Any control and guidance system, from the most basic to the most sophisticated, must contain four distinct elements, or steps:

1. Standards of performance must be established as the starting point. These evolve from the goals to be accomplished and are qualitative and quantitative estimates of the efforts and results expected of the salespeople.

2. Collection of data on actual performance must be a continuous process.

3. Analysis of actual performance against predetermined standards is the evaluation stage.

4. Corrective action is the final step in the control process and is necessary when there is a discrepancy between actual performance and the predetermined standards.

These four steps—standards, collection, analysis and correction—are applied to salesforce activities in order to exercise a degree of control over them. We will briefly consider these in order.

Standards of Performance

Performance standards usually pertain to sales efforts and results. A comprehensive sales control system attempts to relate efforts to results in order to evaluate the profitability of sales results in terms of the amount of effort expended. These ratios of efforts to results also provide a means for evaluating the productivity of sales efforts. In focusing on time utilization, however, as a part of sales control and supervision, the emphasis is on effort standards. Figures 1 through 5 on pages 958 through 963 at the end of this chapter illustrate various sales activity reporting forms that you can adapt for your own use.

In setting effort standards, the areas or activities of the salespeople for which standards should be set are first identified. This may be done by analyzing the salesperson's job description to determine what activities he or she must perform. Next, a review of territorial objectives suggests the activities necessary to accomplish the objectives. The following illustrate standards that may be set to control use of time:

- Number of calls on existing accounts

- Number of calls on potential accounts

- Average time per call

- Total call time

- Average travel time per call
- Total number of hours spent traveling
- Hours spent waiting
- Number of hours spent on nonselling activities
- Number of presentations made
- Number of demonstrations made
- Number of meetings attended
- Number of customers called on
- Number of prospects called on

Data collection is essential to improve time utilization. Before a salesperson can improve the effective use of his or her time, he or she must analyze how it is presently being used. Basically data on actual performance must emanate from the salesperson. The most commonly-used tool to record and communicate performance data is the call report. Firms with effective call reporting systems have the following principles in common:

- The basic approach to call reporting is to find out "how" rather than "what" a salesperson is doing. While these firms recognize that determining "what" a salesperson is doing in the field is important in the case of a new salesperson, or a salesperson experiencing difficulties, in most cases the call report should be used to analyze "how" the person is performing.

- The call report system, accordingly, is seen as a tool of communications. As such, it should allow for two-way communication. At the very least a summary recap of activities reported for a period of time should be tabulated from the reports and returned to the salesperson. In addition, the ideal is some form of comment and suggestions from the managers to the salespeople concerning the data reported.

- A study found that 69 percent of all firms using call reports require the sales force to report on every call made. In many instances, the only rationale for comprehensive reporting is to check on the salesperson's activities to be sure that he or she is working. Some firms have discovered that the exception principle, in which only those activities that require management's attention are reported, can be profitably applied to call reporting sytems. It cuts down the amount of reporting and reading, and results in increased communications, since management's attention is flagged to every important report.

- Effective reporting systems do not require the salespeople to gather and report information that can be obtained from another source. Generally, the salesperson is the most expensive source of information.

- Successful reporting systems look upon the call report as a tool for future planning, rather than simply a historical record.

- Efficient reports are simple to complete, contain a great deal of preprinted information, and employ symbols to facilitate their completion.

(The foregoing conclusions and recommendations result from a study conducted by the Sales Executives Club of New York among its members, plus other firms in the Fortune 500 list not represented in the membership roster. The report was prepared, under the direction of the Research Committee, by Robert F. Vizza, Ph.D., Dean, School of Business; and Thomas E. Chambers, MBA., Dean, School of General Studies, both of Manhattan College, New York.)

Part of the problem of managing a salesperson's time is the amount of other duties the salesperson must perform. Some salespeople are responsible for service. Merchandising, public relations, goodwill, collection, troubleshooting, inventory, reporting on competitors' sales and overdue accounts each receive attention from salespeople. Other duties that salespeople are often involved in are product positioning, quality control, delivery, prospecting, recruiting, market analysis, installation coordination, paperwork, education of store clerks, trade shows, conventions and after sales follow-up.

Table 1, below, shows the breakdown on the amount of time salespeople devote to certain types of calls, according to a Dartnell survey.

Route scheduling is an important factor in salespeople's time management. Forty-eight percent of the routes were scheduled by the individual salesperson. The home office was responsible for scheduling only 3 percent of the routes. Twelve percent of the routes were scheduled on a daily basis and only 1 percent on an hourly basis. Other systems of scheduling routes (3 percent) included a monthly or seasonal basis.

Analysis of Performance

A recent study, in which questionnaires were sent to 380 companies, revealed that more than half of the companies surveyed have not conducted an organized study of salespeople's use of time; 25 percent of the respondents do not have a system of classifying accounts according to potential; 30 percent do not use call schedules for the salepeople and 51 percent do not determine the number of calls it is economical to make on an account.

To provide the sales organization with leadership of the type under consideration (as contrasted with the top-sergeant variety) calls for close supervision in the field. Some companies have found that best results are secured when there is one supervisor for approximately every 10 salespeople. Others figure on the basis of one to 20 salespeople. Just as you pay for sales training, either in what

Table 1.

Type of Call	10% or less	20% or less	50% or less	80% or less	100% or less
Goodwill	20	4	0	0	0
Cold canvass	23	5	5	0	0
Planned sales calls	1	0	10	19	10
Call backs	16	6	4	1	0
Customer services	23	4	4	2	1
Other (totaled 8)					

you spend for the operation or in the loss of profits on the business you lose as a result of inadequate training, so you pay for sales supervision. Since adequately trained supervisors working closely with salespeople in the field usually produce enough extra business to more than carry their expense, it is foolish indeed for management to attempt to get along with half the supervisors needed, and those only partly trained and qualified for sales leadership.

"We try to avoid making the mistake of training our people and then kidding ourselves that they will stay trained," said the sales manager of The Egry Register Company, Dayton. "We cover all districts with personal visits of the sales staff and executives of the company. We also check very carefully on a list of definite points we have prepared.

"We pay particular attention to how our people use the training we have given them during the year. Thus we not only measure the results of the training we have done, but also uncover information which will assist us to plan the next year's training program."

Supervision is conducted through correspondence, telephone contacts, personal interviews in the home office and in the field, bulletins, manuals and sales meetings. Each medium has its advantages and disadvantages.

Personal contact in the field is probably the most effective; the salesperson is more relaxed, and the environments that created the supervisory need is close at hand. However, the supervisor cannot always be on hand when needed, so he or she must sometimes resort to telephone calls and correspondence. They, too, can be effective.

Telephone calls imply importance, immediate action, while letters provide permanent records for study and restudy. Letters carry authority that may easily be forgotten after mere conversation.

Bulletins and manuals provide ready-reference guidance, while sales meetings provide mass supervision and can be strongly inspirational.

One element of supervision is the taking of corrective action, when needed. On such occasions, the sales supervisor must hear both sides of the story, the salesperson's and the customer's, or whoever else may be involved.

Corrective Action

When corrective action is called for, the sales manager should:

- *Discuss the problem in private and not in open meeting or with other salespeople present.* This is vital.

- *Maintain an attitude of fairness and display a desire to be fair.* There should be no snap judgment. Instead, there should be an attempt to reach mutual understanding.

- *Speak quietly, without anger, and permit the salesperson plenty of time to register his or her comments in a like manner.* The salesperson should not be made to feel that he or she is being rushed, and he or she should also be assured that the conversation will be held confidential.

If the salesperson becomes resentful, tries to justify his or her actions, and takes refuge in emotional intensity, time should be taken to calm him or her down and if possible to terminate the conference in a friendly but firm manner. Afterward there must be firm and fair followthrough.

To bawl a person out, give directions for future conduct, and then close one's eyes to infractions is bad for morale and future sound supervision.

Qualities Required of the Sales Supervisor

In many companies the responsibility of supervision and time management of salespeople falls on the district or regional managers. In some companies it is one of the duties of the general sales manager, but most often the field supervisors are responsible. In few organizations are the individual salespeople responsible.

To provide adquate supervisory leadership, the sales supervisor must be familiar with every aspect of each salesperson's job; he or she must have vitality and endurance, as must all staff and assistants who work with and represent the supervisor. Decisiveness and reasonable promptness are required in making decisions.

He or she requires a keen sense of responsibility that must always be retained by management, and must understand the degree to which it can be shared with those being supervised.

There must be integrity, emotional stability, and a sincere regard for the private and personal welfare of all those who are being supervised.

There must be a capacity for intellectual growth that will permit the sales supervisor to handle the increasing complexity of marketing problems; the desire and ability to maintain openmindedness with regard to the suggestions of others, including those who are being supervised; and ambition to advance in the company and provide expanded opportunties for those who are striving to come up in the organization.

Good supervision also requires an awareness of the needs of other departments in the company and a willingness to assist them by every possible means. It should extend also to the development of cooperative willingness by the salespeople supervised.

A field sales supervisor is not only the representative of management in the field; but is also the principal contact point between the field salespeople and top management. He or she interprets the policies and objectives of management to the salespeople and reports the salesperson's attitudes, conditions of work, and problems to management.

The field sales supervisor relates training objectives and programs to the individual personalities of the salespeople, bringing out the strong points in each and correcting their weaknesses. He or she does not try to force everyone into one mold, but intermingles character traits and policy objectives astutely to gain the greatest permanent benefit for both the company and the salespeople.

He or she is the watchdog of local profit attainment, keeping prices in line and expenses under control. Through ability and leadership, he or she improves the effectiveness of the sales force, helping them achieve their results through suggestions and, where needed, through active participation. But he or she takes no undue credit, letting the results of his or her people testify as to his or her leadership.

To discharge his or her responsibilities, the supervisor must have clear-cut objectives established, as well as quotas, goals, standards, and the same type of leadership from above as he or she is expected to give to those under him or her. Policies, duties and responsibilities must be clearly defined.

The Importance of Field Inspections

It is one of the responsibilities of sales executives to keep informed of field conditions and operations through first-hand knowledge—in other words, through personal inspection. Frequently you hear the fear expressed that the field salespeople may feel that the manager is spying on them or doubts their ability to handle their territories when he or she visits them for an inspection. In such cases, the misunderstanding is due to failure of the sale manager to let his or her people know that periodic and thorough inspection is one of his or her duties.

The sales manager should go throughly into each person's operations, reviewing all records the salesperson is supposed to keep, inspecting samples, stocks of literature, the condition of the salesperson's car, and many other pertinent things. If any of these sales tools is sloppily maintained, the manager can blame only himself or herself for permitting the condition to exist.

It is as necessary that well-run territories be inspected as it is to inspect poorly-run ones. The mere act of inspection places a value and importance to that being inspected, which helps contribute to its success.

In addition, the sales manager will usually pick up some good ideas, which he or she can pass on to other salespeople.

Frequently one hears managers say that Salesperson A is a good salesperson and does not need to be visited. The truth might well be that Salesperson A is a lonely person and yearns for some attention from the home office; or he or she might be an even better person if management showed some concern for his or her problems. It is safe to say that erring is more frequent in the direction of too little supervision than too much of it.

Inspection and review of field conditions are needed in sales supervision for four important reasons:

1. To bring management into contact with the realities of performance;

2. To develop morale in the field and respect for authority and for company programs;

3. To assure that proper importance is given to the details of the field work;

4. To determine areas in which corrective action should be taken.

Supervision of salespeople includes consideration in the field, to ascertain the validity of sales objectives. This can be determined only through first-hand knowledge of the territory, its sales opportunities, and the hazards to be encountered in realizing these objectives.

Also included is the element of evaluation, which requires the establishment of standards and the maintenance and study of suitable and meaningful records. Supervisory inspection should culminate in the giving of instructions, encouragement and criticism, in setting examples, in counseling, and, where necessary, in disciplining the salesperson.

Methods of Time Control

The wise sales manager teaches salespeople to learn the buying preferences of their customers and to regulate their calling time accordingly, seeing the "early birds" first.

Two salespersons of the same distributor, on being questioned as to when calls could be made on their customers, gave different replies. One said that since buyers wish to go over their mail the first thing in the morning and to sign their letters late in the afternoon, he made his calls between 9:30 a.m. and 4:00 p.m. The other referred to the same work habit, but said she had a number of customers who would see her at 8:00 a.m. and others who would see her as late as 6:00 p.m. before they closed shop. The first salesperson rationalized a short work day, the second one found a way of making the most of her selling time.

In selling, face-to-face selling time is about the only expendable item. A salesperson improves his or her knowledge by sharing it with customers; the same is true of sales skills and sales personality. Everything used in selling increases by use, except face-to-face selling time; *that* is fully expendable.

It is the sales executive's responsibility to see that the precious, limited, and expendable face-to-face selling time is used to the greatest advantage. Too frequently salespeople are sent out with inadequate preparation as to product knowledge and selling techniques. Knowledge without the ability to convey it to others is useless; selling ability without the strength of product and use knowledge is hollow. Every moment of face-to-face selling time must be put to maximum advantage. Too much time spent in idle chitchat is harmful, as is the monotonous parroting of a "canned" speech. The emphasis here is on "monotonous parroting"; in some lines, prepared sales talks are useful, but they fall flat if they are not given as though they were spontaneous. All sales presentations must be wisely and constructively presented so that every moment of customer contact is productive.

A positive aid to a good sales presentation is the use of a pre-call planning sheet such as the one shown in Figure 6 on page 964.

Routing Salespeople Effectively: The problem of routing salespeople most effectively is one of the perpetual problems of sales supervision. There is no one "solution," but only a number of *approaches* to solutions which have a tendency to "come unsolved" after they have been in effect for a time.

The sales executive who expects to set up a routing plan which his or her salespeople will thenceforward and forever follow implicitly is doomed to a rude awakening.

This does not mean that routing salespeople successfully is an insoluble problem; it merely implies that no system can be depended on to operate automatically in good and bad times and in all sorts of districts. It is an inescapable function of the sales executive to study continually all present and prospective customers and readjust the workload for his or her salespeople accordingly.

Reduced to its simplest terms, the effective routing of salespeople is merely a matter of arranging calls on the most logical basis. A complex, intricate system is not required; even such a simple plan as that of putting the name of individual companies on colored cards and identifying them by corresponding colored tacks on a large road map works well.

Sales managers feel that if a real job is done in correcting sales-people's attitudes towards time losses, the need for specific help is not great. Several who have attempted ambitious time-control plans, such as hour-by-hour routing of salespeople, have not found results sufficient to justify the expenditure. However, some large employers of salespeople, selling established trade channels, have developed home-office routing to a high degree of efficiency. Two such companies are American Brands Inc., of New York and Esmark of Chicago.

Preparing Routing Sheets: A company selling hospital supplies prepares all routing sheets in its home office. Generally four routes are prepared, each covering a week's time; the salespeople are held responsible for abiding by these routes, and are required to send in daily call reports. The company checks their adherance to the program by phoning them from time to time, to give them price information or other important messages along their routes, management knowing approximately where each person should be at any time each day.

It is better for the home office to prepare these route sheets than the salespeople, as the home office maintains historical records, has seasoned judgment, and is not influenced by the personal desires of the salespeople. Of course, all the salespeople are encouraged to offer constructive criticism and suggestions as to route changes, accounts to be dropped, and new prospects to be added. In fact, if a salesperson does not offer such suggestions, management solicits them, calling to the salesperson's attention that the making of constructive recommendations is one of his or her duties and responsibilities.

Helping Salespeople to Route Themselves: There are conditions which sometimes make it desirable to let the salespeople route themselves as, for example, in cases where salespeople are paid a straight commission. Sales managers very often say: "We hold our salespeople responsible for production only; if they make a mess out of routing themselves that is their hard luck." This is short-sighted, however. After all, it makes no great difference whether a salesperson is working on a salary, a commission, or any other kind of compensation plan. The territory assigned to him or her represents a definite volume of potential business. The more of this business he or she gets, the more money the company will make. It is, therefore, up to the company to do all it can to help each salesperson get the maximum production from his or her territory.

The Headquarters "Hounds": In every sales organization there are salespeople who waste a vast amount of time coming back to their homes or headquarters towns far more often than is good for them. Too many of their trips are planned so as to circle out in the morning, then circle back into headquarters in time for the evening meal. It is obvious that such practices use up a lot of gasoline and time which might be better spent face to face with buyers. One company found its salespeople were doing this to such an extent that they were not visiting dealers in the remote sections. The waste of time was terrific. To cut the loss, a plan was devised to send a salesperson half his or her drawing account weekly, then to send the remainder only upon receipt of receipted bills from hotels. In this way the home office could check the salesperson's visits, secure the knowledge that the outlying towns were being worked carefully, because the salespeople could obtain only half their expense money if they did not submit hotel bills to show where they had been during the week. This plan was effective in cutting down the time lost rushing back home two or three times a week.

Sales Reports

To provide management and salespeople alike with a results picture, most companies operate some system of sales reports. Some are quite simple; others are quite involved. In all cases, however, they convey information about territorial conditions useful in sales planning. If they do no more than to make it necessary for a salesperson to sit down at the close of the day and review his or her day's work carefully, the effort is worthwhile. The traditional idea, shared by most salespeople and some sales managers, that daily reports are a kind of portable time clock, has largely disappeared. There are still a few sales executives who will tell you they never require salespeople to make out reports, because all they want from salespeople are orders, but there are not many of that school left.

The essentials of good report forms would include the following:

- Forms should be of convenient size, easy for salespeople to carry, write on, and mail; easy for the recipient to read, process, act upon, and file.

- They should provide check spaces for recurring activities that need merely be recorded, not commented upon.

- They should be so arranged as to discourage any wordy comments about unimportant happenings. It is bad enough for salespeople to spend time writing verbose reports; it is even worse when the reports get to the home office and one or more busy executives have to read them.

- Forms should be instruments of encouragement, motivation, and inspiration. If the salespeople normally average six calls a day, eight or ten spaces can be allowed for recording calls, and the spaces numbered so that the salespeople will automatically see how many calls they have made. As many spaces as possible should appear on the front of the form; if ten spaces are to be provided, at least eight should appear on the front and two on the back of the form. This is better than five on each side, since the salesperson may feel that the day's work is over when the five on the front have been filled.

- Carbons should be required only if the salespeople have no other procedure for recording their activities for their own use. Keeping carbon copies just for the sake of maintaining a file is a waste of time.

- Summaries should be eliminated if possible. Some managers feel that if the salespeople total their number of calls, sales, demonstrations, etc., it will be instructive and motivating. However, if the form is properly prepared, proper motivation will be provided and the salespeople will be saved the chore of doing unnecessary clerical work. If the statistical work is done in the home office by lower-paid but more efficient clerks, monthly summary data can be sent to the salespeople showing how their activities compare with others or with standards.

- Reports should not be too inclusive in communication subject areas. If requests for samples or literature go to separate departments, special forms or perforated sections should be provided.

- Expenses should be recorded on separate reports, as these usually go, after local management approval, to the treasurer's office for reimbursement. If they travel through other departments, they may be delayed or lost. Perforated expense sheets attached to call reports are frequently used; they save time for the salesperson, can be approved by local management and then detached and sent to the accounting department.

- Full instructions and a brief description of the use and purpose of the report should be printed on each form to remind and reinstruct the salespeople after the form has been first explained to them.

- There should be space provided whereby each regular reader or processor of the form initials it and enters the date of completion. This will help assure that the form receives the proper attention.

What Salespeople Should Report

Aside from the transmittal of field activities and market conditions, reports should be used for developing statistics on the number and character of calls, routing, mailing lists, etc. Even when a salesperson makes a call and nothing of particular interest transpires, a record of the call should still be made, to assist in the development of work standards based on such data as the following:

- Calls made per day, week, or month
- Inventories taken
- Displays set up
- Stocks rearranged

- Literature distributed
- Demonstrations made
- Samples give away
- Sales meetings held
- Call-backs required
- Orders taken

Salespeople should be made to understand that these statistics are not only important for good management but are also important for good salesmanship. Reports should flow back to them as to average and standard activities, so they may have a measure of their own activity. Every person with any degree of pride or ambition wishes to know how he or she stacks up with others doing comparable jobs. Scoreboards are necessary, whether for baseball games or for earning a living.

Reports can be written or verbal. The former are probably needed more by medium-sized and large companies than by small ones. A sales executive with only two or three salespeople whom he or she sees often can rely on verbal reports. There probably is little need for written reports other than to obtain historical data for the development of standards of activity. A company that sets its salespeople up as independent operators, without direction or assistance, probably needs no written reports. But as the breadth of coverage and complexity of management increase, written reports are more and more needed for good management.

Written reports should be read and acted upon with promptness so that salespeople learn to rely upon them as an important means of communication with the home office. It is incumbent upon top management to report regularly to the board of directors and stockholders. It receives its information from all segments of the company—from the controller as to profit and losses, from the treasurer as to capital investments, from manufacturing as to production, and from sales as to current results and future projections.

The information on sales stems primarily from field activities, sales results, and information as to competitive and market conditions. Unless the channels of communication from the field are adequate and well used, a comprehensive and accurate understanding of field conditions and the company's competitive position will not be obtained. Thus field reports are an important element in corporation knowledge, and the salesperson should be made so to understand.

What Information Should Be Sent Salespeople?

Practice varies among companies as to what information is sent to the sales force. Some companies send their salespeople copies of all correspondence with present or prospective customers in their territories, copies of all orders as entered, and invoices as issued. Others go farther and send their salespeople summary reports at the end of the month showing dollar value of orders received and shipments made, theoretical profits (if the salespeople are on some profit-sharing plan), expenses incurred by the salesperson, calls made, and other sales data. They may also show a salesperson's standing as compared with a standard or with the average of other salespeople.

What should be sent to the sales force depends on the nature of the business, the complexity of the selling job, the degree to which the salespeople need to be informed in order to best serve their customers, and the degree of authority given the salespeople. Certainly a salesperson needs to be well informed and to be in a position to advise his or her customers about shipments.

If customers send orders directly to the company, the salesperson needs to know about it promptly. It is embarrassing for the salesperson, and a reflection on the company, for the salesperson to ask for an order only to find that the customer has already placed it with his or her firm. It would be better for the salespeople to be able to thank the customers for the order when he or she first walks into the customer's office.

Salespeople also should have copies of invoices to know when shipments are made and to know about the financial details of the transaction; customers may have questions to ask, or errors may have been made in processing the order. It is better for the salesperson to catch these errors than for the customer to find them first.

Some companies rely on copies of invoices to furnish information for their salespeople as to total shipments made during a month to individual customers or for the sales territory as a whole, in which case the salespeople are expected to make their own summations. Some managers, on the contrary, feel that they should not expect their salespeople to do this clerical chore, with all its dangers of error and procrastination, since they may not get around to doing the job.

Summary of Time-Control Planning

The conclusions reached as a result of the study of Time and Territorial Management for Salespeople conducted by the Sales Executives Club of New York, may be summarized as follows:

1. The use of a Time Duty Analysis should be made a regular practice of sales management. It is the first step in a program of improving time utilization. One must know how time is presently being used—or wasted—in order to increase its productivity.

2. Call frequency patterns, including the number, duration, and interval between calls, should be developed based on account potential. These patterns should be established and adopted as standard operating procedure for salespeople.

3. More attention must be given to assisting salespeople in preparing sales calls. This includes gathering marketing intelligence, identifying decision-makers and planning sales presentations, to enable salespeople to save time on calls and to do a more effective selling job, geared to the identified needs of the buyers rather than the obvious needs of the seller.

4. The capabilities of the computer must be recognized and developed in this area.

Sales Expense Control

Top management too often regards sales expense as an unavoidable evil, rather than a profit-returning investment. *The financial executives should never overlook the fact that the purpose of sales expenses is to generate profits.* Of the various practices for handling sales force expenses, the most common are the following:

1. Reimbursement of actual expenses incurred

2. Reimbursement of actual expenses, with top limit

3. Expenses charged to the company

4. Flat expense allowance

Reimbursement of Actual Expenses. This is the most commonly followed practice with salaried personnel and is growing in popularity for commission salespeople.

Table 2, below, from a Dartnell study shows the percent of companies paying all or part of field expenses. It shows the three basic compensation plans and is broken down by company type.

Most marketing executives advance their salespeople a certain

Table 2.

Percentage of Companies Paying All or Part of Expenses (All Companies and by Compensation Plan)				
	All Companies	Salary	Commission	Combination
Automobile (Company-Owned/ Leased/Personal)	76%	90%	49%	86%
Commercial airlines	71%	90%	44%	80%
Railroads	37%	46%	19%	44%
Company plane	21%	27%	11%	24%
Lodging	75%	92%	46%	84%
Telephone	83%	95%	66%	89%
Entertainment	75%	86%	48%	88%
Samples	65%	73%	51%	70%
Promotion	74%	80%	59%	81%
Office and/or clerical	75%	84%	55%	83%

amount weekly or monthly as expense money, then reimburse them as expense reports are submitted. Others require their salespeople to use their own capital for routine selling expenses, reimbursing them weekly or monthly.

However, where salespeople travel from the home office on special trips, it is customary for the company to provide them with air or rail tickets and give them an advance for other expenses, to be accounted for with any balance paid back to the company.

A Company Expense Policy

Properly supervised, the salesperson's expenses are as much an investment as are the expenses incurred in other company operations. It is only by thinking of expenses as *investments for profit attainment* that we bring them into true focus. This is—we repeat— as true of salespeople's expenditures as of any other investment for potential profit. A typical company expense policy is shown in Figure 7, pages 965-967.

Reimbursement of Actual Expenses, with Top Limit

This procedure places a ceiling on expenses. Such plans are useful when reasonable leeway is allowed; but with plans in which the limit is strictly enforced, the program gets away from the basic concept that when expenditures are necessary for increased sales, they should be allowed. Curtailment should not be made on the basis of expenses per se, but of unnecessary expenses.

Expenses Charged to the Company. This is similar to the actual reimbursement plan except that all expenses possible are charged to the company through the use of credit cards. There is considerable merit to this plan because it saves the salesperson from carrying large amounts of cash, avoids the need of frequently cashing checks when traveling, and it provides the company with reliable vouchers for expense allocation.

Flat Expense Allowance. Few companies today follow this method of expense allotment. It has been generally found undesirable, for the following reasons:

1. It ignores the basic concept of expense investment and treats expenses as a necessary evil.

2. It is difficult to apply fairly. Except in rare cases, a salesperson either receives too great an allowance or receives too little and must finance company business from his or her own pocket. In many instances where salespeople have been on flat expense accounts they have not covered their territories as they should because they were temporarily short of cash or wanted to save the money.

3. A flat expense allowance starts out as being money paid to the salesperson for traveling expenses, but quickly it changes its character and becomes part of the salesperson's income. He or she becomes more and more reluctant to spend a part of his or her "income" on company business.

Expense Account Forms

The practice of furnishing salespeople with expense forms is practically universal, whether for social security or for income tax purposes. This arrangement for handling expenses is much more convenient than other methods, as it enables salespeople to note such expenses at the time they are made and thus reduces the chances of error where they are recorded later. To meet the requirements of the Social Security Act, salespeople on a straight commission are required to account for their expenses, so proof is available of net income subject to tax; while salespeople on other types of compensation plans are more than ever expected to keep accurate accounts for reimbursable expense outlays.

In this connection, Dartnell has developed a weekly expense account that is widely used (Figure 8, page 968). It is a composite of a large number of forms submitted to The Dartnell Corporation. Its advangates lie in its simplicity and the manner in which it makes possible an analysis of each salesperson's expenses.

Transportation of Salespeople

The first question to be decided in regard to automobile use in sales work is whether the cars should be owned or leased by the company and all expenses paid by the company, or whether the salesperson should own the car, and the company allow a certain amount for operating it. Both plans meet with favor; both have advantages and both have disadvantages.

Drawbacks to the company-operated fleet plan are that it requires a larger investment on the company's part; that salespeople take better care of their own cars than they do of cars owned by the company; and that they often use company cars on personal business, which in many cases makes the comparative mileage costs shown by the company's records undependable.

The advantages of the fleet plan are that it gives the company more control over the condition of the cars, and in that way reduces the loss of time due to a salesperson's car being out of commission, and that it permits certain economies in operations. It also enables the company to put its trademark or other advertising on the car, which may or may not be of value. With the right kind of automobile allowance plan, the cost of operating salespeople's automobiles in reality is about the same, regardless of whether the salesperson owns the car or the company owns the car.

Company-owned fleets can be handled more economically and with less trouble if you hire a professional fleet manager. There are also management services that can act for a company in this capacity. Figure 9, page 969, is an example of a typical Car Expense Report sheet.

Cost of Operation

For the most current information on the costs of operating and maintaining business automobiles contact the Runzheimer Corporation, Runzheimer Park, Rochester, WI 53167.

Automobile Allowances

The large majority of firms operate larger fleets of company-owned or leased vehicles, but a substantial number of companies pay drivers to operate their own vehicles. There are four methods of payment normally followed to reimburse these drivers:

1. Flat mileage allowance

2. Sliding-scale mileage allowance

3. Fixed allowance plus mileage

4. Fixed allowance

The flat mileage allowance is still the most popular with companies who have driver-owned fleets; however the number is continuing to diminish in favor of the fixed allowance or the fixed allowance plus mileage payment plans. For occasional use of the personal car on business, the IRS will allow driver 24 cents a mile for the first 15,000 miles.

Automobile Insurance Practices

The cost of automobile insurance has climbed steadily. Accident costs are higher, repair bills are higher, new car costs are up, and jury awards are more generous than ever.

What are some of the ways to keep insurance costs controlled? One way, of course, is to self-insure where possible. It is not always easy to tell when this may be the best thing to do, but a common practice is to buy some kinds of insurance from insurance carriers and carry the balance on a self-insured basis.

Another way to keep control of costs is to know how much to buy, when to buy it, and how to buy in combination. This is where many companies say that an insurance manager is worth the cost. He or she will know, for example, that some insurance companies offer rate discounts to policyholders who enforce fleet speed limitations. He or she will know that it is possible to get a 15 percent reduction on combined medical payments, death, and disability coverage. He or she will know, too, that most companies offer low rates where the drivers are young (but not too young) and are well trained.

Every fleet administrator should provide personal or public liability protection for the cars under his or her control. And in 99 out of 100 companies using employee-owned cars, salespeople are required to have the same kind of protection before the car leaves the garage on company business.

Most companies insist on property damage coverage. Nearly all of those owning or leasing cars carry property damage insurance, in amounts reaching $1 million, in umbrella packages.

The limits of per-person and per-accident liability have been rising along with all the other aspects of automobile insurance. A few years ago, Dartnell surveys show, it was common for a company to purchase $50,000/$100,000 coverage and regard itself as thoroughly and completely protected. Now, the most popular liability limits are $100,000 per person and $300,000 per accident. Many companies are carrying the $100,000 umbrella coverage.

Who Pays the Premium?

When asked, "Do you pay the insurance premiums for salespeople who drive their own cars on company business?" two-thirds of the replies were negative. Many companies make indirect payments, however, in that consideration is given to the high cost of insurance when time-and mileage allowances are established. The time element in the reimbursement plan is intended to help out with the fixed costs the salesperson has to cope with, including, of course, his or her annual insurance bill.

The next most common practice among those companies using employee-owned cars is that of supplementing the employee's privately purchased coverage, whether set at a company-required minimum or not, by some sort of blanket liability coverage. This usually has the effect of stepping up the bodily injury and property damage liability limits bought by the employee. While this is a cooperative insurance purchase plan in a sense, it is considered here in a little different light because it involves no agreement between company and employee on the division of the total premium.

On leased vehicles, the terms of the leasing contract determine how insurance premiums are handled. The tendency is for client companies to pay the insurance bill. Situations where lessor and lessee split the cost (with lessor usually paying for collision, fire and theft, and lessee paying for liability coverage) are also common today.

Automobile Trade-in Practices

The variety of trade-in schedules and plans reported by companies that have contributed to Dartnell surveys are almost without limit. The trade-in age most frequently reported, however, is three years. Among the companies that consider only mileage, the figure mentioned most often is 60,000. The margin between the leaders and the rest is not great, though. There are still companies that say every two years is a good time to trade.

Most of the companies taking part in Dartnell surveys used one of the three basic depreciation methods that have specific Treasury Department approval. Only 8 percent say they have developed their own homegrown methods or use combinations of any of the basic plans.

By far the greatest number use the straight-line method of depreciating company cars. Seventy-five percent follow this course. Next most popular were the declining-balance and double-declining-balance methods.

Whatever the method used to figure depreciation, four-year useful life was the basis in most companies. Check with the IRS for the current depreciation schedules.

The vast majority of the companies surveyed give the custodian (generally a salesperson) some authority to have routine repairs made. There is a maximum figure beyond which the user cannot go without permission from the home office. In the case of emergency repairs, companies generally relax this restriction but require a complete report and explanation afterwards.

The ceiling on the custodian's authority to initiate repairs runs from $100. One company with 468 cars in a company-owned salesperson-operated fleet has three ceilings: The salesperson has authority to pay for minor repairs, the district office can authorize some major repairs, and others must be submitted to the automotive department, which will issue a purchase order if it approves the project.

The Peterson, Howell & Heather Expense Control Program

A number of management organizations offer special services to sales executives in companies not set up to analyze their own car expense operations.

As an example of this type of program, Peterson, Howell & Heather (PHH) in Baltimore offers a car expense control program designed to give five benefits to the user:

1. *Reimbursement problem is solved.* Salespeople are repaid only for actual car expenses. Inequities to the salespeople and your company are eliminated. Your people are neither overpaid or underpaid as would happen if salespeople were paid a flat dollar amount per month or so many cents per mile to cover car expenses.

2. *Your paperwork and administrative detail are reduced.* In effect, PHH acts as your fleet manager. They prepare and analyze your reports showing your mileage and expense levels and compare your experience with national and industry trends, with exception limits built into the reports, and highlighting salespeople who are above or below acceptable norms.

3. *Effective control of car expenses is in your hands.* You know what your car expenses are each month, on both a year-to-date and an annual basis. There is no guesswork and no estimating. Discrepancies become obvious and can be immediately acted upon through policy revision or corrective action in the field organization.

4. *Car warranty claims are handled for you.* Each car repair bill is automatically reviewed by PHH for warranty recovery. PHH processes the claims and returns all dollar recoveries to your company.

5. *The program is economical.* Through the use of modern data processing equipment and specialized techniques, PHH can produce these expense control reports at far less

cost than your company can on its own. Warranty recoveries alone will reduce, if not pay for, the cost of the program.

There are three steps in this particular program as follows:

1. Salesperson submits his or her expense worksheet for the period along with receipted bills for repairs and other major expenditures.

2. Salesperson is reimbursed for actual expense as reported.

3. Home office accumulates worksheets from all salespeople and sends them once each month to PHH after checking for accuracy and completeness.

Dartnell Survey on Expense Costs

The total average expense cost (all of the 10 expense items shown in Table 2, page 946) per salesperson currently is about $17,000 and is sure to rise in future years.

CHANGES MADE TO REDUCE EXPENSES

Respondents were asked to comment on changes they have made in salespeople's activities to reduce field expenses. The representative statements that follow didn't track any specific action but rather indicated that every conceivable activity involving expense was examined carefully.

These comments can provide you with possibilities to include in your ongoing cost-reduction program or serve as thought-starters for others.

- More phone calls—*NO* cold calls.

- More phone activity.

- Increase customer contact by inside customer service reps.

- Itinerary planning, electronic mail.

- Restrict travel, use phones more.

- Stop making useless face-to-face calls and replace with phone and direct mail to result in better use of sales rep's time.

- Cut down on overnight trips.
- Personal computer network.
- Calls by appointment. Reduced "cold" personal calls.
- Use phone more from office—reduce field travel.
- Eliminate lunch expense.
- "800" or WATS line installation.
- Reduce non-business lunches and travel expenses.
- Smaller cars, smaller territories.
- Smaller territories, more products.
- Careful review of expense reports.
- Budget for expenses rather than unlimited reimbursement.
- We have a demonstration program—reducing demonstration time.
- More efficient routing—phone coordinators.
- More phone work.
- Limited entertainment, reduced phone calls.
- Changed routing.
- Eliminate telephone credit cards.
- Attempt to increase number of calls made.
- Send fewer people to exhibits and trade shows.
- We are moving salespeople into their markets.
- Better qualified calls.
- Introduce telemarketing.
- Closer supervision on call activity.
- Better routing, less air travel.

- Corporate travel rates on air travel and car rental.
- Teach better routing, provide field help and inside help.
- Allowances for meals—lodging.
- Limits on entertainment, reduced travel.
- Add manufacturer's rep for out-of-state service calls.
- Territory rearrangement—more use of phone.
- Reasonable dinner expenses reimbursed when receipts with customer names are furnished.
- Close tracking of expense: sales ratio, maintain 4 percent (without salary and benefits) at all times.
- Lease cars.
- Adjust expense control to moderate differences in large city versus geographic costs.
- Centralized travel bureau, spending maximums in certain areas (meals, hotels).
- Hope to provide each salesperson with a budget.
- May need to adjust car payment upward.
- Give a flat amount per month or week. Salespeople cover expenses from the amount. Stop paying mileage.
- Increase responsibility. Expenses must be covered by sales profit. They must justify.
- Better monitoring of expense per sale via new computer capabilities.
- Lessen the corporation share of telephone expense.
- Corporate credit cards and central billing—less personal expense report.
- Try to reduce to 21 percent of sales.
- Create travel expense policy.

- Establish expense budgets for sales.

- Require salespeople to purchase own autos and pay them a flat rate per month for all auto costs.

- Expense savings over last year will be paid back to the salesperson by a percentage.

Figure 1. Sales Representative's Progress Report

EMPLOYEE'S NAME _____ LOCATION _____

CLASSIFICATION _____ DIVISION _____

EMPLOYMENT DATE _____

HOW DO YOU RATE SALES REPRESENTATIVE'S PERFORMANCE ON THE FOLLOWING:	PLANS FOR IMPROVEMENT
1. TOTAL SALES VOLUME	
A. FREQUENCY OF CALLS ON PRESENT AND PROSPECTIVE CUSTOMERS. ☐ ☐ ☐ ☐ ☐ ☐ ☐ ☐ BELOW AVERAGE ABOVE AVERAGE	
B. PERSONAL ACQUAINTANCE WITH CUSTOMER'S EMPLOYEES WHO ARE INVOLVED IN BUYING DECISIONS. ☐ ☐ ☐ ☐ ☐ ☐ ☐ ☐ BELOW AVERAGE ABOVE AVERAGE	
C. PLANNING IN ADVANCE TO MAKE SUCCESSFUL SALES PRESENTATION. ☐ ☐ ☐ ☐ ☐ ☐ ☐ ☐ BELOW AVERAGE ABOVE AVERAGE	
D. PROPER SALES PRESENTATION AND CLOSING ABILITY AT TIME OF SALES INTERVIEW. ☐ ☐ ☐ ☐ ☐ ☐ ☐ ☐ BELOW AVERAGE ABOVE AVERAGE	
E. USE OF PROPER SPECIALISTS IN SERVICING ACCOUNTS. ☐ ☐ ☐ ☐ ☐ ☐ ☐ ☐ BELOW AVERAGE ABOVE AVERAGE	
2. EFFECTIVE TIME AND ACTIVITY PLANNING	
A. PLANNING TIME FOR PROPER COVERAGE OF TERRITORY. ☐ ☐ ☐ ☐ ☐ ☐ ☐ ☐ BELOW AVERAGE ABOVE AVERAGE	
C. PUNCTUAL PREPARATION OF REPORTS. ☐ ☐ ☐ ☐ ☐ ☐ ☐ ☐ BELOW AVERAGE ABOVE AVERAGE	
D. KEEPS SUPERVISOR ADVISED OF SITUATION IN THE TERRITORY. ☐ ☐ ☐ ☐ ☐ ☐ ☐ ☐ BELOW AVERAGE ABOVE AVERAGE	
E. EFFECTIVE CORRESPONDENCE AND PERSONAL RELATIONS WITH CUSTOMERS AND COMPANY PERSONNEL. ☐ ☐ ☐ ☐ ☐ ☐ ☐ ☐ BELOW AVERAGE ABOVE AVERAGE	
3. PRODUCT, ORGANIZATION AND POLICY KNOWLEDGE RE:	
A. COMPANY. ☐ ☐ ☐ ☐ ☐ ☐ ☐ ☐ BELOW AVERAGE ABOVE AVERAGE	
B. COMPETITION. ☐ ☐ ☐ ☐ ☐ ☐ ☐ ☐ BELOW AVERAGE ABOVE AVERAGE	
C. CUSTOMERS. ☐ ☐ ☐ ☐ ☐ ☐ ☐ ☐ BELOW AVERAGE ABOVE AVERAGE	

Part of a sales representative's progress report. It is similar to an employee-appraisal form, except that it is tailored to sales work.

Figure 2. Weekly Itinerary

Salesperson _____

Week Beginning: _____

EXISTING ACCOUNTS to be contacted:

ACCOUNT	CITY	CONTACT

TARGET ACCOUNTS to be contacted:

FIRST CALL PROSPECTS to be contacted:

Figure 3. Sales Call Report

SALESPERSON _____ DATE OF CALL ___/___/___

☐ ACTIVE CUSTOMER   ☐ INACTIVE CUSTOMER   ☐ NEW CUSTOMER   ☐ PROSPECT

COMPANY _____ PHONE _____

ADDRESS _____

CITY _____ STATE _____ ZIP _____

TALKED TO _____ TITLE _____

SOLD TO _____ AMOUNT OF ORDER _____

REMARKS AND SPECIAL NOTES

_____

_____

_____

_____

FOLLOW-UP DATE   /   /

ADD TO MAILING LIST: ☐ YES ☐ NO SEND: ☐ CATALOG ☐ PRICE LIST ☐ OTHER

Figure 4. Daily Sales Call Report

SALESPERSON _____ DAY OF WEEK _____ MONTH _____ DAY _____ 19 ___

TERRITORY _____ ROUTE _____ SHEET _____ of _____

ACCOUNT NAME AND ADDRESS	PERSON'S NAME AND TITLE	REMARKS	NEXT CALL		CALL CODE	AMOUNT OF SALE
			DATE	TIME		
1.						
2.						
3.						
4.						
5.						
6.						
7.						
8.						
9.						
10.						
			TOTAL CALLS			
			TOTAL SALES			$

INSTRUCTIONS TO SALESPEOPLE: Mail this report daily. Retain a copy for your file. Use additional sheets as necessary. When writing a supplemental letter or name refer to it in the "Remarks" column. Write a separate letter about each customer or prospect. Code each call as follows: F—for first call on prospect or new account; M—if call was made and person missed; R—Regular call on established account; S—for special call on established account; X—if call planned but not made.

961

Weekly Expense Report (continued)

Number of Calls Made
List Customer On Reverse Side

Number of Hours Worked

State Business Purpose—People Entertained—Place of Entertainment and Time

I Hereby Certify that the Above Expenditures Represent Cash Spent for Legitimate Company Business Only and Includes No Items of a Personal Nature.

Signed _____

DATE	REPAYMENT RECAP	AMOUNT		MILEAGE RECORD	APPROVAL	CASHIER'S MEMO
	Advance Received			End of Trip		Check No.
	Reimbursed			Less Start		
	Total			Miles Per Trip		
	Expense for Week					Date Amount
	Over or Short					

962

Figure 5. Call Report

Pre-Call Plan DATE:_____

SALESPERSON: _____

ACCOUNT: _____

Route:
VP Sales _____
Pres. _____
VP Mktg. _____
Plant GM _____
VP Sales _____

CITY: _____ CONTACT: _____

☐ Existing Account: ☐ Target Account: ☐ First Call Prospect

Objective of call (Be Specific): _____

_____

_____

Anticipated problems (Include any pending service problems): _____

_____

_____

Call Strategy: _____

_____

_____

Post-Call Report

Was objective achieved? ☐ Yes ☐ No If not, why? _____

_____

Amount of order, If written: _____ Date of next Planned Call: _____

OBJECTIVE: _____

Progress toward closing of target account or first call prospect (0% to 100%):_____

   Anticipated closing date: _____

Competitive or Market Condition Information: _____

_____

_____

ATTACHED: ☐ Order   ☐ Target Account Work Sheet   ☐ Customer Data Sheet

Figure 6. Pre-Call Planning Sheet

Name of company _____

Name of individual to be seen _____

Title _____

Type of company _____

Type of product or service _____

Present or prior customer? _____ New prospect? _____

If present or prior customer, when was the last call made? _____

By whom was the call made? _____

Are there now, or have there been difficulties with this account?

What were they? _____

_____

Have we resolved these problems, or are we in a position to do so? _____

What else needs to be considered? _____

Competition? _____

Their advantage, if any _____ Ours _____

What product (service) will gain most ready acceptance? _____

_____Benefit? _____

Second product (service) to introduce? _____

_____Benefit? _____

Opening approach to buyer? _____

_____

_____

Materials needed on call _____

_____

Appointment _____ Date _____ Time _____

Confirm in advance? _____ Secretary/receptionist's name _____

Figure 7. Typical Company Expense Policy

SUBJECT: Business Travel and Expense

PURPOSE

To establish basic policy procedures for authorization and approval for travel and/or other expenses incurred by employees for business purposes.

TRAVEL ADVANCES

Approval of traveler's manager (or approved alternate) must be secured *before* issuance of "permanent" or "temporary" travel advances to meet estimated expenses.

A. Permanent advance amounts are subject to recall at the discretion of management. There will be no permanent advances in excess of $500.

B. Temporary advances are based on estimated expenditures during an agreed period and must be settled before new advances will be authorized. All advances must be settled before final clearance of terminating employees.

CREDIT CARDS

Air travel, telephone, and auto rental cards in the company's name will be issued to authorized employees and are to be used only in conducting company business.

MODE OF TRANSPORTATION

Airline travel for all company employees will be tourist class regardless of flight duration except when specific prior approval for exception is received from the president's office.

Air or railway travel receipts must be attached to the expense report. Any unused company-purchased tickets must be returned to the company or accounted for.

REQUEST FOR CASH ADVANCE

Individuals requiring a travel advance must complete the Request for Cash Advance form. This form must be approved by the individual's manager. Accounting will not honor an advance request that has not been approved.

AUTOMOBILE TRANSPORTATION

A. Automobile mileage for the use of an employee's car to conduct company business will be reimbursed at the rate of 20¢ per mile.

B. Autos should be rented only when necessary and authorized in advance whenever possible. Employees must obtain the 20 percent discount on all auto rentals and should decline the collision damage waiver.

C. The policies as established in the Leased Vehicle Care and Use Manual should be adhered to.

(continued)

Figure 7. Typical Company Expense Policy
(continued)

HOTEL/MOTEL ROOM RENTALS
Hotel/motel accommodations and related expenses should not be billed directly to the company. Travelers should pay for these charges and report them on the Company Business Expense Report (Form 026A) for reimbursement. Receipted copies of hotel/motel bills must be attached to the expense report.

MEAL EXPENSES, INCLUDING GRATUITIES
The actual expenses incurred must be indicated on the expense report. Employees are authorized to incur reasonable expenses for meals.

ENTERTAINMENT EXPENSES
Reasonable entertainment expenses incurred by authorized personnel will be reimbursed. It is required that receipts be attached for any one item $25.00 or over and to note the person(s) entertained (by name and title), company, and business purpose of the expense.

SPOUSES' TRAVELING EXPENSES
Spouses' or other members of employee's families are not permitted to accompany traveling employees at company expense unless specifically and previously authorized by an officer.

APPROVAL OF EXPENSES
Expense reports of Officers reporting directly to the President's office will require the approval of the President or his designated alternate. All other officers or managers will require the approval of their respective superior or their designated alternate. Expense reports of all other personnel will require the approval of the department manager to whom they report or a designated alternate. Names of all designated alternates must be submitted, in writing, to the controller.

REPORTING OF EXPENSES
Expenses incurred by employees in the conduct of company business amounting to $25.00 or more must be reported on the Company Business Expense Report (Form 026A). Miscellaneous expenses incurred that amount to *less* than $25.00 may be reported on a Petty Cash Voucher for reimbursement.

All business expense reports or petty cash vouchers will be submitted promptly for approval and reimbursement upon completion of a business trip and/or at the close of each weekly period.
(continued)

Figure 7. Typical Company Expense Policy
(continued)

VERIFICATION

Prior to reimbursement or application against an outstanding advance, accounting personnel will verify the completed expense report to ensure that:

A. The report has been completed in accordance with this policy.
B. The report is mathematically accurate and includes only bona fide business expenditures.
C. All required receipts are attached.
D. All explanations, where required, are included on the reverse side of the report.

All business Expense Reports containing discrepancies (i.e., improper preparation, lack of receipts and/or explanations, etc.) will be immediately returned to the approving manager for correction and resubmission.

CHANGES IN POLICY AND PROCEDURE

A. Contemplated "out of policy" actions not provided for in this policy and questions regarding interpretation of policy, will be directed to the vice-president of finance for approval prior to any steps being taken.
B. The vice-president of industrial relations will issue approved additions, deletions, revisions, and any other changes in this policy and procedure to personnel policy manual holders after official receipt from the vice-president of finance.

Figure 8. Weekly Expense Report (Attach Receipts)

For Week Ending _____

Time Record
Start Hour _____ Date _____
Return Hour _____ Date _____

		SUN			MON			TUES			WED			THUR			FRI			SAT		Totals for Week
	City	Arrive	Depart	City	Arrive	Depart	City	Arrive	Depart	City	Arrive	Depart	City	Arrive	Depart	City	Arrive	Depart	City	Arrive	Depart	
1	Hotel - Motel																					
2	Breakfast																					
3	Lunch																					
4	Dinner																					
5	Plane - Rail - Bus Fare																					
6	Local Taxis - Bus Fares																					
7	Auto Expense (Repair, etc.)																					
8	Gas - Oil																					
9	Lubrication - Wash																					
10	Garage - Parking																					
11	Tolls																					
12	Phone - Telegrams																					
13	Tips																					
14	Entertainment																					
	TOTALS																					

(continued)

968

Figure 9. Car Expense Report Sheet

MONTH OF_____19___

MILEAGE THIS DATE_____

YEAR_____ MAKE_____ MODEL_____ LICENSE NO._____

FLEET NO._____

(State)   (No.)

1. GASOLINE (Misc. Purchases)

Date	Rec. #	No. of Gals.	Amount
	TOTALS		

2. OIL

Date	Rec. #	No. of Qts.	Amount
	TOTALS		

3. TITLE AND LICENSE EXPENSE

Date	Title State	License No.	Cost

5. AUTO SALES OR USE TAX EXPENSE

Date	Rec. #	%	Taxable Amount	Cost

6. PERSONAL PROPERTY TAX

Date	Rec. #	%	Taxable Amount	Cost

7. TOLL FEES

Tollway	Rec. #	Date	Amount
	TOTALS		

9. PARKING FEES

City	Rec. #	Date	Amount
	TOTALS		

4. MAINTENANCE (As listed below — only)

Description	Date	Rec. #	Amount
Filter Cartridges			
Lubrication			
Tire Rotation			
Tire Repairs			
Align Front End			
Adjust Brakes			
Antifreeze			
Wheel Bearing Pack			
U-Joint Pack			
Steering Gear Check			
Differential Grease			
Transmission Fluid			
TOTALS			

8. OTHER REPAIRS

Description	Date	Rec. #	Amount
	TOTALS		

10. WASH JOBS

Date	Rec. #	Amount
TOTALS		

REIMBURSEMENT CLAIM

	AMOUNT
1. Gasoline	
2. Oil	
3. Title and License Expense	
4. Maintenance	
5. Auto Sales or Use Tax Expense	
6. Personal Property Tax	
7. Toll Fees	
8. Other Repairs	
9. Parking Fees	
10. Wash Jobs	
TOTAL CLAIM	

I CERTIFY THAT THE EXPENSES REPORTED HEREIN ARE MY ACTUAL COSTS OF OPERATING THE ABOVE DESCRIBED AUTOMOBILE DURING THE MONTH REPORTED ABOVE.

SIGNED _____

CHECK TO BE ISSUED TO:

PLEASE PRINT

_____
(Name)

_____
(Street)

_____
(City)   (Zone)   (State)

LEASE COMPANY USE ONLY

Date Paid_____ Check No._____

Amt. Paid_____ Initials_____

NOTE: Reimbursement will be made according to audit within 5 days after receipt of this report. INSTRUCTIONS ARE PRINTED ON REVERSE HEREOF

Chapter 43

Sales Meetings

Sales meetings, conferences, distributors' conventions, and dealer meetings all play a useful and well-adjusted role in the process of stimulating business. Meetings for distributors especially have widened their functions and intensified their sales objectives. In major companies they have become an indispensable part of the launching of new lines on a national basis.

While sales meetings and conventions are good selling tools, one factor that tends to retard their greater use is that of cost. Some conventions staged by large organizations approach the dimensions of a Broadway production, especially if the meeting is tied in with prize incentive trips for dealers and salespeople. Even here, if total cost is in proper percentage relation to the overall volume of business obtained, the expense is justified.

These major meetings may also have additional sales functions by being made the occasion for interviews with the press and open house for local dealers' representatives or salespeople. Too, they afford an excellent opportunity to bring all the elements of a national sales organization together at one place, at one time, with many smaller, private, more intimate contacts between management and the companies comprising its channels of distribution.

What Makes an Effective Meeting?

Having a clear-cut objective in mind when planning any meeting is obviously important. Being able to successfully carry out that objective is directly related to the scheduling and presentation of the content of the meeting. Content involves the effective scheduling and presentation of the material and meeting theme, which is designed to enable the meeting to reach its objective. Figures 1, 2, and 3 on pages 1018 through 1022 at the end of this chapter provide useful forms and checklists to help ensure a successful meeting.

The key element of every meeting is communication. Communication between two individuals is relatively simple, but becomes more complicated as the size of the group increases. Effective communication with a group of individuals can be accomplished if five important communication steps are built into the program. The meeting program, as delivered, must:

• Describe the current conditions or trends

• State the idea behind the meeting—the objective

• Outline techniques and plans for receiving the objective

• Point out the benefits of the objective

• Outline the next steps, and make assignments, if appropriate

An application of these principles was inherent in a series of sales meetings that a chemical company conducted for the sales staffs of its distributors throughout the country. Groups of 12 to 20 salespeople were gathered for two hours on each of three days.

In its meetings, the company *described the conditions* (industry sales are skyrocketing); *stated the idea* behind the meeting (with a little work, the distributors and the company can take the lion's share of increased sales); *outlined plans* (skillfully programmed training program); *pointed out benefits* (increased earnings and greater professionalism in salesmanship); and *made short-term and long-term assignments* (study; calls on problem prospects with a company representative).

So successful was the training sequence in dollars and in attitudes that the company broadened its original program to include a self-help guide for new employees and a rapid-fire group review program. What's more, the company's distributors asked for a similar program on new topics!

For a successful sales meeting, the agenda must answer two questions:

• What was the meeting all about?

• What am I supposed to do about it?

Aims and Purposes

The broad purpose of the sales meeting is to bring about significant improvement in your salespeople's attitudes, knowledge, skills, behavior, and work patterns. The more specific objectives of the sales meeting cover a wide spectrum. Often two or more objectives can be combined in one meeting, especially if it is national in scope (like an annual convention) and lasts for two or more days. Among these meeting objectives are:

- Introducing new products
- Launching new marketing campaigns
- Initiating new incentive programs or contests
- Training in new selling techniques
- Announcing new policies, prices, or programs
- Introducing new compensation or pension plans
- Retraining and reactivating (various sales procedures)
- Slowing current marketing problems
- Awarding honors and contest prizes

There are undoubtedly many other specific objectives endemic to certain businesses and industries. The ideas and suggestions to be developed should, however, have broad enough application to be useful in most any type of meeting, whatever the objectives.

How to Tailor a Meeting to Fit Its Objective

Here are the instructions an oil company insists its sales managers follow when planning a sales meeting:

- Define your objectives clearly and estimate the usefulness of a sales meeting by:
  1. Reducing your objectives to writing;
  2. Determining whether your objectives are worth the time, energy, and money required for a sales meeting;

3. Satisfying yourself definitely that a sales meeting is necessary to put your objectives across.

- Don't attempt to cover more than a few objectives at one meeting.

- Don't hold a meeting unless you can actually accomplish the objectives you set out to accomplish.

- Here are some typical objectives for sales meetings:

    1. To introduce and explain a new product or service, and how to sell it

    2. To review and demonstrate an old product, its quality, and how to sell it

    3. To introduce and explain a new sales campaign

    4. To explain changes in markets for old products

    5. To present best answers to customers' objections

    6. To present and demonstrate the use of new selling tools, advertising, etc., in personal sales contacts

    7. To demonstrate and practice effective sales presentations

    8. To discuss methods of handling competition in sales talks

    9. To discuss ways salespeople can help improve service to customers

    10. To discuss methods of securing new customers and prospects

    11. To assign quotas and discuss use of salespeople's time

    12. To introduce and promote a sales contest

    13. To analyze lost sales and why I lost that sale (clinic)

    14. To discuss credits and collections

    15. To explain company sales policies, objectives, etc.

16. To explain and demonstrate product applications at clinics, e.g., tractor clinics, heating oil clinics, fleet clinics, etc.

17. To explain and demonstrate use of selling aids and services available to dealers

Two Kinds of Meetings

Generally all meetings fall into one of two categories: the national company sales meeting or convention, and the local regional or district sales meeting. These are not necessarily mutually exclusive. Most organizations use both, with the national (or divisional) convention being either the culmination or the pacesetter for the series of monthly or quarterly district meetings.

National sales meetings or conventions can serve many unique and essential functions as methods of communications, if properly planned, structured, and conducted. For the salespeople attending, the meeting affords an opportunity to meet with top management personnel who might otherwise be merely names on the company's letterheads or in its annual reports. In some cases it enables the salespeople to visit the plant and home office and see for themselves how orders are processed and goods produced. It makes it possible for salespeople to meet and chat with their counterparts from other parts of the country, to swap ideas, and to compare experiences. Unfortunately, these inherent advantages are often dissipated. Too many conventions turn into pep rallies. Others are staged as drum-beating extravaganzas that are very costly and, in inverse ratio, produce very limited results. Still others degenerate into sessions of criticism that cause deep resentment in the salespeople. They sulk, "clam up," and fail to participate; morale is damaged and communications are dammed up. Hence too many national conventions fall far short of reaching their objectives and turn out to be merely costly boondoggles.

To repeat and reinforce some of the advantages of national sales conventions:

- They permit the use of top management talent as speakers and as morale boosters.

- They afford opportunity for wider exchange of ideas with salespeople from the various territories.

- They tend to generate greater enthusiasm.

- They often enable the salespeople to visit plant and headquarters offices and to meet top executives.

- They save time for executives who participate in the program.

Generally speaking, national conventions or meetings should be scheduled no more frequently than once a year. In no event should they eliminate or replace the more frequent and generally more effectual local meetings at the district level.

Full scale district meetings should be held at intervals of three months. In this period, enough new reasons for holding another sales meeting have materialized or new problems have developed to make it necessary and desirable. In addition, informal meetings at the field office and (for salespeople in two or more adjoining territories) at some centrally and conveniently located part of a travel territory may be held more frequently. These can be brief enough to be covered at a luncheon or dinner.

District and local sales meetings have these distinct advantages:

- They are geared to handling local problems.

- They permit greater participation.

- They save salespeople's valuable time.

- They are less stilted, more friendly.

- The small groups make training and communications easier.

- They can fulfill specific purposes.

- They cost a lot less.

Types of Meetings

To help regional and district sales managers select the type of sales meeting that will provide the best means to their specific objective, the vice-president of marketing for a large manufacturing company prepared a comparative analysis (see Table 1, page 976).

Table 1.

Objective of Meeting	Type of Meeting Best Suited	Features and Benefits
To disseminate official information; e.g., annual report, etc.	Convention	General session plus committee meetings. Mostly information-giving and voting on official business.
To get facts, plan, solve organization and personal problems.	Work conference	General sessions and face-to-face groups. Usually high participation. Provides more flexible means for doing organization's work.
To train salespeople to gain new knowledge, skills, or insights into problems.	Workshop	General sessions and face-to-face groups. Participants also serve as trainers.
To share experience among experts.	Seminar	Usually a single face-to-face group. Discussion leaders control participants. Provides compact exchange of ideas.
To train in one particular subject.	Clinic	Usually face-to-face grouping but may have general sessions. Staff provides most of training resources and services.
To train in several subjects.	Institute	General sessions and face-to-face groups.
To consider special interests of participants, salespeople, dealers, and others.	Groupings (according to industry, customers, etc.)	Interest generated by discussion of common problems. Usually no action, but findings may be reported.
To apply new skills or information to real-life situations.	Application groups	Mixed composition from total group by interests. Many use trainer to suggest methods. Usually no more than 10. No reporting.

(continued)

Table 1.
(continued)

Objective of Meeting	Type of Meeting Best Suited	Features and Benefits
To help salespeople get acquainted.	Orientation groups	A mixed membership from total group. Member of staff at each group to introduce participants and answer questions. Used only for brief period at start of meeting.
To give participants opportunity to react, make suggestions, etc.	Off-the-record sessions	Mixed membership from total group. Officially scheduled bull session. No reporting but is informal channel to conference staff.
To present information, provide inspiration.	Speech or film	Can convey large quantity of factual information. Residual value must be augmented by takeaway material: lecture outlines, workbooks, booklets, etc.
To present complex information such as new product or service, or details of a new sales and advertising campaign.	Speaker with visuals	More thorough and certain communication with great residual value. Takes more time and money than speaker only.
To present information from diversified points of view.	Symposium	Two or more speakers, each of whom contributes specialized information. Chairman directs and summarizes. Usually a report is published.
To present information from many points of view, sometimes controversial.	Panel	Each member of the panel states his views and discusses with other members. Moderator guides discussion and keeps peace among panelists. Panel members usually hold brief rehearsal. Audience can question and comment.

(continued)

Table 1.
(continued)

Objective of Meeting	Type of Meeting Best Suited	Features and Benefits
To develop or ventilate several different sides of an issue.	Forum	Two or more speakers present different aspects of an issue; address salespeople rather than self. Moderator directs and summarizes.
To help salespeople analyze individual or group action in natural setting.	Situation presentation	Salespeople present role-play or case-history example. Commentator may call attention to specific points as "play" progresses.
To dramatize the outer or inner forces that clash in a selling situation.	Conflict presentation	Salespeople present role-play or staged skits. "Ghost" voice talks out loud, revealing inner thoughts of each character. Salespeople gain insight into emotions of prospects.
To demonstrate skills or techniques and show relative effectiveness.	Skill presentation	Salespeople, supervisors, or trainers demonstrate different ways to handle a selling problem. Salespeople in audience observe and then discuss.

Amoco's Premeeting Guide

The Amoco Corporation provided those responsible for conducting its sales meetings with a premeeting guide containing the following:

1. Plan every sales meeting as far in advance of meeting date as possible

   - Anticipate the need for a meeting before it arrives.

   - Reduce your plan to writing.

   - Discuss your plan with other members of management.

   - Check the need for meeting with sales representatives.

   - Establish time and place when meeting will be most effective.

   - List the objectives to be accomplished at the meeting.

   - Eliminate every nonessential from your meeting plan.

2. Prepare the meeting program

   - List the general subjects to be presented at proposed meeting.

   - Assign subjects to individuals best equipped to present them.

   - Confer with each individual to establish main points that need emphasis in each presentation and to eliminate duplication.

   - Ask for a rough draft of each presentation.

   - Arrange the sequence of subjects to be presented so they will fit into an integrated program that will lend emphasis to each item in proportion to its importance.

   - Study all first rough drafts in terms of materials available for clues to methods of dramatizing their main points.

a. Review your inventory of materials and equipment available for making effective presentations.

b. List materials and equipment available from outside sources that might be helpful in making your proposed meeting more effective.

c. Study trade journals, house journals, and reference materials for showmanship ideas you can adapt to the points needing emphasis.

d. Suggest to each speaker the methods you recommend for emphasizing with showmanship the points he has indicated and you agree need emphasis.

Meetings can sometimes impart incorrect information. This was touched upon in the following memo sent by a company's sales manager to his regional and district sales supervisors:

The sales department spends more time in meetings than any other group in our company. These meetings are costly from point of view of actual expense, the time salespeople lose in selling, and the misdirection or misinformation salespeople may carry away because your message was not sharp and clear. Your company can profit from a better organized and more dramatically presented sales message. Some of the areas to be considered are:

I. *Preparation*

A. Planning (mental activity)

1. Determining needs

a. What

b. How

2. Establish objective

3. People to attend

a. Who should

b. Why should they

      c. Why do they *think* they should

      d. How much do they already know

      e. What are they to do as a result

      f. Who will object

      g. Who will help

  4. Physical aspects

      a. When

      b. Where

      c. How long

      d. Physical setup

      e. Frequency

  5. Take a second look at objectives

  6. Contact necessary personnel

      a. For information

      b. For assistance

      c. To get them concerned

      d. To delegate responsibility

B. Organizing

  1. Determining general areas to be covered

  2. Outline

      a. Opening

         (1) Opening remarks

         (2) Introductions

         (3) Purpose of meeting

       b. Select main topics

          (1) Develop

          (2) Arrange

       c. Select methods and techniques

       d. Closing

          (1) Summarize

          (2) Appeal for action

          (3) End on high note

II. *Presentation*

  A. General factors

    1. Methods and techniques

    2. Motivation and climate

    3. Use of props

    4. Change of pace

    5. Handouts

    6. Notes

    7. Tempo

    8. Level

  B. Individual factors

    1. Personal appearance

    2. Confidence

    3. Enthusiasm

    4. Sincerity

    5. Knowledge of subject

    6. Vocal habits

7. Eye contact

8. Mannerisms

III. *Evaluation*

A. Methods

B. Recommendations for improvement

How to Inject Excitement

Pacesetters is a good theme when you're coming up with an innovation. One sales manager made a list of 10 firms in noncompetitive lines that he regarded as pacesetters, and sent them a letter explaining his plans for his sales meeting. "I'd like to have something from your organization that's a good example of pacesetting, which I'll be glad to return when my meeting is over," he wrote.

"Only three of the ten companies responded," he continued, "but they went all-out. One of the companies sent material they'd put together for an exhibit booth at a trade convention, and it was a graphic display of pacesetting. Another sent, among other things, copies of a handsome little book on finding public needs and satisfying them, to be given to our salespeople. The third actually did a special exhibit tying our pacesetting interest and theirs together. The other seven companies apparently weren't pacesetters in public relations, but I wouldn't have been able to use much more material, anyway."

The opening of the meeting was entitled "A Good Start," with a couple of high school track stars actually demonstrating good and bad techniques with the starting blocks, and a speaker reviewing for the salespeople the elements that the company had assembled for a good start to the coming year.

"The Inside Track" showed the advantage of the inside lane, and then went on to reveal ways in which the salespeople for this particular company had the inside lane—their "edges" over the competition.

"Conditioning" was an intensive session on product information and how best to use it, with considerable role play.

"Protect Yourself" dealt with competition, including some rough tactics on the part of this particular company's competitors.

"Going All Out to Stay Ahead" was the introduction of new products, with instruction on how to sell them.

"The Last Lap" was motivational, showing how the champion had the determination and endurance to repel competition that was breathing down his neck.

"The Winner's Circle" was an excellent pep session on the fruits of victory and the pride that winning stimulates.

Even the dinner menu carried out the theme, with such items as "Puree of Tomato—America's No. 1 Soup," "Blue Ribbon T-Bone Steak—No Losers," "Corn on the Cob—a National Favorite," "All-American Tossed Salad," "Apple Pie a la Mode—Two Pace-setters," and "America's No. 1 Beverage—A Good Cup of Coffee."

"Putting our company in the same class with the pacesetters of industry was part of the idea," the sales manager said, "and the salespeople really believed we belonged in that distinguished company by the time the meeting was over."

Building Advance Interest

Advance interest is an intangible quality that can assure the success of a meeting before the doors are opened. This is the conviction of specialists who have had an opportunity to watch, analyze, and participate in a large number of sales meetings and conventions conducted by some of America's most sales-conscious companies. Here are some remarks about premeeting promotion by a sales-meeting consultant:

"Promotion in relation to sales meetings should not be limited entirely to efforts to lure or increase attendance. Promotional techniques can be very helpful in creating audience interest and receptivity. If, for example, you are assured of maximum attendance because you will have a captive audience of your own sales force, promotion can be used to channel and influence thinking with respect to the meeting. This will give you a valuable head start before your meeting gets underway.

"Successful premeeting promotion will also simplify your programming at the meeting: Instead of facing the double task of creating and sustaining interest, you need only be concerned with the latter problem. And you'll have to admit that it's a big one. What are some ways to promote a sales meeting? A floor-covering company created a corporate character, embodying its trademark, in a meeting it held to introduce its new line, advertising, and sales promotion to its distributors. The corporate character had an important role in the meeting itself, appearing throughout the two days. But he also played an equally important role in the preconditioning promotion. Instead of the usual invitation, a special folder was created. This featured a picture of the corporate character that introduced him to the prospective audience and ensured his recognition when he appeared early in the meeting. Beyond that, however, it titillated the audience's curiosity and served as a teaser, an attention-getter, and helped to increase reading of the explanatory copy that announced the meeting and explained its aims. The promotion did not just invite. It excited interest, too.

"When a bottling company announced a new sales-training program, it used a novel 3D promotion mailing piece to introduce three films that were to be used."

Getting Off on the Right Foot

Here are a few other recommendations for getting the meeting off to a good start:

- Have staff members and company executives greet each person as he or she registers or enters the meeting room.

- If the meeting is an early morning one, serve an informal breakfast.

- Serve coffee near the registration area or the entrance to the meeting room, but shut off the supply well before the first session starts.

- Try to have staff members act as ushers. Don't let hotel employees try to herd your group out of the lobby and into the meeting rooms.

- Pay special attention to those who are attending your meeting for the first time. Assign a host or "buddy" to each. Don't let them get lost or miss events through lack of knowledge.

- In general, try to be the best possible host according to the scale of your operation. Don't overdo things, but consider how you would like to be treated and visualize the guidance needed by a majority of your audience.

- Brief your staff on all arrangements. Make sure they know where to turn for help. Try to have a few extra hands available for special assignments. You can be sure that several unexpected things will happen and that you will need help to run messages, move things, and so forth.

Checklists of Physical Facilities and Plans

To avoid an occurrence of Murphy's Law, the rule is check, check, and check again. Following are three checklists by Amoco, *Industrial Marketing,* and American Express. While some of the points overlap, a composite of all three should produce a foolproof checklist for your meetings.

AMOCO CHECKLIST

1. Are entrance and exit facilities correct for size of audience?

2. Have you provided safety factors—checked fire hazards, floor-load capacity, fire exits, and responsibility of lessor?

3. Have you provided necessary utilities—kinds of electricity, washroom facilities, air conditioning, remote-control switches, adequate fuses, drinking fountains, etc.?

4. Have you made certain that the meeting room is large enough but not too large for the audience and that it has proper acoustics, light, heat, air, comfortable chairs, window blinds for darkening room if slide or motion-picture projector is to be used, space for room displays, projection facilities, and is away from distracting noises?

5. Does meeting room provide adequate space for setting up

and taking down properties planned, and does it have enough height for them? Are backstage entrance and off-stage workroom available if required?

6. Have you obtained necessary house props, such as blackboards, stage chairs, stage lamps, stage desks, carpets, steps to stage, remote-control switch, and P.A. system?

7. Have you made arrangements for necessary house services, such as piano, smoking stands, janitor to clean meeting room, electrician with fuses, porter services for house props, and necessary labor for setting up and tearing down?

8. Have you confirmed in writing:

   • All assignments of speakers to appear on your program?

   • Date(s) and place(s) of meeting(s) to speakers, audience, and to house management where meeting is to be held?

   • *To meeting room crew:* To decorate and clean rooms; to arrange seats for correct sight lines; to handle ventilation, heat, etc., during meeting; to distribute materials to audience; to handle guest registrations; to serve as ushers in handling crowd; to post signs that direct audience to meeting room; to provide drinking water for speaker; and to provide drinking fountains and washroom facilities for audience?

   • *To property staff:* To secure and bring in props; to crate and uncrate props; to help dress stage; to design, build, and set up room displays, product displays, etc.; to know all prop cues for meeting; to check all fuse boxes, carry extra fuses and stand by during meeting; and to troop working tools and repair materials needed for meeting?

   • *To projectionists,* (if projection is being used): To troop projection equipment; to set up projection facilities; to operate projection equipment, signal systems, P.A. system, microphones, remote-control switch on house lights, etc.; to know all projection cues; to correct acoustics, if necessary; and to install window blinds for projection?

- *To stage manager* (if stage is to be used): To set up stage; to dress stage; to handle traveler during meeting; to handle lights during meeting; to change scenery; to handle sound effects; to strike scenes and sets; and to know all stage cues?

- *To utility personnel* (if plans are for a large meeting): To arrange for and handle entertainment, food, refreshments, etc.; to handle emergencies, special props, calls, errands, etc.; to handle special lighting; to serve as prompter on cues; to serve as prompter on stage; to assist in handling crowd; and to assist other departments with special assignments?

INDUSTRIAL MARKETING CHECKLIST

1. Is it agreed that a sales meeting is necessary and that the purpose for the meeting has been well defined? Has a theme been decided on for the meeting?

2. Has management been informed, and is there agreement regarding the program?

3. Have dates for the meeting been established, and has everyone been notified?

4. Has a chairman or coordinator been appointed?

5. Has an agenda been prepared, and have speakers or participants been notified and oriented?

6. Has all transportation been arranged for?

7. Have meeting and sleeping rooms been reserved?

8. Have all arrangements been completed for the meeting to include?

   - Comfortable chairs
   - Name cards
   - Good lighting

- Charts, visuals, etc.
- Blackboard
- Projectors
- PA systems
- Pads, pencils, etc.
- Podium
- Electrical outlets
- Proper ventilation
- Easels
- Coffee and coke breaks
- Restroom facilities
- Coat and hat racks
- Water and glasses

9. Have all speeches and presentations been written out in detail and edited, and have speakers been adequately rehearsed and timed?

10. Have enough supporting visuals been prepared to make each presentation clear and understandable? Are they large enough to be seen at the back of the room?

11. Have dry runs been conducted to familiarize and accustom speakers or assistants with the use of their visuals?

12. Have all sound or movie projectors been checked to see that they are in working order and material presented can be seen and heard by the audience? Has an operator been designated and familiarized with a script?

13. Have all union regulations and procedures regarding shipments, handling, apparatus and trades been cleared?

14. Have all handouts, meeting materials, or follow-ups been prepared and delivered to the meeting site?

15. Has someone been designated to handle properties and to assist with handouts at the meeting?

16. Have plans been made for refreshments and meals?

17. Has an entertainment suite been reserved and provisioned for the evening?

18. Has a budget been prepared and approved to cover all expenses for the meeting?

AMERICAN EXPRESS CHECKLIST

1. Have you set preliminary dates for meeting?

2. Determined how many people will attend?

3. Included spouses, if appropriate?

4. Estimated the budget?

5. Invited the company's top executives?

6. Determined your requirements for a meeting site? (Location? Price? Facilities? Accessibility?)

7. Evaluated potential meetings sites? (Availability? Meeting room facilities? Entertainment and recreational facilities? Liquor licensing? Food and beverage facilities? Music availability? Potential conflicts because of other groups booked at site? Audio-visual availability? Meeting site "house" rules? Firm price quotations? Possible things that could detract from meeting—such as construction noises?)

8. Set final dates for meeting?

9. Selected meeting site?

10. Determined requirements for off site functions? (Price? Facilities needed?) Obtained firm price quotes from outside suppliers?

11. Confirmed arrangements in writing with meeting site? (Dates, price, number of people attending, number and types of rooms required, meeting room requirements, registration procedure, audio-visual requirements, communications needs, menus, coffee break requirements.)

12. Set objectives for meeting? Developed a theme for meeting?

13. Listed subjects to be covered at meeting?

14. Planned program for spouses (if invited)?

15. Company speakers chosen? Appearances at meeting cleared with their superiors? Selected backup speakers?

16. Negotiated with outside speakers? Reached understanding on types and length of speeches?

17. Established audio-visual requirements?

18. Listed all audio-visual equipment needed by speakers? (Lighting, sound, projection equipment?)

19. Listed printing needs?

20. Set up promotion schedule?

21. Liability insurance for meeting?

22. Sent out first general letter announcing meeting?

23. Sent out second letter with mailing and return cards?

24. Do you have *extra* rooms for unexpected guests? Made arrangements for early arrivals, and people staying over *after* the meeting?

25. Made airline travel arrangements? Taken care of ticketing? Method of payment? Notified people concerning flight arrangements and ticket payment?

26. Taken care of ground transportation? (Buses? Limousines? Rental cars?) Provisions for early comers, late-stayers?

27. Transportation planned for emergency situations? (Strikes? Snow? Rain? Breakdowns?)

28. Prepared room list and sent to meeting site?

29. Have bids on decorations and/or special services?

30. Created art theme for mailings and for use in meeting room(s)?

31. Arranged for decorating meeting room(s)?

32. Ordered and sent baggage tags? Ordered name tags? Ordered plaques and pins? Prepared slides?

33. Prepared or ordered signs, banners? Are you prepared to make emergency signs *on the spot*?

34. Arranged for display area?

35. Have you planned, coordinated, and checked menus? Made provisions for *dietary* menus? Decided on plan? (American? Modified American? European?)

36. Determined how much you want to spend on liquor? Use of chits? Cash bar? Open bar? (Price per head? Flat rate? Per drink consumed?) Decided how long bar will be open? How many bartenders at each bar? Exotic drinks, or simple drinks? Waiters walking around with drinks? Determined what hors d'oeuvre you want? (Plain or fancy? How many? Negotiated by head or platter?) Have you confirmed with manager or maitre d'hotel?

37. Planned for *emergency* liquor on hand in case you run out?

38. Planned for formal gala? (Menu? Wine? Entertainment?)

39. Planned for hospitality suite? Do you need a hotel captain or one of your own staff members to manage hospitality suite? Supervise consumption of food and beverages? Accountability?

40. Need additional hospitality suite by pool? Golf course? Tennis courts?

41. Arranged for photographer?

42. City maps obtained for attendees? Agenda made out and printed for attendees?

43. Confirmed all arrangements in writing? (Speakers? Company executives? Suppliers? Meeting site?)

44. Arranged for *tipping*? Is it negotiable? Or is there a union contract that specifies how many people? For check in? Checkout? Food? Hospitality suite? Bar? Open bar?

45. Alerted press (if desired)? Set up a press room? Arranged means of communications for press?

46. Arranged for reproducing papers, charts, lists, etc. *at the site*?

47. Arranged for typewriters, pencils, pens, pads, etc.?

48. Submitted final VIP list to meeting site with instructions?

49. Pre-registration arranged?

50. Submitted detailed list of required materials and services to meeting site?

51. Confirmed specific duties and hours meeting site personnel are needed to service meeting?

52. Established deadline for completion of all supplier and meeting site services?

Getting People to Participate

It is generally agreed among sales executives that it is essential for salespeople to take an active part in meetings. A passive audience is likely to be a disinterested and unreceptive one. Here are some hints from "How to Get Group Participation in Sales Training," prepared by the National Society of Sales Training Executives:

1. *Explain exactly what you want.* This saves breaking in to correct the person's impression of what he or she is supposed to do. When you want a salesperson to do a task, say,

"First I want you to do this; second, this; and third, this. Do I make it clear?" If the person says he or she understands, ask for an explanation of what he or she is going to do and how.

2. *Keep after them until they cooperate.* You can get people to do anything in a meeting if you keep after them. You ask, "Are there any questions?" The group looks at you as if they haven't heard. You ask, "Will someone come up and demonstrate this machine for me?" No one moves. If you want questions or participation, be persistent. Don't give up.

3. *Illustrate what you want.* When you ask a salesperson to take part, illustrate what you want him or her to do. Do the demonstration first. Now say, "I'm going to do this again because I am then going to ask one of you to do it." You then ask, "How many think you can do it now?" If you give them enough illustration of what you want, they feel they can't miss.

4. *Start early in the session.* If you want the group to take part, start asking for it early in the session. The introductions help to do this. Ask for show of hands. Have each answer the question: "How long have you been in selling?" Ask the person to stand and give his or her name, home town, or company. Get some of this into the first 10 minutes.

5. *Use numbers.* In describing certain tasks, use numbers to help you explain. Salespeople seem to respond better when the task is broken down into numbered steps.

6. *Let him or her have the spotlight.* When the salesperson starts his or her performance, step off the stage and take a seat in the audience. Have him or her make the presentation to the group, not to you. When the leader stands beside the participant, many of the group will be watching the leader to see how he or she takes the performance.

7. *Use the compliment.* You can't make a person angry by patting him or her on the back. Be free with honest praise. Note

the word "honest." But when a person volunteers to try a task for you, he or she deserves a compliment just for that willingness to try. Usually the person will do some parts of his or her presentation well. Ask the group if they noticed how well certain points were handled.

8. *Be patient.* When you ask a salesperson to do a task, allow that person to finish without interruption. Watch with interest. Listen intently. Why should the group listen to the salesperson if you show that you are not listening?

9. *Think of his or her self-esteem.* You will note that many of the suggestions for handling participation help the person keep his or her self-esteem. The suggestion of courtesy, the compliment, starting with the small bits and going on to the more difficult—all these are designed to give recognition, and to increase self-esteem. In a sales meeting, if you hurt the feelings of one participant you draw resentment from the group. Always build up and never tear down.

10. *Too much is too much.* While group participation is a big help in meetings, it is possible to use too much. The best meetings are those that have a good balance of all of the methods that help salespeople sell better. Too much audience participation in a session can get tiresome. If the morning is to be given over to practice selling, the wise leader plans so that he or she can break in at a low point with demonstrations, voice exercises, or other such devices to change the tempo of the session.

The Question-and-Answer Period

Participation can be engendered by a lively question-and-answer period. The most common reasons given by sales managers for using such periods in sales meetings are:

1. To get audience participation in the meeting

2. To help the audience relate the information to their own situations back home

3. To rate audience reception and understanding of the information disseminated

4. To observe which presentations are the most effective

Variations of the following basic methods may be used to increase the quantity and quality of questions:

1. *A guide to listening.* Print or photocopy a list of categories or areas in which you feel significant questions should be asked. Leave space under each category listing that each salesperson can write his or her questions. Call for the questions by category.

2. *Audience listening teams.* Divide the audience into teams of approximately equal size, with the number of teams being determined by the specific areas of questions you want "listened for." Assign each team the area in which it will concentrate its questions and instruct each individual to write down questions as they occur to him or her.

   Divide the time allotted for the question period into as many parts as there are listening teams. During this allotted time, team members bring up the questions that concern their particular area.

   Another procedure is to ask each member of the audience to write one question in the area of listening to which he or she has been assigned. These are then picked up, sorted, and answered, section by section.

3. *Buzz groups.* Ask the salespeople to move their chairs into circles of six or eight. Tell the audience that its task in these buzz groups is to select the one or two most important questions in an assigned area of listening. Each group appoints one of its number as a spokesperson to report its findings to the total audience.

   Write the questions on a blackboard or project them on a screen. They are then answered from the platform. An interesting variation is to have the buzz-group spokesperson join the speakers on the platform to discuss the points developed by the listening teams.

Following are a number of suggestions for making the most of the question-and-answer session:

1. *When the leader asks questions.* The quiz session looks easy—all you need is a list of questions. But don't be fooled. The quiz is a discussion tool. You want it to help your salespeople solve their selling problems. A question such as "How many benefits does this plan have?" may seem fine when you write it, but how much help will the answer give the group? A question such as, "How would you use this benefit to sell a prospect?" might be better.

    - *The list of questions.* Let's say you come to the session with a list of questions; you can pass out the list and ask one person which question he or she cannot answer. He or she says, "Number 5." Ask others the same question and write the numbers mentioned on the blackboard. Then ask, "Who can answer Number 5?" Let the volunteer answer. The numbers on the blackboard might indicate which points have not been clarified.

    - *Start with one who can answer.* Some leaders like to start the quiz session by asking the first question of a person the leader feels can come up with a good answer. The quiz might seem unfair if the first few called on fumble in answering. Experience proves that quizzes get off to a better start if the first question is assigned to a person who has a high interest in the subject.

2. *When salespeople ask questions.* "Are There Any Questions?" This is a weak start for a quiz session. It's weaker when the leader gets no immediate response and then follows the question with, "Well, Mr. Ajax, you must have covered the subject mighty well, for there seem to be no questions." If you want questions, plan to get questions. There are a number of devices you can use to get questions started.

    - *When they won't reply.* Let's say you ask, "Are there any questions?" The group sits there looking at you as if it hasn't heard. You ask again, and still no response. You can say, "Well, if you know this subject so well, it won't hurt if *I* ask you a few questions about it." You ask the first question, and say, "Joan, you answer that one, please." Usually you will not have to ask more than three questions before the group has thought of a number of questions it wants to ask.

- *The "plant" can help.* To get questions started give out questions to three or four of the group. After a few of these planted questions, the group will start asking.

- *Have salespeople write out the questions.* Pass out blank cards and have salespeople write out questions that they would like to have answered. Collect these, and sort out the duplicate questions. Have the salespeople sign the cards so that you give credit to the person who asks it. To make sure you get enough questions from the group, write out some yourself.

3. *Getting the question repeated.* This is the most difficult problem you have when questions are asked in a meeting. A question is asked by a person in the front row. The leader starts to answer without repeating. The people in the back rows do not hear the question and they wonder what it is all about. Here are some suggestions for getting the question repeated:

- *The leader repeats it.* The leader opens the quiz session by asking, "Who has the first question?" When a question is asked, the leader repeats it. This assures that everyone hears, and it gives the leader or speaker a few seconds to think about his answer.

- *A sign on the wall:* A sign on the back wall of the meeting room, "Repeat the Question Please," may help. Some companies use a flasher sign. If the speaker starts to answer without repeating, the sign starts to flash. It also helps to have a sign in front of the speaker.

4. *Leader's attitude in quiz session.* In a quiz session, the leader is there to help the group. That attitude should show. You are not there to show how much you know, or to get laughs. If, after the session, the salespeople do not know the answers, whose fault is it? Not theirs!

Thus, when a salesperson asks a question that shows he or she did not understand something, say, "Oh, I guess we did not make that point clear." That wording indicates that you are at fault for not making the point clear. In the quiz session, the leader admits that he or she doesn't know all the answers. It is good to tell the group frankly, "I can answer a lot of them, but not all. I do know where to get the answers, and I'll do my best to get them for you." If you show that you are trying to help, your quiz sessions will go over better.

5. *The leader's plan for answering.*

- *He or she listens to the question, all of it.* Even though the first words indicate the nature of the question, he or she lets the person finish and doesn't show impatience in any way.

- *He or she repeats the question.* This allows all of the group to hear the question, and gives the person who asked it a chance to agree that the leader has understood.

- *He or she answers the question.*

- *He or she checks the answer.* The leader asks the questioner, "Does that answer your question?"

- *He or she asks one of the group to repeat the answer.* This is used as a check on whether or not the answer was clear to the group.

Appeal to the Active Senses

The discussion technique offers another way to give salespeople the important sense of being involved in a meeting. It appeals to active senses of seeing, hearing, and feeling. The participant sees the visuals, he or she hears what others have to say, and gets into the act to ask questions and present ideas. He or she writes notes, and reads the visuals, and quiz sheets. Salespeople like to talk, to express their ideas, and to listen to other salespeople express theirs.

There are some drawbacks, too. The discussion session takes time, more time than a lecture on the same subject. Further, it takes more planning. While most discussion sessions seem to run without much control, that appearance is a result of planning. To set up for a discussion session you need:

- An outline of what will be covered.

- Some notes for opening remarks that sell the group on taking part because of the good each salesperson can get out of the discussion.

- A blackboard or easel pad, with chalk or crayon.

- Notebooks for the participants. Sell the group on using the notebooks. If you see that they are not making notes, say, "Everybody write this down."

- Tables or desks on which the participants can write. Arrange these informally. Don't have too much space between the leader and the participants.

Here are some further points to keep in mind when planning the discussion session.

1. *The chairperson's job in the discussion.* The job of the chairperson is a lot like that of a committee chairperson. He or she starts the discussion, brings up the points in order, and keeps the discussion on the track. He or she makes sure that each point gets the time it should have, and watches to see that one point does not hog all of the time. The chairperson sees that the points are summed up and guides the group in sifting out conclusions.

2. *The discussion outline.* The leader needs an outline of the subjects to be covered. This can be made up by the chairper-

son or can be made up by the group. If you make it up, list the main points to be covered and the minor points under each main point. Even when the group makes up the outline, it is well for the chairperson to have an outline so that he or she can check the group's suggestions to see if any points that should be covered have been omitted.

3. *Building-a-plan session.* This type of session is handled much like the one that builds a sales story. Let's say you want to build a plan for a call on a customer. The leader asks, "What is the first thing you do when you call on a customer?" He or she asks one participant to describe what he or she does first, second, third, and so on. Now the leader asks a second, "Is that the way you do it?" If the person agrees, he or she is asked to describe the procedure in detail. Then the leader asks, "Who does it differently?" Now he or she gets more ideas. Each is discussed and in the end the group winds up with a procedure that is approved by the group, and one that the leader will not have much trouble getting the salespeople to try.

4. *The boasting session.* In this type of session, the salespeople tell how they did a certain job. In organizing such a session, give the people an outline to follow. There never was an unsuccessful boasting session. Salespeople love to tell how they used sales strategy in making a sale. Other salespeople listening to these stories learn from the descriptions of plans that have worked. The leader might ask the salesperson to follow the steps of the standard sales procedure. The salesperson's story might then be organized to answer the following statements:

- My survey showed this . . . .
- Because of this, I used these facts in my approach . . . .
- My presentation covered these points . . . .
- My appeal for action was . . . .

- The objections I got were . . . .
- Here's how I handled each . . . .

It is not absolutely necessary to have such an outline, but it will help organize the stories and it will not handicap the salespeople.

5. *The gripe session.* In this type of session the salesperson gets his or her beefs out in the open. This is good for morale, and out of participation in it a person gets ideas that will help in his or her job. Salesperson A has a complaint. He or she comes to the session and goes to town on it. Much to his or her amazement he or she finds that none of the other salespeople feel that his or her complaint is important. He or she learns, too, that other salespeople have found ways of handling this complaint. He or she goes away resolving to try these ideas and to see if they will work for him or her.

Role Playing in Meetings

The value of role playing for sales training has long been recognized. Usually one salesperson plays the part of a customer, and another plays the salesperson. An alternate plan is to have a sales supervisor take the role of the customer while the salespeople try to sell him or her. Or a top salesperson may use a telephone to demonstrate how he or she secures appointments with hard-to-see prospects.

Several years ago the Brown-Forman Corporation used a larger cast, including a role playing "newspaper reporter," to tell the company story at a regional sales meeting. In the hypothetical situation, the reporter was gathering material for a feature story on the history and operations of the company. The scene was a hotel room. Four members of the company's top management in marketing, bottling, financing, and engineering played themselves.

Keeping closely to an agreed-upon outline, the reporter asked leading questions to which the others could reply from their own broad knowledge and experience. Because the whole setting was informal, the speakers were able to comment upon each other's presentations and reinforce or assist a speaker as he or she went along.

By eliminating a formal speech, which would probably have had to be either read or memorized, these people—experts in their field and with plenty of product knowledge—were able to relax and say what they had to say in their own way. This spontaneity made for sincerity and for really effective communication. The audience was involved and interested instead of being the object of a lot of speechifying.

This was not a skit with a script, but a spontaneous presentation based on an outline that guided the reporter, so that he or she served as the voice of the audience, and as an element with whom the salespeople were able to identify. To reinforce this natural condition, the role of the reporter was played by one of the people in the sales department.

The effectiveness of the presentation was tested by a post-meeting reaction form in which the salespeople were asked to tell how they felt about the meeting and to list the reasons for their likes and dislikes. The most frequent comment from the salespeople related to the number of facts about Brown-Forman products they had gleaned from the presentation. The second most frequent comment dealt with the sincerity, informality, and spontaneity of the presentation. Another comment was, "The meeting gave me a much better understanding of the company and the people who run it."

Films, visual aids, and playlets all play their parts in sales meetings. But whether a sales manager is designing sessions for new recruits or refresher courses for his or her salespeople, he or she cannot do better than to utilize role playing of salespeople. That is the way salespeople master lessons, learn from each other, and obtain experience in selling their products. This in turn will revitalize them and help them to sell more when they are back in their own individual territories.

Planning Your Meetings

Establishing an orderly and logical planning sequence is vital to achieving a successful sales meeting. Here is a plan used by the 3M Company:

1. The date, place, time, and length of the meeting.

2. The specific objectives you hope to accomplish.

3. Information you plan to give to assist in accomplishing your sales-meeting objectives.

4. The method of presentation you plan to use.

5. The visual and other aids you will need at the meeting.

Many meetings fall apart because the meeting planner failed to be concrete in clearly defining his or her meeting objectives. What can you do to ensure against this? First, write down what you want your meeting to accomplish. Then find out what your salespeople would like your meeting to accomplish.

After you have established your meeting objectives, your next step is to determine what subjects should be included on your meeting agenda to accomplish these objectives. For example, if one of your meeting objectives is to sell your salespeople on the need for better territory management, you would want to list, "How to profitably manage your time and your customer," as discussion material.

If another of your meeting objectives is to get your salespeople excited about a current promotion, you would want to list, "How this promotion can build sales and profits for us," to discuss.

If another one of your meeting objectives is to get more effective use of sales tools, advertising, and sales promotional material, you would want to list, "A review of our current selling tools and promotional aids and how their effective use can increase our productivity," as a subject.

If another of your meeting objectives is to get your salespeople to concentrate on selling large-account business, you would want to schedule, "How to approach the big business order—whom to see, what to sell, and how to sell."

Adopt a Theme

Your sales meetings will excite more interest if they are built around a theme. A good meeting theme tied in with a popular trend or event—and this can be either past or present—will give your meeting impact. It will cause immediate interest and will provide a carryover of enthusiasm for applying the conclusions reached at your meeting.

The one main rule for adopting a theme for your meeting is to make certain that it is tied in with your meeting objectives. Your theme should be immediately identifiable with what you want your salespeople to accomplish.

Producing Your Meeting

The first step is to set up a general format for your meeting. A typical meeting day for the 3M Company is divided into seven major time periods. For example:

1. The meeting opening

2. Clinic or workshop session

3. Morning coffee break

4. Luncheon

5. Clinic or workshop session continued

6. Afternoon refreshments

7. Your meeting close

Your meeting format represents your meeting skeleton. It is around this skeleton that you build an agenda of subjects to be presented. A practical format assures that the subjects you wish to present to accomplish your meeting objectives will be presented in the most interesting manner.

Let us consider a few dos and don'ts to observe in conducting your meeting. These dos and don'ts come out of the experience of literally hundreds of sales managers, like yourself, who, over the years, have found out what techniques work best in presenting sales meetings.

1. Don't create competition for yourself. You do just that when you pass out material to your salespeople while you are trying to get across a point. It is physically impossible for anyone to concentrate on two things at once. So tell your story, demonstrate, show your chart presentation, or whatever else you might be presenting, and then and only then pass out any material with reference to what you have just covered. Before going on to your next subject, make certain you pick up any of this material so that it does not compete for attention when you take up your next subject. The same rule applies to your use of any meeting props. After a prop has served its purpose, get it off-stage or cover it up.

2. Follow your script! The control script you have prepared for your meeting will go a long way in preventing interruptions of a non-constructive nature. But, in spite of the best-laid plans, you may still get the person who wants to bring up something irrelevant to the subject or particularly personal to his or her own operation. This requires tactful handling, but your knowledge of these individuals will tell you best how to handle such situations. If, for example, a subject is brought up that your meeting provides for later on in the program, in a nice way inform the individual that you are glad he or she brought the subject up, but as it will be handled later on in the meeting, you would like to press on. The griper or the person who brings up the personal problem can be taken care of by saying in a friendly way—"Tom, I'll be very glad to discuss this with you personally after the meeting. I assure you I am interested in your problem and appreciate your concern."

3. Be easy to listen to, and listen yourself.

4. Whenever a controversial discussion takes place, regardless of how you resolve it, be sure to let your salespeople save face.

5. Keep to your time schedule.

6. Keep each subject on a high note.

7. Try to anticipate interruptions and prepare for them.

8. Don't leave a subject hanging in the air.

And now for a word about the close of your sales meeting. Every good sales meeting, in order to justify the time it took to present it, should ask for action. It should challenge your salespeople to put the ideas and the plans you presented into practice.

Your salespeople should understand that you intend to evaluate their performance following the meeting to determine how successfully they are applying what all of you agreed upon as being necessary to get the results you want.

Develop Good Meeting Leaders

It is an important responsibility of some salespeople to conduct effective meetings in front of groups of customers. The agricultural division of Olin Corporation wanted to improve its field representatives' skills in this area. E. Duane Riffel, manager, manpower development and training, offered this report of what was done to accomplish this:

"Some time ago a conference was held on the subject of conducting educational meetings. The panel of specialists at this conference did an outstanding job in presenting visual aids and other material to support their presentations. This material was reproduced as a text and a copy furnished to each of our sales representatives over the nation.

"Since that time, we have evolved a six- to eight-month orientation program for new sales representatives. This program culminates in a two-and-a-half week training conference. All phases are explored in detail, including organization and preparation of the material to be presented. Finally, the trainees conduct a practice meeting and a critique of their efforts is held, including comments by the trainees and their instructors. A second practice meeting is then held to include the recommendations for improvement brought out by the critiques.

"We have found this intensive treatment of a difficult responsibility has resulted in substantial dividends in increased sales effectiveness over the years."

Meetings for Retailers

Sales of appliance manufacturers depend not only on what their salespeople sell but ultimately on *what their dealer salespeople sell.* One company found very little training material directed toward the retail salespeople, particularly the independents, so it developed its own program.

Clyde Dains, as director of sales promotion and advertising for Oklahoma Natural Gas Company, of Tulsa, supplemented dealer training through a program that he described as follows:

"We assist our dealers with special appliance training meetings conducted by our sales promotion and home service personnel:

- *Kit conferences.* A 15- to 30-minute meeting is held in the dealer's store. The dealer schedules the date and time. Those participating receive a kit of demonstration aids—a sales-presentation summary and a customer-benefit checklist identifying appliance features, functions, and use. Display material and sample appliance ads are also presented.

- *Dealer meal demo.* A one-hour presentation is conducted at an Oklahoma Natural Culino Room—either breakfast, lunch, or dinner. Customer-benefit demonstrations of gas appliance features—how they really work—aid salespeople in "showing and telling" a customer an informed quality-performance story.

- *Special training skits.* For a change of pace, we use training skits to launch major sales promotions. Company home economists and sales promotion representatives make up the cast, with one salesperson overplaying the "don'ts" of good salesmanship, and another smoothly picking up the pieces with benefit selling. These have been well received by dealer salespeople.

Wholesalers' Meetings

A survey reported by the magazine *Jobber Topics* disclosed that, among its wholesaler readers, Saturday is being less frequently used as a day to hold sales meetings, while Monday is gaining in popularity. Only 41 percent of the participants hold sales meetings on Saturday, in contrast to the 54 percent participating in the survey the magazine conducted 10 years before. Friday also is losing ground; five out of eight favored it previously, but only one of eight do so today.

Sales meetings that last for half a day or a whole day are becoming more popular, *Jobber Topics* reports. They are usually a combination of sales-training and sales-promotion meetings. Until recently, few sales managers tried to make any distinction between the two basic types of meetings.

The wholesalers' complaints are instructive. Chief among them is the gripe against the manufacturer's spokesperson for being "inexperienced" or "lacking in knowledge of his or her lines." Sometimes such speakers talk too long or attempt to pass out too much technical and product information instead of sticking to "sales" information. Jobbers think that they can improve the factory representative's talk by finding out in advance the tenor of his or her "pitch" and suggesting various ways to make it apply more to the needs and interests of a specific audience.

Planning the Film Presentation

Film presentations can be ruined because of poor or inadequate equipment, unfavorable room conditions, or simply because of lack of foresight, check-up, and follow-up. The breakdown of the projector or the sound system is disastrous enough without adding problems created by lack of attention to details. The sales executive should charge one person with complete responsibility for supervision of all the physical and mechanical factors necessary to produce a timely, smooth-flowing meeting featuring one or more film presentations. Following is a useful film-presentation checklist:

- Room
    1. Is the room large enough to accommodate the audience you expect and to project the film to the appropriate size without making some of the audience sit almost on top of the screen?

2. Is it possible to group the audience in front of the screen reasonably close to the center?

3. Are there any intervening posts, pillars, or other obstructions to consider?

4. Are the acoustics good enough for your presentation? Don't spoil a good meeting and a fine film with poor acoustics!

5. Can you darken the room properly?

6. Do you know where the light switches are, and do you have someone to operate them at your signal? Did you arrange the cues with that person?

7. Do you know where the electrical outlets are?

8. Is the power correct for your equipment?

9. Is there proper ventilation? Air conditioning? Heat?

10. Have you arranged with the building custodian for adequate ventilation, air conditioning, and heat?

11. Are there proper exits and are they marked as required by law?

12. Have you sufficient chairs arranged properly? Be sure to leave sufficient aisles to exit doors!

13. Is there a speaker's table or podium from which to deliver opening and closing remarks and to hold notes and other materials? Don't forget the water and glass!

14. Do you need a sound system for the room? Have you checked it?

- Projector

  1. Is the projector otherwise in good working order? Have you checked it today?

  2. Is there a table or other furniture on which to place the projector?

3. Is the projector the proper size? 16mm., sound!

4. Is the projector light source powerful enough for the size of the room and screen desired? Check and make absolutely sure under actual projection conditions!

5. Have you checked for extra take-up spool?

6. Do you have an extra lamp?

7. Have you focused the projector so that you can start without any fiddling about to get clarity?

• Sound

1. Have you placed the speaker directly in front of the screen?

2. Is the speaker cord long enough to reach to the projector position?

3. Have you made sure no one will trip over the speaker cord? Loop the cord around the leg of the projector table and cover the cord on the floor with a rug or mat.

4. Is the audio (sound) working clearly and strongly? Have you noted the right position for the volume control for this room? Set and mark it clearly!

5. Can you hear the sound clearly in the rear of the room?

6. Is the speaker large enough or do you need two or more of them?

• Screen

1. How large a screen will the size of room and audience require?

2. How far will the projector be from the screen? Is the projector lens right for this distance? Check and make absolutely sure.

3. Will there be a table or other furniture upon which to place the screen?

4. Would it be better to hang the screen from the wall or from the ceiling?

5. Should the screen be readily portable or have its own stand?

6. Are the front row seats no nearer to the screen than twice the width of the projected picture?

7. Are the rear seats no farther from the screen than six times the width of the projected picture? (If so, you need a larger screen!)

8. Are you sure the heads of your audience won't cast shadows on the screen? Check by sitting in various seats.

9. Can late arrivals take seats without walking in front of the projector?

Show Business in Sales Meetings

Use of music and other entertainment has long played a role in sales meetings. Many sales executives point out, however, that—primarily because of TV—salespeople have become much more sophisticated judges of such presentations and are able to react not only to what is being said and shown, but also to *how* it is being said and shown.

An account director of an organization that plans, creates, and stages sales meetings—had these points to make about the use of professional entertainers:

Professional help in meetings is not a real help if it consists in merely tacking "show biz" or visualization factors onto what is a grueling and disrupting job performed by the executives of the company holding the meeting.

It is undeniable that the audience at a sales meeting—salespeople; district, branch, and regional managers; brokers; distributors; dealers—are all intricately involved with the aims of the host company.

But let's never forget that, aside from being a sales or dealer organization, our audience is a group of human beings.

In the physical planning, creation, and staging of the most effective kinds of meetings—both large and small—SCI has developed a full tool kit of methods, approaches, and systems.

A number of these are presented here, some relatively mechanical in nature, but all essential to a smooth-running and effective sales meeting.

1. *Use cast to enforce, not entertain.* The use of cast for comedy alone is obviously distracting to the communications job a meeting must do. In a meeting in which a live cast is used, it can be used most effectively to introduce speakers, start and wrap up sessions, dramatize important points, show displays, and distribute samples. This requires an integration of all cast material into the meeting subject matter, rather than merely adding on a cast number as a meeting brightener. Even a small cast can contribute excitement and an emotional build up.

2. *Show the real thing wherever possible.* Slides have an important place in any good meeting. However, the more of the real thing—the real packages, the real point-of-sale material, the real product, the real advertising—that can be shown, the better.

   In the case of small items, duplicates can be shown by the cast so that all get a closeup look. The aisles, the sides of the room, the coffee-break area—all are also good spots for a close-up look. In the case of large items, special meeting-room facilities are desirable.

3. *Aim for a tighter, shorter program.* A mistaken notion of "as long as we've got them here, let's make them work," has often led to sales meetings that last from early morning until well into the evening. While, in some cases, this kind of a schedule may be necessary, in our experience, a tight, well-planned meeting that ends at 5 p.m. or before is more effective.

   When people are forced to listen to hour after hour of facts, figures, and inspiration, they tend to become brain-weary. Their attention lags. Their minds wander. They lose more of what they are supposed to be hearing than they retain. A well-paced meeting—with well-timed coffee breaks and adequate lunch period—can usually do the job right and still release the sales force at the end of a seven- to eight-hour day.

4. *Scripted speeches are an important control factor.* If a meeting is to be well planned and run smoothly, it is of prime importance that speakers use scripts. In some cases a point outline—with specific time limit—will be adequate. However, in SCI's experience, scripts for all speakers, with the possible exception of a top management speaker or panel, provide the best insurance of a good meeting.

5. *Advance rehearsal produces the best results.* The speakers should be rehearsed by professionals well in advance of the date of the meeting or of travel to the meeting location. These rehearsals are held in the executives' offices or in a conference room set aside for that purpose.

6. *A slide-check saves confusion, time, and nerves.* At the scene of the meeting rehearsal, a final check of slides is, of course, necessary. However, the business of having all speakers sit around for hours while speeches are read and slides and slide cues are checked is both wearing to all and actually unnecessary.

By taking only those speakers who will use slides into a separate room—and, there, checking quietly and at close quarters only those portions of their speeches in which slides occur—a more accurate check is provided. And, of course, time and nerves are saved.

7. *A walk-through need not be a death march.* By carefully segmenting all elements that need checking or rehearsing on the day before the meeting, and then approaching each one on a scheduled basis, the arduous and endless dress rehearsal is eliminated. Such elements include:

- The slide-check, previously mentioned.

- A test of all speakers' voices for microphone level.

- A walk-through with each speaker of where and when he or she comes up to the lectern or on stage.

- A separate, scheduled rehearsal of each speaker who has cast integrated into his or her session.

8. *The workbook—an effective communication device.* One problem of the one-, two-, or three-day sales meeting is the mass of material to which those in the audience are exposed. In direct reverse ratio to the amount of such material is the ability of the salespeople to absorb and retain the information. Yet it is important that much of it be retained in order to be of value.

SCI has developed a workbook to help accomplish this. The workbook is a simple booklet or looseleaf binder containing pages with headings, some unfinished statements, and many blank spaces.

At the close of segments of the sales meeting, workbook summary sessions are held. In these, the speaker goes over the highlights of the material just covered and asks the salespeople in the audience to write specific key facts, figures, and the like in their workbooks.

In this manner, by getting the audience to participate, several excellent things are accomplished:

- The important points are sifted out and spotlighted.

- The act of listening is broken by an opportunity to participate—in this case, by writing in the books.

- The salespeople remember the points, because they wrote them down themselves.

Another form of workbook is one that is used concurrently with the meeting talks themselves. Workbook writing is integrated into the major speeches. This is particularly effective as a training medium.

The workbook, depending on the need, can vary from a simple booklet or looseleaf book to an elaborate book containing pictures, charts, and graphs, as well as write-in sections.

In any case, added to its obvious advantages, it also provides an excellent take-home piece for any meeting and can be used for further communication in the field.

9. *Follow-through for year-round effectiveness.* No matter how well planned, created, and staged, a sales meeting is only a one-, two-, or three-day period in a selling year of 365 days. To fully achieve what it can achieve, a sales meeting should, in the last analysis, be the starting point of a six-month or year-long communication effort. Planned with the meeting should be the follow-through activities that will carry the effect of the meeting throughout the year.

Microphone Technique

These excellent suggestions for mastering the microphone were prepared by Shure Brothers, Evanston, Illinois, and are excerpts from that company's brochure, "The Microphone in Public Address Systems."

It's amazing how often a speaker, performer, or lecturer "loses" his or her audience simply because he or she doesn't take time to master microphone technique. Using one properly is really just a matter of practice and common sense.

One of the most frequent errors occurs when a speaker turns away from the microphone and keeps on talking. His or her voice is lost—the microphone can't follow him or her. Face the microphone whenever you're talking. If you want to look around at various members of your audience, make the microphone your pivot point.

On the other hand, you should turn away at times. A speaker who clears his or her throat or coughs directly into the microphone may rock an entire audience.

The sure sign of an amateur speaker is blowing into a microphone to see if it's operating. Yes, it indicates whether sound is coming through or not, but it doesn't give you any idea of the volume at which your voice will be reproduced. Test the sound system by talking. "One, two, three, four" is as good as anything else.

All other things being equal, the best sound system is the one that can be operated at minimum volume. Too often, an inexperienced speaker will try to compensate for a bad acoustic condition simply by turning up the volume. This may only result in a disturbing effect for the listeners.

At first, most people in an audience won't complain about sound that is just a little too loud, too soft, or distorted. Unconsciously, perhaps, they will just work harder at listening more carefully, honestly trying to compensate for the inadequacies of the public address system.

But the strain of such careful listening over a period of time takes its toll. Attention wanders and points are missed. Listeners may become generally irritable, and blame the irritation on the speaker or the people in charge of the arrangements. Quite frequently, a sizable proportion of the audience may just finally give up and let their minds wander.

Tips for Speakers

1. Be natural. Good speaking is neither mechanical nor artificial.

   - You need not be a literary genius and use big and unusual words to deliver an effective presentation.

   - You need not use studied and elaborately rehearsed gestures.

   - You need not always have a certain type of posture. Your voice need not be that of an opera star, but need only be adequate.

   - You need not speak so fluently that there are no hesitations or uncertainties.

   - You should not speak as from a memorized, learned script, but should show a large degree of spontaneity.

2. Use the style of speaking that best suits your audience, your subject and the occasion.

3. Absorb the *principles* of effective speech, modifying your natural style in terms of those principles rather than copying them as ideals.

4. Your success as a speaker is directly proportionate to the degree your thoughts and ideas are comprehended by your audience. No other function is paramount. Always be well prepared. There is no excuse for doing less than your best.

Figure 1. Sales Meeting Evaluation

Meeting Topic:_____

Date:_____

To The Salesperson:

This checklist will help us to determine if we have succeeded in our sales meeting presentation. Under each heading *please number 1 - 2 - 3 the most important things you feel you learned.* If you do not feel that anything helpful was presented, leave the entire group blank. If you have comments, write them in the space provided or on the back.

DO NOT SIGN THIS CHECK SHEET.

PRODUCT	AIDS IN SELLING	MARKET
____New Product	____Where to Sell	____Potential
____New Applications	____New Sales Points	____New Users
____Typical Uses	____How to Sell	____Competing Lines
Values to	____New Presentation	____Competing Sources
____Customers		
Product	____Price Advantages	
____Sources—Service		
How Product	____Quality Advantages	
____Is Made		
Inventory	Reasons for Buying	
____Levels—Scope	____the Product (for Customer)	
	Reasons for Buying from Us	
	____(for Customer)	
	How to Sell Against	
	____Competition	
	____Samples	
	____Sales Aids	
	____Related Sales	

COMMENTS:_____

_____

(Filled out by salespeople at the end of the meeting as a check on whether or not meeting objectives were accomplished)

Figure 2. Master Timetable for Annual Meetings

M *minus one year*
Discuss meeting concept with executives directly involved
Consider who will attend
Set objectives
Develop theme
Set date
Consider tentative sites
Estimate time (days) for program
Rough out staff responsibilities

M *minus nine months*
Select hotel
Negotiate with hotel for facilities and services
Make list of printing needs
Set up schedule for promotion
Create list of premeeting assignments
Consider program for spouses (if invited to attend)
List subjects to be covered at meeting
Choose company speakers best qualified to participate on program
Clear company speakers with their superiors
Create list of physical requirements
Create checklist for each meeting segment

M *minus six months*
Invite company top executives
Invite local dignitaries, board members, or VIPs in finance
Negotiate with outside speakers
Reach understanding on types of speeches and length
Get list of audio-visual equipment needed by all speakers
Inventory needs against company supplies
Order buses for special transportation needs
Get bids on decorations and/or special services
Confirm all agreements in writing—speakers, company executives, suppliers, etc.
Confirm all meeting assignments in writing

M *minus six months*
Plan for transportation of attendees to meeting city
Create art theme for mailings and use in meeting room

M *minus one month*
Reproduce materials to be distributed
Make or order final visuals
Send rooming list to hotel
Arrange for photographer
Set timetable for ground transportation
Order necessary signs
Alert press if coverage is desired
Make detailed arrangements chart for each session
Arrange for recording of sessions
Purchase souvenirs or theme giveaways
Arrange for shipping materials
Arrange for typewriters or PCs at site
Arrange for necessary reproductions of papers or forms at site

M *minus two weeks*
Assemble materials for meeting
Submit final VIP list to hotel with instructions for special handling
Check on shipping of materials
Confirm meeting details with suppliers
Contact individuals on program to reconfirm agreements
Submit detailed list of materials and services required to hotel
Confirm specific hours and duties of hotel personnel to service meeting
Establish deadlines for completion of all hotel and supplier services
Assemble list of gratuities to be paid
Order locked storage space at hotel
Arrange for receiving and shipping goods at hotel
Confirm menus, coffee-break timing, receptions, and clarify instructions

(continued)

Figure 2. Master Timetable for Annual Meetings

(continued)

M *minus one week*
Prepare name badges
Rehearse company speakers
Reconfirm date and time for out-
side speakers
Invite outside speakers to major
functions
Prepare releases for invited press
Make up meeting supply package

M *minus two days*
Schedule final rehearsals
Review plans with hotel depart-
ment heads
Check on arrival of shipped
materials
Check on delivery of rented
audio-visual equipment
Place all materials and equipment
in secured storage
Order flowers, wine, fruit as gifts
for outside speakers or VIPs
Alert press again if coverage
desired
Turn over final list of all attendees
to hotel

M *minus one day*
Reconfirm plans for registration
desk
Check weather reports for possi-
ble effect on arrivals
Check out operation of audio-
visual equipment
Review plans with electrician
Check handout materials
Arrange to meet speakers and
guests
Meet with hotel manager to coordi-
nate plans
Distribute duplicate room setup
plans to your staff
Final briefing for your staff on re-
sponsibilities
Reconfirm meal guarantees
Reconfirm coffee-break times and
menus
Reconfirm hospitality room
arrangements
Reconfirm credit and check cash-
ing agreement with hotel

M *minus one day*
Clear system on messages with
telephone operators
Have product displays set up
Dress rehearsal of entire program

M *minus two hours*
Check room setup
Check ventilation and temperature
Check mikes and public address
system
Check audio-visual equipment
Check registration desk setup
Arrange handout material for use
Check for necessary personnel
Check for signs in place

M *minus one hour*
introduce outside speakers to
fellow speakers
Check on photographer
Check on place cards
Have honorariums ready
Check on tape recorder operator
Check lectern light and stage
props
Give last-minute instructions to
program participants

M *day*
Note audience response to content
and meeting format
Record questions raised by
audience
Keep record of attendance at meal
functions
Inventory liquor
Pick up papers and audio-visual
materials left in meeting rooms
Check all bills and record on
budget sheet

M *plus one day*
Hold critique session with hotel
department heads
Check all charges
Arrange for shipping back displays
and materials
Return rental audio-visual
equipment
Issue gratuities

(continued)

Figure 2. Master Timetable for Annual Meetings
(continued)

M *plus one week*
Critique meeting with executives
present or involved
Send answers to field on questions
raised at meeting
Send "thank yous" to meeting
participants

M *plus one week*
Send report of meeting to
company's publication
Make up "Dos and Don'ts" report
for next year's planning committee
Plan follow-up meetings to implement meeting objectives

Reprinted with permission from *Sales and Marketing Management* Magazine

Figure 3. Site Check List.

Date of Meeting _____   Number Attending _____

Features	Site No. 1	Site No. 2	Site No. 3	Site No. 4
HOTEL/MOTEL FACILITIES				
Number of singles				
Number of twins				
Number of suites				
MEETING FACILITIES				
Auditorium				
General meeting room				
Seminar rooms				
Display space				
COMMUNICATION				
Stage size				
Public address system				
AV equipment				
TRANSPORTATION				
Miles from airport				
Car rental				
Limousine service				
Parking rates				
FOOD SERVICE				
Breakfast				
Lunch				
Dinner				
Banquet				
ENTERTAINMENT				
Liquor service				
Dancing				
Nightclub				
RECREATION				
Swimming pool				
Private beach				
Tennis courts				
Green fees				
Horseback riding				
Charter fishing				
NEARBY ATTRACTIONS				
Sports				
Night clubs				
Amusement parks				
REGISTRATION				
Deposit				
Pre-registration				
Late check-out				
Meeting signs				

This chart enables the meeting planner to compare the facilities offered by various hotels. Rates and other costs would be separately analyzed to complete the basis for the final selection.

(Courtesy: Delta Airlines)

Chapter 44

Sales Force Compensation

Compensation is perhaps the most important element in a program for the management and motivation of a field sales force. The question of how to compensate salespeople entails many factors such as the size of the company, its position in its industry, its marketing policies and its approach to product distribution.

Naturally, a high-cost, specialized product requiring selective selling necessitates a different sales compensation program than one merchandised through chain retail stores.

The selection of a compensation plan which meets both company objectives and motivational needs of salespeople is often as difficult as selecting a good salesperson—and is just as important.

A properly designed and implemented compensation plan must be geared to the needs of the company, the products or services sold and must attract and keep good salespeople producing at increasing rates.

Types of Compensation Plans

Three basic compensation approaches are available to sales management: *salary* plan; *commission* plan; and *combination* (salary plus incentive) plan.

Surveys by the Dartnell Institute of Financial Research have shown a trend in American and Canadian companies towards increased use of some form of a combination plan. Table 1, page 1024, shows the popularity of different categories of the three basic plans in 1987.

Salary Plan

Salary includes plans in which salespeople are paid fixed rates of compensation. They may also include occasional additional

Table 1. Percentage of Use of Different Methods of Pay

Salary Plans	27%
Straight Salary	
All Commission Plans	27%
Straight Commission	24%
Commission + Bonus	3%
All Combination Plans	50%
Salary + Commission	11%
Salary + Bonus	28%
Salary + Commission + Bonus	11%
(Note: Total may exceed 100% because more than one plan may be used by a company.)	

compensation in the form of discretionary bonuses, sales contest prizes, or other short-term incentives.

This plan works well when the main objective is missionary work or requires an unusual percentage of time devoted to prospecting, or if the salesperson's primary function is servicing accounts. Secondary objectives of increasing sales from existing accounts and opening new accounts require special incentive treatment.

The salary plan is appropriate in sales activities where it is difficult to evaluate who really makes the sale. This is the team approach to sales—a salesperson's contribution cannot be accurately separated from the efforts of others in the company, such as inside personnel and technical service persons. The sales of technical products commonly involve this form of team selling.

When management finds it difficult to develop adequate measures of performance against which an equitable bonus or commission can be paid, a salary plan is desirable.

Many durable goods industries experience cyclical sales patterns which make a salary plan more compatible to the salesperson's efforts and avoids the sharp swings in income that can occur in a commission plan.

Here are some basic advantages and disadvantages of the salary plan approach:

ADVANTAGES

- Assures salespeople a regular income
- Develops a high degree of loyalty
- Makes it simple to switch territories and quotas or to reassign salespeople
- Ensures that nonselling activities will be performed
- Facilitates ease of administration
- Provides relatively fixed sales costs

DISADVANTAGES

- Fails to give balanced sales mix due to selling products with greater customer appeal
- Provides little if any financial incentive
- Offers few reasons for putting forth extra effort
- Favors those who are the least productive
- Tends to increase direct selling costs over other types of plans
- Creates the possibility of salary compression where the new trainee may earn almost as much as the experienced salesperson

The two lists do not necessarily cancel each other out. Every compensation plan is a compromise. Determination of marketing/sales objectives that will, in turn, determine the role of the sales force, will indicate to the sales executive whether or not the salary plan approach is best for achieving company goals.

Commission Plan

In this type of plan, salespeople are paid in direct proportion to sales made. Such plans include straight commission and commission with draw.

This plan works well with the start of a new business where the market possibilities are very broad and highly fragmented. In such situations, territory boundaries are usually rather fluid and difficult to define. Therefore, quota and customer assignments are difficult to determine, making other types of compensation plans too costly or too complex to administer.

When management has a sincere desire to maximize incentive, regardless of the compensation levels in other company functions, or when management prefers a predictable sales cost in direct relationship with sales volume, the commission plan is appropriate.

However, the straight commission approach has declined in popularity over the past several years and is not currently preferred. In analyzing the reasons for its weak rating, the following comparisons of advantages and disadvantages emerge:

ADVANTAGES

- Pay relates directly to performance and results achieved
- System is easy to understand and compute
- Salespeople are provided with the greatest incentive possible
- Unit sales costs are proportional to net sales
- Company's selling investment is reduced

DISADVANTAGES

- Emphasis is more likely to be on volume than on profits
- Little or no loyalty to the company is generated
- Wide variances in income between salespeople
- Salespeople are encouraged to neglect nonselling duties
- Tendency for some salespeople to "skim" their territories

- Service aspect of selling either bypassed or neglected

- Problems in cutting territories or shifting salespeople or accounts

- Pay is often excessive in boom times and very low in recession periods

- Strong tendency for salespeople to sell themselves rather than the company, and to stress short-term rather than long-term relationships

- Reluctance on the part of high-paid salespeople to move into supervisory or managerial positions

- Turnover of sales personnel tends to be excessive when business turns bad

Two other considerations to keep in mind are:

1. Commission plans encourage salespeople to conduct themselves as though they were in business for themselves, and thus their aggressiveness is increased. At the same time, bad practices may be encouraged that cannot be corrected by management because of the salesperson's attitude of independence and his or her resentment of direction and control.

2. Commission plans attract a type of person who will work hard for high stakes, gambling his or her time and effort for a big return. But they also attract some persons who are less competent than management thinks they are and who overstock their customers, falsely represent the goods, and are inclined to cut corners. The company can do little to correct the situation until after the damage has been done.

Straight commission plans usually pay a commission on shipped orders, with the returns and allowances deducted. The commission varies with different types of products and for different industries. If the product is in great demand and sold in large quantities, the commission rate may be as low as 1 percent or even a fraction of 1 percent of sales. If the product requires intensive selling, or if quantities are small and expenses high, the rate may run as high as 25 percent of sales or higher. Straight commission salespeople usually pay their own expenses.

There is a growing trend for salespeople who work on a commission basis to be given a drawing account, which is deducted from their earned commissions. Some sales managers feel that this gives the salesperson the security of a salary, yet is a hedge against company loss, since no further commissions are paid until earned commissions exceed draws; but in reality there is no protection to the company. If the salesperson is not able to earn his or her draw, the company has two alternatives:

1. Fire the salesperson and absorb the loss

2. Keep the salesperson and continue his or her draw

Combination Plan

This type of plan includes all variations of salary plus other monetary incentive plans. These variations include base salary plus commission on all sales, salary plus bonus on sales over quota, salary plus commission plus bonus, and so on.

Many sound reasons abound for installing a salary plus incentive plan. It permits greater incentive than a salary or commission plan, while providing better control of the incentive or variable income than is possible with the commission plan. Also the much greater degree of flexibility with a wide variation in incentives to work with allows management to develop practically tailor-made plans for each salesperson.

But these plans have a liability side too. Salary plus incentive plans tend to be more complex than the other two methods. Thus, they involve more paperwork, control, and administrative work load. They need more frequent revision because of the interaction of the elements that make up the total plan. One caution to be observed in making individual adjustments over the years is to avoid a gradual loss of uniformity in the plan.

The most important determination in building a sound salary plus incentive plan is the split between the fixed portion (salary) and the variable portion (incentive).

The split is usually determined on the basis of historical sales performance and compensation records. Competitive analysis of other company programs, the base salary needed to keep good people, and an estimate of incentive potential should also be considered. Ceilings on incentive payments are usually included in combination plans.

The most frequent percentage split is 80 percent base salary/20 percent incentive. A close second is a 70 percent/30 percent split, with a 60 percent/40 percent split being the third most frequently used arrangement. As the rewards are closely tied into sales or gross margins, closer supervision and control of the plan is needed as the incentive portion of the plan increases.

Structuring the salary portion of the plan requires establishing salary grades for the sales force. Each salary grade should be supported by a job description and each salesperson assigned according to experience and ability.

In the incentive portion of the combination plan, three basic forms of reward can be considered: a *commission,* a *bonus,* and a *commission* plus *bonus.*

Commission incentives are the most popular. Sales executives use one or more of these typical methods:

- pay a fixed commission on all sales

- pay at different rates by product category

- pay on sales over a determined goal

- pay on product gross margin

The rationale of paying commissions on gross margin dollars is based on the assumption that it will motivate the salesperson to improve both product and customer mix and therefore improve territory gross margin.

One great advantage of the commission incentive is the frequency and regularity of the reward—usually monthly. Salespeople are more quickly motivated to maintain or exceed performance levels with the rapid tie-in between performance and reward.

Bonus incentives are usually paid as a percent of salary and vary by goal performance levels. Although bonuses are paid on a variety of sales results, gross margin goals are used most frequently. Other factors used as a measure for bonus goals are market share, product mix, new accounts, nonsales activities, higher unit sales, and increased sales from existing accounts. Some companies simply make bonus arrangements on a discretionary basis.

Goals may be based on an analysis of the potential of the territory and expected performance against the potential. They may be developed from a moving average of historical sales or gross margin for two or three years, plus a one-year forecast averaged into the moving base.

Bonus payments should be structured to begin at the 70 percent to 75 percent-of-goal level to motivate salespeople toward goal achievement. A lower threshold level works against sustained sales effort. Conversely, by not receiving bonuses until sales effort of 100 percent goal is achieved, many salespeople will become discouraged along the way, making motivation more difficult. While payment rates may be uniform both under and over the 100 percent goal, increasing the rate beyond the 100 percent mark adds an additional incentive with a lower cost factor.

As bonus incentives are usually paid quarterly, it is not recommended that the full amount be paid when due. Withholding a small percentage due each quarter until the end of the year avoids a possible overpayment for the total year bonus. A proper adjustment is made with the final quarter payment.

A bonus incentive plan is more difficult to establish and administer than a commission incentive. Also, rewards paid on a quarterly basis are not as effective motivators as weekly or monthly commission payments.

Another variation of the combination plan is one that pays *salary, commission* and *bonus*. While this approach offers more flexibility than the other two types, it is more complex and more difficult to administer than any other plan.

As we did with the other two basic plans, let's take a look at the advantages and disadvantages of the combination plan.

ADVANTAGES

- Offers participants in this type of pay program the advantages of both salary and commission

- Provides greater flexibility and control over salespeople

- Gives salespeople greater security by providing them with a steady base income

- Makes possible a favorable ratio of selling expense to sales

- Compensates salespeople for all of their activities

- Allows a greater latitude of motivation possibilities so that goals and objectives can be achieved on schedule

DISADVANTAGES

- Often complex and difficult to understand

- Where low salary and high bonus or commission exist, bonus can become too high a percent of earnings. When sales fall, salary is too low to retain salespeople

- Sometimes costly to administer

- Unless a decreasing commission rate for increasing sales volume exists, the "windfall" of new accounts and the runaway of earnings can result

- Tendency to offer too many objectives at one time so that the really important ones can be neglected, forgotten, or overlooked

Which Is the Right Plan?

The right compensation plan for your sales force is dependent upon many factors, such as:

- The life cycle of your company and products

- Your marketing objectives and goals translated into what you want your sales force to accomplish

- Industry and/or relevant labor market pay practices
- The degree of personal selling influence

Regarding this last point, Jerome A. Colletti, president of New York and Arizona-based The Alexander Group, compensation specialists, cites three examples of three degrees of personal selling influence, which he designates as low, medium, and high.

In the *low* category, Colletti gives as an example the grocery products sales rep who calls on individual retail stores and independent operators representing nationally advertised products. The principal objective of the job is to maintain distribution, i.e., point-of-purchase displays and adequate levels of inventory. National advertising, trade promotions, and product appearance are quite important in stimulating sales demand and therefore are more important than personal selling.

As an example of *medium* degree of personal selling influence, he cites a specialty chemicals sales rep who calls on engineers and purchasing agents in the paint, paper, and coating industries to present additive and process chemicals. Product literature, technical service support, and availability/delivery are *as* important as personal selling influence.

In the *high* category, the example given is that of a computer-services sales rep who calls on business managers who have specific application needs that must be met with customized software.

He or she must design the product, if you will, through the sales call process. Personal selling is the most significant factor in creating the sale.

Colletti indicates how the split between salary and incentive pay varies as a function of personal selling influence. When a *low* degree exists, he suggests an average range of 8 percent to 15 percent incentive pay as a percent of total compensation.

When a *medium* degree of personal selling influence exists, he suggests an average range of from 9 percent to 25 percent.

With a *high* degree, an average range of 26 percent to 50 percent is recommended.

Leading sales managers have discovered that sales forces, like business in general, evolve through various stages from infancy to maturity.

If your incentive plan doesn't match your company's stage, you may find that:

- Your sales force is much too comfortable
- Variable pay has become too automatic
- Too much incentive goes toward sale of existing products and not enough toward new products.

As far as sales force compensation plans are concerned, the design and execution of a given compensation plan are too important and too involved to leave to chance. The substantial effect it has on sales productivity, as well as on correct sales behavior, dictates that you should run a compensation audit at least every two years and—dependent upon current business conditions—perhaps every year.

The compensation picture is a dynamic situation, constantly affected by changes in your company's and products' life cycles, your marketing objectives and goals, market labor prices, and general economic conditions.

To quote Colletti again: "The marketing puzzle becomes a lot clearer once you obtain the necessary pieces concerning the best kind of sales incentive compensation plan for your sales force. The questioning process requires some careful judgment concerning the importance of each of the factors. But when you do fit the right plan into the puzzle, it *will* lead to maximum sales force productivity."

The IBM Compensation Plan

The need for constant reappraisal of compensation plans was effectively spelled out by the manager of marketing research and development, International Business Machines Corporation, in a statement to Dartnell. He said:

"Marketing chiefs might look carefully at their sales compensation plan if they are not admired, rewarded, or appreciated by general management to the degree deemed desirable. Without question, this is one area often taken for granted and overlooked in management's constant search for more profit dollars.

"In many companies sales compensation is the largest item in the marketing budget. If marketing expenses are to be materially reduced over a period of time, the sales-compensation expense has to be reduced.

"Perhaps the adoption of a variable-compensation plan that pays a decreasing *percentage* of sales income to the salesperson in succeeding years sounds impractical to many businesses. In fact it may be impossible for a few businesses; but it definitely has not been properly evaluated by all businesses that could benefit by its adoption.

"Several conditions have to be present, or planned for, if sales-compensation plans are to produce the optimum number of extra dollars of profit that drop into the bottom line without endangering sales morale:

1. Salespeople should receive the major part of their income in the form of commissions or bonuses, as opposed to salary.

2. Salespeople have to be given programs and/or products that will increase the yearly amount of total revenue they can individually generate.

3. Total net income for the average salesperson has to increase as revenue generated increases, though not in the same proportion. While it is not absolutely mandatory, the sales force should be conditioned to live with change.

4. The sales-compensation plan should be changed every year as a matter of course.

5. New sales territories should be periodically created and it should not be a traumatic experience for a salesperson to lose part of his or her territory.

"More than one change will be required and many sacred cows will have to be killed before the above concepts can be imposed on an existing sales force operating under a different philosophy.

"The obvious starting point is to make sure that 50 percent to 80 percent of a salesperson's total income is dependent on the volume or type of sales generated. There are many pros and cons to a predominantly commission-based sales plan. Some points that are contrary to most ideas on the subject are worthy of comment:

"It is often said salaried salespeople's activities can be controlled better than commissioned salespeople's activities. However, there are a number of marketing executives who are convinced that: 1) salaried salespeople are more prone to work in "lower gear" than a salesperson who participates in every sale, and 2) overall it is easier to direct, motivate, and control commission salespeople.

"Most statements on the subject stress that sales-compensation plans should be simple and straightforward. This concept has to be challenged if a marketing organization wants to use its sales compensation to give sales direction and get maximum motivation out of its sales force. There is no argument that each part of the plan has to be easily understood, but if you are to be fair to each salesperson regardless of experience, and to each product regardless of its maturity in the marketplace, you need several provisions in your plan that are often interpreted as "complicated."

"Many companies pay the same rate of commission or even a decreasing rate of commission as volume increases. Neither of these systems does much to motivate salespeople to bring in a maximum amount of revenue. They might be pleasantly surprised if they adopted a plan that basically *increased* the average commission paid with each new sale made.

"In addition to a regular sales plan for the bulk of your sales force, four or five special compensation plans should be adopted if sales management is to have the flexibility needed to maximize sales. This point is not really contrary to popular ideas on the subject, but it is included because many businesses apparently have not adopted a predominantly commission-based compensation plan because it is wrong for a small portion of their sales force.

"Once salespeople operate on a plan that has most of the suggested ingredients, management must give careful thought as to what it can do for the salesperson that will allow him or her to increase productivity in his or her assigned territory. This can include such items as:

1. Increased education in sales techniques

2. A broader product line

3. A new generation of products

4. Increased financial tools, such as a company-sponsored lease program

5. Aids to free him or her for more sales time

6. More effective sales tools

"After management makes an investment in a product or a program which will increase a salesperson's productivity, it has to make a careful evaluation of what this will mean to the average salesperson. It is suggested that, for planning purposes, management adopt a philosophy of planning an increase in the average salesperson's income of 1 percent for every 3 percent or 4 percent increase in productivity. This approach, in effect, reduces the percentage of total commissions paid. If the saving is greater than the cost of the program (and it should be if the program is properly evaluated), the difference will be available to offset other costs or, more hopefully, become profit. It will also become acceptable to the salesperson because he or she takes home total dollars rather than a percentage."

Establishing Sales Base and Quotas

Setting the sales base is probably the most difficult part of designing a combination plan. If the base is set too high, salespeople will have too much difficulty in meeting it and the incentive motivation will be lost. If it is set too low, salespeople will earn more extra compensation than is reasonable.

The term *base* refers to the minimum volume that represents a satisfactory job in relation to the salary paid. *Quota* represents the dollar volume, quantity, or other objective expected that the salesperson will sell. It may be the same as the base or it may be higher. Quotas are used in budgetary control. A *goal* is what the salesperson and his or her manager hope to sell if all goes well. It represents their ambitions and is never used for budget controls.

A second difficulty in determining the base arises from cyclical and seasonal variations. In a period of rising economy, it is easy for the salesperson to increase his or her sales. When the economy is declining, he or she may do a good job but still have sales drop.

For the foregoing reasons, the base should be adjusted annually, with careful consideration of cyclical trends and seasonal fluctuations. There are a number of different methods for determining the annual base. These include:

1. *The previous year's sales.* This is not bad when the trend is steadily upward; but as the economy levels off, it becomes more and more difficult for the salesperson to reach his or her base, much less exceed it. The previous year's sales may do for a year or two, or for longer in a newly-opened territory, but usually the program quickly runs out of steam.

2. *A percentage of the previous year's sales (usually 80 percent).* This method poses the same problems as the first, but has the benefit of assuring that the salesperson makes some extra monetary compensation if he or she does a reasonably good job. This money is supposed to whet his or her appetite and motivate him or her to greater effort for more of the same.

3. *A three-year moving average or 80 percent of such average.* For this, the previous three years are averaged for the following year's base; then, for each subsequent year, the sales figures for the first of the three years are dropped and the immediately previous year's sales are added. This plan smooths out any wide year-to-year fluctuations, yet retains the remaining disadvantages of the two previous methods. An additional disadvantage is that there is a year's lag in giving effect to any change in trend. This works to the salesperson's advantage when the trend turns up, but he or she is fighting quite a battle when the trend turns down.

4. *Expenses including salary.* These are sometimes capitalized at about 5 percent and the result used as the base.

5. *A percentage of the amount of available business (potential).* This may not produce any hardship for a well-established

territory, but may be exceedingly difficult to attain in a new or underdeveloped territory.

A constructive variation of this is to establish the desirable amount of business based on potential, then give the salesperson a yearly "grubstake" for five years as he builds the territory to normal realization.

For example, if the base should be $200,000 when the territory has been fully developed, the salesperson might be given a grubstake of $150,000 for the first year, Then, if he or she sold $75,000, that amount added to $150,000 would give him or her credited sales of $225,000, or $25,000 over the $200,000 base; he or she would then receive a commission on the $25,000. The second year the grubstake would be reduced to $100,000, the third year to $75,000, the fourth year to $25,000, and after that the full $200,000 base would apply.

The advantage of a grubstake is that the salesperson always has the $200,000 full potential base before him or her as a goal, whereas if the base were merely raised each year, the salesperson would have lesser figures as motivation.

6. *Break-even volumes.* Usually it is difficult to determine a break-even point for a sales territory or district that includes all elements of expense. Therefore, the company's break-even volume at anticipated gross margin is determined, plus the volume needed for an adequate minimum return on invested capital. This company volume is then apportioned to the sales territories in accordance with the ratios of their previous three years' sales to total company sales.

This establishes the share of the volume of business that each salesperson must attain for the company to reach its break-even point (covering cost of manufacture, overhead expenses, promotional and research expenses, and their own expenses) and to provide a minimum return to the stockholders. The use of the three-year sales figures for the salespeople measures their penetration into their markets. As a salesperson's sales increase, he or she carries a larger share of the break-even volume. The commission paid may be based on dollar sales over base; or, if salaries are equitable, it may be paid as a percentage of salary.

7. *Arbitrary bases.* Here the manager uses his or her best judgment on all factors involved—past sales, future possibilities, economic trends, salesperson's development—and then arbitrarily picks a base. This is dangerous, as biases are bound to creep in, and some salespeople may not feel that the base chosen is fair to them.

Adjusting the Retroactive Sales Base

Companies in industries that have good access to monthly sales data, such as the work-glove industry, for example, frequently adjust their salespeople's base at the end of the year with the trend in the industry's sales.

For example, Salesperson A may have a base of $200,000, which is deemed fair in view of the industry's sales trends. But during the year, the economy had a setback and the industry's sales for the year dropped 10 percent below the previous year's sales. The salesperson's base is also dropped 10 percent, retroactive to the first of the year.

Obtaining Specific Product Sales

Salespeople are past masters at spending most of their effort on what they like to sell or on what is the easiest for them to sell. This may or may not be in keeping with the company's desires. In order to overcome this tendency of favoritism or specialization, many companies use the commission portion of their compensation plans to place emphasis on full product coverage or on special products.

To obtain product-coverage emphasis, companies may divide the products into groups, with a sales base set for each group. To qualify for commissions, a salesperson may have to exceed his or her sales base in certain important groups, in a certain number of groups, or in all groups. Or the company might pay commissions when the sales base is exceeded for each group, but step up the commission rate as more and more group sales bases are exceeded.

For example, a company has established five product groups: group A, the most profitable, carries a commission of 5 percent when the salary base is exceeded; group B, 4 percent; groups C, D, and E, 3 percent. To qualify for any commission, the salesperson must exceed the sales base in group A; even though he or she exceeds the base in groups B, C, D, and E, the salesperson receives no commission unless he or she exceeds the base in group A; if he or she exceeds the base only in group A, the salesperson receives a commission on that group only.

Or the salesperson might receive commissions at the rates specified as each sales base is exceeded; but if he or she qualifies in all three groups, he or she receives an extra ½ percent on sales above base for the three groups; if he exceeds the base in four groups, he or she receives an extra ¾ percent for the four groups; for all five groups, he or she receives an override of 1 percent on all sales over the bases.

Handling Split Credits

The problem of assigning proper sales credit frequently arises when two or more salespeople are involved in a sale. This happens when the buyer of the goods is located in one salesperson's territory, but the shipment is made to the territory of the second, who must service the sale. In such cases, an even split is usually made.

Even more complicated is the situation when the specifications have been written by an architect or engineer in one salesperson's territory, the goods purchased in a second salesperson's and shipment made in the territory of a third. Some companies handle such situations by giving full credit to the salespersons getting the order, reasoning that although the other two salespersons may lose out at this time, they will receive their full credit on similar orders they get signed.

Other sales managers feel this policy is a shortsighted one, and that the company is taking a risk that the two other salespersons involved will not do their jobs properly and the company will stand a loss.

To guard against such a possibility, to treat all salespeople fairly, and to see that due credit is given, many companies split credits. If the situation outlined above is normal, credit is split, with a third to each salesperson; if the specifications are written and the order is placed in one territory with shipment to a second one, the first salesperson would receive two-thirds credit and the second a third credit.

Mail and Telephone Sales

Most sales organizations give credit to territory salespeople for mail and telephone sales; only a very small minority do not.

The prevailing attitude is that the salesperson in the territory has prepared the groundwork for such orders; he or she is responsible for the territory as such; hence he or she should receive credit for the results of his or her work in that territory.

House Accounts

One troublesome problem concerns house accounts, which are reserved for handling by branch or headquarters management. House accounts should be distinguished from the personal accounts of branch or district managers who receive commissions thereon.

A simple way to handle this problem is to spell out any specific house accounts in annual salesperson contracts or agreements. Obviously, house account sales volume should not be included in territory quotas or goals.

Starting New Territories

When starting a new territory, there is a considerable amount of promotional work to be done, and sales volume may not reach a profitable level for a year or possibly five years. Many companies consider such expenses as a capital investment, even though they might expense the cost currently.

They may pay the salesperson assigned to the new territory a larger salary than their other salespeople, knowing that he or she will be unable to obtain the extra compensation that the others do.

As the territory becomes better established, the salary would be brought back to normal level with extra compensation being earned.

Some companies have salespeople particularly adept in opening new territories; these salespeople are moved from one new territory to another. Their superior skill justifies their receiving higher salaries than the company's average salespeople.

The grubstake plan is a useful method of compensation for new territories. The salesperson has a high goal at all times. Understanding the program, he or she feels that the company is providing assistance in getting established. Of course the steps in reduction of the grubstake should be explained in advance so he or she will not feel that the company is changing the rules in the middle of the game.

If a company turns a new territory over to a commission salesperson, expecting him or her to invest time and money in the development of the territory, the salesperson has every right to feel that it is his or her property. The company could hardly take it, or even a portion of it, away without reimbursing the salesperson in some way.

Transferring Territories

It is relatively easy to transfer salespeople from one territory to another when they are paid straight salaries, but it becomes increasingly difficult as the ratio of variable income increases.

When a salesperson who receives a portion of income as a commission is moved to another territory, his or her income may increase considerably due to the purchasing pattern of new customers, or the salesperson's income may decline because the territory must be built up. This latter condition prevails when a territory is split; it may take months for the salesperson to build up the portion of the territory that he or she retains to a point where it will be as productive as was the old full territory. When a salesperson loses territory, some companies guarantee minimum extra compensation to the person for a year, to safeguard against loss while building up the territory.

Other companies follow a split commission program, whereby

the salesperson losing territory and probable income receives credit for a percentage of sales from his or her old territory, such credit being reduced, declining in amount during the year.

A Policy for Older Salespeople

Good management requires that to make room at the top for younger salespeople on the way up, the compensation plan should make it possible for salespeople who have reached normal retirement age to retire.

An alternative is to keep the older salesperson on the payroll at retirement age in a consulting capacity and pay him or her a monthly salary (usually about 40 percent of average earnings for the last three years). He or she can be called upon for advice or counsel at any time, or in the event of an emergency he or she can, if physically able, take over his or her old territory. In accepting such a plan, the salesperson remains a company employee, which precludes the person from going to work for a competitor. It also gives the individual the opportunity to improve his or her Social Security base.

Terminating Salespeople

Companies follow different practices as to termination compensation policies. Some have formal contracts with their salespeople stipulating the program that is to be followed; others have verbal understandings, while many have no stated policy.

With salaried salespeople, many companies expect their salespeople to give from two weeks' to three months' notice before leaving, in order that the company may arrange for replacements. If the salespeople are permitted to leave before that period is up, they receive their full salaries for the period agreed upon. If they leave without notice, many companies merely pay them up to the time of their leaving. Some contracts stipulate that where a salesperson is fired for cause, he or she receives salary compensation up to the time of being fired.

With commission payments, some companies allow commission only on orders that have been shipped prior to the time of the salesperson's leaving the company. Other companies pay commissions on all business written by the salesperson prior to leaving and shipped within a specified time after his departure. The length of time depends on the type of product sold and the amount of work usually required to close an order. It is advisable to get this down on paper.

Commissions to departing salespeople are sometimes paid on sales entered, but usually on sales shipped less deductions and allowance, the thinking being that a sale is not completed until it is shipped or even paid for.

Profitability of Sales

Many different concepts have been voiced, along with many attempted formulas too numerous to describe in detail here. Top management pressures for profitable sales increases. Profitability of sales an be uneasy and unfamiliar ground for many sales executives. It demands new rules and definitions of the cost of doing business in a given sales territory. It requires a long hard look at advertising's role and cost in producing sales. It demands looking at alternate forms of selling, such as direct mail, telemarketing, and servicing. It means accumulating many more facts regarding cost of product and cost of sales activities, and deciding which—if any—home office functions should be included in the cost of a sale (R & D, overhead, order processing, etc.).

In Dartnell's 24th Biennial Survey of Sales Force Compensation, respondents were asked: "Have you introduced a profitability of sales measure in your compensation program? Here is a representative sampling of their responses, which show the irreversible trend away from compensating on sales volume alone.

- We do construction work in industrial plants and pay commissions based on net profits on each job.

- Yes, we have a sliding commission program based on the margin of profit per account.

- Yes, bonus formula is tied to profit index—the better the profit, the larger the multiplier.

- Our commission is set up as a percentage of profit on each sale. Salespeople know the profit of each item sold.

- Part of each bonus (50 percent) will be discretionary, based upon a minimum overall gross profit in the territory.

- The commission percentage increases the profitability of the order increases.

- Yes, we may reduce profit margins on a job to win it. However, the salesperson may also have to take a lower commission. It's up to the salesperson to decide.

- All commission is based on percentage of gross profit of the sales (discounts are charged back).

- We have a graduated commission schedule for increased sales volume.

- Bonus is based on profitability of sales territory.

- We have established a Salesman of Year award with six computerized categories—total sales, percent increase, monthly specials sold, workdays missed/worked, profitability, and costs per cars registered in territory.

- Salespeople get override on their own commissions after meeting quota.

- Commissions are paid on a sliding scale for gross profit margin on lump sum jobs only.

- Our sales compensation program is based on value added (no outside purchases included). Sales volume booked by account and annualized for one year determines salary plus 3 percent to 1 percent commission on contracts sold.

- Salesperson is paid an increasing share of profits after a lease is met.

- No credit is given orders below a certain profit.

- As calculated by computer, under 10 percent profit pays no commissions.

- We measure sales versus expenses versus discounts.

- Yes, based on highest percent of gross margin.

- Yes, sales with less than 20 percent gross profit are paid a lower commission rate.

- It's built in. The salespeople get 20 percent of the gross profit.

- Salespeople are subject to quarterly review showing activity versus results and weekly review during the first 12 months.

- Salespeople are paid through gross profit only—not sales volume.

Chapter 45

Contracts with Salespeople

At one time, the process of hiring a salesperson consisted of the application form, the interview, and the decision. Today, legal considerations are involved.

The enactment of federal and state laws affecting the relationship between the company and its salespeople has made it important that all employment agreements be put in writing. This not only avoids misunderstandings between employer and employee, but establishes the salesperson's status under the law.

Because of the trend of government to regulate employer-employee relationships, some employers utilize salespeople as independent contractors rather than as employees of the company. In such cases both the employment agreement and all correspondence with the salesperson or sales agent must support the independent contractor status, and neither the basic agreement nor subsequent correspondence should attempt in any way to control the salesperson's time. In fact, the agreement should state, "The company does not exercise any control over the amount of time the agent devotes to the sale of its products, the number of other lines handled, or the methods used in canvassing the agent's territory." Such a clause establishes the agent's independence of action.

Another consideration in determining whether salespeople shall operate as regular employees or as independent contractors is the company's liability for acts of the salesperson, as, for example, automobile accidents and injuries. Modern courts hold that the term *independent contractor* signifies one who contracts to do work acording to his or her own methods and without being subject to the broad control of his or her employer. In other words, an independent contractor is a person who contracts with another to do something but who is not controlled by the latter as to how or when he or she does the work. However, the employer has the legal right to discharge an independent contractor who does not perform work satisfactorily, or in accordance with prior agreements.

Not long ago a higher court said that the real test of an independent contractor is whether the employer has any authoritative control with respect to the manner in which the details of the work are to be performed.

For example, in the case of *Peterson* v. *Brinn & Jensen Company,* 277 N.W. 82, it was disclosed that a salesman named Porter used his own automobile and covered his territory about every five weeks. He made sales and collections for his employer. He was paid a commission computed on the gross profit to the company on his orders, and against this he had a drawing account. If at any time the company was dissatisfied with his work he could be discharged.

One day the salesman negligently drove his automobile in collision with another car, seriously injuring the occupants, who sued the salesman's employer to recover damages.

When discussing the distinctions between a legal employee and an independent contractor, the court said that under the above arrangement the salesman was an independent contractor. Therefore, in holding the employer not liable, the court said:

"The ultimate test (of whether a salesperson is an independent contractor) is determined by the control reserved in the employer. However, in some forms of employment the management (employer) reserves the right to give the most detailed instruction as to the manner and form in which the work is accomplished, even though there is no doubt whatever that the person so directed and instructed is an independent contractor."

Therefore, according to this decision, the fact that an employer instructs a salesperson in detail as to how to solicit orders or business does not in the least interfere with their legal relationship of employer and independent contractor.

Notwithstanding the holding of the higher court in this case, there are on record many decisions to the effect that a traveling salesperson is a legal employee although he or she is paid on a commission basis. Among these is *Riggs* v. *Standard,* 130 F. 199. In this case a salesman was paid on a commission basis, but the employer treated him as a salaried employee. Therefore, he was held *not* to be an independent contractor.

Nature of Employment

While the contract must specify the kind of employment to be given, it is well not to be too specific. In general contracts the nature of employment is purposely very vague. In sales agreements it is usual to specify the products that the salesperson is to sell, thus protecting a territory should a new product be brought out later that the company might wish to sell through a different sales organization. The territory is definitely described, and if there are to be any exceptions or limitations as to the type of trade the salesperson is to sell, exceptions should be specifically set forth in the body of the contract.

Many companies have found it good practice to incorporate a clause that the employee agrees to devote his or her full time to the work. While it is possible that the company will never wish to take advantage of such a clause, nevertheless it has a valuable moral effect and would give the company certain rights in that which an employee might develop while in the company's employ. If, however, there is a possibility of that a separate clause should be used to cover that contingency. A full-time clause used in employment contracts of NCR Corporation follows:

"Said employee agrees to devote his or her full time and best endeavor to the business of the company, under the direction of its officers and representatives, and to conform to the rules, regulations, and instructions of the company now in force, or that may hereafter be adopted and mailed to said employee."

Compensation of Employee

It is particularly important that this clause be most specific. There are many opportunities for misunderstandings about compensation. For example, the right of employer to charge commissions on credit losses to salespeople can be challenged, and the courts have held that employers have no right to hold salespeople responsible for credit losses in the absence of a contract covering that point. It should be clearly set forth that the salesperson's commissions are not earned until the sale has been completed (i.e., money collected) and that any commission paid prior to the completion of the sale is in the nature of an advance. The most approved method of protecting the company against paying commissions on incompleted orders is to word the clause as follows:

"Said employee, during his or her continuation in the employment of the company under this contract, shall receive a commission on all monies received from the sales of products sold for the company in the aforementioned territory, as follows:

(Tabulation of Commission Rates)

"Said employee agrees commission shall not be credited to his or her account on the company's books until the purchaser has made settlement in full for cash or acceptable notes, in which case the company may withhold payment of the commission, wholly or in part, until the notes are paid."

The above clauses are taken from a contract used by one of the largest corporations in the country.

It is common practice in drawing contracts with salespeople to agree to pay a commission on sales. Unless the agreement is specific in defining what is meant by sales, the court will construe the agreement in any number of ways. The courts have held that a salesperson completed his or her responsibility by writing up an order and mailing it to the office. This, of course, is seldom what a sales manager has in mind. He or she is thinking in terms of accepted orders, but the order blank does not specify, as it should, that the order is not an order until accepted by a duly authorized officer of the company at the home office. In one case a salesman's contract provided that he receive commissions on all "sales" within a named territory. He had secured orders under this contract that were not filled until after its termination. The employer maintained that "sales" referred to deliveries; that since deliveries were made after the salesman's employment had ended he did not make the sales and was entitled to no commission.

"We do not agree," said the court. "The word 'sale' or 'sales' does not always include deliveries. These words are constantly used as meaning or including a contract to sell or contract to buy. The salesman's duty was discharged when the contracts or orders were closed and forwarded to his employer. It is simply a question whether he shall be paid for services fully rendered before his discharge and it is not material that the commissions did not become due until after the termination of his contract."

From a lack of understanding between employer and salesperson, not only regarding when the commission is earned but when it is payable as well, come the suspicions and distrust that sap the loyalty of any sales organization.

Profit-sharing agreements, both commission agreements with salespeople and agents or profit-sharing agreements with executives and other employees, should carry a clause that requires complaints regarding the commissions or profits shown on the statement to be filed within 30 days. Such a clause is helpful in court, should an employee sue for an accounting after leaving the company's employ.

Authority of Employee

Under the law an employee's position carries with it certain rights of contract. Frequent decisions have held that when a corporation appoints a sales manager and gives him or her the authority to use such a title, it then automatically confers upon that individual the right to enter into contracts necessary in the fulfillment of his or her duties, as, for example, the right to hire salespeople; to enter into advertising contracts; and to do all those things that are essential to managing sales. The same is true in the case of a purchasing agent. The mere granting of the title conveys the authority to enter into purchase agreements, unless a contract limiting the duties of the employee exists.

As a protection to the company against representatives who might be inclined to exceed their authority in such directions, it is well to incorporate a clause in all employment contracts specifically stating that the acts of employees are not binding unless ratified by the company. And in the case of salespeople, it should be clearly set forth that no order is binding until it has been accepted by the company. If this is not done, you may find yourself entangled with state laws that hold that you are doing business in their states and that a portion of your business is subject to certain taxes. In a contract of NCR Corp., a clause is included to cover this point, as follows:

"When an order is taken, the same shall not be binding until accepted by the company. The company reserves the right to reject an order when in its judgment the register may not be suitable to the business of the customer. The company agrees to fill all orders accepted with practical dispatch according to the instructions endorsed thereon, but failure to do so from any cause shall not make it liable for any commissions thereon."

Drawing Accounts

Where the employment contract calls for the establishment of an account to which profits or commissions will be credited periodically, and against which the employee is permitted to make periodic draws, provision should be made to cover the possibility of overdrafts. There have been a number of different rulings, in different states, as to the ability of an employer to collect monies advanced against such drawing accounts.

Generally speaking, an overdraft cannot be collected unless it has been specifically agreed that it would be repaid, that it is in the nature of a personal loan, or where notes have been given. Without such understanding the court is likely to hold that it was a business partnership, in which the company agreed to finance the employee, and any resulting loss was in the nature of a business loss.

If it is the desire or intention of the employer to treat overdrafts against drawing accounts as a loan to be set up on the books of the company as an asset, it is imperative that a note should be secured from the salesperson for the specific amount of the overdraft and, if possible, that it should be endorsed by some responsible person. In that case it is well to cover that point in the contract. The following clause is taken from an agreement used by an oil heating company:

"The company will allow a salesperson to borrow or draw $_____ a week for which he or she will give the company his or her personal note to apply against and be deducted from commission credit. This note is payable on demand and may only be satisfied by payment thereof."

Agreements Covering Reports

While it is obviously foolish to expect that getting a salesperson to sign an agreement to make periodic reports to the office will entirely solve the report problem, it will help materially. If deemed advisable, a clause covering that point, under the broad title of "Absence from Territory," should be inserted just ahead of the clause relating to the employee's duties.

Some agreements are very definite on this point. One reads: "This contract shall be null and void if second party (salesperson) does not make complete and full daily reports of all work on company's regular blank for that purpose."

Duties of Employee

The principal advantage of such a clause is to familiarize an employee with the policies of the company and the objective of the business. In the case of general employees the employee merely agrees to adhere to stated policies. It is in the nature of taking an oath of office. In the case of salespeople and employees engaged to do a specific job, the various phases of that job, in the order of their importance, should be set down, so that there can never be any question as to just what the salesperson is being paid to do.

In addition to living up to the company's standards of practice and its rules and regulations, points to be covered in defining the duties of a salesperson should include: 1) maintenance of price, 2) avoidance of any statements that will incriminate the company, 3) giving the company the benefit of any information that will help other salespeople, 4) care of samples, 5) collection and credit cooperation, 6) advertising cooperation, 7) agreement not to handle side lines, 8) agreement to give fidelity bond if required, and 9) cooperation with the home office in every possible way.

Salespeople's Samples

A matter upon which many disagreements have arisen and which should be clearly defined in an agreement with salespeople is the responsibility for samples. The following clauses, taken from the employment contract of Coopers, Inc., of Kenosha, Wisconsin, may be of interest in that connection:

"Coopers, Inc., will furnish the salesperson on memorandum charge, as it may deem necessary, trunks, sample cases, sample garments, hosiery, swatches of fabric and swatch book covers, price lists with covers, order books with covers, stationery, business cards, and other supplies, which will aid the salesperson in properly exhibiting, soliciting for, and in selling Coopers, Inc., products. All such supplies so furnished by Coopers, Inc., shall at all times remain the property of Coopers, Inc., and shall be returned on demand or upon the termination of this agreement. The salesperson agrees to conduct all correspondence and dealings with customers, in connection with the sale of goods, on stationery furnished by Coopers, Inc.

"The salesperson is obligated to return the sample cases, trunks, and other supplies in good condition and to use his best efforts to protect such supplies from waste, damage, and destruction. Upon demand for the return of such supplies or upon the termination of this agreement, the salesperson agrees to return such supplies to the office of Coopers, Inc., in Kenosha, Wisconsin, including all old or used order books, files of correspondence, original letters received from customers, and copies of letters sent by the salesperson relating to the business of Coopers, Inc. For all supplies not returned, the salesperson will pay to Coopers, Inc., the invoice price thereof."

Stealing Customers

Is it possible to make an agreement governing an employee's actions after he leaves your employ? Will such contracts hold water? The courts do not like these contracts, but will enforce them when they are reasonable, because they afford the only way by which the owner of a business can guard against appropriation by former employees.

It is important, however, that such a clause be so worded that it will not deprive an employee of his or her right of livelihood. For example, if the contract prevents a person from following the only trade he or she knows throughout the entire United States, it could probably not be enforced. But if consideration for the employee's rights were shown by giving him or her the right to follow his or her trade in two states, say Arizona and Utah, then it would have a much better chance to be enforced.

The New York State Court of Appeals upheld the case of *Altschuler-Baterson Company* v. *Markowitz* on a contract containing a clause of this kind. The specific wording of the clause was as follows:

"That for a period of 12 months after the termination of his or her employment, for any cause whatsoever, the party of the second part will not, directly or indirectly as employer, employee, or otherwise, engage in the brokerage business of fire insurance, life, marine, accident, fidelity, employers' liability, burglary, plate-glass insurance, and all other kinds of insurance, and in such other business similar thereto, nor act in aid of the business of any rival or competing person, firm or corporation in the same or similar business within the boroughs of Manhattan, Brooklyn, Bronx, Richmond, and Queens in the city of New York."

Businesspeople should take care, however, not to make such agreements unreasonably stringent. Anything that goes beyond proper protection is a restriction upon the right of an employee to make a living. It must be limited both as to time and territory and the limitations in both cases must be reasonable.

Should a contract get into court, it will have a much better chance of being enforced if it seems to be an instrument in the employee's interest. The natural sympathy of the court and the jury is with the employee. This point is not generally appreciated, and contracts that are preponderantly in the interests of the house are frequently nullified in court as being unduly stringent.

In the case of salespeople's contracts the following points should be covered for the protection of the employee: 1) agreement by the company not to put another salesperson in the specified territory, 2) arrangement of split-commission sales, 3) notice from the company regarding termination of contract, 4) payment of commissions in event of the salesperson's death, 5) cooperation and equipment furnished by the house, and 6) agreement not to reduce territories.

Termination Agreements

An examination of court records discloses that a very large percentage of cases filed against employers by employees who have been dismissed are the result of a misunderstanding as to the termination of employment. Several companies have reported that clauses to cover the matter of a salesperson's leaving the employ of the company are the most important of all clauses that go to make up an employment agreement. In fact, some of them consider this matter sufficiently important to make it the basis of their entire agreement with their salespeople. Hotel expenses in the headquarters town and the payment of any balance due in case of the salesperson's death may be the only other matters covered by such an agreement.

Common practice in all employment contracts that are in the nature of a running agreement is to provide for cancellation by either party giving advance notice in writing. The method of cancellation is important, because it is a point of attack often used by lawyers in breaking down employment contracts. The following points should be incorporated in the termination clause:

1. Thirty days' notice shall begin when the letter or telegram is placed in the hands of the post office or telegraph company.

2. Notice waived if in the sole judgment of the company the employee has been guilty of a breach of trust, neglect of the company's interests, or acts detrimental to the company's interest.

3. Methods of final settlement, in the case of commission salespeople or profit-sharing employees.

In the event the procedure for termination is not specifically covered in the contract, the court will hold, as it has in test cases, that cancellation does not become effective until the *receipt* of the letter of notification. In the famous decision of the Supreme Court of Iowa, *Oldfield* v. *Chevrolet Motor Company of Nebraska,* 199 N.W. 161, the contract did not state the period it would remain in force but contained the wording: "Either party may cancel this contract by five days' written notice to the other."

The company wrote to the salesperson stating: "We are canceling your selling agreement with this company. This is in accordance with Clause No. 8 in your contract, and the cancellation becomes effective *within* five days from the date of this letter." The court held that the method used by the company to effect cancellation was not in accordance with the termination clause of the contract and awarded damages to the plaintiff. In this particular case great importance was attached to the use of the word "within," which was held to be contrary to the spirit of the agreement.

Termination of Commission Contracts

There are probably more lawsuits over unpaid commissions after expiration of a contract than any other one thing. Unless this is covered fully, a large area for misunderstanding between the salesperson and company is left open. A striking instance of this sort arose in a controversy between the Knox Hats Division of New York City and a sales agent for that company. The commissions were 10 percent on all sales up to $150,000 and 2 percent on sales in excess of that amount. The contract provided a definite date for termination. Some months before that time the contract was ended "by the consent and agreement of both parties." At that time about $6,000 of commissions had been earned but were not payable until later.

These the company refused to pay, insisting that the rescission of the contract absolved them from liability, since no stipulation for payment of these items had been made when the contract had been terminated. In this they were sustained by the court.

"When the performance of a contract consists in doing on one side and in giving on the other, the doing must take place before the giving. In all contracts for services, therefore, the presumption is that the performance of the service is a condition precedent to the payment for it."

The obligations, both of the salesperson and the employer, had ended with the cancellation of the contract. The unpaid commissions, then, became a mere gratuity, for which the salesperson was rendering no services to the company and which the former employer was under no obligation to pay.

In every salesperson's commission contract these three essentials must be outlined in unmistakable detailed terms and with scrupulous care: 1) the circumstances that determine when the commissions are earned—whether on receipt of the order by the salesperson, on its acceptance by the employer, on the shipment of the goods, or on whatever incident that may be agreed upon; 2) the event on which commissions are payable; 3) a simple, clear setting forth of the disposition of unpaid commissions on the termination of employment.

Providing Against Contradictory State Laws

Many companies using employment contracts in national operations, knowing the conflicting state laws that exist governing many phases of employee relations, insert in their contracts a clause to the effect that in case of dispute the laws of the state in which the company is incorporated apply.

Exclusive Agency Agreements

While the passage of the Clayton Act made illegal many of the agreements that had been used in establishing exclusive agencies, it is still possible to make exclusive contracts with dealers or agents that are not in violation of the provisions of the statute. If your contract does not "substantially lessen competition or tend to create a monopoly" in your line, it violates no provision of the Clayton Act.

It has been held by the Supreme Court (*Standard Fashion Company* v. *Magrane-Houston Company,* 42 Supreme Court 360) that any contract that limits the dealer to a single line is illegal, provided the dealer still maintains his or her status as an independent merchant. In the case cited above the dealer had entered into an agreement whereby he was to become the agent of the Standard Fashion Company for the sale of dress patterns. As a part of the agreement, the dealer was obliged to take and pay for a certain number of patterns and maintain a certain stock on hand at all times. In the event that any of these patterns were not sold, they could be returned to the original seller and an allowance, less than the original price, was to be credited to the dealer. The dealer further agreed that he would not sell or permit to be sold in his store any other patterns of any competitor while this agreement was in force.

The court held that this was not a joint venture, but that when the dealer bought and paid for the patterns they belonged to him. Any agreement that put any limitation on his freedom as an independent merchant was a direct violation of the act and therefore illegal.

For an exclusive agency agreement to be legal, therefore, it must either make the dealer or representative an agent in fact, or it must be binding only on the manufacturer.

It is possible, however, to appoint a dealer an exclusive agent and still be within legal bounds. Where this is done, the contract must be so drawn as to leave the principal the actual owner of the goods and to limit the action of the dealer to that authorized in the agency agreement. It is possible to stipulate in such a contract that the agent, in return for the agency, may be required to carry a given stock or to meet any other requirement. The point is that the dealer must, under the contract, lose his or her status as a general dealer and become, in fact, an agent. In such an agreement it is possible for the principal to decide whether he wants his or her agent to sell more than one line.

Many firms, however, find that an agency agreement is just as effective when their contracts limit them alone as it was when it used to apply to both parties. Such agreements provide that the manufacturer will grant to a dealer the exclusive right to sell products in a given area, set up the conditions under which this right is granted, and leave the merchant absolutely free to sell any other or as many other competitive lines as desired. If the agreement is carefully drawn as to terms, amount of stock to be carried, and rights to be enjoyed, the ultimate effect of such an agreement is about the same as if the dealer had agreed not to offer a competitor's stock. But, in fact, the dealer is not under any obligations to refrain from doing so, and so long as he remains in that status there is no violation of the Clayton Act.

Sales on Contracts

In many lines of business, such as office appliances, machinery, equipment, musical instruments, and so forth, the ultimate sale to the user is based on a contract, partial payment, or otherwise. In such cases the salesperson or distributor not only sells the goods, but establishes legal relationships between company and its customers. For the protection of the company's rights it is necessary that the acts of its representatives in this respect be rigidly controlled, and in the case of disputes it must be able to show exactly how far the authority of its representatives extended.

The same considerations apply where valuable patent rights are involved. Patent rights are sometimes adversely affected by acts of salespersons or agents, and it is essential to be able to show exactly what authority is delegated and what is not.

Following is a typical sales-representative contract used by a manufacturing company. Other sales contracts will be found in the Ready-Reference Section.

Figure 1. Klinger Sales-Representative Agreement

In consideration of my employment or continued employment by Klinger Manufacturing Company and of the salary, commission, and other benefits received or to be received by me in connection with such employment, it is agreed as follows:

1. During my employment I shall devote my best efforts and full time to the performance of such duties as are assigned to me as sales representative and shall comply with all policies and instructions promulgated by Klinger.

2. I agree to such salary, commission, bonus rates, and methods of payment as may be established from time to time.

3. Although commissions may be paid to me upon shipment of the merchandise, commissions will not be considered as earned until such time as the merchandise has been shipped, installed, and customers' invoices have been paid in full. I shall not be entitled to commissions or bonuses on merchandise returned or refused by a customer and acknowledge that the decision as to accepting any such return or refusal shall be in the sole discretion of Klinger. Further, I shall not hold Klinger liable in any way for failure to meet a delivery date or for defects in merchandise or for any other factor that may

(continued)

Figure 1. Klinger Sales-Representative Agreement
(continued)

create any such return, refusal, or any delinquent account. Any commissions or bonuses that have been paid upon shipment of merchandise shall be charged back against my account in the event of a subsequent return or refusal to accept delivery by the customer or in the event of a customer's delinquency in payment.

4. Upon termination of my employment, I shall immediately return to Klinger all property of Klinger in as good condition as when received by me (normal wear and tear excepted) including records, manuals, promotion materials, equipment, and supplies. For my failure to do so, I shall be liable to Klinger for the following amounts:

   - Equipment and supplies—Klinger list price

   - Sales manuals, brochures, and promotional materials—$50.00

   - Customer lists and records pertaining to customer accounts—the monetary value thereof to Klinger

   I authorize Klinger to charge any such amounts of liability against my account.

5. Upon termination of my employment, my final compensation payments shall be made as follows:

   - My final salary payment, prorated to the date of termination, shall be paid on the next regular pay day following receipt of notification of such termination by the payroll department.

   - My final commission payment shall not be made to me until a reasonable period of time not in excess of 120 days following termination, to make necessary adjustments for returns, cancellations, allowances, delinquent accounts, and any other similar adjustment item. Any merchandise not fully paid for at the end of said 120-day period shall be considered a delinquent account to the extent of the unpaid amount. In the case of orders obtained by me prior to termination but shipped and fully paid for within said 120 days after termination, I shall receive full commission on any such orders for supplies and one-half (½) commission on any such order for equipment (the other one-half commission to be payable to my successor, who shall have the responsibility for installation, instruction, and servicing).

   - No quarterly bonus payments, Director's Club awards, or payments, or sales-promotion contest awards or payments, shall be made subsequent to the date of termination. I understand and

(continued)

Figure 1. Klinger Sales-Representative Agreement

(continued)

agree that I must be employed by Klinger on the payment date of any quarterly bonuses, special payments and awards in order to be eligible to receive such payments and awards.

6. While employed by Klinger, I will acquire a certain amount of confidential information regarding its business, including but not limited to the following: the names and addresses and purchasing history of Klinger's customers; the name and other pertinent data concerning the persons responsible for purchasing for such customers; the particular needs and applications of such customers for Klinger products and other stationery products and business equipment; information relating to Klinger products, whether presently marketed or in the process of development; research developments, marketing practices, and other business data. This confidential information is a valuable property of Klinger and has been developed over a period of years at great expense to Klinger. Accordingly, I agree that I will not at any time either during or after my employment with Klinger disclose any such confidential information to any third party, or to make any use whatever of such confidential information in any manner detrimental to Klinger, particularly the use of such confidential information in connection with any business activities in competition with Klinger.

7. For a period of one year following the termination of my employment with Klinger, I shall not, directly or indirectly, within any sales territory or within a 25-mile radius of any such territory in which I may have worked for Klinger at any time during the 18-month period prior to termination of my employment with Klinger, accept employment, consult with, or become associated or affiliated with any person, sole proprietorship, partnership or corporation, in any capacity, involving activities competitive to Klinger in the laminating or punch-and-bind product industries, or otherwise engage in such competitive activities on my own account.

   Without limiting the generality of the foregoing, it is specifically agreed that during such one year period I shall not call on, contact, or communicate with, for any purpose whatsoever, any customers or former customers of Klinger.

8. I agree and acknowledge that the above confidential information nondisclosure and noncompeting convenants are reasonable in that they give Klinger the protection to which it is entitled and yet do not impair my ability to earn a livelihood. Further, since a violation by me

(continued)

Figure 1. Klinger Sales-Representative Agreement
(continued)

of these covenants would result in immediate and irreparable damage to Klinger, I hereby expressly consent to and waive any objections to Klinger obtaining immediate injunctive relief in a court of law in the event of any such violation, such injunctive relief to be in addition to any rights to damages and any other rights available to Klinger under the law.

9. I understand that I shall have no authority to enter into any contract or agreement on behalf of Klinger or to make collections of accounts for Klinger except where I am given specific written authorization by an officer of Klinger.

10. I agree to abide and be bound by the bylaws and rules and regulations of the Klinger Director's Club as they now exist and as they may be amended from time to time in the future.

11. In the event that any provision of this agreement should be deemed to be unenforceable or void, such invalidity of unenforceability shall not affect the validity or enforceability of any other provision hereof.

12. It is agreed that the provisions of this agreement contain the entire agreement between the parties and cannot be changed, modified, or added to except by a written agreement signed by me and by an officer of Klinger.

Approved and Accepted:

KLINGER MANUFACTURING CO.

By: . . . .

Dated: . . . .

. . . .
Sales Representative

Dated: . . . .

Chapter 46

Motivating the Sales Force

The efforts of the individual members of a sales organization are in direct proportion to their motivation. This aspect of sales management is receiving new and greater emphasis in many companies. It has long been proven that the only true motivation is self-motivation. Motivation calls for creating a climate in which the salesperson becomes motivated by the incentives provided by sales management.

There are many ways to stimulate salespeople to greater effort. As previously pointed out, money is not the sole consideration, although financial reward is a powerful driving force. However, the desire for promotion, the esteem of associates, the yearning for recognition, and the self-satisfaction derived from excellence in any field are all motivating forces.

Motivational incentives can be financial, nonfinancial, or a combination of both:

1. *Security.*

   - The assurance of steady employment

   - Opportunities for advancement

   - Training programs that help to ensure he or she will know what and how to do the job

2. *Advancement.*

   - Salary increases

   - The acquiring of new responsibilities

   - Promotions

   - Increased authority

3. *Success symbols.*

- Recognition in company publications
- Prizes
- Awards
- Titles

4. *Ego-building activities.*

- Special assignments
- Praise for outstanding achievements
- Freedom to try new methods, techniques, and ideas
- Demonstration of respect for the individual's intelligence and initiative

5. *Cordial environment.*

- Acceptance by other employees
- Good rapport with managers and supervisors
- Friendly relations with customers

6. *Personal development.*

- The chance to grow into bigger jobs
- Education and training opportunities

Nonfinancial Methods

Nonfinancial methods of motivation are defined as those techniques that principally provide salespeople with recognition, status, and a sense of group belonging. These types of rewards are generally referred to as *psychic income.*

Periodic or ongoing actions that provide the climate for self-motivation include:

- Distinguished sales award
- Honorary job titles

- Publicity
- Personal letters of commendation
- Published sales results
- Telephone calls of commendation
- Face-to-face encouragement
- Individual help with responsibilities
- Honor societies
- Management by objectives

Respondents to a Dartnell survey were asked to indicate the broad nonfinancial methods used with their sales forces. The results are shown in Table 1 on page 1067.

All companies ranked fairly high in the usual traditional methods. Heading the list is face-to-face encouragement, which 93.5 percent of the companies utilized. This is followed by sales meetings (92 percent) and training programs (72.5 percent). After these methods, the percentages fall off.

Sales executives are not utilizing the many forms of nonfinancial motivational methods to best advantage. Personal recognition and encouragement are potent forces. It would appear that sales executives are not getting the most out of the techniques available to them. While it is difficult to compute the lack of effort, amount of lost sales, and the degree of dissatisfaction of the unmotivated salesperson, it's a safe bet that all three areas would show substantial improvement with increased effort by management.

Motivational Studies

A research study of a respected research firm of 5,000 consumer and industrial salespeople determined that the following management practices are key to the high morale that distinguishes an organization of salespeople who are well motivated.

- The organization must be supplied with the necessary product training, with information updated as external and internal changes occur.

Table 1. Nonfinancial Incentives
Percent of All Companies Using

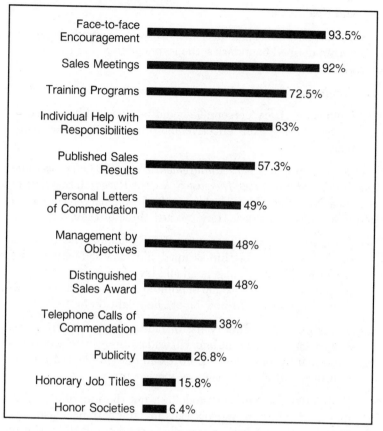

- Salespeople must be trained in the skills of professional selling.

- Salespeople must be given credit and recognition for noteworthy sales performances.

- Salespeople should be offered the opportunity to provide input in sales planning.

- Activities and performance results should be evaluated regularly as a device for informing salespeople of their strengths and weaknesses.

- To the greatest degree possible, salespeople should be given, within defined boundaries, the responsibility and freedom to make their own decisions.

- Compensation should be consistent with sales contribution.

- Field supervisory personnel should be thoroughly trained to enable them to exert effective and professional management techniques.

In a special report, *Sales Management Plus: How to Uncover and Use Hidden Motivators to Increase Sales,* the Research Institute of America, New York, New York, some basic managerial courses of action are recommended. Here are just three of them.

- Act more like a partner than a critic. Remember that problem producers tend to be thin-skinned, have low self-esteem, and resent criticism. Managers should try to treat the weak performer as an equal. Instead of pointed criticism, ask the worker for suggestions on how he or she might do better.

- Never present a laundry list of faults to a poor performer. Such a list is demeaning and will lead more easily to defensiveness than to improvement. Focus on one problem at a time; improvement is also easier by increments.

- Emphasize the work methodology, not the individual's failings. Criticizing the person leads inevitably to backlash. Try changing the worker's approach to the job ("I'd like you to make six appointments a day instead of four," for example). It's more constructive and less threatening.

Another study on motivating salespeople by Halliday Clark, Ph.D. in Business Administration, California Coast University, Santa Ana, California, was reported in Dartnell's *Sales & Marketing Executive Report.* Dr. Clark contends that it is possible to increase the sales productivity of at least 40 percent of the sales force that falls into the gray area between the top one-third of producers and the bottom 20 percent.

The key, says Dr. Clark, lies in communication—how well the sales job is understood and how well the sales rep understands what is expected. The relationship between the sales manager and the salesperson is crucial but often neglected.

How do sales reps view themselves? How do sales managers view sales reps? To answer these important questions, Dr. Clark polled 209 wholesale and industrial sales managers and sales reps. Here are some highlights of the study. Due to multiple answers, percentages frequently total more than 100 percent.

QUESTIONNAIRE ON MOTIVATION FOR SALES REPS

Beyond a satisfying pay scale, sales reps were asked what, in their opinion, offered them the *most* incentive to do their jobs. Of the reps polled, 72 percent said self-esteem was very important, followed by bonus (62 percent), approval of superiors (55 percent), peer approval (47 percent), promotion or new title (45 percent). Seventy percent of the reps viewed special awards as *least* important, followed by "spiffs" (65 percent), extra paid vacations (58 percent), and trips to exotic places (57 percent).

Of the reps polled, 62 percent said they understood company rules very well and 32 percent said they understood company rules moderately well. A whopping 90 percent considered themselves to be motivated. Motivating these reps were economic ambition (73 percent), desire for independence (48 percent), need for achievement of status in the company (35 percent), and a need to be looked up to by the company and peers (33 percent). Only 2 percent of the reps indicated a need for "perks."

When reps were asked what, in their opinion, made it hardest to close the sale, the vast majority said it was hard to know when the buyer was ready. Threat of rejection by the buyer and feelings of insecurity tied for second place.

Interestingly, the reps were quite vocal when asked what the most important ingredients were in making a sale. Timing was rated very important by 73 percent of the reps responding, followed by gaining the buyer's confidence (70 percent), talking to the decision-maker (67 percent), sizing up need for the product or service (60 percent), selling yourself, then the product (55 percent), and laying out a program for the buyer (48 percent). Twenty-five percent of the reps responding said they wanted to do a better job, but needed more help from their superior. Twenty percent said they had many fears about the job and 33 percent wanted to be consulted more on the job and asked more frequently for their opinion.

When asked why they thought some sales reps shy away from big accounts, 58 percent of the reps said "failure to understand how a big account works." Fifty-five percent cited fear of rejection. Not surprisingly, 81 percent of the reps thought "above average income" was very important to them.

The reps appeared to be quite honest in describing themselves as sales reps: 80 percent felt they were economically motivated while only 13 percent thought they were altruistically motivated.

QUESTIONNAIRE ON MOTIVATION FOR SALES MANAGERS

When sales managers were asked what, beyond a satisfying pay scale, offered the most incentive (motivation) to their sales forces, self-esteem was the overwhelming favorite of 85 percent of the managers responding. Bonus was second (58 percent), followed by peer approval (48 percent) and approval of superior (55 percent). Special awards, "spiffs," and trips to exotic places were not considered very important as motivators.

Sales managers felt their top sales reps were very strongly motivated by economic ambition (88 percent) and the desire for independence (47 percent). Factors sales managers thought provided the strongest motivation for most sales reps were, in descending order of importance, extra pay, praise for a job well done, desire to be better than anyone else and a special non-monetary award.

CLOSING THE SALE

The sales managers responding to the question, "Why is it so hard for the average sales rep to close the sale?" ranked "Doesn't know when the buyer is ready, or can't sense it" number one. In second place is "Doesn't know how to ask for the order" followed by "Doesn't know when to stop talking" and "Doesn't lay out all benefits for the buyer."

INGREDIENTS IN A SUCCESSFUL SALE

The most important ingredient in making the sale, according to the managers, is gaining confidence of the buyer (91 percent), followed by sizing up the need for the product or service (61 percent), timing (60 percent), and laying out a program for the buyer (56 percent).

In addition to the questionnaire survey, Dr. Clark interviewed eight corporations on an in-depth basis to determine how they were handling sales force motivation.

MOTIVATION AND TRAINING PROGRAMS

Three out of the eight corporations do not have a formalized motivation program, but all provide training programs of which motivation is a part.

DEFINITION OF MOTIVATION

Each individual company had their own definition of motivation, but five out of the eight felt that motivation "tends to come from within the individual. The individual must motivate him- or herself, providing the company provides the proper climate to encourage growth and achievement." Most companies agreed that communication was something that required constant attention and review.

CONCLUSIONS

In order to increase sales productivity, Dr. Clark says, the manager must get to know a salesperson's likes and dislikes, goals and aspirations. Dr. Clark notes that sales reps want to do a better job but need help from their sales managers. "It is clear," says Dr. Clark, "that sales managers have to be more responsive to the needs of their sales reps."

Non-Cash Incentive Programs

Non-cash incentive programs can be a very effective motivational tool in a number of different areas and applications, according to Bruce Tepper, vice president of Trans Continental Incentives, San Mateo, California, in the following article written for Dartnell's *Sales & Marketing Executive Report*. He said they can help you increase sales, improve productivity and attendance, and reduce accidents.

Why use merchandise and travel?

In psychological research performed in recent decades, much evidence has emerged regarding human response to the environment. Once an individual has satisfied the basic needs (food, shelter, security, etc.), they respond to higher-level needs such as recognition and status. That's where merchandise and travel awards can help you.

Merchandise and travel awards:

1. are more memorable than cash. Your participants receive awards that are identified with your company as the source and remembered. Cash awards are spent on necessities and quickly forgotten.

2. provide a cumulative way to build toward large prizes for up to a year or more.

3. provide a special award that's different from compensation. Everyone gets paid in cash. Not everyone earns merchandise and travel.

4. are promotable. You can talk about the awards and the people who earn them. You cannot discuss pay checks on a public basis.

5. costs you less than cash. To motivate an employee with cash takes a substantial percentage of their income and can, in fact, be confused with their income. Merchandise and travel awards can be cumulative in nature, so that a small amount of money goes a long way.

6. are flexible. You can start and stop your program whenever you like and define very broad or narrow goals without upsetting compensation. Because you're not using cash, you're not likely to make salespeople feel they've lost something when the program is over or run afoul of a union contract in your plant.

There are some important things you should determine first, however, to see if merchandise and travel awards will work for you.

Can you determine precise goals?

To motivate people, they need to know what is expected of them. You'll need to offer precise goals, such as increasing sales by your salespeople, increasing purchasing by your distributors, or reducing accidents in the plant.

Your overall goal then, has to be broken down into individual or group goals for the program participants. If you cannot establish definite goals for a specific period of time, it will be difficult to implement your program.

Can you measure performance objectively?

It doesn't matter what your measurement standard is; it could be units sold, dollar volume of purchases or unit per hour output in the plant. What *is* important is that you establish a uniform and objective measurement system.

Your program participants need to know what progress they're making toward their goals and that they all have an opportunity to share the rewards. Subjective measurements and widely varying performance standards can reduce and defeat your purpose.

Are your targeted participants monetarily compensated adequately?

For merchandise and travel awards to be effective, your participants need to be compensated within general industry standards. If you're including company salespeople, that means a salary, bonus, commission, etc., that is in line with your industry. If it's a sales program for manufacturers' representatives, agents, or distributors, it means a wage and benefit packge in line with industry standards.

A non-cash incentive program is not effective when your participants feel that basic compensation is lacking. They will resent money being applied in this fashion. This doesn't mean you need to offer the highest wages or best commissions, only a package that would be considered competitive in your industry.

Is your product or service saleable?

A non-cash incentive program can help you improve sales. However, your product or service needs to have a useful and some desirability on the part of your customers. Merchandise and travel awards cannot help in getting rid of truly dead stock or pushing a service that seems to have no demand.

If you have a saleable product, adequate compensation package, objectively measurable standards, and specific goals, merchandise and travel awards can help.

How do you set your program in motion?

Program applications are as broad and varied as your imagination permits. Previously, we talked about the need for precise goals that are objectively measurable. Any need you have that meets these criteria is suitable.

Typical sales programs might include:

1. Overall sales increase (measured in percentage over goal, dollars, units, etc.)

2. Promotion of specific products or services

3. Seasonal promotions

4. Better utilization of factory resources

5. Placement of displays for consumer products

6. Training seminar attendance

7. Securing order commitments or bookings

8. Promoting a new product or service

9. Improving collections

10. Making more cold calls or prospecting efforts, etc.

Typical non-sales applications could include:

1. Increased production output

2. Reduced absenteeism

3. Reduced lost time accidents

4. Increased effort on quality control

5. Increased number of employee suggestions

6. Cost containment programs and waste reduction, etc.

Setting the goals and designing the rules.

Your program rules should be designed to accomplish the goals you've selected.

First, you must decide what you want to accomplish.

Then you must determine who can best help you accomplish that goal. Should you target on your production people to increase output, your sales force to increase sales, your distributors to increase purchases, or all of them? Include those who have a direct impact on reaching the goal.

For example, if you need to increase inventories of your product at the distributor level, you might want a program targeted to your distributors to increase purchases and your sales force to promote sales. Can both of these groups help or is one or the other far more important in reaching the goal? Do sales management people have an impact and should they be included? Do you need to reach distributor salespeople as well? These areas can become complex and you might want to seek the advice of one of the professional incentive and motivation organizations to help you determine where your investment can be applied most effectively.

When do you want your program to run and for how long?

Make sure it's timed to meet your special requirements and long enough to accomplish your goals.

Your program should be long enough to allow everyone a chance to reach their goal (and yours), but not too long or it loses its impact. (You can run an incentive campaign indefinitely as long as you update the rules and keep your promotional efforts bright, vibrant, and interesting.)

It should reflect seasonal requirements that may exist and offer a sufficient award to entice your participants. For example, a financial institution would typically want a program of four to six months to pick up one or two rollover periods on certificates of deposit while still making an impact on their employees.

A manufacturing organization might want to run a basic program for a year to match its sales plan and introduce seasonal bonus awards on specific products. A safety program in the plant might run as long as 18 months without change to firmly establish the good habits necessary for an accident-free environment.

Your rules structure should reflect your specific needs, include the people who can contribute, and be timed to run when it's most effective. Again, professional advice is available to you from the major companies in the motivation and incentive industry.

What else is needed to make the program work?

Once you've set your objectives, determined the eligible participants, defined a rules structure, and created your awards package you're ready to roll.

To make sure your program works, you'll need to add two elements: administration and promotion.

Administration. Since we need to measure performance, you'll need to develop a system that accurately measures performance by your participants (perferably on an ongoing regular basis) and reports their performance to them. Your system might be a sophisticated data processing program or a simple manual tabulation once a month.

If you're measuring units sold, you might track sales on a monthly basis. In reporting results to your salespeople, you could:

1. Post results in a monthly mailing.

2. Send certificates of a certain value (cash value—it could be awarded credits toward a goal).

3. Issue checks in award credits with awards having specific values in credits.

4. Create a bank account for each participant and deposit "credits" on a regular basis.

Frequent and regular recognition of credit earned reinforces your program by keeping everyone involved. It is not important to divulge the cash value of the credit earned, as you want everyone to think in terms of work units for a particular award. Select a system that matches your requirements and make sure there is vigorous follow-through.

Promotion. An incentive program requires hype and enthusiasm to sustain interest, particularly if it's six months long or more. A carefully prepared campaign, with mailings reminding your participants of the program, can go a long way to making it a success.

Some tips that can help here are:

1. Send your mailings to the home if possible, as spouses can and do get involved.

2. Send mailings to each individual participant, not just to a team or group.

3. Create a unique campaign that doesn't look like other company bulletins.

4. Establish a campaign that's light and fun for everyone.

Promotion, administration and a carefully planned rule structure can make your program achieve your goals, and more. It allows you to increase your profits with one of the most cost-effective managerial tools available today.

How much should be invested and how should it be used?

We've already discussed program applications, basic criteria for setting up a program, and the necessary supporting elements to make your program work.

Now we'll review establishing the budget and selection of awards.

The Budget. Two factors must be considered in setting up your budget:

1. How much is it worth to achieve the goal?

2. Is the awards package big enough to excite the participants and make it work?

   - Ideally, you should not work with a fixed budget, but rather plan on using a portion of your new profits generated by the program. For example, if you currently have total revenue of $50 million annually and want a 20 percent increase to $60 million through sales, how much of the profit from your $10 million dollar increase will you plow back into the program? How much would it be worth if only a 10 percent gain is achieved? Is it worth an even greater percentage for a 30 percent gain?

     Your program costs can be set up on a variable basis to ensure a precise expenditure for a given result.

   - The award must be sufficient to entice your participants to succeed. A general guildeline follows. (Table 2, on page 1078, is based on merchandise and travel awards and would be inadequate for a direct cash program.)

You should plan on at least 60-70 percent achieving some awards (perhaps only $10-$50) with about 8-15 percent earning near the top level.

Since the income level of your distributor principals is not usually available information, we suggest a slightly different approach. Proceed with step 1 (how much is the increase in your sales worth?) and include a buy-in provision. This ensures an award of meaning for high-income individuals and control of costs for you.

A buy-in provision allows your distributors to supplement the award credit you provide by buying in the award with cash. This still allows you to offer a substantial award at a controllable cost. Unlike employees, distributors generally accept this approach and will still strive for success.

Table 2.

Program Length	*Percent of participants' gross income for the period	
	Top	Avg.
2-4 months	10-15%	5-8%
4-9 months	9-12%	4-7%
10-14 months	8-11%	3-6%
* Sales oriented programs for employees, agents, and distributor sales personnel. Programs for distributor principals and safety and absenteeism programs are handled differently. Safety, absenteeism and productivity programs should run 12-18 months and need only budget $150-200 per person for top performers. So little is done with merchandise and travel recognition in these areas (frequently reserved for white-collar employees) that there is a tremendous impact.		

The Awards. What's right for your program? You have a lot of options.

Merchandising catalogs offer hundreds of items to choose from such as:

- Weekend trips for your top performers

- An exotic trip for your top performers

- A group trip for all who qualify

- Individual gift items (video recorder, computers, watches, etc.)

- Plaques and trophies

- A night on the town or a trip to the ball game

In some cases, you'll use more than one award in a program. You might have a group-travel program that also offers selected merchandise and trophies.

First you need to look at the income level and age of your participants. If they're primarily young and just beginning, they may appreciate some extras around the house more than a trip to Europe. If they're well established and have those things, travel may be more meaningful and memorable.

If you use merchandise, you have the option to select a few very promotable items or use a catalog that offers something for everyone.

You might wish to combine both. Use a catalog for the year and offer special promotions on one or two items seasonally.

In non-sales programs, your budget is generally insufficient for anything beyond limited merchandise programs. We recommend avoiding travel awards other than nearby weekend resorts for safety, absenteeism, suggestion, and productivity programs.

Use group travel when you want to bring your participants together in a nonbusiness, comfortable environment. It's an ideal vehicle to build rapport with salespeople and customers and keep them committed to your goals.

Individual travel awards offer high appeal to the recipient and allow flexibility for action. They're excellent motivators for your participants and can help you increase profits when bringing everyone together would serve little or no purpose.

Selection of travel destinations should reflect your budget and the general nature of your participants. As in other incentive application areas, expert advice is available from a number of companies in the industry.

Your awards are an end to the means and should be established after you've determined your goals, plan, program and budget. In that way, you'll ensure a program designed to make sales, increase productivity, etc., rather than guarantee certain awards.

Merchandise and travel incentive programs can help you increase profitability with a measurable and controllable investment. Used properly, they can be a cost-effective, highly valuable management tool in the competitive environment we face today.

The Power of Tangible Rewards

Granting the value of such ego drives as recognition, pride, and appreciation, these psychological stimulants take more time than sales managers have available when a company must increase sales or introduce a new line of products over a limited period. To produce more immediate results, tangible rewards must be offered to stimulate action.

Over the years, sales contests have proved to be the best means of rewarding those who have helped, through outstanding or unusual performance, to attain their company's sales objectives.

Properly used, a sales contest not only pays, but lays the foundation for future selling. It gives salespeople the urge to go out and exert themselves to the limit. In many cases, it involves not only the sales department, but the entire organization. It is the most advanced form of sales promotion; its effectiveness may be measured, its results are definite, and the returns are faster than anything else short of price reduction or doubling the sales force.

According to Henry B. Ostberg, president, Blankenship and Ostberg, Inc., there are two preliminary steps in setting up a contest:

1. *Establishing the purpose.* Contests can help you accomplish a wide variety of purposes and objectives. An increase in total sales is only one of them. Among some other possible objectives are:

   • Selling a particular line or product

   • Picking up new accounts

   • Reactivating lost accounts

   • Overcoming a temporary sales slump

   • Encouraging salespeople to aid dealers in store promotions

   • Getting salespeople to make more calls

2. *Handicapping.* For one reason or another, one salesperson sells better than another. This may not be due to differences in sales ability, but to the nature of the territory covered, the length of time in which a salesperson has become established, and local economic conditions. Accordingly, it may be desirable to "handicap" the participants. To accomplish this you can:

   • Use a percentage increase in sales over the previous year, rather than total sales, to determine the winner.

   • Set a quota for each salesperson, the winner being the one who exceeds his or her quota by the most.

   • Run a contest in which the salesperson who brings in the largest number of orders (rather than the highest volume of sales) gets the top prize.

- Declare every salesperson a winner who exceeds a minimum standard of performance (say $18,000 worth of sales *during the contest period).*

Forty Incentive Objectives

Following are some broad uses of contests compiled by *Incentive Marketing Facts:*

1. Sustain year-round selling effort.

2. Introduce a new product or a new model.

3. Extend a distribution area.

4. Move slow items in a line.

5. Open new accounts.

6. Stimulate sales force by a change of pace.

7. Encourage full-line selling.

8. Back a special consumer promotion.

9. Revive inactive accounts.

10. Encourage salespeople to close earlier.

11. Push use of literature, other sales tools.

12. Bolster slow-season sales.

13. Push new product uses or combinations.

14. Offset competitive promotions.

15. Teach salespeople product information.

16. Help train salespeople in selling skills.

17. Help train salespeople in sales-service functions.

18. Increase use of retail displays.

19. Back special promotions to dealers.

20. Increase number of calls by salespeople.

21. Help gather market data through salespeople.

22. Support production levels.

23. Stimulate higher unit sales per account.

24. Find new prospects.

25. Get sales help from nonselling personnel.

26. Reduce selling costs.

27. Promote proper use of equipment.

28. Improve use of order and report forms.

29. Improve salespeople's record-keeping.

30. Cut salesperson turnover.

31. Recruit salespeople with present salespeople's help.

32. Encourge safety by route drivers.

33. Extend a peak selling season.

34. Enlist help from salespeople's spouses.

35. Move more expensive or high-profit items.

36. Clear inventory before a model change.

37. Aid in evaluating salespeople's performance.

38. Improve sales-force morale.

39. Stimulate activity by manufacturers' reps.

40. Help collect past-due accounts.

The Essentials of a Well-Planned Contest

The first yardstick that must be used in determining whether to have a sales contest is, "What will it do for the salespeople, besides providing an urge for them to strive for more business?" If the plan is right, a constructive contest should measure up to the following:

1. The contest should be so clearly described that the salesperson will have no doubt as to *what* he or she should do.

2. Care should be taken to show *how* to do it.

3. The anticipated results should be evaluated so that the *cost* of the contest is kept within reasonable bounds.

4. The *objectives* of the contest should be well thought out. Determine exactly what you are trying to achieve whether it be increased market share, penetration into new markets, or an overall increase in sales volume. Caution: In cases where your objective is to simply increase sales, make sure that the added volume achieved isn't "stolen" from sales which would have occurred naturally during the following sales period. Some salespeople may try to convince certain key customers to place their customary orders earlier than usual to give themselves an edge in winning the contest.

5. The contest period should be *short,* so that payoffs come with reasonable quickness. One month to six weeks is usually considered a good period. It is difficult to keep up interest for longer periods.

6. The entire family should be brought into the act, when possible. Pressure at home is often more effective than that from management.

7. The program should be *planned well in advance,* in order that samples, presentation techniques, product literature, production of materials for inventory, promotional bulletins, prize literature, quotas, and goals are ready. If a sales manager is slow in getting a contest underway after it has been announced—if starting dates are made retroactive, or samples are not available, or shipments cannot be made of prize goods—the contest will have two strikes against it at the start.

8. If contests are to be conducted throughout the year, they should be programmed for the full year so that the proper sequence of product or activity promotion can be followed.

9. Why should a trip to the home office be a prize or award? If trips to the home office are beneficial to the salespeople, they should be brought in on some predetermined schedule having nothing to do with any contest. An award trip to the home office seems to the salesperson to be "two for the company and one for the salesperson."

Cash or Merchandise Prizes

An investigation made some time ago showed that only three out of ten companies used cash prizes in sales contests, while seven out of ten preferred merchandise prizes. A smaller group used honor prizes, where some badge of distinction is awarded to those who do a superlative selling job.

In a sales campaign for one of the large eastern insurance companies, the only reward offered was to bind the salespeople's sales reports into a book that was presented to the president of the company.

Money doesn't mean everything to salespeople. Many salespeople will work twice as hard to win a TV set for their families as they will for a check for themselves. One saleswoman has her apartment furnished with prizes which she has earned over a five-year period. That is why the majority of companies reported that merchandise is better than money as a reward for constructive sales acheivements. When you set up a prize appropriation, it will go farther in merchandise upon which you get wholesale prices than it will go if paid to the salespeople in money; although, if you ask ten salespeople which they prefer, nine will tell you "money." Usually, they'll use the money to buy the very things that can be found in any good prize book.

Year-Round Contests

There is a trend toward making competitive activities continuous. Instead of having one or two contests a year, an all-year program of contests is set up and executed, so that there will be a continuing effort behind sales instead of an occasional push. The argument that holding one contest after another dulls interest does not seem to be borne out by experience any more than does having a quota for every month of the year. It is, however, important that there be variety to the competition, so that new interest will be added every month.

To illustrate how a program of sales contests may be set up to provide a year-in-and-year-out sales push, without having them become tiresome, the following outline may be of interest. It was followed by a manufacturer of printers' supplies:

- *January-March: Step Ahead Campaign.* During this period, the sales organization was supplied with new tools and new plans to help it keep out in the front during the new year.

- *April-May: Question Box Contest.* Each week, during the period, salespeople were asked to submit their most effective sales argument for a given product in the line. Those selected as best each week won. The answers, of course, are published and circulated in the company house organ.

- *June: Vacation Campaign.* Five products were selected, which the company desired to push, and quotas were given to each salesperson. Those making quota received a two weeks' vacation at the company's expense, or a proportion of their expenses if they fell short of quota.

- *July-August: Baseball Tournament.* Each branch house constituted a team. Prize points were awarded on prospects reported (hits) and sales (runs), with grand prizes going to the winning team and to the heavy hitters.

- *September: World Series Jamboree.* Carrying forward the interest in the baseball tournament, salespeople who qualified in the ball game and who also made quota in September got a free trip to the World Series.

- *October-November: Bulls and Bears Stock Market Contest.* A novel campaign in which each salesperson is incorporated as a going business, and his stock listed on the "Big Board."

- *December: President's Month.* Sales this month are a testimonial to the head of the business. A banquet is given during

Christmas week to round out the year and make the presentation.

It will be noticed from the foregoing how a variety of interest is maintained. The majority of the contests are educational. Most of them have a definite incentive interest, to permit playing upon salespeople's liking for competitive activities. The schedule is so set up that one contest begins just as soon as the other ends. The successul sales contest—

1. Is built to do a constructive educational job, rather than make a salesperson work harder.

2. Is dramatized with a central theme—but showmanship is not permitted to submerge salesmanship.

3. Is planned well ahead of starting time so that it can be effectively merchandised to those who must promote it.

4. Makes it possible for every salesperson who does a job to win something; it is aimed at the tail-enders rather than the stars.

5. Recognizes all phases of constructive selling as well as the total business obtained by contestants.

6. Is neither too long nor too short—about two months is the best period.

7. Is never allowed to become monotonous. It is a series of surprises that keep interest alive from beginning to end.

8. Teaches better ways to sell, and rewards those who put those methods into operation.

The time-honored conception of a sales contest was a competition in which the salesperson who got the most business during the period of the contest won a prize. But that practice had one great fault. The same salespeople won most of the prizes, and the average salesperson who typifies about 80% of the organization, quickly lost interest.

Since it is more important to stimulate the tail-enders than the few persons at the top, sales managers quickly hit upon the idea of handicapping salespeople having above-average territories, to give the less fortunate salespeople a break. The sales task was developed. Each salesperson was given a definite task, and the prizes went to those who succeeded in showing the largest percentage of increase.

The ideal today is to base competition on percentages so calculated that every salesperson will be able to win some prize, and thus be spurred to do his or her best.

The Connelly Company, of Ann Arbor, Michigan, for example, takes 80 percent of the previous year's sales as the minimum to qualify, and then pays on a small point unit up to 100 percent, with double the point unit for over 100 percent of that year's sales. The company uses points for merchandise prizes. Thus, everyone gets something, since he or she is competing merely with himself or herself. Prize catalogs are sent to the salespeople's homes so that family members are also brought into the picture.

A. W. Chesterton Dealer Travel Contest

A.W. Chesterton, a Massachusetts manufacturer of mechanical seals, credits incentive programs staged for dealers for its success; its volume has risen from less than a million dollars to over $16 million in an 11-year period. Its big prize, too, is travel.

Distributors who exceeded their quota by 10 percent are entitled to a free trip for two to a specific destination; those who exceeded it by 15 percent or more are awarded a trip for four. It is possible to win a trip for as many as eight people by making a maximum effort. Visits have already been made to Madrid, Mexico City, Paris, Rio de Janeiro, Puerto Rico, Hawaii, Rome, and Las Vegas. Quotas, of course, are set to cover the cost of the program. One of the Chesterton dealers has won every trip for which he has been eligible. He maintains that his desire to win such trips is so great it has made him a millionaire, and a well-traveled one at that.

Cudahy Team Incentive Contest

Occasionally, when incentive awards are based on individual effort, the early success of a few sales reps reaching their goals can tend to reduce the effort of the rest of a sales force. To prevent this, Patrick Cudahy, Inc., the meat packer, recently gave its 32 sales reps a team incentive to strive for. In order to gain a trip *for all* to a major vacation site, it was necessary that *each* member of the staff sell 27 truckloads of products in the nine-week period of the promotion. "With a team program they urge each other on," said Art C. Reimann, vice president, sales and marketing.

Example of Treasure Contest

Recently, a drug firm organized a Treasure Hunt contest in which its sales reps assumed the names of ship captains such as Cap'n Long John Silver, Cap'n Bligh, Cap'n Teach, Blackbeard, and other famous legendary sea captains. Each captain was to sail a course toward Treasure Island, each island en route representing a percentage of the sales quota. Achieving Treasure Island meant the sales rep had reached 100 percent of quota, while island hopping back toward home port represented varying percentages over the quota. The three reps whose individual quotas brought them closest to home port within the six-week period of the contest won travel and merchandise prizes.

A Checklist for Sales Contests

The following is useful for planning and implementing sales contests.

1. *Planning your contest*

   - Is the contest timed right? You can pay more for extra volume when sales are below the profit break-even point.

   - Will the contest do a building job as well as get extra business? Or do you regard it merely as a shot in the arm?

   - Is your contest designed to bring out the best in the tailenders, rather than to put a halo on the salespeople at the top of the list?

   - Will everyone have a chance to win if he or she makes the special effort required?

- Is the contest too short? Will you have ample time to promote it properly?

- Is the contest too long? Will the salespeople lose interest so that you can't get up the necessary winning head of steam?

2. *Scoring*

- Is your system of credits worked out so that a permanent benefit will result from the contest?

- Have you arranged to reward salespeople who come through with a constructive sales suggestion that can be passed along to the others?

- Have you provided extra recognition for the salesperson who does the best territory development work, such as opening new accounts during the contest?

- Have you provided points for those contestants who do a particularly good job in getting point-of-sale advertising?

- Have you emphasized the importance of getting window and store displays put in by the customer?

- Have you provided extra points for orders that include the neglected items in the line?

- Is there a period near the end of the campaign when a salesperson gets double points for double effort? Give the weak salespeople a chance to score.

- Is your scoring system fair? The most successful contests require salespeople to beat their normal sales expectancy rather than their fellow salespeople.

- If you give points on volume alone, is there some equalizing factor so that the weaker salespeople will get a break?

3. *Awarding prizes*

- Has each contestant a chance to win a prize of his or her own selection; are all prizes the same?

- Have you provided prizes of some sort for the spouses of the winners, as well as prizes that only the salespeople would use?

- If prize books are to be used, do they feature standard, advertised merchandise or cheap merchandise that will kill interest in prize contests forever?

- Are prizes well displayed in prize book? Remember—the success of the contest depends upon the lure of the prize book.

- If only a first and second prize are awarded, there should be prizes of recognition for at least the top third of the salespeople. The more winners, the more workers you will have next time.

- Will the prize be kept and cherished? Money is seldom as effective as merchandise in the long run.

4. *Staging the contest*

- Is your contest sufficiently different from your last activity to make it novel and interesting?

- Is it dramatic? There should be just enough showmanship and color to awaken interest without detracting from the sales message.

- Does it drive home *one* central selling idea that will stick in a salesperson's mind long after the contest itself will be forgotten?

- Will it click with the salespeople? It should neither be too highbrow nor too clever. One fault is as bad as the other.

- Has the office force been put into the picture so that salespeople will feel the eyes of the folks back home are upon them?

- Is your starting time far enough ahead so you can do the best possible job of promoting the contest with distributors or dealers?

- How about the qualification task? Is it easy to attain so that you will get as many salespeople as possible underway quickly?

- Have you provided suitable recognition for those who meet the qualification task—a lapel button, belt buckle, or certificate?

- Are your mailings timed so as to reach the sales force on Monday morning? Use priority or overnight delivery to far-off points.

- Is there a surprise in every mailing? Nothing is more fatal than to let the tempo of a contest drag.

- Is the office scoreboard so placed that the entire office organization can see it and comment upon it in letters they may be writing to salespeople?

- Is the salesperson's family tied in to the contest? Send them duplicate mailings, or provide in some way to get them involved.

5. *Putting the contest over*

- Is your contest "announcement" sufficiently spectacular? Will it impress your salespeople as it should?

- Do you give each salesperson an opportunity to go on record as wishing to participate by enclosing a registration card with advance announcements?

- Does the advance announcement carry detailed rules, with exact starting and finishing time, what kind of orders count and what kind won't count, etc.?

- Have you some simple method by which a salesperson can notify the office every time he or she scores? Such notification cards can be posted on the scoreboard.

- How frequently do you send progress reports out to the salespeople? Toward the end of the contest they should be mailed daily, using telegrams the last week.

Communicating with the Sales Force

While practically every company operating 10 or more salespeople issues some sort of bulletin, many of these are dull and uninteresting. Although sales managers have abandoned the pepletter technique that characterized the sales bulletin years ago, many still make the mistake of using bulletins to preach to their salespeople, and clutter them up with instructions and material that should properly be issued as loose-leaf pages for an operating manual. They forget that even a bulletin carrying the sales manager's signature is in competition for a busy salesperson's time.

An effective sales bulletin should, above all, be informative. It should be regarded by management as a device for spreading the good news about the business. It should inspire salespeople to renewed effort, strengthen their confidence in the company and its products, bring ideas and suggestions helpful to them in their work, and keep them sold on company policies. It is, in short, the newspaper of the sales organization. And like a good newspaper it should present the news objectively, with a minimum of coloring. It should be well printed and easy to read.

Are bulletins to your salesforce worth the time and expense they take to produce? Many companies have found that sales bulletins perform several useful functions, namely:

- Provide a forum to bestow recognition on individual salespeople, thus boosting morale

- Serve as an adjunct to a well-rounded training program by presenting selling tips and advice

- Enable sales managers to give their salespeople messages that are more effective in print than when presented verbally

- Provide a means to inform the entire sales force of company policy and price changes

- Provide a permanent record of company news for future reference

PREPARING BULLETINS

The secret of writing successful bulletins or house organs to salespeople is to talk *with* them rather than *at* them. Instead of writing articles telling them to do such and such a thing, use a "let us do it" approach. It is a weakness characteristic of sales managers to make these bulletins read like army orders, rather than like intimate, friendly communications designed to help a salesperson do a better selling job.

Another sour touch that spoils many otherwise well-received sales bulletins are signed articles by home-office officials who use the space to talk about the value of loyalty, hard work, and care in spending the firm's money. While these concerns are important and worthy of being kept before every salesperson, it is better to "say it with news" rather than signed articles. Relating selling experiences and plans of other salespeople and the scoreboard, or comparative standings of salespeople, are generally regarded as the two most important features in sales bulletins. The consensus is that the scoreboard comes first. It is one of the greatest sales stimulators ever invented.

A poll of 3,500 salespeople gives preference to stories of sales, salespeople's experiences and plans, and other material of this nature. They also voted for contests to be operated through the sales bulletin. The demand for more photographs, charts, and cartoons having to do with selling was very great. Some kinds of inspirational articles were strongly commended, but poetry, humor, and general articles received "thumbs down." A majority of the salespeople made clear that their second choice of articles was personal stories about salespeople.

One sales manager makes it a practice to watch sales reports for leads. She selects the most likely looking sales and drops the salesperson a line requesting him or her to write on the opposite side of the sheet what argument was used in making the sale, what objections had to be overcome, and what point seemed to carry the most weight in clinching the order. The brief replies usually form the basis for building interesting articles.

PUTTING BULLETINS TOGETHER

Perhaps one of the most important things to bear in mind when putting together a sales bulletin is that there are very few hard and fast rules to follow. Formats of company bulletins vary widely. Some are elaborate, some are simple. Some are printed, while others are reproduced on office copying machines.

1. *How to begin.* Decide what size your publication will be (8½" x 11" or whatever) and how many pages it will average. Decide how it will be reproduced (on your office copying machine, sent to an outside printer, etc.), how often it will be issued, and how many copies of each issue you will need. Figure out how much each issue will cost.

2. *Know what you expect to accomplish.* Make a list of all the kinds of things you should put in the publication, such as ongoing sales achievements, photos of top salespeople, price changes, column for suggestions from the sales force, sales tips, and inspirational material. Make sure this material is readily available.

3. *Experiment.* Have the material set or typed as it would appear in the publication. Use an office copying machine to reproduce it. Cut out all the copy to exact size. Also make sure any photos and illustrations you plan to use are the right size. One way to begin planning your publication is to get a copy of your company logo and put it at the top of the first page. It will serve the same function as the logo on the newspaper: you will attract immediate attention and identify your company. Your company news can begin right under your logo without further introduction. Arrange your copy and illustrations in various layouts until you hit on one you think looks best.

Visually, there are few things that look more formidable than copy that is not broken up into sections for easy reading. Set off type-groups using borders above and below the type to anchor it to the page. You can set off a quotation, an interesting phrase, or even a sentence or two. Make sure you use borders above and below this material to avoid having the type you set off seemingly "float in air." Art supply houses can furnish you with borders that you apply much like scotch tape.

Illustrations can also be used to break up type and add to the publication's attractiveness. Many companies maintain extensive clip art files that contain a wide variety of illustrations. The local graphics supply house can put you in touch with one of these services.

Other techniques sales managers use effectively include:

1. *Use different colors throughout to add variety.* Color attracts attention and is a pleasant change from the standard white page. Also, different color pages enable you to group material by subject matter. For example, use yellow for selling tips, green for sales standings, and pink for price changes and product information.

2. *Use of full-color letterheads to emphasize a specific theme.* These preprinted letterhead sheets can be purchased in a variety of styles. Full-color letterheads give the copy added emphasis without excessive cost.

3. *Use of repetitive headlines in different issues to emphasize recurrent themes and to create departments.* Examples of such "standing" headlines include, "What's New" (short items of general interest), "New Arrivals" (employees who have just joined the company), "The Top Ten" (outstanding sales achievers), and so on.

Properly implemented, your bulletin will open a direct line from the home office to the salespeople in the field. Most sales managers quickly discover that changes in company policy are more readily accepted when presented in the format of a sales bulletin rather than in that of a cold directive from the top office. You can give salespeople immediate recognition for a good sales record and build morale, announce an upcoming sales contest and explain the rules, and offer words of encouragement when things aren't going as well as expected.

How you finally decide to do your publication will depend on your type of company, the size of your sales force, the amount of territory you cover, and other factors that pertain to your organization. Each company is different and the objectives of a company publication will vary.

How Companies Motivate Their Sales Forces

Respondents to a Dartnell survey were asked what has been the most effective way of motivating their sales forces. While the representative replies, which follow, emphasized the most-used techniques cited previously in Table 1, page 1067, many other methods were contributed that might be put to good use.

- Individual one-on-one meetings to set goals, discuss problems, build up emotion and attitude.

- Personalized, ongoing sales training program supervised by me directly.

- Sales contests combined with product specials.

- Special incentives paid in cash, with known goals per agreement with management.

- Recognition—developing a sense of importance.

- Public acknowledgement within company and unlimited commission potential.

- Pride and money.

- Management working with field sales, new products, bonus program.

- Good total compensation package plus occasional special incentive programs.

- Daily conversations showing personal interest in every deal, whether large or small.

- Individual attention and encouragement.

- Prompt support when needed *and* recognition when excellent actions are obtained.

- Benefit programs and bonus.

- Having salesperson set priorities based on expected sales.

- Show interest by getting involved in day-to-day activities of the sales force.

- Interoffice contest, reviewing performance with each salesperson, and traveling with salespeople.

- Daily encouragement, sales board in office, small incentive contests.

- Training salespeople to be *knowledgeable* about their *product*—and knowledgeable about their *customers.*

- Bonus dollars for achievement of special incentive programs.

- Good support staff and company support.

- Personal encouragement and reinforcement.

- Trip incentive to Acapulco.

- Praise and self-recognition.

- Monetary rewards and annual national award program—five days in resort area.

- Trips.

- Realistic objectives with rewards for each.

- Sales contests and quotas.

- Recognition.

- Good incentive plan, achievable sales quota.

- Monetary compensation upon reaching sales goals.

- Recognition and encouragement.

- Close working relationship with manager; frequent encouragement and recognition when objectives are achieved; meeting with presentation of results.

- Showing dollar incentive for commissions on our products plus concept of using our accessory items as "door openers" for reps' capital equipment product lines.

- Treating salespeople like human beings rather than numbers.

- Good compensation plan that rewards salespeople for doing what it is you want them to do.

- Physically showing how to make the big dollar by in-field sales presentations.

- Money, offering specials on different products.

- Regional meeting.

- Recognition of accomplishments.

- Peer pressure and saying "thanks."

- Day-to-day discussion.

- Providing warm sales leads through sales promotion and direct mail, plus trade journal direct marketing.

- Money, contests, threats and praise.

- Short-term contests with quick rewards.

- Commendation and incentives.

- Incentive compensation and recognition, in that order.

- Positive reinforcement—have salespeople believe in what they are selling.

- Personal commendation before peers, annual convention, plaques and trophies.

- Training, monthly newsletters on results, regional meetings, yearly award meetings, management by objectives.

- Exciting the sales force with an exceptionally good item to sell.

- Bonuses and contests.

- Money! Extra commissions, etc.

- Quarterly sales versus plan bonus and recognition.

- Meeting with each individual to set realistic sales goals.

- Meetings, keeping product information up-to-date, circulation of relevant books, newsletters and materials.

- Commission and published sales results.

- A friendly, healthy atmosphere to work in.

- Contests and commissions.

- Monitoring activity, making specific recommendation, pats on the back.

The Ultimate Objective

In stimulating salespeople to achieve higher performance levels, the ultimate objective is not sales volume but profit. In the eyes of top management, the one thing that really counts is the profit figure. As stated by Robert F. Vizza and Thomas E. Chambers in their report *Time and Territorial Management:**

"The focus on sales volume must be shifted to sales profitability. Measurement techniques must be developed to overcome this major obstacle. However, caution must be exercised to assure that this obstacle is not simply a rationalization. Companies are applying the concept of profit contribution to the sales force, despite the lack of an absolute measurement theory. Any measurement technique, if applied equally to all units of operation, will yield a comparison of results, if not an absolute measure. This enables management to compare customer to customer, salesperson to salesperson, product to product, time period to time period, or any combination of these elements. It is a start into the most important measure of effectiveness—profit."

---

*Robert F. Vizza and Thomas E. Chambers, *Time and Territorial Management* (New York: American Management Assn., 1979).

Ready-Reference Section

Bibliography for Sales Executives

This list of publications offers the reader a choice of reference books most closely related to sales management.

Anderson, Robert B.: *Professional Sales Management,* Prentice-Hall, New York.

Bobrow, Edwin E. & Wizenberg, Larry: *Sales Manager's Handbook,* Dow Jones-Irwin, Homewood, IL.

Britt, Steuart Henderson & Guess, Norman, eds.: *Marketing Manager's Handbook,* The Dartnell Corporation, Chicago.

Buskirk, Richard H. & Buskirk, Bruce D.: *Retailing,* McGraw-Hill, New York.

Calvin, Robert J.: *Profitable Sales Management & Marketing for Growing Businesses,* Van Nostrand Reinhold, New York.

Canfield, Bertrand R.: *Sales Administration: Principles and Problems,* Prentice-Hall, Englewood Cliffs, NJ.

Carney, Gerald J.: *The Complete Field Sales Program,* American Management Association, New York.

Cateora, Philip R. & Hess, John M.: *International Marketing,* Richard D. Irwin, Homewood, IL.

Engel, James F., Blackwell, Roger D., and Kollat, David T.: *Consumer Behavior,* Dryden Press, New York.

Fahner, Hal: *Successful Sales Management: A New Strategy for Modern Sales Management,* Prentice-Hall, Englewood Cliffs, NJ.

Fisher, Peg: *Successful Telemarketing,* The Dartnell Corporation, Chicago.

Haas, Kenneth Brooks: *Professional Salesmanship,* Holt, Rinehart & Winston, New York.

Hodgson, Richard S.: *Direct Mail and Mail Order Handbook,* The Dartnell Corporation, Chicago.

Kelleher, Robert F.: *Industrial Marketing & Sales Management in the Computer Age,* Van Nostrand Reinhold, New York.

Kinnear, Thomas C. and Taylor, James R.: *Marketing Research,* McGraw-Hill, New York.

Konikow, Robert B.: *How to Participate Profitably in Trade Shows,* The Dartnell Corporation, Chicago.

Kotler, Philip: *Marketing Management,* Prentice-Hall, Englewood Cliffs, NJ.

Lambert, Clark: *Field Sales Performance Appraisal,* John Wiley & Sons, New York.

Lumsden, George J.: *Building a Winning Sales Force,* The Dartnell Corporation, Chicago.

McCarthy, E. Jerome: *Basic Marketing,* Richard D. Irwin, Homewood, IL.

Michman, Ronald D. & Sibley, Stanley D.: *Marketing Channels and Strategies,* Grid Publishing, Columbus, OH.

O'Connell, William A.: *Dartnell's Biennial Survey of Sales Force Compensation,* The Dartnell Corporation, Chicago.

Odiorne, George S.: *Sales Management by Objectives,* The Dartnell Corporation, Chicago.

Parker, Donald D.: *The Marketing of Consumer Services,* Business Study Series No. 1, University of Washington, Seattle, WA.

Rice, Craig: *Marketing Planning Strategies,* The Dartnell Corporation, Chicago.

Riso, Ovid: *Sales Promotion Handbook,* The Dartnell Corporation, Chicago.

Seltz, David D.: *How to Conduct Successful Sales Contests and Incentive Programs,* The Dartnell Corporation, Chicago.

Seltz, David D.: *How to Franchise,* Addison-Wesley Publishing, Reading, MA.

Shaw, Steven: *Salesmanship: Modern Viewpoints on Personal Communications,* Holt, Rinehart & Winston, New York.

Stanton, William & Buskirk, Richard H.: *Management of the Sales Force,* Richard D. Irwin, Homewood, IL.

Stroh, Thomas F.: *Managing the Sales Function,* McGraw-Hill, New York.

Stroh, Thomas F.: *Salesmanship: Personal Communications and Persuasion in Marketing,* Richard D. Irwin, Homewood, IL.

Thompson, Joseph: *Selling: A Behaviorial Approach,* McGraw-Hill, New York.

Webster, Frederick E., Jr.: *Field Sales Management,* John Wiley and Sons, New York.

Wingate, John: *Fundamentals of Selling,* SouthWestern Publishing Company, Cincinnati, OH.

Wortman, Leon A.: *Sales Manager's Problem Solver,* John Wiley and Sons, New York.

Glossary of Marketing Terms

The following glossary of sales/marketing terms is the result of a report from a joint committee representing principal sales/marketing executive groups. All instances where there is a difference of opinion among the groups are acknowledged and identified in the report.

accessory equipment. See *equipment.*

advertising. Any paid form of nonpersonal presentation and promotion of ideas, goods, or services by an identified sponsor.

It involves the use of such media as the following:

• Magazine and newspaper space

• Motion pictures

• Outdoor (posters, signs, skywriting, etc.)

• Direct mail

• Store signs

• Novelties (calendars, blotters, etc.)

• Radio and television

• Cards (car, bus, etc.)

• Catalogs

• Directories and references

• Programs and menus

• Circulars

This list is intended to be illustrative, not inclusive.

See publicity *for a definition of a kindred activity. It should be noted that retailers often do not regard display as a part of advertising but as a separate activity.*

advertising research. See *market research.*

agent middleman. A middleman who negotiates purchases or sales or both but who does not take title to goods.

The middleman usually performs fewer marketing functions than does the merchant middleman. He or she commonly receives remuneration in the form of a commission or fee and rarely represents both buyer and seller in the same transaction.

Examples: broker, commission merchant, manufacturer's agent, selling agent, and resident buyer.

The Committee recommends that the term agent rather than agent middleman be preferred. The Committee also recommends that the term functional middleman no longer be applied to this type of agent. It is hardly logical or consistent in view of the fact that he or she performs fewer marketing functions than other middlemen.

assembling. The marketing function of concentrating goods or their control to facilitate sale or purchase.

The concentration involved here may affect a quantity of like goods or a variety of goods. It includes the assembling of adequate and representative stocks by wholesalers and retailers.

branch house. An establishment maintained by a manufacturer or a wholesaler, detached from the headquarters establishment, and used primarily for the purpose of carrying stocks of, selling, and delivering the manufacturer's or wholesaler's product.

branch office. An establishment maintained by a seller, detached from the headquarters establishment, and used for the purpose of selling a product or service.

The characteristic of the branch house that distinguishes it from the branch office is that it is used in the physical storage, handling, and delivery of merchandise. Otherwise the two are identical.

branch store. A subsidiary retail business owned and operated by an established store and smaller than, or carrying a much less extensive line of merchandise than, the parent store.

See parent store for a kindred term.

brand. A name, term, symbol, or design, or a combination of them that identifies the goods or services of one seller or group of sellers and distinguishes them from those of competitors.

A brand may include a brand name, a trademark, or both. The term brand is sufficiently comprehensive to include practically all means of identification except perhaps the package and the shape of the product. All brand names and all trademarks are brands or parts of brands, but not all brands are either brand names or trademarks. Brand is the inclusive, general term. The others are more particularized.

brand name. A brand or part of a brand consisting of a word, letter, or group of words or letters making up the name that identifies the goods or services of a seller or group of sellers and that distinguishes them from those of competitors.

The brand name is that part of a brand that can be vocalized. To illustrate, the brand under which the Buick car is sold is the name Buick printed in script and set in the familiar rectangle design that usually appears somewhere on this make of car. This combination also happens to conform to the legal requirements of a trademark. The word Buick used orally or set in any kind of type face, whatever its surroundings, is the brand name. This is true of the pronounceable part of it, regardless of the presence or absence of the usually accompanying designs or symbols.

broker. An agent who does not have direct physical control of goods with which he or she deals, but who represents either buyer or seller and who does business for a principal. A broker's powers as to prices and terms of sale are usually limited by his or her principal.

buying power. See *purchasing power.* Purchasing power is preferred.

canvasser. See *house-to-house salesperson.*

cash and carry wholesaler. See *wholesaler.*

chain store. A group of retail stores of essentially the same type, centrally owned, and with some degree of centralized control of operation.

According to the dictionary, two may apparently be construed to constitute a group. This term may also refer to a single store unit of such a group.

collection period. The number of days that the total of trade accounts and notes receivable (including assigned accounts and discounted notes, if any), less reserves for bad debts, represents when compared with the annual net credit sales. Divide the annual net credit sales by 365 days to obtain the average credit sales per day. Then divide the total of accounts and notes receivable (plus any discounted notes receivable) by the average credit sales per day to obtain the average collection period.

commissary store. A retail store owned and operated by a company or governmental unit to sell primarily to its employees. Nongovernmental establishments of this type are often referred to as company stores or industrial stores.

Many of these establishments are not operated for profit. The matter of the location of the control over and responsibility for these stores, rather than the motive for their operation, constitutes their distinguishing characteristic.

commission house. An agent, transacting business in his own name, who usually exercises physical control over consignments of goods, and who negotiates their sale.

The commission merchant usually enjoys broader powers as to prices, methods, and terms of sale than does the broker, although the commission merchant must obey instructions issued by his or her principal. The commission merchant generally arranges delivery, extends necessary credit, collects, deducts his fees, and remits the balance to his or her principal.

Most of those who have defined the commission merchant state that he or she has possession of goods handled. In its strict meaning, the word possession *connotes the idea of ownership; in its legal meaning it involves a degree of control somewhat beyond that usually enjoyed by the commission merchant. Therefore, the phrase* physical control *was used instead.*

The fact that many commission merchants are not typical in their operations does not detract from their status as commission merchants. While the term merchant *is somewhat of a misnomer when applied to an agent, that fact is disregarded in this definition because this usage is commonly accepted in the trade.*

company store. See *commissary store.*

consumer research. See *market research.*

consumer's cooperative. An association of ultimate consumers organized to purchase goods and services primarily for use by or resale to the membership.

According to this definition, the term applies only to the cooperative purchasing activities of ultimate consumers and does not embrace collective buying by business establishments, industrial concerns, and institutions.

consumers' goods. Goods destined for use by the ultimate household consumer and in such form that they can be used without further commercial processing.

Certain articles, such as typewriters, may be either consumers' goods or industrial goods, depending upon whether they are destined for use by the ultimate household consumer or by an industrial, business, or institutional user.

convenience goods. Those consumers' goods which the customer usually purchases frequently, immediately, and with the minimum of effort.

Examples of merchandise customarily bought as convenience goods are tobacco products, soap, most drug products, newspapers, magazines, chewing gum, small packaged confections, and many grocery products.

These articles are usually of small unit value and not bulky. The definition, however, is based on the method of purchase employed by the typical consumer. Its essence lies in consumer attitude and habit. The convenience involved may be in terms of nearness to the buyer's home, easy accessibility to some means of transport, or close proximity to places where people go during the day or evening, as, for example, downtown to work.

cooperative marketing. The process by which groups composed of producers, middlemen, consumers, or combinations of them act collectively in buying, selling, or both.

This term includes only those collective activities that are more or less directly connected with buying and selling.

cost and freight (C&F [named point of destination]).

Note: Seller and buyer should consider not only the definitions but also the "C&F Comments" and the "C&F and CIF Comments" in order to understand fully their respective responsibilities and rights under "C&F" terms.

Under this term, the seller quotes a price, including the cost of transportation, to the named point of destination.

Under this quotation the seller must:

1. Provide and pay for transportation to named point of destination;

2. Pay export taxes, or other fees or charges, if any, levied because of exportation;

3. Obtain and dispatch promptly to buyer, or agent, clean bill of lading to named point of destination;

4. Where received-for-shipment ocean bill of lading may be tendered, be responsible for any loss or damage, or both, until the goods have been delivered into the custody of the ocean carrier;

5. Where on-board ocean bill of lading is required, be responsible for any loss or damage, or both, until the goods have been delivered on board the vessel;

6. Provide, at the buyer's request and expense, certificates of origin, consular invoices, or other documents issued in the country of origin, or of shipment, or of both, that the buyer may require for importation of goods into country of destination and, where necessary, for their passage in transit through another country.

The buyer must:

1. Accept the documents when presented;

2. Receive goods upon arrival, handle and pay for all subsequent movement of the goods, including taking delivery from vessel in accordance with bill of lading clauses and terms; pay all costs of lading, including any duties, taxes, and other expenses at named point of destination;

3. Provide and pay for insurance;

4. Be responsible for loss of or damage to goods, or both, from time and place at which seller's obligations under 4) and 5) above have ceased;

5. Pay the costs of certificates of origin, consular invoices, or any other documents issued in the country of origin, or of shipment, or of both, which may be required for the importation of goods into the country of destination and, where necessary, for their passage in transit through another country.

C&F Comments

1. For the seller's protection, the contract of sale should stipulate that marine insurance obtained by the buyer include standard warehouse-to-warehouse coverage.

2. The comments listed under the following CIF terms in many cases apply to C&F terms as well, and should be read and understood by the C&F seller and buyer.

cost, insurance, freight (CIF [named point of destination]).

Note: Seller and buyer should consider not only the definitions, but also the "comments" at the end of this section, in order to understand fully their respective responsibilities and rights under CIF terms.

Under this term, the seller quotes a price including, the cost of the goods, the marine insurance, and all transportation charges to the named point of destination.

Under this quotation the seller must:

1. Provide and pay for transportation to named point of destination;

2. Pay export taxes, or other fees or charges, if any levied because of exportation;

3. Provide and pay for marine insurance;

4. Provide war risk insurance as obtainable in seller's market at time of shipment at buyer's expense, unless seller has agreed that buyer provide for war risk coverage;

5. Obtain and dispatch promptly to buyer, or agent, clean bill of lading to named point of destination, and also insurance policy or negotiable insurance certificate;

6. Where received-for-shipment ocean bill of lading may be tendered, be responsible for any loss or damage, or both, until the goods have been delivered into the custody of the ocean carrier;

7. Where on-board ocean bill of lading is required, be responsible for any loss or damage, or both, until the goods have been delivered on board the vessel;

8. Provide, at the buyer's request and expense, certificates of origin, consular invoices, or any other documents issued in the country of origin, or of shipment, or both, that the buyer may require for importation of goods into country or destination and, where necessary, for their passage in transit through another country.

The buyer must:

1. Accept the documents when presented;

2. Receive the goods upon arrival, handle and pay for all subsequent movement of the goods, including taking delivery from vessel in accordance with bill of lading clauses and terms; pay all costs of lading, including any duties, taxes, and other expenses at named point of destination;

3. Pay for war risk insurance provided by seller;

4. Be responsible for loss of or damage to goods, or both, from time and place at which seller's obligation under 6) or 7) above have ceased;

5. Pay the cost of certificates of origin, consular invoices, or any other documents issued in the country of origin, or of shipment, or both, that may be required for importation of the goods into the country of destination and, where necessary, for their passage in transit through another country.

C&F and CIF Comments

Under C&F and CIF contracts there are the following points on which the seller and the buyer should be in complete agreement at the time that the contract is concluded:

1. It should be agreed upon, in advance, who is to pay for miscellaneous expenses, such as weighing or inspection charges.

2. The quantity to be shipped on any one vessel should be agreed upon, in advance, with a view to the buyer's capacity to take delivery upon arrival and discharge of the vessel, within the free time allowed at the port of importation.

3. Although the terms C&F and CIF are generally interpreted to provide that charges for consular invoices and certificates of origin are for the account of the buyer, and are charged separately, in many trades these charges are included by the seller's price. Hence, seller and buyer should agree, in advance, whether these charges are part of the selling price, or will be invoiced separately.

4. The point of final destination should be definitely known in the event the vessel discharges at a port other than the actual destination of the goods.

5. When ocean freight space is difficult to obtain, or forward freight contracts cannot be made at firm rates, it is advisable that sales contracts, as an exception to regular C&F or CIF terms, should provide that shipment within the contract period be subject to ocean freight space being available to the seller, and should also provide that changes in the cost of ocean transportation between the time of sale and the time of shipment be for account of the buyer.

6. Normally, the seller is obligated to prepay the ocean freight. In some instances, shipments are made freight collect and the

amount of the freight is deducted from the invoice rendered by the seller. It is necessary to be in agreement on this, in advance, in order to avoid misunderstanding which arises from foreign exchange fluctuations that might affect the actual cost of transportation, and from interest charges that might accrue under letter-of-credit financing. Hence, the seller should always prepay the ocean freight unless he or she has a specific agreement with the buyer, in advance, that goods can be shipped freight collect.

7. The buyer should recognize that he or she does not have the right to insist on inspection of goods prior to accepting the documents. The buyer should not refuse to take delivery of goods on account of delay in the receipt of documents, provided the seller has used due diligence in their dispatch through the regular channels.

8. Sellers and buyers are advised against including in a CIF contract any indefinite clause at variance with the obligations of a CIF contract as specified in these definitions. There have been numerous court decisions in the United States and other countries invalidating CIF contracts because of the inclusion of indefinite clauses.

9. Interest charges should be included in cost computations and should not be charged as a separate item in CIF contracts, unless otherwise agreed upon, in advance, between the seller and buyer; in which case, however, the term CIF&I (Cost, Insurance, Freight, and Interest) should be used.

10. In connection with insurance under CIF sales, it is necessary that seller and buyer be definitely in accord upon the following points:

- The character of the marine insurance should be agreed upon insofar as being With Average (WA) or Free of Particular Average (FPA), as well as any other special risks that are covered in specific trades, or against which the buyer may wish individual protection. Among the special risks that should be considered and agreed upon between seller and buyer are theft, pilferage, leakage, breakage, sweat, contact with other cargoes, and others peculiar to any particular trade. It is important that contingent or collect freight and customs duty should be insured to cover Particular Average losses, as well as total loss after arrival and entry but before delivery.

- The seller is obligated to exercise ordinary care and diligence in selecting an underwriter that is in good financial standing. However, the risk of obtaining settlement of insurance claims rests with the buyer.

- War risk insurance under this term is to be obtained by the seller at the expense and risk of the buyer. It is important that the seller be in definite accord with the buyer on this point, particularly as to the cost. It is desirable that the goods be insured against both marine and war risk with the same underwriter, so that there can be no difficulty arising from the determination of the cause of the loss.

- Seller should make certain that the standard protection against strikes, riots, and civil commotions be included in the marine or war risk insurance.

- Seller and buyer should be in accord as to the insured valuation, bearing in mind that merchandise contributes in General Average on certain bases of valuation that differ in various trades. It is desirable that a competent insurance broker be consulted, in order that full value be covered and trouble avoided.

dealer's brand. See *private brands.*

department store. A retail store that handles a wide variety of lines of goods, such as women's ready-to-wear and accessories, men's and boys' wear, piece goods, and small wares and house furnishings, and which is organized into separate departments for purposes of promotion, service, and control.

Examples of department stores are: R. H. Macy & Company in New York; Marshall Field & Company in Chicago; J. L. Hudson Company in Detroit; Jordan Marsh Company in Boston; Rich's in Atlanta; Emporium-Capwell in San Francisco; Bullock's in Los Angeles; and Frederick & Nelson in Seattle.

This definition departs from the usual one in that it includes no definite requirement as to classes of goods handled, save only that they shall embrace a wide variety of lines. Most definitions previously suggested for this term set up a list of categories of merchandise that a store must handle before it can be designated as a department store. The emphasis here is placed upon the departmentalization feature, provided a wide variety of lines is handled.

This formula probably more nearly conforms to common usage than do those of the more rigid type and at the same time it includes many stores whose problems and characteristics belong to this group but which do not fall within it if a rigid requirement as to classes of goods handled were applied. This is roughly the definition used by the Bureau of the Census.

direct selling. The process whereby the producer sells to the user, ultimate consumer, or retailer without intervening middlemen.

The Committee recommends that when this term is used, it be so qualified as to indicate clearly the precise meaning intended (direct to retailer, direct to user, direct to ultimate consumer, etc.).

distribution. The Committee recommends that the term *distribution* be regarded and used as synonymous with *marketing*.

For a specialized sense in which it is sometimes used in this field, see *physical distribution*.

In using this term, marketing people should clearly distinguish it from the sense in which it is employed in economic theory, which is, the process of dividing the fund of value produced by industry among the several factors engaged in economic production.

distribution cost analysis. The study and evaluation of the relative profitability or costs of different marketing operations in terms of customers, marketing units, commodities, territories, warehouses, or services.

drop shipment wholesaler. See *wholesaler*.

equipment. Those industrial goods that do not become part of the physical product and which are exhausted only after repeated use, such as major installations, or installation equipment, and auxiliary accessories or auxiliary equipment.

Installation equipment includes such items as boilers, linotype machines, power latches, and bank vaults.

Auxiliary equipment includes such items as trucks, typewriters, filing cases, and most small tools.

ex (point of origin). This term includes the named point of origin and may be expressed as *Ex Factory, Ex Mill, Ex Mine, Ex Plantation, Ex Warehouse, etc.*

Under this term, the price quoted applies only at the point of origin, and the seller agrees to place the goods at the disposal of the buyer at the agreed place on the date or within the period fixed.

Under this quotation the seller must:

1. Bear all costs and risks of the goods until such time as the buyer is obliged to take delivery thereof;

2. Render the buyer, at the buyer's request and expense, assistance in obtaining the documents issued in the country of origin, or of shipment, or both, that the buyer may require either for purposes of exportation, or of importation at destination.

The buyer must:

1. Take delivery of the goods as soon as they have been placed at his or her disposal at the agreed place on the date or within the period fixed;

2. Pay export taxes, or other fees or charges, if any, levied because of exportation;

3. Bear all costs and risks of the goods from the time when he or she is obligated to take delivery thereof;

4. Pay all costs and charges incurred in obtaining the documents issued in the country of origin, or of shipment, or of both, that may be required either for purposes of exportation, or of importation at destination.

ex dock (named port of importation).

Note: Seller and buyer should consider not only the definitions but also the "Ex Dock Comments" at the end of this section, in order to understand fully their respective responsibilities and rights under "Ex Dock" terms.

Under this term, seller quotes a price, including the cost of the goods and all additional costs necessary to place the goods on the dock at the named port of importation, duty paid, if any.

Under this quotation the seller must:

1. Provide and pay for transportation to named port of importation;

2. Pay export taxes, or other fees or charges, if any, levied because of exportation;

3. Provide and pay for marine insurance;

4. Provide and pay for war risk insurance, unless otherwise agreed upon between the buyer and seller;

5. Be responsible for any loss or damage, or both, until the expiration of the free time allowed on the dock at the named port of importation;

6. Pay the costs of certificates of origin, consular invoices, legalization of bill of lading, or any other documents issued in the country

of origin, or of shipment, or of both, that the buyer may require for the importation of goods into the country of destination and, where necessary, for their passage in transit through another country;

7. Pay all costs of landing, including wharfage, landing charges, and taxes, if any;

8. Pay all costs of customs entry in the country of importation;

9. Pay customs duties and all taxes applicable to imports, if any, in the country of importation, unless otherwise agreed upon.

The buyer must:

1. Take delivery of the goods on the dock at the named port of importation within the free time allowed;

2. Bear the cost and risk of the goods if delivery is not taken within the free time allowed.

Ex Dock Comments

This term is used principally in United States import trade. It has various modifications, such as "Ex Quay," "Ex Pier," etc., but it is seldom, if ever, used in American export practice. Its use in quotations for export is not recommended.

General Notes of Caution

1. As foreign trade definitions have been issued by organizations in various parts of the world, and as the courts of countries have interpreted these definitions in different ways, it is important that sellers and buyers agree that their contracts are subject to the latest revised edition of *American Foreign Trade Definitions, Revised,* and that the various points listed are accepted by both parties.

2. In addition to the foreign trade terms listed herein, there are terms that are at times used, such as Free Harbor, CIF&C (Cost, Insurance, Freight, and Commission), CIFC&I (Cost, Insurance, Freight, Commission, and Interest), CIF Landed (Cost, Insurance, Freight, Landed), and others. None of these should be used unless there has first been a definite understanding as to the exact meaning thereof. It is unwise to attempt to interpret other terms in the light of the terms given herein. Hence, whenever possible, one of the terms defined herein should be used.

3. It is unwise to use abbreviations in quotations or in contracts that might be subject to misunderstanding.

4. When making quotations, the familiar terms "hundredweight" or "ton" should be avoided. A hundredweight can be 100 pounds of the short ton, or 112 pounds of the long ton. A ton can be a short ton of 2,000 pounds, or a metric ton of 2,204.6 or a long ton of 2,240 pounds. Hence, the type of hundredweight or ton should be clearly stated in quotations and in sales confirmations. Also, all terms referring to quantity, weight, volume, length, or surface should be clearly defined and agreed upon.

factor.

1. A type of commission merchant who often advances funds to the consignor, identified chiefly with the raw cotton and naval stores trades.

2. A specialized commercial banker, performing the function of financing for producers of and dealers in many varieties of products and occasionally combining this function with that of selling.

The term factor *was formerly synonymous with* commission merchant.

FAS (Free Alongside)

FAS VESSEL (named port of shipment).

Note: Seller and buyer should consider not only the definitions but also the "comments" given at the end of this section, in order to understand fully their respective responsibilities and rights under FAS terms.

Under this term, the seller quotes a price, including delivery of the goods alongside overseas vessel and within reach of its loading tackle.

Under this quotation the seller must:

1. Place goods alongside vessel or on dock designed and provided by, or for, buyer on the date or within the period fixed; pay any heavy lift charges, where necessary, up to this point;

2. Provide clean dock or ship's receipt;

3. Be responsible for any loss or damage, or both, until goods have been delivered alongside the vessel or on the dock;

4. Render the buyer, at the buyer's request and expense, assistance in obtaining the documents issued in the country of origin, or of shipment, or of both, that the buyer may require either for purposes of exportation, or of importation at destination.

Buyer must:

1. Give seller adequate notice of name, sailing date, loading berth of, and delivery time to, the vessel;

2. Handle all subsequent movement of the goods from alongside the vessel.

   • Arrange and pay for demurrage or storage charges, or both, in warehouse or on wharf, where necessary;

   • Provide and pay for insurance;

   • Provide and pay for ocean and other transportation;

3. Pay export taxes, or other fees or charges, if any, levied because of exportation;

4. Be responsible for any loss or damage, or both, while the goods are on a lighter or other conveyance alongside vessel within reach of its loading tackle, or on the dock awaiting loading, or until actually loaded on board the vessel, and subsequent thereto;

5. Pay all costs and charges incurred in obtaining the documents, other than clean dock or ships receipt, issued in the country of origin, or of shipment, or of both, that may be required either for purposes of exportation or of importation at destination.

FAS Comments

1. Under FAS terms, the obligation to obtain ocean freight space, and marine and war risk insurance, rests with the buyer. Despite this obligation on the part of the buyer, in many trades the seller obtains ocean freight space, and marine and war risk insurance, and provides for shipment on behalf of the buyer. In others, the buyer notifies the seller to make delivery alongside a vessel designated by the buyer and the buyer provides his or her own marine and war risk insurance. Hence, seller and buyer must have an understanding as to whether the buyer will obtain the ocean freight space, and marine and war risk insurance, as is his or her obligation, or whether the seller agrees to do this for the buyer.

2. For the seller's protection, the contract of sale should provide that marine insurance obtained by the buyer include standard warehouse-to-warehouse coverage.

fixed assets. The sum of the cost value of land and the depreciated book values of buildings, leasehold improvements, fixtures, furniture, machinery, tools, and equipment—valued at cost or appraised market value.

funded debt. Mortgages, bonds, debentures, gold notes, serial notes, or other obligations with maturity of more than one year from statement date.

free on board. *(FOB [named inland carrier at named inland point of departure]).*

Note: Seller and buyer should consider not only the definitions but also the "Comments on All FOB Terms" given at end of this section, in order to understand fully their respective responsibilities and rights under the several classes of FOB terms.

Under this term, the price quoted applies only at inland shipping points, and the seller arranges for loading of the goods on, or in, railway cars, trucks, lighters, barges, aircraft, or other conveyance furnished for transportation.

Under this quotation the seller must:

1. Place goods on, or in, conveyance, or deliver to inland carrier for loading;

2. Provide clean bill of lading or other transportation receipt, freight collect;

3. Be responsible for any loss or damage, or both, until goods have been placed in, or on, conveyance at loading point, and clean bill of lading or other transportation receipt has been furnished by the carrier;

4. Render the buyer, at the buyer's request and expense, assistance in obtaining the documents issued in the country of origin, or of shipment, or of both, that the buyer may require either for purposes of exportation, or of importation at destination.

Buyer must:

1. Be responsible for all movement of the goods from inland point of loading, and pay all transportation costs;

2. Pay export taxes, or other fees or charges, if any, levied because of exportation;

3. Be responsible for any loss or damage, or both, incurred after loading at named inland point of departure;

4. Pay all costs and charges incurred in obtaining the documents issued in the country of origin, or of shipment, or of both, that may

be required either for purposes of exportation, or of importation at destination.

FOB (named inland carrier at named inland point of departure); freight prepared to (named point of exportation).

Under this term, the seller quotes a price including transportation charges to the named point of exportation and prepays freight to named point of exportation, without assuming responsibility for the goods after obtaining a clean bill of lading or other transportation receipt at named inland point of departure.

Under this quotation seller must:

1. Assume the seller's obligations, as under "Free on Board," except that under 2) he or she must provide clean bill of lading or other transportation receipt, freight prepaid to named point of exportation.

Buyer must:

1. Assume the same buyer's obligation as under "Free on Board," except that buyer does not pay freight from loading point to named point of exportation.

FOB (named inland carrier at named inland point of departure); freight allowed to (named point).

Under this term, the seller quotes a price including the transportation charges to the named point, shipping freight collect and deducting the cost of transportation, without assuming responsibility for the goods after obtaining a clean bill of lading or other transportation receipt at named inland point of departure.

Under this quotation seller must:

1. Assume the same seller's obligations as under "Free on Board," but deducts from his or her invoice the transportation cost to named point.

Buyer must:

1. Assume the same buyer's obligations as under "Free on Board," including payment of freight from inland loading point to named point, for which seller has made deduction.

FOB (named inland carrier at named point of exportation).

Under this term, the seller quotes a price including the costs of transportation of the goods to named point of exportation, bearing any loss or damage, or both, incurred up to that point.

Under this quotation seller must:

1. Place goods on, or in, conveyance, or deliver to inland carrier for loading;

2. Provide clean bill of lading or other transportation receipt, paying all transportation costs from loading point to named point of exportation;

3. Be responsible for any loss or damage, or both, until goods have arrived in, or on, inland conveyance at the named point of exportation;

4. Render the buyer, at the buyer's request and expense, assistance in obtaining the documents issued in the country of origin, or of shipment, or of both, that the buyer may require either for purposes of exportation, or of importation at destination.

Buyer must:

1. Be responsible for all movement of the goods from inland conveyance at named point of exportation;

2. Pay export taxes, or other fees or charges, if any, levied because of exportation;

3. Be responsible for any loss or damage, or both, incurred after goods have arrived in, or on, inland conveyance at the named point of exportation;

4. Pay all costs and charges incurred in obtaining the documents issued in the country of origin, or shipment, or of both, that may be required either for purposes of exportation, or of importation at destination.

FOB vessel (named port of shipment).

Under this term, the seller quotes a price covering all expenses up to, and including, delivery of the goods upon the overseas vessel provided by, or for, the buyer at the named port of shipment.

Under this quotation seller must:

1. Pay all charges incurred in placing goods actually on board the vessel designated and provided by, or for, the buyer on the date or within the period fixed;

2. Provide clean ship's receipt or on-board bill of lading;

3. Be responsible for any loss or damage, or both, until goods have been placed on board the vessel on the date or within the period fixed;

4. Render the buyer, at the buyer's request and expense, assistance in obtaining the documents issued in the country of origin, or of shipment, or of both, that the buyer may require either for purposes of exportation, or of importation at destination.

Buyer must:

1. Give seller adequate notice of name, sailing date, loading berth of, and delivery time to, the vessel;

2. Bear the additional costs incurred and all risks of the goods from the time when the seller has placed them at the buyer's disposal if the vessel named by the buyer fails to arrive or to load within the designated time;

3. Handle all subsequent movement of the goods to destination:

   • Provide and pay for insurance;

   • Provide and pay for ocean and other transportation;

4. Pay export taxes, or other fees or charges, if any, levied because of exportation;

5. Be responsible for any loss or damage, or both, after goods have been loaded on board the vessel;

6. Pay all costs and charges incurred in obtaining the documents, other than clean ship's receipt or bill of lading, issued in the country of origin, or of shipment, or of both, that may be required either for purposes of exportation, or of importation at destination.

FOB (named inland point in country of importation).

Under this term, the seller quotes a price including the cost of the merchandise and all costs of transportation to the named inland point in the country of importation.

Under this quotation seller must:

1. Provide and pay for all transportation to the named inland point in the country of importation;

2. Pay export taxes, or other fees or charges, if any, levied because of exportation;

3. Provide and pay for marine insurance;

4. Provide and pay for war risk insurance, unless otherwise agreed upon between the seller and buyer;

5. Be responsible for any loss or damage, or both, until arrival of goods on conveyance at the named inland point in the country of importation;

6. Pay the costs of certificates of origin, consular invoices, or any other documents issued in the country of origin, or of shipment, or of both, that the buyer may require for the importation of goods into the country of destination and, where necessary, for their passage in transit through another country;

7. Pay all costs of landing, including wharfage, landing charges, and taxes, if any;

8. Pay all costs of customs entry in the country of importation;

9. Pay customs duties and all taxes applicable to imports, if any, in the country of importation.

Note: The seller under this quotation must realize that he or she is accepting important responsibilities, costs, and risks, and should therefore be certain to obtain adequate insurance. On the other hand, the importer or buyer may desire such quotations to reduce the risks of the voyage and to provide assurance of landed costs at inland point in country of importation. When competition is keen, or the buyer is accustomed to such quotations from other sellers, seller may quote such terms, being careful to protect himself in an appropriate manner.

Buyer must:

1. Take prompt delivery of goods from conveyance upon arrival at destination;

2. Bear any costs and be responsible for all loss or damage, or both, after arrival at destination.

Comments on All FOB Terms

In connection with FOB terms, the following points of caution are recommended:

1. The method of inland transportation, such as trucks, railroad cars, lighters, barges, or aircraft should be specified.

2. If any switching charges are involved during the inland transportation, it should be agreed, in advance, whether these charges are for account of the seller or the buyer.

3. The term *FOB (named port)*, without designating the exact point at which the liability of the seller terminates and the liability of the buyer begins, should be avoided. The use of this term gives rise to disputes as to the liability of the seller or the buyer in the event of loss or damage arising while the goods are in port, and before delivery to or on board the ocean carrier. Misunderstandings may be avoided by naming the specific point of delivery.

4. If lighterage or trucking is required in the transfer of goods from the inland conveyance to ship's side, and there is a cost therefor, it should be understood, in advance, whether this cost is for account of the seller or the buyer.

5. The seller should be certain to notify the buyer of the minimum quantity required to obtain a carload, a truckload, or a bargeload freight rate.

6. Under FOB terms excepting *FOB (named inland point in country of importation)*, the obligation to obtain ocean freight space, and marine and war risk insurance, rests with the buyer. Despite this obligation on the part of the buyer, in many trades the seller obtains the ocean freight space, and marine and war risk insurance, and provides for shipment on behalf of the buyer. Hence, seller and buyer must have an understanding as to whether the buyer will obtain the ocean freight space, and marine and war risk insurance, as is his or her obligation, or whether the seller agrees to do this for the buyer.

7. For the seller's protection, the contract of sales should provide that marine insurance obtained by the buyer include standard warehouse-to-warehouse coverage.

general store. A retail store that carries a variety of nonrelated items of merchandise, usually including groceries, hard goods, and soft goods, and that is not departmentalized.

The type is most generally and most typically found in country districts. However, the term is not confined to stores serving the country and village trade, but includes retail establishments in cities as well. This conforms roughly to the usage of the Bureau of the Census.

Some country general stores in Western states are departmentalized. It is possible that they are departmentalized specialty stores instead of general stores, although the term general stores *is applied to them as a matter of custom.*

grading. Grading is the process of sorting individual units of a product according to predetermined standards or classes.

This term is often defined so as to include the work of setting up classes or grades. This work is really a part of the standardization.

gross profit. Sales less Cost of Goods Sold (adjusted for inventory depreciation and merchandise shortages).

house-to-house salesperson. A salesperson who is primarily engaged in making sales direct to ultimate consumers in their homes.

The term canvasser is often employed as synonymous with house-to-house salesperson. Due to its extensive use in fields other than marketing, as for instance in public-opinion polls, this usage is not recommended.

independent store. A retail store controlled by its own individual ownership or management rather than from without, except insofar as its management is limited by voluntary group arrangements.

This definition includes a member of a voluntary group organization. It is recognized that the voluntary group possesses many of the characteristics of and presents many of the same problems as the chain store system. In the final analysis, however, the members of the voluntary groups are independent stores, cooperating, perhaps temporarily, in the accomplishment of certain marketing purposes. Their collective action is entirely voluntary and the retailers engaging in it consider themselves to be independent.

industrial goods. Goods destined for use in producing other goods or rendering services, as contrasted with goods destined to be sold to the ultimate consumer.

They include land and buildings for business purposes, equipment (installation and accessory), maintenance, repair and operating supplies, raw materials, fabricated materials.

The distinguishing characteristics of these goods is the purpose for which they are destined to be used, in carrying on business or industrial activities rather than for consumption by individual ultimate consumers or resale to them. The category also includes merchandise destined for use in carrying on various types of institutional enterprises.

Relatively few goods are exclusively industrial goods. The same article may, under one set of circumstances, be an industrial goods and under other conditions, a consumers' goods.

industrial store. See *commissary store.*

installation equipment. See *equipment.*

inventory. The sum of raw material, material in process, and finished merchandise. It does not include supplies.

jobber. This term is now widely used as a synonym of *wholesaler.*

Formerly the jobber was a dealer in odd lots, but this usage has practically disappeared. The term is sometimes used in certain trades and localities to designate special types of wholesalers. This usage is especially common in the distribution of agricultural products. The characteristics of the wholesalers so designated vary from trade to trade and from locality to locality.

Most of the schedules submitted to the Bureau of the Census by the members of the wholesale trades show no clear line of demarcation between those who call themselves jobbers and those who prefer to be known as wholesalers. Therefore, it does not seem wise to attempt to set up any general basis of distinction between the terms in those few trades or markets in which one exists. There are scattered examples of special distinctive usage of the term jobber. The precise nature of such usage must be sought in each trade or area in which it is employed.

limited function wholesaler. See *wholesaler.*

limited price variety store. See *variety store.*

mail-order house (retail). A retail establishment that receives its orders and makes its sales by mail.

Other types of retail stores often conduct a mail-order business, usually through departments set up for that purpose, although this fact does not make them mail-order houses. On the other hand, some firms that originally confined themselves to the mail-order business now also operate chain store systems. For example, Sears, Roebuck and Company and Montgomery Ward & Company are both mail-order houses and chain store systems.

mail-order wholesaler. See *wholesaler.*

major installations. See *equipment.*

manufacturer's brand. See *national brand.*

manufacturer's store. A retail store owned and operated by a manufacturer.

Such stores may serve as a channel for the distribution of the manufacturer's products; in other cases they may be used for experimental or publicity purposes.

manufacturers' agent. An agent who generally operates on an extended contractual basis; sells within an exclusive territory; handles noncompeting but related lines of goods; and possesses limited authority with regard to prices and terms of sale.

market.

1. An aggregate composed of a prospective buyer (or buyers) and a seller (or sellers), and that brings to focus the conditions and forces that determine prices.

2. The aggregate demand of the potential buyers of a commodity or service.

3. The place or area in which buyers and sellers function.

4. (As a verb) To perform business activities that direct the flow of goods and services from producer to consumer or user.

   In defining this term the Committee sought to include the usages of it commonly found in business, in marketing literature, and in economic theory. It is recommended that when the term is used, the context indicate clearly the sense in which it is employed.

   Examples of the usage described in 2) of the definition are the New England Market, the College Market, the Professional Market, and the Medical Market, as applied to any product or service.

market analysis. A subdivision of market research involving the measurement of the extent of a market and the determination of its characteristics.

   See also market research. *The activity described above consists essentially of the process of exploring and evaluating the marketing possibilities of the aggregates described in 2) of the definition of* market.

marketing financing. That part of the general business function of providing and managing funds and credit that is directly related to the transactions involved in the flow of goods and services from producer to consumer or industrial user.

   This definition includes the provision and management of funds needed to finance the carrying of stocks and the granting of mercantile and retail credit, including installment credit. It does not include the provision of funds to purchase a building in which to carry on a marketing enterprise nor does it embrace consumer borrowing on a personal basis. Roughly it embraces financial operations that are undertaken to control or modify the direction of the flow of goods and services in marketing but excludes those of a more general nature.

market potential. The expected sales of a commodity, a group of commodities, or a service for an entire industry in a market during a stated period.

The use of this concept should be considered in relation to that of sales potential.

marketing. The performance of business activities that direct the flow of goods and services from producer to consumer or user.

This definition seeks to exclude from marketing those semimanufacturing activities that result in changes in the form of merchandise which represent material modifications in its characteristics or uses. It seeks to include such activities when they result in changes in form primarily designed to make the product more salable and only incidentally to affect its use, such as packaging.

The task of defining *marketing* may be approached from at least three points of view.

1. *The* legalistic, *of which the following is a good example:*

   "Marketing includes all activities having to do with effecting changes in the ownership and possession of goods and services." It seems undesirable to adopt a definition that throws so much emphasis upon the legal phases of what is essentially a commercial subject.

2. *The* economic, *examples of which are:*

   "That part of economics dealing with the creation of time, place, and possession utilities."

   "That phase of business activity through which human wants are satisfied by the exchange of goods and services for some valuable consideration."

   Such definitions are apt to assume somewhat more understanding of economic concepts than are ordinarily found in the marketplace.

3. *The* factual or descriptive *of which the definition suggested by the Committee is an example. This type of definition merely seeks to describe its subject in terms likely to be understood by both professional economists and businesspeople without reference to legal or economic implications.*

marketing facilities agencies. Those agencies which perform or assist in the performance of one or a number of the marketing functions, but which neither take title to goods nor negotiate purchases or sales.

Common types are banks, railroads, storage warehouses, commodity exchanges and markets, stockyards, insurance companies, graders and inspectors, advertising agencies, firms engaged in marketing research, cattle loan companies, furniture marts, and packers and shippers.

Writers on marketing at one time classified these agencies as functional middlemen, including also in that classification all types of non-title-taking middlemen. This mixture of incongruous elements hardly seems desirable. The groups included in the definition above are not middlemen *as that term is defined by the Committee.*

marketing function. A major specialized activity performed in marketing.

There is no generally accepted list of marketing functions. Probably those most generally recognized are transportation or traffic management, physical distribution, storage, market financing, risk management, selling, grading, assembling, standardization, and buying. Merchandising is sometimes included in the list, although many students regard it as a broader business function lying between marketing and production.

Some of these activities are broad business functions having special marketing implications. Others are peculiar to the marketing process. In the first category are traffic management, physical distribution, market financing, and risk management. In the second group are buying, selling, and assembling.

Under this term students of marketing have sought to squeeze a heterogeneous and inconsistent group of activities. For example, the functions of assembling and dividing, if such functions exist, are performed through buying, selling, and transporting. Grading, standardization, and packaging are adjuncts of selling. Such functions as assembling, storage, and transporting are broad general economic functions, while selling and buying are essentially individual in character. All these discrete groups we attempt to crowd into one class and label marketing functions.

marketing plan. A program covering all methods and procedures for marketing the product or products of a company.

marketing policy. A course of action established to secure consistency of marketing procedure under recurring and essentially similar circumstances.

market research. The gathering, recording, and analyzing of all facts about problems relating to the transfer and sale of goods and services from producer to consumer.

Among other things market research involves the study of the relationships and adjustments between production and consumption, preparation of commodities for sale, their physical distribution, wholesale and retail merchandising, and financial problems. Such research may be undertaken by impartial agencies or by specific concerns or their agents for the solution of their marketing problems.

Market research *is the inclusive term that embraces all research activities carried on in connection with the management of marketing work. It includes various subsidiary types of research, such as* market analysis, *and* sales research, *which is largely an analysis of the sales records of a company;* consumer research, *which is concerned chiefly with the discovery and analysis of consumer attitudes, reactions, and preferences, and* advertising research, *which is carried on chiefly as an aid to the management of advertising work. The term* marketing research *is often used as synonymous with* market research.

merchandising. The planning involved in marketing the right merchandise or service at the right place, at the right time, in the right quantities, and at the right price.

This term has been used in a great variety of meanings, most of them confusing. The usage recommended by the Committee has the advantage that it adheres closely to the natural and essential meaning of the word. The activity described here might also be called merchandise, or product, planning. Included in the activity are such tasks as selecting the article to be produced or stocked and deciding such details as the size, appearance, form, dressing of the product (packaging, etc.), quantities to be bought or made, time of purchase or production, price lines to be made or carried, etc.

merchandising control. The collection and analysis of statistical data of sales, stocks, and pricing practices as a guide to the profitable purchase and sale of merchandise.

merchant middleman. A middleman who takes title to the goods he or she stocks and sells. Such middlemen usually perform most or all of the distributive functions.

The distinctive feature of this middleman lies in the fact that he or she takes title to the goods handled. The extent to which he or she performs the marketing functions is incidental to the definition. Wholesalers and retailers are the chief types of merchant middlemen.

merchant's brand. See *private brand.*

middleman. A business concern that specializes in performing functions or rendering services immediately involved in the purchase and/or sale of goods in the process of their flow from producer to consumer.

Middlemen are of two types: merchants, or merchant middlemen, and agents, or agent middlemen.

The essence of the middleman's operation is that he or she plays an active and prominent part in the negotiations leading up to transactions of purchase and sale. This is what distinguishes the middleman from a marketing facilitating agent who, while performing certain marketing functions, participates only incidentally in negotiations of purchase and sale.

This term is very general in its meaning. The Committee recommends that whenever possible more specific terms be used, such as agent, merchant, retailer, wholesaler.

missionary salesperson. A salesperson employed by a manufacturer to make contact with and work with the customers of his or her distributors, usually for the purpose of developing goodwill and stimulating demand, helping or inducing them to promote the sale of his or her employer's goods, helping them train their salespeople to do so, and often taking orders for delivery by such distributors.

This term has been used to designate any sort of salesperson who is primarily engaged in goodwill work. The definition above gives it a much narrower meaning. The term should not be confused with the so-called "missionary" sales work which usually covers a much more varied type of sales activity than that done by the missionary salesperson. Missionary salespeople are sometimes called "detailers." Medical drug salespeople calling on physicians and hospitals are called "detail persons."

national brand. A manufacturer's or producer's brand, usually enjoying wide territorial distribution.

The usage of the terms national brand *and* private brand *while generally current and commonly accepted, is highly illogical and nondescriptive. It is recommended that whenever possible more specific and descriptive terms be used, such as* manufacturer's brand *or* producer's brand.

net income. Final income available for proprietary accounts (either before or after deduction of federal and state income taxes). It includes *operating profit* together with *net other income.*

Net profit *is recommended as the preferred term among the three.*

net profit. Profit after full depreciation on buildings, machinery, equipment, furniture, and other assets of a fixed nature; after reserves for federal income and excess profit taxes; after reduction in the value of inventory to cost or market, whichever is lower; after charge-offs for bad debts; after miscellaneous reserves and adjustments; but before dividends or withdrawals.

net sales. The dollar volume of business transacted for 365 days net after deductions for returns, allowances, and discounts from gross sales.

net sales to inventory. The quotient obtained by dividing the annual net sales by the statement inventory. This quotient does not represent the actual physical turnover, which would be determined by reducing the annual net sales to the cost of the goods sold, and then dividing the resulting figure by the statement inventory.

net working capital. The excess of the current assets over the current debt.

operating profit*. Gross margin (gross profit) less operating expenses (including salaries of managers, whether proprietors or employees), fixed plant and equipment cost, and sometimes interest on invested capital.

Obviously this definition includes only the profit accruing from the trading operations of a mercantile business.

organized market. A group of traders operating under recognized rules for the purpose of buying and selling a single commodity or a small number of related commodities.

Examples are the Chicago Board of Trade, the New York Cotton Exchange, and the New York Produce Exchange.

parent store. A retail store that owns and operates a *branch store* or a group of *branch stores.*

personal selling. Oral presentation in a conversation with one or more prospective customers for the purpose of making sales.

This definition embraces the idea that the presentation may be either formal (as a "canned" sales talk), or informal, although it is more likely to be informal, either in the actual presence of the customer or by telephone.

**For purposes of marketing.*

physical distribution. The movement and handling of goods from the point of production to the point of consumption or use.

The word distribution *is sometimes used to describe this activity. In view of the technical meaning of the word* distribution *in economic theory and of the fact that it is used by the Bureau of the Census and increasingly by marketing students and businesspeople as synonymous with* marketing, *the Committee recommends that its use as a synonym of or substitute for* physical distribution *be discouraged.*

price cutting. Offering merchandise or a service for sale at a price below that recognized as usual or standard by the buyers and sellers in a market.

One obvious criticism of this definition is that it is indefinite. But that very indefiniteness also causes it to be more accurately descriptive of a concept that is characterized by a high degree of indefiniteness in the mind of the average person affected by price cutting.

Traders' ideas of what constitutes price cutting are so vague and indefinite that any precise or highly specific definition of that phenomenon is bound to fail to include all its manifestations. If you ask a group of traders in a specific commodity to define price cutting, you will get as many conflicting formulas as there are traders. But if you ask those same traders at any particular time whether selling at a certain price constitutes price cutting, you will probably get a considerable degree of unanimity of opinion. It is precisely this condition which the definition is designed to reflect.

private brands. Brands sponsored by merchants or agents as distinguished from those sponsored by manufacturers or producers. In the food industry, sometimes called *private label.*

This usage is thoroughly illogical, since no seller wants his or her brand to be private in the sense of being secret and all brands are private in the sense that they are special and not common or general in use. But the usage is common in marketing literature and among traders.

It is recommended that, whenever possible, more specific terms, such as wholesaler's brand, retailer's brand, dealer's brand, *or* merchant's brand *be used.*

producer's brand. See *national brand.*

producer's cooperative marketing. That type of cooperative marketing that primarily involves the sale of goods or services of the associated producing membership.

Many producer's cooperative marketing associations both buy and sell for their members. This fact does not subtract from their status as producer's cooperatives; this is especially true of the farm cooperatives. The term does not include those activities of trade associations that affect only indirectly the sales of the membership. Such activities are the maintenance of credit rating bureaus, design registration bureaus, and brand protection machinery. It does include, however, such things as cooperative advertising.

publicity. Any form of commercially significant news about a product, an institution, a service, or a person published in print, television, or radio that is not paid for by the sponsor.

In the retail trade this term is often used to include such activities as advertising and display work.

The term free publicity *is often used as a synonym or substitute for* publicity. *The Committee does not recommend this usage because it is a misnomer. It is doubtful if any publicity is ever entirely free.*

purchasing power. The capacity to purchase possessed by an individual buyer, a group of buyers, or the aggregate of the buyers in an area or a market.

raw materials. Those industrial goods which in part or in whole become a portion of the physical product but which have undergone no more processing than is required for convenience, protection, or economy in storage, transportation, or handling.

retailer. A merchant or business establishment that sells mainly to the ultimate consumer.

The retailer is to be distinguished by the conditions surrounding the sale rather than the procurement of the goods in which he or she deals. Attempts to define the retailer on the basis of the size of units of sale prove indefensible. The size of sales unit is an incidental rather than a primary element in the character of the retailer. The essential distinguishing mark of the retailer is the fact that a typical sale is made to the ultimate consumer.

retailer cooperative. A group of independent retailers organized to buy cooperatively either through a jointly owned warehouse or through a buying club. Their cooperative activities usually include operating under a group name, joint advertising, and cooperative managerial supervision.

retailer's brand. See *private brand.*

retailer. The activities incident to selling to the ultimate consumer. The goods sold may be produced, bought, or carried in stock by the seller.

This definition includes all forms of selling to the ultimate consumer. It embraces the direct-to-consumer sales activities of the producer, whether through his or her own stores, by house-to-house canvass, or by mail order. It does not cover the sale by producers of industrial goods, by industrial supply houses, or by retailers to industrial, commercial, or institutional buyers for use in the conduct of their enterprises.

risk management. The function of reducing, spreading, or avoiding the loss of pecuniary value of goods and services during their marketing. Such losses may occur through physical deterioration, obsolescence, theft, damage, waste, changes in supply or demand, or through changes in the price level.

Some criticism may attach to the designation of this function as risk management *since it often happens that not much can be done in the way of managing risks. They come as they will regardless of attempts to manage them.*

The term has many advantages, however, over risk bearing, *which is often applied to this type of activity. Not all risks arising in distribution are borne by those engaged in it. Many of them are avoided and many others are changed in character or intensity as a result of good management on the part of marketing concerns. Losses are of two types, those that are insurable, such as fire and accident, and those that are not insurable, such as the losses from changes in price.*

sales budget. An estimate of the probable dollar sales and probable selling costs of a specified period.

The use of this term is sometimes confined to an estimate of future sales. This does not conform to the general use of the term budget, *which includes schedules of both receipts and expenditures. If the sales budget is to be used as a device to facilitate sales control and management, it should include the probable cost of getting the estimated volume of sales. The failure to allow proper weight to this item in their calculations is one of the most consistently persistent and fatal mistakes made by American business concerns. It has led to much of the striving after unprofitable volume that has been so costly.*

sales control. A system of supervision involving the use of such devices as records, statistical analyses, correspondence, and personal contact for the purpose of carrying out or adjusting marketing policies and plans.

The application of this term is often confined to the operation of a system of records and forms from which a picture of sales operations may be obtained. The recommended usage goes much farther and includes the practical use that may be made of such a picture once it is obtained.

sales forecast. An estimate of dollar or unit sales for a specified future period under a proposed marketing plan or program.

The forecast may be for a specified item of merchandise or for an entire line; it may be for a market as a whole or for any portion thereof.

Two sets of factors are involved in making a sales forecast:

1. *Those forces outside the control of the firm for which the forecast is made that are likely to influence its sales;*

2. *Changes in the marketing methods or practices of the firm that are likely to affect its sales.*

   In the course of planning future activities, the management of a given firm may make several sales forecasts, each consisting of an estimate of probable sales if a given marketing plan is adopted or a given set of outside forces prevails. The estimated effects on sales of a number of marketing plans may be compared in the process of arriving at that marketing program which, in the opinion of the officials of the company, will best promote its welfare.

sales management. The planning, direction, and control of personal selling, including recruiting, selecting, training, equipping, assigning, routing, supervising, paying, and motivating as these tasks apply to the personal sales force.

sales manager. The executive who plans, directs, and controls the activities of salespeople.

This executive may and often does perform broader functions in the marketing work of his or her company, but the essential nature of this position lies in its relation to the personal selling work of the firm.

sales planning. The work of setting up objectives for marketing activity and of determining and scheduling the steps necessary to achieve such objectives.

This term includes not only the work of deciding upon the goals or results to be attained through marketing activity, but also the determination in detail of exactly how they are to be accomplished. The result of this work is a sales plan.

sales potential. The share of a market potential that a company expects to achieve.

The portion of the total expected sales of an industry which the managers of a firm expect that firm to get is the sales potential *for that firm. By means of market research a firm may establish a market potential for the industry of which it is a part. Through the use of one or more sales forecasts its managers may determine upon a sales potential for the firm. From this may be derived the sales budget and a sales quota for the entire company or any part of it.*

sales promotion.

1. In a specific sense, those sales activities that supplement both personal selling and advertising and that coordinate them and help to make them effective, such as displays, shows and expositions, demonstrations, and other nonrecurrent selling efforts not in the ordinary routine.

2. In a general sense, sales promotion includes personal selling, advertising, and supplementary selling activities.

This definition includes the two most logical and commonly accepted among the many confusing and conflicting usages of this term. It is the consensus of the Committee that insofar as possible the use of the term should be confined to the first of the two definitions given above.

sales quota. A sales goal assigned to a marketing unit for use in the management of sales efforts.

It applies to a specified period and may be expressed in dollars or in physical units.

The quota may be used in checking the efficiency, stimulating the efforts, or in fixing the payment of individual salespeople or groups of salespeople or other personnel engaged in sales work.

A quota may be for a salesperson, a territory, a branch house, or for the company as a whole. It may be different from the sales figure set up in the sales budget. Since it is a managerial device, it is not an immutable figure inexorably arrived at by the application of absolutely exact statistical formulas but may be set up with an eye to its psychological effects upon the sales personnel or any part of it. Two salespeople, working in territories of identical potential, may be assigned different quotas in accordance with the anticipated effects of this variation on their sales efforts because of differences in their characters or personalities.

sales research. See *market research.*

selective selling. The policy of selling only to dealers and distributors who meet the seller's requirements, such as size of orders, volume of purchases, profitability, or area or type of operations.

While accounts are selected on a variety of bases, probably the most common are size and the kind and amount of reselling service the account is willing and able to give to the goods or services of the seller. Possibly the soundest basis is that of the amount of potential net profit to be derived from the business placed by the account.

selling. The personal or impersonal process of assisting and/or persuading a prospective customer to buy a commodity or a service or to act favorably upon an idea that has commercial significance to the seller.

This definition includes advertising and other forms of publicity and sales promotion, as well as personal selling.

selling agent. An agent who operates on an extended contractual basis; sells all of a specified line of merchandise or the entire output of his or her principal, and usually has full authority with regard to prices, terms, and other conditions of sale. The selling agent occasionally renders financial aid to his or her principal.

service wholesaler. See *wholesaler.*

services. Activities or anticipated satisfactions offered for sale either as such or in connection with the sale of goods.

Examples are amusements, hotel service, electric service, transportation, the services of barber shops and beauty shops, repair and maintenance service, and the work of credit rating bureaus. This list is merely illustrative and no attempt has been made to make it complete. The term also applies to the various activities, such as credit extension, advice and help of salespeople, and delivery, by which the seller serves the convenience of his or her customers.

shopping goods. Those consumers' goods that the customer in the process of selection and purchase characteristically compares on such cases as suitability, quality, price, and style.

Examples of goods that most consumers probably buy as *shopping goods* are millinery, furniture, dress goods, men's and women's ready-to-wear, shoes, jewelry, and residential real estate (not bought for purposes of speculation).

It should be emphasized that the same articles may be bought by one customer as shopping goods *and by another as* specialty *or* convenience goods. *The general classification depends upon the way in which the average or typical buyer purchases. See* specialty goods.

simplification. The process of reducing the varieties of goods within a line offered for sale.

It involves reducing the number of articles, parts, materials, models, styles, grades, colors, sizes, price lines, brands, designs, etc.

specialty goods. Those consumers' goods on which a significant group of buyers characteristically insist and for which they are willing to make a special purchasing effort.

Examples of articles that are usually bought as specialty goods are specific brands of fancy groceries, watches, men's shoes, and possibly automobiles.

There seems to be room for considerable doubt as to whether the distinction between shopping goods *and* specialty goods *is any longer valid or useful. There is less doubt of the validity of the class* shopping goods *than of* specialty goods. *The term is included here because many students of marketing appear still to find it useful and to desire its retention.*

specialty salesperson. A salesperson, other than retail, who specializes in the sale of one product or a few products of a seller's line.

A specialty salesperson should be contrasted with a general salesperson *who handles an entire line. He or she does not necessarily sell specialty goods.*

specialty shop. See *specialty store.*

specialty store. A retail store that makes its appeal on the basis of a restricted class of shopping goods.

Large specialty stores, if organized into departments, are called *departmentalized specialty stores.* Small specialty stores in certain trades are sometimes called *specialty shops.*

This term should not be used to include stores handling one or a few lines of convenience goods, such as staple groceries, hardware, stationery, or tobacco.

standardization. The determination of basic limits or grades in the form of specifications to which manufactured goods must conform and classes into which the products of agriculture and the extractive industries may be sorted.

This term does not include grading, *which is the process of sorting units of a product into the grades or classes that have been established through the process of* standardization.

storage. The marketing function that involves holding goods between the time of their production and their final sale.

Some processing is often done while goods are in storage. It is probable that this should be regarded as a part of production rather than of marketing.

store unit. A single retail establishment of a chain store system or other group, such as a voluntary, cooperative, or ownership group.

supplies. Those industrial goods which do not become a part of the physical product or which are continually exhausted in facilitating the operation of an enterprise. Examples are fuel, lubricants, stationery, typewriter ribbons, cleaning materials, etc.

tangible net worth. The sum of all outstanding preferred or preference stocks (if any) and outstanding common stocks, surplus, and undivided profits, less any intangible items in the assets, such as goodwill, trademarks, patents, copyrights, leaseholds, mailing lists, treasury stock, organization expenses, and underwriting discounts and expenses.

trademark. A brand that is given legal protection because it is capable of exclusive appropriation; because it is used in a manner sufficiently fanciful, distinctive, and arbitrary, because it is affixed to the product when sold, or because it otherwise satisfies the requirements set up by law.

Trademark *is essentially a legal term and includes only those brands or parts of brands which the law designates as trademarks. In any specific case a trademark is what the court in that case decides to regard as a trademark.*

trade name. The name by which an article or a certain type or grade of an article is known among buyers and sellers. The name under which a business is conducted.

Credit acknowledged to Webster's International.

trading area. A district whose boundaries are usually determined by the economic buying or selling range for a commodity or group of related commodities from a center of distribution.

Trading areas are not static but are in a constant state of flux. A wholesale trading area may be distinguished chiefly by the economic selling and delivery range of the firms in it; a retail trading area is usually distinguished by the area from which the center draws the buying trade of consumers in significant amounts.

traffic management. The planning, selection, and direction of all means of transportation involved in the movement of goods in the marketing process.

This definition is confined to those activities in connection with transportation that have to do particularly with marketing and form an inseparable part of any well-organized system of distribution. It includes the movement of goods in trucks owned by the marketing concern, as well as by public carrier. It does not include the movement of goods within the warehouse of a producer or distributor or within the store of a retail concern.

truck wholesaler. See *wholesaler.*

turnover of tangible net worth. The quotient obtained by dividing annual net sales by the tangible net worth.

turnover of net working capital. The quotient obtained by dividing annual net sales by the net working capital.

ultimate consumer. One who buys and/or uses goods or services to satisfy personal or household wants rather than for resale or use in business, institutional, or industrial operations.

There seems to be a growing tendency to drop the word ultimate *from this term. The Committee recommends that this tendency be encouraged.*

The definition distinguishes sharply between industrial users *and* ultimate consumers. *A firm buying and using an adding machine, a drum of lubricating oil, or a carload of steel billets is an industrial user of those products, not an* ultimate consumer *of them; under the developing usage it is not even a* consumer *of them. A vital difference exists between the purposes motivating the two types of purchases, which in turn results in highly significant differences in buying methods, marketing organization, and selling practices.*

variety store. A retail store that handles a wide assortment of goods, usually of a low or limited price.

Examples are what used to be called five-and-ten-cent stores.

This is often called a limited price variety store. *The validity of these terms and of the limited price feature of the definition is being dissipated by the tendency of these establishments to handle merchandise within a broader price range.*

voluntary group. A group of retailers, each of whom owns and operates his or her own store, and who is associated with a wholesaler to carry on joint merchandising activities; members are characterized by some degree of group identity and uniformity of operation. Such joint activities have been largely of two kinds—cooperative advertising and group control of store operation.

wholesaler. A merchant middleman who sells to retailers and other merchants and/or to industrial, institutional, and commercial users but who does not sell in significant amounts to ultimate consumers.

In the basic materials, semifinished goods, and tool and machinery trades, merchants of this type are commonly known as *dealers, distributors,* or *supply houses.*

Generally these merchants render a wide variety of services to their customers. Those who render all the services normally expected in the wholesale trade are known as service wholesalers; *those who render only a few of the wholesale services are known as* limited function wholesalers. *The latter group is composed mainly of* cash and carry wholesalers *who do not render the credit or delivery service,* drop shipment wholesalers *who sell for delivery by the producer direct to the buyer,* truck wholesalers *who combine selling, delivery, and collection in one operation, and* mail-order wholesalers *who perform the selling service entirely by mail.*

This definition ignores or minimizes two bases upon which the term is often defined; first, the size of the lots in which wholesalers deal, and second, the fact that they habitually sell for resale. The figures show that many wholesalers operate on a very small scale and in small lots. Most of them make a significant portion of their sales to industrial users.

wholesaler's brand. See *private brand.*

Directory of Sales Training Aids

For a free copy of the *Dartnell Directory of Sales Training Films* write:

Susan Cariato, Customer Relations Manager
The Dartnell Corporation
4660 North Ravenswood Avenue
Chicago, Illinois 60640
312/561-4000 - 800/621-5463

Dartnell 16mm Films or Videocassettes

Sell Proud (featuring Earl Nightingale)

Second Effort (starring Vince Lombardi)

Second Effort II (starring Ron Masak)

Charge (featuring golf's great Arnold Palmer)

Take Command (featuring Wally Schirra)

Make It Happen (starring Julius Boros)

Put It All Together (starring Janet Guthrie, Gene Cernan, and Joe
   Paterno)

Think Win (featuring George Blanda)

Salesman (starring Wayne Tippit)

Sell Like an Ace—Live Like a King (with John Wolfe)

The Professional (featuring Van Johnson and Forrest Tucker)

The Tough-Minded Salesmanship Film Series
   (featuring Joe Batten)

   Ask For the Order and Get It

   Your Price Is Right—Sell It

   Manage Your Time To Build Your Territory

   When You're Turned Down—Turn On

   Sharpen Your Sales Presentation—Make It a Winner

Dealing With Price Resistance

Wickersham

Stand Out

Keep Climbing

Salesmanship on the Line

Professional Selling (six interrelated videocassettes)

Audiocassettes

New-Call Selling

What a Sales Professional Should Know About . . . (series)

Time to Sell

Film Distributors and Dealers

UNITED STATES

Eastern Region

Monad Trainers Aide
163-60 22nd Avenue
Whitestone, NY 11357
718/352-2314

Resource Communications
1616 Soldiers Field Road
Boston, MA 02135
617/783-3400

Sagotsky Multi Media
Office Suite 8,
The Village Shopper,
Route 206
Rocky Hill, NJ 08553
609/921-8778

Videolearning Systems, Inc.
354 W. Lancaster Avenue
Haverford, PA 19041
215/896-6600

Southern Region

**Thompson Mitchell
& Associates**
3384 Peachtree Road, NE
Atlanta, GA 30326
404/233-5435

Midwest Region

Masterco
11485 Pleasant Shore Drive
Manchester, MI 48158
313/428-8300

Roa's Films
914 N. 4th Street
Milwaukee, WI 53201
414/271-0861

Sportlite Films
230 N. Michigan Ave., Suite #525
Chicago, IL 60601
312/236-8955

Swank Motion Pictures, Inc.
2800 Market Street
St. Louis, MO 63166
314/534-1940

Western Region

National Business Films
7111 Garden Grove Blvd.
Garden Grove, CA 92641
415/828-9450

MDP Training Media
3250 Wilshire Blvd., Suite #900
Los Angeles, CA 90010
213/380-1653

Video Training Centers
1407 116th Avenue N.E.
Bellevue, WA 98004
206/453-1555

CANADA

International Tele-Film Enterprises
47 Densley Avenue
Toronto, ON M6M 5A8
416/241-4483

International Tele-Film Enterprises
4364 Rue St. Denis
Montreal, PQ H2J 2L1
514/844-1058

International Tele-Film Enterprises
1200 West Pender Street
Suite #601
Vancouver, BC V6E 2S9
604/685-2616

Equipment Directory

The equipment section of this directory lists manufacturers, not distributors. By writing directly to a number of manufacturers for literature, prices, and distributors' names, the sales executive can shop for the equipment best suited to his or her specific needs.

The same shopping process can be employed when choosing the services of a sales-training consultant or a film producer.

This directory was designed to be a starting point from which wise buying decisions can be made.

Although the editors have attempted to make this directory as complete as feasible, it is always possible that some firms and individuals will have been missed. Such omission is, of course, no reflection on the firm, nor does inclusion necessarily imply an endorsement by Dartnell.

We invite your comments on the usefulness of this directory, as well as suggestions for its improvement in future editions.

FOR ADDITIONAL HELP

A guide to local distributors of audio-visual equipment is available from the International Communications Industries Association (ICIA), 3150 Spring Street, Fairfax, Virginia 22031-2399. Write directly to the association. The Yellow Pages of your phone book are also an excellent source of information regarding audio-visual equipment retailers.

Projection Equipment

16 mm. Motion Picture Projectors

Bell & Howell, AV Division
7100 McCormick Road
Chicago, IL 60645

Bergen Expo Systems Inc.
1088 Main Ave.
Clifton, NJ 07011

Eastman Kodak Company
343 State Street
Rochester, NY 14650

Eiki International Inc.
27882 Camino Capistrano
Laguna Miguel, CA 92677

Hokushin/Rangertone
115 Roosevelt Ave.
Belleville, NY 07109

8 mm Motion Picture Projectors

Buhl Inc.
5 Paul Keaner Place
Elmwood Park, NJ 07407

General Audio-Visual Inc.
333 W. Merrick Road
Valley Stream, NY 11580

Xetron Corporation
10 Saddle Road
Cedar Knolls, NJ 07927

Filmstrip Projectors
(Silent)

AIV Concepts Corporation
756 Grand Blvd.
Deer Park, L.I., NY 11729

Apollo Audio-Visual
60 Trade Zone Court
Ronkonkoma, NY 11779

Dukane Corporation
2900 Dukane Drive
St. Charles, IL 60174

(Sound)

Apollo Audio-Visual
60 Trade Zone Court
Ronkonkoma, NY 11779

Dukane Corporation
2900 Dukane Drive
St. Charles, IL 60174

T.M. Visual Industries
212 W. 35th Street
New York, NY 10001

Telex Communications
9600 Aldrich Ave., South
Minneapolis, MN 55420

Slide Projectors

Atlantic Audio-Visual Corp.
630 Ninth Ave.
New York, NY 10036

Bergen Expo Systems Inc.
1088 Main Ave.
Clifton, NJ 07011

Eastman Kodak Company
343 State Street
Rochester, NY 14650

Hokushin/Rangertone
115 Roosevelt Ave.
Belleville, NJ 07109

Sound Slide Projectors

Creaton Inc.
504 Cherry Lane
Floral Park, NY 11001

RMF Products
1275 Paramount Parkway
Batavia, IL 60510

Sharp Electronics
Sharp Plaza
Mahwah, NJ 07430

Telex Communications Inc.
9600 Aldrich Ave., South
Minneapolis, MN 55420

Overhead Projectors

American Coated Products Inc.
1603 W. Algonquin Road
Arlington Heights, IL 60056

Audiscan Products Company
1414 130th Ave. NE
Bellevue, WA 98009

Bell & Howell Company
7100 McCormick Road
Chicago, IL 60645

Front Projection Screens

Apollo Audio Visual
60 Trade Zone Court
Ronkonkoma, NY 11779

Da-Lite Screen Company
PO Box 137
Warsaw, IN 46580

The Screen Works
3925 N. Pulaski Road
Chicago, IL 60641

Rear Projection Screens

Da-Lite Screen Company
PO Box 137
Warsaw, IN 46580

Draper Shade & Screen Company
411 S. Pearl Street
Spiceland, IN 47385

Video Tape Recorders and Players/Video Cameras/ Camcorders

JVC Company of America
41 Slater Drive
Elmwood Park, NJ 07407

Panasonic Industrial Company
One Panasonic Way
Secaucus, NJ 07094

Sony Corporation
Sony Drive
Park Ridge, NJ 07656

Video Monitors and Receivers

Audiotronics Corporation
7428 Bellaire Ave.
North Hollywood, CA 91605

Electrohome Limited
809 Wellington Street North
Kitchener, Ontario N2G 4J6
Canada

JVC Company of America
41 Slater Drive
Elmwood Park, NJ 07407

Panasonic Industrial Company
One Panasonic Way
Secaucus, NJ 07094

RCA Service Company
Rt. 38, Bldg. 203-3
Cherry Hill, NJ 08358

Sharp Electronics Corp.
Sharp Plaza
Mahwah, NJ 07430

Sony Corporation
Sony Drive
Park Ridge, NJ 07656

Sales and Marketing Executives International Directory

Sales and Marketing Executives International, an association for sales management and marketing professionals, has affiliated associations in the following listed areas. Anyone interested in joining can contact the local association or Sales and Marketing Executives International (SMEI). A direct membership with SMEI is available when an affiliated association is not in the member's area. Contact SMEI for details:

Sales and Marketing Executives International
Statler Office Tower
Cleveland, Ohio 44115
216/771-6650.

SMEI Affiliated Associations

ALABAMA

Birmingham
Sales and Marketing Executives
    of Birmingham
3107-C Independence Drive
Birmingham, AL 35209

Mobile
Sales and Marketing Executives
    of Mobile
P.O. Box 8391
Mobile, AL 36689

Montgomery
Sales and Marketing Executives
    of Montgomery
2067 Commodore Circle
Montgomery, AL 36106

North Alabama
Sales and Marketing Executives
    of North Alabama
250 Governors Drive, S.E.,
Suite J
Huntsville, AL 35801

ARIZONA

Greater Phoenix
Sales and Marketing Executives
    of Greater Phoenix
3104 E. Camelback Road
Suite 156
Scottsdale, AZ 85016

ARKANSAS

Little Rock
Sales and Marketing Executives
  of Little Rock
8023 Cantrell Road
Little Rock, AR 72207

Northeast Arkansas/Jonesboro
Sales and Marketing Executives
  of Northeast Arkansas/
  Jonesboro
P.O. Box 74
Jonesboro, AR 72402

CALIFORNIA

Long Beach
Sales and Marketing Executives
  of Long Beach
P.O. Box 2643
Long Beach, CA 90801

Los Angeles
Sales and Marketing Executives
  of Los Angeles
16529 Arminta Street
Van Nuys, CA 91406

Orange County
Sales and Marketing Executives
  of Orange County
12431 Lewis Street, Suite 203
Garden Grove, CA 92640

San Diego
Sales and Marketing Executives
  of San Diego
3888 Genesee Avenue, Suite 110
San Diego, CA 92111

San Francisco/Bay Area
Sales and Marketing Executives
  of San Francisco
649 Mission, #324
San Francisco, CA 94105

DISTRICT OF COLUMBIA

Metropolitan Washington
Sales and Marketing Executives
  of Metropolitan Washington
1331 P Street, N.W., #105
Washington, D.C. 20005

FLORIDA

Jacksonville
Sales and Marketing Executives
  of Jacksonville
1919 Beachway Road, Suite 6J
Jacksonville, FL 32207

Orlando
Sales and Marketing Executives
  of Orlando
P.O. Box 803
Winter Park, FL 32790

Pinellas-Suncoast
Sales and Marketing Executives
  of Pinellas-Suncoast
8832 Fifteenth Way, N.
St. Petersburg, FL 33733

Polk County
Sales and Marketing Executives
  of Polk County, Inc.
P.O. Box 2365
Lakeland, FL 33806

Tampa
Sales and Marketing Executives
  of Tampa
P.O. Box 10603
Tampa, FL 33679

GEORGIA

Atlanta
Sales and Marketing Executives
  of Atlanta
4360 Georgetown Square,
  Suite 805
Atlanta, GA 30338

Hawaii

Honolulu
Sales and Marketing Executives
of Honolulu
1088 Bishop Street, Suite 702
Honolulu, HI 96813

Idaho

Boise
Sales and Marketing Executives
of Boise
P.O. Box 1251
Boise, ID 83701

Pocatello
Sales and Marketing Executives
of Pocatello
P.O. Box 1501
Pocatello, ID 83204

Illinois

Chicago
Sales and Marketing Executives
of Chicago
1411 Peterson Avenue
Park Ridge, IL 60068

Rockford
Sales and Marketing Executives
of Rockford
P.O. Box 7616
Rockford, IL 61107

Kansas

Topeka
Sales and Marketing Executives
of Topeka
P.O. Box 2691
Topeka, KS 66601

Wichita
Sales and Marketing Executives
of Wichita
P.O. Box 48025
Wichita, KS 67201

Louisiana

Baton Rouge
Sales and Marketing Executives
of Baton Rouge
P.O. Box 67063
Baton Rouge, LA 70896

Shreveport
Sales and Marketing Executives
of Shreveport
Box 699
Shreveport, LA 71162

Michigan

Jackson
Sales and Marketing Executives
of Jackson
P.O. Box 1564
Jackson, MI 49204

Lansing
Sales and Marketing Executives
of Lansing
500 Marsh Road, Suite 14
Okemos, MI 48864

Minnesota

Minneapolis/St. Paul
Sales and Marketing Executives
of Minneapolis/St. Paul
2626 E. Eighty-second Street,
Suite 235
Minneapolis, MN 55420

MISSISSIPPI

Hattiesburg
Sales and Marketing Executives
of Hattiesburg
P.O. Box 1593
Hattiesburg, MS 39401

Jackson
Sales and Marketing Executives
of Jackson
P.O. Box 6926
Jackson, MS 39212

MISSOURI

St. Louis
Sales and Marketing Executives
of St. Louis
8816 Manchester, #202
St. Louis, MO 63144

NEBRASKA

Midlands
Sales and Marketing Executives
of Midlands
10908 Forrest Drive
Omaha, NE 68144

NEW YORK

Buffalo/Niagara
Sales and Marketing Executives
of Buffalo/Niagara
1552 Hertel Avenue
Buffalo, NY 14216

NORTH CAROLINA

Cape Fear
Sales and Marketing Executives
of Cape Fear
P.O. Box 1424
Wilmington, NC 28402

Charlotte
Sales and Marketing Executives
of Charlotte
P.O. Box 36186
Charlotte, NC 28236

Durham
Sales and Marketing Executives
of Durham
P.O. Box 1113
Durham, NC 27702

Greensboro
Sales and Marketing Executives
of Greensboro
2300 W. Meadowview Drive,
Suite 208
Greensboro, NC 27407

Raleigh
Sales and Marketing Executives
of Raleigh
3301 Woman's Club Drive,
Suite 105
Raleigh, NC 27612

Salisbury
Sales and Marketing Executives
of Salisbury
115 Pine Hill Road
Salisbury, NC 28144

Winston-Salem
Sales and Marketing Executives
of Winston-Salem
P.O. Box 24442
Winston-Salem, NC 27114

NORTH DAKOTA

Fargo-Moorhead
Sales and Marketing Executives
of Fargo-Moorhead
P.O. Box 1321
Fargo, ND 58078

OHIO

Akron
Sales and Marketing Executives
 of Akron
P.O. Box 602
Hudson, OH 44236

Cincinnati
Sales and Marketing Executives
 of Cincinnati
P.O. Box 39535
Cincinnati, OH 45239

Cleveland
Sales and Marketing Executives
 of Cleveland
Statler Office Tower, Room 303
Cleveland, OH 44115

Stark County
Sales and Marketing Executives
 of Stark County
P.O. Box 35982
Canton, OH 44735-5982

OKLAHOMA

Oklahoma City
Sales and Marketing Executives
 of Oklahoma City
P.O. Box 12419
Oklahoma City, OK 73157

OREGON

Portland
Sales and Marketing Executives
 of Portland
P.O. Box 986
Portland, OR 97207

PENNSYLVANIA

Lancaster
Sales and Marketing Executives
 of Lancaster
P.O. Box 7071
Lancaster, PA 17604

Lehigh Valley
Sales and Marketing Executives
 of Lehigh Valley
P.O. Box 2512
Lehigh Valley, PA 18001

Reading
Sales and Marketing Executives
 of Reading
P.O. Box 199
Reading, PA 19603

York
Sales and Marketing Executives
 of York
P.O. Box 1982
York, PA 17405

SOUTH CAROLINA

Columbia
Sales and Marketing Executives
 of Columbia
P.O. Box 5777
Columbia, SC 29250-5777

Greenville
Sales and Marketing Executives
 of Greenville
P.O. Box 5191
Greenville, SC 29606

Spartanburg
Sales and Marketing Executives
 of Spartanburg
c/o: Grier & Company, Inc.
P.O. Box 5139
Spartanburg, SC 29304

SOUTH DAKOTA

Sioux Falls
Sales and Marketing Executives
  of Sioux Falls
5901 Silver Valley Drive
Sioux Falls, SD 57106

TENNESSEE

Memphis
Sales and Marketing Executives
  of Memphis
5100 Poplar, Suite 3115
Memphis, TN 38137

Nashville
Sales and Marketing Executives
  of Nashville
210 Twenty-fifth Avenue, N.
  Suite 512
Nashville, TN 37203

TEXAS

Dallas
Sales and Marketing Executives
  of Dallas
8585 Stemmons, Suite 914, S.
Dallas, TX 75247

Fort Worth
Sales and Marketing Executives
  of Fort Worth
609 N. Retta, P.O. Box 7002
Fort Worth, TX 76111

San Antonio
Sales and Marketing Executives
  of San Antonio
P.O. Box 691252
San Antonio, TX 78269

Wichita Falls
Sales and Marketing Executives
  of Wichita Falls
P.O. Box 1860, Hamilton Building
Wichita Falls, TX 76307

VIRGINIA

Richmond
Sales and Marketing Executives
  of Richmond
7103 Pinetree Road
Richmond, VA 23229

Roanoke Valley
Sales and Marketing Executives
  of the Roanoke Valley
3217 Pasley Avenue, S.W.
Roanoke, VA 24014

Tidewater
Sales and Marketing Executives
  of Tidewater
700 Independence Boulevard,
  Suite 103
Virginia Beach, VA 23455

WASHINGTON

Seattle
Sales and Marketing Executives
  of Seattle
217 Ninth Avenue, N.
Seattle, WA 98109

Tacoma
Sales and Marketing Executives
  of Tacoma
P.O. Box 921
Tacoma, WA 98401-0921

WISCONSIN

Madison
Sales and Marketing Executives
 of Madison
P.O. Box 56135
Madison, WI 53705

Milwaukee
Sales and Marketing Executives
 of Milwaukee
3333 N. Mayfair Road, Suite 308
Milwaukee, WI 53222

Northeastern Wisconsin
Sales and Marketing Executives
 of Northeastern Wisconsin
1004 S. Oneida Street
Appleton, WI 54915

Racine/Kenosha
1303 Douglas Avenue
Racine, WI 53402

CANADA

Toronto
Sales and Marketing Executives
 of Toronto
24 Denby Court
Unionville, Ontario L3R 4P6

Vancouver
Sales and Marketing Executives
 of Vancouver
1250 Homer Street
Vancouver, British Columbia
 V6B 2Y5 Canada

Victoria
Sales and Marketing Executives
 of Victoria
P.O. Box 4214
Postal Station A
Victoria, British Columbia
V8X 3X8

Winnipeg
Sales and Marketing Executives
 of Winnipeg
634 Riverwood Avenue
Winnipeg, Manitoba R3T 1K2
Canada

International Associations

Contact SMEI for addresses of specific associations.

HONG KONG

Ms. Nora Leung
Sales and Marketing Executives
 Club
c/o: Hong Kong Management
 Association
14/F Fairmont House
8 Cotton Tree Drive
Central, Hong Kong

JAMAICA

Ms. Rita Girvan
HQ Sales and Marketing
 Executives of Jamaica

Export House
13 Dominica Drive
Kingston 5, Jamaica
West Indies

JAPAN

Mr. Hiroh Kuno
International Marketing Council of
 Japan
#405, Bildo Yoshida
4-30-23, Yotsuya, Shinjuku-ku
Tokyo, Japan

Legal Data and Contract Forms

Legal Data

The following information includes references to significant court decisions.

BULK SHIPMENTS

Statement contained in first paragraph hereof is also true where the merchandise ordered is sent to the salesperson or to some other representative in bulk, to be broken up and delivered to purchasers according to their individual orders. Caldwell vs. N.C., 187 U.S. 622. Rearick vs. Pa., 203 U.S. 507. Crenshaw vs. Arkansas, 227 U.S. 389. Rogers vs. Arkansas, 227 U.S. 401. Stewart vs. Michigan, 232 U.S. 665. 12 Corpus Juris, Pages 106-107. Jewel Tea Co. vs. Lees Summit, 189 Fed. 280. In re Tyerman, 48 Fed. 167. In re Spain, 47 Fed. 208. In re Nichols, 48 Fed. 164.

A salesperson or dealer may take a number of orders for future delivery, and after such orders are taken may purchase for shipment from another state the exact merchandise ordered, have it shipped to him or her in bulk, break open the bulk shipment, and fill individual orders, without being liable for the payment of any local license, fees, or other charges. (Same cases, except the last two.)

PHYSICAL EXAMINATIONS INVALID

State laws or municipal ordinances which seek to interfere, burden, or regulate interstate sales, by requirement of permits, physical examinations, health certificates, elaborate reference and personal information, or other conditions or restrictions, even though a tax or license is not charged, are invalid and unenforceable. Real Silk Hosiery Mills vs. City of Piedmont, 274 U.S. 723. Jewel Tea Co. vs. City of Norman, Equity Case No. 219, U.S. District Ct., Western District, Oklahoma, decided 10-23-17. Jewel Tea Co. vs. Mapleton, Equity Case No. 294, U.S. District Ct., Northern District Iowa Western Division, decided 6-27-31. Shaffer vs. Grain Company, 268 U.S. 189. Buck Stove Company vs. Vicars, 226 U.S. 295. Textbook Company vs. Pigg, 217 U.S. 91. Lemke vs. Grain Company, 258 U.S. 50. Also Ex Parte Edwards, 37 Fed. Supp. 673 (Fla.). Pictorial Review Co. vs. Alexandria, La., 46 Fed. (2d) 337. Nippert vs. Richmond, 327 U.S. 416, 427 66 S. Ct. 586. McCarter vs. Florence, 104 So.

806 (Ala.). Best & Co., Inc., vs. Omaha, 33 N.W. (2d) 161 (Neb.); cert. denied 336 U.S. 935.

RESIDENCE OF SALESPERSON IMMATERIAL

The United States Supreme Court has repeatedly held that the taking of orders for the future delivery of merchandise which is at the time located in another state, constitutes interstate commerce. The residence of the salesperson makes no difference whatever, nor does the method of delivery of the merchandise have any bearing on the question. It may be delivered in person by the individual who took the order, or by some other representative or person, or by mail, freight, or express. Brennan vs. Titusville, 153 U.S. 289. Caldwell vs. North Carolina, 187 U.S. 622. Stewart vs. Mich., 232 U.S. 655. Crenshaw vs. Ark., 227 U.S. 389.

POLICE POWER NOT TO RESTRICT INTERSTATE COMMERCE

A state or municipality cannot, under the guise of police power, impose licenses, burdens, or other requirements as a condition precedent to engaging in or entering into interstate commerce. See the first paragraph listing court decisions, above. Also: Brennan vs. Titusville, 153 U.S. 289, 300. Shaffer vs. Grain Co., 268 U.S. 189. Lemke vs. Grain Co., 358 U.S. 50. Buck Stove vs. Vicars, 226 U.S. 295. Crutcher vs. Kentucky, 141 U.S. 47. Textbook Co. vs. Pigg, 217 U.S. 91. Real Silk Hosiery Mills vs. Portland, 268 U.S. 325.

WHEN INTERSTATE COMMERCE ENDS

Once the character as interstate commerce attaches to a movement of goods, such character continues until the goods reach the point where the parties originally intended that they should arrive. Caldwell vs. N. C., 187 U.S. 622. Illinois Central R.R. Co. vs. Louisiana R.R. Comm., 236 U.S. 157. Western Union Tel. Co. vs. Foster, 247 U.S. 105. Western Oil Refining Co. vs. Lipscomb, 244 U.S. 346. Jewel Tea Co. vs. Camden, 172 S.E. 307 (S.C.).

ADDITIONAL INTERSTATE COMMERCE DECISIONS

Nicholson vs. Forrest City, 228 S.W. (2d) 53 (Ark.). Olan Mills vs. Tallahassee, 43 So. (2d) 521 (Fla.). Wilk vs. Bartow, 86 Fla. 186. Graves vs. Gainesville, 51 S.E. (2d) 58 (Ga.). Winchester vs. Lohrey Pkg. Co., 237 S.W. (2d) 868 (Ky.). Cordell vs. Commonwealth, 254 S.W. (2d) 484 (Ky.). State vs. Best & Co., 195 So. 356 (La.). Waseca vs. Braun, 206 Minn. 154, 288 N.W. 229. Craig vs. Mills, 33 So. (2d) 810 (Miss.). W. K. Vantine Studio vs. Portsmouth, 59 A. (2d) 475 (N.H.). Dimmig vs. Mann, 200 A. 545 (N.J.). Bossert vs. Okmulgee, 260 P. (2d) (Okla.). Leibold vs. Brown, 71 So. (2d) (Ala.). Gadsden vs. Roadway Express, 73 So. (2d) 765 (Ala.). Myers vs. Miami, 131 So. 375 (Fla.). Olan Mills vs. Tallahassee, 43 So. (2d) 521 (Fla.). Olan Mills, Inc., vs. Maysville, 272 S.W. (2d) 460 (Ky.). Olan Mills, Inc., vs. Cape Girardeau, 272 S.W. (2d) (Mo.). Best & Co., Inc., vs. Omaha, 33 N.W. (2d) 161 (Neb.); cert. denied 336 U.S. 935. Commonwealth vs. Olan Mills, Inc., 86 S.E. (2d) (Va.).

CUSTOMARY METHOD GOVERNS

Salespersons who customarily take orders for the future delivery of merchandise at the time located in another state and who occasionally sell or dispose of a sample or rejected merchandise are still within the scope and protection of interstate commerce and may not be required to take out a license. Commonwealth vs. Farnum, 114 Mass. 267. Kansas vs. Collins, 342 U.S. 344. In re Houston, 47 Fed. 539. Powell vs. Roundtree, 247 S.W. 389 (Ark.). Smith vs. Dickinson, 142 Pac. 1133 (Wash.) Penn. Collier Company vs. McKeever, 87 N.Y.S. 869. Frank vs. State, 42 Tex. Crim. 222, 58 S.W. 1015.

CUSTOMER'S REFUSAL OF COD

Where a customer rejects a COD shipment, such action constitutes a breach of contract, and the customer is not entitled to recover from the salesperson or the company the deposit which he or she paid. In fact, the company could properly sue the customer for damages for such breach. Bullard vs. Eames, 106 N.E. 584 (Mass.). Carle vs. Nelson, 130 N.W. 467 (Wis.).

BRANCH OFFICES NO BAR

A direct selling company or district agent may maintain a branch office in a state other than that where the home office is located, for the purpose of facilitating interstate business, without being compelled to pay a license. Crutcher vs. Ky., 141 U.S. 47. Cheney Bros. vs. Mass., 246 U.S. 146, Railroad Company vs. Pa., 136 U.S. 114. Textbook Company vs. Pigg, 217 U.S. 101. Myers vs. City of Miami, 131 So. 375 (Fla.).

ORDER TAKERS NOT PEDDLERS

Even when a person taking orders for the future delivery of merchandise is not engaged in interstate commerce he or she cannot be required to pay a peddler's license which does not specifically include order-taking or sales by sample. Crenshaw vs. Arkansas, 227 U.S. 389. State vs. Bristow, 131 Ia. 664. St. Paul vs. Briggs, 85 Minn. 290. DeWitt vs. State, 155 Wis. 249. 40 Am. Jur. p. 916.

EXCESSIVE LICENSE FEES INVALID

Even when a salesperson is not engaged in interstate commerce he or she can not be made to pay a license fee which is so excessive as to constitute an indirect prohibition of the business. Such an ordinance is void as being confiscatory, as prohibiting a lawful occupation, and as constituting an illegal discrimination. Real Silk Hosiery Mills vs. Bellingham, 1 Fed. (2d) 934. State vs. Wilson, 249 Ill. 195, 94 N.W. 141. 40 Am. Jur. p. 948.

PEDDLER ORDINANCES DO NOT APPLY

Power granted to a city to license and regulate peddling does not give it power or authority to license or regulate order takers. Village of Cerro Gordo vs. Rawlings, 135 Ill. 36. Ideal Tea Company vs. Salem, 150 Pac. 852 (Ore.). Emmons vs. City of Lewistown, 132 Ill. 380. Village of South Holland vs. Stein, 26 N.E. (2d) 868 (Ill.).

PROHIBITION OF LAWFUL BUSINESS IS ILLEGAL

The power to license or regulate does not carry with it the power to prohibit. A city council cannot, under any powers, pass an ordinance absolutely prohibiting a lawful business. Adams vs. Tanner, 244 U.S. 590. Ralph vs. City of Wenatchee, 209 Pac. (2d) 270 (Wash.).

GREEN RIVER ORDINANCE INVALID

The so-called Green River or nuisance-type ordinances are invalid in these states: Wilkins vs. City of Harrison, 236 S.W. (2d) 82 (Ark.). Prior vs. White, 180 So. 347 (Fla.), 116 A.L.R. 1176. DeBarry vs. City of LaGrange, 8 S.E. (2d) 146. C. B. Garrison vs. City of Cartersville, 8 S.E. (2d) 154 (Ga.). City of Osceola vs. Blair, 2 N.W. (2d) 83 (Ia.). City of Derby vs. Betty Hiegert, 325 Pac. (2d) 35 (Kans.). City of Mt. Sterling et al. vs. Donaldson Baking Co., 155 S.W. (2d) 237 (Ky.). Jewel Tea Co. vs. Town of Bel Air, 192 A. 417 (Md.). Excelsior Baking Co. vs. City of Northfield, 77 N.W. (2d) 188 (Minn.). Jewel Tea Co. vs. City of Geneva, 291 N.W. 644 (Nebr.). McAlester vs. Grand Union Tea Co., 98 Pac. (2d) 924 (Okla.). Orangeburg vs. O. R. Farmer, 186 S.E. 783 (S.C.). Ex parte Faulkner, 158 S.W. (2d) 525 (Tex.). White vs. Culpeper, 1 S.E. (2d) (Va.).

OFFICIALS LIABLE FOR DAMAGES

A police official or other person actively participating in causing or making an arrest under a void ordinance can be personally held for general and specific damages. Scott vs. McDonald, 165 U.S. 58 (89). U.S. Code, Title 42, Section 1983.

Registration of Trademarks under Lanham Act

Service marks may be registered. A service mark is one used in the sale or advertising of services and includes marks, names, symbols, titles, designations, slogans, character names, and distinctive features of television, radio, or other advertising used in commerce.

Collective marks may be registered by persons exercising legitimate control over their use. A collective mark is a trademark or service mark used by the members of a cooperative, association, or other collective group or organization.

Certification marks may be registered by persons exercising legitimate control over their use, but who do not themselves engage in the production or marketing of any goods or services to which the mark is applied. A certification mark is one used upon or in connection with the products or services of one or more persons, other than the owner of the mark, to certify regional or other origin, material, mode of manufacture, quality, accuracy or other characteristic of such goods or services, or that the work or labor on the goods or services was performed by members of a union or other organization.

Related companies may use a *registered mark,* such use inuring to the benefit of the registrant, provided the public is not deceived. A "related company" is one legitimately controlling or controlled by the registrant in respect to the nature or quality of the goods or services in connection with which the mark is used.

Concurrent registration of the same mark to more than one registrant is authorized in cases of concurrent lawful use prior to any filing date; conditions and limitations as to mode, place, or goods are to be prescribed by the Commissioner of Patents and Trademarks.

Registered marks are automatically canceled after six years, unless within the sixth year the registrant files an affidavit showing that the mark is still in use, or excusing nonuse. Abandonment may be presumed after two consecutive years of nonuse.

Assignment of a registered mark, or of a mark for which application to register has been filed, may be made with that part of the goodwill of the business connected with the use of the mark. Assignments should be recorded in the Patent and Trademark Office.

The requirement for use of the notice "Registered in U.S. Patent and Trademark Office" or "Reg. U.S. Pat. and Trademark Off." still stands; but as an alternative it is now optional to display the letter "R" within a circle. No such notice should appear on a mark, however, until it has, in fact, been registered in the Patent and Trademark Office.

Any mark distinctive of the owner's goods in commerce may be registered, if not immoral, deceptive, scandalous, confusingly similar to a mark in use, etc., and this is true even though the mark is descriptive or geographical or a surname.

Registration is constructive notice of the registrants claim of ownership of the mark. The purpose of this provision in the law is to make a registrant's rights coterminous with the territory of the United States; thus it becomes impossible for a later comer to acquire, in good faith, adverse rights in a mark in a section of the country (embracing parts of at least two states) where the registrant has not actually used his or her mark.

Registered marks may become incontestable after any five-year period subsequent to registration on the filing, within the sixth year, of an affidavit setting forth that the mark has been in continuous use for such five years, that there has been no final decision adverse to registrant's claim of ownership, and that no proceeding involving his or her rights is pending. But "no incontestable right shall be acquired in a mark or trade name of any article or substance, patented or otherwise." An incontestable registration is conclusive evidence of the registrant's exclusive right to use the registered mark. However, incontestability may, paradoxically, be contested on numerous grounds (one being "that the mark has been or is being used to violate the antitrust laws of the United States," and others including fraud and abandonment), and so is limited at best.

To register a trademark, a written, verified application in the form prescribed by the Commissioner of Patents and Trademarks must be filed in the Patent and Trademarks Office. The application must be accompanied by a drawing which complies with the Commissioner's requirements; by five specimens or facsimiles; and by a filing fee per class of goods. Goods are classified for registration purposes under the International Classification System.

Certificates of Registration remain in force 20 years (if an affidavit of use is filed during the sixth year). A registration may be renewed for successive 20-year periods.

Contracts and Agreements

While the documents reproduced in this book are excellent examples of their kind, they are by no means *representative* examples. The purpose of the collection was not to make a statistically reliable inference of national practices, but to obtain salesperson's agreements that could serve as models for companies seeking to design or redesign employment contracts for their own sales force.

CAVEAT

These forms are not intended to encourage sales executives to practice law. This is a "do-it-yourself" project that holds many dangers. The whole subject of employment contracts is one over which seasoned lawyers differ. Even an expertly drawn agreement with a salesperson might prove full of holes when put to a legal test. The forms following are designed only to serve as a source of format and language suggestions useful to an attorney for drafting documents tailored to the specific needs of your company.

CONSIDERATIONS

A good contract can save a lot of time, money, and misunderstanding. Here is a list of factors that especially need to be considered when a contract with a salesperson is being drafted:

1. What product(s) and/or service(s) are to be covered by the agreement.

2. Detailed description of the territory or prospect list to be covered by the salesperson, including any right the company will retain to split the territory and/or reassign accounts.

3. The established policies and practices to which parties to the contract will agree to adhere at all times.

4. The method of compensation to be used. Where applicable, state policy for handling write-offs of uncollectable bills; whether commissions are to be paid when order billed, or when bill collected; frequency of payment; and the handling of commission overdrafts. Here are some considerations peculiar to each method of compensation:

   a. *Straight Salary:* Include provision to switch to another method of compensation under certain conditions and after certain period;

   b. *Straight Commission:* State clearly the method of computation that will be the company's normal and accepted accounting method;

   c. *Combinations Involving Draw, Quota:* Include amount of salary or "guaranteed" draw; percent of commission and override; when and how commissions are to be paid; when they are subject to review and revision.

5. Procedure for compensating for orders received from office in salesperson's territory but originating from another salesperson's territory. Generally these "split accounts" can be handled in one of two ways:

   a. Commission shared by both salespeople at some predetermined rate;

   b. Commission assigned in full to one salesperson or the other.

6. Conditions under which contract can be terminated.

   a. Immediately "for cause";

   b. Action of one or the other parties, with advance notice, usually from 30 to 90 days;

   c. Disposition of commissions, if any, earned after termination.

7. The life of the agreement. Standard wording: "The term of this agreement shall be for _____ month(s) or year(s), commencing _____, and shall automatically be renewed for similar periods unless written notice of termination be sent by either party to the other not less than _____ days prior to the expiration of any such period. Company agrees to accept orders until termination date."

8. Policy regarding expenses, reimbursable and not reimbursable, including clear statement of limitations of authority regarding extraordinary expenses, obligations, or liability of any kind in the name of, or for, or on account of the company.

OVERALL COMPANY POLICY: Thomas Truck & Caster Company, Keokuk, Iowa

The basic marketing program of the Company is designed to provide a thorough sales coverage for all products manufactured, in all areas of each Territory, as well as nationally. The overall growth and strength of the Company, its national competitive position, and the value of Thomas to Representatives, all require adherence to these basic principles.

The basic manufacturing program of the Company, for efficiency of production and all other internal operations, requires an adequate volume of business from every existing and potential surface, ranging from manufacturers who can use Thomas products on the equipment they make, to the homeowner who may only be a one-time, one-item buyer.

The basic problem for the Company resolves itself to the obtaining of an adequate, proportionate, and profitable volume of business for all its products, which requires more than one phase of marketing to produce that result.

The most important and the principal marketing method is by direct sales to the user through commission Representatives, assigned a definite, exclusive territory, and given adequate territory protection and commission compensation in return for their agreement and performance in actively promoting the sale of Company products assigned to them, on that basis.

The other marketing methods used by the Company, in order to obtain an adequate overall volume, are aimed at sources of business which experience has demonstrated requires other methods of selling, except in rare, individual situations. These exceptions to the principal marketing method are specified in the Company Sales Policy and made a part of each Territory Agreement.

Territory

The territory outlined in the Sales Agency Agreement is yours on an exclusive basis for direct sales to users, except as otherwise noted in this Agreement.

The territorial area may be revised by mutual agreement of the Sales Representative and the Company, or by the Company in the event of necessity.

You are not to solicit business, make calls, or in any way attempt to secure orders for Thomas products in any area outside your exclusive territory, except with written permission from the Company. Commission credit will not be given on any order which violates this rule.

SALES AGENCY AGREEMENT: Thomas Truck & Caster Company, Keokuk, Iowa

Date_____

This agreement is between THOMAS TRUCK AND CASTER COMPANY of KEOKUK, IOWA, hereinafter called the "COMPANY" and_____
of_____, an independent contractor, hereinafter called the "SALES REPRESENTATIVE."

The COMPANY and the SALES REPRESENTATIVE agree as follows:

A.—The COMPANY hereby appoints_____
its exclusive District Sales Representative in the territory defined in Section B, for the period of time beginning with the date hereto, until otherwise terminated in accordance with this agreement.

B.—The territory is defined as follows:

C.—It is agreed that the SALES REPRESENTATIVE and the COMPANY will comply with the rules and regulations as set forth in the "SALES POLICY" of the COMPANY.

D.—This Sales Agency Agreement will be terminated by the COMPANY or the SALES REPRESENTATIVE upon not less than thirty days written notice. This agreement may also be terminated, effective on date written notice is received and without the thirty day notice because of:

1. Failure of the SALES REPRESENTATIVE to comply with or perform any of the requirements or provisions of the SALES POLICY.

2. Legislation, court decision, or Government ruling which contravenes any provision of this Agreement.

After aforesaid written notice terminating this agreement, the COMPANY shall not be liable to pay commission on any order accepted by the COMPANY, except orders mailed to the COMPANY by the SALES REPRESENTATIVE, prior to date of termination, and accepted by the COMPANY and paid for by the customer. Payment of commissions, after notice of termination, will be made after collection of customer's account by the COMPANY.

E.—This Sales Agency Agreement is approved by the COMPANY at its home office, KEOKUK, IOWA and is acceptable to the SALES REPRESENTATIVE.

THOMAS TRUCK AND CASTER COMPANY

_____   _____

Representatives Signature

_____   _____

Date

Exceptions

Railroad Business
   Due to the procedure of selling railroads, the company has special railroad representatives, and other sales representatives do not receive commission, except on sales to railroads by resale dealers in their territory.

U.S. Government Business
   The company has a special government representative, and other sales representatives do not receive commission credit on Government business originating and contracted for at or from Washington, D.C., or the Military General Supply Agency, Richmond, Virginia, except as follows:
   U.S. Government and local or area government business, purchased in a sales representative's territory, is handled like any other customer. If the purchase on any quotation is transferred to Washington, D.C., the company is to receive a copy of the quotation and full information without delay, for transmission to the government representative. Otherwise, the sales representative may not participate in the commission.

Export Business
   All inquiries and sales for equipment for export are handled by the company and our exclusive export sales representatives, except purchases made by a customer in your territory for its own use in a foreign location.

National Accounts

The company, upon due notification to the sales representative, may establish commission rates payable for certain established national accounts, or may, due to a lack of interest by the sales representative in working such accounts, discontinue payment of commission on orders from such accounts.

Other

Any items or products manufactured and sold by the company which are not cataloged or otherwise offered for sale through the representative are exempt from commission credit.

Sales Activities

Quotations

Copies of all written quotations on Thomas products are to be sent to the home office for checking of prices and specifications.

Promotion

In return for sales privileges in your territory, we expect you to actively and aggressively promote the sale of Thomas products. We expect you to produce a sales volume satisfactory to the company, on the entire line, and to do this in accordance with the rules of the sales policy.

The sales representative agrees not to sell items made by another manufacturer that are competitive to items available in the Thomas line of equipment, and will continue to receive exclusive commission protection on those items.

You are an independent contractor and we do not exercise any control over the amount of time you devote to the sale of Thomas products, nor the number of noncompetitive lines you handle, nor in any way intend to regulate you or your activities in such a way as to place you in the category of a direct employee of the company.

It is agreed that the sales representative will make every effort to attend and/or send other personnel when requested or deemed advisable to product training sessions, sales meetings, or other legitimate activities at the home office, or at such regional locations as are announced.

Terms of Sale

Prices are FOB Keokuk, Iowa. No freight is allowed. Freight charges will not be prepaid, unless the company agrees in writing to do so, and will be added to the invoice.

Terms for all items are net 30 days from the *date of the invoice.* No deviation is permissible.

Purchase Orders

All orders must be signed, and made out to the company at Keokuk,

Iowa, and are subject to approval and acceptance at that point.

Orders should be *complete* and correct as to terms, price, specifications of product, and shipping instructions. Verbal instructions must be confirmed in writing. The sales representative will be charged the cost of all errors in an order for which he or she is responsible, and the company will stand the cost of any errors for which it is responsible.

An acknowledgment copy of each order, except orders for items to be shipped immediately from stock, will be mailed promptly to both the customer and representative. The latter should carefully *check* the acknowledgment and immediately notify the company if not in accord with the sale. In the case of orders for items from stock, your acknowledgment copy is in the form of a commission credit copy, as the item will be shipped promptly.

Credit

The company's credit department checks the credit rating of all customers in Dun & Bradstreet. If the customer is not listed or adequately rated, the order is not passed for shipment until the credit department is satisfied as to the customer's ability to pay the invoice.

When the sales representative has reason to believe the customer is too new in business or otherwise not properly rated, he or she should send credit references and full information as to the customer's credit standing with the order. Or, attach the customer's check made out to the company for the full amount of the order. This will avoid delay in entering the order.

The company reserves the right to debit back all or part of the sales representative's commission on an unpaid account. The commission will be reinstated if the customer pays the invoice in full at a later date. If the account has to be given to an attorney for collection, commission will be prorated on the net proceeds.

Trial Orders

Only certain standard items are available for trial, per specified trial period. A signed purchase order must be obtained from the customer stating: "Subject to return for credit after _____ days' trial, FOB Keokuk, Iowa." Consult the company before offering to submit equipment for trial. Special trucks will not be furnished for *free* trial.

Special Sample Trucks

On an order for special trucks, the customer may desire to purchase a sample for approval before we proceed with construction of the entire order. In this case, the sample truck will be shipped and invoiced at the first user discount. Later, when the entire order is shipped, price adjustment will be made to allow the correct quantity discount to apply on the price of the sample. *Sample special trucks cannot be returned for credit,* and this must be agreed to by the purchaser.

Special Finish and Marking

The company does not furnish equipment with a special finish or special marking different from its standard finishes and identifying marks, except at an extra charge based upon the extra labor, material, and equipment required.

Guarantee

The products of the company are designed and built for the capacities given in the catalog or quotation, which are based on smooth floors and normal operating conditions. Under such conditions, parts claimed defective within 60 days after shipment and returned prepaid for inspection will be replaced at no charge only if found defective in material or workmanship. All other parts will be sold in the regular way.

Breakage or failure because of defect in our products is rare. It is found that, in most cases, overloading and abuse are common practices, and with uneven elevator entrances, holes in floors or other obstacles which truck wheels or other parts are pushed up against with sharp, heavy impact, breakage may result, which is no fault of the equipment. Sales representatives should carefully investigate all breakage complaints with these factors in mind, remembering that defects would normally occur within 60 days after shipment.

No payment or credit is allowed for repair work or materials furnished by others, except on *written authority* from the company, after full investigation.

An order becomes the property of the customer when delivered to the carrier. If breakage or damage occurs in transit, *the customer* should immediately have a damage notation made on the freight bill to support his or her claim for damage. Parts to repair such damage will be sold in the regular way.

Returned Goods

The sales representative is not to authorize a customer to return goods to the factory without first getting authorization and shipping instructions from the home office. In the event such authorization is given and goods are returned to the factory, there will be a refinishing and restocking charge of at least 10 percent to cover actual costs. The sales representative will be debited for full commission on any goods returned.

Advertising

Publication

The Company conducts an outstanding national advertising program through its advertising agency at its own expense. This advertising is designed for the benefit of all territories, and inquiries resulting are referred to sales representatives for follow-up.

Direct Mail

From time to time, certain direct mail material is supplied by the company to any territory at no cost or on a mutual cost basis, as announced at the time of the program.

Local

The company does not share any part of the expense of local territory advertising of any kind which is not a part of its own advertising program.

Telephone Directory

The company handles and pays for all Thomas classified telephone-directory advertising through its advertising agency on a *national basis,* using a regular-type, boldface Caster listing, and a trade name listing under "Trucks-Industrial," except in cities where a trademark heading under "Trucks-Industrial" is deemed advisable. In territories where the classified directory has a material handling equipment section, the trade name listing is usually preferred under this section in place of under "Trucks-Industrial."

Cost of the above telephone-directory advertising is divided equally between the company and the sales representative at the time the directory order is placed, and is debited against commission accounts.

Proper notification of a new directory deadline will be sent each territory by the company in advance, in order that any change necessary can be made.

The representative is *not to contract locally* for the above telephone-directory advertising.

The *full* name of Thomas Truck & Caster Co. cannot appear in telephone-directory advertising or similar local publications in such a way as to make the company liable for any local, city, county, state, or federal tax.

Use of Company Name

The sales representative shall have no right to use the company name in such way as to make the company liable for any local, city, county, state, or federal tax contribution or expense of any kind.

The full company name is not to be placed on office doors or building directory. Proper listing is, "Sales Representative for Thomas Trucks, Casters, and Wheels."

The company must be consulted and its instructions followed in each case where the sales representative desires to use the company name for any publications or listings within his or her territory.

Operating Expenses

The company does not pay any part of the sales representative's operating expenses.

Types of Accounts—Defined

Regular User Sales

All customers' sales are subject to the *suggested* product quantity discounts of the discount schedule for all items except skids and allied products (see below for skids). Commission rates paid are based on the discount allowed by the sales representative.

Sales at discounts other than the user discount specified will carry a commission applying to the next lower user discount.

Orders received by the company without price will be invoiced at the net figure for the quantity and discount applying, with the appropriate commission rate for that discount.

Skids and allied products discounts for users apply only to one item of one size and specification, and not to a miscellaneous assortment. Two or more orders for a single buyer, but for shipment to two or more destinations, may be grouped together to obtain a higher quantity discount, *provided* the orders are for items *of identical specifications* and can be manufactured and shipped on the same date.

Resale Dealers

A resale dealer is a person or organization engaged in buying products for sale through them to others, either with shipment direct to the ultimate user, or to the dealer.

Any account in this classification must be approved by the company, and will be rated as either Class AA, Class A, or Class B, and will have to maintain a satisfactory credit standing.

Credit AA: those dealers who do a substantial volume and who stock or catalog our products, and those who deal in a particular product line on a regional or national basis and who are directly competitive with a sales representative.

Class A: those dealers who regularly buy Thomas products, are generally operating in a normal territorial area, and who work the Thomas line actively and regularly.

Class B: all other dealers, not otherwise rated, who occasionally buy Thomas products and who are qualified by the representative and the company to receive a dealer discount.

The representative in whose territory the resale dealer is located will receive the sales commission if qualified, regardless of the destination of the shipment.

Discounts applicable to this classification will be determined by the company, and will be published discounts.

Sales Representatives' Stock Purchases

Qualified sales representatives who purchase company products for their stock. Prices are FOB Keokuk, Iowa; terms net 30 days.

No special terms, deferred payments, or consignment arrangements are available. The sales representative assumes full responsibility for invoicing, collection, and taxes on sales made from his or her stock.

Discounts applicable are as shown, or as otherwise published or established.

Original Equipment Manufacturers (OEM)

An OEM is a manufacturer who *regularly* purchases wheels, casters, or other parts for use as an auxiliary or integral part of machinery or products manufactured by such purchaser for sale or lease.

The company must approve any account in this classification, and will establish discounts and commission rates where applicable.

General

Sales Supplies

The company furnished the sales representative with an adequate supply of catalogs, bulletins, and sales literature on its products. The company supplies interoffice letterheads and company letterheads imprinted with the sales representative's name and address at no cost to the sales representative.

Telephone and Telegraph

The sales representative must pay for all telephone calls and telegrams to the company. The company will pay for all telephone calls and telegrams originating from the company.

When necessary to place collect calls or wires, same will be accepted, but charged back to the sales representative as a debit against his or her commission account.

Compensation

Compensation to the sales representative is in the form of commission paid on shipments. Commission is credited at the time the customer is invoiced, and is paid on the 20th of each month on all shipments made during the previous month.

Interterritory Commissions

When two or more territories share in a user order, the commission will be divided in proportion to the effort and influence exercised in securing the business.

Commission on jobber or resale dealer sales is paid to the sales representative in whose territory such dealer is located, based on billing address and qualification.

The factors that will be used as evidence to substantiate the decision of the company will be the following:

1. Point at which our equipment is specified

2. Point at which requisition is issued

3. Point of issuance of purchase order

4. Destination of shipment where equipment will be used

5. Point or points at which specifications are drawn, engineering performed, and selling done

6. Evidence of sales work by territory being considered because of 3 and 4

In deciding each of the above factors, the company will be guided entirely by the file of the transaction in our office at the time the order is received. This file will consist of correspondence and quotations, sales representative's reports, the formal purchase order, and all other data regarding the sale.

To protect himself or herself, a sales representative who has reason to believe that the job he or she is quoting on may be ordered in another territory, should immediately send full information and the price quoted to the home office. The sales representative must not mail a quotation directly to another territory. Interterritory quotations must clear through the home office of the company.

The commission will be divided as follows:

1. One-third to the territory in which the formal purchase order is issued, except on certain national accounts which merely clear orders of all their plants on an informal basis, and which are not influenced by a sales representative at that plant;

2. One-third to the territory in which the equipment is used;

3. One-third to the territory in which the selling and engineering performed causes the company's product to be purchased.

Exceptions to the above may be made at the discretion of the company providing the file of the complete transaction clearly proves that two territories equally share part 3, or where buying formalities in certain national firms make part 1 of no consideration.

Sales Reports

Monthly reports of sales and the territory position as to sales volume and number of orders will be sent to each territory approximately 15 days after the close of each month. Cumulative reports will be issued in conjunction with the monthly report. Advertising results are also included in this report.

Office Bulletins

There are three main types of data on general letters sent at various times to each sales representative. They are:

1. *"T" Sheet.* Designed for the person who sells Thomas equipment; a *weekly* news and special feature letter with information of interest, including changes in personnel, personal news items, etc., of sales representatives;

2. *"G" Letter.* A "general" letter embodying general material regarding sales, meetings, announcements, etc., issued when required;

3. *"D" Sheet.* A data sheet embodying technical and price data on the company's line of equipment, issued when required.

DISTRIBUTOR'S SALES AGREEMENT: Westinghouse Air Brake Company, Pneumatic Equipment Division*

THIS AGREEMENT, executed as of the _____ day of _____, 19_____, by WESTINGHOUSE AIR BRAKE COMPANY, Pneumatic Equipment Div., hereinafter referred to as the "Manufacturer," and

a _____ of
      (State whether individual, corporation or copartnership)

_____
          (Street address, City and State)

hereinafter referred to as the "Distributor," shall constitute the Agreement governing their business relations.

1. Right to Purchase and Sell Products

   A. The Manufacturer grants to the Distributor the right to purchase from the Manufacturer for resale the following described products of the Manufacturer (hereinafter called "Products"):

Class A Products

_____

_____

Class B Products

_____

_____

*Absorbed into WABCO Fluid Power Div., American Standard, Lexington, New York

The right to purchase granted herein to Distributor is non-exclusive as to both Class A Products and Class B Products, but it is the Manufacturer's intention that, insofar as is practicable, no corresponding rights to purchase Class A Products for resale to the Industries listed in paragraph 1.C. below will be granted to other distributors within the Territory described in paragraph 1.C.

B. The Manufacturer grants to the Distributor the right to purchase from the Manufacturer for resale, service parts for the aforesaid Products (hereinafter called "Service Parts").

C. It is expected that Distributor will concentrate his or her efforts in promoting and making sales of Products and Service Parts to customers engaged in the following Industries within the following described territory (hereinafter referred to as "Territory"):

INDUSTRIES:

_____

_____

TERRITORY:

_____

_____

D. The Manufacturer reserves the right to sell any Product or Service Parts to anyone, either within or outside the Territory, without liability to the Distributor, and specifically reserves the right, without in any respect limiting the generality of the foregoing, to sell to the United States or to any State or local government or to any of their agencies or instrumentalities, or to any other vendee for ultimate use by any such governmental authority pursuant to original specifications of that authority, and to sell to purchasers which the Manufacturer classifies as national accounts and which in his or her opinion can only be served via direct sales.

2. Discounts, prices, and terms

Prices to the Distributor shall be the Manufacturer's list price in effect at time of shipment, less the applicable discounts and subject to the Manufacturer's terms. All orders are subject to Credit and Sales Department approval and acceptance by the Manufacturer at Sidney, Ohio and not elsewhere. Unless otherwise stated, prices are FOB plant of Manufacturer. Delivery of Product by the Company to a common carrier or to Distributor's own, leased, chartered, or authorized conveyance, shall constitute delivery to Distributor. Title and risk of loss shall pass to Distributor upon such delivery, regardless of whether shipments are freight collect, allowed, or prepaid and charged back, except as title may be retained by the Manufacturer as security for payment of the purchase price. The Manufacturer may change list prices, discounts, and terms, in whole or in part, at any time without notice. Any sales, use, excise, or other tax applicable to the manufacture, sale, delivery, or use of merchandise sold to Distributor shall be added to the price and paid by Distributor. No more than one discount or commission will be allowed on any one sale, and any dispute between the Distributor and other distributors of the Manufacturer, or dealers or supply houses, concerning rights under this or similar agreements relating to the Product shall be determined by the Manufacturer, if he so elects, and any such determination, expressed in writing, shall be final and conclusive.

3. Warranty

A. The Manufacturer warrants each new Product sold by the Manufacturer to be free from defects in material and workmanship for six (6) months from date of shipment by Manufacturer but not to exceed ninety (90) days of service, or such other period of time as Manufacturer may agree to in writing except as pertains to unit type air compressors.

B. The obligation under this warranty, statutory or otherwise, is limited to the replacement or repair at the Manufacturer's factory, or at a point designated by the Manufacturer, or such part as shall appear to the Manufacturer, upon inspection at such point, to have been defective in material or workmanship.

C. This warranty does not obligate the Manufacturer to bear the cost of labor or transportation charges in connection with the replacement or repair of defective parts, nor shall it apply to a Product upon which repairs or alterations have been made unless authorized by the Manufacturer.

D. The Manufacturer makes no warranty in respect to accessories, such being subject to the warranties of their respective manufacturers.

E. The Manufacturer shall in no event be liable for consequential damages or contingent liabilities arising out of the failure of any Product or parts to operate properly.

F. No express, implied, or statutory warranty other than herein set forth is made by the Manufacturer.

G. The Distributor shall make no warranty or representation on behalf of the Manufacturer with respect to the Product unless authorized in writing by Manufacturer to do so.

4. Lists and Sales Manuals

The Manufacturer issues to the Distributor one or more Sales Manuals, parts and price lists, and/or Schedules setting forth current prices and trade discounts, all of which are subject to change by the Manufacturer at any time. All of this material as revised from time to time is by reference incorporated into and agreed to be made a part of this agreement whether or not attached hereto. Sales Manuals, parts and price lists, unless specifically sold to the Distributor, remain the property of the Manufacturer and shall be returned on termination of this agreement.

5. Delivery Delays or Shortages

The Manufacturer shall not be liable to Distributor or any of Distributor's customers for any loss, damage, detention, or delay resulting from fires, strikes, lockouts, delays in manufacture, delays in transportation or delivery of materials, embargoes, insurrections or riots, civil or military authority, car shortages, acts of God, acts of the Distributor, or any other cause beyond its reasonable control. Any claims against the Manufacturer for shortages in shipment shall be made in writing within five (5) days after receipt of shipment.

6. Trademarks

The Distributor agrees not to use the Manufacturer's name or registered trademarks or those of Westinghouse Air Brake Company or any marks closely resembling any of them (or the translation of such names or trademarks into any foreign language), as part of the corporation or business name of the Distributorship, or in any manner which the Manufacturer considers misleading, detrimental, or objectionable.

7. Relationship of Parties

The relationship contemplated by this agreement is one in which the Manufacturer is vendor and the Distributor is vendee. The Distributor is not an agent, employee, or legal representative of the Manufacturer for any purpose whatever, and shall have no power or authority to incur or create any obligations or liability of any kind for or on behalf of the Manufacturer. The Distributor shall conduct his or her business as an independent contractor and all persons employed in such business shall be employees of Distributor and all costs and obligations incurred by reason of any such employment shall be for the account and expense of Distributor even though employees of Distributor may be regarded as employees of Manufacturer under a particular law or regulation.

8. Facilities and Sales Efforts

A. The Distributor, to the satisfaction of the Manufacturer, will:

   1. Make adequate sales and sales promotion efforts;

   2. Maintain adequate and suitable sales and display facilities;

   3. Maintain at all times adequate service facilities and stocks of genuine Le Roi service parts. The adequacy of the Distributor's stock of genuine Le Roi service parts shall be determined by the Manufacturer upon the basis of the Product populations in the Territory. Obsolete parts in the Distributor's stock shall be purchased, replaced, or allowed as a credit by the Manufacturer to such extent and upon such terms as it may determine;

   4. Maintain sufficient qualified sales and service personnel to cover all sources of orders for the Product within the scope of this agreement and to render prompt and adequate service at reasonable prices to all users of the class of Product covered by this agreement within his or her Territory regardless of when, where, or by whom sold.

   5. Avoid in every way such activities or trade practices as may be injurious to the Manufacturer's good name and goodwill, or detrimental to public interest.

B. The Manufacturer will make available to the Distributor such facilities for training of personnel and other assistance as it may deem necessary for adequate distribution and service of the Product.

9. Advertising

A. The Manufacturer shall furnish, without charge to the Distributor, such catalogs, circulars, and other advertising material as are, in the judgment of the Manufacturer, necessary or desirable.

B. The Distributor's advertising shall be at his or her own expense, and shall include placing an appropriate classified advertisement in his local telephone directory, in the form acceptable to Manufacturer.

10. Termination

A. This agreement shall remain in full force and effect until terminated by either the Manufacturer or the Distributor. Either shall have the right to terminate the agreement at any time upon written notice to the other by registered mail, which termination shall become effective _____ days after mailing of such written notice. After termination, the sale or purchase of any Product by the Distributor, or the referring of prospective purchasers by the Manufacturer to the Distributor, shall not be construed as a renewal of this agreement.

B. This agreement shall terminate, at Manufacturer's option and without any notice to Distributor, as of any date on which:

1. Distributor shall become insolvent.

2. Distributor shall become subject to any liquidation, receivership, bankruptcy, reorganization, or creditors' proceedings, either voluntary or involuntary, if such proceeding shall not have been dismissed within thirty (30) days after commencement.

3. Distributor shall attempt to assign this agreement without Manufacturer's written consent.

4. Distributor shall fail to perform any obligation hereunder.

5. Distributor or a partner thereof, if a partnership, shall die or become disabled.

11. Effect of Termination

A. In case the Manufacturer terminates this agreement otherwise than by reason of circumstances stated in paragraph B of paragraph 10, the Manufacturer shall purchase from the Distributor, and the Distributor agrees to sell to the Manufacturer, all new and unsold Products and Service Parts then owned by the Distributor and previously purchased by the Distributor from the Manufacturer, which are, in the opinion of the Manufacturer, unused, undamaged, and not obsolete, at 85 percent of the net prices originally charged the Distributor.

B. The Product and Service Parts shall be considered not obsolete for the purpose of this paragraph 11 if it has been produced or sold in like type and size by the Manufacturer within the 12-month period immediately preceding the effective date of termination of this agreement. All Products and/or Service Parts so purchased by the Manufacturer shall be immediately shipped by the Distributor, freight collect, to the destination designed by the Manufacturer.

C. In case the Distributor terminates this agreement, or the agreement is terminated by Manufacturer by reason of circumstances stated in paragraph B of paragraph 10, this paragraph 11 shall apply, at the option of the Manufacturer, to all Products and Service Parts then owned by the Distributor previously purchased by the Distributor from the Manufacturer.

D. Distributor shall be entitled to receive a discount or commission only on orders received and accepted by Manufacturer prior to the date of termination or on orders resulting from outstanding quotations by Distributor which orders are received and accepted by Manufacturer within thirty (30) days following the date of termination, provided, that the Distributor shall have filed written notice with Manufacturer within five (5) days of the date of termination specifying the quotations or orders on which a discount or commission is or will be claimed.

12. Assignment

Neither this agreement nor any interest therein is assignable by the Distributor. The benefit of this agreement shall ensure to and be binding upon the successors and assigns of the Manufacturer.

13. No Other Agreement—Acceptance by Manufacturer—Law of Performance

This agreement contains the full and entire agreement between the parties hereto, and replaces all previous agreements between Manufacturer and Distributor or Distributor's predecessor in interest or assignor. No agent or representative of the Manufacturer has any authority to make any representations, statements, warranties, or agreements not herein expressed. This agreement shall become valid and binding when signed by a duly authorized representative of Manufacturer at its office at Sidney, Ohio, and when so accepted, this agreement shall be an Ohio contract and shall be construed, enforced, and performed in accordance with the laws of the State of Ohio. If it shall be found that any provision hereof violates the law of any government or governmental division having jurisdiction in the premises, such provision shall be of no force and effect and this agreement shall be treated as if such provision had not been inserted herein.

(Name of Distributor)

By_____

Title_____

Originated by_____

Recommended by_____

Accepted and executed at Sidney, Ohio

WESTINGHOUSE AIR BRAKE COMPANY, Pneumatic Equipment Div.

By_____

Title_____

SALES AGREEMENT, SALARY PLUS COMMISSION:
Blackhawk Manufacturing Company*

It is our policy to outline in detail our compensation plan each year. This is an employment contract—the agreement between you and the Company which specifies how you will be paid for services you render.

Compensation is divided into "direct" and "supplementary." Our direct compensation plan includes a good base salary, a reasonable expense account, a company leased automobile, and an attractive bonus opportunity.

In addition we provide you with a supplementary compensation plan which includes hospitalization insurance, health and accident policies, major medical, surgical, accidental death, and life insurance. When you have been with the company for five years and have reached the age of 30, you are also eligible for the Blackhawk Retirement Plan.

In order to familiarize yourself again with this insurance, we are enclosing the booklets describing it in detail. We have also spelled out your actual coverage on page nine. Be sure to read this over carefully and then determine how much it would cost to provide this same protection for you and your family.

Often we have a tendency to overlook the importance of supplementary compensation. We may look upon it as "fringe benefits" or believe it is standard procedure with all companies. This is not true in either case. Supplementary compensation is intended to take care of those emergencies which most of us could not otherwise afford and also to build that all-important security for our later years.

Many companies have some form of supplementary compensation but few even approach our plan. Our insurance programs are the most complete available.

From time to time we also offer an opportunity to earn important additional money in the form of special contests, which help to provide those "extras" that make life more enjoyable.

It is our desire to provide an overall program which will allow you to live comfortably now, provide for the future, and, most important, give you the opportunity to grow in proportion to your capabilities.

This covers our agreement with you for the period beginning January 1, 19_____, and ending December 31, 19_____.

---

*Now known as Blackhawk Automotive Inc., Div. of Hein-Werner Corp., Milwaukee, Wisconsin

1. *Employment.* You are employed by the Blackhawk Mfg. Company, A Division of Applied Power Industries, Inc., hereinafter referred to as "Blackhawk Mfg. Company," as its salesperson to sell to the jobbing trade our products exclusively in accordance with prices, terms, conditions, policies, and regulations as specified and directed by us from time to time. You are to devote your entire time during business hours to this work, and to use your best efforts and energies to promote the sale of our products in your territory.

2. *Definitions.* The term "our products" wherever used in this agreement shall cover only those standard terms of manufacture regularly offered for sale through jobbers and for which distributor price lists are issued.

   The term "specials" wherever used in the agreement shall cover 1) items of manufacture made according to customers' specifications, 2) items embodying changes in our standard items, 3) products of Dynex, Incorporated (Hydraulic Control products), 4) and specific items of Blackhawk Industrial Products Company.

   The term "shipments" as used in this agreement shall mean gross shipments of our products to jobbers only, less deductions for returns, allowances, credits, including redistribution credits, less freight if paid by us. The term "shipments" shall not include shipments to anyone of repair parts or repair tools and equipment, specials, or shipments to the United States Government or any of its departments or divisions.

3. *Territory.* Under this agreement you will cover the following territory for the sale of Blackhawk Products as indicated:

4. *Compensation.* Your compensation for your services under this agreement will be calculated and paid on the following basis:

   (a) For each month of the contract term you will be paid a salary of $_____.

   (b) In addition, in the event shipments of Lifting Equipment into your territory for the period from January 1, 19____, to December 31, 19____, exceed $_____; and the shipments of Porto-Power Equipment into your territory for the period from January 1, 19____, to December 31, 19____, exceed $_____, which amounts are hereinafter referred to as "base shipments," you will be paid a bonus of 4 percent of such excess shipments. This means you must exceed the bases on both Lifting Equipment and Porto-Power Equipment before you are eligible to receive any bonus. This bonus will be paid as follows:

   At the end of the contract term the bonus to which you are entitled shall be determined, and shall be paid to you on or before February 15, 19____.

(c) To carry this out properly, we expect you to spend 10 percent of your time on Lifting Equipment and 90 percent of your time on Porto-Power Equipment. We expect you to work out your schedule in accordance with this.

5. *Compensation on sales of specials.* On any government business or any business involving specials we reserve the right 1) to deal directly with the government or customer concerned regardless of how or where the business originated, 2) to determine in our discretion what, if any, discount shall be allowed to the jobber; what, if any, special commission shall be allowed to you as a salesperson; and what, if any, shipments on such business shall be included in the calculations referred to in paragraph 4 (b) above. If any shipments on such business are not included in the calculations referred to in paragraph 4 (b), and if any special commissions be allowed on such shipments under the provisions of this paragraph 5, said special commission shall be considered earned and payable when the customer's payment has been received in full by us.

6. *Expenses.* It is agreed that the Company will pay the normal expenses you incur in covering your territory away from home. To assist you in determining what should be covered by this expense program, the following information is provided.

(a) *Personal expenses.* We will pay for meals and lodging away from home. Hotel receipts must be included with your expense report. If you use transportation other than the car we furnish you, prior permission must be received from your Regional Manager.

(b) *Car expense.* We will provide you with a car, as outlined on pages 10 through 15. We will pay for all gas and oil to operate this car for business purposes. This is the only car expense for which the Company is responsible, and receipts must be included with your weekly expense report.

All other service and repairs for these cars are the responsibility of the leasing company, and should be handled directly by you with them.

Your car must be kept clean, and it is your responsibility to see that it is.

(c) *Miscellaneous expenses.* Any expenses in addition to those listed above must be described and receipts provided where possible. This can include such items as: telephone expense, customer entertainment, tolls, parking, cab fares, and postage.

(d) *Submitting expenses.* It is necessary to submit expense reports only when expenses have been incurred. They must be sent to the Sales Manager for approval, with a copy to your Regional Manager.

(e) *Expense allowance.* We think your expenses should average $_____ per month.

(f) *Expenses for which you are responsible.* In managing your territory, you will find that there are some expenses that are not covered by our expense allowance. These normal operating expenses are your responsibility and include such items as routine stationery, office supplies, Christmas greeting cards, luggage, brief cases, etc. There may be other expenses that you incur in managing your territory in addition to those itemized above.

7. *Acceptance of orders.* All orders solicited in your territory are subject to acceptance by an executive of the Company at the home office, and we reserve the right to reject, for any reason whatsoever, any or all orders solicited by you or by any Company salesperson in your territory, or any or all orders received at the home office from any jobber located in your territory. Failure of the Company to make shipments on any order or orders whether for causes within or without its control shall not entitle you to compensation with respect to the amount of such order or orders.

8. *Sales literature and samples.* The Company will furnish you from time to time such sales literature, samples, and data as the Company shall deem sufficient to exploit the sale of its products properly. Samples will be charged to your account at our standard jobbing price. All samples furnished to you shall be returned to the Company by you when requested by the Company, and you will be given full credit for all samples returned. In no case shall any samples be sold to anyone.

9. *Termination.* This agreement, unless sooner terminated as hereinafter provided, shall terminate at the close of business on December 31, 19_____.

(a) Either of us shall have the right to terminate this agreement at any time, by giving 30 days' prior written notice of intention to terminate.

(b) In the event that the total shipments into your territory as of March 31, 19_____, are 10 percent or more under 25 percent of the base shipments, or in the event that your total shipments as of June 30, 19_____, are 10 percent or more under 50 percent of the base shipments, or in the event that your total shipments as of September 30, 19_____, are 10 percent or more under 75 percent of the base shipments, then we reserve the right to terminate this agreement forthwith.

(c) We reserve the right to terminate this agreement at any time for cause. Cause shall include, but shall not be limited to, your failure or inability for any reason to furnish regular full-time services to the Company.

(d) Upon the termination of this contract for any reason, you are to account for all samples furnished to you, and all samples you cannot account for shall be paid for by you at the price charged on your account by deducting said amount from any amounts due you from the Company. In the event the amount you owe for samples exceeds the amount which the Company owes you, you shall pay for the balance in cash. In addition, you agree to immediately return to the Company all sales literature and other data in your possession.

(e) Upon termination of this contract for any reason, you shall receive your salary for the full calendar months which have transpired since the beginning of the contract term, plus the proportion of the salary for the month in which the termination occurs which the part of the month worked bears to the full month, less any amounts previously paid to you. In the event you have received on account your salary in an amount in excess of that which you are entitled to under this sub-paragraph, you shall promptly remit the difference to the Company. Payment of any balance of the drawing account due you, which the Company is required to make by the terms of this sub-paragraph shall be made as soon as you have returned or accounted for all of the property of the Company previously delivered to you.

(f) In case of the termination of this agreement by either party prior to December 31, 19_____, you shall not be entitled to receive and the Company shall not be liable to pay to you the bonus provided for in paragraph 4.

10. *Construction.* This agreement is executed at West Allis, Wisconsin, and shall be construed and interpreted under the laws of the State of Wisconsin.

11. *Effective Date.* This agreement shall not be binding on either party until accepted by you in writing as provided in the form of acceptance endorsed at the end of this agreement, and returned to the Company's office at 5325 West Rogers Street, West Allis, Wisconsin, within 45 days of the date hereof. When so accepted and re-

turned this agreement shall be effective as of January 1, 19____,
and shall supersede and annul all former agreements between the
Company and yourself.

BLACKHAWK MFG. COMPANY

A Division of
APPLIED POWER INDUSTRIES,
INC.

By_____

I hereby acknowledge receipt of the above agreement, and the same is
approved and accepted by me.

Date_____ (Signed)_____ (Seal)

BRANCH MANAGER CONTRACT

MEMORANDUM of Agreement by and between _____ COM-
PANY, and _____ corporation, duly licensed to do business in
_____, and with an office at _____, _____, party of the first part,
and _____, party of the second part, made and entered into this _____
day of _____, A.D. 19____.

WITNESSETH:

_____ COMPANY employs the second party as Branch Manager of
the _____ territory at a salary of _____ dollars per month, and his
or her legitimate traveling expenses when absent from his or her home
and engaged upon the business of _____ COMPANY, and second
party accepts such employment and agrees to give his or her entire time
and undivided attention to the interest of _____ COMPANY, and to
be governed by and to carry out the instructions of the company, whether
embodied in standing rules or special instructions that may be issued
from time to time.

As a special incentive to increase activity and watchfulness on the part
of the second party, the _____ COMPANY agrees to pay the second
party a special bonus of _____ percent on the net profit of above-
mentioned territory, if earned, under and in accordance with the following conditions:

1. The net profit of business obtained from the _____ territory shall
   be ascertained by deducting from orders obtained, which orders
   have been accepted and filled and for which payment has been received by the company, the total of the following items:

   (a) Marginal cost

   (b) Commissions

(c) Policy allowances

(d) Interest of one-half of 1 percent per month on the total inventory of goods on hand and in the hands of the agents in said territory on the first of each month, based upon the marginal cost price established for such goods.

(e) All expenses incurred upon the authority and for the benefit of the _____ Branch as recorded on the books of the company in accordance with their regular accounting practice.

2. The marginal costs shall be determined by extending all shipments, upon which credit may be due to second party under paragraph 1 hereof, at the standard list price, less the discount shown on separate sheet hereto attached, marked "Marginal Cost Discounts."

3. The bonus, if earned, to be calculated monthly and to be accumulated for the six months' period ending _____ and _____ of each year, and shall be payable semiannually on _____ and _____ of each year.

4. It is understood and agreed by the parties hereto that this contract, so far as it pertains to the payment of a special bonus, shall be retroactive to _____, 19_____.

5. This contract may be terminated by either party hereto giving to the other two weeks' notice in writing, and in case of termination, any amounts earned as bonus shall be calculated as of the date of termination of this contract.

By_____

Accepted_____

INFORMAL LETTER OF INTENT*

Dear Mr. or Ms._____:

This letter constitutes your agreement of employment and itemizes all major details of duties, responsibilities, and compensation.

Effective _____, you will be employed as sales representative for _____ in that territory described as the Chicago area. This area is defined as that portion of the state of Illinois north of and including the counties of Vermillion, Champaign, Platt, De Witt, Logan, Menard, Mason, Schuyler, and Hancock; that portion of the state of Wisconsin south of and including the counties of Door, Brown, Kewaunee, Outagamie, Winnebago, Waushara, Adams, Juneau, Monroe, and

_____

*Actual figures used in this example are for illustrative purposes only and have been intentionally simplified.

Vernon; the counties of Dubuque, Jackson, Clinton, and Scott in the state of Iowa; plus Lake County in the state of Indiana.

Your initial training period of _____ through _____ will be divided into two periods: the first at _____ main office and factory in _____; the second in the Chicago area. During this preliminary training period your compensation will be based on a $900.00 per month salary prorated over the training period.

Effective _____, you will assume all normal activities as our sales representative in the Chicago area and your compensation will be based on the following.

$600.00 per month salary plus:

Commissions on all orders dated on or after February 1 (which are shipped to some point within the Chicago area) as follows:

0 —$100,000.00	Annual Sales at 3 %
$100,000.00—$200,000.00	Annual Sales at 3½%
$200,000.00—$300,000.00	Annual Sales at 2½%
Over $300,000.00	Annual Sales at 2 %

You will be compensated for expenses incurred in the interests of _____ on the basis of actual detailed expenses during the period of _____ through _____. Effective _____, you will receive an expense allowance of $400.00 per month.

It is definitely understood that your services will be devoted exclusively to the promotion and sale of _____ products and that you will assist in any special activity in the company's interest when required.

This Agreement may be terminated by either party, only upon receipt of 30 days advance notice in writing.

_____

Sales Manager

_____

Executive Vice-President

_____

Sales Representative

Promotion Law

The Tax Reform Act of 1986 joins our summary of laws, regulations, and court decisions affecting promotion. What follows is an in-depth article by Raymond M. Patt reprinted with the permission of *Incentive Marketing*.

Although 1986 was a relatively quiet year with respect to legislative changes, there was one significant enactment—the Federal Tax Reform Act of 1986.

After a long and difficult battle, the Incentive Federation, with significant support by trade associations in the promotion field, achieved a signal victory. The new law, unlike the previous existing statute, specifically creates an income tax exemption for both employers and employees for employee recognition awards that come under the purview of this legislation. Thus, a struggle that began in December 1982—when the Internal Revenue Service ruled that such gifts were taxable to employees and proposed severe restrictions on the nature of such awards—ended successfully for the incentive industry. A detailed discussion appears under the heading of Employee Service Awards.

The following pages are a compendium of laws, regulations, and court decisions affecting the field of promotion. It is important to bear in mind that a summary such as this should never be substituted for consultation with knowledgeable counsel. The subject matter is much too complex to be covered in its entirety in this article.

Also, laws and regulations change, and court interpretations affecting them are made. This can alter the information set forth in this summary.

Alcoholic Beverages

Both federal and state regulatory bodies and statutory enactments have jurisdiction in this area.

Federal. The Federal Alcohol Administration Law regulates distribution of dealer gifts, articles of nominal value, and advertising specialties by alcoholic beverage suppliers.

The Bureau of Alcohol, Tobacco and Firearms of the Department of the Treasury, which administers the law, issued new regulations in 1980. The major ones are as follows:

1. Advertising specialties—coasters, napkins, clocks, thermometers, calendars, etc.—may be furnished by a wholesaler or manufacturer to a liquor retailer, with a limit of $58 per year per brand.

2. Wholesalers or manufacturers may furnish consumers with coupons redeemable by retailers, and retailers may be paid by the wholesaler or manufacturer a "customary handling fee."

3. Wholesalers or manufacturers may offer contest prizes, premiums, refunds, and the like directly to consumers.

4. Consumer advertising specialties may be furnished, given or sold to a retailer by a wholesaler or manufacturer for unconditional distribution by the retailer to the general public.

5. In-pack premiums, such as glasses packed with an alcoholic beverage in a gift box, are allowed.

State. Every state has some form of legislation or regulation covering the sale of alcoholic beverages, including beer and wine, and many of those rules restrict the use of premiums or chance promotions. However, there appears to be a trend toward easing long-standing restrictions. Nevertheless, careful checking must be made to ensure that the proposed promotion does not run afoul of restrictions in any state in which the promotion is contemplated.

Bank Premiums

Federal. In 1980, the Depository Institutions Deregulation Committee (DIDC) was established by Congress for the purpose of phasing out restrictions on the amount of interest that banks and thrift institutions were permitted to pay depositors.

After initially indicating an intention to prohibit the use of premiums and incentive promotions by depository institutions, the committee announced rulings that not only allowed such promotions but even raised gift limits.

Regulations, effective October 1, 1980, removed restrictions on the value of premiums that may be offered to depositors on super NOW accounts, money market accounts, and time deposits of more than 31 days. Some premium limits still apply to passbook savings accounts and time deposits of 7 to 31 days requiring a minimum deposit of less than $2,500.

State. At the state level, bank boards or banking superintendents, either by regulation or persuasion, establish guidelines for premium usage. Note should be made of special restrictions existing in Texas and California.

Iowa permits banks to conduct self-liquidator promotions with merchandise selling for not more than $15. Idaho allows state-chartered savings and loan associations to offer premiums in the same manner as is permitted by the DIDC.

Coupons and In-Pack Promotions

In the past, coupons have been regulated mostly by the federal government. Recently, states have begun to enact legislation, especially with respect to those coupons not enclosed with a manufacturers' packaged goods.

Federal. The Food and Drug Administration limits the type of premium merchandise that may be inserted in food or confectionery packages. Premiums must be packed separately in FDA-approved materials unless the premium is made of materials that are FDA-approved for direct contact with food and are designed so that there is no possibility of accidental ingestion of a premium component. Any printing on the insert container must be done with FDA-approved inks.

The Federal Trade Commission has held it to be a deceptive practice when the insertion of a premium in a package results in a decrease in the normal amount of product in that package.

The FTC policy statement of 1969 requires full disclosure on the product package of all terms of the offer on enclosed coupons. It also bars unreasonably short expiration dates on coupons. The FTC requires disclosure if the coupon is good for a price reduction on the next purchase of the same item or on a purchase of a different product.

State. Kansas permits a manufacturer or packer to issue a premium coupon redeemable for any product it manufactures or packs or for one specified product it does not manufacture or pack. The coupon may offer a premium free or with no limit on the cash requirement, which previously was set at $5. The manufacturer or packer also may issue a coupon redeemable for cash.

A retailer may issue a merchandise premium coupon redeemable by the retailer, with or without a cash requirement, provided the coupon is redeemable for a product that the retailer sells in its regular course of doing business.

An Illinois statute provides that any retail seller who publishes or issues coupons for use by consumers for the purchase of specific merchandise in the retail outlet and who represents that coupons permit the purchase of the merchandise for less than the regular price shall clearly state the discount or the fact that the coupon-featured price is a sale price to which the presenter is entitled.

In 1985, Wyoming increased the cash discount allowed on a manufacturer's coupon from $5 to $50.

A prohibition on discounting of milk products via coupons or rebates was repealed in Iowa last year.

Employee Service Awards

According to the Tax Reform Act of 1986, effective in 1987:

1. Employee achievement awards are defined as items of tangible personal property other than cash which an employer gives to an employee for either length of service or safety achievement. Awards for productivity are excluded. There may be some question as to whether "tangible personal property" includes gift certificates or travel awards. Clarification will have to await the issuance of IRS regulations.

2. Length-of-service awards of more than nominal value can be given to any one employee only once every five years and not during the first five years of his or her employment.

3. Safety achievement awards of more than nominal value can be given to no more than 10 percent of eligible employees in any one year. Managers, administrators, clerical workers, and other professional employees are not deemed eligible for this type of award.

4. Qualified plan awards are defined as employee achievement awards provided for under an established plan or program of an employer that does not discriminate in favor of highly compensated employees.

5. In non-qualified plans, awards are deductible to the employer and excludable from the income of the employee for tax purposes to the extent that the aggregate cost to the employer of all awards to any one employee does not exceed $400 during a tax year. Other restrictions apply.

6. Qualified plan awards are deductible and excludable for tax purposes to the extent that the aggregate cost to the employer in a tax year for all employee achievement awards to any one employee does not exceed $1,600 and that the average cost of all awards given by an employer during the year does not exceed $400. Other restrictions apply.

7. Employee achievement awards that are deemed excludable from the employee's income tax are also excludable for social security tax purposes.

Free, Two-For-One, Half-Price and Similar Offers

These retail promotions are regulated by the FTC "Guide Concerning Use of the Word 'Free' and Similar Representations," effective since 1971.

The guide prohibits use of "free" or similar offers on products or services usually sold at a negotiated price and on introductory offers, unless the offerer intends in good faith to commence selling the promoted product at the same price after a limited time; requires clear and conspicuous disclosure of terms and conditions in advertising or on-pack representation; and limits frequency of such offers to no more than three promotions at least 30 days apart in a 12-month period.

Note that some states have rules on "free" offers that differ from federal rules.

Games and Sweepstakes

This is perhaps the most comprehensive area of regulation in the field of incentive law. While games and sweepstakes do not have the same "crazy quilt" of regulatory controls as exists for alcoholic beverages, here, too, various federal and state statutes play a major role.

FEDERAL

Lottery and postal laws prohibit the operation of a lottery and forbid carrying in the mails, newspapers and advertisements containing information of lotteries. However, the federal government interprets the term *lottery* liberally, so that if a consumer is not required to part with material consideration for participation in a contest or sweepstakes, the promotion generally will not be considered a lottery.

Food stores and gasoline stations that conduct promotional games of chance can observe a shortened interval between games and have less required information to post under 1981 modifications to a 1980 FTC rule.

The games-of-chance rule, adopted in 1969, required a waiting period between the end of one game and the beginning of the next equal to the length of the first game. In July 1978, the FTC granted a temporary exemption from the hiatus provision of the rule, allowing a new game to begin 30 days after completion of a preceding game that had a duration of more than 30 days.

Another amendment revises the requirements with respect to posting and reporting. Rather than posting the name, address, and prize value for every game winner as had previously been required, retail outlets are required only to post information on those winners who redeem their prizes at that outlet. The amendment also eliminates the requirement that a complete winners list be forwarded to the FTC at the conclusion of each game. Other posting requirements are preserved, including disclosure of the number of game pieces distributed at all participating outlets, the number of prizes offered, and the number awarded.

For protection of sponsors of games and sweepstakes, all advertisements, broadcasts, coupons, entry blanks, and tickets should contain a nullification clause voiding the offer wherever the promotion is prohibited or otherwise restricted.

STATE

Bonding or trust account deposits are required in Florida and New York, and registration is necessary in Florida, New York, and Rhode Island, with the following exceptions.

Florida, as of 1981, provides that bonding or trust accounts can be waived for operators who have conducted promotions for at least five years and who have not had an action instituted against them for violations within that period. In 1983, the law was further amended to provide for a filing fee and to exempt from registration those sweepstakes in which the value of prizes is $5,000 or less.

Promotional games are prohibited at gasoline service stations in Delaware, Maine, Maryland, Massachusetts, New Jersey, and Virginia, and they are restricted in New Hampshire.

If a planned promotion involves sales of cigarettes, or dairy or milk products, be certain to check out state laws that may be applicable in the locality where the promotion is taking place.

Michigan, Missouri, and Texas now require users of some game card promotions to make free game cards available at the retail site to non-purchasers as well as purchasers, rather than only through the mail by request.

A number of states prohibit notifying people that they have won or are eligible for prizes or premiums when the awards are conditioned upon rental or purchase of merchandise or property or upon submission to a sales presentation. Florida, Louisiana, and Tennessee enacted such legislation in 1983, and California did so in 1984. Maryland, Missouri, Texas, and Vermont followed suit in 1985.

Since 1982, New York has required written disclosure to consumers at the time they are offered an award as part of a promotion that they must submit to a sales presentation in order to claim the prize. The written disclosure also must include all terms and conditions attached to the prize.

Maryland enacted similar legislation, effective January 1, 1985, with respect to the purchase of time shares.

Georgia enacted sweeping legislation in 1986 which, among other things, requires disclosure of need to submit to sales presentation in order to receive a prize or gift.

Another recent trend in many states is to mandate disclosure of comparable retail value of prizes being awarded. It would therefore be advisable for all promotional games and sweepstakes to set forth this information in order not to run afoul of the requirement.

Following are specific highlights of recent state enactments or rulings concerning games and sweepstakes:

Maryland. By legislation enacted in 1985, promotions must, among other requirements, disclose the manufacturer's suggested retail price or comparable retail price of each prize offered.

Minnesota. In 1983, this state's lottery statute was amended by exempting from the definition of a lottery an in-pack chance promotion if certain requirements were met, including free participation without purchase, a clear statement on the package or related advertisement of the method of participation and the termination date, and no misrepresentation of a participant's chances of winning.

Missouri. Liquor regulations were amended in 1982 to permit chance promotions on premises of retail stores that are licensed for the sale of alcoholic beverages as long as no consideration is required, liquor is not an element of the promotion, and the promotion is sponsored by the retail store or by a manufacturer whose principal product is not liquor.

This removed previous restrictions with respect to chance promotions in supermarkets, which sell liquor products in Missouri.

New York. Retailers are prohibited from conducting games that are similar to bingo.

State legislation enacted in 1986 prohibits use of any intangible personal-property free incentive in the sale of consumer goods having a value of $500 or more without written disclosure of the actual retail value of the incentive at the time of sale and of whether any tax obligations may be incurred by the consumer as a result of owning the incentive.

In a discussion of this legislation that appeared in the *New York Law Journal,* Assistant Attorney General Stephen Mindell stated that it was intended to protect consumers who receive zero-coupon bonds as premiums. However, the vagueness of the statute may create problems with respect to other intangible personal property offered as a premium.

Last year, New York also passed a law prohibiting the giving or offering of live animals, other than purebred livestock or fish, as prizes in any promotion.

North Carolina. In 1979, a statute that prohibits false representation with respect to prizes supposedly won in connection with sales promotion was enacted. It requires, among other things, that the recipient of a prize be selected by a method in which no more than 10 percent of the names considered are selected as winners and that the recipient receive the prize without any obligation.

Ohio. The former opinion of the attorney general holding it to be a violation if store visit is necessary to enter a chance promotion appears to have been reversed in 1985.

Pennsylvania. As of 1984, any offering by mail or telephone of a prize in relation to the offering for sale of real property, including time sharing, must be accompanied by a statement of the fair market value—not suggested retail price—of all prizes offered, plus a statement of the odds of receiving any of the prizes.

Utah. The Supreme Court, in October 1979, reversed a ruling by the state attorney general and lower court decisions that had upheld restrictions on retail games of chance. As a result of this Supreme Court decision, chance promotions are legal in Utah provided no purchase or payment is required.

Washington. By amendment in 1985, frequency of supermarket retail promotions is still limited to one per year but for a maximum duration of fourteen consecutive days instead of seven.

Wisconsin. In 1982, this state enacted a sweeping revision of its lottery and promotion statutes, liberalizing its definitions with respect to certificates, coupons, and sweepstakes promotions. Store visits to obtain entry blanks for a game or promotion are legal, provided there is no purchase necessary.

Insurance

Generally there are few restrictions with respect to offering premiums or incentives to consumers or insurance agents. New York, however, prohibits prizes or awards offered to agents in addition to commissions.

Mail-Order Rules

The FTC's mail-order rule provides consumers who shop by mail with important protection. Under the rule a mail-order company must send ordered goods within the time period specified in its ads or within 30 days if no shipping date is specified. The time requirements go into effect when the company has received a completed order. This means that the company has received the consumer's cash, check, or money order, or charged a credit account, and that it has all the information needed to process and ship the order. Failure to specify essential information, such as the size or color of an ordered item, would delay the start of the time period until such information was received. If the goods cannot be shipped within the time period, the company must notify the customer and give the customer the opportunity to cancel the order.

California statute regulates mail order and catalog merchandise sales, and other California laws regulate warranties. The FTC has held that, where the state law affords greater consumer protection than federal regulations, the state's more stringent requirements prevail.

The FTC and the Direct Mail/Marketing Association offers a free pamphlet entitled "Make Knowledge Your Partner in Mail-Order Shopping." Copies may be obtained by writing to Public Reference Branch, Department DCE, Room 130, Federal Trade

Commission, Sixth Street and Pennsylvania Avenue N.W., Washington, D.C. 20580.

Meat-packers

Revised regulations issued in 1982 by the Packers and Stockyards Administration removes policy statement 203.3, which had prohibited meat-packer dealer sales promotions.

State and Local Sales and Use Taxes

This is a sticky subject, and incentive suppliers must be especially watchful. Because of the increase in exchanges of information among state authorities, many premium suppliers add taxes to products supplied.

Bill S.1510 was introduced in the U.S. Senate to eliminate restrictions on the taxing powers of the various states to impose, collect, and administer state and local sales and use taxes on sales in interstate commerce, but the bill failed to pass. If enacted, any state, or political subdivision, would have had the power to impose a sales or use tax on any interstate sale of tangible personal property by a person located outside such state.

Telephone Solicitation

This is an issue of growing concern in various state legislatures.

In Nebraska, a 1979 law provides that no automatic dialing/announcing device shall be connected by any person to any telephone line without a permit from the Public Service Commission. Written application must be submitted to the commission providing information as to the type of automatic dialing/announcing device proposed to be placed, the anticipated number of calls, the average length of a completed call and such additional information as the commission may require. Each applicant also must agree to include on all calls made on the automatic device a statement of the nature of the call and the name, address, and telephone number of the business being represented.

In Michigan, a law was approved in 1980 proscribing telephone use for recorded commercial advertising messages without permission of the telephone subscriber. Florida enacted similar legislation in 1984, Texas in 1985, and Arizona, Tennessee, Virginia, and Washington in 1986.

Trading Stamps

Various states have statutory requirements regulating trading stamps. Except for IRS rulings on taxes and unredeemed stamps, there is no federal involvement.

Kansas and Puerto Rico prohibit trading stamps.

Bonding and registration statutes exist in California, Connecticut, Florida, Maine (no bond required), Maryland, Massachusetts, New Hampshire, New Jersey, New Mexico, New York, South Dakota, Utah, and Vermont.

Optional cash redemption is required in all above states and Indiana, Nebraska, North Dakota, Ohio, and Wisconsin.

Cash redemption only is required in Washington and Wyoming.

A question as to the applicability of the cash redemption requirement in the state of Washington arose in connection with controlled markdown promotions. In these programs, consumers are issued trading stamps or coupons by a retailer when purchasing merchandise, and stamps or coupons are redeemed for normally stocked merchandise marked down significantly for coupon recipients.

The state's statutes require that trading stamps either be redeemed in cash or that the issuer obtain a license for a fee of $6,000 per store if stamps are redeemable for merchandise. The state attorney general indicated in response to an inquiry by this writer that the law does apply to such promotions. This, in effect, makes prohibitive the use of such promotions in Washington, if the statute is enforced.

In South Dakota, sales of trading stamps are exempted from sales provisions.

Unsolicited Mail Merchandise

The FTC holds that there is no obligation on the part of recipients to return or pay for unsolicited merchandise received in the mail and warns that companies sending consumers such merchandise and attempting to collect may be liable for civil penalties of up to $1,000 for each violation.

Under the Postal Reorganization Act of 1970, only two kinds of merchandise can legally be sent through the U.S. mail without the consumer's prior agreement. These are free samples, clearly marked as such, and merchandise that is mailed by a charitable organization seeking contributions.

Warranties

The Magnuson-Moss Warranty Act became effective in 1975, and the FTC promulgated rules for its implementation. The act and the rules require that warranties be made available for consumers to read and compare before purchase.

Under the law, a written warranty offered for any consumer product costing more than $10 must clearly state whether it is *full* or *limited*. *Full* refers to the range of consumer rights under the warranty, such as the right to choose a replacement or refund if a defect is not repaired after a reasonable number of attempts. Limited warranties give consumers fewer rights than full warranties.

Anyone offering written warranties for consumer products costing more than $15 must make the text available to prospective buyers and must disclose certain information, including:

1. A clear description of products, parts, or characteristics covered by or excluded from the warranty;

2. A statement of what the warrantor will do in the event of a product defect or malfunction, specifying items or services the warrantor will pay for or provide;

3. A date or event upon which the warranty begins, if different from the purchase date, and

4. A statement saying, "This warranty gives you specific legal rights, and you may also have other rights which vary from state to state."

The FTC has prepared a booklet to assist businesses in complying with the warranty requirements. For copies of the booklet, entitled "Warranties, Making Business Sense Out of Warranty Law," write to: Public Reference Branch, Department MM, Room 130, Federal Trade Commission, Sixth Street and Pennsylvania Avenue N.W., Washington, D.C. 20580.

How to Advertise Consumer Credit*

The Truth in Lending Act and Advertising

The main purpose of the Truth in Lending Act is to assure the meaningful *disclosure* of consumer credit and lease terms so that consumers can compare those terms and shop wisely. Certain provisions of the Act apply to advertisements.

Prior to the passage of the Act, an advertiser might have disclosed only the most attractive credit (or lease) terms, thus distorting the true cost. For example, an advertisement might have read, " '63 Chevy, only $30 per month." Whether this is a bargain depends upon information missing from the advertisement, such as the down payment and the number of payments. The advertisement also fails to disclose the annual percentage rate or even whether the transaction is a credit sale or a lease. The Act requires that the advertisement tell the whole story.

If an advertisement contains any one of a list of terms specified in the Act, then that advertisement must also include a number of prescribed disclosures. In other words, the specified terms "trigger" the disclosures.

Thus, if you choose to use a "triggering" advertising claim, you must use the disclosures. If you steer clear of the "triggering" claims, you need not make the disclosures.

The type of transaction advertised (open-end credit, closed-end credit, or a consumer lease) determines the triggering terms as well as the disclosures. In all cases, the required disclosures must be made "clearly and conspicuously." Sometimes specific terminology is required.

The Act also prohibits "bait and switch" advertising of consumer credit and leases. That is, you cannot advertise credit or

---

*A Federal Trade Commission Manual for Business

---

lease terms that are not, in fact, available. No advertisement may state that a specific amount of credit or a specific installment payment or a specific down payment term can be arranged unless the creditor will make those arrangements.

Who Must Comply

Anyone placing a consumer credit or lease advertisement (that is subject to the Act) must comply. Thus, *advertisers,* not just creditors and lessors, must comply. Associations, manufacturers, and even government agencies (such as the Federal Housing Administration) must comply with the Act when they place consumer credit and lease advertisements.

Others who may be subject to the Act's advertising provisions are real estate brokers advertising private homes and builders advertising new housing developments. If the advertisement promotes credit, then the broker, the seller, the builder, or anyone who places the advertisement must comply with the Act.

There is no liability under the Act for the media in which advertisements appear. The media can, however, protect their customers by screening advertisements to make sure that they comply with the law.

Definitions

1. *Advertisement.* An advertisement subject to the Truth in Lending Act is *any commercial message* that promotes consumer credit or a consumer lease. Advertisements may appear:

   • in newspapers, magazines, leaflets, flyers, catalogs, direct mail literature, or other printed material;

   • on radio, television, or a public address system;

   • on an inside or outside sign or display, or window display;

   • in point-of-sale literature or price tags.

   A commercial message is any message that promotes sales or leases. Thus, materials that are only educational or that are required by law are not "advertisements." For example, a brochure issued by a bank explaining FHA mortgage rates is not a commercial message. Nor is a state-required sign posted by a finance company explaining credit terms. On the other hand, a brochure or sign which combines a sales message with educational or state-required information is an advertisement. A sales ticket which accompanies merchandise and does not contain credit information is not an advertisement.

2. *Consumer credit.* Consumer credit is any credit that is primarily for personal, family, or household purposes. It excludes business and agricultural loans and must be arranged or extended by a creditor. A creditor is a person or organization that regularly* arranges or extends consumer credit a) for which a finance charge is required or b) which is repayable in more than four installments even without a finance charge.

There are two types of consumer credit: open-end credit and closed-end credit.

3. *Open-end credit.* Examples of open-end credit are bank and gas company credit cards, stores' revolving charge accounts, and cash-advance checking accounts. In open-end credit:

- the creditor reasonably expects the customer to make repeated transactions;

- the creditor may impose a finance charge from time to time on the unpaid balance;

- as the customer pays the outstanding balance, that amount of credit is, generally, once again made available to the customer.

4. *Closed-end credit.* Closed-end credit includes all consumer credit that does not fit the definition of open-end credit. Closed-end credit consists of both sales credit and loans. In

---

*Credit is extended regularly if it is extended more than 25 times during the preceding year (or more than 5 times for transactions secured by dwellings).

a typical closed-end credit transaction, credit is advanced for a specific time period, and the amount financed, finance charge, and schedule of payments are agreed upon by the lender and the customer.

5. *Consumer lease.* A consumer lease is a lease of personal property to a private individual. The lease must be for personal, family, or household purposes and must be for a term of more than four months. (Renting a car for a weekend is, therefore, not a consumer lease.) The term includes leases when the customer has the option to buy at the end of the lease;* however, it does not include leases where the customer will have to pay more than $25,000.

6. *Annual percentage rate.* The annual percentage rate is the total charge for credit stated as a percentage, calculated on an annual basis.

7. *Finance charge.* The finance charge is the total dollar amount charged for credit. It includes interest and other costs, such as service charges, transaction charges, buyer's points, loan fees, and mortgage insurance. It also includes the premiums for credit life, accident, and health insurance, if required, and property insurance, unless the buyer may select the insurer.

Clear and Conspicuous Disclosure

All disclosures required by the Truth in Lending Act must be printed "clearly and conspicuously." That is a vague term, but Congress made it that way on purpose. To be safe, advertisers should aim for large and plain disclosures.

---

*However, a lease in which the payments equal or exceed the value of the property and where the consumer may, without further payment, or with only a nominal payment, buy the property in the end, is actually a credit sale (closed-end credit) and not a consumer lease.

Oral Rate Disclosures

If a consumer orally asks for information regarding the cost of either open- or closed-end credit, the only rate the creditor may give in response is the annual percentage rate. If, in closed-end credit, the annual percentage rate cannot be determined at the time the consumer asks the question, then the creditor shall disclose the annual percentage rate of a sample transaction and give the consumer other cost information which applies to the consumer's specific transaction.

Liability for Violations

The FTC may 1) rule that an advertiser has violated the law and 2) order the advertiser to cease and desist from further violations. *Each violation* of that order may result in a $10,000 civil penalty *each day the violation continues.*

In addition, if advertisers engage in advertising practices which they know the Commission has previously determined to be unfair or deceptive, the Commission may file a court action seeking penalties.

Finally, anyone who is actually harmed by an illegal consumer lease advertisement may sue the advertiser for:

1. Actual damages

2. Twenty-five percent of the total amount of monthly payments under the lease (but not less than $100 nor more than $1,000)

3. Court costs and a reasonable attorney's fee

Open-End Credit Disclosures

TRIGGERING TERMS

If an advertisement promoting open-end credit contains any of the following triggering terms, then three specific disclosures must also be included in the advertisement. The *triggering* terms are:

1. *A statement of when the finance charge begins to accrue, including the "free ride" period (if any).*
   Examples: "Up to 30 days of free credit if you pay in full each month"

   "We charge interest from the date we receive notice of your purchase"

2. *Either the periodic rate used to compute the finance charge or the annual percentage rate.*
   Examples: "Less than two percent per month"

   "Periodic rate — one and one-half percent per month"

3. *The method of determining the balance on which a finance charge may be imposed.*
   Examples: "A small monthly service charge on your remaining balance each month"

   "Interest will be charged on your average daily balance each month"

4. *The method of determining the finance charge, including a description of how any finance charge other than the periodic rate will be determined.*
   Examples: "You only pay $1.00 each time you write an overdraft check"

   "Minimum finance charge: 50¢ per month"

5. *The amount of any charge, other than a finance charge, that may be imposed as part of the plan.*
   Example: "There is a $35 annual membership fee to get your card"

6. *The fact that the creditor will acquire a security interest.*
   Examples: "A security interest will be taken on all goods purchased"

   "Secure your credit with a $1,000 certificate of deposit"

The following are examples of terms which do *not* trigger the required disclosures:

- Charge accounts available

- Open a revolving budget account

- Just say "Charge It"

- All major credit cards honored

- Pay monthly

- Charge some cash

REQUIRED DISCLOSURES

If any triggering term is used in an open-end credit advertisement, then the following three *disclosures* must also be included in that advertisement:

1. Any minimum, fixed, transaction, activity, or similar charge that could be imposed;

2. Any periodic rate that may be applied, expressed as an annual percentage rate.* The term *annual percentage rate* must be used. If the plan provides for a variable periodic rate, that fact must be disclosed;

3. Any membership or participation fee.

SAMPLE DISCLOSURES

The following is an example of the required disclosures for an open-end credit advertisement that would comply with the Truth in Lending Act *if printed clearly and conspicuously:*

"Your ABC Credit Card monthly bill will include a 50¢ transaction charge for each purchase you make during the month. In addition, a finance charge at the rate of 1 percent per month will

---

*The annual percentage rate is found by multiplying the periodic rate by the number of periods in a year. For further information on the finance charge and annual percentage rate, see sections 226.4 and 226.14 of revised Regulation Z.

be imposed on your unpaid balance. This is an annual percentage rate of 12 percent. The annual membership fee is $35."

CATALOG AND MULTI-PAGE ADVERTISEMENTS

A catalog or other multi-page advertisement may, under certain circumstances, be considered a single advertisement—which means only one set of disclosures is necessary. In such cases, all the disclosures required by Regulation Z may be set forth in a single table, clearly and conspicuously. However, any triggering term appearing elsewhere in the advertisement must include a clear reference to the page on which the table of disclosures appears. The table must include disclosures for amounts up to the level of the more commonly sold higher-priced items or services.

Not every open-end advertisement consisting of more than one piece of paper qualifies as a multi-page advertisement. As used in the Truth in Lending Act, "catalogs and multi-page advertisements" consist of a *series of numbered pages,* such as a newspaper supplement. Thus, separate pieces of paper, even those mailed in the same envelope, are separate advertisements. For example, if a mailing consists of several pieces of paper, each of which promotes a different item of merchandise sold on credit, each piece of paper containing a triggering term must include a full set of disclosures.

OTHER CONSIDERATIONS

All required disclosures must be specific. For example, a general statement, such as "the finance charge will be imposed on the opening balance less all appropriate credits," is not adequate. (Such a statement does not inform the consumer of the size and nature of the credits.)

Some creditors impose a minimum finance charge on unpaid balances that are below a certain dollar amount. (For example, a plan which normally charges 1½ percent per month might charge 30¢ for all balances below $20.) Under the Truth in Lending Act, if disclosures are triggered, this minimum charge must also be disclosed. If the creditor does *not* impose a finance charge when the outstanding balance is less than a certain amount (for example, a plan which normally charges 1½ percent per month might not charge for balances less than $10), the advertisement need *not* disclose this fact.

Closed-End Credit Disclosures

TRIGGERING TERMS

If an advertisement promoting closed-end credit contains any of the following triggering terms, three specific disclosures must also be included in the advertisement. The *triggering* terms are:

1. *The amount of the down payment* (expressed either as a percentage or as a dollar amount).
   Examples: "10 percent down"
   　　　　　"$25 down"
   　　　　　"90 percent financing"

2. *The amount of any payment* (expressed either as a percentage or as a dollar amount).
   Examples: "Monthly payments less than $67"
   　　　　　"Pay 5 percent each month"
   　　　　　"$9 per month"

3. *The number of payments.*
   Examples: "36 small payments are all you make"
   　　　　　"48 monthly payments and you're all paid up"

4. *The period of repayment* (the total time required to repay).
   Examples: "5 years to pay"
   　　　　　"36 months to pay"
   　　　　　"4 year loans available"

5. *The amount of any finance charge.*
   Examples: "Financing costs less than $100"
   　　　　　"Less than $100 interest"
   　　　　　"$100 financing"

The following are examples of terms that do *not* trigger the required disclosures:

- No down payment

- 18 percent annual percentage rate loans available here

- Easy monthly payments
- Loans available at 5 percent below our standard annual percentage rate
- Low down payment accepted
- Pay weekly
- Terms to fit your budget
- Financing available

REQUIRED DISCLOSURES

If any triggering term is used in a closed-end credit advertisement, then the following three *disclosures* must also be included in that advertisement:

1. The amount or percentage of the down payment;
2. The terms of repayment;
3. The annual percentage rate.

If the annual percentage rate may be increased after consummation of the credit transaction, that fact must be disclosed.

SAMPLE DISCLOSURES (GENERAL)

The following example, which promotes the credit sale of a $1,000 car, illustrates the required disclosures for a closed-end consumer credit advertisement which would comply with the Truth in Lending Act *if printed clearly and conspicuously:*

"No down payment. Twelve monthly payments of $100 each; annual percentage rate: 35 percent"

In displaying the down payment, the words "down payment" need not be used. For example, "10 percent cash required from buyer" or "credit terms require minimum $100 trade-in" would suffice.

Repayment terms may be expressed in a variety of ways in addition to the exact repayment schedule. For example, a creditor who offers loans might use unit cost to disclose repayment terms: "48 monthly payments of $25 per $1,000 borrowed."

RATE DISCLOSURES

If the finance charge in a closed-end credit advertisement is expressed as a rate, it must be stated as an annual percentage rate, using that term. If the annual percentage rate may increase after consummation of the credit transaction, that fact must be stated. If a component of that finance charge is interest computed at a simple annual rate, that rate *may* also be included. However, it must not be displayed more conspicuously than the annual percentage rate. For example, an advertisement for mortgage credit may include the contract rate of interest* together with the annual percentage rate.

If the finance charge is computed by applying a periodic rate to the unpaid balance, the periodic rate may also be stated along with the annual percentage rate. As with the simple annual rate, the periodic rate may not be stated more conspicuously than the annual percentage rate.

Except as noted above, no closed-end consumer credit advertisement may include any rate of finance charge other than the annual percentage rate. An advertiser may *never* include an add-on rate (for example, "$6 per $100 per year") or a discount rate in an advertisement. These rates are misleading since they are significantly lower than the corresponding annual percentage rate, and their use violates the Truth in Lending Act.

REAL ESTATE ADVERTISEMENTS

Real estate advertisements that also promote consumer credit must comply with the advertising provisions of the Truth in Lending Act.

---

*The annual percentage rate may include insurance, discounts, and points that may not be included in the contract rate. For further information on the finance charge and annual percentage rate, see sections 226.4 and 226.22 of revised Regulation Z.

Rate Disclosure Examples. As with other advertisements of closed-end consumer credit, if only the annual percentage rate is disclosed, additional disclosures are not required. An advertisement may simply state, "Assume 12 percent annual percentage rate mortgage" or "14 percent annual percentage rate mortgages available."

If the annual percentage rate offered may be increased after consummation of the transaction, the advertisement must state that fact. An advertisement for a variable rate mortgage with an initial annual percentage rate of 14 percent that may vary after settlement without any limit could be advertised as "14 percent annual percentage rate, subject to increase after settlement." This disclosure may be used for any type of mortgage instrument with a variable interest rate, including a renegotiable rate mortgage and a shared appreciation mortgage.

It may not be used in advertisements of graduated payment mortgages that have a fixed interest rate and payments that may increase during the loan. Fixed-rate buydowns and step-rate mortgages are also *not* variable rate mortgages. These mortgages involve different interest rates in effect during the life of the loan, all of which are known at settlement. A variable rate transaction involves future interest rates unknown at settlement.

The simple interest rate may *never* be displayed in lieu of the annual percentage rate. Where more than one simple interest rate is applied to the transaction (such as in a step-rate or buydown mortgage*), these rates may be advertised if all the interest rates and the limited term during which each rate applies are disclosed and

---

*However, in buydown mortgages, the interest rate that must be used, *for purposes of calculating and disclosing the annual percentage rate,* is contingent on the legal obligation of the consumer. Assume the seller or a third party pays an amount to the creditor to reduce the consumer's payments for the first 3 years of a 30-year loan from 15 percent to 12 percent. If the lower rate is stated in the credit contract between the consumer and the creditor, the annual percentage rate should take the buydown into account. If the lower rate is not in that agreement, the annual percentage rate should not reflect the buydown. The latter situation can occur, for example, when the seller agrees separately with the consumer to subsidize the consumer's payments.

the annual percentage rate is stated. For example, assume a step-rate mortgage in which the credit contract provides for 13 percent interest the first year, 14 percent the second year, 15 percent the third year, and 16 percent for the remainder of the term. In this transaction, the following is an acceptable rate disclosure:

- 13 percent 1st year

- 14 percent 2nd year

- 15 percent 3rd year

- 16 percent remainder of loan

- 15¾ percent annual percentage rate

Although an advertiser may disclose the different interest rates which are in effect during the loan, each loan has only one annual percentage rate. Thus, in the above example, it would not be proper to disclose any annual percentage rate other than 15¾ percent.

Triggering Terms. The following are examples of triggering terms that might be used in real estate advertisements:

- 20 percent down

- Pay only $550 per month

- Only 360 monthly payments

- Pay less than $600 per month

- 30-year mortgage available

The following are examples of terms that do *not* trigger the required disclosures:

- No down payment

- 12 percent annual percentage rate mortgage available

- Easy monthly payments

- Graduate payment mortgages available

- Terms to fit your budget
- VA and FHA financing available
- 100 percent VA financing available

Whenever an advertisement displays triggering terms, the same three disclosures are required in a real estate advertisement as in other closed-end consumer credit advertisements.

The following example, for a house with a $55,000 sales price, illustrates the required disclosures for a real estate advertisement that would comply with the Truth in Lending Act *if printed clearly and conspicuously:*

> "Down payment—$5,000; 360 monthly payments of $592.44; 14 percent annual percentage rate."

Graduated Payment Loans and Mortgage Insurance. If an advertisement requiring disclosures promotes a mortgage in which the payments vary (either due to the inclusion of mortgage insurance premiums or because of a graduated payment feature), it is not necessary to disclose all of the different payments that will be required during the term of the mortgage. However, the advertisement must state the number and timing of the payments, the largest and smallest payments, and that other payments will vary between those amounts. The following example, for a house with a $60,000 sales price, illustrates the required disclosures that would comply with the Truth in Lending Act *if printed clearly and conspicuously:*

> "Down payment—$10,000; annual percentage rate—9 percent; 360 monthly payments. The first 60 payments vary from $303.94 to $405.96. The remaining 300 payments are $436.35."

Wraparound Loans. If an advertisement promoting a wraparound mortgage states the annual percentage rate, that rate should be determined by treating the transaction as a refinancing. If triggering terms are advertised, the required disclosures should also be calculated based upon an amount financed that equals the principal balance remaining on the initial obligation plus the new amounts advanced.

For example, assume a borrower has a first mortgage for $36,800 at 7 percent for 30 years with monthly payments of $245. The borrower wants an additional $20,000 for home improvements and applies for a $20,000 loan. (At this time, the balance remaining on the first loan is $30,000.) The wraparound lender would require the borrower to sign a note for $50,000 to mature in 30 years at the current 15 percent interest rate with equal monthly payments of $632.22. The wraparound lender would agree to make each monthly payment on the first mortgage. In an advertisement, disclosures for this transaction would be based upon a $50,000 amount financed, a 30-year term, and a 15 percent annual percentage rate (assuming no credit costs in addition to interest), and the monthly payments would be determined accordingly.

ADVERTISING TYPICAL TERMS

In some cases, it may be appropriate for advertisements to include examples of typical credit terms. For example, a home builder may want to advertise credit terms, but each house has a different price. Or a bank wishing to advertise mortgage loans may make loans in varying amounts with different repayment terms. In these situations, if disclosures are required, the advertiser may advertise one or more examples of typical credit transactions as long as all the terms that apply to each example are disclosed. These examples must be typical of the credit that is actually available. Table 1, below, illustrates disclosures for an advertisement that uses the *typical example* disclosure method:

Table 1. Homeowner's Secondary Financing

Amount Financed	6 Year Financing 72 Monthly Payments of	Annual Percentage Rate
$2160	$ 42.23	12.00%
$3160	$ 62.32	12.25%
$4160	$ 82.41	12.50%
$5160	$103.05	12.75%
$6160	$123.66	13.00%
Other terms and amounts upon request		

CATALOG AND MULTI-PAGE ADVERTISEMENTS

Under certain circumstances, a catalog or other multi-page advertisement may constitute a single advertisement, meaning that only one set of disclosures may be necessary. In such a case, the disclosures must be clearly set forth in a table sufficiently detailed to show all the disclosures required by the Act. However, any credit or lease terms appearing elsewhere in the advertisement must include a *clear and conspicuous reference* to the page on which the table of disclosures appears.

Not every closed-end advertisement consisting of more than one piece of paper qualifies as a multi-page advertisement. As used in the Truth in Lending Act, "catalogs and multi-page advertisements" consist of *a series of numbered pages,* such as a newspaper supplement. Thus, separate pieces of paper, even those mailed in the same envelope, are separate advertisements. For example, if a mailing consists of several pieces of paper, each of which promotes a different item of merchandise sold on credit, each piece of paper containing a triggering term must include a full set of disclosures.

OTHER CONSIDERATIONS

Even though advertising the period of repayment or the amount of the down payment will trigger disclosure, statements such as "take years to pay" or "no closing costs" do not trigger further disclosure because they do not specifically state or imply the period of repayment or down payment cost. However, the statement "Move-in costs $600," which implies that the required cash down payment is no more than $600, does trigger full disclosure. Similarly, "up to 48 months to pay" limits the period of repayment and thus triggers disclosure. In general, the more specific a particular statement, the more likely it is to trigger disclosure.

Consumer Lease Disclosures

CONSUMER LEASES IN GENERAL

The Truth in Lending Act regulates consumer leases because they represent an alternative to buying on credit. Also, unless certain information is provided, a consumer might easily confuse leasing with purchasing on credit.

TRIGGERING TERMS

If an advertisement promoting a consumer lease contains any of the following triggering terms, then five specific disclosures must also be included in the advertisement. The *triggering* terms are:

1. *The amount of any payment.*
   Example: "Pay a mere $128 per month"

2. *The number of required payments.*
   Examples: $133 a month ... 36 month lease"
   "Low monthly payments on our four-year auto leases"

3. *A statement that any or no down payment, or other payment, is required at the beginning of the lease.*
   Examples: "Lease now and make no payments for three months"
   "Only a small down payment"
   "Leave your pocketbook behind and return home in your leased '88 Chevy"

The following are examples of terms which do *not* trigger the required disclosures:

- Low monthly payments

- Lease for less than it costs to buy

- We lease to anyone

REQUIRED DISCLOSURES

If any triggering term is used in a consumer lease advertisement, then the following five *disclosures* must also be included in that advertisement:

1. A statement that the transaction advertised is a lease;

2. The total amount of any payment (such as security deposit or capitalized cost reduction) required at the beginning of the lease, or a statement that no such payment is required;

3. The number, amounts, due dates, or periods of scheduled payments, and the total of such payments under the lease;

4. A statement of whether the customer has the option to purchase the leased property and at what time and price (the method of determining the price may be substituted for disclosure of the price);

5. A statement of the amount (or method of determining the amount) of any liabilities the lease imposes upon the customer at the end of the term; and, if the customer has such liability, a statement that the customer shall be liable for any difference between the estimated value of the leased property and its realized value at the end of the lease term.

SAMPLE DISCLOSURES

The following is an example of the required disclosures for a consumer lease advertisement that would comply with the Truth in Lending Act *if printed clearly and conspicuously:*

"36 month lease. No payments at the beginning of the lease, 36 monthly payments of $128 totaling $4,608. Customer has no option to purchase at the end of the lease. Customer will have no further liability unless auto has depreciated to less than 40 percent of its new car price. If so, customer is liable for that additional depreciation."

CATALOG AND MULTI-PAGE ADVERTISEMENTS

Consumer lease advertisements that appear in catalogs or other multi-page advertisements are subject to the special provisions described earlier in this manual.

MERCHANDISE TAGS AND MULTIPLE ITEM LEASES

If a merchandise tag for an item normally included in a multiple item lease contains any triggering term, it must either a) include all required disclosures or b) *clearly and conspicuously* refer to a sign or display prominently posted in the lessor's showroom that includes all required disclosures.

Principal Business Directories

Adweek Agency Directory. A quick-access guide to more than 4,500 ad agencies, 1,500 public relations firms, and 300 media-buying services. Published in six regional editions. Published annually. ADWEEK AGENCY DIRECTORY, 49 E. 21 Street, New York, NY 10010.

Advertising Specialties Directory. Directory contains entries of approximately 12,000 names and addresses of suppliers and services. Includes brands carried, specialties, or franchises held. Published by AMERICAN BUSINESS DIRECTORIES, INC., 5707 S. 86th Circle, Omaha, NE 68127.

Air-Charter Guide. A guide to business, individual, and cargo charter of aircraft. Contains maps, distance tables, airport and aircraft references necessary to supplement specific listings of air-charter operators. Published semi-annually. BOSTON AVIATION, INC., 55B Reservoir Street, Cambridge, MA 02138.

Air Freight Directory. A listing of motor carriers for delivery and pick up of freight. Bimonthly. AIR CARGO, INC., 1819 Bay Ridge Ave., Annapolis, MD 21403.

American Export Register. This annual directory lists over 40,000 United States firms exporting products and services, American chambers of commerce abroad, and financial and transportation companies. THOMAS INTERNATIONAL PUBLISHING COMPANY, INC., One Penn Plaza, 250 W. 34th Street, New York, NY 10119.

American Motor Carrier Directory. Directory contains listings of licensed general commodity carriers. Refrigerated carriers, heavy haulers, bulk haulers, riggers, and specified commodity carriers are also included. Published semi-annually. GUIDE SERVICES, INC., P.O. Box 72055, Atlanta, GA 30338.

American Stock Exchange Guide. Lists approximately 1,375 member companies listed as traders with the American Stock Exchange, and floor officials. Published annually. COMMERCE CLEARING HOUSE, INC., 4025 W. Peterson Ave., Chicago, IL 60646.

Apparel Trades Book. Provides information on over 125,000 apparel retailers and wholesalers in the United States, which are rated by Dun & Bradstreet's Credit Clearing House. Published quarterly.

DUN & BRADSTREET CORPORATION, One Diamond Hill Road, Murray, NJ 07974.

AT&T Toll Free 800 Directory for Business. Contains a business products and services section which gives in-depth information by product and service categories. Includes company name, city and state, product specifications, areas of specialization, hours of operation, and credit cards accepted. Also includes an alphabetical listing of business, government, and other organizations with 800 numbers for quick reference when the name is known. Published annually in October. AMERICAN TELEPHONE & TELEGRAPH COMPANY, 550 Madison Ave., New York, NY 10022.

Audio Video Market Place. Provides more than 4,500 companies that create, supply, or distribute A/V equipment and services for business, education, science, and government. Features contact information for state and local film and TV agencies plus A/V trade associations, award sponsors, meetings, and conventions. "Names & Numbers" directory to 13,000 A/V firms and personnel are also given. R. R. BOWKER COMPANY, 245 West 17th Street, New York, NY 10011.

Bank Automation Directory. Lists more than 225 suppliers of data processing software and equipment, bank service bureaus, consultants, and correspondent banks. Directory is classified by software, hardware, or service supplier. AMERICAN BANKERS ASSOCIATION, 1120 Connecticut Ave., N.W., Washington, DC 20036.

Bank Systems and Equipment. This annual directory lists more than 2,000 manufacturers, distributors, and suppliers of equipment to the banking industry. Listing includes company name, address, names of key personnel; and product descriptions are given for many companies. GRALLA PUBLICATIONS, 1515 Broadway, New York, NY 10036.

Best's Safety Directory. This directory lists over 2,500 manufacturers and distributors of safety, industrial hygiene, security, and pollution control products. Published annually in November. A. M. BEST COMPANY, INC., Oldwick, NJ 08858.

Business America—Worldwide Business Opportunities Section. Contains details about licensing and joint venture proposals, opportunities to sell to foreign enterprises, and major construction and expansion projects. Compiled by Dept. of Commerce representatives and Dept. of State foreign commercial service officers worldwide. Published biweekly. SUPERINTENDENT OF DOCUMENTS, U.S. Government Printing Office, Washington, DC 20402.

Business Forms & Systems Reference Yearbook. A listing of more than 600 manufacturers of business forms and 500 suppliers of equipment used to manufacture business forms. Entries give company name, address, phone, executive and manager names, products and services. Published annually each December. NORTH AMERICAN PUBLISHING COMPANY, 401 N. Broad Street, Philadelphia, PA 19108.

Business Organizations, Agencies, and Publications Directory. The third edition of this guide gives approximately 20,000 new and established organizations, agencies, and publications concerned with business, trade, and industry. GALE RESEARCH CO., Book Tower, Detroit, MI 48226.

Business Software Database. Lists the publishers of more than 5,500 business software packages for microcomputers and minicomputers. Entries include software title, name, address, and phone of publisher, name and title of contact, description of product, program language, type of documentation available, and other services. 1983. Updates issued quarterly. DATA COURIER, INC., 620 S. Fifth Street, Louisville, KY 40202.

Canadian Advertising Rates & Data. This monthly publication lists daily and weekend newspapers, business publications, advertising agencies, radio and television stations. Includes names, addresses, key personnel names, advertising rates, copy regulations, closing and publication dates. Published monthly. MACLEAN HUNTER LTD., 777 Bay Street, Toronto, ON M5W 1A7, Canada.

Canadian Business Information, Browning Directory of. This directory covers the publishers of over 800 directories, market surveys, trade guides, association publications, and special periodical issues that are sources of Canadian business information. Title and subject indexes. Published annually each September. BROWNING ASSOCIATES, 105 Browning Avenue, Toronto ON M4K 1W2, Canada.

Canadian Premiums & Incentives—Buyers' Guide & Source Directory Issue. This directory provides a list of over 1,500 suppliers and manufacturers of incentive premiums and merchandise. Covers automobiles, appliances, and travel packages. Also includes company name, address, telephone, and lists key personnel. Published annually. CP&I, INC., 777 Bay Street, Toronto, ON M5W 1A7, Canada.

Canadian Trade Index. A listing of over 15,000 manufacturers in Canada. Includes company name, address, names of key executives, products, brand names and trade names. Published each January.

CANADIAN MANUFACTURERS ASSOCIATION, One Yonge Street, Toronto, ON M5E 1J9, Canada.

Canadian Transportation Safety Professionals, Directory of. Contains an alphabetical listing of transportation-safety professionals. Indexes identify the professionals by province, organization, and current research activities. ADDICTION RESEARCH FOUNDATION, 33 Russell Street, Toronto, Canada M5S 2S1.

Chase's Annual Events: Special Days, Weeks, and Months. Over 4,500 special days and events given. Worldwide dates are also included. Published annually each November. CONTEMPORARY BOOKS, INC., 180 N. Michigan Ave., Chicago, IL 60601.

Congressional Handbook. Publication contains a list of members of Congress arranged by state, member's party, and home city. Also includes committee assignments, office building, room and phone numbers. Published annually. CHAMBER OF COMMERCE OF THE UNITED STATES, Dept. of the Legislature, 1615 H Street, N.W., Washington, DC 20062.

Construction Associations, Directory of. Provides name, address, and phone number for approximately 3,500 local, regional, and national professional societies, technical associations, trade groups, labor unions, and government agencies. Publications also included. Third edition. METADATA, INC., 310 E. 44th Street, New York, NY 10017.

Consultants Directory, Corporate Services. This directory contains a select list of management consultants and their services. Arranged alphabetically by subject. Published semi-annually. BUSINESS RESEARCH & COMMUNICATIONS, 203 Calle del Oaks, Monterey, CA 93940.

Conventions, Directory of. More than 19,000 listings of meetings and conventions held by United States and Canadian organizations are given. This directory is cross-indexed by 82 industries, businesses, and professions. Midyear supplement available in July. BILL COMMUNICATIONS, INC., 633 Third Avenue, New York, NY 10017.

Corporate Affiliations, Directory of. Provides information on who owns whom for 4,500 United States parent companies and over 47,000 domestic divisions, subsidiaries, and affiliates. Published annually in January. NATIONAL REGISTER PUBLISHING CO., 3004 Glenview Road, Wilmette, IL 60091.

The Corporate 1000. A directory of who runs the top 1000 United States corporations with executive names and titles, addresses, phone numbers, and a description of each company's business. Published annually. MONITOR PUBLISHING COMPANY, 1301 Pennsylvania Ave., N.W., Suite 1000, Washington, DC 20004.

Direct Marketing Marketplace. Provides company name, address, phone, description of services and products, and key personnel for over 5,000 direct marketing companies, suppliers, and creative and consulting services firms. Published annually in January. HILLARY HOUSE, 1033 Channel Drive, Hewlett Harbor, NY 11557.

Directory of Directories. The fourth edition lists 9,600 business and industrial directories, professional and scientific rosters, and guides of all kinds. GALE RESEARCH COMPANY, Book Tower, Detroit, MI 48226.

Dodge Reports. Reports on new building and construction sites, major additions and renovations, and estimated cost of projects. Useful information for general contractors, subcontractors, suppliers, dealers, and manufacturers' reps. F. W. DODGE DIV., MCGRAW-HILL INFORMATION SYSTEMS CO., 230 W. Monroe Street, Chicago, IL 60606.

Encyclopedia of Associations. This directory contains information about active associations, organizations, clubs, and other non-profit groups. Published annually. GALE RESEARCH COMPANY, Book Tower, Detroit, MI 48226.

Exhibits Schedule: Directory of Trade and Industrial Shows. This annual directory lists trade, industrial, and public shows, worldwide. Published annually each January. BILL COMMUNICATIONS, INC., 633 Third Ave., New York, NY 10017.

Fly-Rights. A guide to air travel in the U.S. This booklet will explain your rights and responsibilities as an air traveler. Areas covered are reservations and tickets, delayed and cancelled flights, overbooking, baggage, smoking, and tips on how to complain to resolve individual complaints. Revised periodically by the U.S. Department of Transportation. SUPERINTENDENT OF DOCUMENTS, U.S. Government Printing Office, Washington, DC 20402.

Foreign Manufacturers in the United States, Directory of. This third edition lists 4,800 companies in the United States that are 10 percent or more foreign-owned and provides name, address of each firm, zip code, name and address of parent company, list of products produced and SIC product classification numbers. GEORGIA STATE UNIVERSITY, Business Publishing Division, College of Business Administration, University Plaza, Atlanta, GA 30303-3093.

1226

Fortune-Service 500 Issue. Lists top 100 companies in finance, commercial banking, and diversified service, and top 50 firms in life insurance, transportation, utility industry, and retailing. Entries include company name, headquarters city, net income, sales, employees, and comparative earnings per share for 10 years, and other financial information. Published each June. TIME, INC., 1271 Avenue of the Americas, New York, NY 10020.

Franchise Annual. Lists names and addresses of over 2,700 franchisors, distributors, licensors, franchise consultants, and joint ventures. Published annually in January. INFO PRESS, INC., 728 Center Street, Lewiston, NY 14092.

Gold Book of Multi-Housing. This directory covers about 3,100 major builders, developers, owners, and managers of apartments and condominiums, and managers of rental property. Published annually in December. LSI SYSTEMS, INC., 11-A Village Green, Crofton, MD 21114.

Graphic Arts Marketplace. Includes pictures and specifications of printing presses and equipment. Published annually. NORTH AMERICAN PUBLISHING COMPANY, 401 N. Broad Street, Philadelphia, PA 19108.

Hardware Age—Who Makes It Buyer's Guide. Lists the names, addresses, phone numbers of over 5,600 manufacturers of automotive, electrical, plumbing products, lawn and garden products, and warehouse equipment. Published annually in December. CHILTON COMPANY, Chilton Way, Radnor, PA 19089.

Highway Emergency Manual. Includes approximately 650 truck stops, primarily on interstate highways, that are open 24 hours per day. Formerly titled "Highway Assistance Directory." Published annually. HIGHWAY SERVICE ASSN., 1425 Lakeland Drive, Jackson, MS 39216.

Holidays and Anniversaries of the World. Arranged by month and day, this book covers: special days, weeks, and months, national holidays, birthdates of famous people, and historical anniversaries. Also included is a perpetual calendar covering the years 1753 through 2100 and a ten-year projection of all movable feasts, such as Easter and Passover. GALE RESEARCH COMPANY, Book Tower, Detroit, MI 48226.

Housing Manufacturers, Red Book of. Publication contains approximately 1,100 prefabricated home manufacturers, modular home manufacturers, mobile home manufacturers, and major firms which erect production homes. Published annually in February. LSI Sys-TEMS, INC., 11-A Village Green, Crofton, MD 21114.

Industry Surveys. Provides continuous economic and business information on all major U.S. industries and numerous related industries. Financial data on more than 1,300 companies is included in the 22 surveys now published. Available in loose-leaf binders as well as permanently bound volumes. STANDARD & POOR'S CORPORATION, 25 Broadway, New York, NY 10004.

Insurance Adjusters, Hine's Directory of. Gives company name, office address and phone, areas of occupational specialization for over 1,300 independent insurance adjuster offices in the United States and Canada. Published every December. HINE'S LEGAL DIRECTORY, INC., Box 71, Glen Ellyn, IL 60138.

Insurance Almanac. Classified by insurance lines and type of activity. Over 2,100 companies that write fire, casualty, accident and health, life, and Lloyd's policies are listed. Published annually in July. UN-DERWRITER PRINTING & PUBLISHING CO., 291 S. Van Brunt Street, Englewood, NJ 07631.

Law and Legal Information Directory. The new 1986 edition offers sources of legal information, from state bar associations to law schools. Biennial. GALE RESEARCH COMPANY, Book Tower, Detroit, MI 48226.

Local Chambers of Commerce Which Maintain Trade Services. Provides approximately 265 listings giving names, addresses, and phone numbers. Arranged geographically. CHAMBER OF COMMERCE OF THE UNITED STATES OF AMERICA, International Div., 1615 H Street, N.W., Washington, DC 20062.

Magazine Industry Market Place. Describes more than 3,400 consumer, trade, professional, literary, and scholarly periodicals. Published annually in February. R. R. BOWKER, 245 West 17th Street, New York, NY 10011.

Mail-Order Sales, Guide to U.S. Provides a listing of mail-order conglomerates, parent companies, and subsidiaries. Published annually in July. HOKE COMMUNICATIONS, 224 Seventh Street, Garden City, NY 11530.

Malls, Directory of Major. Provides a list of existing and planned shopping centers in the United States and Canada. Published annually in January. MJJTM PUBLICATIONS CORPORATION, Box 2, Suffern, NY 10901.

Management Consultants. Geographically arranged directory, lists over 16,000 consultants plus names, addresses, and phone numbers. AMERCIAN BUSINESS DIRECTORIES, INC., 5707 S. 86th Circle, Omaha, NE 68127.

Marketing Information. Part I contains over 2,000 names, addresses, and phone numbers of businesses, agencies, and other organizations in the marketing field. Part II is an annotated bibliographic guide to 3,100 marketing books, periodicals, and other sources of marketing information. GEORGIA STATE UNIVERSITY, Business Publishing Div., College of Business Administration, University Plaza, Atlanta, GA 30303-3093.

National Directory of Addresses and Telephone Numbers. Lists names, addresses, phone numbers, zip codes, and business classifications for leading U.S. corporations, banks, credit unions, accounting and law firms, computer firms, colleges and universities, government agencies, restaurants and hotels. Over 150,000 listings in the current edition. GENERAL INFORMATION, INC., P.O. Box 3299, Kirkland, WA 98083.

National Trade and Professional Associations of the United States. The 22nd edition lists about 6,500 trade associations, labor unions, professional, scientific, or technical societies, and other national organizations composed of groups for a common purpose. COLUMBIA BOOKS INC., 1350 New York Ave., N.W., Washington, DC 20005.

On Cassette. More than 15,000 titles are listed and described in title, author, subject, reader/performer, and producer indexes. A comprehensive bibliography of spoken word audio cassettes. Annually. R.R. BOWKER, 245 West 17th Street, New York, NY 10011.

Package Printing—Who's Who of Suppliers Issue. Company name, address, description of goods and services given for suppliers to the package printing, converting, and die cutting fields. Published annually in August. NORTH AMERICAN PUBLISHING CO., 401 N. Broad Street, Philadelphia, PA 19108.

Paper Year Book. Provides a listing of suppliers and manufacturers of paper and paper-related equipment, and products. Published annually in June. HARCOURT BRACE JOVANOVICH, INC., 7500 Old Oak Blvd., Cleveland, OH 44130.

Physical Distribution Directory. Publication contains entries on transportation services, freight forwarders, motor carriers, railroad firms, and air cargo. COLUMBUS AREA CHAMBER OF COMMERCE, 37 N. High Street, Columbia, OH 43215.

Planning Forum. This annual membership directory lists over 7,000 corporate planners. Alphabetical listing by chapter. Company names, addresses, and telephone numbers are also given. Published annually. PLANNING EXECUTIVE INSTITUTE, 5500 College Corner Pike, Oxford, OH 45056.

Plant Location. An annual reference guide for plant and office locations. Lists names, addresses, and industrial development managers in the United States and Canada. PLANT LOCATION, 345 Hudson Street, New York, NY 10014.

Plants, Sites & Parks. Listing of professional contacts in the private and public sector throughout the U.S. and overseas. Published seven times per year. PLANTS, SITES & PARKS, 10240 West Sample Road, Coral Springs, FL 10240.

Public Affairs Officers, Directory of. Contains an alphabetical and geographical listing of 250 executives with public affairs responsibilities. Biennial, July of odd years. PUBLIC AFFAIRS COUNCIL, 1225 23rd Street, N.W., Suite 750, Washington, DC 20037.

Radio Co-op Sources. Provides information on over 3,740 manufacturers who provide cooperative allowances for radio advertising. RADIO ADVERTISING BUREAU, 304 Park Ave. S., New York, NY 10010.

Railroad Officials, Pocket List of. Publication contains entries of officials and equipment of railroads, including transit systems, private car companies, and railroad-owned truck lines. Issued quarterly. NATIONAL RAILWAY PUBLICATION COMPANY, 424 W. 33rd Street, New York, NY 10001.

Research & Development Directory. Publication contains firms that have received research and development contracts from the federal government during the preceding 12 months. Published annually in September. GOVERNMENT DATA PUBLICATIONS, 1616 McDonald Ave., Brooklyn, NY 11230.

Resorts & Parks Purchasing Guide. Provides information on manufacturers and suppliers of services and products for national parks, winter and summer resorts, and ski areas. Published annually in April. KLEVENS PUBLICATIONS, INC., 7600 Avenue V, Littlerock, CA 93543.

Rubber Red Book. Lists manufacturers of rubber located in the United States, Canada, and Puerto Rico. COMMUNICATION CHANNELS, INC., 6255 Barfield Road, Atlanta, GA 30328.

Sales & Marketing Management in Canada—Directory of Canadian Business Publications Issue. Lists Canadian business and trades periodicals. Over 575 publications are given plus addresses, telephone numbers, editors, and advertising rate per page information. Published annually. STANFORD EVANS COMMUNICATIONS LTD., 3500 Dufferin Street, Suite 402, Downsview, ON M3K 1N2, Canada.

Scott's Directories: Ontario Manufacturers. This reference source provides almost 19,000 manufacturers in Ontario, Canada. Entries include company name, address, phone, telex, names and titles of key personnel, SIC numbers, and parent or subsidiary companies. Published every 18 months. Latest edition September 1986. SOUTHERN COMMUNICATIONS LTD., 75 Oakville, Ontario L6J 3A3, Canada.

Security Dealers of North America. Lists over 14,000 brokerage and investment banking houses in the United States and Canada along with an executive roster of over 45,000 individuals and 8,000 branch offices. Published twice a year. STANDARD & POOR'S CORPORATION, 25 Broadway, New York, NY 10004.

Small Business Sourcebook. Lists federal and state government agencies, trade associations, publishers of reference works, publishers of trade periodicals, sponsors of trade shows and conventions, and consultants. GALE RESEARCH COMPANY, Book Tower, Detroit, MI 48226.

Standard & Poor's Register of Corporations, Directors, and Executives. Corporation volume gives executive rosters and business telephone numbers of 45,000 companies, plus principal products, SIC codes, number of employees, and annual sales. The Directors and Executives volume includes biographies-in-brief of 70,000 officers and directors with business and home addresses. The Index volume includes breakdowns by SIC (industry) and a geographical index, plus Corporate Family Indexes linking subsidiaries and affiliates to their parent companies in the Register. Published annually. STANDARD & POOR'S CORPORATION, 25 Broadway, New York, NY 10004.

Standard Directory of Advertising. Includes over 17,000 advertiser companies. Classified edition and geographical edition with monthly supplements. Published annually. NATIONAL REGISTER PUBLISHING COMPANY, 3004 Glenview Road, Wilmette, IL 60091.

Standard Industrial Classification Manual. This manual was developed for use in the classification of establishments by type of activity in which engaged; for purposes of facilitating the collection, tabulation, presentation, and analysis of data relating to establishments; and for promoting uniformity and comparability in the presentation of statistical data collected by agencies of the United States Government, state agencies, trade associations, and private research organizations. Latest edition published September 1987. SUPERINTENDENT OF DOCUMENTS, U.S. Government Printing Office, Washington, DC 20402.

Standard Rate & Data Service-Business Publication Rates & Data. Covers more than 4,400 United States business, trade, and technical publications, and 250 international publications. Includes publisher's editorial statement, advertising rates, contract and copy regulations, mechanical requirements, issuance and closing dates, and circulation statements. Published on the 24th of each month. SRDS, 3004 Glenview Road, Wilmette, IL 60091.

Strout Real Estate Values. Lists thousands of small town businesses, rural properties for sale, and farms. Published quarterly. STROUT REALTY, INC., Plaza Towers, Springfield, MO 65804.

Target Marketing Directory: U.S. Paint and Coating Manufacturers. Lists over 1,500 coating and paint manufacturing companies and key personnel. Published annually in July. MANNSVILLE CHEMICAL PRODUCTS CORPORATION, Box 230, Cortland, NY 13045.

Telephony's Directory & Buyers Guide. Lists Bell System companies, officers, and exchanges in the United States and Canada. Published annually in September. TELEPHONY PUBLISHING CORPORATION, 55 E. Jackson Blvd., Chicago, IL 60604.

Thomas Register of American Manufacturers and Thomas Register Catalog File. Alphabetical listing of 140,000 United States companies and 5,000 Canadian firms. Provides company name, address, phone number, sales offices, service locations, corporate affiliations, cable/telex numbers, and distributors. Also included is an alphabetical listing of over 108,000 brand names and trademarks in the "Brand Names" section. Revised annually each February. THOMAS PUBLISHING COMPANY, One Penn Plaza, New York, NY 10019.

Toll-Free Hotline Directory. Lists name, description of service, and toll-free number of over 100 federal government and private agency toll-free hotline services. PUBLIC CITIZEN, 2000 P Street, N.W., Washington, DC 20036.

Toll-Free Numbers, Directory of. A guide to over 25,000 free telephone numbers in the United States. Areas covered include businesses, service organizations, hotels, airlines, auto rentals, cable

TV, business supplies, colleges, insurance agents and brokers, and health and allied services. SIMON AND SCHUSTER, INC., Pocket Books Division, 1230 Avenue of the Americas, New York, NY 10020.

Trade Names Dictionary. A two-volume guide to over 220,000 consumer-oriented trade names, brand names, product names, coined names, model and design names, with names and addresses of their manufacturers, marketers, or distributors. GALE RESEARCH Co., Book Tower, Detroit, MI 48226.

Trade Show & Convention Guide. A guide to current conventions and trade shows, worldwide, for up to seven years into future. Show entries are arranged by industry or subject; facility and supplier entries are geographical. Published annually each June. BILLBOARD PUBLICATIONS, INC., Box 24970, Nashville, TN 37202.

Traveler's Toll-Free Telephone Directory. Contains a listing of auto rental agencies, hotels, motels, airlines, and other travel related businesses. Published annually in January. LANDMARK PUBLISHING COMPANY, Whipple Road, South Hero, VT 05486.

Video Source Book. More than 420 subject areas are covered in this new eighth edition. Over 2,300 pages listing 50,000 video titles, distributor's names and addresses, cast listing index, and producers and descriptions are included. GALE RESEARCH COMPANY, Book Tower, Detroit, MI 48226.

Walker's Manual of Western Corporations. Divided into two volumes, this manual describes publicly owned corporations headquartered in 13 western states. Company profiles give up to 10 years of income statements, balance sheets, per share data, plus earnings and price ranges. Published annually in November. WALKER'S MANUAL, INC., 14032 Lake Street, Garden Grove, CA 92643.

Water Quality Association Directory. Lists retailer, individual, and allied members, member manufacturers and suppliers. Personal name index is also included. Published annually. WATER QUALITY ASSN., 4151 Naperville Road, Lisle, IL 60532.

Who's Who in Advertising. Lists over 11,000 advertising agency executives, corporate advertising executives, and teachers of advertising. Published biennially. REDFIELD PUBLISHING COMPANY, INC., Box 42535, Houston, TX 77042.

World Commodity Markets, Guide to. About 90 exchanges for commodities and futures trading worldwide are listed. Published at irregular intervals. Latest edition May 1985. NICHOLS PUBLISHING COMPANY, Box 96, New York, NY 10024.

Word Processing Buyer's Guide. Gives a description of commercially available programs and describes ease of use, safety, and editing power. MCGRAW-HILL BOOK COMPANY, 1221 Avenue of the Americas, New York, NY 10020.

Index

A

profitability of sales, 1044–46
qualified bonus compensation plan, 85–86
salary plan, 1023–25
for sales force, 1023–46
for sales managers, 68–69, 73
sales' share of the sales dollar, 69
starting new territories, 1041–42
telephone sales, 1041
terminating salespeople, 1043–44
transferring territories, 1042–43
types of plans, 1023–31
and variations in makeup of sales expense, 72
Competition
cornering merchandise of, 587
disparaging, 587
getting information on, 359–63
recruiting through salespeople of, 810–11
Computers
applications of, 463–65
benefits of, 460–61
development of, 459–60
and marketing decisions, 460
for ordering, 18, 779–80
portable personal, 468–69
in sales, 458–59
in small firms, 461–62
Concessionaires, 688
Conference Board, 58
Confidence Interval (C.I.), 357
Congressional Information Index, 361
Consignment, legal pitfalls in, 534–35
Constant costs, 399
Consultants
in international trade, 737–38
in outside training, 868–69

value of, in making hiring decisions, 841–42
Consumer(s). *See also* Customer(s)
functional, 634–35
shifts in value structure of, 22
Consumer affairs, director of, 579
Consumer attitudes, 20
Consumer co-ops, 707–8
Consumerism, wave of, 579
Consumer market, 19–20
Consumer pricing, versus industrial pricing, 502
Consumer-product wholesalers, 647
Consumer testing, 321. *See also* Market research; Test marketing
Contact selling programs, evaluation of, 44–50
Container premium, 266
Contest(s), 266. *See also* Sales contest(s); Sweepstakes
Contingent compensation, 69, 79–80
Continuity program, 266
Contracts. *See also* Employment contracts
government, 312–14
need for, in exclusive distribution outlets, 547
termination of commission, 1057–58
Controlled pricing, 500
Convenience sample, 356
Convictions, legal restrictions concerning, in application form, 823
Coolen, Ronald B., 614
Cooperative advertising, 686–87, 694
Coopers, Inc., 1054

Mills, James T., 771
Mineral Yearbook, 373
Minicomputer, 459
Misleading names, using, 587
Misrepresentation, 589
Mister Donut, 769
Mitchell management systems, 464
Mitsubishi International Foods Division, 487
Mobil Oil Corp., 686
MOM (middle of month) terms, 523–24
Monopoly, 584
Monsanto Polymer Products, 465
Monthly Catalog of U.S. Government Publications, 375
Monthly Catalog of U.S. Public Documents, 374
Monthly Product Announcement, 375
Monthly Wholesale Trade Report: Sales and Inventories, 375
Moore, Benjamin, and Company, 465
Motivational studies, 1066–72
Motivation of sales force, 1064–99
   and communication, 1092–96
   and incentive objectives, 1081–82
   methods of, 1096–99
   motivational studies, 1066–72
   non-cash incentive programs, 1072–79
   nonfinancial methods, 1065–66
   power of triangle rewards, 1079–81
   preparing sales bulletins, 1093, 1094–96
   questionnaire on, for sales reps, 1069–70
   research on, 320–21, 325

sales contest, 1082–84
   checklist for, 1088–92
   essentials of well-planned, 1082–84
   prizes for, 1084
   representative, 1087–88
   year round, 1084–87
Motley, Red, 851
Motorola, 579
Multi-marketing, 12
Multinational company, 724
Multiple interviews, 841
   company policy on, 834–35
Multi-sales force marketing organization, 101, 102, 103, 105
Murtha, Joseph M., 490

N

Naisbitt, John, 718
National Association of Textile and Apparel Wholesalers, 677
National Association of Wholesalers (NAW), National Wholesale Distribution Associations affiliated with, 673–78
National Directory of Manufacturers' Representatives, 178
National account manager, 125
   position description for, 137–38
National Aeronautics and Space Administration, 310
National Association of Electrical Distributors, 649–50
National Association of State Development Agencies (NASDA), 734
National Automotive Parts Association (NAPA), 654
National Biscuit Company, 654

O

Observation, increasing powers of, 901–2

O'Connor, Michael, 3

Odiorne, George S., 53, 55, 852

O'Donnell, Joseph J., 280

OEM (original equipment manufacturer), 637

Office of Economic Growth and Employment Projections (OEGEP), 15

Office of Transportation (USDA), 733

Oklahoma Natural Gas Company, 1008

Oldfield v. *Chevrolet Motor Company of Nebraska*, 1056–57

Olin Corporation, 1007

On-line computer systems, development of, 460

On-pack, 267

Open account terms, 522

Organization, evaluation of, 50–52

Organizational assignment, marketing functions by, 107–8

Ormsby, T. Edward, 286

Osco Drug, 709

Ostberg, Henry B., 1080

Outside training consultant, 868–69

Owens-Illinois, 256

Ozanne, U. B., 766

P

Pacesetters, 983

Pacific Mills, 437

Packaged goods salespeople, training of, 866

Package enclosure, 267

Packaging
designing, 487–88
federal regulation of, 484–87, 587–88
and product failures, 492–93

Palmer, Arnold, 888

Part-cash redemption, 267

Participating ownership voluntary chains, 705–6

Partners in Export Trade, 744

Patent, 591

Patent and Trademark Office, 606

Patented products, trademarks on, 600

Patent rights, 1060

Patents, General Information Concerning, 375

Patronage, bribing, 586

Payment requirements, 522–24
advertising allowances, 531–32
AOG (arrival of goods) terms, 524
cash discounts, 530
COD (cash on delivery) terms, 523
dating ahead terms, 523–24
early order discounts, 529
EOM (end of month) terms, 523–24
extra terms, 524–25
FAS (free alongside ship) terms, 523
FOB (free on board) terms, 523
freight allowances, 532–33
MOM (middle of month) terms, 523–24
net terms, 522
open account terms, 522
proximo terms, 524
ROG (receipt of goods) terms, 524